THE
DEMOCRATIC
DEBATE

THE DEMOCRATIC DEBATE

An Introduction to American Politics

Bruce Miroff
State University of New York—Albany

Raymond Seidelman
Sarah Lawrence College

Todd Swanstrom
State University of New York—Albany

HOUGHTON MIFFLIN COMPANY Boston Toronto
Geneva, Illinois Palo Alto Princeton, New Jersey

To our teachers, who taught us to take democracy seriously:

Walter Dean Burnham, Norman Jacobson, Isaac Kramnick, Theodore J. Lowi, Grant McConnell, Michael Paul Rogin, Sheldon S. Wolin

Sponsoring Editor: Jean Woy
Senior Associate Editor: Fran Gay
Editorial Assistant: Colleen Shanley
Senior Project Editor: Janet Young
Editorial Assistant: Marybeth Griffin
Senior Production/Design Coordinator: Jill Haber
Senior Manufacturing Coordinator: Marie Barnes
Marketing Manager: Pamela Shaffer

Cover Designer: Catherine Hawkes

Photo Credits

p. 4: Jacques Langevin/Sygma; p. 9: J. P. Laffont/Sygma; p. 20: Library of Congress; p. 29: "James Madison" by Charles Wilson Peale. From the collection of Gilcrease Museum, Tulsa (registration #0126.1005); p. 58: UPI/Bettmann; p. 64: UPI/Bettmann; p. 70: Mark Cullum/Copley News Service; p. 90: TOLES copyright 1992 The Buffalo

Credits continue on p. A-113

Printed in the U.S.A.

Library of Congress Catalog Card Number: 94-76528

ISBN: Student Copy 0-395-56086-1
     Complimentary Examination Copy 0-395-71726-4

123456789-DH-98 97 96 95 94

BRIEF CONTENTS

PART ONE   FOUNDATIONS

PART TWO   PARTICIPATION

CONTENTS

PART ONE
FOUNDATIONS

1
Introduction: The Democratic Debate   3

2
The Revolution and the Constitution: Origins of the Democratic Debate   17

The Dilemma of American Federalism 47

The American Political Economy 78

PART TWO
PARTICIPATION

5

Where Have All the Voters Gone? 113

6

Public Opinion: Does it Matter? 141

The Media: Setting the Political Agenda   172

Where's the Party?   200

PART THREE
INSTITUTIONS

Presidential Leadership and the Democratic Debate   352

Congress: Between Elite and Popular Democracy   319

Bureaucracy: Myth and Reality   382

The Judiciary and the Democratic Paradox   412

PART FOUR
POLICY

16   Civil Liberties and Civil Rights   447

17   Economic Policy: Growth versus Equality?   479

20 Afterword: The Prospects for Popular Democracy 571

"A CLOSER LOOK" BOXES

FIGURES

PREFACE

In the summer of 1988 the authors of this book set out on an ambitious backpacking trip in New York's Catskill Mountains but instead wound up waterlogged in a rundown motel room. With the steady patter of rain for company, the three of us talked through the night about many topics. Finally, the conversation settled on a topic that bothered us all: how difficult it was to motivate beginning students to take seriously the issues and questions that had prompted us, as political activists, to become college teachers in the first place. We agreed that part of the problem was political science textbooks. Although they claimed objectivity, the mainstream textbooks in fact presented a consensus interpretation of American politics that supported the status quo and deadened the students' critical sensibilities. Worse, they often made politics seem boring and distant, as if the important debates were over.

We also felt ambivalent about the critical point-of-view texts that had been produced since the 1960s. These books raised critical issues and challenged the status quo, but after using them we noticed that they did little to counter student cynicism about politics. Most of these texts argued that American political institutions were corrupted by the structures of global capitalism. After documenting the economic forces that overwhelm democracy, these texts often turned around in the last chapter and called for radical change or even revolution. As teachers, we felt the unintended consequence was to reconfirm student cynicism about all politics, even the democratic kind.

With the Cold War rapidly coming to a close, we felt the time was ripe for a new type of critical theme text. That night we sketched out an outline that six years later evolved into this textbook. Instead of writing a text that took its critical standard from European socialism or utopian democratic theory, we decided to write a point-of-view text that drew its standard from homegrown traditions of participatory democracy in America. We talked of the Antifederalist critics of the Constitution, of Populists, progressive unions, the civil rights struggle, and the current battles over race, gender, and class. *The Democratic Debate* was born that night. While we have come a long way since then, we have never wavered from our conviction that an introductory book on American government ought to draw its critical standard from the ongoing struggles for democracy in the United States.

THEMATIC FRAMEWORK

Beginning students easily become overwhelmed and confused by the sheer volume of facts presented in most textbooks on American politics. They need a framework to make sense of the facts. Since our initial discussion, we have developed a sophisticated yet simple framework for analyzing American politics. In *The Democratic Debate* the facts of American politics are organized around the theme of democracy. Specifically, each chapter examines the debate between what we call elite democracy and popular democracy, showing how that debate has impacted on the particular institution, process, or policy covered in the chapter. The overall goal is to assess the prospects and possibilities for the extension of democracy in the United States.

Our goal has caused us to treat the conventional topics of American politics differently from other textbooks. Some textbooks, for example, treat the Framers as a brilliant group of men who gave the country a Constitution that created a consensus about democracy that has persisted to this day. Because they lost the debate on the Constitution, the Antifederalists are viewed by most textbooks as backward-looking opponents of progress who were relegated to the dustbin of history. We treat the Founding period differently. In our view, the Founding period did not end debate but *began* a debate about American democracy between the tradition of elite democracy, as founded by the Federalists, and popular democracy, as founded by the Antifederalists. To emphasize that point, we include an Antifederalist work in the Appendices of the book.

Although the basics of the democratic debate were laid down at the Founding, both the elite and popular democratic positions have evolved over the years. We define elite democracy as a system in which elites acquire the power to rule by a free competition for the people's votes; between elections the elites are given substantial autonomy to govern as they see fit. Over the years, the increasing complexity of society has been used to buttress elite rule, aided by technical experts. The evolution of corporate capitalism has also been used to justify the power of private economic elites over the economy. Times of international crisis and war, which extended for decades during the Cold War against communism, were used to justify giving power over foreign policy to tough and experienced elites in the executive branch. Too much democracy would only weaken us, elites argued.

Popular democrats have not been without resources and influence, however. Since the first ten amendments to the Constitution were added, partly at the insistence of the Antifederalists, popular democrats have succeeded in amending the Constitution in a more democratic direction, including winning the vote for women and African-Americans. The inclusionary logic of democracy, based on the language of equal rights and equal participation, has proven hard to resist. Popular democrats have used that language repeatedly to revive the spirit of protest that began with the Revolution and extend democracy to new arenas. Throughout American history, then, we have seen periods of elite domination and consolidation followed by periods of mass upsurge and democratization.

In addition to organizing the facts of American politics, the theme of the democratic debate helps students to become personally engaged in the material. The book challenges students to examine their own beliefs about democracy. At the most basic level, the democratic debate revolves around different conceptions of human nature. Elite democrats view most people as private and self-interested; with the exception of a well-educated elite, people are not well-suited to make public policy decisions. Popular democrats, on the other hand, view people as political beings by nature; once involved in democratic participation, people are capable of transcending their narrow parochial interests and becoming responsible and intelligent participants in governance. *The Democratic Debate* introduces students to this debate and challenges them to devise their own democratic philosophy based on their own view of human nature.

While we present both sides of the democratic debate, we make no pretense of impartiality; in the pages ahead we develop a popular democratic critique of American politics. We constantly ask the question, How is it possible to increase democratic participation in American politics? By using as our standard of criticism American traditions of grassroots democracy, we can be critical without leaving students wallowing in cynicism or hopelessness. We identify the sources of democratic reform in the American context and we show how popular democratic forces have constantly reasserted themselves, often overcoming what appeared to be overwhelming odds. At the same time that it engages in a hard-hitting critique of the elitist elements in American politics, *The Democratic Debate* ultimately provides a hopeful, and we believe realistic, analysis of the prospects for democracy in the United States.

COVERAGE AND ORGANIZATION OF THE BOOK

The Democratic Debate is organized along conventional lines similar to that of the mainstream texts. We cover the conventional topics, however, in an unconventional manner. We do not sacrifice coverage to develop our theme; rather, we use the theme to draw the reader along, examining all the essential facts and concepts that are covered in other texts. One of the main purposes of a textbook, we believe, is to cover all the important institutions and processes of American politics that should be addressed in an introductory course, thus freeing the instructor to lecture on themes of particular interest that supplement the text.

We also discuss a number of unconventional topics that are not covered in most mainstream texts. We felt, for example, that a book with democracy as its central theme must have a chapter on nonvoting, probably the most serious flaw in American democracy. Chapter 5, "Where Have All the Voters Gone?" examines why so many Americans don't vote and how voters might be mobilized. We have also included a chapter (Chapter 11) on mass movements—their history, tactics, and achievements, and their importance to American democracy.

The book is organized in four parts. Part One deals with the foundational rules and structures of American politics. After a short introductory chapter that lays out the theme of the democratic debate, we go on to examine the Revolution and the struggle over the Constitution. In this book, the chapter on the Founding is not just of historical interest in explaining the Constitution, as it is in most texts; instead, it lays down the basic contours of the democratic debate that has persisted to this day. Chapter 3 then examines the system of federalism, so important to understanding the peculiar nature of American politics. Part One concludes with an analysis of political economy, showing how the private system of wealth formation affects the public system of democratic governance.

Part Two covers the basic processes of participation in American politics. As befits a book that is focused on the issue of democracy, this section is longer than in most texts, spanning seven chapters. Part Two is designed to acquaint students with the basic patterns of participation and the literature in political science that helps explain why some people are well represented in the political system and others are not. In the absence of strong political parties, we argue, other institutions, such as the mass media and interest groups, take over important political functions, with questionable effects for democracy. While fully documenting the phenomenon of nonvoting and other obstacles that lie in the path of increased democratic participation, Part Two ends on a hopeful note by examining the power of mass protest movements in American politics.

Part Three covers the basic institutions of American politics—Congress, the presidency, bureaucracy, and the courts. In Chapter 2, we showed how the original Constitution set up institutions that were quite elitist in nature, with the House of Representatives being the only institution directly elected by the people. Since then, democratic struggles have made the major institutions more responsive to popular pressure. They still contain many elitist elements, however, as we demonstrate. A theme of Part Three is that institutions have an independent effect on political outcomes and on the democratic debate.

Part Four explores the democratic debate further by looking at four policy areas: civil rights and civil liberties, economic policy, social policy, and foreign policy. The democratic debate concerns not just processes and rules but the distribution of rights, resources, and services. Part Four examines contemporary public policy debates through the lens of democracy, concentrating on the question, Does a particular policy enhance or undermine democratic participation?

The Democratic Debate concludes with a short Afterword on the prospects for popular democracy. Although the resources of elite democracy are considerable, we conclude that popular democracy, rooted in deeply held American beliefs, is on the march. The end of the Cold War, in particular, presents an opening for the extension of democracy.

SPECIAL FEATURES

We have included a number of special features to help students learn from the book and deepen their understanding, but we have tried not to clutter the text with too many distractions from the central theme.

To give students a roadmap through the book, we have included an outline at the beginning of each chapter. Important terms are boldfaced, listed at the end of the chapter, and defined in a glossary, and an annotated bibliography follows each chapter.

A boxed feature called "A Closer Look," found in chapters 2–19, provides students with a contemporary example of the democratic debate. In Chapter 5 on voting and nonvoting, the feature is "Mobilizing the Latino Vote"; in Chapter 7, "The Media," we look at "The Information Superhighway: Freeway or Toll Road?". In Chapter 15 on the judiciary we take up "Clarence Thomas and the Politics of Judicial Selection." We hope that "A Closer Look" will encourage students to be more critical consumers of the news media.

TEACHING AND LEARNING AIDS

- An *Instructor's Resource Manual with Test Items*, written by Lance Denning and Christopher Grill, graduate students at the State University of New York—Albany, accompanies the text, providing ideas for lectures and innovative classroom exercises. The text's focus on the debate over models of democracy will, we believe, help to stimulate class discussion. The manual includes a wide array of test questions, including multiple choice, identification, and essay; the test questions are available on computer disk as well.

- A set of 25 acetate transparencies is available to instructors upon adoption of the text.

- Also available to instructors is the *Houghton Mifflin Video Program in American Government*, a series of six 30-minute videos produced by Professors Ralph Baker and Joseph Losco of Ball State University. The videos, on subjects including the 1992 election, the Clean Air Act, and the Webster case, include interviews with journalists and political scientists. Accompanying the videos is a video guide that provides shot lists, transcripts, and test questions.

- New in 1994 is a 60-minute videodisc of archival material. There are four parts—the presidency, civil rights, campaigns, and Watergate—and the disc is accompanied by a video guide that describes each segment and provides barcodes for use in illustrated lectures.

ACKNOWLEDGMENTS

Like democracy itself, this text has benefited from the participation of many people. We were fortunate to have a series of dedicated professionals to guide the project at Houghton Mifflin. Gregory Tobin worked with us at the inception and Margaret Seawell helped us though most of the process of development. Jean Woy's sound judgment was a comfort to us in the latter stages of the project.

Fran Gay helped guide the book through production. Naomi Kornhauser helped select appealing cartoons and photos. A special thanks goes to Janet Young, whose untiring patience and attention to detail made this book much more attractive and accurate than it otherwise would have been.

Our friends and colleagues Walter Balk, Susan Christopherson, Marty Edelman, Anne Hildreth, and Steve Wasby provided insightful feedback on a number of chapters. A number of graduate students at SUNY—Albany, including Marty Shaffer and David Filbert, helped us with research on the text. Michael Gizzi and Lance Denning wrote the glossary and assisted with the research.

The book benefited greatly from the comments of many political scientists across the country. Fortunately, these outside reviewers did not spare us in their criticisms, and although we squirmed, the book was ultimately much better because of their efforts.

The following individuals gave us valuable criticism on the manuscript: Gordon Alexandre, Glendale Community College; Judith A. Baer, Texas A&M University; Sue Davis, University of Delaware; Dennis J. Goldford, Drake University; Steven Hoffman, University of St. Thomas; James Hogan, Seattle University; Robert Kerstein, University of Tampa; Kenneth Kennedy, College of San Mateo; James Meader, Augustana College; Jerome O'Callaghan, State University of New York at Cortland; Mark P. Petracca, University of California, Irvine; George Pippin, Jones County Junior College; Ted Radke, Contra Costa Community College; Leonard Ritt, Northern Arizona University; and John Squibb, Lincoln Land Community College.

An additional seven reviewers provided criticism of our original prospectus: Theodore S. Arrington, University of North Carolina at Charlotte; Jim Bromeland, Winona State University; John P. Burke, University of Vermont; Allan J. Cigler, University of Kansas; Henry Flores, St. Mary's University; Dr. Virginia G. McClamm, City College of San Francisco; M. Elliot Vittes, University of Central Florida.

We especially want to acknowledge the work of our editor, Ann West. Like the best editors, Ann entered into the spirit of the project and helped us to write the kind of book we wanted to write. She constantly fed us new ideas and prodded us to put our thoughts in plain English. Ann responded to our anxieties with unflappable good humor and optimism that helped us to persevere. The book is immeasurably better because of her efforts. Thanks, Ann.

Finally, we want to thank our families for their support and love: Melinda, Nick, Anna, Fay, Eva, Rosa, and Jessica.

B.M., R.S., T.S.

Bruce Miroff (Ph.D. University of California, Berkeley, 1974) is a professor of political science at the State University of New York, Albany. He is the author of *Pragmatic Illusions: The Presidential Politics of John F. Kennedy* and *Icons of Democracy: American Leaders as Heroes, Aristocrats, Dissenters, and Democrats*, along with numerous articles on the presidency, political leadership, and American political theory.

Raymond Seidelman (Ph.D. Cornell University, 1979) has taught American politics at Sarah Lawrence College in Yonkers, New York, since 1982. Seidelman is the author of *Disenchanted Realists* and the coeditor of *Discipline and History*, books about the development of political and social science in America.

Todd Swanstrom (Ph.D. Princeton University, 1981) teaches at the State University of New York at Albany. Specializing in urban politics and public policy, he is the author of *The Crisis of Growth Politics: Cleveland, Kucinich, and the Challenge of Urban Populism* and coauthor of *City Politics: Private Power and Public Policy*.

THE

DEMOCRATIC

DEBATE

PART

·ONE·

FOUNDATIONS

The foundations of American politics do not reflect an uncompromising commitment to democracy. Instead, they reflect a tension between elitist and democratic tendencies. This essential tension was present at the American founding, and even though it has changed form over the years, it animates a democratic debate that still shapes American politics. Part One looks at the basic political rules and structures that lie behind this tension.

Chapter 1 advances the theme of the book—that American politics can be understood as an ongoing debate between "elite democracy" and "popular democracy." This democratic debate serves as a framework for organizing and evaluating the facts of American politics.

Chapter 2 covers the Revolution and the Constitution. It describes how the democratic debate began in the struggle between the Federalists and Anti-federalists over the ratification of the Constitution. It is essential to study the founding period not only to understand the Constitution but also to grasp the basic contours of the democratic debate.

American politics grows out of a system of federalism that divides power among federal, state, and local governments. Chapter 3 examines the changing balance of power among these levels of government over the years, showing how the rules of federalism help determine who wins and who loses in American politics.

The foundational rules of American politics govern the private sector as well as government. Part I ends with Chapter 4 on political economy that traces the emergence of large corporations and investigates the challenge that they present for democracy.

Introduction:
The Democratic Debate

M en, by their constitutions, are naturally divided into two parties: 1. Those who fear and distrust the people, and wish to draw all powers from them into the hands of the higher classes. 2. Those who identify themselves with the people, have confidence in them, cherish and consider them as the most honest and safe, although not the most wise, depository of the public interests. . . . The appellation of Aristocrats and Democrats is the true one, expressing the essence of all.

Thomas Jefferson, *Writings*, Vol. XVI, p. 73

A mericans view themselves as a model democracy for the world. As long-time democrats, we cheer the new democratic movements struggling to overcome the entrenched elites in China, Latin America, Eastern Europe, and the former states of the Soviet Union. The media treatment of these movements has been reassuring, even self-congratulatory: Aren't these countries struggling to create the same democratic free market societies we created in this country? As this text will show, the struggle for democracy actually is taking place in the United States *at the same time* that it is taking place in these other countries.

A democratic debate lies at the heart of American politics. The central idea of democracy is quite simple. Democracy originated in the fifth century B.C. in the small city-states of Greece. The word *democracy* comes from the Greek words *demos*, meaning "the people," and *kratein*, meaning "to rule." Democracy, therefore, means simply "rule by the people." Defined as "rule by the people," democracy, Americans agree, is the best form of government. Americans disagree, however, about what democracy means in practice and how far democratic decision making should be extended.

One of the fundamental disagreements is over who is best suited for democratic decision making: the masses or political elites. *Elites* are small groups of people who possess extraordinary amounts of power. Throughout history, advocates of elite rule have argued that ruling is too difficult for ordinary citizens. Elites dominate many political systems—including communist, aristocratic, and even democratic ones—controlling ordinary citizens. Elitism comes in various forms, with claims to rule based on different criteria. A totalitarian regime, for

Before being violently evicted by the army from Tiananmen Square on June 4, 1989, strikers protesting for democracy in Beijing, China, constructed a plaster statue. Called the Goddess of Democracy, the statue is reminiscent of the American Statue of Liberty.

instance, is ruled by an elite few with unlimited power to control the daily lives of the citizens; a theocracy is a system run by religious elites. Although these are among the most extreme forms of elitism, even U.S. democracy is seen by some as controlled by a group of highly educated and wealthy elites. This was C. Wright Mills's central argument in *The Power Elite.* Many Americans would support the representation of citizens by a well-heeled and -educated few, who are best qualified to make important decisions.

Few Americans are classical elitists, however; a strong democratic impulse pervades American culture and politics. Anyone who argued that family genes, religious training, or even wealth automatically qualified a person to rule would not be taken seriously in the U.S. Americans believe in the democratic principle that political power ultimately should stem from the people. Americans also agree on certain basic principles of democratic government, including the importance of a written constitution, representative institutions, and basic rights such as freedom of speech and press. Throughout American history, political movements have risen to extend democratic citizenship to blacks, women, and other excluded groups. Political equality is a strong value in American politics.

A deep elitist strain, however, also pervades our politics. Americans believe in rule by the people, for example, but every time we cede power over war and peace to an executive elite on the grounds that "the president knows best," Americans buy into elitism. Americans generally support elitism not because they believe elites are inherently superior to the common people, but because they believe elites have the specialized knowledge and experience to make the best decisions. In a modern high-tech world, democracy must often defer to specialized expertise, whether in government or private corporations. Democracy is a fine ideal, many people argue, but to be realistic and effective, "the people" must cede much of their power of decision making to elites.

The thesis of this text is simple: American politics is characterized by a fundamental conflict between elite democracy and popular democracy. **Elite democracy** is a political system in which elites acquire power by a free and fair competition for the people's votes.[1] Once elected, elites should be given the freedom to rule as they see fit. If the people do not like the results, they can vote them out at the next election and put a different elite into office. Under elite democracy, the people are not expected to participate in the day-to-day affairs of governing.

Popular democracy has its roots in **direct democracy,** in which all citizens gather in one place to vote on important matters. In the Greek city-states, where democracy originated 2500 years ago, democracy meant face-to-face debate and decision making by all citizens, with offices rotating among the citizens. Some examples of direct democracy still exist in the United States, such as the New England town meeting, where all town citizens gather in one hall to debate and decide important issues.

Popular democracy is the adaptation of direct democracy to a large country with a modern economy and society. **Popular democracy** can be defined as a political system in which the people are involved as much as possible in making the decisions that affect their lives.[2] Popular democrats maintain that ordinary citizens can be closely involved in governing and that, in the long run, they will govern more wisely than elites. In a large country, popular democrats admit, everyone cannot meet in one place to make decisions. Political representatives are needed, but they should remain as close as possible to the people who elected them, accurately reflecting their values and interests. Between elections, citizens should be involved in political affairs, holding representatives accountable and making sure that the experts, who are necessary in a complex modern society, serve the needs of the people and not the needs of elites.

It is important to recognize that popular democracy is not the same as majority rule. Ironically enough, majorities have often supported elite rule and undemocratic values. For example, ordinary citizens often defer to corporate elites in the private marketplace, and for much of American history a majority opposed giving full civil rights to blacks and women. Popular democrats believe that democracy requires more than majority rule; it requires basic levels of toleration, respect for individual rights, and equality. There is no guarantee that the people will always choose wisely in a democracy, but in the long run we are better off with rule by the people than rule by elites. The greatest threat to democratic values comes from elites, not from the masses.

At the heart of American politics lies an essential tension. We are not the first to present a conflict interpretation of American politics. Marxists have long focused on the "contradictions" of capitalism, particularly the conflict between workers and capitalists. Although class inequalities have caused division in American politics, the fundamental conflict has been between elite democracy and popular democracy. The United States does have a radical political tradition, but it is rooted in home-grown ideas of popular democracy rather than in European socialist concepts.

As we flesh out the principles of elite and popular democracy that serve as the framework of this text, we begin in the 1780s, the founding period when the U.S. Constitution was written and approved.

ORIGINS OF THE DEMOCRATIC DEBATE: THE FOUNDING

Normally, the founding period is treated as a celebration of the American consensus on democracy as embodied in the Constitution. As Chapter 2 shows, however, the U.S. Constitution was born in conflict, not in consensus. The ratification of the Constitution did not end debate but began a new debate about the meaning of democracy. The terms of this debate, which were laid down over two hundred years ago, continue to influence American politics to this day.

Our Constitution was not written by lofty statesmen who offered their eternal truths to a grateful nation. The men who wrote the Constitution were practical politicians with pressing political objectives. The framers distrusted popular democracy, especially the power of the majority.[3] The supporters of the U.S. Constitution in the late 1780s' debate over ratification, known as **Federalists,** were the founders of elite democracy in the United States. The Constitution they wrote and ratified was mixed, containing elements of both elitism and democracy. The original Constitution placed severe limits on majority rule and contained many elitist elements; neither the president nor senators, for example, were to be elected directly by the people. (In the original Constitution, senators were chosen by state legislatures and presidents were elected by an elite, the Electoral College, appointed under procedures chosen by the state legislatures.)

The ratification of the Constitution was bitterly opposed by a group known as the **Anti-federalists.** The Anti-federalists were the founders of popular democracy in the United States.[4] The Anti-federalists denounced the proposed Constitution as a betrayal of the democratic spirit of 1776 and the American Revolution itself. The new Constitution, they protested, gave too much power to the central government and took too much away from the states and localities. In the long run, they charged, it would erode the face-to-face participation necessary for a healthy democracy. The Anti-federalists were not a marginal group; many state conventions ratified the Constitution by only the narrowest of margins.

Federalists and Anti-federalists disagreed about the most basic questions of human nature, society, and politics (see Chapter 2). In the eyes of the Federalists, the mass of Americans were passionate and selfish creatures. In a small republic where simple majority rule prevailed, nothing would stop this mass from taking away the rights or the property of the minority. But in a national republic, where the majority could not rule directly, minority rights would be protected. Elite representatives, likely to be drawn from the wisest and most virtuous segment of society, would rise above selfish conflicts and pursue the common good. Should these elites themselves go astray, other elites would check them through the ingenious constitutional system of checks and balances.

Anti-federalists had more faith in the common people. They believed that most people could be educated into civic virtue, overcoming their selfish inclinations and learning to pursue the common good. They wanted representatives who would not claim superiority over the masses, but who would faithfully reflect ordinary citizens' grievances and aspirations. To the Anti-federalists, the main threat to democracy came not from majorities but from selfish and powerful elites. Instead of elites checking elites, they wanted ordinary citizens to check elites and hold them accountable. The best way to protect against tyranny of an aristocratic elite was to have the people participate in the political process.

The original debate between Federalists and Anti-federalists had its limitations. In contemporary terms, neither the Federalists nor the Anti-federalists were true democrats. Many on both sides owned slaves, for example. Neither advocated citizenship rights for women, African Americans, Indians, and other excluded groups. Both Federalists and Anti-federalists supported property qualifications for voting.

Although the Federalists and Anti-federalists were limited by the prejudices of their times, they laid down the basic principles of the democratic debate that have animated American politics to the present. Even though the principles have remained the same, the debate between elite and popular democrats has evolved dramatically in response to the changes in American society over the past two centuries. Understanding this evolution is necessary to understand the contemporary democratic debate.

EVOLUTION OF POPULAR DEMOCRACY: THE LOGIC OF INCLUSION

The Anti-federalists are normally viewed as losers who had little impact on American politics. This is false. Although the Anti-federalists lost the initial struggle over the Constitution, their perspective has had a tremendous influence on American politics.

If the founding document of elite democracy is the Constitution of 1787, the founding document of popular democracy is the Declaration of Independence of 1776. With its bold statement that "all men are created equal" and are "endowed by their Creator with certain unalienable Rights," the Declaration laid down the basic principles of popular democracy. The Declaration of Independence proclaimed a radical idea: If the government violates people's rights, they have a right "to alter or abolish it." This "Spirit of '76"—based on political equality, rights, and rebellion—has inspired popular democrats ever since.

The democratic faith of Americans, as expressed in the Declaration of Independence, has given popular democrats an ideological advantage and frequently placed elite democrats on the defensive. In 1791, for example, two years after the Constitution was ratified, the first ten amendments—the Bill of Rights—were added, mostly at the insistence of the Anti-federalists, who wanted to ensure protection of their political rights. (Chapter 16 discusses the importance of civil rights and civil liberties for popular democracy.) Nearly all the amendments to the Constitution since then have moved it in a popular democratic direction, including the Fifteenth Amendment, which extended the legal right to vote to blacks in 1870; the Seventeenth Amendment, which required the direct election of senators in 1913; the Nineteenth Amendment, which extended the right to vote to women in 1920; and the Twenty-sixth Amendment, which gave the vote to eighteen- to twenty-year-olds in 1971.

Popular democratic influence, however, has not been limited to amending the Constitution. It has also affected how we interpret the Constitution. Elected in 1800, Thomas Jefferson, who shared many of the beliefs of the Anti-federalists, can be viewed as our nation's first popular democratic president. As such, Jefferson could have proposed writing a new constitution. Instead he decided to infuse democratic content into the Constitution of 1787 by expanding the participation of common people in governmental decision making. Jefferson supported a narrow interpretation of the powers of the federal government, preferring that as many decisions as possible be made by state and local governments that were closer to the people. Jefferson's attempt to read popular democratic views into the Constitution was pivotal in American history and helps explain why Americans love the Constitution, but disagree so vehemently about how to interpret it.

Although politicians like Jefferson, at the top of the political system, sometimes championed popular democracy, more often its impulses came from ordinary citizens. Throughout American history, popular democrats have mobilized the masses to expand democratic decision making. Periods of elite dominance have given way to periods of mass participation and popular democratic upsurge, such as the 1890s, the 1930s, and the 1960s.[5] During the last period, the civil rights, feminist, environmental, and neighborhood organizing movements, among others, challenged the power of entrenched elites and forged landmark legislation such as the 1964 Civil Rights Act and the 1970 Environmental Protection Act.

In mobilizing people for mass movements, popular democrats have appealed to the ideas of political equality and rights found in the Declaration of Independence. In 1848, for example, Elizabeth Cady Stanton used the language of the Declaration of Independence to write a women's declaration of independence.

Following a long tradition of protest in American politics, demonstrators gather in New York City on April 8, 1969, to protest the war in Vietnam.

Her Declaration of Sentiments is considered the founding document of the women's rights movement, which won the right to vote in 1920 and flowered into a modern feminist movement in the 1960s. In the 1950s and 1960s, Martin Luther King, Jr., used the popular democratic language of rights and equality to energize the civil rights movement and appeal successfully to a broad white audience. The civil rights movement, examined in Chapter 11, shows how protest politics goes beyond electoral politics and uses the techniques of direct action to empower the powerless.

EVOLUTION OF ELITE DEMOCRACY: THE LOGIC OF EXPERTISE

Elite democrats have not stood still while popular democrats pushed for extending democracy. Throughout American history, elite democrats have been immensely resourceful, devising new arguments for limiting democracy. In the early years of the republic, many openly defended elite values. The democratization of American values, however, has rendered such naked appeals to elitism illegitimate. Elitism is no longer defended on the grounds that elites are inherently superior to the masses or that certain people are destined to rule. In contemporary American society, elites profess democratic values but maintain that elite rule is necessary in many spheres of modern society. Elite democrats would not admit they are elitist; they would simply say they are realistic.

The elite democratic position cannot be easily dismissed. When we ride on an airplane, for example, we do not take a vote to see how high the plane will fly or who will serve as pilot. Everyone acknowledges that democratic decision making must defer to rule by experts, or technical elites, in particular situations. But where do we draw the line? Elite democrats believe that in a rapidly changing, technologically complex, and dangerous world more and more power must be ceded to elites—elites whose power is justified not by birth or wealth, but by their knowledge, expertise, and experience. Democracy is viewed as a kind of luxury that we cannot "afford" too much of, especially given our desire for economic growth and the necessity to compete with other nations for economic, political, and military advantage.

The elite democratic position has evolved over the years, especially in response to changing economic conditions. At the time of the debate over the Constitution, few private corporations existed and those that did were small and family owned. By the late nineteenth century, huge railroad and industrial corporations controlled national markets and employed thousands of workers. These private corporations were run in a top-down fashion by wealthy elites. Elite democrats argued that the owners of capital should be free to run the corporations as they saw fit. Corporations would be held accountable by market competition; by giving free rein to the corporations, government would encourage economic growth that would, in the long run, benefit everyone. This argument for elite autonomy based on free market capitalism has continued into the present period of multinational corporations. Chapter 4 examines the argument for free market capitalism that is so important for contemporary elite democrats, as well as the popular democratic response that corporations exert power over the marketplace and thus must be held directly accountable by democratic means.

A popular democratic movement emerged in the late nineteenth century, called populism, that challenged the control of corporate elites over the economy. In the crucial election of 1896, however, the populist candidate, William Jennings Bryan, was defeated by the candidate of big business, William McKinley. Drawing on huge corporate contributions, McKinley is credited with having pioneered the first modern campaign using mass media techniques of persuasion. McKinley's victory ushered in a long period of declining party competition and voter turnout. Chapters 7, 8, and 9 document the power that money can exert over the electoral process when parties decline and their functions are taken over by the mass media.

In the political struggles produced by economic changes, elite democrats and popular democrats have reversed some of their original positions. One of the most important shifts concerns whether power should be centralized in the national government or decentralized into the states and localities. At the time of the founding, elite democrats like Alexander Hamilton favored a strong national government, while popular democrats wanted states and localities to retain most powers. The rise of powerful corporations and the generation of tremendous inequalities in the private economy caused popular democrats to reverse their position and favor expanded powers for the federal government. Popular democrats increasingly have turned to the federal government as a counterweight to the power of private corporations and to ensure action on behalf of the disadvantaged. This happened during the Great Depression of the 1930s. When the states and localities failed to respond adequately to the desperate needs of the poor and unemployed, Franklin Roosevelt dramatically expanded the powers of the federal government.

Present-day elite democrats have often appealed to the popular democratic value of states rights or local control in order to defend elite privileges. States rights was used for many years to prevent the federal government from intervening to guarantee blacks the right to vote. The need to expand the powers of the federal government, however, has placed popular democrats on the horns of a dilemma: Although an expanded federal government is necessary to address inequalities and curb the powers of entrenched elites, the result is a government removed from popular democratic participation. Chapter 3 examines this dilemma of federalism.

Although elite and popular democrats have nearly switched positions in domestic policy, in foreign policy elites continue to favor decision making by the few whereas popular democrats remain suspicious of centralized power and its potential for elite tyranny. In the twentieth century, many argue that trends in this country and in the world justify concentrating power in the hands of experienced elites. These trends include the increasing complexity of social relations, the mobility of capital in an international economy, and the alarming speed of modern warfare in a rapidly shrinking globe. Just as the Anti-federalists feared, the president has gained substantial powers at the expense of Congress, which is often viewed as too slow to act effectively in the modern world. In particular, the Cold War against communism was used to justify the creation of what we call in Chapter 19 the "national security state"—a shadow government, led by an elite in the executive branch, that has substantial power over American foreign policy with little congressional oversight. Popular support for the national security state demonstrates that elitism has not been supported only by elites; ironically, elitism has often enjoyed widespread popular backing.

SUMMARIZING THE DEMOCRATIC DEBATE

Because Americans agree on democracy, everyone who runs for elected office uses the myths, symbols, and rhetoric of democracy. Everyone supposedly agrees that democracy is the American way. According to the consensus view of American politics, there are no more burning debates about the rules of the game. If Americans disagree, it is over specific policies, not the structure of politics.

This consensus view of American politics fundamentally distorts reality. Americans do disagree about the rules of the game. In particular, Americans disagree about the meaning of democracy and how far democratic decision making should be extended into society. This text argues for a conflict, not a consensus, approach to American politics. American politics is best understood as embodying an essential tension, or conflict, between two different conceptions of democracy: elite democracy and popular democracy. The essential points of both can be summarized as follows:

Elite Democracy

1. With the exception of an educated, largely white male, elite, most people are uninterested in politics and uninformed about issues; most people are more interested in their own private lives than in politics.

2. When the masses do get involved in politics, they tend to be highly emotional and intolerant; the main threat to democracy comes from the masses, not from elites.

3. Democracy basically means free and fair elections in which elites acquire the power to rule by competing for people's votes.

4. The main goal of democracy should be to protect the right of individuals to pursue their own interests. Because of varying talents and ambitions, democracies must tolerate a great deal of inequality.

5. Political representatives should filter the views of the people through their superior expertise, intelligence, and temperament.

6. Reforms in America almost always come about gradually, through the actions of elites.

Popular Democracy

1. People are naturally inclined to participate in the decisions that affect their lives; if they don't participate, something must be wrong with the democratic system.

2. Through democratic participation people can overcome their parochial interests and become public-spirited citizens. When their powers and privileges are threatened, elites often respond by curtailing democracy; the main threat to democracy comes from selfish elites, not from ordinary citizens.

3. Democracy means more than fair elections; it means the participation of ordinary citizens in the decisions that affect their lives in an atmosphere of tolerance and trust.

4. The main goal of democracy should be to strengthen community; inequalities that divide the community should be minimized.

5. Representatives should stay as close to their constituents as possible, accurately reflecting their views in the political system.

6. Meaningful reforms in American politics have almost always come about because of political pressure from below by ordinary citizens.

‖ NTERPRETING POLITICAL FACTS: THE PROBLEM OF PARTICIPATION

It is easy to become confused by the complexity of American politics. Magazines, newspapers, radio, and TV bombard us with facts about political negotiations in Congress, interest-group bargaining, maneuverings of the political parties, the state of the economy and its effect on political fortunes, key decisions by the Supreme Court, and the actions of foreign countries. The sheer volume of political facts threatens to overwhelm our ability to comprehend them. Students of American politics need an organizing framework to make sense of these facts—to identify patterns, decide which facts are important, and evaluate political outcomes.

The ideas of elite and popular democracy can serve as an interpretive framework to help us make sense of American politics. To understand how this framework is used in the text, apply it to one example: the different ways people interpret basic facts about political participation in American politics (a topic covered in Chapter 5).

The facts of political participation in the United States are well known. Voting is the most common political act, yet only a little over one-half of the eligible electorate voted in the most recent presidential election; the turnout rate in off-year congressional elections is only about one-third.[6]

Although these facts are straightforward, making sense of them is more difficult. For example, how do we assess the simple fact that about half of the eligible electorate votes in presidential elections? Is the glass half full or half empty? What you see depends as much on your interpretation of the facts as on the facts themselves.

For elite democrats the glass of democratic participation is half full. According to this view, the fact that only about half the people participate in elections is a sign of a healthy democracy. People are not inclined to participate in politics; most prefer to spend their time in private pursuits: making a living, raising children, or watching TV. The fact that many people do not participate in politics is a sign of satisfaction. After all, nothing is stopping them from voting— legal barriers to voting have been eliminated (property qualifications, poll taxes, literacy tests). If the masses of nonvoters felt their interests were threatened by government, they could mobilize their slack resources, including the vote, and influence the system. Moreover, because we know that nonvoters tend to be less educated, we should be happy that many do not participate in politics. As *Newsweek* columnist George Will put it: "The reasonable assumption about electorates is: smaller is smarter."[7]

Popular democrats contest the elite democratic interpretation of the facts of participation on every count. For them, the glass of democratic participation is at least half empty. They see low levels of political participation as a sign of a sick democracy. Popular democrats believe that people are naturally inclined to participate in the governance of their societies. When they don't participate, something must be wrong. Although there are no legal barriers preventing Americans from participating in the political process, popular democrats argue, many people are so alienated from politics that they view their own participation as meaningless. They see the decisive role of money in elections and conclude that ordinary citizens can have little influence. Moreover, when they see the limited choices on the ballot, they think who wins doesn't matter. In short, those who fail to participate in politics are not satisfied, they are *discouraged*.

Who is right? As the example of participation shows, political facts do not speak for themselves. The same facts can be seen from radically different perspectives. Interpreting the facts of American politics is like viewing a Gestalt drawing (Figure 1.1); what is seen depends on the observer. Do you see a vase or two faces? You can see one or the other, but you cannot see both at the same time. As with the Gestalt diagram, we must interpret the facts of American politics to give them meaning. Elite and popular views of democracy are the two frameworks we will use to interpret the facts of American politics.

There is an important difference, however, between interpreting the Gestalt drawing and interpreting political facts. What you see in the Gestalt diagram does not affect anyone's interest. In politics, interpretations of the facts are hotly contested because they directly affect people's interests. Consider the different interpretations of nonvoting. If nonvoting is an expression of satisfaction, then the system is legitimate—those in power are viewed as having the right to rule. On the other hand, if nonvoting is an expression of alienation, then the government loses legitimacy and political protests outside of normal channels, such as street demonstrations and civil disobedience, are justified. Our interpreta-

FIGURE 1.1

Gestalt Drawing

tions of political facts shape our evaluations of right and wrong, and what should and shouldn't be done.

CONCLUSION: JOINING THE DEMOCRATIC DEBATE

We must end this Introduction with a warning: The authors of this text are not neutral observers of the democratic debate. Although we present both sides, we defend popular democracy and develop a popular democratic critique of American politics. We do so to redress an imbalance that is unconsciously embedded in most treatments of American politics, both in scholarly texts and in the mass media.

Finally, we invite readers not to accept our bias but to critically examine their own views toward democracy. In short, we invite you to join the democratic debate.

KEY TERMS   elite democracy   Federalists
                direct democracy   Anti-federalists
                popular democracy

SUGGESTED   Robert A. Dahl, *Who Governs? Democ-*   govern cities with little input from the
READINGS   *racy and Power in an American City*   masses of ordinary citizens.
                (New Haven, Conn.: Yale University
                Press, 1961). An influential community   Robert A. Dahl, *Democracy and Its Crit-*
                power study arguing that plural elites   *ics* (New Haven, Conn.: Yale University

Press, 1989). Moving in a popular democratic direction, Dahl argues here that democratic decision making should be extended into all areas of the society and economy.

G. William Domhoff, *Who Really Rules? New Haven and Community Power Reexamined* (Santa Monica, California: Goodyear, 1978). A critique of Dahl's *Who Governs?* arguing that private elites dictated policy with few democratic checks and balances.

Frances Moore Lappe, *Rediscovering America's Values* (New York: Ballantine Books, 1989). Written as a dialogue between two points of view that correspond closely to elite and popular democracy, the book synthesizes a great deal of information on American value conflicts.

C. Wright Mills, *The Power Elite* (New York: Oxford University Press, 1956). The classic statement that America is ruled by a small elite that occupies the command posts at the top of the economy, the polity, and the military.

The Revolution and the Constitution: Origins of the Democratic Debate

W hen modern American politicians hope to establish their noble aspirations and to wrap themselves in the mantle of higher authority, they invariably turn to the founders of the Republic—even to those whose ideas seem very different from their own. Proclaiming a new national beginning after the dark days of Watergate, President Gerald Ford, a conservative, quoted radical Thomas Paine on our revolutionary beginnings. President Bill Clinton, an advocate of an activist national government, is fond of citing Thomas Jefferson, who favored local action and feared national power. Probably the most remarkable recent use of the authority of the founders came from President Ronald Reagan, who called the Nicaraguan *contras*, counterrevolutionaries notorious for their brutal deeds, "the moral equivalent of our founding fathers." Republicans or

Democrats, conservatives or liberals, American political leaders speak in hushed tones of the founders as our political saints.

Ford, Clinton, and Reagan drew on assumptions about the founders that most Americans hold: that the founders agreed among themselves about the fundamental premises of politics and government; that they believed in the same kind of democracy that we profess; and that they were above the petty desires for power and wealth that seem to drive most present-day American political leaders. All of these assumptions are essentially false. The founders of the Republic did not agree among themselves; they argued vehemently about fundamental issues of human nature, society, and government. Many were skeptical about democracy and its values, and held to an elitist conception of government that no contemporary American politician would dare to profess openly. Struggles over power and wealth were as central to their politics as to our own.

This chapter demonstrates how the American political system was born not in consensus but in conflict. The Revolution and the Constitution did not settle the basic issues at stake in the democratic debate; rather, they began that debate and established the terms in which later generations would carry it forward. The Constitution did not enshrine democracy as we know it today; its framers wrote a mixed constitution that contained both popular and elite elements. American political life at the time of our founding was characterized by an essential tension between popular and elite democracy—a tension that has driven our politics ever since.

To understand our founding, we must follow a story with many twists and turns. The chapter begins as Americans cast off their colonial past and launch a bold experiment in republican politics. Next, we observe the hopeful political spirit of 1776, expressed in the philosophy of the Declaration of Independence and the political institutions of the first state constitutions and the Articles of Confederation. But this revolutionary beginning, marked by popular democratic assumptions, becomes caught up in economic conflict and political controversy. Rejecting popular democracy, the advocates of a new constitution establish a political order in which elite democratic assumptions are predominant. The ratification of the new constitution in turn provokes a fundamental and wide-ranging argument between elite democrats and popular democrats.

The aim of this chapter is to explain how Americans came to have the political system under which we have lived for over two centuries. The focus is not only on institutions and processes but also on values, ideas, and political philosophies. The era of the Revolution and the Constitution shaped the ways Americans would practice politics. But it also shaped the ways Americans would *think* about politics. This shared attitude—our political identity—cannot be understood until we explore the story of our founding.

That story had no final victory for either elite democrats or popular democrats. From the start, American political identity was contested and debated. In studying the Revolution and the Constitution, we witness the origins of this democratic debate. Particularly in the argument over the new Constitution, which pitted

Federalists against Anti-federalists, the democratic debate was launched with a depth and passion that still echo in today's politics.

FROM COLONIALS TO REVOLUTIONARIES

In 1763, the idea that the American colonies of Great Britain would declare their independence, start a revolution, and shape a political system unlike any then known would have seemed absurd. In the first place, the colonists enjoyed their status as outposts of a glorious empire. England, their "mother country," was nurturing and permissive. The colonies flourished economically and possessed a considerable degree of liberty and self-government under the relatively lax British administration. Second, the colonists not only thought of themselves as English people but also resembled them in many respects. Historian Gordon Wood has written that colonial America was, like Britain, a "monarchical" society, hierarchical in character and dominated by a small elite of "gentlemen."[1] Americans felt a strong allegiance to the King and liked to celebrate his birthday with rousing alcoholic toasts.

But in 1763, the British had just defeated the French and Spanish in the Seven Years' War and established their dominance in the New World. They needed revenues to pay off the debts incurred in this war. As beneficiaries of the British efforts, the American colonists seemed the obvious targets for new taxation. This assumption proved, however, to be disastrous for the British. Colonial America responded to the first British tax levies, the Sugar Act and the Stamp Act, with spirited resistance. While American writers denounced taxes imposed by a Parliament in which the colonies were not represented, American "patriots" formed organizations known as the Sons of Liberty and mobbed stamp collectors until they resigned their royal commissions.

For the next decade, a political dynamic developed that led the Americans toward independence. When the British eased their attempts at taxation, peace returned. But every time they tried to reassert their authority, the American spirit of resistance grew stronger. It was not that Americans rushed eagerly into revolutionary politics; even the leaders of the patriot forces continued to swear allegiance to the (unwritten) British constitution and to claim that they were only seeking to preserve the rights of all Englishmen. Yet the increasingly bitter conflict wore away old loyalties and fostered a growing sense of an independent American identity.[2]

Two events epitomized the colonists' growing radicalism. One was the famous Boston Tea Party in 1773, as Boston patriots, disguised as Indians, dumped a shipload of tea into the harbor in protest of a tax on the beverage. Notable here was the colonists' militance, their reliance on direct popular action to redress a grievance. A second event was the fiery rhetoric of the most widely read pamphlet calling on Americans to declare their independence, Thomas Paine's *Common Sense*, published early in 1776. Paine poured scorn on a monarch that Americans

After listening to a reading of the Declaration of Independence, a New York crowd of soldiers and civilians pulls down a statue of King George III. The picture dramatizes the overthrow of monarchism (rule by one) by republicanism (popular rule).

customarily had revered. By sending his troops to enforce his taxes with bayonets, George III deserved to be called the "Royal Brute of Britain." Monarchy itself, Paine thundered, was a crime; if we could trace the origins of kings, he wrote, "we should find the first of them nothing better than the principal ruffian of some restless gang. . . ."[3] A decade of resistance and protest had undermined much of the hierarchical thinking of colonial Americans; reading Tom Paine, many of them became filled with a bold and hopeful spirit that was ready to launch a grand revolutionary experiment in popular democracy.

Birth of Republicanism

To understand this revolutionary experiment, we need to look beneath questions of taxation and representation. Contemporary historians have identified a deeper level of thought that transformed loyal colonials into defiant revolutionaries. This body of thought shaped the political activities of Americans and infused them with the revolutionary "spirit of '76." The name historians have given to this body of thought is **republicanism.** (The republicanism of the Revolution should not be confused with the ideas of the Republican party, formed in the 1850s.) Eighteenth-century republican ideas led Americans to interpret the actions of the British government as a sinister threat to liberty. They also propelled Americans to seek new and more popular forms of government to replace the British model.[4]

What were the central ideas of republican ideology and how did they shape the thinking of the American revolutionaries? We focus on four interrelated ideas: liberty versus power, legislatures versus executives, virtue, and the small republic.

Liberty versus Power. Eighteenth-century republicans saw the struggle between liberty and power as the core of political life. *Power* meant dominion or control. Although necessary for the maintenance of order, power was, by its nature, aggressive. Its tendency was to exceed legitimate boundaries and to invade the sphere of liberty. By *liberty,* republicans meant both private liberty—such as property rights—and public liberty—the right of the people to have a collective say in government. This view of politics made the actions of the British government especially frightening to the American colonists. The taxes imposed by London, the flood of new royal officials to rule over the colonists, and the troops eventually sent to America to support both were read not as limited measures but as steps in a comprehensive plot to reduce Americans to servility and slavery.

Legislatures versus Executives. Republican theory identified power largely with executives. Executives were entrusted with enforcing the laws, but they had a natural inclination to arbitrary rule and self-aggrandizement. Thus, executives were seen as the most likely threats to liberty. Legislatures, on the other hand, were the most likely defenders of liberty. Closer to the people, mirroring the people's desires, cherishing the people's liberties, the legislature was the natural adversary of the executive. This view helped Americans make sense of their quarrel with Britain. Executives—the royal governors appointed by London, the ministers of the King, ultimately George III himself—were assailing American liberty; American colonial legislatures and later the Continental Congresses were championing it.

Virtue of the American People. Why were republicans so optimistic about the people and their representatives in the legislature? If all individuals had selfish desires that would be expressed if unchecked power was granted to them, might not the people, under some circumstances, also prove dangerous? Republicans conceded that liberty could go too far and become anarchy. But they hoped for a people characterized by virtue rather than lawlessness. By *virtue,* they meant the willingness of individuals to subordinate their private interests to the common good. Virtue was a passion for the public good superior to all private passions. Americans believed that the British effort to introduce tyranny into the colonies showed that the British government and even the British people had become corrupt; selfishness had destroyed their traditional commitment to liberty. But America—peopled by those who had fled the Old World in search of liberty—was a land where virtue still resided.

The Small Republic. What conditions encouraged virtue? As good republicans, the American revolutionaries stressed such things as simplicity and frugality. But the single most important condition necessary for republican virtue was the small republic. In a large republic, diverse economic interests and dissimilar ways of life would produce factional conflicts, encouraging selfishness and eroding virtue. In a small republic, however, a genuine common interest could be found, for the people would be more homogeneous and united. To the Americans of 1776, the British empire proved how a large republic became hostile to liberty and the common good. The revolutionaries' goal was not to build a large republic of their own but small republics that would nurture virtue and the public good. Their principal political efforts were focused on the governments of the thirteen new states, not on the national government.

Thus, the revolutionary assumptions of 1776 were the danger of power and the need to safeguard liberty, the threat of executives and the confidence in legislatures, the hope for a virtuous people, and the stress on small republics and political decentralization. On the basis of these assumptions, Americans began shaping their own independent governments in 1776. However, each of these assumptions would be challenged in the decade that followed and debated at length in the struggle over the Constitution.

The Spirit of '76

The American Revolution exploded in 1776 with political energy, excitement, and creativity. The institutions it first shaped were soon replaced by others, but the ideals it espoused were to form the base of America's democratic creed. Both the successes and the failures of revolutionary creativity are evident in the Declaration of Independence, the constitutions of the new states, and the Articles of Confederation.

The Declaration of Independence. When the Second Continental Congress finally decided that the moment had arrived for the decisive break between America and Britain, it appointed a small committee to prepare a justification for such revolutionary action. This committee of five wisely turned to its best writer, the young Thomas Jefferson of Virginia. The **Declaration of Independence,** the document that Jefferson drafted and that the Congress adopted with some revisions on July 4, 1776, has become, along with the Constitution, the most hallowed of all American political texts. Its opening words are very familiar, so familiar that we usually do not read them with the care and reflection they deserve.

When in the course of human events, it becomes necessary for one people to dissolve the political bands which have connected them with another, and to assume among the powers of the earth the separate and equal station to which the Laws of Nature and of Nature's God entitle them, a decent respect to the opinions of mankind requires that they should declare the causes which impel them to the separation.

We hold these truths to be self-evident, that all men are created equal, that they are endowed by their Creator with certain unalienable rights, that among these are life, liberty, and the pursuit of happiness. That to secure these rights, governments are instituted among men, deriving their just powers from the consent of the governed. That whenever any form of government becomes destructive of these ends, it is the right of the people to alter or to abolish it, and to institute new government, laying its foundation on such principles and organizing its powers in such form, as to them shall seem most likely to effect their safety and happiness.

Scholars argue about the sources of Jefferson's ideas in the Declaration of Independence. The most common view is that he was influenced by an English philosopher, John Locke. Several of Locke's central themes are evident in the Declaration: that the primary objective of government is the protection of life, liberty, and property, and that all legitimate political authority derives from the consent of the governed and can be taken away from rulers who betray the will of the people. These ideas of Locke are considered central to the political philosophy of liberalism.

If Locke's liberal philosophy is found in the Declaration, the democratic Jefferson gives it a more revolutionary interpretation than the English philosopher intended. The Declaration of Independence establishes equality as the basis for American political thought and makes "life, liberty, and the pursuit of happiness" universal rights. It dethrones government as a higher power and renders it subject to the consent of the people. In its argument, and even in its form, it transforms the nature of political life, supplanting the commands of a king with the discussion and persuasion suitable to a free people.[5]

Like most great documents, the Declaration of Independence bears the marks and limits of its time. Its words about equality and rights were not meant to include women or African Americans. The American revolutionaries used universal terms but restricted them in practice to white males. Still, the Declaration created a standard to which later popular democrats would appeal in efforts to include those who had originally been excluded from its promises. Battling the spread of slavery, Abraham Lincoln grounded his opposition on the words of the Declaration, proclaiming in 1859 that the "principles of Jefferson are the definitions and axioms of free society."[6] Feminist and African-American movements for emancipation have also rested their cases on the Declaration of Independence.[7]

The Revolutionary State Constitutions. The revolutionary ideas of 1776 were also embodied in the first state constitutions. In 1776, ten states established new constitutions to replace their old colonial charters. These constitutions reflected both the struggle with Britain and the core ideas of republicanism. Three features of the new constitutions were noteworthy: the inclusion of a bill of rights, the weakening of executive power, and the enhancement of legislative power.[8]

After years of fighting against British invasions of their rights, Americans wanted to make it clear that these rights were sacred and inviolable, beyond the reach even of the governments that they themselves were establishing. So most of the new constitutions contained a bill of rights; several began their constitutions with such declarations. The most influential of the bills of rights of 1776, that of Virginia, began like the Declaration of Independence: "That all men are by nature equally free and independent, and have certain inherent rights. . . ." The Virginia Bill of Rights also appealed to the republican concept of virtue: "That no free government, or the blessings of liberty, can be preserved to any people, but by a firm adherence to justice, moderation, temperance, frugality and virtue, and by frequent recurrence to fundamental principles."[9]

Colonial experience and republican theory had identified executive power as the chief threat to liberty. Therefore, the revolutionary constitution-makers sought to guard against the return of executive despotism. Revolutionary executives were, intentionally, weak executives. In the first state constitutions, executives were chosen by the legislature and held office for a term of only one year. They were stripped of the executive powers traditionally exercised by the British monarch and left with only modest duties of law enforcement.

The revolutionary mistrust of executives was matched by a trust in legislatures. In the eyes of the constitution-writers of 1776, the legislature would not threaten liberty because it would be close to the people, even an embodiment of the people. Legislators were expected to act as mirrors of the people's views and interests. Therefore, legislatures could safely be granted most of the powers that had been taken away from executives. American revolutionaries were not, however, completely optimistic about legislative politics. The bills of rights they wrote were designed to limit what the legislatures could do. Equally important, the revolutionaries attempted to make the state legislature, particularly the more popular lower house, genuinely representative. This required annual elections so that legislators would frequently be returned to live among the people and feel the effects of the laws they had passed. It also required a large and equal representation so that all areas of a state would be fairly reflected in the deliberations of the legislature.

The Articles of Confederation. The states, not the nation, were seen as the centers of political life in 1776. More than a holdover from colonial experience, the primacy of the states reflected the belief that republics were workable only in a small territory. Consequently, the first American system of national government was a confederation, a loose association of states that agreed to join in a compact for common ends (especially foreign relations and the conduct of war). In a confederation, the individual units remain sovereign, so each state had supreme power within its borders. The **Articles of Confederation,** adopted by

A Revolutionary Experiment in Popular Democracy

The state constitutions written in 1776 reflected the revolutionary desire to restrict the power of rulers and to place government more directly in the hands of the people. No state carried this impulse further than Pennsylvania. The Pennsylvania Constitution of 1776 was the boldest revolutionary experiment in popular democracy.

In most states the struggle for independence created a coalition between the social and economic elite and common people. In Pennsylvania, however, the elite clung to the hope of reconciliation with Britain. Encouraged by champions of independence in the Continental Congress, middle and working-class Pennsylvanians—small merchants, shopkeepers, and artisans—pushed this elite aside. Aiming to shift political control to the people and prevent wealthy gentlemen from resuming their traditional rule, they drafted a constitution whose character was, for its day, remarkably democratic.

The principal institution in the new government was a unicameral (one house) legislature. Pennsylvania democrats saw no need for an "upper" house, which would be dominated by the elite. To ensure that this legislature would represent all the people, the constitution established the easiest suffrage requirement in any of the states. To ensure that it did what the people wanted (and did not become a new elite with interests of its own), it provided for annual elections and prohibited any representative from serving for more than four years out of every seven. Even more fearful of executive despotism than constitution writers in the other states, popular democrats in Pennsylvania eliminated the office of governor,

putting in its place an executive council of twelve, elected directly by the people and holding very limited powers.

Critics complained that this simple form of government placed no checks on the power of the unicameral legislature. Defenders of the constitution responded that it was designed to make the people themselves the check. The constitution made government in Pennsylvania more open to public knowledge and involvement than any other state government. It required that the legislature be open for public attendance and votes be published weekly for public scrutiny. Once the legislature passed a bill, it could not become law until the next session, allowing the people time to consider it and, if they chose, to reject it through their election of new representatives.

Was this popular democratic experiment in government workable? The question is hard to answer because the experiment never had a clear trial. Opponents of the constitution, many from the old social and economic elite, fought from the beginning to obstruct and overturn it. Their powerful resistance gained ground as the revolutionary spirit of 1776 faded. In 1790, Pennsylvania adopted a new constitution, setting up a government similar to those in other states, and ended its revolutionary experiment in popular democracy.

Sources: The Pennsylvania Constitution of 1776; David Hawke, *In the Midst of a Revolution* (Philadelphia: University of Pennsylvania Press, 1961); Gordon S. Wood, *The Creation of the American Republic, 1776–1787* (New York: Norton, 1972).

the Continental Congress in 1777 but not finally approved by all thirteen states until 1781, left little power in the hands of a centralized authority.

Congress under the Articles of Confederation was an assembly of delegates from the states, each of which had one vote. It had the authority to levy taxes and raise troops but had to requisition each state to supply its assigned quota; should a state fail to meet its duty, the central government could do little about it. The suspicion of the states toward national authority was displayed most dramatically in the provision of the Articles of Confederation regarding amendments: No alterations in the Articles could be made until the legislature of *every* state agreed to them.

That this first national authority was not a real central government was evident in its fundamental differences from the first state governments. The national government could not tax the people directly. There was no provision in the Articles for either an executive or a judiciary. All of this government's limited and closely watched powers were left in the hands of the Congress.

The deficiencies of the Articles of Confederation became increasingly obvious once it was put into practice. Supporters of the 1787 Constitution based their strongest arguments on the inadequacy of the Articles of Confederation to meet America's need for an effective national government. Alexander Hamilton, in particular, heaped scorn on the Articles of Confederation as weak and futile, and his sarcasm has shaped the way later generations have regarded them. Yet it should be remembered that the Articles of Confederation were not designed to create a strong national government. The framers of the Articles, adhering to the revolutionary spirit of '76, believed that local liberty—and not national power—was the true source of republican strength and virtue.

FROM REVOLUTION TO CONSTITUTION

What happened to the political institutions established by the American revolutionaries? Why did the spirit of '76, the hopeful experiment in liberty and virtue, give way to a more somber spirit a decade later, as reflected in the Constitution and in the arguments that upheld it? To answer these questions, we must look at the years between the Declaration of Independence and the Constitution, some of the most fateful years in American history.

In 1776, the American revolutionary cause attracted a broad coalition. The struggle for independence and self-government united wealthy merchants, slave-owning planters, and lawyers with yeoman farmers, urban artisans, and unskilled laborers. But during the war for independence, and even more in the years immediately following the war, major economic and social tensions emerged in the revolutionary coalition. Revolutionary unity broke down, and with the new economic and social divisions came divisions over both government policies and fundamental matters of political philosophy. The result was a sense of crisis in the new American republic that engendered a move to reconstitute American politics on a different basis than that of 1776.

Economic and social tensions in the revolutionary coalition that had begun during the war with England grew much worse after the fighting stopped. A short-lived boom in imports from England produced a depression that spread from commercial areas to the countryside. As prices for both manufactured and agricultural goods fell, money became scarce, especially specie or "hard money" (gold and silver). Hardest hit during this depression were the small farmers, who constituted the majority of Americans at the time. With falling prices and a shortage of specie, farmers could not pay off their creditors. Because many states were levying taxes to pay off wartime debts, the farmers also faced demands for specie payments from the tax collector. The combination of debt and taxes threatened many small farmers with foreclosure—the loss of their tools, livestock, or land. Some faced prison, for in this period one could be jailed for a failure to pay debts.

Not surprisingly, small farmers faced with such dire losses became the main source of political agitation in the mid-1780s. They wanted their state legislatures to relieve their distress. They petitioned for "stay laws" to postpone foreclosures and "tender laws" to allow payment of debts and taxes in agricultural commodities. Most of all, they sought paper money—a new and inflated currency that would make paying their debts and taxes easier.

In some states legislators were not responsive to these demands. In Massachusetts, the failure of the legislature to do anything about the plight of the rural majority led to an explosion. The counties in the western part of the state repeatedly petitioned for relief, but the legislature, dominated by the merchants and moneylenders of the coastal cities, ignored them. By the fall of 1786, conditions were ripe for rebellion. Under the leadership of Daniel Shays, a former revolutionary army officer, farmers in the western counties banded together to close down the local courts and prevent further foreclosures. When Shays and his followers marched on the state armory in Springfield, they were dispersed by the state militia. Shays's Rebellion, as this event came to be called, was hardly a revolution; it was a disorganized campaign by desperate farmers who felt they were losing everything that the American Revolution had promised them.

To the more conservative and propertied American republicans, Shays's Rebellion was a disturbing yet familiar phenomenon. Just as republican theory had warned that power, if not properly checked, led to despotism, so it had also maintained that liberty, if not properly contained by power, led to lawlessness. But in the 1780s, what most troubled the conservative and the propertied was not the people's rebellions against the state governments. Rather, they were troubled that the majority of the state governments, with their strong legislatures and weak executives, *were* responding to popular grievances. Seven states, for example, passed paper-money legislation; stay and tender laws were also put into effect. Attempts by the agrarian majority to alter contractual obligations and to interfere with what conservatives defined as the sacred rights of property were now obtaining the force of state law.[10]

Why were the legislatures in the majority of the states so responsive to mass grievances? One reason was the democratic nature of these revolutionary governments. With annual elections and with large and equal representation, the legislatures were quick to grant their constituents' requests. A second reason was the character of the representatives themselves. Before the Revolution, colonial assemblies had been dominated by an upper class of merchants, lawyers, and large landowners. But the Revolution had brought new men into politics from the middle class, and the composition of the legislatures had changed. Now, when yeoman farmers petitioned their state legislatures, they were heard in many states by people like themselves.[11]

To conservative and propertied republicans, the new state laws (such as paper-money legislation) and the new state legislators called into question the assumptions about politics that had been shared by all republicans in 1776. These men, looking fearfully at developments in the states, no longer believed the core ideas of 1776. In their eyes, power was no longer the problem; liberty was. Executives were no longer the major threat; legislatures were. Shays's rebels and debtors seeking paper money aroused concern about the virtue of the American people. The turmoil in the states seemed to invalidate the capacity of a small republic to arrive at a common good. Condemning the "Vices of the Political System of the United States," the young James Madison, soon to play the leading role at the Constitutional Convention, placed them at the doorstep of "the representative bodies" and "the people themselves." To Madison, the heroes of 1776 had become the culprits of 1787.[12]

The Constitutional Convention of 1787 assembled largely in response to these developments in the states. The delegates who came to Philadelphia agreed that efforts in the states to block what was happening had been unsuccessful. They also agreed that the weak national government under the Articles of Confederation, with its dedication to state sovereignty, provided no recourse. If they hoped to restore stability and protect property, the answer was in a new set of national institutions. These delegates were still republicans, but they no longer hoped to base the American republic on the virtue or public spirit of the people. As they saw it, if republicanism was to survive in America—without subverting either order or property—only a proper constitution could save it.

THE CONSTITUTIONAL CONVENTION

The Constitutional Convention of 1787 was a lengthy affair, lasting from May 25 to September 17. For nearly four months of a sweltering Philadelphia summer, fifty-five delegates from twelve states (Rhode Island refused to send a delegation) orated, debated, and negotiated the creation of a new American political system. Their proceedings were secret, and our knowledge of what took place rests mainly on notes of several delegates (particularly James Madison). In considering the Constitutional Convention, we focus on the creation of a strong national government, the shaping of new national institutions, and the political values that guided the delegates.

James Madison was the leading figure at the Constitutional Convention. His essays in *The Federalist Papers* are the most brilliant exposition of the political theory of elite democracy.

A Strong National Government

Forging a new national government was a complex process whose eventual outcome no one really anticipated. Most of the principal figures at Philadelphia—the delegates who took leading roles—wanted a far stronger national government than the Articles of Confederation provided. But the actual features of this government would emerge only gradually through the debates, votes, and compromises of four months.

As the debates commenced, the delegates were subject to conflicting pulls. On the one hand, these mostly propertied and conservative men were representatives of the tradition we call elite democracy, and they were eager to end the upsurge of popular democracy that had been manifested in paper-money legislation and Shays's Rebellion. Furthermore, they hoped that a lofty new national government, elevated high above local democracy, would be dominated by people like themselves rather than by the more ordinary folks who had gained prominence in the state legislatures. On the other hand, they knew that whatever they might consider the best plan of government, the new Constitution would have to obtain the approval of the American people. Frequent references were made during the proceedings to the values or "genius" of the American people, which could not be ignored or overridden. As historian Alfred Young has observed, the leading figures at the convention were "accommodating conservatives," who "made democratic concessions to achieve conservative ends."[13]

The Virginia Plan. The initial agenda for the convention was set by the **Virginia Plan,** introduced on May 29 by that state's governor, Edmund Randolph, but principally the handiwork of James Madison. The Virginia Plan aimed to establish a strong national government. Where the Articles of Confederation had been based on the sovereignty of the states, the Virginia Plan made national government primary and reduced the states to a subordinate position. It envisioned the United States as a large republic—the kind of centralized political order that the American revolutionaries had opposed as inconsistent with liberty.

With the favorable reception accorded the Virginia Plan, it was evident that the convention would ignore its limited mandate from Congress to revise the Articles of Confederation and would frame a wholly new political system. Yet if the shell of the convention's final product is visible in the Virginia Plan, a look at some of its features indicates how much of the substance was different. The Virginia Plan called for three branches of government: legislative, executive, and judicial. Representation for each state in *both* houses of the bicameral legislature was to be based on either taxes paid to the national government or the number of free inhabitants—provisions that would favor the large states. Members of the upper house of the legislature would be selected by members of the lower house from lists submitted by each state legislature. The national legislature would choose the national executive, which was allowed only one term. The length of the term was left blank, and the Virginia Plan did not even specify whether the executive would be one individual or a committee. The provision that most strongly indicated how authority was to be shifted from the state governments to the national government was one crafted by Madison that empowered the national legislature to veto state legislation.

The New Jersey Plan. Although the Virginia Plan dominated the initial debate, it leaned so far in the direction of the large states that the smaller states took alarm. On June 15, they countered with an alternative framework, introduced by William Paterson of New Jersey and thus known as the **New Jersey Plan.** The New Jersey Plan was essentially a reform of the Articles of Confederation rather than a wholly new constitutional order. It retained from the Articles a unicameral legislature in which each state would have equal representation. It strengthened the Articles by bestowing on Congress greater powers over revenues and commerce, and by establishing a plural executive and a national judiciary. The New Jersey Plan never had enough support to gain serious consideration, but the concerns of the small states that it raised had to be addressed if the convention was to arrive at sufficient agreement to present a new constitution to the nation.

The Great Compromise. The quarrel between large and small states over representation was finally settled through a compromise proposed by the delegation from Connecticut and known as the Connecticut Compromise, or **Great Compromise.** Under the terms of this compromise, the House of Representatives would be apportioned according to the populations of the various states, while each state would have two members in the Senate. Senators would be selected by their state's legislature. The origination of revenue acts would be an exclusive right of the House. Through this compromise, the large states had the dominant position in the House and a more favorable position with regard to taxation, yet the small states were well protected by their equal representation in the Senate.

The delegates who were most eager to build national power at the expense of the states had to make compromises that pained them. Equal representation for the states in the Senate was one blow to the "nationalist" position; another was the defeat of Madison's plan for a national veto power over state legislation. Rather than drawing clear lines of national dominance and state subordination, the constitution that began to emerge by midsummer drew uncertain boundaries between national and state powers. The Constitution of the United States is celebrated for creating a novel system of **federalism** under which power is divided between the central government and the states. Alexander Hamilton and especially James Madison applauded the virtues of this federalism in *The Federalist Papers,* considered later in this chapter. The irony is that this system of federalism was not what Hamilton, Madison, or their allies wanted. If they had not needed to compromise on representation and had not lost on the veto over state laws, we would have had a far more centralized government.

National Institutions

The Articles of Confederation had provided only a single legislative branch. But the Constitutional Convention intended to create a more complex government, possessing a bicameral legislature, a national executive, and a national judiciary. Molding these institutions and determining the appropriate relationships between them occupied much of the convention's time. In framing new national institutions, most of the delegates rejected the assumption that had dominated constitution-making a decade earlier: that the lower house of the legislature—the branch closest to the people—should be entrusted with the most power. Recent actions of the state legislatures had soured most of the men at Philadelphia toward the virtues of the people's representatives and made them look more favorably at traditional organs of power.

The Legislature. The House of Representatives proved to be the least complicated of the institutions to fashion. The delegates were clear that this branch would directly reflect the people's opinions and interests. But they were also clear that a legislative body so closely representing popular democratic sentiments would need strong checks. The House was seen as the most democratic part of the new system—and for that very reason the part most feared and constrained.

The nature and shape of the second legislative body, the Senate, occasioned greater controversy. Many delegates envisioned the Senate as an elite assemblage, a forum where the nation's economic, political, and intellectual aristocrats would constrain the more democratic House and supply wisdom and stability to the process of law-making. As James Madison put the argument, the people should recognize "that they themselves, as well as a numerous body of representatives, were liable to err . . . from fickleness and passion. A necessary fence against this danger would be to select a portion of enlightened citizens, whose limited number and firmness might seasonably interpose against impetuous counsels."[14]

Those who wanted a cool, deliberative, elite legislative body fought hard against making the Senate a forum for state interests. Madison bitterly opposed the Great Compromise, saying it would turn the Senate into a copy of the inept Congress under the Articles of Confederation. Yet even though the Senate that emerged, with its special protection for the small states, fell short of the elite national body that Madison and his allies urged, it was viewed by all as more selective, conservative, and stable than the House. As a consequence, it was given deliberative functions and prerogatives denied to the House: the judgment of treaties and of presidential nominations to the executive branch and the judiciary.

The Executive. If the fashioning of a Senate gave the convention its share of pains, the shaping of the executive was a continual headache, not relieved until the closing days of the proceedings. The Virginia Plan had left open the question of whether the United States would have a single or a plural executive. To some delegates, the idea of a single man exercising executive powers over so vast a country as the United States conjured a disturbing likeness with the King of Great Britain. Thus, when James Wilson of Pennsylvania proposed on June 1 that "the Executive consist of a single person" who would provide "energy, dispatch, and responsibility to the office," Madison's notes observe "a considerable pause ensuing. . . ." Attacking Wilson's proposal, Governor Randolph of Virginia claimed that a single or "unitary" executive would be the "fetus of monarchy," and suggested instead that the executive consist of three men.[15]

After vigorous debate, Wilson's proposal for a unitary executive carried, but another of his proposals—election of this executive by popular vote—failed. For most of the remainder of the convention, the prevailing view was that the national executive should be selected by Congress. However, legislative selection ruled out more than a single term for the executive, because the desire for reelection would have made the executive too dependent on legislative favor. If the executive was to be restricted to one term, many delegates wanted that term to be lengthy. In the debates of July 24, one delegate proposed an eleven-year term for the executive; another suggested fifteen years; and a third, perhaps jokingly, called for twenty.

The convention moved, gradually and fitfully, to strengthen the executive office. Revolutionary fears of executive power were waning, especially among conservative and propertied republicans; a more favorable view of executives as pillars of order and stability was gaining ground. The willingness of the delegates to create the kind of powerful American executive that would have been unthinkable in 1776 was furthered by the universal assumption that George Washington would be the first president. The final key decision of the convention on the executive—selection by electors rather than by Congress—added greatly to executive independence and strength.

The Judiciary. The third branch of the new national government provoked surprisingly little debate. Given the suspicions of the smaller states, one of the few contested issues involved the relation between federal courts below the Supreme Court and the courts in the states. The idea of "judicial review"—that federal courts have the authority to judge a law by the standard of the Constitution and to declare it null and void should it be found incompatible—was not stated in the Constitution but was discussed by the delegates. Although they did not agree universally on the subject, their comments about judicial review suggest that most delegates did assume that the federal courts would have this authority.

Values, Fears, and Issues

The Constitution was gradually shaped by the convention as institutions were formed, their powers defined, and their relationships to one another determined. In this process a number of values, fears, and issues drove the work of the framers. The next sections consider the interrelationship of one value, property; one fear, democracy; and one issue, slavery, in the development of the Constitution.

Property. Ever since historian Charles Beard charged in 1913 that the Constitution of the United States was written for the direct economic benefit of its framers, a debate has ensued about the role of property in the constitutional convention. Although Beard's specific arguments about the framers' personal economic gains have been successfully refuted by other historians, considerable evidence remains in the record of the convention debates that the general protection of property was an objective for many of the framers. The new national government was designed to make property far more secure than it had been under the state constitutions. The convention bestowed on the national government new powers that holders of substantial property desired, such as the means to pay off public debts, disproportionately held by the wealthy. Equally important, it prohibited the state governments from coining money, issuing paper money, or "impairing the obligations of contracts," thus putting an end to the popular democratic efforts of the 1780s to aid the many at the expense of the few.

The "Threat" of Democracy. In the eyes of most of the framers, democracy was the chief threat to property. Democracy had a somewhat different meaning in 1787 than it has today; it meant direct rule by the people. When the framers talked about democracy, they usually meant the lower house of the legislature, where the people's interests and feelings were directly represented. Some delegates assailed democracy on the grounds that the people were ignorant, subject to fits of passion, and prone to pursuing their own economic interests at the expense of a minority of the most industrious, successful, and propertied citizens. Others feared the people less because of their inherent flaws than because they were so easily duped by demagogues, selfish leaders who stoked the flames of popular passion to gain power.

Most delegates at the convention agreed that the crisis of American politics in the 1780s stemmed from an "excess of democracy" in the states. Typical was the view expressed by Governor Randolph of Virgina, who observed that "the general object was to provide a cure for the evils under which the United States labored; that in tracing these evils to their origin every man has found it in the turbulence and follies of democracy. . . ."[16] Given this perspective, it is not surprising that the delegates aimed many of the checks and balances they were writing into the constitution at democracy. Only the House of Representatives would be directly democratic, and it would be restrained by the Senate, president, and judiciary, all of which would be selected in an elite rather than a popular fashion.

Slavery. The delegates at Philadelphia concurred on the importance of promoting property and averting the dangers of democracy. But they were sharply divided on another issue: slavery. The words *slavery* or *slaves* do not appear in the Constitution. A document written in the most enlightened terms of the day should not, most of the framers thought, make reference to such a barbaric institution as slavery. Nonetheless, the issue of slavery haunted the convention, at times threatening to destroy its precarious harmony.

Four positions on slavery were advanced during the debates. Some northern delegates opposed giving slavery any protection in the Constitution on economic grounds; if slaves were property, why should this form of property alone gain special safeguards? Other delegates—from both northern states and the upper South—denounced the institution itself on moral grounds. Against these two positions, delegates from South Carolina and Georgia insisted that slavery was indispensable to their economies, and repeatedly warned the convention that if slavery was not given special protection their states would not join the Union. The fourth and ultimately decisive view was put forward by delegates from New England, who expressed dislike for slavery but suggested that the convention should not meddle with this topic and should accept the compromises necessary to keep the most southerly states in the Union. In accordance with this position, slavery was given three special safeguards in the Constitution: (1) to apportion direct taxes and representation in the House, slaves would count as three-fifths of free persons, thereby enlarging southern representation; (2) the slave trade could not be banned for at least twenty years; (3) fugitive slaves would be returned to their owners.

The framers of the Constitution compromised in this case for the sake of harmony and union, justifying their moral lapse with the belief that slavery would gradually die out without any forceful effort against it. The Civil War would show this pious hope to have been their greatest error. Remarkably, one delegate uttered a chilling prophecy of just such a catastrophe as the Civil War. In words that foreshadowed Abraham Lincoln's Second Inaugural Address at the close of the Civil War, George Mason of Virginia, an opponent of slavery (and soon to become an opponent of the Constitution itself) warned his fellow delegates that "by an inevitable chain of causes and effects providence punishes national sins by national calamities."[17]

The full text of the Constitution is in the appendix. Table 2.1 summarizes the features of the Preamble and the seven Articles. The final article stated that ratification by conventions in nine of the thirteen original states would be sufficient to put the Constitution into effect. It began one of the most important contests in American history—a political and philosophical struggle to determine nothing less than the basis on which all subsequent American political life would be conducted. It is to this debate that we now turn.

RATIFICATION STRUGGLE AND THE DEMOCRATIC DEBATE

Most contemporary Americans assume that the greatness of the Constitution under which we have lived for two hundred years must have been obvious from the start. In reality, the ratification of the Constitution required a long and sometimes bitter struggle whose outcome was by no means certain. Although some states ratified the Constitution swiftly and with little dissent, in a number of the larger states the contest was close. In Massachusetts, the vote in the ratifying convention was 187 to 168 in favor of the Constitution. Virginia ratified by the narrow margin of 89 to 79; New York endorsed the Constitution by a vote of 30 to 27.

The closeness of these votes becomes less surprising when we recall that the Constitution largely reversed the political verdict of 1776 by ending the revolutionary experiment in state-based popular democracy. Historians have suggested that the agrarian majority in many of the states was, at least initially, opposed to the Constitution. If the Constitution was a defeat for popular democracy and a victory for an elite democracy (moderated by concessions to the democratic spirit), how did its supporters, who called themselves *Federalists*, win popular approval?

The Federalists enjoyed a number of political advantages over opponents of the Constitution, who came to be known as *Anti-federalists*. Perhaps most

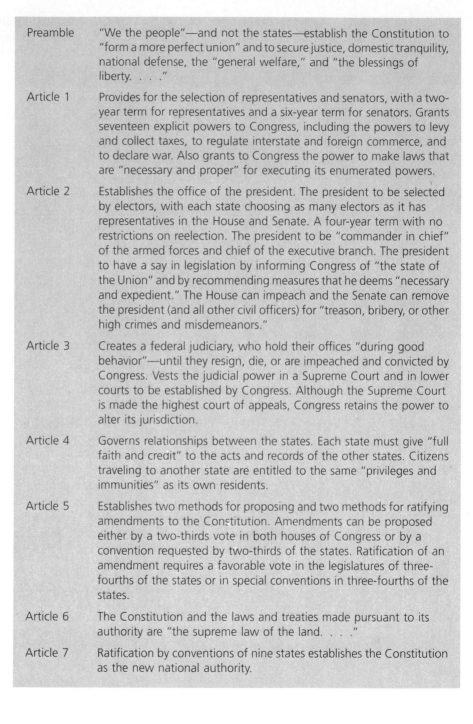

TABLE 2.1		
Preamble and Articles of the Constitution	Preamble	"We the people"—and not the states—establish the Constitution to "form a more perfect union" and to secure justice, domestic tranquility, national defense, the "general welfare," and "the blessings of liberty. . . ."
	Article 1	Provides for the selection of representatives and senators, with a two-year term for representatives and a six-year term for senators. Grants seventeen explicit powers to Congress, including the powers to levy and collect taxes, to regulate interstate and foreign commerce, and to declare war. Also grants to Congress the power to make laws that are "necessary and proper" for executing its enumerated powers.
	Article 2	Establishes the office of the president. The president to be selected by electors, with each state choosing as many electors as it has representatives in the House and Senate. A four-year term with no restrictions on reelection. The president to be "commander in chief" of the armed forces and chief of the executive branch. The president to have a say in legislation by informing Congress of "the state of the Union" and by recommending measures that he deems "necessary and expedient." The House can impeach and the Senate can remove the president (and all other civil officers) for "treason, bribery, or other high crimes and misdemeanors."
	Article 3	Creates a federal judiciary, who hold their offices "during good behavior"—until they resign, die, or are impeached and convicted by Congress. Vests the judicial power in a Supreme Court and in lower courts to be established by Congress. Although the Supreme Court is made the highest court of appeals, Congress retains the power to alter its jurisdiction.
	Article 4	Governs relationships between the states. Each state must give "full faith and credit" to the acts and records of the other states. Citizens traveling to another state are entitled to the same "privileges and immunities" as its own residents.
	Article 5	Establishes two methods for proposing and two methods for ratifying amendments to the Constitution. Amendments can be proposed either by a two-thirds vote in both houses of Congress or by a convention requested by two-thirds of the states. Ratification of an amendment requires a favorable vote in the legislatures of three-fourths of the states or in special conventions in three-fourths of the states.
	Article 6	The Constitution and the laws and treaties made pursuant to its authority are "the supreme law of the land. . . ."
	Article 7	Ratification by conventions of nine states establishes the Constitution as the new national authority.

important, they were united around a common and positive program. With a solution in hand to the nation's distresses (which they often exaggerated for rhetorical purposes), they possessed the political initiative. The Anti-federalists, on the other hand, could not agree among themselves either about what was wrong with the Constitution or about what should take its place. The Federalists also had an advantage in disseminating their ideas. Based largely in the cities and supported by most of the wealthy, they had better access to newspapers than the Anti-federalists.

The Federalist cause was also blessed with exceptional intellectual talent. A majority of the distinguished, learned, and articulate men in America argued for the ratification of the Constitution. Among them, none presented the case for the Constitution so brilliantly as Alexander Hamilton, James Madison, and John Jay in *The Federalist Papers.* These eighty-five papers laid out the arguments for the new constitutional order so profoundly that they transcended their immediate aim and became the most famous American work of political theory. (Some of their arguments are presented later in this chapter.)

Although a number of able writers opposed the Constitution, no single Anti-federalist writing was comparable to *The Federalist Papers.* Moreover, the Anti-federalists can be said to have lost the intellectual debate because their side lost the political contest. *The Federalist Papers* thus overshadowed Anti-federalist thought. Yet both sides were important in the debate over the Constitution. As political theorist Herbert J. Storing has written, "If . . . the foundation of the American polity was laid by the Federalists, the Anti-Federalist reservations echo through American history; and it is in the dialogue, not merely in the Federalist victory, that the country's principles are to be discovered."[18]

The dialogue Storing mentions is what we call the democratic debate. In the following, we pay equal attention to both voices in the debate—Federalist and Anti-federalist, elite democrat and popular democrat. We consider six issues on which the two sides differed: human nature, the proper scale of political life, the character of representation, separation of powers and checks and balances, the purpose of government, and stability and change. The debate over these six issues deserves careful study. The arguments between the elite democratic position and the popular democratic position recur throughout this book; they form the essence of the democratic debate.

Human Nature: Its Dangers and Its Possibilities

The basic issue of the democratic debate is human nature. The Federalists held a pessimistic view of human nature. In the most famous of *The Federalist Papers,* number 10, James Madison wrote that people were "much more disposed to vex and oppress each other than to cooperate for their common good."[19] Alexander Hamilton's view of human nature was even more bleak: Men, he wrote, are "ambitious, vindictive, and rapacious."[20] Although Madison could also write that "there are other qualities in human nature which justify a certain portion of esteem and confidence,"[21] the Federalist view was that good government could not be founded on the idea of goodness in its participants.

Any goodness in human nature, the Federalists believed, was most likely to be found in elites. Madison argued that the new national government would bring to power the relatively few citizens who were both wise and public spirited. Hamilton claimed that his favorite institution, the presidency, would be filled by men "preeminent for ability and virtue."[22] The Federalists recognized that the dangerous qualities in human nature might also show up in the governing elite. But their greater fear was the raw human nature of the masses. The history of experiments in popular democracy had, in the eyes of the Federalists, demonstrated that most ordinary people were prone to passion, selfishness, and disorder. To the Federalists, any attempt by the people to assemble and debate affairs in a face-to-face or direct democracy would inevitably degenerate into mob rule.

The Anti-federalists were not naive optimists who held a rosy view of human nature. They, too, wrote vividly of the ambition and greed that could disfigure the human character. Yet they differed profoundly from the Federalists on where virtue and vice were most likely to be found. Ordinary individuals, most Anti-federalist writers believed, had modest aspirations: They wanted to live a life of comfort, decency, and dignity. Moreover, whatever natural tendencies existed toward selfishness and quarreling could be counteracted through instruction in morality and religion. Virtue could be taught by republican institutions, laws, and customs, and would grow as citizens participated in the politics of their communities.[23]

The Anti-federalists feared human nature among elites. Power, they claimed, was intoxicating, especially when the connection between governors and citizens grew distant and the instruments for abuse and corruption were nearby. Human nature at its worst was not a lawless people, the Anti-federalist Patrick Henry of Virginia proclaimed. Rather, it was "the tyranny of rulers."[24]

Scale of Political Life

From this initial difference between Federalists and Anti-federalists over human nature flowed a further difference over the proper scale of political life. Federalists favored a large republic (the national government); Anti-federalists favored small republics (the state governments).

In the view of the Federalists, the small republic brought out the worst in human nature. In the face-to-face political space of the small republic, a majority of selfish but like-minded individuals would form a "faction" or political group and try to oppress a minority, such as those who owned large amounts of property or those who held unorthodox religious beliefs. Irrational and violent passion would spread among this majority like an infectious disease, and politics in the small republic would degenerate into turbulence, injustice, and misery.

But in the large republic, the Federalists claimed, the selfish passions of the people could not have this unhappy result. There would be so much diversity in the large republic that a powerful and unjust majority faction was unlikely to form. James Madison explained the logic of the large republic: "Extend the sphere and you take in a greater variety of parties and interests; you make it less probable that a majority of the whole will have a common motive to invade the rights of other citizens; or if such a common motive exists, it will be more difficult for all who feel it to discover their own strength and to act in unison with each other."[25]

Given their view of human nature, the Anti-federalists favored the small republic and feared the large republic. The Anti-federalists saw the small republic as the home of liberty rather than oppression. It was only in the small republic, they argued, that citizens were close enough to their representatives in government to have confidence in them and to hold them accountable for their actions. Further, only in the small republic could citizens participate in political affairs and, through the practice of active citizenship, develop a broader and less selfish understanding of the common good.[26]

The Anti-federalists saw the large republic as bringing out the worst in human nature. Above all, they mistrusted the national elites on whom the Federalists were banking their hopes. As a New York Anti-federalist who used the pseudonym of Brutus (killer of the tyrant Caesar, who had destroyed the Roman Republic) put it: "In so extensive a republic, the great officers of government would soon become above the control of the people, and abuse their power to the purpose of aggrandizing themselves, and oppressing them."[27]

Representation

Federalist and Anti-federalist understandings of representation also followed from their differing views of human nature. Because ordinary people were prone, the Federalists believed, to selfish, factional, and even violent passions, the task of the elected representative was to filter out these bad impulses and seek the people's true welfare. In a large republic, James Madison argued in *Federalist* number 10, the process of representation would "refine and enlarge the public views by passing them through the medium of a chosen body of citizens, whose wisdom may best discern the true interest of their country and whose patriotism and love of justice will be least likely to sacrifice it to temporary or partial considerations."[28] The Federalist claim was that representatives, as a distinctive elite, would both know better and do better than the people themselves.

The Anti-federalists denied that representatives should act the part of the people's superiors. Representatives, they argued, should not filter out what the people wanted; they should mirror the people's exact hopes and goals. In the words of New York Anti-federalist Melancton Smith: "The idea that naturally suggests itself to our minds when we speak of representatives is that they resemble those they represent; they should be a true picture of the people; possess the knowledge of their circumstances and their wants; sympathize in all their distresses, and be disposed to seek their true interests."[29]

Separation of Powers and Checks and Balances

Although the Federalists entertained high hopes for a talented and virtuous elite to run the new national government, they were aware that concentrated power could be abused. Their remedy was to separate the powers of government into three branches—legislative, executive, and judicial—each of which would have the constitutional weapons to check the others. Thus, the president could check the legislature with his veto, the Senate could check the executive with its power over appointments, and the judiciary could check the other two branches by its authority over the meaning of the Constitution and the laws. Members of each branch were expected to defend their rightful powers against the others, James Madison explained, less out of virtue than out of a regard for their own interests. To guard against an oppressive concentration of powers within government, he wrote in one of his most famous sentences, "ambition must be made to counteract ambition."[30]

The Federalists did not, however, see all branches as equally dangerous. They worried most about the popular democratic body, the House of Representatives. The more elite institutions were expected to hold the House in check and thereby ensure wiser and more stable governance. Madison and Hamilton preferred institutions that were more remote than the House from the pressures of popular democracy. Madison described the Senate as a select body that would provide cool deliberation even in the heat of passionate political controversies. Hamilton placed his greatest hopes on the presidency. Perhaps his most famous sentence in *The Federalist Papers* proclaimed "Energy in the executive is a leading character in the definition of good government."[31]

The Anti-federalists viewed the institutions of government in a different light. Some preferred a simpler structure of government than that provided in the Constitution, arguing that its complex arrangement of conflicting powers would leave the people confused about whom to hold accountable for abuses. The more common Anti-federalist perspective, however, accepted the idea of separation of powers and checks and balances, but complained that the Constitution was checking the wrong people. It was not the democratic House that needed most closely to be watched, but rather the elite branches. Patrick Henry thus warned that Hamilton's energetic executive "squints toward monarchy."[32] Anti-federalist writers also denounced the constitutional alliance between a monarchical president and an aristocratic Senate in making treaties and appointing civil officers, judges, and ambassadors.

Purpose of Government

What was the purpose of government? Both Federalists and Anti-federalists agreed that government must protect and promote the liberty of the people. Yet they meant different things by *liberty*. To James Madison, liberty was primarily a private possession—private property or private convictions. Liberty in this sense needed to be protected from oppressive majorities that would take away property or force the same religious faith on everyone. If liberty was protected, individuals would, Madison believed, succeed or fail in accordance with their own abilities. A free society would inevitably be marked by a substantial amount of economic inequality that resulted from the natural differences between people and was therefore just.[33]

Alexander Hamilton thought of liberty in slightly different terms, as the freedom to acquire greater property and power. He wanted a powerful national government that would promote the economic growth and develop the military potential of the United States. The purpose of government was to steer the United States in the direction of national greatness. In the right hands, he suggested in *The Federalist Papers*, this bold young nation "might make herself the admiration and envy of the world."[34] Hamilton's vision of a prosperous and mighty America was beyond the sight of most of his fellow Federalists. But he shared with them the idea that inequality in wealth and power inevitably accompanied liberty.

To the Anti-federalists, liberty was equally precious. But they emphasized the political rights of the people as much as the people's right to property. Understood in this way, liberty was endangered less by oppressive majorities than by oppressive rulers. The most common Anti-federalist complaint against the Constitution—that it contained no bill of rights to safeguard the people against government oppression—is considered in the next section.

The Anti-federalists also disagreed with the Federalists about how liberty related to economic life and national defense. Although desiring a prosperous America, they hoped for a simpler and more egalitarian society than the Federalists. If wealth became highly unequal and Americans began desiring luxurious goods, they feared, the republic would lose its anchorage in the civic virtue of the people. The public good would be neglected once Americans cared only about getting rich. Anti-federalists also worried about the rise of a powerful military that might be used by rulers for domestic tyranny or foreign aggression.

The Anti-federalist view of the purpose of government looked back to the vision of popular democracy that had fired the hopes of American revolutionaries in 1776. Their protest against turning America away from its original democratic dream and making it more like the undemocratic governments of Europe was eloquently expressed by Patrick Henry:

> If we admit this consolidated government it will be because we like a great splendid one. Some way or other we must be a great and mighty empire; we must have an army, and a navy, and a number of things. When the American spirit was in its youth, the language of America was different. Liberty, Sir, was then the primary object.[35]

Stability and Change

The final critical area of difference between the Federalists and the Anti-federalists involved their perspectives on stability and change in American politics. Responding to the upsurge of popular democracy in the Revolution and its aftermath, Federalists looked for sources of stability in a new constitutional system. Their chief answer to the danger of radical economic and social change through popular democracy lay in the complex mechanisms of the Constitution itself. In the vastness and diversity of a large republic, majorities desiring radical change were unlikely to form; should they overcome the problem of distance and gain power in the democratic branch—the House of Representatives—the more elite branches would check their progress and protect the status quo. Federalists were not averse to all change—witness Hamilton's program for economic development—but they wanted change guided by an elite.

Among the Federalists, James Madison was particularly insightful in recognizing a more profound basis for stability. He saw that if the Constitution could prevail over its initial opposition, its status as the foundation of American politics would eventually cease to be questioned. It would gain "that veneration which time bestows on everything, and without which perhaps the wisest and freest governments would not possess the requisite stability."[36] Madison foresaw that Americans would come to love the Constitution. Forgetting the original debate over it, they would revere the document—and the ideas—produced by the winning side.

What the Federalists desired as stability looked to the Anti-federalists like the most dangerous form of change: political corruption and decay. The Anti-federalists were not worried that the people would become unruly; they feared that the people would become apathetic about public affairs. Under the new constitutional order, they predicted, arrogance and corruption would grow among ruling elites, while the people would become preoccupied with the scramble for riches. Unless ordinary citizens were called to remember their political rights and to exercise them, liberty was sure to be lost.

The Anti-federalist view continued the spirit of protest and resistance that had marked the American Revolution. No one expressed this spirit so strongly during this period as Thomas Jefferson. Strictly speaking, Jefferson was neither Federalist nor Anti-federalist; as the American minister to France during the years in which the Constitution was written and debated, he stood at a distance from the conflict over it. Yet his support for popular protest, expressed in letters to friends in America, dramatically opposes the Federalist dread of popular action. Whereas the Federalists reacted in horror to Shays's Rebellion as a signpost of impending anarchy, Jefferson wrote to Madison: "I hold it that a little rebellion now and then is a good thing, and as necessary in the political world as storms in the physical."[37] Jefferson, like the Anti-federalists, believed that only an alert and active citizenry could preserve the democratic values of the American Revolution. (See Table 2.2.)

THE BILL OF RIGHTS

When farmers in the backcountry of South Carolina heard that their state had ratified the Constitution, they "had a coffin painted black, which borne in funeral

TABLE 2.2

Differences
Between the
Federalists and
Anti-federalists

Issue	Federalists	Anti-federalists
Human Nature	Ordinary people basically selfish; capacity for virtue greater among elites	Ordinary people moderately ambitious and capable of virtue; dangerous ambitions found among elites
Scale of Political Life	Favored a large republic (national government)	Favored a small republic (state governments)
Role of Representatives	To refine the public views	To mirror the people's hopes and goals
Separation of Powers	Favored checks and balances, with particular eye on the House of Representatives	Believed in checks and balances, with particular eye on the president and Senate
Purpose of Government	To protect liberty, especially private rights; expected inequality as just result	To protect liberty, especially political rights; sought to prevent large inequalities that threatened values of a republic
Stability and Change	Stability found in complexity of Constitution and in public reverence for it	Feared political decay and corruption; favored spirit of protest embodied in the Revolution

procession, was solemnly buried, as an emblem of the dissolution and interment of public liberty."[38] Such Anti-federalist fears—that the Constitution would become a monstrous mechanism for oppressing the people—strike us today as absurdly exaggerated. Yet in one crucial respect, the fears of the Anti-federalists were fortunate and productive. Without them, we would not have gained the Bill of Rights.

Among the Anti-federalists' objections to the Constitution, none was as frequently voiced, as popularly received, and as compelling in force as the complaint that the Constitution lacked guarantees of the people's basic liberties. Most of the state constitutions, Anti-federalist writers and debaters pointed out, expressly protected the fundamental personal and political rights of the people against arbitrary and invasive government. Yet this new national constitution contained no such guarantees of liberty. Anti-federalists at the state ratifying conventions thus began to propose various amendments to the new Constitution as safeguards of the people's fundamental rights.

Some Federalists resisted the call for amendments, fearing that they would weaken the new political system. But the more moderate supporters of the Constitution increasingly recognized that amendments that guaranteed the rights of the people would conciliate opponents of the Constitution and thus give the new system a better chance to survive and flourish. The leader of these moderates was James Madison. To win election to the House of Representatives, Madison had pledged to the voters in his district that he would introduce amendments in the first Congress. Fulfilling his promise, he became the principal drafter and legislative champion of what became the Bill of Rights. The greatest thinker in the American tradition of elite democracy thus became one of the greatest contributors to the American tradition of popular democracy.[39]

The Bill of Rights adds to the original Constitution a commitment to the personal and political liberties of the people. It safeguards the rights of religious conscience, free speech, a free press, and political activity; it protects the people against an invasion of their homes and papers by an intrusive government; it guarantees a fair trial and a freedom from excessive punishment. If the Constitution proved to be the great charter of American government, the Bill of Rights was the great charter of American liberty. It stands as an enduring testament to the vision and values of the Anti-federalists. Today, when Americans think of the U.S. Constitution, the Bill of Rights seems as much a part of its original composition as the seven articles drafted at the Philadelphia convention of 1787. The original democratic debate had made the Constitution a better—and a more democratic—document.

CONCLUSION: BEGINNING THE DEMOCRATIC DEBATE

The Constitution represented a victory for elite democrats in the original democratic debate. Not only did this victory lie in the creation of lofty national institutions in which elites would control most of the offices. Even more, it lay in the impediments to popular democracy that the constitutional system established. The growing size of the national republic tended, as Madison had argued, to fragment potential popular democratic movements and encourage in their place the narrower struggles of interest-group politics. The complexity of national institutions tended to stalemate democratic energies for social change. The remoteness of national institutions tended to undermine the civic virtue nourished in local, face-to-face political participation.

Elite democrats also won a philosophical victory in 1787. Embodied in many of the clauses of the Constitution and brilliantly argued in the pages of *The Federalist Papers*, the premises of elite democracy have come down to Americans with the sanctity of the highest political authority.

The constitutional victory of the elite democrats did not, however, mean that the popular democrats were vanquished in the era of the American founding. Later generations of popular democrats have looked back to the founding for authority and inspiration—but to the Revolution more than to the Constitution. The American tradition of popular democratic protest and struggle finds its roots in the Sons of Liberty, the Boston Tea Party, and the revolutionary war militia. The popular democratic vision of equality and self-government rests on the opening paragraphs of the Declaration of Independence. Echoing the revolutionaries of 1776 (and the Anti-federalists as well), popular democrats balance their fears of remote and unaccountable power with hopes for democratic community and public-spirited citizens.

Popular democrats not only can claim the revolutionary heritage, they also can point to concessions obtained from elite democrats in the constitutional system itself. The framers of the Constitution had to include elements of popular democracy in order to win ratification. Subsequent to ratification, popular democrats won an even larger victory when the Bill of Rights was added to the Constitution. Later amendments have also made the Constitution more compatible with popular democracy. The Thirteenth, Fourteenth, and Fifteenth amendments, products of the Civil War and Reconstruction era, established the rights of African Americans to participate in the American political system. The Nineteenth Amendment established women's right to the suffrage. Products of long struggles by popular democratic movements, these amendments opened doors that the founders had kept shut. They established the equal right—although not the equal chance—of all Americans to exercise the political rights and enjoy the political rewards that had originally been reserved for white males alone.

The Revolution and Constitution engendered a great democratic debate, but they did not resolve it for all time. Throughout this text, we point out how the democratic debate continues to flourish in American politics. Should large corporations, for example, be regarded as the indispensable engines of economic growth, or should we instead discourage concentrated economic power and favor smaller economic enterprises and a more equal distribution of economic resources? Do contemporary elections foster civic virtue or bury it under a blizzard of media spectacles financed by elite money? Is the modern president the "energetic executive" that Alexander Hamilton applauded or the arrogant "monarch" that Patrick Henry dreaded? In these and many other forms, the democratic debate still animates American politics. As we study its contemporary expressions, we need to recall the fundamental terms of the debate set down by the founders of the American Republic.

KEY TERMS

republicanism
Declaration of Independence
Articles of Confederation
Virginia Plan

New Jersey Plan
Great Compromise
federalism

SUGGESTED READINGS

Ralph Ketcham, ed., *The Anti-Federalist Papers* (New York: New American Library, 1986). An anthology of the leading Anti-federalist critics of the Constitution.

Clinton Rossiter, ed., *The Federalist Papers* (New York: New American Li-

brary, 1961). Hamilton's and Madison's brilliant defense of the Constitution—and the foremost work in the history of American political thought.

Herbert J. Storing, *What the Anti-Federalists Were For* (Chicago: University of Chicago Press, 1981). A brief yet profound explanation of the Antifederalists' political ideas.

Garry Wills, *Inventing America: Jefferson's Declaration of Independence* (New York: Vintage Books, 1978). An unconventional look at the hallowed text that proclaims America's democratic creed.

Gordon S. Wood, *The Creation of the American Republic, 1776–1787* (New York: W. W. Norton, 1972). The leading work on the transformation of American political thought from the popular democracy of the Revolution to the elite democracy of the Constitution.

The Dilemma of American Federalism

W hen the fifty-five delegates to the Constitutional Convention convened in Philadelphia in 1787, their purpose was to revise the Articles of Confederation to hold the union together. The delegates were dissatisfied with the weaknesses of their loose confederation, which had become all too apparent once the country achieved independence. As we saw in Chapter 2, however, the delegates soon changed their mandate from revising the Articles of Confederation to writing a new Constitution that would form a strong national government. In the process, a completely new political form—federalism—was created. Born in compromise, the Constitution signalled an end to one revolutionary experiment and the beginning of another.

Federalism is a system of government that divides power between a central government and state and local governments. It combines elements of a confederation with elements of a **unitary government,** in which all significant powers rest in the hands of the central government, and state and local governments derive their authority from the central government. (Over 90 percent of all countries in the world today, including France and the United Kingdom, are governed by unitary systems.)

Born in compromise between elite and popular democrats, federalism is at the heart of the fundamental dilemmas of political life. Complex federal programs often are necessary to address national problems like poverty and racism. On the other hand, Americans prefer state and local governments, and frequently criticize federal programs for being overly bureaucratic and lacking democratic accountability.

This chapter examines the dilemma of federalism in the context of the democratic debate. In the American political system, disagreements over *what* policies should be chosen are often played out as disagreements over *where* policy decisions should be made—at the national, state, or local level. Conflicts over federalism are not surprising because the division of powers between levels of government is not politically neutral. Where decisions are made determines the scope of conflict, and the scope of conflict, in turn, helps determine who wins and who loses.

FEDERALISM AND THE FOUNDING

As we saw in Chapter 2, the framers of the Constitution, led by Madison and Hamilton, favored a centralized or unitary system that would correct the weaknesses of the Articles of Confederation. They knew, however, that the country would not accept a unitary state. The rank-and-file soldiers who had fought in the Revolution would not vote for a government that reminded them of their subservience under the British. The Federalists thus were forced to compromise with Anti-federalist sentiment, creating a mixed system that gave some powers to the federal government and left others to the states.

In shaping this compromise, even the framers disagreed as to how the powers should be divided. As a result, the Constitution is full of vague language that papers over these disagreements, especially on the issue of federalism. In the words of Supreme Court Justice William J. Brennan, Jr., the framers "hid their differences in cloaks of generality."[1] The Constitution, to cite just one example, gives the federal government the power to "regulate commerce . . . among the several States" (ARTICLE I, SECTION 8). But nowhere is this power defined. As a result, the definition of "interstate commerce" has repeatedly been the center of a heated controversy in the Supreme Court and elsewhere.

As skilled politicians, however, the framers who argued for ratification put their best "spin" on the new Constitution. They did not admit that the federalism of the Constitution had grown out of tactical political compromises. On the contrary, they argued that the proposed Constitution was based on a new theory of government that carefully balanced the powers of the central government and the state governments. Madison referred to the new Constitution as a "happy combination" between a centralized and a decentralized system: "the great and aggregate interests being referred to the national, the local and particular to the State legislatures."[2] The Federalist proponents of the Constitution argued that it embodied what we have come to call **dual federalism.** Under dual federalism, the national government and the states each have separate spheres of authority, and "within their respective spheres the two centers of government are 'sovereign' and hence 'equal.' "[3] Each level of government relates directly to the citizens, and the other level of government cannot interfere within its legitimate sphere of authority.

Under dual federalism, the federal government has only those powers specifically granted in the Constitution, called **enumerated powers** (see Table 3.1). Seventeen such powers are given to the national government, or Congress, in ARTICLE I, SECTION 8, including the power to "regulate commerce with foreign nations and among the several States," "coin money," and "provide for the common defence." All powers not given to the national government are **reserved** to the states by the Tenth Amendment. In cases where both levels of government possess the power to act—so-called **concurrent powers**—the **Supremacy Clause** (ARTICLE VI) states that the national laws supercede the state laws. (Local

TABLE 3.1	Power	Definition	Example
Principles of Dual Federalism	Enumerated	Powers specifically granted to Congress	Coin money
	Concurrent	Powers exercised by both Congress and the states	Taxation
	Reserved	Powers not mentioned in the Constitution and therefore left to the states	Police powers (e.g., land-use regulation)

governments are not mentioned in the U.S. Constitution; they are essentially creatures of the states.)

The Federalists tried to reassure people that the new Constitution carefully balanced the powers of the federal and state governments. Madison argued that the powers of the federal government were "few and defined," while those reserved for the states were "numerous and indefinite."[4] As you might imagine, the Anti-federalists did not accept Madison's reassurances. Drawing on classic writings in political theory from Aristotle to Montesquieu, the Anti-federalists argued that Madison's extended republic was a contradiction in terms; democracy was only possible in a small homogeneous republic. Placing so much power in the hands of a distant central government, they warned, would ultimately foster a despotism as oppressive as the British monarchy. The Anti-federalists also had a practical political reason for opposing the new federal system: Their political base was in the state legislatures, and they believed that placing more powers in the central government would weaken them politically.

After the Pennsylvania Convention ratified the Constitution by a vote of 46 to 23, twenty-one persons in the minority signed a statement that expressed the fears of the Anti-federalists about centralized power:

> We dissent . . . because the powers vested in Congress by this constitution, must necessarily annihilate and absorb the legislative, executive, and judicial powers of the several states, and produce from their ruins one consolidated government, which from the nature of things will be an iron handed despotism, as nothing short of the supremacy of despotic sway could connect and govern these United States under one government.[5]

Just as the Federalists were not above exaggerating the flaws in the Articles of Confederation, the Anti-federalists did not shy away from rhetoric to criticize the Constitution.

The Anti-federalists were concerned about the taxing power of the federal government, the vague wording of the Constitution, and the role of the Supreme Court. By giving the national government concurrent powers over taxation with the states, the Anti-federalists argued that the national government would come to monopolize the taxing power and force the states to withdraw. The Anti-federalists were also suspicious of the vague language in the Constitution, such as the clause that gave the national Congress the power "to make all Laws which shall be necessary and proper for carrying into Execution the foregoing Powers" (the so-called Necessary and Proper, or Elastic, Clause). The Federalists answered that the Necessary and Proper Clause did nothing but state the obvious. The Anti-federalists, however, smelled a rat here; if this was the case, then why was it included at all?

Finally, the Anti-federalists pointed out that the institution that would interpret the vague language of the Constitution was itself a part of the federal government and would therefore be biased. Moreover, the justices of the Supreme Court would be appointed by the president for life and therefore could not be held democratically accountable.

Although exaggerated for rhetorical effect, the concerns of the Anti-federalists about the powers of the federal government have proven well founded. The superior taxing power of the federal government did give it an advantage (especially after the income tax amendment was passed in 1913) and ambiguous clauses were interpreted by the Supreme Court to expand the powers of the federal government into areas previously reserved for the states.

Despite the Federalists' claims, no comprehensive theory of American federalism is expressed in the Constitution. One of the shortest constitutions in the world, the U.S. Constitution is so vague on division of powers between governmental levels that conflict over interpretation is inevitable. Although present-day players in the democratic struggle defend federalism in terms of the framers' intent, their positions are tenuous because even the framers disagreed on the meaning of federalism. The Constitution essentially deferred conflict over federalism to future generations.

EARLY CONFLICTS OVER FEDERALISM

This distinctive pattern of American politics—that political struggles are transformed into constitutional struggles over federalism—was laid down early in the American republic in the conflict over the National Bank. It resulted in the most important Supreme Court decision on federalism: *McCulloch* v. *Maryland* (1819). The decision laid the groundwork for major expansions of federal power in the twentieth century.

Marshall's Doctrine of Implied Powers

The National Bank was the subject of heated conflict between elite and popular democrats from the time it was chartered during the administration of George Washington.[6] In 1816 the National Bank became the center of a political struggle between Federalists and Jeffersonian popular democrats. Jeffersonians accused Federalists of using the Bank for political purposes to line the pockets of their friends. They charged that the Bank was part of the hated "money trust" that was ruining the nation's economy. Popular demands for legislative controls on the Bank arose, and eight states passed laws or constitutional amendments restricting the activities of the Bank or imposing heavy burdens on it.

Maryland passed a law that required the National Bank to either pay the state a $15,000 annual tax or issue all bank notes on special stamped paper obtained from the state upon payment of a heavy tax. James McCulloch, the cashier of the Baltimore branch of the Bank of the United States, issued notes without complying with Maryland's law. The state of Maryland took McCulloch to court to recover the penalties.

John Marshall, Chief Justice from 1801 to 1835, and a brilliant advocate of a strong national government, delivered the opinion of the Court. Marshall admitted that no enumerated power enabled Congress to establish a corporation or create a bank. The Constitution did, however, state that Congress had the power to collect taxes, issue currency, and borrow funds. Marshall broadly interpreted the Necessary and Proper Clause as implying the power to charter a national bank:

> Let the end be legitimate, let it be within the scope of the Constitution, and all means which are appropriate, which are plainly adapted to that end, which are not prohibited, but are consistent with the letter and spirit of the Constitution, are constitutional.[7]

Marshall's doctrine of **implied powers** became a cornerstone of the expanding powers of the federal government.

Following his conclusion that the Bank was constitutional under the doctrine of implied powers, Marshall went on to argue, under the Supremacy Clause, that the National Bank must be immune from attack by the states. Coining the famous phrase, "The power to tax involves the power to destroy," Marshall declared that states could not tax any federal instruments. The Maryland law, therefore, was unconstitutional.

The States Fight Back

Marshall's decision unleashed a storm of protest by popular democrats who controlled many state governments. Ohio defied the law and continued to collect a tax on the National Bank, but it was later forced to cease. President Andrew Jackson, a fierce opponent of the National Bank, vetoed the bill for the recharter of the Second Bank in 1832, defiantly rejecting the Supreme Court's reasoning on the bank's constitutionality. In 1836, Jackson appointed Roger B. Taney, a strong advocate of states' rights, to succeed Marshall as chief justice. Led by Taney until 1864, the Court chipped away at federal supremacy by upholding state laws that probably would have been struck down by the Marshall court—ushering in a long period of state domination in domestic policymaking. In the infamous *Dred Scott* decision (1857), the Taney Court ruled that the federal government had no power to prohibit slavery in the territories.[8]

The conflict between states' rights and national supremacy came to a head over the issue of slavery. Led by John C. Calhoun of South Carolina, southern states resisted tariffs to protect northern industries and efforts by the federal government to restrict slavery. Calhoun argued for the doctrine of **nullification**—that states have the right to nullify, or declare null and void, federal laws that they believe violate the Constitution. Eventually, the issue was settled by the Civil War. Although many people believe the Civil War was fought over slavery, it actually broke out over fundamental issues of federalism. Only in the middle of the war, when Lincoln issued his Emancipation Proclamation, did slavery become a central issue. The Civil War settled the issue: The federal union is indissoluble, and states do not have the right to declare acts of the federal government unconstitutional or secede from the union.

The Struggle over Dual Federalism

Although the Civil War settled the issue of state secession, virtually every other aspect of federal–state relations was still subject to debate. In the late nineteenth century, popular democrats still had power in many state legislatures and they used that power to regulate corporate elites. These efforts were frustrated by the Supreme Court, however, which often ruled against the states when they threatened the rights of private property. Concerned by rate discrimination against areas not served by competing railroads, for example, popular democrats united behind the Granger movement in the early 1870s and passed laws setting maximum rates. In the celebrated Granger cases in 1877, the Supreme Court upheld the constitutionality of these laws (*Munn* v. *Illinois, 94 U.S. 113*). In 1886, however, the Supreme Court reversed itself and ruled that the Constitution placed power to regulate interstate railroad rates exclusively in the federal government, even for segments of the journey lying entirely within one state.[9] This provided an impetus for the creation by Congress in 1887 of the Interstate Commerce Commission (ICC), the first attempt by the federal government to regulate the economy through means other than general control over money and credit. Additional impetus for the ICC, however, came from the railroads, who feared the rising power of popular democrats in the state legislatures. They saw federal railroad regulation "as a safe shield behind which to hide from the consequences of local democracy."[10]

In short, elite and popular democratic forces tried to shift policymaking authority to the federal or state level, respectively. In the late nineteenth and early twentieth centuries, the Supreme Court generally acted to protect private property and was suspicious of governmental efforts, at all levels, to regulate private property. From a late-twentieth-century viewpoint, the Court construed the powers of the federal government very narrowly. It struck down the federal income tax, for example;[11] restricted the powers of the ICC to set railroad rates;[12] and declared federal laws to regulate child labor unconstitutional.[13]

For almost the first 150 years of the U.S. Constitution—until the New Deal in the 1930s—something like dual federalism prevailed in American government. The powers of the federal government were construed narrowly, and Congress did not legislate in domestic policy areas that we now take for granted. Government was small, but in domestic policy state and local governments raised more taxes, spent more money, and provided more services than the federal government. There were important exceptions to this pattern of federal reluctance, particularly the assertion of federal power following the Civil War during Reconstruction in the South and federal regulation of business during the progressive era. Nevertheless, until the New Deal the federal government was the junior partner in domestic policy.

STATE COMPETITION: SURVIVAL OF THE UNFIT?

Although states, under dual federalism, possessed sole authority to act in many domestic policy areas, they often had difficulty exercising that authority because of profound changes in the economy and society. Three broad trends diminished the effectiveness of state and local governments: (1) the increased mobility of capital; (2) the creation of national markets and the growing interdependence of different regions of the country and parts of society; and (3) the emergence of huge private corporations with national connections. These trends increased the competition between state and local governments for outside resources, particularly corporate investment, thus limiting their ability to exercise their constitutional powers.

Growth of Corporations

The weakness of the states is illustrated by state chartering of private corporations. Corporations are not mentioned in the Constitution, but it was assumed that both the federal government and the states had the right to charter them. In its landmark *Dartmouth College* decision in 1819, the Supreme Court ruled that the charters of private corporations were protected under the clause in the Constitution that prohibited states from "impairing the obligation of contracts" (Art. I, Sec. 10). The sanctity of contracts is crucial to the development of American capitalism. Thus, state laws could not interfere with corporations, once established as contracts between private individuals.

Corporations could be limited, however, by their state charters. Nineteenth-century corporate charters were different from today's. They were used by popular democrats, who controlled state legislatures, to limit the powers of private corporations. Limitations were placed, for example, on capital and indebtedness. Corporations were forbidden from holding stock in other corporations. Corporate charters were limited in time, and many states prohibited corporations from owning property outside the state of their charter. Furthermore, shareholder democracy was guaranteed by the state charters. A majority of shareholders chose the board of directors, who, in turn, appointed executives to run the day-to-day affairs of the corporation.[14]

Throughout the nineteenth century the number of corporations grew, but most of them were small, served local markets, and were constrained by competition. Railroads changed all that. They became the nation's first big businesses—truly national corporations that linked different regions of the country together. For the first time, producers could contemplate winning monopoly control not just over a local area but over an entire national market. John D. Rockefeller, for example, in a blatant violation of state incorporation laws, set up Standard Oil of Ohio, which placed controlling interest of the stock of supposedly competing companies in a trust run by a single board of directors. The Standard Oil trust enabled Rockefeller to control 95 percent of all refined oil shipments in the nation. Trusts were soon organized in other industries: the Cotton Oil Trust in 1884 and the Whiskey Trust, the Sugar Trust, and the Lead Trust in 1887.

A furious popular democratic movement arose to challenge the growing powers of corporate elites. Popular democrats used state incorporation laws to declare the trusts illegal. All of the early national trusts were dissolved, except the Standard Oil Trust. In 1892, the Supreme Court of Ohio ruled that the Standard Oil Trust was "organized for a purpose contrary to the policy of our laws" and therefore "void."[15] For five years, Standard Oil simply refused to obey the ruling. In 1898, Ohio's attorney general brought a contempt citation to revoke Standard Oil's charter. Standard Oil survived by skipping to New Jersey, a state which had put out a welcome map to corporations with a permissive incorporation law.

New Jersey: The Traitor State

In 1891, New Jersey, sensing a profitable opportunity, passed a new state incorporation statute that legalized trusts by enabling New Jersey corporations to control stock or assets in their competitors. New Jersey, which came to be known as "The Traitor State," went further in 1896 by allowing unlimited corporate size and concentration; legalizing stock watering, which enabled corporations to purchase competitors without any cash; and gutting shareholder democracy by placing power in the hands of directors and management. Other states could do little because, according to the Constitution (ART. IV), states must give "Full Faith and Credit" to the laws of other states.

New Jersey got rich with its new incorporation laws, as corporations flocked there and incorporation fees flooded state coffers. By 1902, New Jersey was able to abolish all property taxes and pay off its entire state debt. In 1905, the governor bragged that "Of the entire income of the government, not a penny was contributed directly by the people. . . ."[16] Subsequently, Delaware surpassed New Jersey, passing "enabling acts" that allowed corporations to do as they pleased without interference from state regulation.[17] By 1988, nearly eighteen thousand corporations were chartered in the tiny state of Delaware.[18]

The elite democratic justification for permissive incorporation laws was that corporations should be free to engage in unrestrained competition. In the words of John D. Rockefeller, "The growth of a large business is merely the survival of the fittest. . . . The American Beauty Rose can be produced in the splendor and fragrance which bring cheer to its beholder only by sacrificing the early buds which grow up all around it."[19] Liberal state incorporation laws, however, allowed anticompetitive practices to proliferate, enabling corporate elites to accumulate vast wealth and power. According to one commentator, competition under dual federalism promoted not the best state laws but the "survival of the unfit."[20]

Present-Day State Competition

The case of state incorporation laws illustrates that states can have formal constitutional powers to act—for example, to regulate corporations—and yet be unable to exercise those powers. As capital has become more mobile in the twentieth century, states have moved beyond competing for chartering fees to competing for corporate investment. The competition for mobile investment has placed distinct limits on what cities and states can do.[21] State and local governments provide incentives to attract capital investment into their jurisdiction. Increased capital investment fattens the tax base, thus enabling the government to either reduce taxes or take in more revenues at the same tax rate. If states and cities do not create a favorable "business climate," the argument goes, they experience a downward spiral of disinvestment and fiscal crisis.

The competition between states for industrial investment was pioneered by southern states after World War II and then spread to northern states in the 1970s. States have now developed a vast array of incentives, including property tax abatements, investment tax credits, exemptions on business equipment, loan guarantees, and land writedowns (purchasing and clearing land for private investors at the public expense). When northern states began to suffer from extensive *deindustrialization* (the loss of industrial jobs) in the 1970s, they began a fierce competition with Sunbelt states for industrial investment. In 1976, *Business Week* called the spread of northern business incentives "a counterattack in the war between the states."[22]

A good example of how far states and localities will go in the competition for investment is the decision by General Motors to build a new Cadillac plant in Detroit. To get the $600 million investment, the Detroit city government had to purchase and clear a 500-acre site in the city, "the largest land-assemblage and clearance program in United States history."[23] A viable neighborhood known as Poletown had to be gutted, with 3,200 people forced from their homes, many churches torn down, and 160 community businesses eliminated. In addition, the city had to invest over $250 million of its own money and offer tax breaks worth hundreds of millions of dollars.

Many people question whether this type of "smokestack chasing" is really beneficial. The authors of a major study on Poletown concluded that "the project has not paid for itself"—it cost the city more than it gave back in additional tax revenues.[24] In another example, New York City and New York State gave Chase Manhattan a package of incentives worth $235 million to stay in New York rather than move to New Jersey. The incentive package was worth $47,000 per job, raising the question of whether the costs to the city exceeded the benefits.[25]

The literature on state and local incentives for business indicates that they are often not effective. Studies show, for example, that tax incentives are usually insufficient to alter corporate location decisions.[26] As a result, such incentives may provide windfall profits to corporations that would have invested there anyway. Nevertheless, mayors and governors often pursue incentives as a way of signalling to voters that they are doing something about economic decline and unemployment. The proliferation of tax incentives, however, erodes the ability of state and local governments to raise revenues. Preoccupied with the competition for economic development and concerned that generous social welfare benefits will attract the poor, states and localities fail to adequately address social problems and poverty. Fortunately, in the 1930s, the federal government initiated social programs, in conjunction with state and local governments, to address these problems.

THE NEW DEAL: FROM DUAL FEDERALISM TO INTERGOVERNMENTAL RELATIONS

Until the twentieth century, popular democrats, following the tradition established by the Anti-federalists, favored leaving most powers in the hands of state and local governments. Increasingly, however, popular democrats found that the competition for mobile wealth hindered the ability of states to address the basic problems of industrialism. Large corporations, with national networks and lobbying powers, were able to play one state against another to avoid being regulated and paying for the costs of industrialization. Moreover, state legislatures were often dominated by rural representatives who had little concern for the problems of cities. Because of the way district lines were drawn, cities, where mobilization on the issues of industrialism and poverty was centered, were grossly underrepresented.

Popular democrats, who favored grassroots solutions, were forced to turn to the federal government to address problems of inequality and corporate abuse of power. The dilemma of American federalism was born. It is reflected in the tremendous expansion of the federal government during the New Deal, which grew out of the inability of states and localities to manage the problems of the Great Depression.

The Great Depression posed a serious crisis for American economic and political institutions. It began with the stock market crash on October 24, 1929—Black Thursday. The effects of the crash rippled out from Wall Street to paralyze the entire nation. The unemployment rate soared from 3 percent in 1929 to over one-quarter of the work force in 1933. Those who were lucky enough to have jobs saw their average incomes fall 43 percent from 1929 to 1933. The collapse of the economy spread to the financial system; by the end of 1932, 5,096 commercial banks had failed.

The initial response of the political system to the Depression was halting and inadequate. Under the system of dual federalism, almost all social welfare functions were left to the states and localities. Before the New Deal, the American welfare state was based on the Elizabethan Poor Law of 1601, which was transplanted to the colonies from England.[27] Governmental efforts to care for the destitute were financed and administered locally. In 1929–1930, local governments provided 95 percent of the costs of general relief.[28] The American welfare state was incredibly fragmented, with Ohio, for example, having 1,535 different poor relief districts.[29] Burdened by a crazy quilt of jurisdictional responsibilities, welfare was poorly administered and inadequately funded.

The local welfare state had other characteristics that hindered its effectiveness. The system was based on a sharp distinction between the deserving and the undeserving poor, generally excluding all able-bodied men from receiving aid.

A loser in the stock market crash of 1929 puts his car up for sale.

Strict residency requirements excluded many others. Finally, the system was based on almshouses, where the poor were warehoused under wretched conditions and often made to work. On the eve of the Depression, almshouses and workhouses were the dominant methods for aiding the poor.[30]

Even though donations to private charities increased when the Depression hit, the system was incapable of keeping up with the soaring needs. In 1932, less than a quarter of the unemployed got any relief at all. For those who did, relief payments were inadequate. In New York City, families received an average grant of $2.39 per week.[31] The cities with the worst problems had the fewest resources to deal with them. With nearly one-third of its industrial work force unemployed, Detroit made a heroic effort to provide relief, spending more per capita than any other city in the country. Detroit's compassion, however, soon surpassed its tax base. Under pressure from the city's creditors, Detroit was forced to cut already inadequate relief appropriations in half in 1931–32.[32]

Adhering to the principle of dual federalism, President Herbert Hoover refused to sanction an expansion of federal relief activities. Speaking in 1932, Hoover asserted

I hold that the maintenance of the sense of individual responsibility of men to their neighbors and the proper separation of the functions of the Federal and local Governments require the maintenance of the fundamental principle that the relief of distress rests upon the individuals, upon the communities and upon the states.[33]

Hoover, who remained in office until 1933, held steadfastly to the position that capitalism would right itself, so long as the federal government did not interfere.

Roosevelt's New Deal: The Dilemma of Dual Federalism

Franklin Delano Roosevelt assumed the presidency on March 4, 1933, in an atmosphere of profound political crisis that cried out for decisive federal action. The unemployed were taking to the streets to vent their frustrations. Violent confrontations occurred in many cities between police and workers trying to organize unions. Communists were increasingly effective in organizing demonstrations against the government.

Roosevelt's past gave little indication, however, that he would preside over one of the greatest expansions of federal power in history. He won office not so much because voters endorsed his program, which was consummately vague, but because they rejected Hoover's handling of the economy. Roosevelt was a shrewd politician, however, known for bold experimentation. In his speech accepting the Democratic Party's nomination for the presidency in 1932, Roosevelt declared: "It is common sense to take a method and try it. If it fails try another. But above all, try something."[34] Roosevelt would give voters the action they wanted, but the exact roles of various levels of government depended more on practical politics than on settled doctrines of federalism.

Roosevelt faced a dilemma. The situation called for decisive federal action, but he knew that any attempt to expand federal powers into areas that had previously been reserved for the states would meet crippling opposition in the Supreme Court and in Congress, which strongly represented local interests. A Supreme Court veto was no idle threat. The Supreme Court was dominated by conservative justices who accepted the tenet of dual federalism that there were certain functions that were off limits for the federal government. In 1935, in the "sick chicken" case, the Supreme Court struck down the National Industrial Recovery Act, asserting that the regulation of wages and hours fell outside the powers of Congress to regulate interstate commerce.[35] Emboldened by Supreme Court rulings, by late 1935, lower court judges had issued sixteen hundred orders to prevent federal officials from implementing acts of Congress.[36] In perhaps the biggest blow to the New Deal expansion of federal power, in 1936 the Supreme Court struck down the Agricultural Adjustment Act. Rejecting an expansive definition of the General Welfare Clause, Justice Owen Roberts wrote:

From the accepted doctrine that the United States is a government of delegated powers, it follows that those not expressly granted or reasonably to be implied from such as are conferred, are reserved to the states or to the people. . . .

None to regulate agricultural production is given, and therefore legislation by Congress for that purpose is forbidden.[37]

Frustrated by the Supreme Court's opposition, Roosevelt attempted to "pack the court" by adding justices friendly to the New Deal. He failed. Although most Americans opposed Supreme Court limitations on the New Deal, they also opposed tampering with the checks and balances of the Constitution.

Roosevelt's Solution: Grants-in-Aid

Realizing that strong national programs and standards were politically infeasible, Roosevelt gradually embraced an approach advocated by Supreme Court Justice Louis Brandeis. In a famous dissenting opinion in 1932, Brandies praised the federal system for allowing a state to "serve as a laboratory, and try novel social and economic experiments without risk to the rest of the country."[38] Brandeis recommended to Roosevelt that the federal government encourage the states to assume more active policy roles in addressing the crisis.

The Brandeis position was essentially a "third way" that attempted to slip between the horns of the dilemma of state inaction and federal domination. The new approach combined federal funding with state administration. The federal government enacted a series of conditional **grants-in-aid**—monies provided by one level of government to another to fulfill certain functions. Usually states are required to put up some of their own money (these are called **matching**

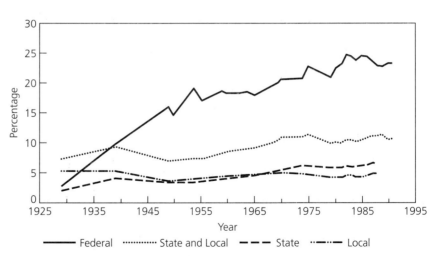

FIGURE 3.1

Government Spending as a Percentage of GNP, 1929–1991

Federal ·········· State and Local ▬ ▬ State ▬··▬ Local

Note: Separate state and local figures unavailable after 1988. Shown as "own source" spending, i.e., before intergovernmental transfers.

Source: Stanley, Harold W., and Richard G. Niemi, *Vital Statistics on American Politics,* Fourth Edition. Copyright © 1994 CQ Press. Used with permission.

grants), and they have to meet minimal federal standards for the program. Grants-in-aid had been in existence for many years, and as early as 1923, the Supreme Court had declared them constitutional on the ground that they were not obligatory but simply offered "an option which the state is free to accept or reject."[39] Federal grants-in-aid expanded rapidly during the New Deal, from $217 million in 1932 to $744 million in 1941.[40]

The New Deal revolutionized American federalism, moving the federal government into domestic policy functions previously reserved to the states. At the same time, the new federal system preserved many of the powers of state and local governments. As Figures 3.1 and 3.2 show, although federal spending has soared, most public employees work for state and local governments. Under the system of federal grants, relations between governmental levels are worked out by specific legislation and negotiations. Hence, the new federalism is called **intergovernmental relations** to distinguish it from dual federalism, which was based on separate spheres of authority.

Intergovernmental Relations as a Political Compromise

The New Deal represented a historical shift for popular democrats. Until then, popular democrats had generally favored action through state and local governments. The failure of states and localities to address the problems of the

---

FIGURE 3.2

Number of Federal, State, and Local Government Employees, 1929–1991

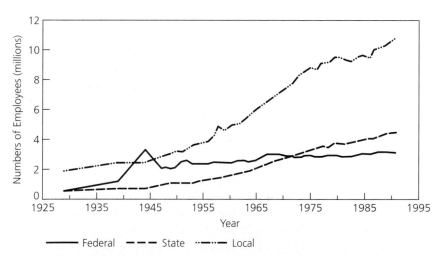

Source: Stanley, Harold W., and Richard G. Niemi, *Vital Statistics on American Politics,* Fourth Edition. Copyright © 1994 CQ Press. Used with permission.

Depression, however, dramatically illustrated the need to expand the powers of the federal government. Popular democrats turned to the federal government, but they were forced to compromise with elite democrats who now turned to state and local governments to protect their powers and privileges.

The shifting positions of elite and popular democrats over New Deal programs are evident in the 1935 Social Security Act, probably the most important piece of domestic legislation in American history. (The politics of Social Security are examined more extensively in Chapter 18.) Popular democrats succeeded in including in the law a system of old-age insurance run entirely by the federal government. Because Social Security old-age insurance covers most American workers and is administered nationally, it has proven to be politically popular and benefits have risen much more rapidly than inflation. As a result, poverty among the elderly has fallen significantly, enhancing their ability to participate in the political system and be heard.

To get the Social Security Act through Congress, however, Roosevelt was forced to compromise on welfare and unemployment insurance with southern white elites who controlled key congressional committees. Southern elites feared that a federally run welfare and unemployment insurance system with high uniform payments would disrupt race relations in the South and threaten the low-wage labor market that was central to the southern economy. Both for welfare and unemployment insurance, therefore, the Social Security Act set up systems that gave substantial discretion to the states. In the case of welfare, the law set up federal matching grants that gave states considerable freedom to set benefit levels and eligibility. Unlike old-age insurance, welfare, which is administered by the states, has suffered from uneven, inadequate, and (since the 1970s) declining benefit levels. To this day, southern states still provide low benefit levels. In 1991, for example, under Aid to Families with Dependent Children (AFDC) average monthly benefits ranged from $691 in Alaska to only $122 in Mississippi.

In 1937, the Supreme Court, without any change in membership, narrowly approved the Social Security Act, arguing that the purposes of the act fell under the powers of the federal government to "promote the general welfare."[41] Had the Social Security system been run entirely by the federal government, it probably would not have been approved by the courts.

The expansion of the federal government under the New Deal had elements of both elite and popular democracy. In part, the system of federal grants deferred to the power of entrenched state and local elites. (It should be noted that Roosevelt did not challenge the racist practices in the South that prevented most blacks from voting. Black voting rates remained low until the federal government directly intervened after passing the 1965 Voting Rights Act.) On the other hand, the New Deal did use the powers of the federal government to address problems of economic inequality. Annual public expenditures for relief, welfare, and social security increased twenty-five-fold from 1929 to 1939.[42] As we discuss in Chapter 8, federal programs also mobilized urban working-class ethnics in the New Deal coalition.

Strains in the New Deal Coalition: The Problem of Race

By the 1960s, conflicts over issues of federalism threatened the New Deal coalition. The coalition was partly held together by deferring to southern white elites' wishes to uphold states' rights in key areas such as education and voting. The 1954 *Brown* decision, in which the Supreme Court ordered southern states to desegregate their schools, set in motion the civil rights movement that raised the expectations of African Americans around the country. (Chapter 11 discusses the civil rights movement in depth.) The migration of blacks to northern cities, where they voted in greater numbers, created a dilemma for the Democrats. Winning the urban black vote was key to winning the large industrial states that were decisive in the electoral college, but appealing to the black vote risked alienating southern Democrats. In 1960, John Kennedy made a strong appeal to the urban black vote, promising federal assertiveness on poverty and civil rights; partly as a result, the States' Rights Party won Mississippi and Alabama and the Republicans won Florida, Tennessee, Kentucky, and Virginia. At the same time, huge black majorities in key cities in major industrial states helped vault Kennedy into the presidency.

Kennedy's successor, Lyndon Johnson, went much further, giving up southern segregationist white votes in exchange for black votes in the cities. When Johnson signed the 1964 Civil Rights Act, which put the force of the federal government behind integration in public accommodations, employment, and schools, he confided to an aide that he believed he had "delivered the South to the Republican Party for a long time to come."[43] Johnson's opponent in 1964, Senator Barry Goldwater, voted against the Civil Rights Act, taking the dual federalist position that the federal government had no power to legislate in the area of education. Even though Goldwater was trounced by Johnson, he carried the states of the Deep South, signalling the end of the "Solid South" for the Democratic party.

EXPANDING FEDERAL GRANTS: LBJ'S CREATIVE FEDERALISM

The system of grants-in-aid put in place by the New Deal expanded slowly until the 1960s. President Eisenhower did not roll back the welfare state established by the New Deal but, with the exception of interstate highways, he initiated few major new grants. But major expansion occurred in the 1960s. By the end of Eisenhower's presidency in 1960, grants-in-aid totalled only $7.0 billion; by 1970, they had more than tripled, to $24.1 billion, representing 19 percent of total state and local outlays (see Figure 3.3). To understand this tremendous expansion, it is necessary to understand the political context and goals of the key actors.

After his victory in the 1964 presidential election, Johnson saw the need to tie restive urban blacks to the national Democratic party. The obvious strategy was to expand the system of grants-in-aid targeted to urban problems, which Johnson did. During his five-year presidency, Johnson created hundreds of

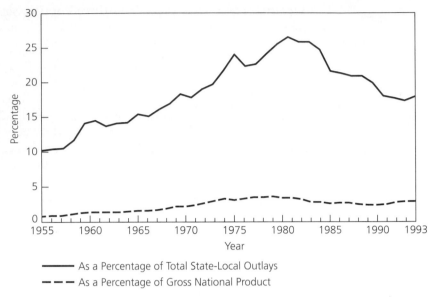

Source: Adapted from Advisory Commission on Intergovernmental Relations, *Significant Features of Fiscal Federalism, 1991,* vol. 2 (Washington, D.C.: Author, 1991), p. 50.

FIGURE 3.3

Federal Grants-in-Aid in Relation to State and Local Outlays and Gross National Product, 1955–1993

President Lyndon Johnson greets a group of youngsters in the White House Rose Garden to announce the first grants for Head Start (May 18, 1965). The program gave grants to local organizations to help children from underprivileged backgrounds prepare to enter school on a more equal basis.

categorical grant programs—which required recipients to apply for funding under specific categories, detailing how the money would be spent and subjecting themselves to strict federal monitoring—aimed at urban problems (see Figure 3.4). At the same time, Johnson was keenly aware that these programs would help tie urban voters, especially blacks, to the Democratic party.

The shortcoming of the conventional grants-in-aid strategy was that most of the money went through state and city governments, which had little black influence. State governments were still usually dominated by suburban, small-town, and rural interests, and many city governments were controlled by white ethnics who resisted black efforts to gain power. Johnson called his solution **creative federalism:** The federal government would bypass state and city governments and give grants directly to community and nonprofit organizations in the ghettos. The Economic Opportunity Act of 1964, for example, created expensive new categorical grants to fight urban, largely black, poverty, and included programs such as Head Start (an early education program for disadvantaged children), the Job Corps, and community action agencies. Approximately 75 percent of the community action agencies were nongovernmental.[44] They provided service centers for the urban poor and became political advocates for the disadvantaged, often attacking municipal governments.

THE DEBATE OVER FEDERAL GRANTS

The expansion of federal grants in the 1960s and 1970s initiated a debate about American federalism that continues to this day. Many argued that the system had

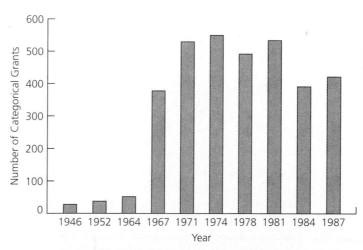

FIGURE 3.4

Growth of Categorical Grants

Source: Janda, Kenneth, Jeffrey M. Berry and Jerry Goldman, *The Challenge of Democracy: Government in America,* Second Edition. Copyright © 1989 by Houghton Mifflin Company. Used with permission.

become overloaded. The federal government funded grants for every conceivable purpose—from rat control to crime control, from urban gardening to home insulation. Every grant required detailed regulations that became increasingly burdensome to the recipients. The pages in the *Federal Register*, which prints new regulations, increased from 14,479 in 1960, to 20,037 in 1970, to 71,191 in 1979.[45] Red tape, it was called. Implementation became complicated, as each program required the cooperation of different agencies and governments. One study of a federal program in Oakland, California, concluded that it required seventy separate agreements between different agencies, making successful implementation nearly impossible.[46]

The expanding system of federal grants was criticized not only for being inefficient but also for undermining democratic accountability. With hundreds of grants, each involving numerous actors at the federal, state, and local levels, the voters had difficulty pinpointing responsibility. Complex federal grant programs, critics argued, took power from elected representatives and gave it to staff experts, issue specialists, and bureaucrats. Grantsmanship (the ability to write successful grant applications) biased the allocation of funds. Members of Congress began to ignore state and local needs to favor national lobbies situated in Washington, D.C. Every special interest seemed to have its own categorical grant, benefitting narrow constituencies at the expense of the public interest.

Often, criticisms of the expanding federal powers resonated with the Antifederalist warnings of a distant central government. Sometimes, however, popular democrats favored federal action. Federal action was necessary, for example, to break the elite stranglehold on electoral power in many southern states. Many people criticized the 1965 Voting Rights Act as interference by the federal government in the internal affairs of states. The act, however, precipitated a democratic revolution in southern politics, enabling millions of blacks to vote for the first time.

Although the federal Voting Rights Act clearly supported popular democracy, popular democrats often disagreed about the expanded system of federal grants-in-aid. Many federal grants were too complex and placed power in the hands of experts and federal bureaucrats who were unfamiliar with local conditions. Criticisms of the system, however, were based as much on practical politics as on democratic principles.

As we noted earlier, many of Johnson's new categorical grants bypassed state and local governments and gave power over funds directly to ghetto residents. The community action program called for "maximum feasible participation." The War on Poverty programs helped poor ghetto residents mobilize politically. In some ways, Johnson's creative federalism was the epitome of popular democracy. Mayors and city officials, who often bore the brunt of angry demonstrations, however, did not see it this way. Local Democratic parties were often dominated by white ethnic politicians who had always been at the center of the New Deal coalition. They were outraged that the federal government was funding their political opponents. By mobilizing poor blacks, which resulted in a countermobilization of white ethnics, Johnson's War on Poverty programs strained the Democratic coalition. Johnson got so much political grief for the War on Poverty programs that he suspected it was being orchestrated by his political enemies, led by Robert Kennedy.[47]

NIXON'S NEW FEDERALISM

Just as Johnson's creative federalism was shaped by calculations of political advantage, the Republican response also was based on political calculations. The Republicans took advantage of the perceived bias of federal grant programs. Many federal grant programs were targeted to inner cities, the poor, and blacks.[48] The number of families on welfare (AFDC) soared 237 percent from 1965 to 1975.[49] Although most welfare recipients were white, the public viewed welfare as a black program. The expansion of welfare took place at a time of rising racial tensions worsened by the urban riots of the 1960s. During this period, federal courts began calling for busing to achieve integration in the schools and affirmative action to correct historical bias in the workplace. Busing was to the North what the Voting Rights Act had been to the South: It evoked a white backlash against federal intervention.

Republicans were in a position in the 1960s to take advantage of this backlash and appeal to lower-middle-class white voters who perceived that their hard-earned tax monies were going, under Democratic-sponsored federal grants, disproportionately to the inner-city poor and minorities. Direct opposition to the objectives of these programs, however, would risk alienating traditional Republican voters repelled by any taint of racism. Richard Nixon found a brilliant way out of this dilemma that helped him win the presidency in 1968: He supported the goal of racial equality but opposed federal intervention to achieve it in education, employment, and voting rights. Advocating decentralization of power to states and localities provided a way for Republican (and sometimes Democratic) politicians to appeal to white voters, who felt threatened by racial change, while not appearing racist.[50]

In 1969, President Nixon proposed what he called "the first major reversal of the trend toward ever more centralization of government in Washington. . . . It is time for a New Federalism in which power, funds, and responsibility will flow from Washington to the States and to the people."[51] Nixon's **new federalism** was politically appealing because it weakened the power of Washington-centered liberal lobbies which would now have to divide their attention among fifty state and hundreds of local governments. Nixon, however, did not reject the goals of the welfare state and the system of federal grants that had originated with the New Deal. Unlike a later Republican president, Ronald Reagan, Nixon did not aim to shrink government. His goals were basically managerial: to rationalize the system of grants by shifting responsibilities within the intergovernmental system.

After a series of political defeats on his new federalism, Nixon succeeded in making important changes in the grant system. Until then, nearly all grants had been categorical grants. In 1972, Nixon won passage of **general revenue sharing,** which provided for the distribution of about $6 billion a year in federal grants to state and local governments with few strings attached. The distribution of funds was weighted to give more money to governments that had poor tax bases and were already taxing themselves heavily. General revenue sharing was popular with governors and mayors who felt that the federal government should share its superior taxing ability. It was not popular with members of Congress who had little control over how the money was spent compared to traditional categorical grants.

Nixon also proposed a series of **block grants**—grants in which federal involvement is midway between the tight controls of categorical grants and the minimal controls of general revenue sharing. Under this method, a number of related categorical grants are consolidated into one block grant. Instead of competing for the funds, governments are allocated monies according to a formula based on need. The recipients spend the grant as they see fit within the broad purposes of the block grant.

Nixon enacted two major block grants: the Comprehensive Employment and Training Act (CETA) in 1973 and the Community Development Block Grant (CDBG) in 1974. CDBG, which was actually signed into law by President Ford, folded seven categorical grant programs into one block grant—becoming the major successor to the poverty programs of the 1960s. Although the act required that each locality "give maximum feasible priority to activities which will benefit low- or moderate-income families," the rules were sufficiently vague to give local governments freedom to spend the money on a wide range of urban priorities.

THE COUNTERREVOLUTION: REAGAN'S NEW FEDERALISM

Contrary to conventional wisdom, cuts in federal grants actually began during the administration of Democrat Jimmy Carter. Carter ran for the presidency in 1976 promising to reduce the size and cost of the federal government. As Figure 3.3 shows, Carter reversed the growth of federal grants, which reached their peak in 1978 and began a downward trend in the last two years of his presidency. But it was Carter's Republican successor, Ronald Reagan, who really challenged the system of intergovernmental grants initiated by Roosevelt's New Deal.

Compared to Nixon, Reagan was a radical on federalism issues. His goal was to go back to the system of dual federalism that had existed before the New Deal. As Reagan put it in his First Inaugural Address (January 20, 1981):

> It is my intention to curb the size and influence of the Federal establishment and to demand recognition of the distinction between the powers granted to the Federal government and those reserved to the states or the people. All of us need to be reminded that the Federal government did not create the states; the states created the federal government.

Reagan's rhetoric against federal grants invoked the values of popular democracy, such as making government more democratically accountable and returning power to the grassroots. Reagan's commitment to decentralizing governmental power was sincere, but it was secondary to his commitment to private markets. Reagan had a firm ideological commitment to the market as a better allocator of goods and services than government. By removing restraints on corporate elites, Reagan's new federalism favored elite democracy over popular democracy. His goal was not to revitalize state and local governments but to shrink governmental programs across the board.

Reagan and his aides thought that decentralizing power to states and localities would achieve their goal of shrinking government. There were three reasons for this belief: (1) Liberal lobbies, which had been centered in Washington, D.C. for a generation, would be less influential at the state and local levels; (2) being closer to the voters, state and local governments would be less inclined to increase taxes to pay for social programs; and (3) economic competition between states and localities for mobile investment would force them to limit tax increases. In practice, decentralization of power did not always lead to shrinking government, and when the two goals of shrinking government and decentralizing power conflicted, decentralization was sacrificed.

In 1981, shortly after he assumed office, Reagan won congressional approval to eliminate sixty categorical grants and to merge another fifty-seven into nine block grants. State officials, initially enthusiastic about having greater control over the monies, lost some of their enthusiasm when they realized that funding for the programs was cut 25 percent. Buoyed by this initial success, Reagan proposed an ambitious swap of programs between the states and the federal government. Reagan's proposed swap provoked intense opposition from state officials who felt it would saddle them with new financial burdens and it failed to win congressional support.

After the failure of his swap proposal, Reagan turned to a more incremental approach, proposing cuts in existing grant programs. Reagan's popular tax cuts in 1981 and 1986 undermined the revenue base of the federal government. Facing serious deficit problems, Congress was generally receptive to his proposed cuts in intergovernmental grants. Federal spending on payments to individuals, like Social Security, increased 22 percent from 1980 to 1987 after controlling for inflation. At the same time, total grants-in-aid to state and local governments declined 15 percent.[52] In 1986, Congress killed general revenue sharing. The Reagan cuts in intergovernmental grants hurt poor people the most, especially minorities and those living in cities. Reagan knew he did not need the urban vote to win reelection; in 1984, he trounced Walter Mondale, even though he won only about a third of the big-city vote.

When the Reagan administration's new federalism goals came in conflict with its goals of enhancing private decision-making power, the federalism goals were sacrificed. Big businesses generally oppose shifting regulatory authority from the federal government to state and local governments. Businesses have trouble keeping track of regulations in fifty different states and thousands of local governments. Moreover, sometimes states pass more restrictive regulations than the federal government. To forestall these limits on business, the Reagan

The federal government often requires state and local governments to take certain actions, such as cleaning up the environment, but does not provide them with the money to pay for the new responsibilities. Unfunded mandates place fiscal burdens on state and local governments.

administration advocated pro-business federal regulatory expansion in many areas, including trucking, nuclear power, offshore oil exploration, and coastal zone management.

Violating his commitment to governmental decentralization, Reagan frequently supported the preemption of state and local regulatory powers. **Preemption** is the ability of the federal government to assume total or partial responsibility for a function designated for concurrent authority. Under the Supremacy Clause of the Constitution, federal regulations preempt, or supercede, state laws. In 1982, for example, Reagan supported uniform national truck standards that gave large new trucks access to 38,000 more miles of highway than state highway departments had deemed suitable. States that refused to comply with the new standards were threatened with loss of federal highway funds.[53] Reagan signed 106 bills in which the federal government preempted the powers of states or local governments; he vetoed only two preemption statutes.[54]

SURPRISING RESURGENCE OF THE STATES

Reagan strategists calculated that the decentralization of governmental policy-making would lead to an overall reduction in governmental activities. The actual record is mixed. Some states and localities aggressively filled the gaps in social programs hurt by Reagan cuts; others did little. Neither conservative hopes nor liberal fears were confirmed. As in the 1920s, during a time of conservative dominance at the national level, some states became laboratories of democracy, experimenting in diverse ways to address social and economic problems.

In many ways, the economic pressures that limit state policy options are more intense now than they were in the nineteenth century. The development of truck transportation, enhanced by the federal interstate highway system, gives manufacturers greater freedom to locate their factories anywhere around the country. The increased mobility of capital makes states reluctant to increase taxes to pay for redistributive policies for fear of hurting the business climate. States are also reluctant to provide generous welfare benefits for fear of becoming "welfare magnets."[55]

On the other hand, political factors that limited state responsiveness were greatly reduced in the postwar period. Politically, states are now more capable than ever of exerting leadership within the federal system. A quiet revolution has swept the states, making them both more capable of effective action and more responsive to a variety of interests:

1. State constitutions have been streamlined.

2. The powers of governors have been strengthened through constitutional provisions and statutory enactments.

3. State bureaucracies have been professionalized and made more representative.

4. State legislatures now meet annually and are aided in their work by more efficient procedures and more professional staffs.[56]

5. Following Supreme Court mandates, beginning with *Baker* v. *Carr* (1962), state legislatures have been reapportioned to reflect population, making them more responsive to metropolitan and minority interests.

The response to the Reagan cuts in intergovernmental aid varied significantly among programs and states. In general, programs targeted to the poor, such as AFDC (welfare), suffered the largest federal aid cuts. Moreover, states did little to protect these programs. On the other hand, programs with politically active state and local constituencies, such as social services for the elderly, tended to have federal cuts replaced or delayed by state funds. The responses also varied by state. Generally, states with strong fiscal conditions and liberal political traditions did more to replace the cuts. Massachusetts and New York, for example, were assertive in replacing the Reagan cuts, whereas California, limited by a powerful tax revolt, did little.[57]

New State Ventures

Many states did not just wait to respond to the Reagan cuts; they embarked on their own ambitious public sector experiments in the 1980s. In the area of economic development, for example, entrepreneurial state governments stepped

A CLOSER LOOK

Linkage Policies: Robin Hood Responses to the Reagan Cuts

It wasn't just the states that became laboratories of democracy in the 1980s in response to the federal cuts. Cities also responded with innovative programs, proving that popular democracy is still alive at the grassroots.

One of the areas in which cities became the most innovative was housing. Of all the major federal policy areas, housing suffered the deepest cuts, falling from $30 billion in authorized spending in 1981, at the start of the Reagan administration, to less than $10 billion by 1986.

At the same time as the federal cuts, housing problems were worsened by a boom in downtown office construction. The high-income professionals who occupied the gleaming new office towers competed with low-income inner-city families for available housing, driving up rents and displacing the poor. The process was called gentrification. Further evidence of a housing crisis was the dramatic rise in homelessness in the 1980s.

To make up for the federal cuts, many cities began to experiment with innovative ways to link downtown commercial development to the provision of affordable housing. The reasoning behind "linkage" policies was simple: New downtown office buildings bring additional office workers into the city who compete with city residents for existing housing, driving up rents for low-income families, often forcing them to move. Thus, downtown office developers should be required to contribute to affordable housing; office development should be linked to housing.

San Francisco was the first city to pass a linkage policy in 1981. By 1990, 10 percent of a sample of 133 major American cities had enacted linkage policies.

Corporate elites attacked linkage policies as unfair and ineffective. An article in *Fortune*, entitled "Robin Hood Subsidies: A Dubious New Fad," faulted linkage policies for "making builders scapegoats for forces beyond their control." In addition, developers warned that linkage fees would discourage investment in downtowns, "killing the goose that lays the golden eggs."

There is little evidence, however, that linkage policies have hurt investment. They are simply too small a factor in the overall costs of development. "We've checked with economists and real estate people," said Dean Macris, Director of San Francisco's Planning Department, "and we can't find any evidence that it's been harmful."

Announcing Boston's expanded linkage program in 1984, populist mayor Ray Flynn stated: "The paradox of prosperity in our downtowns and poverty in our neighborhoods can now be addressed." By the end of 1992, Boston's linkage policies had raised almost $70 million, helping to provide ten thousand affordable housing units. Linkage policies can contribute to affordable housing, but they cannot make up for the huge federal cuts.

More important than the economic contribution is the symbolic message that linkage sends: Those who draw on the commonwealth of the city have an obligation to help those who are hurt by their profit-making activity. As a report on linkage by the Boston Redevelopment Authority put it: "The critical issue is economic justice."

Sources: Edward G. Goetz, *Shelter Burden: Local Politics and Progressive Housing Policy* (Philadelphia: Temple University Press, 1993); Douglas Porter, ed., *Downtown Linkages* (Washington, D.C.: Urban Land Institute, 1985); Gurney Breckenfeld, " 'Robin Hood' Subsidies: A Dubious New Fad," *Fortune,* March 21, 1983, pp. 148–52.

into the vacuum of economic planning left by the federal government and developed aggressive strategic plans for development. Instead of engaging in smokestack chasing with mindless incentives, states have tried to expand markets for existing industries or supplied venture capital for small and innovative businesses. In addition, many states have made special efforts to increase the number of well-paid jobs.[58]

Attempts to Fill the Health-Care Gap

Even though about 37 million Americans had no health insurance and costs in the system were soaring beyond inflation, the federal government enacted no major health-care legislation in the 1980s. Tired of waiting, many states stepped into the breach. Hawaii developed a plan, enacted in 1974, that provided nearly 100 percent coverage. It worked surprisingly well; Hawaii's citizens enjoyed one of the lowest infant mortality rates and chronic disease rates in the nation. Oregon developed a plan to expand eligibility for Medicaid, require employers to buy coverage for their workers, and ration medical services. In 1992, the Bush administration vetoed the plan, arguing that the rationing would discriminate against people with disabilities.

In 1993, the Clinton administration proposed a comprehensive program of national health insurance that borrowed from health-care reforms initiated in the states. The plan was modelled on the Social Security System, with states organizing their own delivery systems and minimum national standards mandated by the federal government. The interests threatened by Clinton's plan—insurance companies, drug companies, small businesses, and doctors—attacked it for creating a new coercive federal bureaucracy. (The health-care debate is covered extensively in Chapter 18.)

Since the 1970s, the states have led the federal government into new program areas. In areas like economic development, health care, welfare reform (for example, requiring welfare recipients to get jobs), and air pollution standards (where California has led the way) the states have experimented with a range of innovations. Nevertheless, many problems, especially those caused by economic restructuring, such as unemployment, poverty, and homelessness, will never be adequately addressed by states and localities without substantial federal help.

CONCLUSION: IS THERE A WAY OUT OF THE DILEMMA?

From the original debate on federalism between the Federalists and Anti-federalists, changing intergovernmental relations in the United States have been influenced as much by calculations of political advantage as by theories of federalism. Different approaches to federalism determine where decisions are made, influencing who wins and who loses. It is distinctive to American politics that political conflict often is over how power should be distributed between the federal, state, and local governments.

Although conflicts over federalism have been driven by practical politics, important democratic principles also are at stake. Popular democrats value both equality and participation. At the founding, Anti-federalists argued that equality and participation could be maximized by decentralizing decision-making power as much as possible. The Anti-federalists warned that the U.S. Constitution gave too much power to a distant central government and that the system would eventually become unbalanced in favor of the central government.

The Anti-federalist fears have turned out to be well-founded, but in ways that they would find ironic. Since the New Deal, it has primarily been popular democrats who have urged that the powers of the federal government be expanded to address economic inequalities and racial injustice. The results have been mixed. Sometimes the expansion of federal power enhanced popular democracy. The 1965 Voting Rights Act, for example, made it possible for millions of blacks to vote for the first time. Federal programs, begun during the New Deal, have lessened inequalities and given poor people more of a stake in democratic government. On the other hand, the complicated system of federal grants has distanced citizens from government through bureaucratic red tape. Present-day popular democrats appear to be trapped in a dilemma: Decentralizing policy to the grassroots will reinforce inequalities, but dealing with those inequalities through federal programs will undermine democratic accountability.

What aspects of American society have created this dilemma? Is there any way out of it?

One reason we face the dilemma of federalism is that growing concentrations of power in the marketplace require countervailing concentrations of power within government. (Corporate power in the marketplace is examined in the next chapter.) Until private corporations are made more democratically accountable to shareholders, workers, consumers, and especially their communities, we will need powerful federal bureaucracies, such as the Environmental Protection Agency (EPA) and the Securities and Exchange Commission (SEC) to regulate them in the public interest.

Another reason state and local governments find it difficult to address many problems is the tremendous inequalities in resources among governments. The tax capacities of states (how much a state would raise if it applied a common bundle of taxes to its tax base) vary significantly. During the 1992 campaign, Bill Clinton was criticized for not having done more as governor to clean up the environment and address social ills. As Figure 3.5 shows, however, if Arkansas applied the same tax *rate* to its tax base as Connecticut, it would raise only about half as much revenue. Thus, states like Arkansas, which have the greatest need to address problems like poverty, possess the fewest resources.

Within states, inequalities between central cities and suburbs are growing. In 1960, for a sample of sixty-two cities, the per capita income of central-city residents was 105 percent of the income of people living in their suburbs. By 1989, the ratio of central-city to suburban income had fallen to 84 percent. For many central cities the gap with the suburbs is even greater: In Newark the ratio is 43 percent, in Cleveland 53 percent.[59] Central cities thus face pressing

FIGURE 3.5 State Fiscal Capacity, 1988

Source: Adapted from U.S. Bureau of the Census, *Statistical Abstract of the United States: 1992*, 112th ed. (Washington, D.C.: U.S. Government Printing Office, 1992), p. 292.

demands to help their impoverished populations, but they lack sufficient tax bases to meet those needs. At the same time, federal aid to cities has dropped precipitously. Not surprisingly, many cities find themselves perpetually on the edge of fiscal crisis. Geographical inequalities cripple local democracy.

Federal programs to promote greater equality among different jurisdictions would empower state and local governments to address their own problems. Most federal grants distribute money on the basis of population, not need. Other federal systems, including Germany, Australia, and Canada, have well-developed national laws designed to equalize the tax capacities of subnational governments.[60] In the United States, a general revenue sharing program distributed on the basis of need could significantly reduce fiscal constraints on state and local governments. Even more important, many nations have national programs to equalize economic conditions in different areas of the country. A federal program to reduce economic inequalities among regions and between central cities and suburbs would do more than anything else to revitalize our federal system.

In short, the dilemma of federalism is not inevitable. Democratizing corporations and reducing inequalities among jurisdictions would free state and local governments for democratic experimentation. It should be noted, however, that many present-day states have more people than the entire country had in 1789; therefore, the ultimate goal of popular democrats must be to empower local governments and communities, not state governments.[61] Of course, revitalizing state and local governments also requires political reforms such as reducing the power of money in elections, strengthening local political parties, and increasing voting turnout. Economic and political reforms could help realize the popular democratic dream of state, and especially local, governments becoming laboratories of democracy.

KEY TERMS

unitary government
dual federalism
enumerated powers
reserved powers
concurrent powers
Supremacy Clause
implied powers
nullification
grants-in-aid

matching grants
intergovernmental relations
categorical grant
creative federalism
new federalism
general revenue sharing
block grants
preemption

SUGGESTED READINGS

Ann O'M. Bowman and Richard C. Kearney, *State and Local Government*, 2nd ed. (Boston: Houghton Mifflin Company, 1993). Comprehensive treatment of state and local governments that shows why they are more capable than ever of handling major responsibilities in the federal system.

Timothy Conlan, *New Federalism: Intergovernmental Reform from Nixon to Reagan* (Washington, D.C.: The Brookings Institution, 1988). The best treatment of the new federalism initiatives, arguing that Nixon and Reagan actually had very different goals and politics.

Grant McConnell, *Private Power and American Democracy* (New York: Vintage Books, 1966). An influential statement that the decentralization of power under American democracy leads to tyranny by private elites.

Michael D. Reagan and John G. Sanzone, *The New Federalism*, 2nd ed. (New York: Oxford University Press, 1981). A comprehensive text on federalism that makes the case for expanding federal power and responsibility.

David B. Robertson and Dennis R. Judd, *The Development of American Public Policy* (Glenview, Illinois: Scott, Foresman and Company, 1989). Argues that American federalism biases the policy process in a conservative direction, favoring the status quo.

CHAPTER

4

The American Political Economy

In December 1989, the world watched in awe as ordinary Germans hacked at the Berlin Wall with sledgehammers. Freed from Soviet domination, the fledgling democracies of Eastern Europe began dismantling the command-and-control economies that had failed to deliver the quality of life and levels of consumption taken for granted in the West. The collapse of the planned economies in Eastern Europe and the former Soviet Union and their replacement by market economies seem to have closed a monumental conflict in human history—the conflict between capitalism and communism. Capitalism, it seems, has triumphed.

The events in Eastern Europe exposed the failures of centrally planned, state-controlled, and Communist party–dominated economies. Yet to declare that capitalism has triumphed and that debates over the fundamentals of economic organization are finished is too simplistic. In reality, the collapse of communism has aroused conflicts about the meaning of democracy and the forms that capitalism can and should take. In the post-communist world, the differences among various forms of democracy and capitalism are just as important as the similarities. In Japan, capitalism seems to mean planning by big business and government together. In Sweden, "welfare state capitalism" provides high levels of benefits and equality along with high taxes. In Great Britain and the United States, the market seems more important than either conscious planning or high levels of social benefits.

Important differences between countries should not hide the fact that debates about respective political economies continue within all democratic countries. The United States is no exception. For at least a century Americans have engaged in spirited conflict about how to organize economic life. For the most part, the debate has not been between those who favor capitalism on the one side and Eastern European–style communism on the other. Most Americans have usually agreed on certain principles of a market economy: Private goods and services in society should be distributed primarily not by governments but by markets; people should be allowed to accumulate private property by their own efforts so long as no one else is harmed. What Americans have deeply disagreed about, however, is where to draw the line between the private market and democracy. The economic debate in the United States has been between elite democrats and popular democrats about how far the claims of democratic citizenship should be extended into the market economy. They have not debated over merely a certain policy or who should get what particular benefits. They have debated over the rules of the game. This chapter explores their democratic debate on the economy.

THE SILENCE OF THE CONSTITUTION

For all the divisions between Federalists and Anti-federalists about how to organize *political* power, the U.S. Constitution is strangely silent about *economic* power. The silence of the Constitution does not mean that the opponents in the original democratic debate lacked strong views about the relationship of politics and economics. The Anti-federalists feared propertied elites and their power to use government to oppress common citizens. They warned about the concentration of power in a central government and in the hands of a unitary executive. The Federalists, led by Madison and Hamilton, feared tyranny by a property-hungry majority, especially in radical state legislatures. For this reason they inserted a clause in the Constitution (one of the few that directly address economic relations) forbidding states from "impairing the Obligation of Contracts" (The Constitution, ARTICLE I, SECTION 10). When governments or private organizations and individuals made contracts, the Constitution was to ensure that their terms were obeyed.

Yet the debate on political economy at the founding never touched on issues that are central to present-day economic debates. Both the Federalists and the Anti-federalists concentrated on government alone as the source of potential tyranny. They were *not* concerned with how private institutions might invade the rights of others. The reason is simple: Big private institutions were relatively weak and underdeveloped. Government was by far the most powerful institution and was thought to represent the biggest potential threat to liberty.

Times have changed. Consider the differences between 1787 and the present. Then, as now, there were great economic inequalities. In 1787, many of the richest white men made their money by exploiting the labor of slaves. Merchants and bankers enjoyed luxurious lifestyles in the trading cities of New York, Philadelphia, and Boston. Yet for the vast majority of common citizens, life was very different. Most people lived on farms or in small villages. Most whites owned neither slaves nor plantations but worked for themselves as independent farmers or artisans. Farm families often produced most of their own provisions. What farmers couldn't make themselves would very likely be produced by an artisan in a nearby village. The few people who worked for someone else generally were apprentices in small shops. Almost all businesses were family owned and run. In many cases, producers, buyers, and sellers knew each other personally. There were no large factories organizing the labor of millions or producing for a national and international market.

With property, land, and tools widely distributed throughout the white population, the general sentiment that government should protect private property could have a popular democratic basis. The production and exchange of goods did not seem to threaten individual liberty or democracy. Although there were sizable inequalities in the amount of owned property, nearly all white citizens had some independence and some property—usually farmland, a shop, or tools. With the very important exception of black slaves, most citizens therefore had some measure of control over how they worked and what they produced. Quite naturally, the terms of the democratic debate in 1787 thus took the form of arguing about the relative political power of different kinds of independent property owners.[1]

The Saga of General Motors

Consider present-day America, governed by the same Constitution. Consider North Tarrytown, New York, the village where "the headless horseman of Sleepy

Hollow" made his legendary rides. The scene is the General Motors (GM) Tarrytown plant. The factory makes minivans and is part of a company whose worldwide operations employ 715,000 people. GM employs a work force larger than the entire population of seven of the original thirteen states. GM alone accounts for 1.5 percent of the entire U.S. economy, down from 5 percent in the 1950s. To make its cars, GM in 1992 spent more money than the entire U.S. government at the turn of the century. The company's profits in good years have far exceeded the U.S. gross national product in 1787 and surpass the current net worth of all the exports of at least forty foreign countries.

Inside the plant, 2,000 workers assemble the minivans from parts that come from smaller factories in the United States, Japan, and Mexico. The GM plant workers perform specialized functions, while others ensure that robots assembling the vans function well. Both robots and workers are watched by supervisors. In turn, Tarrytown supervisors and workers are coordinated by an army of executives and managers in far-off Michigan. The managers take their orders from a board of directors, who are ostensibly under the direction of thousands of ever-changing institutions and individuals who buy and sell GM stock on Wall Street.

Two centuries after the founding, most Americans work for large bureaucratic institutions and are completely dependent on the market to meet their basic needs. GM employees belong to a union, the United Auto Workers (UAW), itself a large bureaucracy with about 900,000 members. Organized in bitter struggles with the auto companies in the 1930s, the UAW once formed a counterweight to managers and owners by significantly enhancing the bargaining power of workers. In the 1950s and 1960s, when GM was doing well and the UAW was relatively strong, GM paid relatively good wages. In those years, a small plurality of workers were able to buy modest homes scattered from Tarrytown itself to fifty miles away in the outer reaches of the New York City suburbs. GM's wages and benefits must provide all of life's necessities, which are bought largely from companies that, like GM itself, are owned and controlled by unknown managers and stockholders in far-off places.[2]

Capitalism: New and Old

Are the differences or the similarities between the two eras in the American political economy more important? Both political economies are based on the principles of **capitalism.** In both 1789 and the 1990s, the means by which goods are produced and distributed—land, tools, workshops, factories, and stores—are in *private*, not public, hands. Owners of eighteenth-century farms and the board of directors of GM both work according to the *profit motive*; they want to make more money from the goods they sell than the amount they initially put into their enterprises. In both epochs, *contracts* between buyers and producers are essential and protected by law. In both, *market competition* exists: The prices received for GM minivans in 1995 and plantation tobacco in 1787 are at least in part determined by the tastes of consumers and the actions of other producers. The same basic rules of the game seem to characterize both eras: private property, production for profit, protection of contracts, and the existence of markets. In the broadest sense, the political economy of current American capitalism seems to be a natural extension of the political economy at the founding.

Actually, however, such massive changes have occurred in our political economy that it strains the historical record to call both societies capitalist. We can see this transformation by comparing the lives of Tarrytown workers with those of average eighteenth-century citizens. On the positive side, farmers and artisans in the eighteenth century did not have the relatively high standard of living of today's GM workers. The GM employees also have millions more consumer products from which to choose. Moreover, slavery is gone. GM nevertheless is not the same as a family farm or even a plantation, nor is it organized like the corner grocery store. GM is among thousands of large, global organizations that make group decisions about what to produce, how to produce it, whom to employ, and what to pay them. Its sales and purchases cross the boundaries of nation-states. Its business activity greatly depends on the attitudes of the governments of these nation-states toward corporate prosperity. Although GM workers can buy TV sets and cars, they are, in ways that would bewilder eighteenth-century citizens, utterly dependent on the decisions of a gigantic bureaucratic corporation for their livelihoods.[3]

The saga of GM and its contrasts with the political economy of 1787 demonstrate the need for a new label to describe the changes that have occurred over two centuries. After the Civil War, the simple capitalism of the eighteenth century began evolving into the **corporate capitalism** of the late twentieth century. The rise of corporate capitalism has posed new problems and challenges for democratic politics, transforming the terms of the eighteenth-century democratic debate about the American political economy.

THE DEMOCRATIC DEBATE ON THE ECONOMY

The debate between elite and popular democrats revolves around where to draw the line between the market economy and democratic politics. Both sides generally agree on the terms of the debate: If an economic transaction is purely private, does not have significant public effects, and is not characterized by relations of power or authority, then government should stay out of it. If, on the other hand, economic transactions have broad public effects involving power or coercion, then they should be subject to public decision making. What elite and popular democrats disagree about is to what degree economic relations are private and nonpolitical, and to what extent they should be. From electric utilities proposing rate increases to decisions to promote fuel economy in cars, the lines between what is private and public are hotly contested.

The Marketplace: Elite Democratic View

Modern elite democrats argue that it is precisely the voluntary character of most exchange relations that enables them to serve the public interest without any interference from government. Because private individuals are said to be the best judges of their own interests, they don't enter into an exchange unless they think they'll benefit from it. In this way, each economic exchange leads to efficiency; producers must give consumers what they want to stay in business. According to Adam Smith, the eighteenth-century theorist of capitalism, a marketplace of many consumers and producers is guided by an "invisible hand" to bring about the greatest good for the greatest number of people.[4]

For modern elite democrats, the free market is responsible for the high standard of living many Americans enjoy. But in addition to maximizing economic growth and efficiency, elite democrats argue that markets are the form of economic organization most conducive to freedom and democracy. Perhaps the most elegant modern defense of a political economy of markets and limited government has been made by economists Milton and Rose Friedman. They wrote:

> By enabling people to cooperate with one another without coercion or central direction, it reduces the area over which political power is exercised. . . . by dispersing power, the free market provides an offset to whatever concentration of political power may arise. The combination of economic and political power in the same hands is a sure recipe for tyranny. . . .[5]

Thus, like democracy in politics, free markets in the economy are said to increase the number of choices available to everyone.

However, free markets require government protection of private property. Without it, people would have no incentive to either make products or buy them. Private property provides a bulwark of freedom, a potential check on tyranny by government. The major opponents of private property and a free market tend to be governments and monopolies. When either become too meddlesome, too much power falls into the hands of the few, everyone's choices are reduced, and democracy itself is threatened.

Elite democrats use the language of political democracy to justify their faith in free markets. Terms like *consumer sovereignty* are used to suggest that the whole system is driven by the preferences of consumers who "vote" with their dollars for the products they want. From this point of view, corporations are like elected representatives who are required by the market to obey the desires of consumers, speaking through their purchases.

Although democratic language is used to legitimize the market, underneath its surface are many qualifications about how far democracy should extend. Like the Federalist case for checks and balances and the importance of representatives in politics, elite democratic arguments for markets don't maintain that consumers and workers should run corporations directly. In the contemporary marketplace, elite democrats cede this power to competing corporate elites. Corporate executives are viewed as experts on organizing production and applying advanced technologies. Instead of being held accountable by direct democratic processes, corporate elites check other corporate elites through market competition. Ultimately, they are held accountable by the necessity of competing with each other for consumer dollars. Just as the three branches of American government pit ambition against ambition, the marketplace is said to pit corporation against corporation.

Modern elite democrats do not conclude that markets always work perfectly or that they can be completely self-regulating. Somewhat more than their eighteenth-century predecessors, they acknowledge that government should play an important, if limited, role in the political economy. Yet the primary role for government is as umpire, not participant, preserving the rules that ensure fair competition in the marketplace. Government should punish those who attempt to overcome the checks and balances of the marketplace by replacing voluntary and free exchanges with power and coercion.

Accordingly, modern elite democrats accept, at least in theory, government measures to ensure that producers and consumers compete and cooperate freely and voluntarily. Nowadays, elite democrats even accept some governmental measures to correct dramatic failures of the market system, such as economic depressions. Government also supplies public goods that the market cannot provide, such as highways, water systems, and limited public services. Moreover, governments must provide military protection against countries that threaten political and economic freedom. Last but not least, elite democrats have come to accept that some people—such as the aged, children, and the disabled—can't compete in the marketplace and that government has some responsibility to care for them. Philosophically, few elite democrats will go beyond this concession.

Power and the Political Economy: Popular Democrats

Popular democrats do not disagree with the theory of free markets. If economic exchanges are purely private and do not harm anyone, they should be allowed to proceed without interference from government. Popular democrats agree that it would be a big mistake to do away with private property or to have government take over the means of production. They disagree with elite democrats, however, on the possibility of drawing a strict line between economics and politics, between the private and public spheres. Popular democrats see a great deal more power wielded through the market processes that elite democrats label as private and voluntary. Instead of individuals cooperating and competing by the laws of supply and demand, popular democrats see large organizations and rich individuals doing most of the voluntary cooperating and deciding. The rest of the population—wage workers and small businesses—are generally forced to take part in a game they neither created nor benefit from.

In place of a strict separation between freedom of the market and the potential tyranny of government, popular democrats see increasing tendencies toward connections between the politically and economically powerful in *both* arenas. Far from dispersing political and economic powers, our modern political economy concentrates them. The economic elites who head large corporations are not held accountable to democratic citizens through competition, and they often prevent political elites from serving citizens as well.

For popular democrats, the way U.S. markets have developed has produced severe economic inequalities. These inequalities are not necessary for the efficient functioning of a market economy. More important, economic inequalities translate into inequalities in political power, undermining citizenship and democracy themselves. Because of their place within the economic hierarchy, many citizens become dependent and powerless. In a system where producers and consumers "vote" for what they want with dollars, those with more dollars have more power than others. By defending an economy with such vast inequalities in power and wealth, elite democrats undermine their own arguments about freedom and choice.

Finally, popular democrats argue that the free market often leads to dire consequences and wrenching instability. In the 1930s, our market system collapsed, throwing a quarter of the country out of work and establishing the conditions for World War II. In the modern political economy, recessions and economic stagnation often follow boom years. Can democracy survive a market political economy in which millions are threatened with continued instability?[6]

The key difference between elite and popular democrats on political economy is about the scope of democratic citizenship. Elite democrats want to limit democratic decision making, arguing that many decisions are best left to the impersonal processes of the private market. By excluding certain issues from the public agenda, popular democrats argue, elites are exercising a form of power called **nondecision making.** The democratic debate is limited to issues that are comparatively unthreatening to the economic elites.[7] Certain issues, such as more democratic control over the economy, never even make it onto the public agenda. In this way, the market economy often excludes democratic politics and citizenship.

The democratic debate about the political economy is not only about how markets work in practice. It is also about values, human nature, and the capacities and intelligence of ordinary citizens. For elite democrats, market capitalism is consistent with human nature. Individuals are interested primarily in their own well-being and that of their immediate family. The market-driven race to acquire and consume property is said to be the essence of human freedom, whereas participation in public life is unnatural. Given the narrow focus of most peoples' concerns, it is better for them to relinquish crucial decisions to business elites who have the experience, wisdom, and expertise to make the economy work. Ultimately, these businesspeople will be held accountable by the self-interested decisions of ordinary consumers in the marketplace.

The popular democratic view of citizenship is more expansive: If inequalities of power have developed in our political economy, why shouldn't decisions that affect the public be made by the affected citizens? Moreover, popular democrats believe that a democratic economy corresponds to the complexity of real human beings; for them, the calculating property seeker of elitist market theory is too abstract. People are capable of participating in the economy as more than passive consumers or cogs in a corporate bureaucratic hierarchy. By nature, people are social; they want to participate in the institutions that govern their lives. Given the chance, ordinary citizens can transcend narrow self-interests and participate directly in the governance of economic institutions where they work and live. Excluding them from economic decision making hinders citizenship and limits democracy.

ECONOMIC RECORD OF CORPORATE CAPITALISM

The way to test the competing claims of elite and popular democrats is to establish some facts about our twentieth-century political economy. How great are the inequalities, and are they growing? Do corporations, workers, and consumers have equal bargaining power in the marketplace? How does our political economy treat children, the elderly, minorities? Does the market provide a basic level of security for most Americans? In examining these facts, we should observe whether the organization of our political economy encourages or retards effective democratic citizenship.

Economic Growth

Corporate capitalism seems to have made the United States a rich country. Since the emergence of the modern corporation in the late nineteenth century, the United States has experienced tremendous overall economic growth. With only about 5 percent of the world's population, America has a gross domestic product that far exceeds that of any other nation, including Japan and the combined countries of western Europe. The American economy produces and consumes more goods and services than any other in the world.

American economic growth has, however, always been *cyclical*—subject to booms and busts, spurts of economic growth followed by periods of recession and, as in the 1930s, depression. In addition, the American economy has lagged since 1973, the year of the first Arab oil boycott. As Figure 4.1 shows, the United States had the highest per capita gross domestic product in 1963, but by 1990 a number of western European countries had surpassed us.

The average weekly earnings (in constant dollars) of private-production workers increased 61 percent between 1947 and 1973, but between 1973 and 1989 average weekly earnings fell 16 percent.[8] Since 1973, median household income has remained about the same in constant dollars, but mainly because more women have entered the work force. Although present-day Americans no longer enjoy the highest growth rates or the highest per capita income, the overall growth record of the American economy is still superb. America is a much richer country economically than it was when your grandparents or great-grandparents were young.[9]

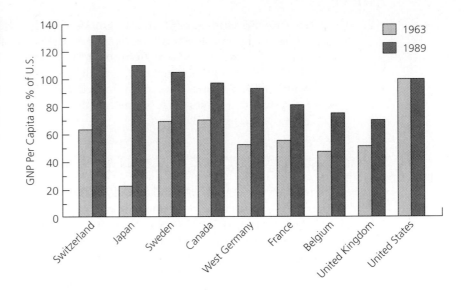

FIGURE 4.1

Per-Capita GNP of Other Nations as a Percentage of the United States, 1963 and 1989

Source: From *The Struggle for Democracy* by Edward S. Greenburg and Benjamin I. Page. Copyright © 1993 by HarperCollins College Publishers. Reprinted by permission.

Social Mobility

Free market capitalism has always justified itself through the claim that the top corporate positions in America were open to anyone with talent and energy. Rags-to-riches stories abound in capitalist America; we supposedly live in a land of boundless opportunities for **social mobility** where many people like Ross Perot have ascended from relatively poor circumstances to great wealth and power.

The facts, however, indicate otherwise. Throughout American history, most people have been able to improve their economic situation over the previous generation's standard. In addition, goods once reserved to the elite—college education, cars, and appliances—are now more widely diffused among the population than they were in the 1930s and 1940s. America is a country of *mass consumption* of many goods once reserved for the elite.

Mass consumption of goods is, however, far different from social mobility. Most Americans experience little, if any, social mobility. Only about 10 percent of the children of manual workers manage to become white-collar professionals. Compared to western Europe, this is a high figure. But huge leaps from poverty to wealth are extremely rare: Of the country's richest four hundred citizens, 60 percent inherited their wealth. Most of the others came from middle- to upper-middle-class families and went further "up" from there. The majority of Americans do not move up very much: At present, most people born before 1930 have made small steps up the social mobility ladder from the places where their great-grandparents or grandparents were. Very few have gone from rags to riches, although many have ascended from poverty to the possession of a relatively stable job, more education, and a modest home.[10]

In the 1970s and 1980s, however, even these small upward steps almost ceased. During this period, more Americans moved *down* the ladder—an ominous trend for a system that prides itself on the fact that each generation can be better off than its predecessors.[11]

Distribution of Income

From World War II until the early 1970s, most Americans experienced steady and real gains in their yearly income and purchasing power, even taking inflation and increased taxes into account. Yet even in years when the benefits of economic growth were distributed proportionately among various income groups, **income inequality**—the gap between those with the highest and lowest incomes—in America remained close to the highest among Western industrialized nations. Income inequality was greater in America than in many countries where living standards were much lower. America may be richer than Indonesia, Tanzania, and Malaysia, but it has higher levels of income inequality than those nations.

In the 1980s, America became first in income inequality among rich countries by surpassing France. As Figure 4.2 shows, between 1977 and 1990 average

---

FIGURE 4.2

Change in Income for Sectors of the U.S. Population, 1977–1990

~~~~~

Each decile represents 10 percent of income earners. The first decile represents the lowest 10 percent; the tenth decile represents the highest.

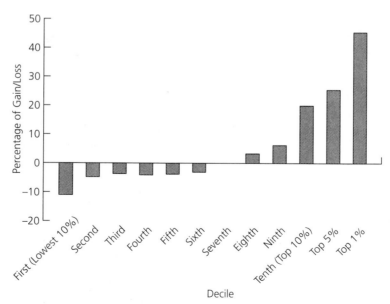

Source: Kevin Phillips, *Boiling Point: Democrats, Republicans, and the Decline of Middle-Class Prosperity* (New York: Random House, 1993), p.21.

family income, adjusted for inflation, fell for the bottom 60 percent of the population. The top 10 percent increased their average family income by almost 20 percent, while the top 1 percent posted an approximately 45 percent increase. In the words of Donald Bartlett and James Steele: "The total wages of all people who earned less than $50,000 a year—85% of all Americans—increased an average of 2 percent a year over the last 10 years. At the same time, the total wages of all millionaires shot up 243% a year."[12]

Distribution of Wealth

The distribution of wealth is even more unequal in the United States than the distribution of income. (Wealth is defined as the dollar value of all the assets a person or a household owns, minus what they owe creditors.) Wealth inequality is important because very wealthy people can accumulate power to make decisions that affect others through their investments and purchases. Wealth inequality has become more pronounced in recent years. In 1986, the Joint Economic Committee of Congress reported the results of an exhaustive study: The top 0.5 percent of America's households held 27 percent of the nation's total wealth. The top 10 percent held 68 percent. The top 20 percent owned 90 percent of the wealth. The remaining 80 percent of the population was left to divide 10 percent of the wealth. Of this, the bottom 30 percent of Americans were indebted, and thus held no net wealth at all.[13]

Economic Insecurity

In the 1950s and 1960s, one of the proudest achievements of American capitalism was the creation of the largest and what was thought to be the most stable middle class in world history. During those years, most American families expected few long bouts with unemployment. Most could buy a modest home, save for their children's education and their own retirement, and count on slowly but steadily rising wages as they aged. Moreover, many families had only one wage earner, who worked about forty hours a week to provide all this for the family. In the heyday of corporate capitalism, income equality was not achieved but a measure of stability seemingly had been.

Yet middle-class stability has proven to be the exception rather than the rule in our history. Before World War II corporate capitalism had been anything but stable, and since the 1970s the conditions of well-being and stability have radically changed. The numbers again tell the story. Between 1973 and the present, the purchasing power of average workers has either stagnated or declined. In part to compensate for the decline, many new workers—especially women—have entered the work force. By 1990, two-thirds of married women held jobs; employed women with children averaged sixty-five work hours a week, including time for housework.[14] In recent years, even though most families now

have two breadwinners and are working more than ever, the median family income has remained essentially flat.

Have two incomes brought the American family much peace of mind? To earn enough money to buy a new home, American wage earners have to work almost twice as many years now as they did in the 1960s. Homeownership rates declined in the 1980s, as mortgage foreclosures rose. How about a secure retirement? Almost half of American workers were covered by private pension funds in 1980. Since then corporate pension plans cover fewer people, and the payouts to retirees have diminished. As the health-care debate raged in 1994, one out of six Americans didn't have medical insurance, with growing numbers in danger of losing theirs. In 1970, keeping one child in a four-year private college took 30 percent of a family's income, but by the early 1990s the figure was up to 43 percent. Paying for day care and the expenses of two cars, besides finding the time to take children to the doctor, dentist, and after-school activities has created time and financial pressures on American families, as well as stress. To deal with these realities, most American families have acquired more and more debt to maintain the standard of living in which they were raised. Yet even as they accumulate debt, these families face increasing job insecurity, making it harder to pay the money back.[15]

Struggling for Respect in the New Service Economy

The new service economy has generated millions of jobs. The airline travel business provides an excellent example of a growing occupation for primarily women workers. Four in five flight attendants are female. Do these new jobs provide dignity, and are the wages and benefits adequate to support a family?

Once called stewardesses, flight attendants have shaken their 1960s image as young, over-sexed jet setters employed to serve male passengers. In the 1970s, flight attendants formed unions and integrated their ranks by introducing men and nonwhite women. They won respect as skilled and competent professionals. The new unions fought to keep their members' jobs even as flight attendants married, had children, put on a few pounds, or refused to wear eye shadow. As their number grew with the explosion of mass airline travel, however, flight attendants were increasingly blamed for the low profit margins of the big airlines and their continuous price wars. During the 1980s, in the wake of huge airline losses, flight attendants at the "big four"—United, American, Northwest, and Delta—agreed to wage and benefit concessions, and new work rules that allowed the airlines to control everything from their hairstyles to their dwindling paychecks.

After further concessions to bolster sagging profits, average pay by 1993 had sunk to $23,000 a year for flight attendants at the industry's leader, American Airlines (AA). New flight attendants had even lower salaries and no regular days off. Female attendants were forced to enroll unpaid in "Commitment to Courtesy" classes, in which they were instructed about personal hygiene, politeness, food presentation, and the evils of oversized earrings. Although AA's ads praised its employees to consumers, airline management gave flight attendants less respect when it came to working conditions and contracts.

1993 turned out to be a profitable year for AA. It was also a year in which the flight attendants' contract was up for negotiation. Its CEO Robert Crandall insisted on a new series of concessions. He proposed more employee cuts, increased employee contributions for health insurance, and even stricter work rules to get more work out of fewer employees. AA's management was betting that in a tough job climate, the unions would buckle. In the words of one flight attendant, Crandall's offer meant that "on the one hand, management says you're #1. Then a contract comes along. Then they say 'We can get rid of you just like that.' "

A week before the lucrative 1993 Thanksgiving holiday, the flight attendants' union at AA, 21,000 strong and 85 percent women, went on strike. Holiday travel for AA's 200,000 daily passengers was disrupted. Scorning both negotiations and the union, CEO Crandall promised that most of the planes would run anyway. By the fifth day of the strike, the airline was losing $10 million a day and most planes were flying without passengers. Airline pilots threatened to strike in sympathy. At President Clinton's urging, AA management finally agreed to submit the strikers' demands to an outside arbitrator, who immediately ruled against Crandall's cutbacks. Just in time for Thanksgiving, the flight attendants went back to work—with a new contract showing that women workers in service industries can struggle for respect against big corporations, and *win*.

Sources: Peter Kilborn, "Strikers at American Airlines Say the Object Is Respect," *New York Times,* November 22, 1993, pp. A1, 9; Michael Riley, "Fasten Your Seatbelts," *Time,* November 29, 1993, p. 62; Marc Levinson, "On a Wing and a Prayer," *Newsweek,* November 29, 1993, p. 53.

Poverty

Given the wide disparities of income and wealth in the United States, it is not surprising that large numbers of people live in poverty. How many poor people live in our rich country? In 1990, 33.6 million Americans had incomes below the federally designated poverty level of $13,359 for a family of four. Using a more realistic definition of poverty (an income of below $16,699 for a family of four), about 45 million Americans, or 18 percent of us, are poor.[16]

The U.S. poverty rate far exceeds those of western Europe, Canada, and Japan. Poverty rates fluctuate somewhat with economic cycles and with the extent of governmental programs. Yet even in periods of rapid economic growth and relatively heavy governmental expenditures, the extreme poverty rate has not fallen much below 10 percent. Still, it could be worse: During the Great Depression an estimated 40 percent of the country was poor.

The vast majority of adults in poor families work, and the majority of the poor don't receive either food stamps or welfare payments. An ominous trend of the 1980s was an increase in the number of *working poor*—people who labored at full-time jobs but didn't earn enough to feed, clothe, and house their families adequately. In 1989, almost 40 percent of all full-time workers did not earn a "living wage" sufficient in itself to keep a family of four out of poverty.[17]

American children are the chief victims of poverty. In 1992, the percentage of American poor children was lower than it had been in the 1981–82 recession. But during the last two decades, the overall percentage of children who live in poverty has increased from 14 percent to over 20 percent.[18]

Race, Gender, and Inequality

Most people in the U.S.'s racial and ethnic groups are not poor, and there are more poor white people in America than poor blacks or Hispanics. Yet African-American and Hispanic families have a much greater chance of being poor than white families. In 1990, nearly one-third of all black families were poor, compared to only one in ten white families.

Ethnicity and race also are significant in determining income levels for people who do work. On average, the per capita income of blacks is only 59 percent that of whites, barely any increase at all since 1973 (see Figure 4.3). The per capita income of Hispanics is only 55 percent that of whites, a slight decline since 1974.

At the same time, the median income of full-time employed women edged closer to that of men, increasing from 60 percent in 1980 to 71 percent in 1990.

Still, the statistics reveal a significant **feminization of poverty.** Of all poor families, one in three are headed by women. If women's incomes were improving in relation to that of men, it was because the income of men was falling.[19]

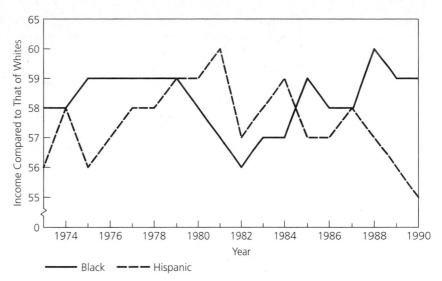

FIGURE 4.3

Per Capita Income of Blacks and Hispanics as a Percentage of White Income, 1973–1990

Source: U.S. Bureau of the Census, Current Population Reports, Series P-60, No. 174, *Money Income of Households, Families, and Persons in the United States: 1990* (Washington, D.C.: Government Printing Office, 1991), Table B-8.

ASSESSING THE FACTS: THE DEMOCRATIC DEBATE ON INEQUALITY

The American political economy comprises great wealth and poverty and profound inequalities, more than other advanced industrial countries. Over the past twenty years, the trend has been toward even greater inequality. Does inequality threaten American democracy by undermining equal opportunity, political fairness, and effective citizenship? Everything depends on how you interpret the facts. As we have already seen, an underlying debate about the facts of American politics exists between elite and popular democrats.

Elite democrats defend inequalities by saying that they fairly reflect varying individual abilities and efforts. Because market outcomes reflect ability and effort, elite democrats argue, the resulting inequalities help to make the whole system function justly and well. Inequalities provide the incentives to ensure that the most important and difficult tasks in society are performed by the most motivated and talented people. Few have the talent to be brain surgeons; fewer still have the motivation to endure six years or more of medical school and residency after college. That brain surgeons make $500,000 a year ensures that at least some competent people will be drawn to this important task.

Elite democrats hold that inequality's rewards and punishments are necessary to motivate people to work hard, save, and invest. If government taxed away some accumulations of wealth and reduced high incomes, the ambitious and talented would have little incentive to work hard or invest in new enterprises. On the other hand, if unskilled work led to high incomes, people would have no reason to work harder or increase their skills. As a result, economic growth would slow down, eventually making the poor—the very people who were supposed to benefit from redistribution—even poorer. In other words, elite democrats argue that democratic efforts to pursue equality are limited by the dynamics of a market economy that generates what economists call the *tradeoff between equality and efficiency.*[20]

In contrast, popular democrats do not deny that a certain amount of inequality is necessary. The problem is that the present inequalities go far beyond those necessary for a well-functioning market economy and democracy. Popular democrats cite the fact that almost all other capitalist democracies have less inequality than the United States, most of which have performed better economically over the last twenty years. Greater equality can improve economic performance by stimulating consumer demand, reducing crime and antisocial behavior by the poor and homeless, and increasing the motivation of people at the bottom by giving them a chance to achieve a more secure life.

Popular democrats oppose inequalities not just because they hurt economic performance but also because they demean citizenship. Current inequalities do not accurately reflect people's talents, efforts, and potentials, but rather the undue power of corporations and wealthy individuals in the marketplace. Do corporate CEOs, who sometimes make one thousand times more than ordinary workers, really deserve their wealth? Moreover, those who make investment decisions and set wages often discriminate on the basis of gender and race. Truck drivers, for example, make many times what daycare workers make. Is this because driving a truck is more difficult and important than caring for young children or because most truck drivers are men and most daycare workers women? To cite another example, research suggests that getting a mortgage from a bank is more difficult for an African-American family than for a white family buying an equivalent house with the same credit history and resources.[21]

According to popular democrats, what's at stake in promoting greater equality is not only levels of income and consumption but, more important, who has a say in making the decisions that affect everyone. Severe inequalities in income and wealth damage democratic citizenship and participation. In the modern political economy, those inequalities are determined largely by the decisions made by two institutions—corporations and government. We now examine these two powerful economic and political actors.

CORPORATE KINGDOMS: PRIVATE POWER AND PUBLIC EFFECTS

As we saw in Chapters 2 and 3, the modern corporation hadn't been born when elite and popular democrats fought over the Constitution. Corporate power and control grew through its ability to play one state against another, achieving a great deal of legal autonomy and independence from government control. By the late nineteenth century, corporations had attained national scope in their operations. Since then, corporations have come to own almost everything in the private marketplace—land, buildings, tools, factories, stores, and office buildings. Yet the way they use their "private" property has countless, and growing, public effects. Legally, corporations are persons, having the same rights as citizens.[22] But they are very large individuals with the potential to speak much more loudly than ordinary citizens. According to one prominent political scientist: "The large corporation fits oddly into democratic theory and vision. Indeed, it does not fit."[23]

Corporate Organization: Management Control

Large corporations have three characteristics that set them apart from unincorporated businesses owned by individuals:

1. *Joint stock ownership.* Corporations pool the resources of a number of investors, called stockholders. The stock can be freely bought and sold.

2. *Limited liability.* Corporations can attract investment more freely because no owner is financially responsible for more than his or her own investment.

3. *Continuous legal identity.* Corporations do not dissolve with the death of any owner; like the Energizer rabbit, they just keep on going no matter what.

The way corporations organize themselves presents a problem for democracy. Americans are citizens of the United States and the official masters of their government. Yet our major employers, the corporations, are run more like aristocracies or monarchies than democracies. With their own king and court, called the chief executive officer and the board of directors, corporations also have layers of officials, called managers, who implement orders and monitor activities. At the bottom, there are the commoners—ordinary workers who usually have no power to elect either their immediate bosses (supervisors) or the distant managers. In their purest forms, corporations are thus highly structured and bureaucratized hierarchies with little room for free speech or voting.[24]

Corporations often claim they are democratic because they take their orders from a large group of shareholders who are the ostensible owners. But who are the actual owners of American corporations, and who benefits from ownership?

In the late 1980s, only about 20 percent of all American families did own stocks or corporate bonds directly. Of that 20 percent, one in four owned stock in the company for which he or she worked, through so-called employee stock ownership plans. Moreover, $1.3 *trillion* in investment capital is indirectly owned by ordinary Americans through their employee pension funds. Much of it is invested in corporate America in the form of stocks and bonds. GM's employees alone had $22.9 billion in their pension funds in 1990.[25]

Sometime in the future, the workers who own pension funds may gain some control over them. Yet at present, the number of people who own shares in

American companies is less impressive than the concentrations of most stocks and bonds held by very rich individuals and institutions. Of all individually owned stock, 50 percent is owned by the top 2 percent of income recipients—that slender slice of Americans who make $250,000 a year or more. The rest of the pie is owned not by the super-rich but by the very well-off. Just one in every two hundred American families makes over $500,000 annually. But they obtain most of their income from collecting stock dividends or trading shares on the stock market. Only 2 percent of the U.S. population earn more than $10,000 a year by owning property of *any* kind, including stocks and bonds.[26]

If only about one in fifty Americans has a direct stake in owning American corporations, then shareholder democracy is no democracy at all. Moreover, even those who do own stocks often have little control over the modern corporations. This is particularly true with difficult-to-organize small shareholders. Other types of ownership confer few privileges. Workers' pension funds are collected and controlled by trusts or are supposedly held for the workers by the corporation who paid into them in the first place. Most pension funds are thus controlled by a company's management, and often are lent back to the corporation itself or invested in other companies. Management is generally able to obtain enough stockholder *proxies* (the right to vote others' shares of stock) to control the annual stockholders' meeting and elect a board of directors who will cooperate with management. Because management controls most of the information about the company, dissident shareholders find mobilization difficult. Shareholders dissatisfied with management generally sell their stock.

Some people maintain that labor unions have given workers the ability to check the power of management within the corporation. It is true that the *Wagner Act* of 1935 guaranteed workers the right to organize unions and bargain collectively. Union membership soared, reaching a peak of 31.8 percent of the nonagricultural work force in 1955 (see Figure 4.4). In addition, union contracts negotiated with management often gave workers certain rights within the corporation. Personnel rules, for example, gave factory workers the right to work breaks and the right to refuse overtime work, and protected workers against arbitrary dismissal.

Overall, however, present-day unions provide only a limited countervailing force to the power of management within the corporation. American unions have basically been "bread and butter" unions, concerned mostly with wages and benefits while conceding control over the shop floor and investment to management. In typical elite democratic fashion, unions have generally deferred to management as possessing the technical expertise and experience to maximize efficiency and growth. In return, most unions have asked simply for a portion of the growth dividend in the form of productivity and cost-of-living increases.

More important, as Figure 4.4 shows, the union presence in the work force has declined since the 1950s, and most workers are not protected by a union. Surprisingly, America has one of the lowest unionization rates among all capitalist democracies. As of 1991, only 16.1 percent of the nonagricultural work force was unionized in the United States, compared to 90 percent in Sweden, 62

FIGURE 4.4   Membership in Labor Unions, 1900–1991

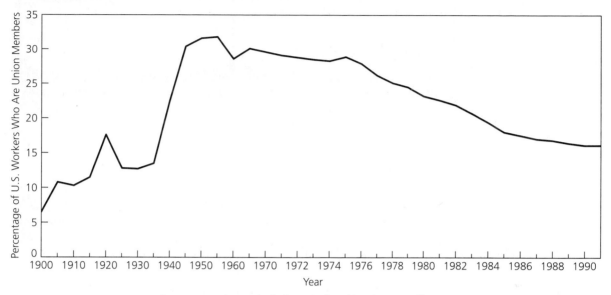

Percentages do not include agricultural workers or self-employed workers whose businesses are incorporated.

Source: Harold W. Stanley and Richard G. Niemi, *Vital Statistics on American Politics,* 4th ed. (Washington, D.C.: Congressional Quarterly Press, 1994), p. 190.

percent in Australia, and 30 percent in Canada.[27] The bargaining strength of unions has deteriorated rapidly since the 1970s. Most current bargaining doesn't consist of workers making demands, but of management demanding concessions in the forms of wage freezes and cuts; "downsizing"; rollbacks on health, pensions, and other benefits; and pledges to not strike.[28]

As institutions, corporations are controlled by their top managers, not by the official owners or by union workers. Management generally controls not only the corporation's direction and structure, but also its own successors. In recent years, managers have often awarded themselves official control of their own corporations by paying top executives in the form of stock.[29] If workers eventually come to control their own pensions, perhaps corporate elitism will change. As of now, opportunities for worker control are severely limited.

Does Market Competition Hold Corporations Accountable?

How are the powers of corporate management defended? The old defense is that because the corporation is private property, its activities are no one's business.

Yet, corporate actions often have broad public effects. Although corporations claim the same rights as private individuals, they often act very much like little governments.

A newer way of defending corporate hierarchy is in terms of its functions—as the best way to promote economic growth, efficiency, and innovation. In today's highly competitive marketplace, corporations must act quickly to meet changing consumer demand and to implement new technology in the most efficient manner. Any corporation that engaged in lengthy democratic consultations with shareholders, workers, consumers, and communities would soon fall behind in the competitive race. The real claim behind this defense is that corporations are not democracies. They are elite hierarchies because they must compete for consumer dollars. Market research tells them what people want, and corporate elites make the important technical decisions to supply it.

The way corporations respond to consumers reveals how much discretion and power they really have. Decisions about the organization of work, plant location, and salaries and benefits have little to do with market research.[30] To prosper, corporations sometimes act like the former communist governments. They engage in long-term planning, a practice elite democrats reject whenever they defend the free market. Corporate managers use long-term plans to allocate shareholders' capital—if, where, and when factories are to be built; workers employed; and research conducted. Corporations also plan by influencing consumer behavior, in addition to responding to it. Through modern advertising, the corporation tries to control consumers in order to provide a predictable, stable, and loyal demand for products. When strong unions are absent, corporations also plan the sizes and conditions of their work forces—the number of jobs, their organization, and who fills them.[31]

Thus, although corporations may respond to consumer demand, one important way they do so is by concentrating their power to control the costs of labor, machinery, and the products they sell. Good corporate planning uses power to predict and control all the factors that affect products and sales. Most present-day corporations do not have monopoly power. But in the hope of driving out competitors, modern corporations attempt to "control . . . not only prices, but costs, labor supply, government action or intervention . . . and consumer and buyer response."[32]

Although in theory competition justifies the marketplace, in practice most corporations still seek to concentrate their power and reduce competition. Ironically, at many times in American history the theory of competition has turned into the practice of monopoly or oligopoly (when one or a few corporations control a market). Since the formation of large industrial firms and banks in the late nineteenth century, periods of intense rivalry have been followed by years of oligopoly and monopoly in which one or a few firms dominated the marketplace for specific goods. In the 1950s and 1960s, for example, a few hundred large and seemingly stable American corporations dominated much of the world's trade, production, and banking. The "Big Three" automakers dominated car sales, while General Electric and Westinghouse monopolized the electrical equipment and machine tool industry. Even small entrepreneurs in the newborn computer industry were quickly gobbled up by the industry's then-giant, IBM. Oil production was controlled largely by a few firms like Mobil, Standard Oil of New Jersey, and Texaco. As late as 1983, the top ten commercial banks in the United States (there were 14,500 in all) controlled more than one-third of all U.S. bank deposits. During this period, corporate capitalism appeared extremely stable. Competition from either new or foreign companies was limited. Major corporations had achieved their central aim—power over the marketplace. Satisfied with stability through predictable profits and sales, many corporations bought peace with their workers by promises of job stability and steadily increasing wages.[33] The cost was higher prices for consumers and relatively low wages for most small-business employees.

Competition, Corporate-Style: The 1980s and 1990s

As it turned out, the easy life of corporate oligopoly didn't last. Beginning in the 1970s, American corporate capitalism has been transformed by events both beyond and within its control. The stimulus for change *has* been competition—from western European and Japanese corporations in the mass production, research, and banking industries, and from East Asian and Latin American nations in the textile, shoe, clothing, steel, toy, and other industries. This economic competition, based on consumer demand, initially cut into the profits of U.S. corporations. The way American corporations responded reveals some of the effects of corporate decision making.

Return for a moment to Tarrytown, New York, and its GM plant. When we last visited this corporate kingdom, GM employees in Tarrytown had won relatively high wages, and the company was prospering. Corporate hierarchy seemed to be working. But a string of bad decisions and investments made by management in the 1970s and 1980s in response to increased competition from foreign automakers led to declining profits for GM. In 1992, the GM managers

United Auto Workers members gather at GM's Manhattan offices to protest the company's decision to close its Tarrytown plant. GM justified its decision as necessary for the company's future profitability.

decided to close the Tarrytown plant. Even though minivans had become profitable for GM, the company's managers wanted to consolidate minivan production in fewer factories.

In its public statements, GM placed the blame on everyone but itself: Japanese competition, the economic recession, government over-regulation, and the high cost of American labor were the most visible targets. Most workers found some of these rationales hard to believe. Ten years earlier, GM had won wage and benefit cuts from workers by promising that the Tarrytown plant would stay open. New York State and Westchester County taxpayers had supplied GM with subsidized electric power and had paid for the renovation of the local railroad to speed GM shipments. The Tarrytown school board had even lowered property taxes on the GM factory, recognizing their dependence on the large corporation's goodwill. Even as GM managers announced the plant's closure (along with many others), GM raised the pay of the top executives who had led GM into crisis. In the 1980s, GM managers received stock and salary increases of over 300 percent, and Roger Smith, the CEO who had led the company into crisis, retired with an annual pension of $1 million.[34]

In one sense, GM was defeated by Japanese competition—worldwide consumers preferred Japanese cars. Yet in our political economy, the choices about how corporations like GM compete are left to the holders of investment capital and the managers of American industry, not to ordinary Americans who depend on these companies. American corporations could have chosen to compete through new investments, in people, products, and factories. But since the late 1970s, they've generally made very different decisions.

"Leaner and Meaner" Workplaces. One response to the new international competition by American corporations has been what corporate chieftains politely call making their companies "leaner and meaner" in the marketplace. In manufacturing, this has usually been bad news for American workers. Corporate strategies have included layoffs, plant closings, wage freezes or rollbacks, and benefit cuts. Some companies, like Greyhound, have "busted" unions by refusing to negotiate with them or by building new factories in locations where unions are weak.

But the most revolutionary response to international competition has spawned thousands of new companies, satellites revolving around the leaner and meaner corporate goliaths. Through **outsourcing,** America's large companies avoid wage and benefit costs by contracting out many operations to smaller companies hiring cheaper, often part-time labor. Outsourcing has helped shape a new economy made of part-time and temporary workers. From the corporate perspective, such workers are preferable to the old work force because they labor for less, are easily hired and fired, and receive no fringe benefits like health insurance and pension contributions. At least in many manufacturing industries and in clerical, secretarial, and other service work, the corporate strategy for beating the competition is not to invest more but to spend less, particularly on labor.[35]

American companies based on innovation, on the other hand, have been successful in devising systems of production that enable constant development of new products and production in small batches for specialized niches in the marketplace. This process is called **flexible specialization**.[36] Increasingly, successful competition in many markets is based not on high-volume, low-cost production but on high-value production that tailors products to specific needs. For example, by 1990, 80 percent of the cost of a computer was in the software services it contained.[37]

In this sector, hierarchical corporations have often been replaced by enterprise webs, concentrated in specific geographic areas, that feed on each other to produce constant innovation in product and design. Good examples in the United States are the movie industry in Los Angeles, the computer industry in Silicon Valley, and Route 128 around Boston. In these new areas large corporations have lost their dominant position. Moreover, between 1975 and 1990 America's five hundred largest industrial companies failed to create a single net new job. The massive layoffs by GM and IBM in the early 1990s are testimony to the problems of the corporate giants. Most of the new jobs in the economy are being created by small businesses, many of which are highly innovative.

In short, the restructuring of the American economy has had a twofold effect: For workers in routine manufacturing, the effect has been devastating. For those in innovative industries engaged in research, the effect has sometimes been a less hierarchical and more participatory workplace. Unfortunately, the innovative industries involve only a minority of American workers—what Robert Reich calls the "fortunate fifth."[38]

"If you can't beat 'em, join 'em." Another response of American corporations to new international competition has been to build new plants in foreign countries, invest heavily in foreign corporations, or replace American-made parts and products with foreign-made ones. The corporate phrase for this strategy is "going global." It means that American corporate capitalists have tried to increase profits by shifting capital and investments abroad and by becoming the intermediaries for foreign companies trying to sell their own products under old American brand names. In the 1980s, the American economy shed over 1.3 million manufacturing jobs through this strategy. Companies often abandoned the communities that depended on them, moving their operations to Mexico, China, and other locales where labor was cheaper. Akio Morita, chairman of Japan's Sony Corporation, comments: "The result is a hollowing of American industry. The U.S. is abandoning its status as an industrial power".[39]

The Casino Economy. The third corporate response to competition and decline has formed the casino economy. Money that could have been used for productive investments is instead used in the new high-stakes "crapshoot" of buying, selling, merging, and sometimes dismantling corporations or parts of them. Between 1983 and 1986—the height of merger mania—over 12,200 companies and parts of companies changed hands in the United States. At a cost of over half a trillion dollars, merger mania's price tag was about 40 percent of the total annual expenditures of the U.S. government. Some—like the Wall Street lawyers, accountants, bankers who arranged the deals, and major shareholders—made big money through such transactions. British tycoon James Goldsmith, for instance, "earned" a quick $90 million when he bought huge quantities of Goodyear Tire stock in a takeover bid, and then sold it back to Goodyear's management at wildly inflated prices as Goodyear struggled to maintain control of its own operations. But in the end, the competitive race to make a quick buck left many companies (like Goodyear) much less competitive. Many smaller companies at the cutting edge were bought, sold, traded, and moved according to the rhythms of the world merger roulette wheel. To finance mergers or to protect themselves from them, many American corporations went into debt by borrowing hundreds of billions of dollars at high rates of interest. "Junk" bonds and other ways of getting quick loan money left many companies heavily indebted and unable to finance new investments.

Although individuals like Goldsmith and Michael Millken made millions through the casino economy, ordinary Americans hardly benefited. In 1985, the peak year of casino economics, $41 billion was spent on the eight biggest mergers, among them GE with RCA, GM with Hughes Aircraft, and R. J. Reynolds with Nabisco. The total amount of money spent on upgrading all companies in the same year was only $133 billion. The $41 billion spent on eight mergers alone would have boosted investment in new machines and labor education by 30 percent.

Nor did the casino economy increase the number of corporate players: Merger mania created even larger, although less stable and healthy, corporate giants. In 1961, the top one hundred industrial corporations controlled 44 percent of the total assets of all nonbanking corporations, but by the end of the feverish 1980s, those same corporations, many with new, hyphenated names like RJR-Nabisco—controlled over two-thirds of all such assets.[40]

In sum, the discipline of market competition affected American and global corporations. Yet corporate behavior in the 1980s indicates that its effects differed from those the discipline of democracy might have had. Most Americans had no say in how the challenge of competition was met, just as in the near past they had had little say in the decisions that led to the original competition crisis. As a result, the search for quick profits generally took precedence over investment and careful nurturance of new products. Workers, communities, and the American political economy suffered as a result. Although the renewed market competition has sometimes spurred corporations on to investments that create good jobs, major decisions are made by the top of the corporate hierarchy, not by those who need the jobs. The political economy of corporate capitalism thus does not so much expand choices as constrict them.

If neither the internal democracy of the corporation nor the external discipline of the marketplace can hold corporations accountable, is there a force that can?

Recently the democratic debate has refocused on the other powerful engine of our political economy—government.

GOVERNMENT: SUSTAINING OR CHECKING CORPORATE AMERICA?

Judging from our current political dialogue, it often seems that Americans are divided into two camps: "liberals," who favor "big" government to achieve high levels of social equality, and "conservatives," who want to minimize the role of government in favor of "free markets." Chapters 14, 17 and 18 explain why this view of the debate is misleading. For now it is enough to note that through most of the nation's history, government has been less a democratic check on business power than a helpmate, director, and servant to American capitalism. Government has always been a powerful player in the free market. Even in the nineteenth century, when policymakers claimed they favored **laissez-faire** (or "leave alone") economic policies, government helped companies build railroads through land subsidies; protected American industries through tariffs; built canals, roads, and other parts of the economy; and helped bankers and lenders by backing the American dollar with gold. The real question about the American government concerns not so much *whether* it is powerful in our economy but *whom* it helps, hurts and hears as it makes decisions.

Current government spending and activity have expanded to the point that finding a free market is difficult. In part, this is because American business demands, and often gets, government assistance. None of the corporate activities of the 1980s—from merger mania to massive foreign investment—would have been possible without friendly governmental policies. Business power in America is partially related to corporate ability to translate wealth and power in the private economy into specific political interests. Corporate groups have a great advantage over less moneyed groups in hiring the lawyers and experts who lobby congressional committees and maintain friendly relationships with government bureaucracies. As the most powerful interest in America, corporate business poses a problem for democracy. Its power in politics is often a vicious circle. Successful business interests use their economic resources to influence public policies. The resulting policies enhance corporate economic success and provide even more resources. This money, in turn, enhances business power over public policies, as the cycle of economic success feeding political success continues. The result is the economic corruption of democracy.

Perhaps the best example of the power of corporate economic interests entrenched in government is the **military-industrial complex.** Currently, with approximately $260 billion to spend every year, the Pentagon and many of America's largest companies have created a privileged island in the American economy. This island is largely sheltered from the free market and competition, as the military often provides a guaranteed demand for the bombs, fighters, uniforms, and rations supplied by Pentagon contractors. Despite some cuts in military expenditures, that government spending perhaps does not so much reward economic success in the marketplace as it creates it outright. Companies like Lockheed, Rockwell International, and United Technologies have intricate ties with the Pentagon, which guarantees their profits on commodities sold to government.[41]

The Privileged Position of Business

Corporations in the military-industrial complex and elsewhere influence government in more ways than as interest groups. Whatever their goals, government policymakers and institutions often recognize what Charles Lindblom calls the "privileged position" of business in politics. Because businesses have the "freedom" to invest or not invest, and to lay off or hire workers, they have an important impact on the deliberations of government. Policymakers must always be concerned about their effect on corporations, which are the keys to the entire economy. Through its attention to the **business confidence factor,** government often shies away from policies that will offend corporate America because policymakers don't want to be blamed for harming investment and economic growth. What is interesting about this aspect of business power is that corporations do not even have to lobby to make it effective. On their own, policymakers will attend to the interests of corporations.[42]

The federal tax code provides a good example of another business privilege. Overall, Americans are taxed less than the citizens of any other nation in the industrialized world. Yet the joy of low taxes is not shared equally. Those who spend investment capital and make profits are often given special treatment. Over the last thirty-five years, tax rates for corporate profits have been drastically reduced—they currently constitute less than 10 percent of federal revenues, whereas in 1960 they averaged about 28 percent. At the same time, the government has engineered hundreds of tax loopholes and writeoffs of losses, allowing businesses to reduce their tax payments even further. Through tax deductions on everything from top executives' salaries to lobbying expenses, corporations have become privileged institutions.

Government's special tax treatment of corporations is not a conspiracy, but a philosophy. By reducing corporate taxes and levies on wealthy individuals, policymakers hope that private investment will increase and that everyone will benefit. The Reagan administration was highly successful in pushing tax breaks for the wealthy under the guise of **supply-side economics,** or what critics called trickle-down economics. Through the tax reforms of 1981 and 1986, taxes on income and capital gains were slashed, benefitting the wealthy. The Tax Reform Act of 1986, for example, cut taxes for those making less than $10,000 an average of $37, or 11 percent, while slashing taxes for those who made more than $1 million an average of $281,033, or 31 percent.[43] At the same time, the Social Security tax, which falls most heavily on the middle class and poor, was raised dramatically. Senator Daniel Patrick Moynihan has commented, "No other democratic country takes as large a portion of its revenue from working people at the lower ends of the spectrum and as little from persons who have property or high incomes".[44]

Government Priorities: The Popular Democratic Agenda

The privileged position of business before government is not always invulnerable. Government activity in the American political economy has also been shaped, if only partly and haltingly, by the claims of democratic citizenship. The aims of popular democrats have always been to extend the rights of democratic citizenship into the economy and to guarantee the level of economic equality necessary for a healthy democracy.

The case for democratic control over the private economy has been enhanced by frequent *market failures*, which occur when basic requirements of a free and fair market are violated. Market failures sometimes spur and justify government intervention, and enhance the claims of popular democrats.

One example of dramatic market failure was the disappearance of meaningful competition and the appearance of monopolies and oligopolies in the early twentieth century. During those years, many corporations themselves demanded government regulation to protect them from the power of other corporations and from the instability caused by either too much or too little corporate competition. Since then, government has assumed the role of regulating competition in a range of industries, from communications to the airlines, from the stock market to the production of oil and gas.[45]

Government has grown in the face of another kind of market failure. Elite democrats include voluntary cooperation and competition in their definition of a free market. But what happens when the public is affected *involuntarily* by a market exchange? Such side effects are called **externalities** by economists. Examples include everything from air, ground, and water pollution in American cities to the damaging effects of overgrazing and soil erosion in the Great Plains and West. When the private economy produces a mess, cleaning it up becomes an important governmental task. Laws that mandate pollution controls are often the products of citizen demands and organizations that have challenged the privileged position of business.

Economic depressions are the most dramatic market failures of all. Next to providing military strength, government's expansion can be seen as an attempt to avoid depressions. Our government has evolved aggressive taxing and spending policies (called **fiscal policy**) to prevent the market economy from failing as a whole. In addition, during the New Deal and in later periods, **deficit spending** has been used as the primary tool to avoid depressions by injecting dollars into the market economy. Both innovations were spurred largely by the theories of British economist John Maynard Keynes and his American followers. Government also acts through its control of interest rates and the supply of currency (**monetary policy**). By regulating both, it can encourage or discourage borrowing, consumption, and investment, as well as curbing inflation.[46]

The cumulative effect of market failures has been to raise the broad question of governmental accountability for the political economy. Before the Great Depression and the intense political controversies it unleashed, the American federal government denied in practice that there was a political economy at all. Yet since the New Deal, the stresses and strains of our economy have generally been seen as having political roots, and therefore can be modified by public policies. In a broad sense, then, the great victory of popular democracy in the twentieth century is the idea that responsibility for the American economy is too important to be left entirely to corporations and the free market.

The most enduring basis of popular democratic intervention into the political economy has been the idea of equality. The power of equality in American politics can serve as an ideological counterweight to the privileged position of business. Corporate elites have an advantage, for reasons outlined earlier, in interest-group politics. It would seem, however, that popular democrats have an advantage in electoral politics, because voting influences governmental willingness to counterbalance the consequences of a market economy. Popular coalitions are often motivated by resentment against rising inequalities.[47] In addition, policymakers respond not only to threats at the ballot box but also to threats of disruption and even violence as citizens vent their frustrations.[48] In their ability to take to the streets or vote to dramatize political grievances, popular democrats have a political resource that enables them, at least sometimes, to counter the power of economic wealth wielded by elite democrats.

Popular protests and electoral mobilizations produced the greatest progress for economic equality in the 1930s and 1960s. Through the Wagner Act of 1935, workers won the right to organize into unions. Through public employment and unemployment compensation, government relieved the worst excesses of market failure. Probably the most important development was the growth of the **welfare state.** American government was pressed to provide some protection against the ravages of unemployment, poverty, old age, and disease. The most important event in the development of the American welfare state was the passage of the Social Security Act of 1935, targeted to the poor as well as the unemployed, the elderly, the disabled, and the widowed at all income levels. Bitterly resisted by business at the time, the existence of Social Security now is relatively noncontroversial, possibly because one in six Americans is a beneficiary.

More controversial have been government efforts to create a universal standard of living below which citizens cannot be allowed to fall. In the early and mid-1960s, when the postwar American corporate capitalist economy was at its most prosperous, nearly one in five Americans was still poor. Sparked by the civil rights protests of the South and by riots and peaceful demonstrations in the North, the Johnson administration initiated Great Society programs that extended federal support to the reduction of hunger and the provision of public housing, health insurance, and other benefits to the elderly, to children, and to the poor. Through the Job Corps and other programs, Great Society programs trained a limited number of poor youth for jobs. Judged in terms of reduced poverty levels—a 60 percent reduction in the eleven years the programs were in full operation[49]—the Great Society was a success.

At their most aggressive, the Great Society programs involved American government in checking the worst inequalities of a market economy. Still, the Great Society programs never supplied direct benefits to the majority of the poor; at best, they prevented greater inequalities rather than removing old ones. Since 1974, many Great Society programs have been frozen, cut back, or eliminated altogether. Under the Reagan and Bush administrations, the elite democratic argument that welfare spending is a drag on the economy once again gained precedence, and the percentage of the federal budget dedicated to the alleviation of poverty was sharply reduced. In the 1980s, the market economy produced higher poverty rates, even in the midst of an economic boom and the generally growing incomes that resulted.

Although popular democratic success in promoting economic equality and extending the rights of democratic citizenship into the economy has been spotty, many economic issues have been placed on the public agenda that had once been excluded. Unemployment, poverty, air pollution, energy consumption, housing availability, and other issues are no longer seen by Americans as private concerns to be left only to corporations and their experts. Once such questions have moved into the democratic debate, it has proven difficult to move them entirely back into the realm of the private economy.[50]

CONCLUSION: CORPORATE CAPITALISM VERSUS DEMOCRATIC CAPITALISM

The democratic debate about the American political economy pits elite democratic faith in markets and corporations against popular democratic advocacy of equality and the importance of citizenship. It is difficult to make the case for corporate capitalism by using the language of popular democracy, for almost all modern corporate behavior and organization reflect hierarchy and inequality. Yet some measure of the hold of elite democracy in America can be gained by noting that both business and government somehow use the language of equality to justify large-scale inequality in wealth and income.

Popular democrats, of course, argue that corporate capitalism is a drag on the promises of democratic citizenship. The inequalities generated in the market corrupt political power and go beyond the inequality necessary for a well-functioning market economy. Greater equality would improve the economy by decreasing the social costs of poverty and increasing ordinary workers' stake in the system. Government should not only uphold corporate priorities but also attempt to expand democratic control over the economy.

Popular democrats view corporate capitalism as a distortion, not a reflection, of human nature. A more democratic political economy would nurture the natural desire of most people to participate in the economic institutions that govern their lives. Policies that strengthened families and communities would help people meet more of their needs outside of the marketplace. If corporations were governed more democratically, they would be more concerned about the broad effects of their decisions on workers, communities, and the environment. Worker-owned factories would be more democratic and probably more efficient. Work does not have to be organized in a top-down fashion, with each worker performing a mindless task in a minute division of labor. If workers were given more responsible roles in production, as we have seen recently in quality circles and job rotation, efficiency would improve at the same time that democratic participation was nurtured.

Each reader must come up with his or her own assessment of human nature. What level of democratic participation is the average American both capable of and inclined toward? Your assessment of human nature will determine to a great extent the level of democratic participation in the economy you deem appropriate. The organization of the political economy lays the foundation, or lack thereof, for democratic participation. Part Two of the text examines the extent of democratic participation in American politics.

KEY TERMS

capitalism
corporate capitalism
nondecision making
social mobility
income inequality
feminization of poverty
outsourcing
flexible specialization
laissez-faire

military-industrial complex
business confidence factor
supply-side economics
externalities
fiscal policy
deficit spending
monetary policy
welfare state

SUGGESTED READINGS

Bluestone, Barry and Harrison, Bennett, *The Great U-Turn* (New York: Basic Books, 1988). A provocative account of how corporate restructuring and public policies hurt ordinary Americans.

Friedman, Milton, *Capitalism and Freedom* (Chicago: University of Chicago Press, 1962). The now-classic defense of the relationship between markets and freedom.

Lindblom, Charles, *Politics and Markets* (New York: Basic Books, 1977). A Yale political scientist shows how and why business becomes the most privileged interest in any capitalist society.

Phillips, Kevin, *Boiling Point: Democrats, Republicans and the Decline of Middle Class Prosperity* (New York: Random House, 1993). A former Nixon aide and contemporary political commentator argues that both political parties are ill prepared to address the economic concerns of the American middle class.

Reich, Robert, *The Work of Nations* (New York: Random House, 1992). The Harvard economist and current Secretary of Labor argues that increased training and benefits for the new working class are the key to future economic growth.

PART

TWO

PARTICIPATION

Forged in the democratic debate, shaped and reshaped by succeeding generations, do our federalist Constitution and Bill of Rights provide citizens with the ability to control most political decisions? How do citizens use their potential power to shape the behavior of government and the modern corporation? Are some people more likely than others to get involved in politics, and if so, why? What actions do people take when they try to shape the democratic debate?

Part Two provides answers to these questions by examining the nature and extent of political participation in America. The balance between elite and popular democracy can be seen in who does and does not participate in American politics and in how ordinary citizens act on their own opinions.

The discussion begins, in Chapter 5, with what may be the most important, if often neglected, fact about American democracy: Many, and sometimes most, Americans just do not vote. Analyzing and interpreting the phenomenon of nonvoting tells us much about the contemporary character of the democratic debate.

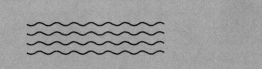

Voters or not, citizens have opinions about each other and about institutions and policies. Active public opinion is a cornerstone of American democracy, and the extent to which it is seen as rational or irrational serves as a major dividing line between elite and popular democrats, as examined in Chapter 6. But public opinion today is often influenced by the mass media, and their influence on the setting of the political agenda is the subject of Chapter 7.

Chapters 8 and 9 are concerned with political parties, voting, elections and campaigns. These chapters examine how well—or poorly—these institutions and practices serve elite and popular democracy, and discuss their enormous potential to shape government policies.

Joining an interest group or a social movement is an increasingly important way that citizens participate in politics. Chapters 10 and 11 look at the goals of both, chronicling the very large differences between interest groups and movements.

The chapters that follow invite students to think of participation as the keystone of effective democracy. Who's afraid of popular participation, and who welcomes it?

CHAPTER

5

Where Have All the Voters Gone?

F ree elections have been called "the crown jewel of American democracy." For the majority of Americans, the right to vote is the prime confirmation of our identity as a free people. Yet facts about recent American elections tarnish the jewel. In presidential election years, a little more than half of the American voting age population goes to the polls. In off-year elections, only a little more than a third of the eligible electorate turns up. Although the 1992 presidential race saw a rise in the number of voters, voter participation had been declining for thirty years before 1992. It couldn't go much lower. Despite the recent rise, America still has lower overall turnout rates than nearly any country in the world that holds free elections.

The scale of American nonvoting is a noteworthy feature of the nation's twentieth-century history. In the early 1900s, political, economic, and intellectual elites made conscious efforts to tame what many of them saw as "dangerous elements" in the American electorate. In the South, almost all blacks and many poor whites were disenfranchised through the introduction of literacy tests, poll taxes, and Ku Klux Klan terror (see Chapter 8). Only the civil rights movement

113

of the 1960s removed most of these barriers to participation. In the rest of the country, many working-class citizens were effectively disenfranchised by stiffened registration and voting laws, also enacted in the early 1900s. As Chapter 8 also shows, urban political parties and their ability to mobilize followers on election day were also weakened through new state laws that regulated parties, prosecuted many party officials, and deprived them of patronage jobs.

It has now been over twenty-five years since most of the extraordinary legal impediments to registration and voting have been removed in the South and elsewhere. Although registering to vote is still harder in the United States than it is in many other countries, it is much easier in most American states than it was several decades ago. In 1993, after a decade of partisan infighting, President Clinton signed a "Motor Voter" bill, making it possible for citizens to register as they visited many federal and state government offices. If citizens want to register, they are now able to do so without huge obstacles. Yet despite the continuous easing of registration requirements, voter participation has continued to be very low.

Who doesn't vote is as important as who does. This chapter tries to solve a mystery: Why is voter turnout so low even though many of the old legal obstacles have disappeared? With half to two-thirds of the American voting age citizenry absent from the polls, our leaders are chosen by a remaining electorate that although diverse and various, still is not representative of the American citizenry. For elite and popular democrats alike, the issue of who votes and who doesn't raises similar questions: Are American elections legitimate expressions of the popular will? Would it make a difference if nonvoters voted? Would popular democracy in America be advanced and would elite democracy be challenged if current nonvoters came to the polls in much greater numbers? Do nonvoters have more in common with each other than they do with people who do vote? Some answers to these questions follow.

THE MYSTERIOUS FACTS ABOUT NONVOTING

As Figure 5.1 shows, voting turnout in America declined sharply in the early twentieth century, recovered somewhat from the onset of the Great Depression until 1960, declined again for 32 years thereafter, then rose a little in 1992. Figure 5.1 includes only data from presidential elections, which generally provoke the highest turnout of any contests. Off-year congressional and state races have even lower turnout rates. Figure 5.2 displays participation rates for recent off-year elections.

Party primaries held to nominate candidates for public office draw even fewer voters. The total number of voters participating in the 1988 Republican and Democratic presidential primaries was 35.5 million, less than a fifth of the voting age population. Four years later in 1992, party primary totals dropped further, to 32.5 million, or less than a sixth of the voting age population. Remarkably,

FIGURE 5.1

Voter Turnout in Presidential Elections, 1884–1992

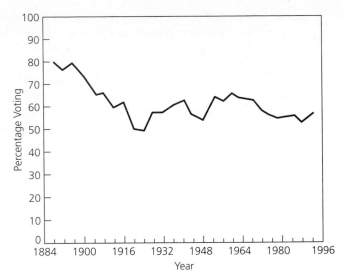

Source: Richard Niemi and Harold Stanley, *Vital Statistics on American Politics* (Washington, D.C.: Congressional Quarterly, 1992).

these low totals occurred in years of substantial competition for the presidential nomination in both parties.[1]

Local elections for mayor, city council, school boards, and the like are frequently not held at the same time as state and national elections. For that reason,

FIGURE 5.2

Voter Turnout in Off-year Elections, 1946–1990

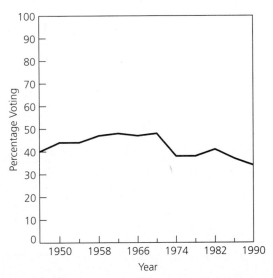

Source: Election 1990, Committee for the Study of the American Electorate, Washington, D.C., 1991.

participation rates are generally even lower than the already low totals reported for presidential and congressional elections. About 10 percent to 25 percent of the voting age population comes to the polls in the big city elections in Los Angeles, New York, Houston, and elsewhere.[2]

Observing the size of the nonvoting citizenry reveals some surprising numbers. In 1980, Ronald Reagan defeated Jimmy Carter and John Anderson in what was then called a decisive victory. Yet Reagan received the support of a smaller percentage of the voting age population than Republican Wendell Willkie did in 1940, as he was defeated by the immensely popular Franklin Delano Roosevelt. Although the media and the Republicans, as well as many Democrats, proclaimed that Carter's defeat was large enough to justify the subsequent "Reagan Revolution," they might have forgotten the 1940 loser Willkie, who actually received a proportion of support higher than Reagan. The dynamics of a modern three-candidate race, like that of 1992, provide further evidence that electoral mandates are often not what they seem to be. President Clinton defeated George Bush by 4 percent and Ross Perot by 24 percent, but his 43 percent of the vote translates into the support of less than a quarter of the voting age population. Both Reagan and Clinton won respectably, but only within the confines of a narrowed electorate.[3]

What sorts of people do and do not vote? The U.S. Census Bureau provides some interesting answers to this question in their postelection reports. Table 5.1

TABLE 5.1

Which Groups Vote the Most and Which the Least? The 1992 Presidential Election

Groups Most Likely to Vote	Percent Turnout	Groups Least Likely to Vote	Percent Turnout
Whites, $50,000+ income	74.3	Whites, income less than $5000	24.8
People with advanced degrees	75.9	People with less than 8th grade educations	31.6
People ages 45–64	63.6	People ages 18–24	38.4
White executives and managers	70.6	Hispanic farm workers	7.8
Homeowners	61.6	Renters	36.1
Government workers	71.2	All farm workers	32.9
The employed	62.4	The unemployed	46.2
College students, 18–24	49.8	People not in college, 18–24	28.6

Percentages are of voting age population, adjusted to reflect average over-reporting of survey respondents.

Source: Voting and Registration in the Election of 1992, Bureau of the Census, Series P-20. (Washington, D.C.: U.S. Government Printing Office, 1993), p. 466.

compares the voting participation rates of Americans most likely to vote with those least likely to vote in the 1992 presidential election. Four major characteristics—age, income, race, and education—delineate the vast social divide between voters and nonvoters. Table 5.2 reports the voting participation rates of different kinds of American citizens in recent presidential elections.

People of non-European descent, or who have less formal schooling, or who are younger and poorer than the norm tend to vote the least in America. Voting participation among Hispanics has always been low and is getting lower, despite their enormous growth in the population. African Americans showed notable increases in 1984 and 1988, but blacks still lag behind whites in national participation rates. Asian American voting rates have risen in some cases but are still very low.

Yet race, education, and income don't indicate the whole story. Since 1960, almost all Americans, including highly educated and wealthy whites, have voted less. The most dramatic decline in voting turnout is among America's **new working class**—people who work as bank tellers, clerks, hospital orderlies, secretaries, and in restaurants. More is said later about why this group, so

TABLE 5.2

Participation by Group in 1992 Election, as Percentage of Voting Age Population

Group	Percent Turnout	Group	Percent Turnout
Race		*Income (family)*	
Whites	57.2	<$5,000	24.9
Blacks	47.6	$5,000–$10,000	32.0
Hispanic origin	22.5	$10,000–14,999	39.3
		$15,000–20,000	48.2
Gender		$20,000–25,000	55.0
Males	53.8	$25,000–35,000	62.0
Females	55.9	$35,000–50,000	67.2
		$50,000 +	72.4
Age			
18–24	38.4		
25–44	51.9		
45–64	63.6		
65 +	63.7		
Education			
Less than 5th grade	15.1		
5th–8th grade	32.7		
9th–12th grade, no diploma	34.8		
High school graduate	51.1		
Some college	62.3		
Bachelor's degree	72.1		
Advanced degree	75.9		

Source: Compiled from U.S. Bureau of the Census, "Voting and Registration in the Election of 1992," Series P-20 (Washington, D.C.: U.S. Government Printing Office, 1993).

increasingly numerous in the population, is declining among the active electorate.

People of all races, educational levels, ages, and incomes are voting less. At the same time, a huge gap remains between races, generations, educational levels, and social classes. As Table 5.3 shows, these realities translate into odd disparities within metropolitan areas, between inner cities and outer suburbs. In America's central cities, neither the Democrats, Republicans, nor independents are a majority. The *party of nonvoters* is. In Bedford Stuyvesant, Brooklyn, 90,000 voters elected Major Owens to Congress in 1986, even though there were 348,000 eligible voters. Less than twenty miles away, in the suburbs of much wealthier and whiter Westchester County, 210,000 voters from a potential 388,000 elected a conservative Republican to office in the same year.

The overall national decline of voting participation also disguises important differences between regions. Generally, southern states have witnessed a rise in voting participation since 1960, while northeastern, midwestern, and western states have experienced steep drops. For instance, in the 1986 New York gubernatorial race, Mario Cuomo defeated his Republican challenger by the biggest plurality in New York State history. But the percentage of the adult population that actually came to the polls was among the lowest in that state's history. The election featured only a slightly higher rate of voting participation than the election of 1820, when the voting electorate was restricted to men and to those who owned property. Impressive as it was, Cuomo's New York landslide came from a mini-electorate.

Voting turnout has not always been so low. Over a hundred years ago, in 1888, it was at its highest in the Republic's history. Although high turnout was sometimes due to illegal and corrupt practices like paying people to vote, citizens

TABLE 5.3

Inner-city vs. Outer-suburb Rates Compared, 1992 Congressional Elections

Number Voting in House Contests		Suburban Advantage
California, Los Angeles Area		
District 29 (suburb)	228,000	
District 35 (inner city)	118,000	+110,000 votes
Georgia, Atlanta Area		
District 5 (inner city)	204,000	
District 6 (suburbs)	262,000	+58,000 votes
Illinois, Chicago Area		
District 2 (inner city)	210,000	
District 6 (suburbs)	251,000	+41,000 votes
New York, NYC Area		
District 11 (inner city)	80,000	
District 20 (suburbs)	210,000	+170,000 votes

Source: New York Times, Nov. 5, 1992, p. B19.

still voted in greater numbers—regardless of their race, education, social class, or age—than they do now. Under different circumstances, American citizens turned out in very different proportions indeed. Since 1888, the proportion of nonvoters to voters has fluctuated, but it has never come close to the earlier standard. Moreover, social class, age, race, and educational level did not make a difference in 1888. Yet for some reason these characteristics matter greatly now.

Some say that the decline in voting is associated with the increasing modernization of our country and the general prosperity of the American people. As people become more satisfied with private life, they are said to have fewer reasons to get excited about politics. With the temptations of consumer items, the pressures of work and raising a family, and the diversions of vacations and the mass media, many people have neither the time nor sufficient enthusiasm to go out and vote.

However, it is those with the *fewest* reasons to be satisfied—people with low incomes and insecure jobs, and the unemployed—who are the most likely to stay away from the polls, while those with high levels of income and education turn out in fairly large numbers. Another interesting fact is that other modern countries like Japan, Sweden, France, and the former West Germany have much higher participation rates than the United States. As these countries have become wealthier since World War II, voting participation rates have risen, not fallen. Table 5.4 on p. 120 shows that U.S. voting participation ranks next to last in comparison with other advanced industrial democracies.

WHY MANY AMERICANS DON'T VOTE

Current voting participation rates of Americans are peculiar and even mysterious. Historically, we have had higher participation rates, at one time even leading the world in enfranchisement. Currently, however, U.S. participation rates rank among the lowest of all democracies. The high rates of American nonvoting are not like historical and foreign trends. How can such massive nonvoting be explained? Does massive nonvoting detract from our democracy or does it really matter?

Elite Democratic Theories of Nonvoting

There are many schools of thought about why so many Americans fail to vote. They follow elite and popular democratic interpretations of American political life. The first view would have been appreciated by elite democrats throughout American history. Its essentials are well captured by ABC commentator and columnist George Will. "The fundamental human right," Will claims, is not to the vote, but to "good government." To Will, there is no necessary relationship between good government, democracy, and high voting rates. Why, Will asks, should people who are more interested in watching TV soap operas be urged

TABLE 5.4		Percent Turnout
Participation Rates in Selected Democracies, by Rank	Australia (1993)	90
	Austria (1986)	87
	Canada (1988)	75
	East Germany (1990)	93
	France (1988)	81
	Hungary (1990)	64
	Italy (1991)	85
	Japan (1993)	75
	South Korea (1992)	79
	Switzerland (1987)	46
	United States (1992)	**55**

Sources: Ruy Texeira, *The Disappearing American Voter* (Washington, D.C.: The Brookings Institution, 1992), p. 8; updates from *The New York Times* for Japan, Hungary, South Korea, Australia.

to vote at all, and why should we be sad if they refrain? Will argues that high turnout may be dangerous, because many people who don't vote are ill-informed. Like Alexander Hamilton and other elite democrats, Will fears the passions of a highly mobilized citizenry. As evidence, he recalls Germany's Weimar Republic of the 1920s. Germans turned out in high numbers, but the result was political divisions so large that they paved the way for the rise of Adolf Hitler and the Nazis. In short, high voter turnout may endanger democracy.[4]

Nonvoting as a Rational Act

Many scholarly arguments explain away low turnout without Will's frank distrust of the nonvoting population. Still, like him, they tend to see nonvoting not as a big problem for democracy; rather, it results naturally from the psychological and social characteristics of many individual voters. Professors Raymond Wolfinger and Steven Rosenstone note that nonvoters are less educated than voters, and they have less political knowledge and less interest in politics. Because of their lack of formal education, current nonvoters know less about the political process, are less likely to follow campaigns closely, and are less likely to feel a sense of political **efficacy**—the belief that they can have an impact on the political process. Instead of simply noting a relationship between lack of schooling and voting, these writers argue that one causes the other.

These interpretations find it natural that poor, relatively uninformed, young, and uneducated people do not show up at the polls. This way of seeing nonvoting is closely allied to what political scientists call the **rational actor approach. Voters** are viewed as individual, self-interested consumers. Citizens select candidates for public office much the way consumers select products in the supermarket, on the basis of candidates' past and future performance, and on the time and effort required to discover a "bargain" that matches their wants.

One implication of the rational actor approach is that candidates for public office, in order to collect the largest number of consumer votes, appeal to **swing voters**—those who are least committed to either party or to specific candidates. In marketing themselves to swing voters, candidates become blander as they move toward the political center to attract voters with few opinions. But by getting blander, candidates confuse large numbers of voters who "can discern no utility difference at all among the rival candidates or parties," and therefore withhold their support on election day.[5]

Rational actor analysis also tries to explain why increased education is so highly correlated with increased levels of voter participation. Less educated citizens have to work harder to find meaningful differences between rival candidates or parties. In addition, acquiring information about the candidates, learning how to register to vote, and getting to the polls are more difficult than for more educated people. After all that, they often can't sort out the contrasts among candidates and don't care enough to inform themselves. Not knowing enough about politics to care very much, and believing that the effort to know more isn't worth the effort, many Americans become nonvoters.

The logical consequence of this explanation of nonvoting is that uneducated people's low turnout is understandable and no real cause for alarm. Registration laws might be relaxed and more attempts made to educate citizens about the political process. These measures would lessen the perceived costs of voting, and more citizen-consumers might show up to vote. Whatever the outcome, though, nonvoting cannot be blamed on defects in our institutions. Given human nature and the diversity of its expression, some people simply are more interested in politics than others.

Scholars who support the above analyses share many assumptions about human nature with the approaches pioneered by the Federalists. Then and now, elite democrats start with the premise that ordinary people are more interested in individual rewards and gratifications than in the satisfactions of participating in the political life of the community. Citizens are seen as bundles of desires, and entrepreneurs in politics compete to satisfy those desires. Self-interested people need individual material incentives to participate in politics, and they vote only when they can see something in it for themselves personally. Some highly educated people are more attuned to the finer things in life, including a view of politics as meaningful in and of itself, which perhaps explains why they vote and participate more in politics. In Will's words: "Thought must be given to generating a satisfactory (let us not flinch from the phrase) governing class. That there must be a class is, I think, beyond peradventure." Nonvoting is thus not a problem, because it allows such a "governing class" to more easily form.[6]

Popular Democrats and Nonvoting:
The Registration Problem

Many other analysts and activists *do* worry about the rise of nonvoting. They attribute it not to human nature, but to various features of our political system and its laws.

Some scholars and many "good government" groups such as the League of Women Voters and Common Cause explain low turnout by criticizing the continuing difficulty citizens face when they try to register and vote. Almost alone among the citizens of Western nations, each American is personally responsible for the sometimes complicated process of registering. Most of us take for granted that we are responsible for locating the local board of elections, finding a registration form, and completing it correctly. When we move, we are often responsible for re-registering. If we don't vote in one presidential election, we sometimes must re-register. If we are not home on election day, it's up to us to apply for an absentee ballot and fill it in.

The American system of personal registration favors those who are not intimidated by its sometimes cumbersome and time-consuming process. To make things more complicated, individual states and counties often have different forms and procedures for registering. In some areas, voter registration forms in which an *i* is not dotted or a *t* not crossed are invalidated by election officials.[7]

In most other countries the situation is simpler because the national government is responsible for registering citizens. British and Canadian governments must maintain up-to-date voter lists by keeping track of who has moved and who has not. In Italy, registration isn't even an issue, because the possession of a national identity card is enough. Belgium and Australia exact minor penalties from those who do not vote.

There is no doubt that duplicating these methods in the United States would raise voting levels. The great majority of people in the United States who are registered to vote do vote, so making registration a governmental responsibility would boost turnout. Moreover, although personal registration might seem to be the only way to compile voting lists, it has been used only in the last hundred years. The personal registration system is not one of America's oldest political traditions, but a twentieth-century innovation.

Analysts agree that changing registration laws and voting procedures (by changing election day to a Sunday, for instance) would probably raise American turnout. However, Republicans have generally resisted registration reform, and many Democrats have favored it for partisan reasons. Republicans believe that easing registration requirements would bring to the polls more Democrats among low-income and minority voters. In some states—most recently in New Jersey's 1993 gubernatorial race—Democrats have suspected Republicans of suppressing the votes of African Americans and other heavily Democratic groups. Republicans counter by saying that they don't try to weaken turnout, but that they are concerned about the potential for fraud when registration laws are eased.

With Republican George Bush's defeat in 1992, Congress finally passed and President Clinton signed a watered-down version of the so-called **Motor-Voter bill,** which mandated that registration forms and voter assistance be available in motor-vehicle and other governmental offices, and that mail-in registration be allowed in all states. To get majority support, the original provisions calling for automatic registration of all people who apply for drivers' licenses or public assistance were dropped. In the 1980s, though, many states had already enacted some parts of the motor-voter initiative, and some, like Wisconsin and North Dakota, went much further by allowing voters to register on election days. Other states have enacted laws that make it difficult for county officials to "purge" voter rolls after each election, so that people remain registered even if they miss one election.

Most analysts agree that a combination of all the measures, including automatic registration, would probably boost actual voter turnout by about 5 percent to 10 percent—a notable improvement. Still, even the most optimistic expectations of far-reaching legal changes would bring voter turnout only back to that of 1960, a year when registration laws were tough. Under the most radical proposals, twenty million more people would probably vote in the next presidential election—a significant number—but America would still have one of the lowest turnout rates.[8]

The problem with registration reform is that nonvoting is seen in isolation from other important features of elite democracy that we shall detail below and in other chapters in Part Two. Change rules and procedures, reformers say, and all will be well—or at least as well as can be expected. If the rules and procedures are loosened and people still do not come to the polls, maybe it is because nonvoters just don't care.

Although registration and voting impediments are important in America, evidence shows that removing them would not make a decisive difference. Why? Voter turnout in the United States outside the South has been declining *even as* easier registration procedures were introduced. Historically, no clear-cut relationship has been apparent between easing registration laws and increasing turnout. In 1988, registration laws were relatively lax, but voter turnout was far below that of 1940 and 1960, election years when turnout was relatively high and registering to vote was much more complicated.

Thus, despite reforms in registration procedures, voter turnout still has continued to decline. No doubt, it would have declined even further if registration laws had not changed. But other explanations are needed to tell why, in the face of much attention to the difficulties of personal registration, voting turnout continues to be so low.

Nonvoting: Historical and Political Explanations

Voter turnout in the United States *is* a serious concern, because people who don't vote often have the fewest economic and educational resources to defend themselves in political struggles. Moreover, the view that American government should be based on popular consent is undermined if consent comes disproportionately from those with higher levels of wealth, income, and education who are whiter and older than most Americans. Changing registration laws does not change that reality.

Freedom Summer

In America, voting and nonvoting are more properly seen as related to the strength and weakness, respectively, of grassroots democratic associations among people who are not particularly wealthy or highly educated. For example, in the late 1950s and early 1960s, African Americans organized against the system of white domination and segregation that had existed in the South since the end of Reconstruction. Aided by their churches and by many young black and white students, black people took on the system of racial apartheid through boycotts, sit-ins, marches, and demonstrations.

In the summer of 1964—**Freedom Summer**—hundreds of young civil rights workers of both races travelled to the South to assist the movement. A few of these workers were murdered. Others were met by mobs or gangs and severely beaten. Still, the work of organizing continued. At great personal risk, people who had never been political began to organize as well. Through their churches and in their neighborhoods, they held meetings to persuade others to join the struggle. They held peaceful mass marches from one southern city to another, talking to tenant farmers, sharecroppers, janitors, maids, and construction workers, who also began to organize.[9]

The movement attracted Fannie Lou Hamer, who had worked as a maid for a white plantation owner in Mississippi all her life. Before the civil rights movement, she had thought little about politics. But after she talked to a civil rights worker, she decided to try registering to vote. After three attempts and a beating, she passed the highly biased literacy test administered by a hostile white county official. When she got back to the plantation, her boss fired her for what she had done. Hamer then became a full-time political organizer and a leader of the Mississippi Freedom Democratic Party. In 1964, her party challenged the all-white Democratic party of Mississippi, prompting a civil rights revolution in the national Democratic party.[10]

Hamer's experience was not very different from hundreds of thousands of others in the South. Civil rights activists urged blacks to vote, a right they had been almost totally denied. These African Americans not only registered to vote, often at great personal risk. Registration was one act in a much larger political drama in which they were the protagonists—the political empowerment of ordinary people through the shared struggle for political and social equality. This drama changed many people as it had Fannie Lou Hamer. African-American farmers and workers in 1950 might have said that politics and voting were for white people and that it was safer not to get involved. But the advance of democracy in the South changed that attitude. For example, Hamer learned

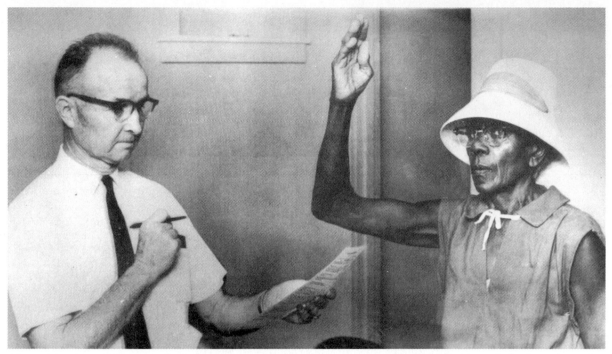

After seven tries and as many rebuffs by county officials, 68-year-old Mississippian Joe Ella Moore is finally registered to vote by a federal official in 1965. The Voting Rights Act of 1965 required federal supervision of voter registration in most Southern states.

that her experience on the plantation was a reality shared by millions of others. More important, she learned that it could be changed, that skin color and schooling weren't requirements for intelligent citizenship.

Under pressure from this movement, Congress passed and President Johnson signed the **Voting Rights Act of 1965.** The act swept away ninety years of racist legal impediments to black registration and voting. Federal inspectors were sent to the South to supervise the registration of black voters. Literacy tests, poll taxes, and other mechanisms of electoral apartheid fell. In Mississippi, the partial removal of these barriers made a tremendous difference, as thousands of previously unregistered blacks voted. But even before passage of the Voting Rights Act, people like Fannie Lou Hamer, participants in a powerful political movement, had won some of these rights themselves. Although registration laws were a barrier to popular democracy and to voting, the civil rights movement had removed a more important psychological barrier before 1965. The movement gave people the courage to come together to fight the political and economic system of which registration laws were only a part. They gained the sense that popular democracy was possible and found personal meaning in voting.

We will never know what would have happened in the South if registration laws had been magically removed by the federal government without the urging of a strong political movement. In other places where registration laws were made more accommodating without a strong democratic movement, voter turnout did not rise significantly. Before 1965, New York City had low turnouts in its black community, although not nearly as low as those in Mississippi. But New York did not have a Freedom Democratic party in every neighborhood. For many reasons, many blacks in New York City were not well organized politically in the 1960s. Low black voter participation in New York brought Federal inspection of its registration and election procedures. But the black turnout hardly increased. In the early seventies it began to decline and did not begin an upswing until Jesse Jackson ran for president in the Democratic primaries in 1984 and 1988.[11]

In short, registration laws do matter. But overturning them makes a difference only when accompanied by a strong political movement that engenders a sense of registering and voting as parts of a larger political cause. Only when the civil rights movement established a strong connection between popular democracy and voting did registration—and voting—really increase.

Nonvoting and Grassroots Politics

Social movements like the civil rights struggle demonstrate that nonvoting and voting are really consequences of elite democracy. Although registration laws and education about candidates affect voting participation rates, organization of people in their neighborhoods and workplaces may be the most important feature. As we'll see in Chapter 11, social movements often boost voting, precisely because they encourage many types of political participation and mobilization. Meetings, marches, boycotts, sit-ins, *and* voting go together in these movements. They help to form a democratic political culture among people who are otherwise isolated from one another.

Are experiences like the civil rights movement exceptions in American political life? Elite democrats from the Federalists onward have feared the consequences of "too much" political activity by ordinary people, and have tried to check, balance, and discourage it. As we saw in Chapter 2, the framers of the Constitution designed a set of political procedures to prevent "tyranny of the majority." They designed American government to be complicated, slow, and distant from "passions," to prevent these passions from overwhelming liberty. Elite democrats hoped social movements would be the exception and not the rule in American politics, for such movements incited people to question the basic rules and practices that bolstered political "stability."

How different are things today? Now, probably not a single elected official would argue against popular participation in politics. Yet actions speak louder than words. Chapters 8 and 9 detail the vast amount of money and expertise that contemporary politicians throw into the electoral process. Only a tiny percentage of it goes toward voter registration or to mobilizing new voters. However, when politicians really want to supply organizational muscle toward voter registration and turnout, their efforts pay off. In 1991, turnout rose as both the national Democratic and Republican parties mobilized to defeat the former Ku Klux Klan leader David Duke as he ran for governor in Louisiana.

Why are most elected officials reluctant to use their power to drastically increase voting turnout? One reason is that they feel they can't. Organizing new voters takes time and energy, and it is not easily achieved through the normal means of political communication, such as TV. A greater reason might be that elected officials got where they are within the *existing* electorate. Why bring newcomers into the electorate with all their new demands and claims? As Ted Lowi and Ben Ginsberg comment, "Both sides (parties) prefer to compete for power without engaging in full-scale popular mobilization".[12]

Elite democratic reluctance to encourage high levels of participation has not been unchallenged. When popular democratic associations are strong and members sense their group effectiveness, political participation in America is robust. Since the country's birth, Americans have been joiners and participants, not just passive spectators or avid property seekers. In the 1880s and 1890s, the farmers of the Great Plains and South organized *Farmer's Alliances* whose goals were not to assert the power of property but to contest the unequal distribution of wealth and power. To them, farming was more than an effort to get rich, it was a way of life that taught people how to work together, cherish the land, and build a future. Alliance men and women resisted the concentrated power in banks and railroads on the grounds that people were more important than money. The strength of the Farmer's Alliance led to the greatest of all modern

Kansas farm families harvest their wheat crop in the 1890s. Western and Southern small farmers provided most of the votes for the Populist Party in 1892 and 1896.

American political movements, *populism*, and its call for a republic based on the dignity of labor and government by the people. In America's cities in the same period, workers joined to protect themselves against the factory and wage labor system that denied them dignity and rights. Mass strikes and trade union activism abounded during the 1890s, prompted by the strength of grassroots associations like the Knights of Labor.

Often such associations provided the camraderie, social services, and community that distant government and big business didn't. The Farmer's Alliance, Populist party, and Knights of Labor, each in its own way, reduced the isolation of work life in farm and factory. They helped their members pool their resources to protect themselves in times of hardship, protected families who got in trouble with the police, and resisted bankers and their foreclosures. The Alliance and American ethnic and labor associations also provided public meeting places that were often shelters from the awesome prospect of facing the complex world of modern America alone. Such groups sprang from what sociologist Ray Oldenburg calls "third places"—public spaces like taverns, churches, coffee houses, clubs, and restaurants where people could be away from home and work, and that "provided frequent engagement in the most basic of all political activities—*talk*".[13]

It is not a coincidence that when American social, economic, political, and religious associations among ordinary people have been strong, voting and other forms of political participation have been robust. What individual workers and farmers lacked in money, formal education, leisure time, and social status made them second-class citizens. But with the collective power of their common associations, people compensated for their disadvantages in a political system dominated by elite democratic principles. Numbers, energy, and enthusiasm balanced money, media power, and college degrees. In the 1890s, the tops of America's political parties were dominated by businessmen, lawyers, and professional politicians. But at the grassroots level, the parties brought people together, sheltering them from the very worst effects of their status as workers, farmers, or immigrants, and even forcing some accountability from leaders to their needs and cultures.

Some argue that associational life is still strong—that Americans are still joiners. Although this is true to some extent, the kinds of people who participate and their activities differ. The original farmers' and workers' associations were made up of individuals with little economic or political clout and with few resources besides their numbers, their time, and their ability to organize and educate themselves. Their strength was based on face-to-face conversations and relationships. In contrast, many present-day associations are organized from the top down, managed by professionals, and composed mostly of middle- and upper-class people. Rather than encouraging widespread talk and grassroots organization, many are composed of members who never meet, don't know each other, and participate in politics only in the isolation of their own homes. Such **mail-order politics** means that computer direct mail, post office boxes, and fat checkbooks finance professional lobbyists who "do" politics for others in Washington.[14]

Such mail-order politics, one recent study concludes, means that political activism "largely remains the province of those with higher incomes and better education," and that "money is fast replacing time as the most valuable commodity in political campaigns." Although 18 percent of American adults gave money to political campaigns in 1992, more than a quarter of it was donated by that tiny proportion of Americans who make over $125,000 annually. Mail-order politics is generally too expensive and not very interesting to people with fewer financial resources, and consequently they participate in such organizations much less. Ironically, their lack of participation creates a kind of self-fulfilling prophecy: As activism involves more and more of the wealthy and well-educated, the political agenda becomes controlled by well-heeled activists and Washington-centered organizations. The rest of us find few places where our participation could really make a difference. Consequently, many citizens come to believe, just as Fannie Lou Hamer did in the 1950s, that "politics is for someone else."[15]

The relative weakness of bottom-up organizations in U.S. politics sparks a counter-reaction by the unorganized to their loss of effective citizenship. But the reaction can take the form of "tuning out" politics not from apathy but from a sense of resignation and impotence. Nonvoting is one such response. Walter Dean Burnham has called nonvoting a "silent vote of no confidence" by millions of people on American politics. Regardless of the good or bad points of the American political debate, nonvoters tend to see it as someone else's, not their own. To many, our politicians are literally speaking a foreign language.[16]

Could popular democratic activity be revived on a large scale? Next, we provide evidence that popular democracy is still very much alive in some places. But it faces new obstacles unknown to the Populists, the Knights of Labor, or the civil rights movement of the past.

Consider, for example, the obstacles faced by what we have called the new working class, that fast-growing part of our population who work as bank tellers, child-care workers, restaurant employees, word processors, janitors, hospital orderlies, and health aides. Many of the new working class are vulnerable to unemployment, job insecurity, and low wages. Most of them don't have the middle-class incomes and fringe benefits that America's older, unionized blue-collar workers once had. Nor do most of them have prospects to move up the job ladder to better positions. These new workers are also younger than the norm, and most are women. The new working class would seem to have the most to gain from voting and political organization.

Yet, with some notable exceptions, it is precisely among this growing part of the population that voter turnout and political organization have declined the most since the 1960s. Why? Neither registration difficulty, apathy, nor ignorance accounts for their low voter turnout. The problem is the new working class has few associations and organizations to call its own. Traditionally, American labor unions concentrated their attention on male workers in the now declining manufacturing industries. The new working class, however, has few opportunities to join unions because their workplaces have never been organized by unions. The Populist, Knights of Labor, and civil rights movements thrived in the closeness and intimacy of small towns, urban neighborhoods, and church congregations. Present-day service workers who work in one place are likely to live in locations scattered throughout metropolitan areas. Without organizations to bind them together, their encounters "beyond the narrow range of families and friends [are] limited to the passive receipt of goods and information" through TV, the mall, and the supermarket. Taken together, the absence of labor unions and the fragmentation in residence make forming political associations more difficult than it once was. Members of the new working class often have difficulty getting together at all, especially for political reasons. Thus, it is no wonder that service workers vote less than the working class of the past.[17]

Is this situation permanent in American politics? Elite democratic explanations of nonvoting bypass the difficulties of the new working class. Yet in doing so, they neglect historical changes in our political economy that have isolated ordinary people from politics. In America, formal education, income, and age correlate more than they ever have with high participation in elections. But are these the actual reasons for massive nonvoting? Only in a polity that makes all three necessary for effective participation can this cause-and-effect relationship be a possibility. It may be that nonvoters haven't dropped out of our political system, but rather that our political system has become insulated from their voices. Whatever its cause, the gap separating nonvoters from our political system makes them confused and cynical, and their political participation all that more difficult.

MOBILIZING NONVOTERS: WOULD IT MAKE A DIFFERENCE?

What difference would it make if nonvoters came to the polls? Nobody can be sure, but researchers have conducted extensive surveys of nonvoters and their political attitudes. Such surveys have to be viewed with caution, though, because they try to predict the political actions of people who are not politically active. It is possible that an event or experience that brought many nonvoters to the polls would change their political perspectives, as the civil rights movement did in the case of Fannie Lou Hamer. If, for instance, nonvoters had been surveyed during the low-turnout election of 1924 and then resurveyed after the Great Depression had begun five years later, different attitudes and behaviors would no doubt have been found. Working-class people who had been silent in the 1920s were by 1936 organizing and joining trade unions as well as voting in large numbers, generally for the Democratic party of Franklin Roosevelt. If popular democratic activities revived, participation in them would change the opinions of the politically inactive. Nevertheless, surveys are worth considering as snapshots of nonvoters as they are, and as the survey researchers see them through the questions they ask.

Very few American nonvoters say that they don't vote out of principle. By large majorities, current nonvoters tell pollsters that voting is an important right and a civic duty that they should undertake sometime in the future. In 1992, younger people were less likely than older nonvoters to feel this sense of civic duty. Still, so many nonvoters apparently feel guilty about not going to the polls that about 10 percent report voting when they actually haven't. At first sight, it would seem that nonvoters have no special attitudes about politics that distinguish them from voters. Both groups feel that voting is important, but for some reason the former simply don't.[18]

Nonvoters are much more critical of the American political system than people who vote consistently. In a 1984 University of Michigan study and a 1988 *New York Times* poll, nonvoters were much more likely than voters to agree with statements like "I don't think public officials care much about what people like me think," "Things go on as before no matter who is elected," and "The government doesn't care about people like me." A majority of nonvoters in both polls said that there are no significant differences between Republicans and Democrats. Their general views of our parties were not very favorable; only one in five identified strongly with a political party at all.[19]

More extensive survey evidence about the basic political beliefs of voting and nonvoting Americans is provided by William Maddox and Stuart Lilie. Their surveys confirm that procorporate policies are furthered by massive nonvoting, while candidates and policies that favor increased economic equality are hurt. In their research, American opinion is divided into the four categories of libertarian, conservative, populist, and liberal. Respondents are not divided primarily on their beliefs in more or less government. The four opinion groups disagree mostly about whom government now serves and what its activities should be.[20] (See Chapter 6 for more discussion of opinion groups.)

Lilie and Maddox find that about half of all Americans are either **populists** or **liberals.** Both groups share a deep disdain for government ties to corporate business and for the high level of economic inequality it produces. They desire increasing regulation of business behavior, and favor measures to redistribute wealth and provide more social services in medical care, housing, and daycare. Populists, however, differ from liberals in that they are suspicious of civil rights legislation, hard-line on crime, and hostile to freedom of choice on social issues like abortion and sexual preference.

Only a third of those surveyed fall into the **libertarian** or **conservative** groups. Conservatives are generally against governmental interference with private property but favor government intervention to control social behavior, much like the populists. Libertarians, a sixth of the citizenry, are the only group that opposes most governmental intervention, whether in the corporate capitalist economy or the private behavior of individuals.

Lilie and Maddox find that people with populist and liberal views are much more likely than libertarians and conservatives to be nonvoters. While about two-thirds of the latter regularly vote, only half of the populist-liberals report voting. As a result, the groups most hostile to the existing distribution of power and wealth are not represented very well in the voting electorate. Conversely, the groups most friendly to corporate capitalism are overrepresented. Given the "class gap" that we've noted between voters and nonvoters, these differences shouldn't be surprising.

With their resentments of economic inequality, their prevalence in the American population and their very low turnout, the populists could trace the future of a new American politics. What could bring them back into the electorate? If they came back, what kind of politics might they bring? The political scientist Kenneth Dolbeare argues that populists could return to the political scene, and

> that crisis conditions and a believable alternative would provide necessary ingredients for an unusual turnout, but the direction is far less predictable. Based on past experience, economic issues or events would bring populists to the side of the Democrats, national security threats or racial issues would send them to the Republicans.[21]

Do we really need a war or an economic depression to bring about a higher populist turnout? The social makeup and opinions of many nonvoters suggest that their powerful grievances and energies could be tapped in less dramatic circumstances. If their energies are to be used democratically, then face-to-face, grassroots political organizations have to be rebuilt. Repairing the social and political organizations of the American citizenry is the necessary solution to nonvoting. The following sections probe cases in which the mobilization of nonvoters has already occurred.

Chicago, 1983: Case Study in Mobilizing Nonvoters

In some places, political life has been enlivened and nonvoters attracted to the polls, with real effects on public policies and the political agenda. Where such repairs in the social and political fabric have been made, elite democrats and their claims about the ignorance of nonvoters can be disputed.

In 1983, for example, something of an electoral revolution occurred in Chicago. Harold Washington, a Chicago congressman, led a coalition of African-Americans, Latinos, women's-rights advocates, labor union members, and white liberals into power at City Hall, defeating both the incumbent mayor, Jane Byrne, and the son of Richard J. Daley, the longtime Chicago boss, in the Democratic Party primary. In a tense campaign where voters were polarized along racial lines, Washington later defeated Bernard Epton, the Republican nominee, in the general election. In 1987, Washington was reelected and brought a clear majority with him into the City Council. The next year, Washington died of a heart attack, and the coalition he helped to build suffered internal splits. Today, Richard M. Daley, Jr. is Chicago's mayor, but he directs a city with a radically different political makeup than it had before Washington and his movement appeared on the scene.

A working-class supporter of Chicago mayoral candidate Harold Washington makes his views known. Washington, who became the city's first black mayor in 1983, successfully forged a coalition of union members, African Americans, Latinos, and the poor.

There are a number of reasons that Washington's victory was remarkable. First, it had been preceded by what might be called a transformation of political life in the city's black neighborhoods, featuring a revival of grassroots politics and associational life. Church congregations, labor unions, educational groups, community organizations, and even high school students combined their resources and got others to think about why they had been excluded from political power under the Democratic party's machine. New, locally owned radio stations were formed and newspapers started by people in the black community, balancing the news coverage of commercial TV and Chicago's daily newspapers with hard-hitting stories about the city's housing projects, social services, and education. People with low levels of formal education suddenly not only voted in large numbers, but also became participants in the political life of their neighborhoods and workplaces. Table 5.5 shows the dramatic rise in African-American participation in Chicago elections.

TABLE 5.5

White and African-American Voters in Chicago Elections, 1975–1983

Election	Percent African-American Turnout	Percent White Turnout
Democratic Primary, 1975	34.1	46.5
Democratic Primary, 1977	27.4	44.8
Democratic Primary, 1979	31.5	48.9
General Election, 1982	55.8	54.0
Democratic Primary, 1983 (Washington vs. Daley and Byrne)	64.2	64.6
General Election 1983 (Washington vs. Epton)	73.0	67.2

Source: Paul Kleppner, *Chicago Divided; The Making of a Black Mayor* (DeKalb, Ill.: Northern Illinois University Press, 1984), p. 149.

The emergence of high levels of organizational activity and voting among Chicago's African-American population was remarkable for a second reason. Although constituting a near majority in the city, Chicago's blacks could not win a citywide race alone. To win, they needed to build coalitions in the Latino and white communities. Lest high levels of African-American voting spur fear among other races, the Washington coalition also organized heavily in the Puerto Rican and Chicano neighborhoods, and among the liberal and more affluent whites in neighborhoods surrounding the University of Chicago and bordering Lake Michigan. In addition, Washington drew many labor union activists of both races to his candidacy.[22]

The vehicle for mobilizing the Washington constituencies was his populist stance on issues. The Washington forces attacked big real estate developers and talked about decentralizing city services to neighborhood control, appointing new people to positions at city hall, improving public housing, fighting drug dealers, and rebuilding public education. Washington's campaign also linked Chicago's problems to the national scene: His criticisms of the Reagan administration's treatment of the working class and poor, his opposition to bloated military budgets, and his pro-choice stance on abortion made his candidacy into a national crusade.

The Washington victory changed the political agenda in Chicago by forging a new coalition around issues that had been largely smothered in Chicago politics. A third remarkable aspect is that while Washington brought thousands of new voters into the electorate, his very success prompted a counter-mobilization among some whites. Emotions ran high in the general election campaign, perhaps the dirtiest and most passionate in Chicago's colorful political history. Thousands of white voters—in wards that had been largely Democratic for fifty years—abandoned their party's nominee and voted for the Republican, Bernard

Mobilizing the Latino Vote

Are people who don't vote not interested in politics? In the Southwest, Mexican Americans have shown that voting participation rises dramatically when nonvoters believe that they can make a difference.

"You feel empowered when you see the politicians come to our accountability night," San Antonian Marilyn Stavinoha told others at a meeting. "Instead of politicians talking to us, we talk to the politicians." A member of Communities Organized for Public Service (COPS), Ms. Stavinoha is a long-time activist in San Antonio politics. She's part of a movement throughout the Southwest to build democratic activity in poor neighborhoods and towns. The movement focuses on issues that give average citizens a sense of their democratic political power.

For Ms. Stavinoha, COPS, and other organizations, it's been a long struggle. Back in 1974, Mexican Americans in San Antonio were ignored by the Anglo-monopolized city government. Poorer westside neighborhoods were flooded because the city hadn't built storm drains there. Streets weren't paved or lit, and parks were nonexistent. Schools in the neighborhood were underfunded compared to the wealthier northside. In Clovis, New Mexico, Mexican Americans were a quarter of the population. Smiley Gallegos, now thirty-eight, remembers that in his boyhood "you couldn't cross Main and you couldn't cross Seventh, not even to shine shoes." Mexican Americans had never elected one of their own to any city, county, or even school board post. District lines had been drawn to exclude them from power, and most didn't vote as a result.

In San Antonio, COPS—at first a loose coalition of groups attached to Catholic parishes—formed in the flood's aftermath. COPS first organized "tie-ups" at downtown banks and department stores to gain the attention of city authorities. Westsiders demanded that city officials come to their neighborhood and meet with new community groups. The local elites eventually got the message, and COPS moved on to register thousands of Mexican-American voters for a city council election in which the westside finally won representation. COPS then joined forces with Anglo environmentalists to limit development that polluted the city's water supply. In 1981 a Mexican American, Henry Cisneros, was elected Mayor. He is now Secretary of Housing and Urban Development. By the early 1990s, ten Texas cities had organizations similar to COPS; these groups focused on new initiatives to redress funding inequalities between and within Texas's school districts.

Another active group has been the Southwest Voter Registration Project (SWVRP), which has spearheaded over one thousand voter registration drives in California, Texas, and New Mexico and has initiated legal challenges to Anglo gerrymandering of electoral districts. In the last fifteen years, their efforts have borne fruit, doubling the number of Mexican-American officeholders in Texas and making real inroads in other states.

As a result of all those efforts, Latino voter registration in the Southwest has increased by over 50 percent in the last fifteen years. In Clovis, Smiley Gallegos became a New Mexico state representative, and the county board and school board now have Mexican-American representation.

The big test, though, remains urban California, where Latinos are almost a quarter of the population but less than 10 percent of the voters. SWVRP has helped to register over a half-million new Latino voters, but they still have a long way to go.

Sources: Carl Abbott, *The New Urban America* (Chapel Hill: University of North Carolina Press, 1987); Craig Quintana "Group Seeks Political Clout for Latinos," *Los Angeles Times,* June 13, 1987; Daniel Pedersen, "All These Guys Owe Wille," *Newsweek,* March 16, 1987; William Greider, *Who Will Tell the People?* (New York: Simon and Schuster, 1992).

Epton. Epton had been almost unknown until Washington's victory in the Democratic primary. His willingness to use racist appeals in his campaign (one famous TV advertisement ended with the slogan "Epton: Before it's too late") indicated the extent of Republican desperation. Table 5.5 shows the increased *white* voter turnout over previous mayoral elections. Most of these wards overwhelmingly supported Epton.

Washington's victory illustrates that when people feel that politics matters, it becomes something no longer monopolized by professionals and experts. Because involvement in politics changes people, people change the political agenda—voting becomes an expression of deeper thoughts and emotions and more than an abstract duty. Politics is no longer ignored as imposed, foreign, distant, and boring. The Chicago election of 1983 definitely was not boring. Fundamental issues of political power were at stake.

Given the realities of American society, the Chicago election of 1983 also presented an uglier side. The generally white city machine that Washington defeated had thrived off low voter turnouts in African-American and Latino sections of the city. Many in those neighborhoods had seen elitist white dominance of city hall as an unchangeable fact. Through the political organization of the Washington campaign, people began to view existing structures of political power as subject to discussion and change. But when nonvoters are mobilized, they don't all speak with one voice. Due to the racial polarization in Chicago, many white nonvoters who had interests in common with their black counterparts nonetheless came to the polls with the perception that race, rather than social class, was the central political dividing line. Although Washington emphasized class themes and appealed to voters in the white working-class wards, his efforts were generally unsuccessful.[23]

The Chicago case casts doubts on conventional explanations for nonvoting. Levels of education and income did not determine voter turnout. Registration barriers were not very important. With political organization, the unique barriers posed by Chicago's system of personal registration were overcome. Difficulties of voter registration lose importance when politicians fully address the divisions rooted in American society. At the very least, Chicago nonvoters were given a reason to go to the polls.

Mobilizing Voters in Presidential Elections

Chicago isn't the only recent example of what happens when nonvoters enter the electorate. In 1984 and 1988, Jesse Jackson's campaign for the Democratic nominations seemed to provoke higher turnouts in Democratic primaries. The 1992 presidential election also saw a 5 percent boost in turnout. In different ways, these three contests speak to the possibilities, limits, and consequences of nonvoter mobilization.

The Rainbow Coalition The Reverend Jackson is the only presidential candidate in recent times who tied his campaign's success explicitly to the mobilization of nonvoters. With his call for a **Rainbow Coalition** composed of "outcasts"—racial minorities, the poor, women, workers, environmentalists, and others—Jackson tried to reverse both the Democratic and the Republican parties' tilt toward the political right.

Jesse Jackson gained a substantial proportion of the total vote in the 1984 and 1988 Democratic primaries, much of it from new voters. In the four states where 1984 voter participation in the Democratic primary was 50 percent or higher than it had been in 1980, Jackson received the lion's share of new voters' support. In 1988, Jackson's candidacy became a serious quest for the nomination, and Democratic primary turnout figures increased again—by a total of six million over 1984. Jackson did remarkably well among young black and white voters participating in their first election, helping to bring to the polls hundreds of thousands of them. Yet at the same time, the presence of Jackson on the ballot seemed to stimulate a backlash in some states, prompting higher than normal turnouts and negative reactions to his candidacy in many. Whether positive or negative, the presence of an interesting candidate like Jackson stimulated increased voter turnout.[24]

What consequences did Jackson's efforts have? Many continue to see Jackson as a political liability for the Democrats, stimulating hostility among some white voters. Although it is true that many white Democrats don't like Jackson, he undeniably increased both black and Latino influence in the Democratic party. Equally important, he pushed the party, and 1992 candidate Clinton, to be much more critical than it had been of the economic policies of the Reagan/Bush years—toward the interracial populism that some say became effective for the Democrats four years later in 1992. Jackson may remain unpopular among many white voters, but the activities of the Jackson movement have spurred the formation of interracial coalitions in many cities and states. In 1992, such a coalition in Illinois helped elect Carol Moseley Braun to the Senate. These victories and others to a great extent resulted from the influx of new black voters, as well as the formation of effective coalitions with whites.

The 1992 Election

The 1992 election was a departure in many ways from the politics of the 1980s. The extent of the departure awaits the outcomes of future elections. (In Chapters 8 and 9, its long-term impact is assessed.) With its 5 percent increase in voter turnout, the 1992 contest needs to be examined for the limited light it sheds on the effects of new voters coming to the polls. Although the increase was not huge, it did reverse years of participation decline.

What accounts for the turnout rise in 1992? In part, the 1992 election featured widespread citizen disenchantment with Washington politics, and with politicians and institutions. The electorate registered worry about the nation's economic future and its spiritual health. Yet despite their hostility to politics and institutions, Americans were much more interested in and knowledgeable about the 1992 election than they had been about the 1988 contest. At least in part, citizens demanded new moral standards and precise policies from presidential candidates. With varying success, Bush, Perot, and Clinton responded to the electorate's intensity, making the contest a more genuine example of the democratic debate than it had been in years.

Of the three candidates, Ross Perot seemed best suited to excite new voters. Through his "infomercials", electronic town halls, and stinging one-liners, he posed as the champion of all outsiders to politics. Spurning both political parties and castigating Congress, Perot promised to get the country moving "without breaking a sweat." Garry Wills called him a "candidate by immaculate conception"—seemingly untainted by politics, Perot sometimes appeared to be the perfect lightning rod for the discontents that had been building among many voters and new voters alike.[25]

Yet Perot's movement bore scant resemblance to either the Populism of the 1890s, the civil rights movement of the 1960s, or the Chicago organization of Harold Washington. The Perot movement was organized largely from the top down, not the bottom up. During and after the election, many volunteers in Perot's electoral organization and in its successor United We Stand America (UWSA) complained that they were prevented by Perot's Dallas operatives from forming statewide groups with their own identities and issues. They also complained that the volunteers could communicate with each other only through Perot's Dallas-based headquarters. Many quit, claiming manipulation of the movement by Perot and his personal entourage. Moreover, Perot's undeniable personal appeal never led to many specifics on policies. His vision of popular participation through electronic town halls was not really very democratic, because the participants didn't so much talk and decide among themselves as they did shout support for issues and slogans that Perot had decided were important. Rejecting coalition politics and the older traditions of populism, Perot appealed more for personal loyalty than new citizen activism. He often said "I'm doing this for the American people because they can't do it for themselves."[26]

Perot's 19 percent of the vote and his continued prominence after the election do, however, indicate that he tapped powerful sentiments of resentment. But this resentment was diffuse, and Perot did little to focus any of it either in a concrete organization or around specific issues other than reducing the budget deficit. Perot got about the same amount of support from the very wealthy as he did from the very poor, the highly schooled, and the poorly schooled. His support was more or less uniform across America's regions. Among Asian, Latino, and African Americans—important blocs of nonvoters—Perot support was quite low, while among Protestant whites it was higher.

Perot helped to shake many citizens loose from their old political moorings. Yet with the exception of very young voters, in 1992 he did not gain significant support among any of the social categories least likely to vote. Among all new voters in 1992, Perot received only a quarter of the total—a little more than George Bush.[27]

Like Perot, Bill Clinton ran as something of a populist outsider, but as a candidate who could refresh the Democrats' coalition with new appeals to the forgotten ordinary American. While often sounding like a middle-class champion of Jesse Jackson's ideas, Clinton consciously sidestepped many of the social and racial issues that divided middle-class and poorer Americans in the 1970s and 1980s. (See Chapters 8 and 9 for more on Clinton's appeal.) His strategy was to build a broad coalition based on change from the policies of the Reagan/ Bush years. Clinton concentrated on new jobs, a universal health care system, and public investments to get the country moving economically. By appearing as the serious candidate of change, Clinton won the majority of people voting for the first time and people who had sat out the 1988 election. Twice as many of these new voters chose Clinton over either Bush or Perot, and Clinton's effects were greatest in elevating white and low-income Protestant turnout, an important part of the party of nonvoters. Sixty percent of the poorest Americans voted for the Democrat Clinton, and at least part of his victory margin can be attributed to his popularity among the social groups that usually voted the least.[28]

CONCLUSION: NONVOTING AND THE DEMOCRATIC DEBATE

With its increased turnout and populist themes, the election of 1992 could be just a lone exception to recent trends or a harbinger of new things to come. Wilson Carey McWilliams has suggested that future citizens "may lapse into their old indifference. . . . Consistent participation presumes a fuller participation in community life." The evidence in this chapter suggests that McWilliams is at least half right. Whether an increase in voter turnout can be sustained in future elections depends on building democratic grassroots organizations.[29]

Yet is it really the indifference of citizens that causes nonvoting? Many nonvoters are not so much indifferent as they are helpless in a political system that seems controlled by others. Nevertheless, in Chicago, in the Deep South, in the Democratic primaries of 1984 and 1988, and in the 1992 election, the cycle of powerlessness was partly broken by citizen activism and its leaders. In all of these cases, surges in voting participation were accompanied by a wider and deeper democratic debate that responded to existing conflicts and rifts in the American citizenry.

We have argued that nonvoting is so central to present-day American politics that no discussions of our politics can start without confronting it. Yet nonvoting is not necessarily a permanent or natural characteristic of American democracy. It is, rather, a symptom and a cause of *elite* democracy, serving it by suppressing public passions and concerns and reducing citizens' power to control the political agenda.

A massive reentry of nonvoters into politics would not magically solve all the nation's problems. The evidence in this chapter suggests that any large upsurge of nonvoters would probably, although not necessarily, result in real changes—in public opinion, in the media, and in our party and interest-group systems. Some of these changes might be for the better, and some might bring out the worst elements in American politics. The promise of popular democracy in America is thus not to end political debate, but to widen it—to welcome political participation as the essence of democracy, not fear it as an intrusion.

What are the prospects for a return to a full democratic debate? The chapters that follow discuss American politics as it is, as a basis from which to answer this important query.

KEY TERMS

new working class
efficacy
rational actor approach
swing voters
Motor-Voter bill
Freedom Summer
Voting Rights Act of 1965

mail-order politics
populist
liberal
libertarian
conservative
Rainbow Coalition

SUGGESTED READINGS

Burnham, Walter Dean, *The Current Crisis in American Politics* (New York: Oxford University Press, 1982). A leading scholar of American electoral history explains how non-voting grew with the decline of our political parties.

Kleppner, Paul, *Chicago: The Making of a Black Mayor* (DeKalb, Ill.: Northern Illinois University Press, 1984). The story of how Chicago politics were transformed through the mobilization of new voters, primarily in African-American neighborhoods.

Piven, Frances Fox, and Richard Cloward, *Why Americans Don't Vote* (New York: Pantheon, 1986). Two scholars make a compelling argument telling why increased voter registration is the key to voter turnout and fundamental political change.

Rosenstone, Steven, and John Mark Hansen, *Mobilization, Participation and Democracy in America* (New York: Macmillan, 1993). An exhaustive study of data on electoral and other forms of political participation and an effort to explain their fluctuation.

Texeira, Ruy, *The Disappearing American Voter* (Washington, D.C.: Brookings Institution, 1992). An important mainstream work arguing that low motivation is the central cause of non-voting.

Public Opinion: Does It Matter?

Ordinary people's beliefs and expressions about politics and policies is called **public opinion.** When it is formed through intelligent and wide-ranging democratic talk, public opinion is supposed to have a large role in shaping governmental decisions and policies. The requirement for effective public opinion is thus a wide variety of information and an opportunity for citizens to sort it all out. Most of all, to reflect and to judge, ordinary people must have some knowledge about politics, politicians and policies.

In this light, consider these rather sobering findings, drawn from recent surveys:

Only a tiny minority of Americans can name the current Chief Justice of the Supreme Court (William Rehnquist).

Asked which party controls the House and Senate, most Americans either do not know or answer incorrectly (as of 1992, the Democrats have a majority in both). Moreover, most people cannot name their representatives in Congress.

Even at the height of the Iran–*contra* scandal of 1987, most Americans did not know that the Reagan administration had aided the government in El Salvador and the *contra* rebels in Nicaragua.

College students fared somewhat better than the mass public in similar surveys. Yet most still couldn't pick out Vietnam, Iraq, Somalia, or Bosnia on a world map, despite America's historic and current involvements in these countries.[1]

PUBLIC OPINION AND THE DEMOCRATIC DEBATE

Such findings seem to indicate widespread public ignorance about American government. They highlight the central question of the democratic debate: Should and does public opinion matter very much? From the founding to our own times, elite democrats have answered that the power of public opinion ought to be limited. To Alexander Hamilton, the public was not only ill informed, but also subject to "sudden breezes of passion." In the 1920s, one of the first students of the subject, Walter Lippmann, wrote that modern public opinion is made up of "manufactured images" and "stereotypes" produced by advertising and governmental propaganda. Later, many social scientific studies seemed to confirm Lippmann's fears. In the 1950s and 1960s, a prominent scholar of the subject concluded that "large proportions of the electorate do not have meaningful beliefs," and that their opinions shifted so much that it was as if people were deciding by "flipping a coin."[2]

Ill-informed, inconsistent, and passionate, modern public opinion often appears as a great beast to be respected for its strength but only if it is controlled. Lippmann concluded that individual liberty and democracy had to be protected "from the roar and trampling" of what he called "the bewildered herd."[3]

To popular democrats, the view that public opinion has to be contained seems very strange. Their claim is that public opinion is the strongest and indispensable ally of what Lincoln called a government "of, by and for the people." Among the most articulate defenders of the integrity of public opinion was the philosopher and educator John Dewey. Writing in a debate with Lippmann in the 1920s, Dewey conceded that most Americans were not knowledgeable about the details of governance or specific policies. He nevertheless maintained that the public was quite wise about most important and long-term questions of governance. If there was a "bewildered herd," it was because both citizens and democracy were threatened by the two premier institutions of elite democracy, the modern corporation and the bureaucratic state. Both institutions possessed imposing machinery to disguise, withhold, and shape information available to the public, and to limit the democratic debate by making decisions in secret. If there was a debasement of public opinion, its cause lay in institutions that insulated elites from democracy.[4] The major struggle, Dewey thought, was to maintain public access to different points of view and to preserve "public spaces" where people could talk, deliberate, and maintain their dignity and independence.

Perhaps the prime example of Dewey's perspective is the way public opposition to the Vietnam War grew and finally forced the American government to sue for peace. Most Americans didn't know as many details about the conflict as Presidents Johnson and Nixon and their advisers. Yet over time, the public learned enough to sense that the entire venture had been a mistake and that the government's justifications were more fiction than fact.[5] Present-day popular democrats thus echo Dewey's sentiments, arguing that in its essentials public opinion is neither ignorant, inconsistent, nor whimsical. From this perspective, public opinion is not just a bunch of individual uninformed impressions and stereotypes. What makes public opinion greater than the sum of its parts is that it is often the product of free deliberation and debate. When public opinion has a chance to develop (as it eventually did throughout the Vietnam War) it can be quite informed and capable of making fine distinctions between different policies. It responds, reasonably in most cases, to new information and new events. For popular democrats, the key task is to preserve and extend the conditions under which citizens can make informed judgments. Far from threatening liberty and democracy, the power of public opinion is their essence.[6]

The democratic debate about public opinion is long-standing. In our age of information networks, advertising, and high technology, it has a new urgency. This chapter gives some basic facts, and addresses important questions, about public opinion. Are elite democrats justified in worrying about public opinion intruding on governmental decisions and on the individual's basic freedoms? Is public opinion independent, or an echo of what elites in the media and government say? Do most Americans think consistently and coherently about politics?

We answer these questions by first outlining what Americans believe about our political institutions, our economic system, and each other. Because Americans have much in common, they show a good deal of consistency in their opinions on many issues. But Americans often interpret the world very differently, depending on their positions in the social order. Second, we trace the basic orientations to politics and government most citizens use as they think about public policies. Third, we examine which forms of organizing public opinion are and are not effective in influencing governmental officials. Throughout this section, we also ask why public opinion changes.

WHAT AMERICANS BELIEVE

The durability of our Constitution for over two hundred years suggests that Americans have long shared what might be called **core beliefs.** An "American creed" seems to define the outer limits of political debate. Since public opinion surveys began in the 1930s, almost all Americans have given support to the ideas that democracy is the best form of government and that political rulers ought to be chosen by a majority vote of the people. Freedoms of speech, religion, and the press are supported by almost all Americans, as is the idea that minorities have a right to criticize majority views and governmental policies. Very few say they do not support the Constitution and the Bill of Rights. The core beliefs extend to a free enterprise economy, equality of opportunity, and a deep faith that the United States "has a very special role to play in the world."[7]

Table 6.1 lists the most important core beliefs. Compared to the people of Japan or western Europe, the American consensus about the basic design of major social, political, and economic institutions is remarkable. Americans are also overwhelmingly proud of their country, and express a great deal more confidence in its future than foreigners have in theirs.[8]

Since the 1960s, there has been one notable addition to the core beliefs. By a ratio of more than 9 to 1, Americans now voice objections to overt gender and race discrimination. The longevity and depth of American core beliefs make the United States seem like a haven of consensus in an otherwise torn world. Although the once nearly universal confidence has weathered with recent recessions, scandals, and economic decline, American public opinion remains remarkably stable.

TABLE 6.1	
Core Beliefs of Americans	**At least eight in ten Americans agree to the following:** 1. Free speech should be granted to everyone regardless of how intolerant they are of other people's opinions. 2. Freedom to worship as one pleases applies to all religious groups, regardless of how extreme their beliefs are. 3. The private enterprise system is generally a fair and efficient system. 4. A party that wins an election should respect the rights of opposition parties to criticize the way things are being run. 5. Forcing people to testify against themselves in court is never justified. 6. Our elected officials would badly misuse their power if they weren't watched and guided by the voters. 7. A minority family that wants to move into a particular neighborhood shouldn't have to check with anyone before doing so. 8. Everyone in America should have equal opportunities to get ahead. 9. Children should have equal educational opportunities. *Source:* Reprinted by permission of the publishers from *The American Ethos: Public Attitudes Toward Capitalism and Democracy* by Herbert McClosky and John Zaller, Cambridge, Mass: Harvard University Press, Copyright © 1984 by the Twentieth Century Fund, Inc.

When Core Beliefs Clash

Unlike many other peoples, Americans don't usually debate the basic design of their political, economic, and social institutions. Yet our bloody Civil War shows that the consensus has not been continuous. What does adherence to the core beliefs actually mean? Consensus in favor of the Bill of Rights, the Constitution, free enterprise, and civil liberties often translates into sharp disagreements about public opinion's meaning, importance, and application to specific policies and governmental actions.

Civil Liberties and Political Tolerance

It is in the realm of civil liberties and political tolerance that the consensus about American core values turns into divisions over particulars. For the last forty years, public opinion surveys reveal a difference in the support that elite and ordinary citizens give to civil liberties. Although support for freedom of speech and thought is very high among all parts of the population, in practice restrictions are sometimes more popular than liberty. Restrictions on free speech are more popular among people who have less schooling, while respect for absolute freedom of speech and religion rises among the highly educated.[9]

At the height of the Cold War in the 1950s, Samuel Stouffer found that levels of popular support for freedom of speech by atheists were 37 percent and for communists only 27 percent. Only 6 percent believed that communists should be allowed to teach in colleges. Support for freedom of speech rose with level of education: Among those Stouffer called "opinion leaders," levels of toleration were almost half again as high as they were for those with high school diplomas.[10]

Public opinion, though, can change. Since the 1950s, levels of support for freedom to speak and teach have dramatically increased. People who lived through the McCarthy era remained less tolerant of cultural and political non-conformists than younger people who came of age during and after the civil rights, feminist, and antiwar movements of the 1960s and 1970s. However, as Figure 6.1 shows, Americans are still sharply divided about the rights of specific political and cultural minorities.[11]

The survey results on civil liberties can be interpreted differently. Commenting on the split between the highly educated and less educated, Thomas Dye and Harmon Ziegler argue that the "active" masses are "antidemocratic, extremist, hateful and violence prone." In contrast, political elites and highly educated individuals "give greater support to democratic values than do masses."[12] Are these statements justified?

In recent history, the split between democratic elites and extremist masses does not stand up well. It is true that elites often profess high levels of tolerance, while the mass public is at best split between tolerance and intolerance. Yet in practice, ordinary people have not been the instigators or even the participants in recent political repression. In the 1960s and 1970s, it was the federal govern-

FIGURE 6.1

Civil Liberties for
Political and Cultural
Minorities,
1954–1990

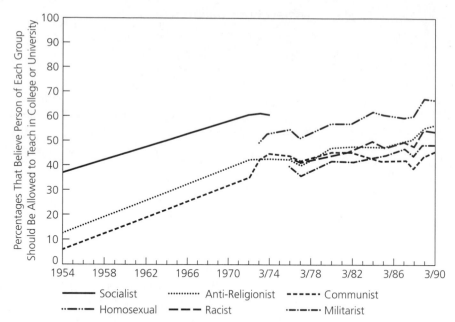

Source: Page, Benjamin and Robert Shapiro, *The Rational Public.* Copyright © 1992 by The University
of Chicago Press. Used with permission.

ment and some state and local political agencies that initiated secret plans of
repression. The targets were political dissenters, antiwar activists, and organizations such as the Black Panthers and the Native American Movement. The
COINTELPRO (short for counter-intelligence and propaganda) program during the Nixon years deployed federal agents from the FBI and CIA as plants in
numerous legal political organizations. Few ordinary citizens were recruited in
the spy network. It was the Nixon presidency, and not the so-called bewildered
herd, that tried to prevent the publication of the "Pentagon Papers," the secret
history of governmental deception about the Vietnam War.

Because all of these operations were conducted secretly, they could hardly
have been caused, or even supported, by a "tyrannical majority" and a "bewildered herd" motivated by "breezes of passion." Polls at the time revealed widespread public opposition to such measures. It was the lopsided majority against
governmental covert action that helped to prompt Nixon's near impeachment
and eventual resignation in 1974.[13]

Even during the hysteria of the McCarthy era of the early 1950s, it was
generally not ordinary Americans who informed on fellow workers and teachers.
Alleged communists in unions, Hollywood, and universities were, rather, targeted by Congress's notorious House Un-American Activities Committee, the
Federal Bureau of Investigation (FBI), and other governmental institutions. Such
activities *were* generally supported in public opinion, but the public was not as
concerned about communism as governmental leaders and elites were. In Joseph

McCarthy's home state of Wisconsin, support for the Senator's anticommunist crusade came primarily from the well-off and well-educated voters, not from uneducated working-class voters. Rather than underscoring the dangers of popular democracy, these episodes of repression seem to indicate the dangers to democracy when elites control information and the political agenda, and public opinion is mostly organized by government agencies.[14]

Economic Power and Distribution

In Chapter 4, we outlined the high levels of economic inequalities in the United States and traced how they were sustained by corporate power. Most Americans seem to ratify this situation through their core belief in free enterprise. Yet do Americans perceive the economic distribution of wealth and income as fair? Why do Americans think some people are poor? What do Americans think government, business, and unions should be doing about it?

Americans seem to be of two minds about economic equality and the political economy. Wide majorities of Americans translate their favorable views about free enterprise into support for what Stanley Feldman calls **economic individualism.** Most Americans believe that hard work is the ingredient necessary to get ahead in life and that ample economic opportunities are available for those who seek them. Following from this core belief, Americans respect small businesspeople more than any other American leadership group. Eighty percent agree that "freedom is more important" than the idea "that social class differences should not be so strong." Large majorities oppose the idea that wages and salaries should be equal.[15]

This economic individualism is countered by another core belief in **equality of opportunity.** Although pro-capitalist in theory, many Americans reject the actual consequences of free enterprise. Even before the gigantic salaries and benefits of corporate chieftains became a political issue in 1992, large majorities of Americans saw top executives as vastly overpaid. They also believe that too much power is concentrated in the hands of big business and that corporations don't usually balance the pursuit of profit with protecting the public interest. Similarly large majorities agree that rich people and institutions are not paying their fair share of taxes compared to the middle classes and the poor.[16]

Many jobs are seen as socially worthy but underpaid by governmental and corporate America. They include teaching, nursing, assembly line work, hospital orderly services, and waiting tables. In addition, the vast majority of Americans blame American business and governmental policies for the recent decline of the middle class. Nor are Americans, regardless of their incomes, ignorant or uncaring about the contrasts of poverty and wealth in their midst. Most Americans think that *more* people live in poverty than the government's statistics say. Finally, a majority believe that being born into a wealthy family confers unequal opportunities for advancement, while being born poor greatly limits one's life opportunities. As Table 6.2 indicates, American beliefs in equality of opportunity have translated into high levels of support for governmental actions that promote

TABLE 6.2				
Public Support for Government Influence	Question: Are we spending too much, too little, or the right amount on . . .			
		Too Much	**Too Little**	**Right Amount**
	Improving and protecting the nation's health care system?	3	66	28
	Assistance to big cities?	10	46	29
	Improving the nation's education system?	4	64	29
	Assistance to the poor?	7	68	23

Sources: Richard Niemi, John Mueller, and Tom Smith, *Trends in Public Opinion* (Westport, Conn.: Greenwood Press, 1989), pp. 77–92; Benjamin Page and Robert Shapiro, *The Rational Public* (Chicago: University of Chicago Press, 1992), pp. 126, 128, 130, 133, 136.

economic security and reduce existing levels of inequality, even if those actions deepen the national debt. In recent years, Americans have reversed their hostility toward labor unions. While a majority suspect excessive union power, they also believe unions are a good influence on the country.[17]

Americans hardly accept the idea that everyone ought to receive the same income, but they think the ever-widening gaps in incomes during the 1980s and 1990s are unfair. Although most Americans, regardless of their personal incomes, see themselves as members of the middle class, they are still conscious of class differences. Aware of poverty, they are apt to make distinctions, valid or invalid, between the working poor (with whom they are sympathetic) and what they call the "undeserving poor"—able-bodied people who refuse to get a job.[18]

What does this mix of opinions mean in relation to free enterprise? Considering the resources of corporate capitalism to influence public opinion, it is not surprising that large majorities support economic individualism and free enterprise. However, the extent to which Americans disagree with the idea that what's good for business is good for everyone *is* surprising. Opposed to measures that simply redistribute income from the rich to everyone else, big majorities of Americans nonetheless favor governmental intervention to supply jobs and train people for them. They favor higher taxes to finance such programs and support regulation of corporate power. Enthusiasm for the core belief of free enterprise doesn't translate into a simple ratification of corporate capitalism.[19]

Government: The Confidence Gap

American core beliefs indicate tremendous support for our form of government. Yet in recent years, a *confidence and trust gap* has developed around all institutions. The highly paid professions, the clergy, the media, big business, and unions have all suffered from increased popular distrust. The greatest distrust, however, has been of the federal government and its elected officeholders and personnel.[20]

Since Richard Nixon's presidency, public trust in government has been high only immediately after elections, during brief military actions abroad, or in other moments when national honor was at stake. As Figure 6.2 shows, these blips hardly balance the long-term rise in political alienation.[21]

Rocked by scandal and gridlock, Congress is the most distrusted national institution. In the wake of the "Rubbergate" check-cashing scandal of 1992, confidence in Congress sank to a record 18 percent. Three-fourths of Americans believed that most members of Congress were *personally* corrupt. Popularity of the president depends on events, but none since Nixon has enjoyed continuous positive ratings for more than six months. Respect for the federal bureaucracy declined steeply in the 1980s and has never recovered.[22]

According to surveys, government has been tagged with spending too much on the "wrong" programs and too little on the "right" ones. It's seen as wasteful, inefficient, meddlesome, and prone to silly regulations. Yet although most Americans have low expectations of current government, they hope that it can regain its integrity, direction, and democratic character. Americans don't want so much to limit government as to apply it in a newly energetic form to pressing tasks, including environmental regulation, consumer protection, and leadership in education and energy conservation.

Dissatisfaction with governmental performance has risen with the decline in middle-class economic security. Accompanying drops in confidence is the widespread sense that the problems of U.S. society—from the deficit to high

FIGURE 6.2

Individual Trust in Government, 1956–1992

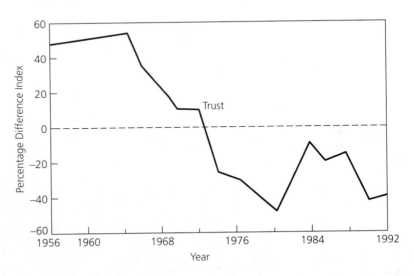

Question: "How much of the time do you think you can trust the government in Washington to do what is right—just about always, most of the time, or only some of the time?" The percentage difference index is calculated by subtracting the percentage giving a trusting response from the percentage giving a cynical response.

Source: Stanley, Harold, and Richard Niemi, *Vital Statistics on American Politics,* Fourth Edition, Copyright © 1993 CQ Press. Used with permission.

crime—are getting out of control. From Watergate to Iran–*contra*, spectacular scandals have reduced confidence and trust in all politicians.[23]

Ideologies: Old and New

Great turbulence exists under the placid surface of the American consensus. Yet is there any consistency in the way people think—or complain—about government? Do people reason in systematic and interrelated ways about politics and governmental activity? Do they link their beliefs together according to a comprehensive understanding about the way the world should work?

Particular world-views that are used to form opinions on political questions are called **ideologies.** Scholars and activists have long debated what ideology is and whether it is a desirable quality of democratic public opinion. Ideologies usually originate with intellectuals and political activists, but they have often taken root in social and economic groups that forge broad political goals. In their most positive form, ideologies help to make sense out of confusing events. Socialist ideology, for instance, has an elaborate way of explaining history and the role of the working class in new forms of democracy. In their most negative forms, ideologies can encapsulate individuals in a rigid and unexamined set of beliefs; Stalinism and Nazism are good examples. In Europe, politics has been divided along ideological lines between socialists, communists, aristocratic conservatives, religious advocates, economic liberals, and even fascists and monarchists. At least since the 1950s, scholars have claimed that these large differences in world-view do not characterize American politics or public opinion. Whether American public opinion is seen as either pragmatic or inconsistent, many studies indicate that European ideologies have not travelled well across the Atlantic.[24]

Instead of the large conflicts besetting European politics, American politics is said to be divided over the lesser differences of liberals and conservatives. *Liberals* are believers in a government that is active in spending to promote social and political equality. *Conservatives*, in contrast, are said to resist governmental intervention and spending in favor of free enterprise. Pollsters have been asking people whether they are liberals or conservatives for a long time. The responses, which have been fairly consistent, are summarized in Table 6.3.

TABLE 6.3

Liberals and Conservatives in U.S. Public Opinion

	% Liberal	% Moderate	% Conservative	% Don't Know
1973	31	36	29	6
1978	26	36	31	5
1985	24	37	35	4
1991	26	39	27	4

Source: Adapted from Harold Stanely and Richard Niemi, *Vital Statistics in American Politics.* Copyright © 1993 by Congressional Quarterly. Used with permission.

Yet there are problems with dividing American public opinion into liberal and conservative camps. Only about half of Americans even recognize the terms, and only the most educated and politically active respondents can identify some of the policies and principles scholars associate with either. Forty percent are reluctant to choose between either position out of choice, ignorance, or confusion. Although members of Congress and political officeholders (and many pollsters) think in liberal–conservative terms, most average citizens simply don't. When they do use them, they often don't agree about what they mean.[25]

For most citizens, the meaning of either ideology seems unclear, which shouldn't be surprising. American liberals and conservatives have much in common. Both ideologies support corporate capitalism and free enterprise, although liberals do so with a few reservations. Both have advocated an anticommunist foreign policy; both have come to agree about basic programs like Social Security and Medicare.

Moreover, political leaders have often muddied the historic meaning of the two ideologies, mixing and matching diverse principles as they campaigned for office. Ronald Reagan—supposedly the most conservative president of modern times—was the self-designated heir of the god of American liberalism, Franklin Roosevelt. Contrary to most definitions of conservatism, Reagan's administration ran up the largest budget deficits in American history; supported low taxes even as the deficit grew; and urged governmental intervention in decisions about abortion, gay and lesbian sex, and a host of other matters. His was hardly a "hands-off" government.

The story is similar for "liberal" leaders. Both Michael Dukakis and Bill Clinton refused to be called liberals and refused to associate programs like universal medical care with liberal doctrines. Jimmy Carter and Walter Mondale called for cuts in social programs, attacked budget deficits, and didn't even mention full employment—a basic goal of traditional liberalism—as an aim of their political careers. In contrast to Franklin Roosevelt, Harry Truman, and John Kennedy, these recent liberal leaders let their political opponents define the term.[26]

It's small wonder that most of the public doesn't know what either term means. However, that the public doesn't apply these ideological labels to itself doesn't mean that American public opinion isn't divided into consistent, coherent, and relatively stable ways of thinking. Students of public opinion have suggested numerous new ways of categorizing public opinion. Rather than revolving around fixed ideological doctrines, they reflect general orientations people use to make sense of the political world. We have produced the following five basic opinion formations, each based on a particular way of thinking about politics and policies.[27]

Populists. Around a quarter of Americans see politics through a populist lens. (See Chapter 5.) A modern *populist* world-view is hostile to all concentrations of economic and political power, especially when exercised distantly in far-off Wall Street or Washington, D.C. Stressing the virtues of common, hard-working citizens, populists oppose snobbishness in any form, be it in culture or in economics and politics. Thus, populists tend to be equalitarians, in favor of public policies that further rights to a job, rights to adequate food, medical care, relief to the aged, and tax fairness to those who want to work. Given their perspectives on the political economy, populists are hardly antigovernment. Yet they also resent alleged special treatment, such as tax breaks for the rich or affirmative action policies for women, African-Americans, and others. Unlike traditional liberals, many populists resist rapid cultural and social change; nonconforming lifestyles and behavior are sometimes seen as threats to ordinary working people. More than many other groups, populists generally oppose complete freedom of choice on abortion. The standard of equality populists apply is directed both upward and downward on the social scale.

Since the 1970s populist public opinion has been harnessed for disparate causes and by radically different political leaders. Pro-business Republicans from Richard Nixon through Dan Quayle have directed populist resentments against allegedly unpatriotic "cultural elites" in the media and in universities, and have appealed to populists for tough anticrime legislation, including the death penalty for capital crimes. Democrats from Jimmy Carter through Bill Clinton have tapped populist public opinion against new economic inequalities, greed, and the corporate arrogance of the 1980s. Ross Perot tried to direct populist public opinion against Washington "politics as usual." Although populist public opinion can result in different voting patterns, its positions on American society and government remain fairly constant.

The New Liberals. The huge baby-boomer generation that came of age during the 1960s is composed of many races and income groups. But many of their attitudes were forged in the common climate of cultural and political protest that spawned the antiwar, environmental, and feminist movements. We label such people **new liberals,** and they make up about a sixth of the population. Like populists and traditional liberals of the 1960s, new liberals favor government programs to promote economic equality. But new liberals give priority to social, cultural, and international questions rather than purely economic ones. In contrast to populists, they are often strong environmentalists, feminists, and defenders of civil liberties for nonconforming groups. Before the Cold War ended, new liberals aimed their criticisms at American foreign policy and what they saw as "militaristic" stances in El Salvador, Nicaragua, and elsewhere. Like populists, they favor strong measures to reduce abuses of power by politicians and believe the political process is corrupted by money.[28]

Libertarians. Between a fifth and a sixth of adult Americans might be called *libertarians.* Unabashedly pro-business, libertarians believe that economic growth is more important than equal distribution of income and wealth. Opposed to much government regulation of the workplace or industry, libertarians are skeptical about governmental intervention in society. In their concern for individual freedom and privacy, they join new liberals in their opposition to governmental regulation of private and personal behavior. On questions such as abortion, sexual preference, and drug use inside the home, libertarians oppose governmental restrictions.[29]

New Conservatives. Unlike libertarians, *new conservatives* don't object to big government in itself. When it comes to maintaining U.S. military power, increasing police and criminal justice forces, prohibiting abortion, and promoting prayer in public schools, new conservatives (unlike many old conservatives) support activist government. What this sixth of the population resists is higher taxes, environmental regulation, and increased governmental spending on entitlement and welfare programs. Despite the Reagan Revolution of the 1980s, many new conservatives remain part of a protest movement—they resist what they see as continued liberal domination of American politics and culture under Presidents Bush and Clinton.[30]

Bystanders. Last, there are those (about one-fifth of the public) who lack consistent views about politics and don't think it would make any difference if they did care. Views of government, regardless of policies, seem to be entirely negative in this group. In their dogged determination to shun politics, **bystanders** do not confirm the elite democratic fears about "sudden breezes of passion" by an ignorant people. Yet their inactivity hardly lives up to the hopes of popular democrats. As we saw in Chapter 5, only dramatic political efforts might bring them back into political activity.

These five formations in American public opinion aren't lodged in ideological cement. Few individuals fit any of the categories with perfection, and many move in and out of or straddle the blocs. Important conflicts in American public opinion—most notably, race and religion—are left out of our categories, except by implication. Depending on the political context, certain features of each political ideology can become more politically salient, or important, than others. Yet the divisions described here show that American public opinion is not simply a collection of loose, haphazard, and momentary impressions. Although views of presidents, political parties, and policy priorities change with particular events, with the exception of bystanders public opinion is often grounded in real perceptions and experiences of the political world, as well as dissatisfactions and hopes.

WHERE DOES PUBLIC OPINION ORIGINATE?

We are not born with intact core beliefs, political ideologies, or views of civil liberties, individualism, equality, and government. Public opinion is formed through a complex interaction among peoples' life experiences and by personal, national, and international events. The formation of public opinion is thus a lifelong process, sometimes involving change and learning.

In the next chapter we discuss how the mass media have become the most important shapers of public opinion. But political opinions—especially the core values—are formed quite early in life in a process called **political socialization.**

The family is the first part of the political socialization process, but it is not the most important. In most families, politics is not discussed much. Yet in families, people learn basic orientations toward neighbors, strangers, and government. The learning that happens may be indirect: Observing a parent struggling with tax forms or through a period of unemployment probably has important but subtle effects on later political attitudes. Family has an important influence in the choice of a political party. Six in ten adult Americans develop the same allegiances to a political party (or nonallegiance in the case of independents) as their parents. However, there is reason to believe that the family is less important than it used to be as a determinant of people's later opinions as adults. Even in the area of inherited party affiliation, the family is apparently a weaker influence, as party affiliations become less important.[31] (see Chapter 8).

Schooling is the second shaper of political orientations. For many, schools provide the initial exposure to people of different races, creeds, and religions. Grade school children are introduced to basic civic rituals like the pledge of allegiance and the national anthem; rudimentary and highly favorable renditions of the Bill of Rights and the Constitution are taught, along with biographies of national heroes. Ideas about one's eventual place in the social and economic hierarchy are often reinforced through the school routines and regimens. Science and social studies curricula currently teach students about environmental questions. Schools teach most of what adult Americans know about their own history and that of other countries, and in recent years multicultural curricula have been designed to teach toleration and diversity.

The specific effects of schooling before college on particular opinions is unclear. What is clear is that schools instill the core beliefs of the American creed. By the time people reach their twenties, some of their political preferences are already formed. College students, especially graduate students, tend to favor more expansive civil liberties for nonconforming groups than those who never attended college.[32]

Social Differences and American Public Opinion

Political socialization occurs in families and schools. But what seems to matter even more are the particular social and cultural contexts in which families and schools operate. How we see society, government, and each other depends on our position in the social and economic order. Shared conditions and experiences generate later public opinion similarities and contrasts. Next, we explain how social class, race, religion, and gender shape divisions in public opinion.

Social Class Differences. Since the rise of corporate capitalism in the late nineteenth century, **social class** has often been the major dividing line both in public opinion and in politics in most democratic countries. Scholars and activists disagree about the definition of social class. Is *class* simply a group with higher or lower income and wealth? Or is it a broader term that includes collective experiences concerning where and how people work, how they are educated, how much schooling they have, and how much control they have over themselves and others?[33]

Chapter 4 presents evidence supporting the broader definition of social class. What the upper classes of owners, managers, and many professionals do with their money and how they use their power in economic and political institutions have enormous effects on democracy, culture, and the life chances of others in society. The majority of citizens neither own nor control these institutions. That important fact influences the way they think about politics and other aspects of life. Indeed, it would be surprising if social class did not have effects on people's opinions about matters such as culture, family, education, and the nature of the "good life."[34]

However, some scholars have seen America as the great exception to this rule. German sociologist Werner Sombart wrote of America at this century's beginning: "On reefs of roast beef and apple pie, socialist utopias of all kinds meet their doom." Rich, poor, or in between, most Americans tend to see themselves as part of the middle class. Yet, as we observed in Chapter 4, the United States has the highest income and wealth inequality among advanced economies. Women of all races and most people of color are especially affected by class inequality; even among white, male wage and salary earners, huge gaps that have long existed have expanded during the 1980s and 1990s.[35]

Social class makes a difference in American popular opinion, more in the 1980s and 1990s than since World War II. People with incomes below the median, who have not completed college, and who labor in nonprofessional blue- or white-collar jobs feel more vulnerable to the workings of the corporate economy than wealthy professionals and managers. They are much more likely to be populists, favoring governmental programs and laws that create jobs, establish standards of occupational safety and health, and increase the difficulty of workers' being fired at will. They are more dissatisfied with conditions in the workplace and are advocates of governmental measures to promote universal medical care and equal education. People with incomes and levels of formal education below the median are more concerned about high unemployment than about high inflation. They are also more likely to favor labor unions (although in recent years not so likely to be able to join them). For the same issues, levels of support and concern among the top fifth of income earners are predictably much lower—generally by about 15 percent to 20 percent.

Although social class help form opinion differences, it doesn't make as much of a difference in America as in many other countries. The poorest Americans are the most populistic and support many measures to promote greater economic equality through governmental spending. Nevertheless, Europeans would be surprised at the great numbers of lower-income people who oppose changes in the tax code and resist efforts to redistribute wealth. On the other hand, people with the highest incomes are not universally libertarians or new conservatives. Both predominate among the wealthiest 40 percent of Americans, but upper-income groups have significant numbers of new liberals and even a few populists.

Where social class makes a profound difference is in levels of political efficacy. Americans with high incomes and good education have a strong sense of political efficacy. They believe that their political participation gets results. Poor and working-class Americans tend to have low political efficacy. They believe that their participation doesn't matter. As we've seen in Chapter 5, significant variations in voter turnout may result from such feelings. Given the way elite democracy has structured American politics and the economy, the disparity in feelings is understandable. It is one reason that bystanders are so numerous in low-income groups and become rarer as the social scale rises.[36]

Racial Differences. One measure of the power of elite democracy stems from its ability to obscure wide class differences and questions of economic equality by highlighting other divisions in American society. Racial fears and hatreds have probably been much more effective than an abundance of "roast beef and apple pie" in diluting social class differences in public opinion.

Nearly thirty years after the civil rights revolution, whites and African Americans differ on a host of political questions, including racial equality and its definition. Contrasts between whites' and African Americans' views of the political world may be the most pronounced in American society between whites of European origin and Latinos and Asian Americans, the differences are less pronounced but still important.[37]

Not surprisingly, the opinions of African Americans and whites diverge most on questions of racial equality and race relations. Great strides have been made over the last three or four decades in white opinion regarding race. Around "questions concerning equal treatment of blacks and whites in the major public spheres of life, there has been a strong and steady movement of white attitudes from denial to affirmation of equality. . . ."[38]

Whites reject organizations like the Ku Klux Klan in numbers as high as African Americans. Large majorities of whites say they would vote for qualified African Americans for the presidency and lesser offices. At least in principle, the proportion of whites believing that segregation in the workplace, public accommodations, neighborhoods, and schools is wrong has reached over 90 percent. Four decades ago, only a small minority of whites disapproved of segregation. Nowadays opposition to segregation has become so universal that most pollsters have stopped asking questions about it. Very few whites say they oppose sending their own children to schools where black children attend, working in the same office as blacks, or eating in the same restaurants.[39]

Although both whites and blacks oppose segregation in principle, significant differences remain. Seventy-eight percent of whites think that African Americans are more likely than whites to prefer living on welfare, and 53 percent believe blacks are "less intelligent." In addition, overwhelming white opposition to segregation should not be read as unqualified support for integration. Whites almost unananimously find no problem with schools, neighborhoods, and work-places where *some* blacks are present. Yet as Figure 6.3 shows, white support for integration decreases when blacks equal or outnumber whites.[40]

Moreover, although huge majorities of whites object to discrimination, they barely support governmental efforts to use law to enforce integration. Racial divisions in public opinion are pronounced when it comes to busing to achieve school integration. Preferential treatment in hiring and promotion is opposed by two-thirds of whites and supported by two-thirds of African Americans. This white resistance to governmental mandates to achieve integration does not appear to be caused by resistance to big government alone. A large majority of whites support laws that ban discrimination in restaurants, hotels, and other public places.[41]

Apart from opinions about race and race relations, African Americans and whites differ most in their opinions about policies to reduce economic inequalities. African Americans of all incomes are much more likely to believe that many features of the American political economy are unjust not only for people of their own race, but for many whites and other racial minorities as well. They're much more likely than whites—even low-income whites—to challenge elite democratic principles and practices supporting economic and status distinctions. African Americans see poverty as much more prevalent—and unjustified—than whites, and they estimate the size of the middle class as much smaller than do whites.[42]

FIGURE 6.3

Public Opinion of Whites About School Integration

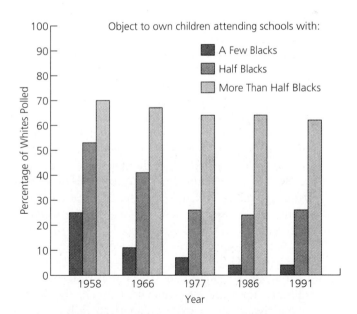

Note: Figures don't add up to 100 because of "Don't know" answers.

Source: Richard Niemi and Harold Stanley, *Vital Statistics on American Politics,* (Washington, D.C.: Congressional Quarterly), p. 398.

Given these opinion differences and similarities, how important is race as a dividing line in public opinion? Racial divisions in America are hardly manufactured by the political system alone, but elite democracy is certainly helped when lower- and working-class whites turn their attention to racial rather than class issues. Many whites are vulnerable to appeals designed to divide people on the basis of race rather than class. In the words of one prominent scholar, the commitment of many whites to desegregation and racial equality may be "cosmetic."[43]

At the same time, low- and middle-income Americans of all races share certain circumstances and vulnerabilities, which in turn often emerge in public opinion. When it comes to access to affordable health care, and the risks of unemployment, underemployment, homelessness, environmental pollution, hunger, and other maladies, low- and middle-income blacks, whites, and Latinos express similar views.

This similarity is reflected in surveys of low- and middle-income people of all races. The African-American population supports populist programs most strongly. Among Latinos, support is also quite strong, with the exception of more affluent and staunchly anticommunist Cuban Americans. Low-income whites' populist views are also strong, but weaker than African Americans' and Latinos'. The future of American politics may depend on whether populism becomes an interracial, interethnic struggle for economic justice or remains mired in racial divisions.

Gender Differences and Public Opinion. The birth of the modern feminist movement has had an important impact on women's political attitudes and on attitudes *about* women's rights by both genders. Although a **gender gap** has probably always existed in expressed public opinion, in the 1970s and 1980s it expanded into new terrain.

Surprisingly, the gender gap is barely evident in opinions about abortion. Majorities of both men and women favor legal abortions in most circumstances and oppose it by narrow margins "on demand" (see Table 6.4). Nor were there differences between men and women over the Equal Rights Amendment (ERA) in the 1970s and 1980s. Although the amendment failed, majorities of both sexes supported it. In contrast, the opinions of men and women do differ on other feminist issues, like comparable worth, legislation regarding sexual harassment, and affirmative action, but even these poll results are not dramatically different. However, as with race, for men to state opinions regarding gender issues that are similar to those of women does not indicate the intensity of those views in real life.

The gender gap widens over policies on the use of force and violence by the military, the state, or criminals. First, in the 1980s, women were much more likely than men to oppose American military intervention and high defense budgets. Second, although a majority of women are in favor of the death penalty, they are less supportive of it than men. Third, women favor gun control by margins of 10 percent to 15 percent over men.

TABLE 6.4

Men's and Women's Opinions on Abortion

~~~~~~~~~~

Should abortion be possible . . .

	% Men			% Women		
	Yes	No	Don't Know	Yes	No	Don't Know
If the mother's health is endangered?	89	10	2	84	12	4
If the woman is married and wants no more children?	40	57	3	38	60	3
for any reason?	34	51	4	35	62	4

Source: Adapted from Richard Niemi et al., *Trends in Public Opinion: A Compendium of Survey Data* (Westport, Conn.: Greenwood Press, 1989), pp. 210–13.

Women are also much more likely to favor support and protection for the weaker members of society, including the homeless, the ill, and most especially children. They are more inclined than men to favor higher governmental spending for education, the environment, health care, and social welfare. And they are more likely to favor laws that curb the use of pornography.[44]

The gender gap in public opinion has been translated somewhat, but not entirely, into women's voting behavior. In 1992, women voters were slightly more likely than men to support female candidates for public office, and provided most of the victory margin for the five new women Democratic senators elected that year. Yet in many races where women candidates lost, women were not much more likely to support female candidates. Since 1980, women have been more prone than men to support the Democratic candidates for president. In 1992, women gave Bill Clinton a 9 percent margin; men supplied only a 3 percent edge.

Although gender does not divide U.S. politics as much as race and social class, it has the potential to do so. The political consequences of the growing economic independence of women from men, spawned by women's massive entry into the work force, the feminist movement, and the rapidly growing number of women who head households, are likely to be substantial. Among wage-earning and unmarried women, the gender gap is pronounced. Unmarried women gave Clinton a seventeen-point margin over Bush in 1992; at 86 percent, black women supplied the highest support for Clinton of any demographic group.[45]

Religious Differences. Along with social class, religious beliefs and traditions continue to shape political attitudes in America. Religious preferences sometimes reinforce historic divisions and alliances based on class, race, and ethnicity. The ancestors of American Jews and Catholics generally arrived in America later than the families of white Protestants. The discrimination they suffered, as well as the fact that many became industrial workers, may account for their relative liberalism on questions of economic inequality. Doctrines of both religions have sometimes stressed social justice and community over personal salvation and individualism, which may account for their economic equalitarianism as well. But as the barriers of discrimination have dropped and class distinctions between religious groups have faded, the political attitudes of Jews and, particularly, Catholics have come to more closely resemble those of the white Protestant population.

Fundamentalist born-again Christians make up the most rapidly growing religious groups in the country, although at 18 percent they still are a distinct minority. Neither the doctrines of fundamentalist Christianity nor the fact that many fundamentalists have less education and income than the norm explains their growing allegiance to Ronald Reagan, Pat Buchanan, and the right wing of the Republican party. The "revivalism" of the 1980s was led by ministers like Jerry Falwell, Pat Robertson, and Jimmy Swaggart, preachers whose power stemmed from the idea that the family, religion itself, and "Americanism" were threatened abroad by communism and at home by homosexuality, feminism, and other cultural and political changes. White fundamentalist public opinion has moved steadily into the new conservative camp, focusing on antiabortion activity. White fundamentalists may often be populists in economics, but their criticisms of feminism, the gay and lesbian movements, and the supposed secular humanism of American culture make them a significant component of the new conservative opinion group.

In the midst of scandals that rocked the TV preacher world in the late 1980s, the political fortunes of Christian fundamentalism seemed to be waning. But in the wake of Democratic victories in 1992, some fundamentalist groups achieved new militance and visibility in anti-abortion struggles and school board battles, and in state Republican parties in Virginia, Iowa, Oregon, and elsewhere. Yet while Christian fundamentalists seem to be united in certain opinions regarding the family, abortion, and school prayer, on other questions their opinions vary. Often concentrated in occupations and income groups vulnerable to economic insecurity, fundamentalists have yet to speak with one voice.[46]

Social Differences: Where's the Bewildered Herd?

Other social differences such as age and region often seem to cause divergent opinions. But public opinion does not form out of thin air; it grows from long-standing and persistent social differences. In addition, the most noticeable changes—mainly about race and gender—have occurred slowly. Both conclusions provide very little evidence that the public is a mindless mass that changes opinions as easily as it does clothes.

HOW PUBLIC OPINION IS ORGANIZED

All the opinions we've discussed so far would be meaningless unless they were put onto the political agenda for debate about various public policies. To be effective, public opinion must be organized. Parties and elections are the most important organizational vehicles, and we'll return to them in Chapters 8 and 9.

Here we are concerned with an equally important matter: How is public opinion organized *outside of* the electoral process? If public opinion is only a collection of the vague impressions of isolated individuals, then it has little power. If it is a reflection of information that government and corporate elites want to give to the public, then it's nothing but an echo.

The Potential Tyranny of Polls

These days, public opinion is frequently organized by the act of polling itself. Writing in 1940, George Gallup, the founder of systematic public opinion polling, wrote that his invention "means that the nation is literally in one great room. . . . After one hundred and fifty years, we return to the town meeting. This time the whole nation is within the doors."[47] Virtually all the manifestations of public opinion used in this chapter derive from public opinion polls of the kind developed by Gallup and his successors. Even the casual observer of American culture would find we are a poll-driven society. The public's opinions on everything from the quality of toilet paper to Bill Clinton's hairstyles are constantly checked and rechecked.

As Table 6.5 shows, there is method to "poll mania." Most polls initiated by academics and the largest national polling organizations, such as Gallup's and the CBS/*New York Times* poll, strive for professionalism. Much care is taken to conform to objective standards and techniques of sampling, question wording, and answer coding. Yet even sophisticated polling has its built-in biases. Polling on a mass scale may lead the entire industry of public opinion sampling to become a powerful organizer of public opinion rather than simply its scientific recorder.

Polling is not the same thing as a town meeting because it is not a meeting at all. People who are asked questions in a poll have no control over which questions are asked. In most polls, they have no way of telling pollsters that they think the questions being asked are not the right ones. By asking a particular question and not another, polls increase what scholars call the **salience,** or priority, of what they do ask.

Polling leaves little time for people to reflect on their answers. Moreover, people who answer poll questions can't engage in two-way conversations with pollsters. They can't listen to others, or participate in a debate before they answer, nor can they control the way their answers are recorded and used. In most polls they can't give the open-ended and qualified answers that constitute independent and thoughtful public opinion in a democratic society. Thus, insofar

TABLE 6.5
Methods and Problems in Public Opinion Sampling

Formulating the questions: Polls conducted by professional organizations and academics strive for "objectivity" in question wording. Questions cannot be vaguely worded, nor should a hidden or obvious bias be contained in them. Moreover, pollsters often err in designing questions and eliciting answers about issues that respondents neither know, care, or have thought about. In one way or another, questions must be carefully tested to avoid bias and forced choice. In practice, both problems plague many polls.

Drawing a sample: Through various means, pollsters try to select a small number of people to interview that can be said to "stand in" for the opinions of a much larger group. Population sampling is the science of developing an exact and small replica of an entire population in terms of income, education, race, gender, religion, and other social characteristics.

Selecting an interview format: Modern pollsters may contact interviewees by mail, phone, or in person. While polling by mail is the cheapest method, it is the most unreliable because it "oversamples" those people who are strongly interested in responding to questionnaires. Personal interviews used to be the major way that pollsters contacted their sample, but it is very expensive. Most political polls today are conducted by telephone through random digit dialing.

Interpreting the results: If mistakes are made in any of the above areas (and they often are), poll results are unreliable. If respondents have been forced to choose between alternatives about which they know or care little, if random digit dialing excludes poor people or people who work during certain parts of the day, or if questions are biased or vague, than poll results can be faulted.

as polls replace other means of understanding public opinion, they can be deceptive.

One of the simplest examples of *poll bias* is in question wording. Through bias, public opinion polls can mislead. In the summer of 1987, officials high in the Reagan administration were being investigated for lying to Congress and the public by selling arms to the Iranian government and diverting the proceeds to *contra* rebels fighting the Nicaraguan government. Yet, Lt. Colonel Oliver North, who had directed much of the operation, appeared before Congress in his full-dress Marine uniform, claiming that patriotism had been his major motive. Polls following his testimony asked the biased question "Do you believe Colonel North is a patriot?" Given Colonel North's reliance on patriotism as the only justification for illegal acts, it was not surprising that most people said yes. Such favorable poll numbers on "patriotism" were then used by the Reagan administration and its supporters to limit the congressional investigation.

Senseless questions can often alienate otherwise concerned respondents or force them to choose between equally unacceptable alternatives. Using the same questions as the professionals, a reporter named Christopher Hitchens tried to conduct his own telephone poll during the 1992 New Hampshire primary campaign. Here's the transcript of Hitchen's experience:

The first three voters hung up in my face when I announced myself to be from the "New Hampshire poll." Making contact on my fourth call, I quickly established that the respondent was over-eighteen and a likely Democratic voter. As I read her the list of candidates and asked how she "leaned," she said it was equal between Clinton and Tsongas.

There was no real provision for that answer.

"Who do you think has the best likelihood of beating George Bush?"

"Who knows? It's only January. There might be another of his wars between now and November."

No designated space for that answer, either. I was trembling when I hung up, and trembling too when I thought to what mush her spirited and warm answers would be reduced. . . .[48]

Public opinion polling has distinct political uses for those who commission them, conduct them, and then deploy them in political struggles. The essential power of such polls is in how, when, and in what context the results are used. Often, they stress the public's immediate reaction to an event and dramatic but short-lived changes in the public's mood. "Spasms of mood" are often used to characterize public opinion about particular people or "hot-button" issues, even though on most matters we've seen that public opinion actually moves quite slowly.

On the other hand, valuable information can be ignored or buried in questions that are *not* asked or not reported, even when asked. Those who commission polls are in a position to decide which results are "important." In November 1991, the *Wall Street Journal* reported on a massive study of public opinion.

Although they highlighted rising "negative" feelings about Jesse Jackson and growing "positive" feelings about Dan Quayle, the paper chose not to report that a majority of middle-income respondents agreed that "the economic and political systems of this country are stacked against people like me."[49]

At their simplest, public opinion polls are quests for common denominators among diverse individuals; when used in this way, they are harmless. But they are no substitute for public opinion that is expressed through the activity of democratic participation and deliberation. Polls thus have their uses and abuses. When used in certain political contexts and employed by partisan strategists and interest groups, they can distort public priorities and shape the political agenda.

Public Opinion as a Government Product

On rare but important occasions, government itself can achieve almost uncontested power to organize public opinion. This is particularly true when the U.S. government engages in sudden military actions abroad. In 1983, U.S. troops invaded the tiny island nation of Grenada. In 1989, the U.S. government sent troops to overthrow the government of Panama. In 1991, the United States mounted a huge and successful effort to drive Sadaam Hussein from Kuwait. In each invasion, the Pentagon tightly controlled access by the press to the battlefield. In each, the U.S. government reserved the right to censor photos. In each, U.S. victories were quick and achieved with few American deaths. In each, Congressional critics were largely silent because U.S. forces were engaged in combat and had to be supported.

In circumstances where public knowledge is low, the issue involves foreign policy, and American lives and prestige are directly at stake, government is able to *"manufacture consent."* In each military effort just mentioned, public opinion registered quick and lopsided support for the president's actions, even though most Americans knew little about the involved countries or the history of U.S. foreign policy regarding them. In 1991, George Bush broke all polling records when, in the wake of the Gulf War, he achieved approval ratings of 90 percent.[50]

Do such instances cast doubt on the democratic character of public opinion? In part, yes. But they also show the dark side of elite democracy. In all three cases, the president and the executive branch developed initiatives in secret, insulated from a nonexistent democratic debate.

The ability to create public opinion and sustain it over time is limited, and is much more pronounced in foreign than in domestic policy. George Bush's unprecedented popularity evaporated a short time after Desert Storm, and by 1992 he was unable to use it effectively when he ran for reelection. When the public hears new facts, opinions tend to become more divided. Democratic public opinion needs time to mature.[51]

Distorting Public Opinion

Public opinion can become distorted when it is not well organized from the bottom up. *Distortion* means that elites are able to organize and use public opinion for the achievement of their own policy goals, about which the public

A CLOSER LOOK

Marginalizing Public Opinion: Reagan and the Contras

The press often saw President Ronald Reagan as a "great communicator" for his supposed ability to shape public opinion. Yet when the Reagan "magic" didn't work and the administration's desires differed from public opinion, which prevailed?

In 1979, a popular revolution led by the Sandinistas overthrew the Nicaraguan dictatorship of Anastasio Somoza, a regime long backed by the United States. Beginning in 1981, President Reagan began a long campaign to undermine the new Sandinista government. Trade and economic sanctions were imposed. The CIA secretly mined Nicaragua's harbors, an act later condemned by the International Court of Justice. Finally, the president engaged in a long effort to supply military support to a *contra* army intent on the violent overthrow of the Sandinistas and the Nicaraguan constitution.

The Reagan administration's efforts were accompanied by a public relations and "disinformation" blitz designed to convince ordinary Americans and Congress that tiny and poor Nicaragua posed an immense security threat to the United States. Reagan officials claimed that Nicaragua could become a new Soviet base. They accused Sandinista leaders of involvement in the drug trade (a claim later proven false). Reagan himself warned that Harlingen, Texas, was a mere four hundred miles from Nicaragua. The Sandinistas, who received aid from nations as diverse as West Germany, Sweden, and the former Soviet Union, were labelled "marxists" and then "communists" in Reagan administration press releases, even though many were neither. In Reagan speeches, the *contras*—who had been censured for atrocities, human rights abuses, and terrorism—were rechristened as "freedom fighters" and the "moral equivalent of the Founding Fathers."

Despite these efforts, public opposition to covert operations and *contra* aid remained consis-tent. By 2 to 1 margins, the public opposed aiding the *contras*. By 7 to 2, Americans opposed sending U.S. troops to Nicaragua under any circumstances. After much debate and very close votes, Congress imposed some restrictions on direct military aid to the Nicaraguan *contras*.

Yet Reagan was able to marginalize public opposition by dominating the Washington and media debate with new charges against the Sandinistas. Poll results hostile to government policy largely disappeared from the mass media's reporting. Public opinion was replaced by a debate between Washington insiders in the foreign policy community. As the debate narrowed, one scholar found that public opinion was largely excluded from the Washington discussion as irrelevant, ignorant, and fickle, or was falsely reported as favorable to the Reagan position. Placing public opinion on the margins helped prompt the Iran–*contra* scandal. Working against the law, Reagan's aides funded the *contras* by using profits from equally illegal arms sales to Iran.

The Nicaraguan case raises important points about the democratic debate: On the popular democratic side, it shows that public opinion can remain independent of elite control, despite governmental propaganda. Yet unless public opinion is organized and vocal, elite government officials will often ignore it. For Nicaraguans, the consequences were a devastating civil war. For American democracy, the result was a scandal that further eroded popular faith in institutions.

Sources: W. Lance Bennett, "Marginalizing Public Opinion," in Michael Margolis and Gary Maurer, eds., *Manipulating Public Opinion* (New York: Brooks Cole, 1987); Michael Parenti, *Inventing Reality: The Politics of the Mass Media* (New York: St. Martin's Press, 1986), pp. 200–1; Scott Armstrong, "Iran–Contra; Was the Press Any Match for All the President's Men?" *Columbia Journalism Review*, May/June, 1990, pp. 27–35.

is only dimly aware. The story of the "Great Anti-Tax Revolt" in public opinion is a case in point.

In the late 1970s, polls showed that a growing number of middle-income Americans believed that the tax system was grossly unfair. The dollar amounts of their wages were rising, but larger proportions were eaten away by both inflation and the higher tax brackets into which they had moved. Property taxes on middle-income homeowners were rising as well. In California, Massachusetts, and elsewhere, large majorities approved initiatives that limited property tax rates. Nationwide, the tax issue moved onto the political agenda with a vengeance.

Corporate leaders and the very wealthy were concerned about taxes, too, but mostly as part of a larger effort to roll back the federal government's "intrusion" into the business of profit making. The perfect marriage of the middle- and upper-class tax revolt occurred when Ronald Reagan was elected president in 1980. He promised large tax cuts for everybody and rode public opinion to victory by talking about a return to tax fairness.

As president, Reagan delivered on all of his promises to corporations and the wealthy. For middle-income earners, Reagan initiated cuts in income taxes. But he—as well as cooperative Republicans and Democrats in Congress—coupled income tax cuts with large Social Security tax increases. By 1984, a family making the median income was actually paying $138 more each year in taxes. Those making over $200,000 gained $17,000 a year in tax relief.

Given these figures, public opinion in the mid-1980s still was strongly concerned with tax relief. Enter the Federal Tax Reform Act of 1986. It was advertised to the public as a plan to cut tax rates further for all individuals, raise them for corporations, plug all tax loopholes, and simplify tax laws. Reagan led the "tax reform" fight in 1986, but the legislation that emerged was also supported by many Democrats. Public opinion was confused about the details, but supported the tax plan by big majorities.

By 1991, tax "reform" had been in effect long enough to warrant judgment. The average American family's Federal taxes had been reduced by 7 percent, but state and local taxes had risen more than that amount. People making between $500,000 and $1 million gained $75,000 in annual tax cuts, thirty times more than the average member of the middle class.[52]

Tax reformers in the 1980s put themselves in the vanguard of public opinion favoring middle-class tax justice. The resulting reform did little except juggle and even raise tax rates for the middle class, while the rich were awarded handsomely. Public opinion had been distorted and used by wealthy elites. Because the middle-class wasn't organized independently, its opinions were used to implement a kind of tax relief that hurt them. Not surprisingly, after twelve years of tax reform, public opinion called for still more in the 1990s.

When Public Opinion Matters

The conditions essential to create, distort, or marginalize public opinion, although not rare, are not particularly common. In the tax reform example, public opinion was not well informed about actual governmental policies. Opinions about tax relief were intense, but the complexity of the Washington debate about tax reform did not promote public knowledge. In the case of military invasions, the public was temporarily susceptible to appeals to patriotism. But given time to reflect and subsequent access to a fuller range of information, unqualified and manufactured support for government actions dwindled. More fundamental public opinion toward the actions of the government were expressed after the invasions had been undertaken, when many ordinary citizens began to have second thoughts. Some studies indicate that in about two-thirds of cases, public opinion can have important effects on changing governmental policies.[53]

On important occasions public opinion has been organized and active. The sleeping giant does wake up. The civil rights, women's, and antiwar movements of the 1960s were small at first. But with patience and time, each became important in changing public opinion about race, gender, and war, respectively. As a result, many barriers fell. In recent years the forces that back reproductive freedom as well as those who oppose abortion have mounted powerful campaigns to mobilize public opinion. On the abortion debate, no one doubts the importance of public opinion. Conflict about abortion is largely not managed by entrenched political elites. Given a choice, most politicians would probably wish that the whole issue would go away. In these examples, public opinion counts because the range of public choice is broad and public debate moves outside of elite circles.[54]

Public Opinion and Nuclear Power

In the last two decades, the battle over nuclear power plants has revealed some important democratic possibilities of public opinion. The nuclear power debate should be heartening to everyone who retains faith in popular democracy. Its story is about the growth of public knowledge, awareness, discussion, organization, and power. Knowledge about nuclear power as well as self-interest in its expansion or elimination has brought bitter political divisions. Yet it has forced some of the most powerful American political interests to modify and in some cases reverse its policies. The issue is still very much on the agenda, and is a real contest between elite and popular democracy.

In the 1950s and 1960s, the interests supporting nuclear power plants forged a seemingly unstoppable elite coalition. From President Eisenhower and his "Atoms for Peace" program through Kennedy, Johnson, Nixon, Ford, Carter, Reagan, and Bush, the federal government, the leadership of both congressional political parties, a host of experts, America's largest corporations and private utilities, and construction unions propagated unqualified faith in nuclear power. The public was told that nuclear power would provide cheap, safe, and abundant electricity. Later, in the midst of the oil embargoes and crises of the 1970s, nuclear power was sold as the path away from dependence on foreign oil. Nuclear power was peddled to a then-passive public as the only solution to accelerating demand for electricity and the keystone of future economic growth.[55]

Protesters try to dramatize the effects of a potential nuclear accident in an effort to prevent the opening of a Seabrook, New Hampshire, plant. Although the Seabrook plant eventually did open, anti-nuclear groups generally moved public opinion their way in the 1980s and 1990s.

Through the Nixon administration, the debate about nuclear power was no debate at all. Hundreds of government reports and elite-dominated fact-finding commissions dominated public awareness and public opinion. As late as 1968, opposition to nuclear power was just about nonexistent. Even in 1972, the Atomic Energy Commission could confidently predict that 60 percent of America's electricity would be generated by nuclear power plants in the year 2000—up from the 3 percent of that year, a whopping 17 percent annual growth rate.[56]

How was the pro-nuke coalition brought down to size? Events like the accident at Pennsylvania's Three Mile Island and Ukraine's Chernobyl helped turn millions against nuclear power. But the lines to channel opposition had already been laid because antinuclear citizens' groups had brought the criticisms of nuclear power to public consciousness.

The transformation of passive into active and independent public opinion proceeded in four stages. In the first, local and largely isolated citizens' groups raised questions about the environmental effects, safety, and need for *particular* nuclear power plants. Victories were won against three proposed plants, two in New York State and one at Bodega Bay, near San Francisco. In the second stage, the questioning was broadened to include expert criticism of general government and industry claims about all nuclear power plants. Grassroots groups used the new information in their local struggles and in legal actions. By 1975, a plurality of Americans still favored nuclear power plants, but a substantial minority opposed them and growing numbers didn't want one built near them. Doubts were growing. In the third stage, antinuclear groups "went electoral": Referenda were held on nuclear power expansions in seven states. Although all were defeated in struggles where industry outspent the antinuclear forces by up to 50 to 1, the campaigns put nuclear power on the political agenda. In addition, the referenda placed local and state officials under new pressures to resist nuclear power plants, to fund programs to conserve energy, and to find alternative energy sources. Most of all, the credibility of industry and government claims about the expense, safety, and necessity of nuclear power was put in doubt. Even before the 1979 accident at Three Mile Island, public opinion had turned against plant construction anywhere near urban areas, and the public was equally divided about nuclear power plants anywhere (see Figure 6.4).

Since the Three Mile Island disaster, opposition to the expansion of nuclear power has become the majority position in America. Even some who viewed nuclear power favorably now doubt its safety and hope other forms of energy and conservation are tried first. Most citizens, moreover, have lost faith in government and industry reports testifying to its safety.[57]

But has growing opposition been effective? Nuclear power has not been rolled back, but its expansion has been halted, its regulation more carefully scrutinized, its operations made more expensive, and its future as a major U.S. energy source jeopardized. While nuclear power plants that were ordered fifteen years ago continue to come on line, they do so at enormous expense and with new restrictions imposed by state and local governments. In the case of the Shoreham nuclear power plant on Long Island, New York, a brand new facility was refused an operating license in the wake of enormous local protests. Even though the Reagan administration made efforts to restrict lawsuits and local government influence over the licensing and operation of plants, the "nuclear future" foreseen in 1970 will probably not come to pass. Even more important is the fact that no new nuclear power plant has been ordered by any utility in

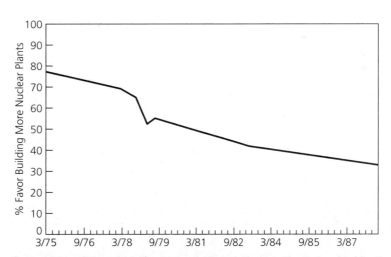

Source: Adapted from Page, Benjamin and Robert Shapiro, *The Rational Public.* Copyright © 1992 by The University of Chicago Press. Used with permission.

FIGURE 6.4

Changing Opinions About Nuclear Power

over twelve years. From the standpoint of electricity companies, the prospect of years of struggle with protesters and local governments and courts has become daunting.

The democratic debate about nuclear power is far from resolved. Yet it is a genuine debate that now takes place on equal terms. The political resources used most often by elite democrats—control of information, the media, and money—remain important. Popular democrats, however, have employed the powers of numbers, of organization, and of solid arguments to pose an alternative. In this way, the ongoing debate demonstrates the potential power and independence of public opinion.[58]

CONCLUSION: THE SENSIBLE PUBLIC

American public opinion is not always right, is frequently ill informed about policy details, and is especially subject to "sudden breezes of passion" when aroused by dramatic and rapid presidential acts abroad. Yet there is little evidence to support the elite democratic view of the public as a bewildered herd. Most of the public holds coherent beliefs, many of which are rooted in institutions such as families and schools, as well as in personal experiences and other identities. Moreover, public opinion responds to new information and new events by modifying, albeit slowly, its views. Public opinion reveals its best qualities when it is free to organize and is exposed to many sources of information about politics. Contrary to many elite democrats' views, it is elites themselves who are the most likely to debase the independence and effects of public opinion when they try to manufacture opinion.

But can the public get reliable information that is crucial in the formation of active and independent opinion? Because the mass media play such an important role in shaping and interpreting public opinion, they are examined at length in the next chapter.

KEY TERMS		
public opinion	bystanders	
core beliefs	political socialization	
economic individualism	social class	
equality of opportunity	gender gap	
ideologies	salience	
new liberals		

SUGGESTED READINGS

Erikson, Robert, Norman Luttbeg, and Kent Tedin, *American Public Opinion: Its Origin, Content and Impact*, Second Edition (New York: Wiley, 1980). An exhaustive and comprehensive account of the social science literature on the subject.

Kluegel, James, and Eliot Smith, *Beliefs about Inequality* (New York: Aldine de

Gruyter, 1986). A subtle examination of contrasting definitions of equality offered by Americans of different social classes, races, and genders.

Lippmann, Walter, *The Phantom Public* (New York: Harcourt Brace Jovanovich, 1925). A classic work on the emergence of modern public opinion and the problems it presents.

McCloskey, Herbert and Alida Brill, *The American Ethos* (Cambridge, MA: Harvard University Press, 1984). Two political scientists present a strong case for the importance of core beliefs.

Moore, David, *The Superpollsters: How They Measure and Manipulate Public Opinion in America* (New York: Four Walls, Eight Windows, 1993). A spirited critique of how pollsters and their sponsors distort public opinion.

Page, Benjamin, and Robert Shapiro, *The Rational Public* (Chicago: University of Chicago Press, 1992). Two scholars of the subject argue for the reasonableness and democratic character of American public opinion.

CHAPTER

7

The Media: Setting the Political Agenda

W hatever its various fates, modern public opinion is highly influenced by how the mass media define and cover political events. In the 1990s, newspapers, radio, magazines, and especially TV are more important than they ever have been in both shaping opinions and setting the political agenda. Rather than just passive recorders of political events and people, news organizations have become part of the political debate and are often called the "fourth branch of government." More than political parties or even interest and advocacy groups, the mass media are the major sources of information about politics both here and abroad for most Americans.

The mass media can determine the fate of other political actors. Presidents, members of Congress, candidates, governors, social movements, and corporate interests depend on the media as the most important arenas in which their actions are reported, ignored, analyzed, praised, or blamed. In turn, political and economic authorities attempt to influence the media. What the media deem newsworthy and inconsequential is crucial, for these decisions establish the boundaries of political debate. In a world in which very few people can have direct knowledge of the forces that shape their lives, the media relay and interpret events.

The power of the media shouldn't cause conflict or concern. Jefferson once wrote that he'd rather live in a country that had many newspapers but no government than in a country with a government but no newspapers. He assumed that newspapers would help citizens to reflect and to act, especially against government violations of rights. Enshrined in the Bill of Rights, press freedom and its importance are perceived by elite and popular democrats alike as synonymous with a democratic society. (Chapter 16 deals with questions of press freedom.)

Few would disagree that the mass media should be diverse and various, a true "marketplace of ideas." Yet just as in the political economy, it is important to ask, if power is concentrated in the American media marketplace and, if so, just how that power is used. Do new political ideas get as much attention in the media marketplace as new comedians or musicians? Are the mass media independent from other centers of power in America? A market has many producers and buyers who compete with one another. In what sense is this true in the media?

Elite and popular democrats give different answers to these questions. Long after Jefferson, the sociologist C. Wright Mills observed in the 1950s that the modern media had furthered the destruction of that "community of publics" essential to both diversity and the ability of citizens to "answer back" to authority. For Ben Bagdikian, a former editor at the *Washington Post*, the idea marketplace of the 1980s and 1990s is not much more than a corporate-dominated exchange of news products supportive of the status quo. And for William Greider, a working journalist critical of his own profession, the mass media have reduced politics to entertainment, forcing citizens into cramped roles as "sullen spectators." Instead of speaking truth to power, Greider observes that top journalists have "secured a comfortable place for themselves among the other governing elites."[1]

Defenders of the present arrangements have responded to critics by arguing that the media marketplace, minus some exceptions, is professional, responsible, and diverse. With an expanding array of magazines, newspapers, cable TV stations, and news sources from which to choose, how could anyone claim otherwise? Such optimistic accounts are most prevalent among notables in the media themselves.[2]

Others, like former Vice President Dan Quayle, have charged that the media marketplace is too diverse and elitist. Failing to reflect family values and patriotic sentiments, the major media are said to be controlled by a liberal "cultural elite" in Hollywood, New York, and Washington. This elite, Quayle claims, is out of step with most Americans. According to Quayle and others, the national media are irresponsible antagonists of American business and government, not their allies.[3]

Although the present-day media are powerful and omnipresent, surveys suggest that they are not widely trusted by Americans. The reasons for distrust are often contradictory. The media have been accused of systematic ideological bias, superficiality, sensationalism, catering to governmental and corporate power, and excessive investigative zeal. In the face of so many critics, most working journalists probably share NBC anchorperson Tom Brokaw's view that, all in all, "the press must be doing something right."[4]

This chapter explores the charges against the media and examines the typical media defenses. The most important questions concern the media's role in the democratic debate. Has the growth in media power fulfilled the hopes of those, like Jefferson, who saw the wide diversity of newspapers as the prerequisite for democratic citizenship? Or do the media squelch active citizenship, substituting their voices and muffling the democratic debate? Although occasionally critical of particular individuals in power, do the media nonetheless act to protect elite democracy?

MEDIA POWER AND AMERICAN HISTORY

Two fundamental historical developments help sort out these arguments. First, as discussed in Chapter 6, the media have often displaced other ways of getting information about politics and other people. While the family, the school, the local community, the tavern, the church, or the political party used to be the chief foci for political knowledge and conversation, most of Americans' current knowledge about politics comes from TV, radio, magazines, and newspapers. Face-to-face conversations and strong group associations are not as important in shaping public opinion as they used to be. Second, media power and influence have followed the same tendencies as the political economy. Political communications in America have almost never been owned or operated by government. But over time, private ownership of the media has passed from single individuals and small organizations into the hands of large corporations with direct material stakes in shaping government's economic, social, and foreign policies. Do these trends affect our marketplace of ideas? How did this situation develop?

Newspapers

American newspapers have always been published by private individuals and organizations. Yet in their early days, their principle purpose was not to make money. In 1787, the *New York Packet* printed the entire text of what became *The*

Federalist Papers. The hundreds of local dailies in the new Republic were forums for the equally long-winded and sometimes eloquent writings of local Anti-federalists. Although we'd think it odd if *USA Today* contained high-brow discussions about human nature and the role of government, political discussion was once a staple of America's privileged form of communication.

The purpose of the early American newspaper was thus not objectivity, or news or sports coverage, but political commentary, propaganda, and partisanship. Thomas Jefferson might have praised them because he had helped start one as a mouthpiece for his Democratic-Republican party. His political rival, Alexander Hamilton, began the *New York Post* not as a tabloid but a political forum for his views. Early newspapers were often synonomous with frank partisanship. Often financed by political loyalists or parties, newspapers were locally owned. They represented the democratic debate in towns, villages, and small cities of the early Republic.[5]

Although born partisan, American newspapers from the late nineteenth century until the present have gradually lost their openly political and propagandistic character. By the mid-nineteenth century, the strictly partisan press had begun to be challenged by a new generation of owners whose aims were profits and the highest possible circulation. Politics was hardly ignored, but papers like the *New York Sun* and *New York Times* redefined the news. Reporting on natural disasters, robberies, murders, society galas, and real estate transactions made newspapers longer and more popular, even as it reduced their political content.[6]

It was not until well after the Civil War that urban newspapers became big businesses, increasing profits through the introduction of extensive advertising. As news became a commodity to be bought and sold, newspapers like Joseph Pulitzer's *New York World* and William Randolph Hearst's *New York Journal* began to compete with each other not only by reporting on events, but by actually creating them to boost influence and circulation. For example, in the 1880s, The *World* sent a woman around the world in a hot air balloon. In the 1890s, one of the most famous and frightening moments in U.S. journalism occurred. William Randolph Hearst dispatched the young painter and illustrator Frederic Remington to Cuba to report on what Hearst hoped would be a revolution against Spanish rule of that island. When Remington wired Hearst that there were few signs of war, Hearst telegraphed back "Please remain. You furnish the pictures, and I'll furnish the War." Later, with screaming headlines and the offer of a $50,000 reward for the capture of the perpetrators, the *Journal* implicated the Spanish government in the sinking of the U.S. battleship *Maine* in Havana Harbor. Soon thereafter, Hearst got his war.[7]

Newspapers at the turn of the century were money-making operations as well as vehicles for the ambitions of their owners. Hearst and Pulitzer used their newspapers for political crusades and saw themselves as champions of the ordinary person. Hearst nearly became governor of New York, crusading for the eight-hour day and woman's suffrage.

Since the beginning of the century, however, these dashing and often outrageous figures of what came to be called **yellow journalism** (named for the "yellow kid," a comic strip character in Joseph Pulitzer's papers) were replaced by the corporate boardroom and new standards of professionalism and objectivity among reporters. Profitable big-city newspapers began to use their gains to expand and eliminate smaller dailies in medium-size cities. "Chains" were born, and with them the number of individually owned and locally controlled newspapers has declined. In 1923, 502 U.S. cities had two daily newspapers, and a few, like New York, had three. By the early 1990s, only one city had three papers, and fewer than thirty had two.[8]

Radio and TV

One reason for the consolidation of newspaper ownership was the stiff competition it began to face first from radio, and then TV. From the start, both media were quite suited to the chain idea, rechristened as the "network." David Sarnoff's Radio Corporation of America (RCA), built with money from AT&T, Westinghouse, General Electric, and the United Fruit Company, was the pioneer network. Yet when RCA began in the 1920s, news programming was not a high priority; radio started with amateur hours, concerts, soap operas, and Westerns.

Only with the onset of the war in Europe did radio become a prime vehicle for news. The two men most responsible for the development were William Paley, the young owner of the new CBS Radio Network, and CBS's European correspondent, the legendary Edward R. Murrow. Through live reports from London, Murrow dramatized the story of the Nazi bombardment in a way that newspapers couldn't. By the end of World War II, RCA's National Broadcasting Company, along with CBS and the newborn ABC, rivalled newspapers as a source of political information. Papers met the challenge by further diversifying their "product" to include articles about cooking, extensive sports coverage, and entertainment.[9]

NBC, CBS, and ABC also dominated TV, the new medium of the 1950s. Yet much like radio in its early days, TV in its childhood was not news oriented. Corporations produced their own programming for networks, and news was not considered to be a big seller if it had to compete with programs such as Ronald Reagan's *General Electric Theater*. A notable exception was again Edward R. Murrow, who produced the highly acclaimed *See It Now* and some hard-hitting investigative reports on McCarthyism, farm workers, and the tobacco industry.[10]

The growth of TV news as the most watched and thus most profitable form of news coverage occurred only in the 1960s. Technological advances accounted for part of the surge. With smaller, hand-held cameras, satellite transmission, and videotape, TV journalism could move out of studios to where the live action was. There was plenty of political action to be recorded. The televised presidential debate between Richard Nixon and John Kennedy during the 1960 campaign perhaps began the trend. After that date, TV became the medium for political candidates to influence, and the coverage of presidential campaigns from the early primaries through the November elections became the most important source of campaign images. Politicians, in turn, began to realize that

TV was the premier instrument to influence public opinion. In Kennedy's case, televised press conferences reflected the importance the young president assigned to TV-generated images and news. His assassination, as well as the civil rights protests, the Vietnam War, antiwar demonstrations, and urban riots were all well suited to the immediacy and drama of TV coverage. Through TV, images of war, political conflict, and social unrest were broadcast nightly.[11]

The increasing importance of TV news departments also began to make celebrities and political figures out of TV journalists. When the networks expanded their nightly news coverage from fifteen to thirty minutes in the 1960s, Chet Huntley and David Brinkley for NBC and Walter Cronkite for CBS became the best-known, highly paid journalists in the country.

Today, the networks remain the major sources of national news. Yet, both the expansion of local and national cable channels and the prospect of greatly expanded news services through a new "**information superhighway**" linking home computers with specialized news and information services and people all over the world give Americans an astounding variety of choices. More than ever, news is addressed to particular audiences—young people have MTV's occasional news programs; sophisticates, C-SPAN and PBS; news addicts, CNN. Local cable stations and network affiliates provide extensive news feeds to particular communities. From the perspective of media owners, the popularity of TV news programs makes them a profitable business, drawing large audiences and advertising revenues (see Table 7.1).

TABLE 7.1

Use and Trustworthiness of Various Media, 1959–1992

Source of most news	1959	1968	1978	1992
TV	51	59	69	75
Newspapers	57	49	49	39
Radio	34	25	20	15
Magazines	8	7	5	4
Other people	4	5	5	6
Most believable				
TV	29	44	47	57
Newspapers	32	21	23	21
Radio	12	8	9	7
Magazines	10	11	9	4
Don't know/no answer	17	16	11	12

Figures do not add up to 100% because of multiple responses.

Source: Harold Stanley and Richard Niemi, *Vital Statistics On American Politics* (Washington, D.C.: Congressional Quarterly, 1993) p. 74.

A CLOSER LOOK

The Information Superhighway: Freeway or Toll Road?

By the year 2000, a new information superhighway combining computer, TV, and telephone signals will revolutionize worldwide media. Almost every home, organization, and business will be equipped to access, send, and receive information in written and video form, from books in the Library of Congress, to E-mail, to shopping catalogs and political conversation. The superhighway promises no less than a revolution in the scope, substance, and manufacture of communication, and even a redefinition of *conversation* itself.

But will the superhighway be a corporate-sponsored, limited-access toll road or a freeway with many on- and off-ramps? Will corporate control of the media be increased or lessened through new forms of "interactivity"? Many see today's Internet as the model for the future. Access to the Net is cheap and uncensored, and any member can communicate with any other member worldwide. Through "bulletin boards," those interested in any kind of politics (as well as Chaucer enthusiasts, particle physicists, and Tantric Buddhists) constantly exchange thoughts. The goal is maximum interaction between users. If the new information superhighway were built like Internet, universal and cheap public access, noncommercial and nonprofit programming, and free speech would be top priorities. "We don't want to build a highway eight lanes wide one way and a footpath the other way," says Mitchell Kapor, a media activist and software entrepreneur.

One-way communication from corporations to consumers may be just what American business orders, however. Creation and operation of the superhighway have been left largely to the marketplace. In recent years, merging telephone, cable, entertainment, computer, and other companies have begun to compete for control of the superhighway. Although corporations claim that a competitive market is the only way to finance it, corporate ownership could turn it into a five-hundred-channel shopping mall in which the chief interactions are corporate selling and consumer buying. If media conglomerates like Time-Warner and AT&T own the cable lines, they may be able to control what goes over them. Superhighway users could have to pay high fees, and system administrators could censor "objectionable" material or monitor messages.

President Clinton and Vice President Gore have pledged federal dollars to "nurture" the new technology and construction of the superhighway. In return, the superhighway has to guarantee competition, open access, no censorship, and cheap rates. Yet the battle of the decade may be to determine how much power users, government, and media conglomerates get. According to John Berry (*Library Journal* editor), we must regulate potential monopolies "to make sure that some of our public space is reserved for the truly free exchange of ideas and messages, uncorrupted by money changers, unpolluted by influence peddlers, undiluted by mass market junk food for the mind. . . . We need some public cyberspace." Stay tuned.

Sources: Robert Wright, "Life on the Internet," *New Republic,* September 13, 1993; Kevin Cooke and Dan Lehrer, "Who Will Own the Information Superhighway?" *The Nation,* July 12, 1993; Howard Rheingold, *The Virtual Community* (Menlo Park: Addison Wesley, 1992).

The average American watches TV about seven hours a day, and over half of all adults watch some TV news daily. Every evening, the networks, including CNN and PBS, draw fifty million viewers. Although most people still read newspapers and listen to the radio, TV has become the premier medium for news, especially among younger people.[12]

Powers of the Mass Media

Does gaining the nation's attention for seven hours a day spell real power? Scholars have studied the question of the media's power to shape public opinion. Back in the 1940s, researchers found that most people didn't "swallow whole" the content of media messages. In the 1970s, political scientists found that TV news didn't do much to change opinions or behavior. People tended to tune in messages and stories they cared about and tuned out messages they didn't want to hear. In many studies, media viewers were found to be skeptical about what they saw and heard.[13]

Have things changed since then? It may be comforting to believe that the media, despite their rapid growth, are still contained by people's natural

THIS MODERN WORLD by TOM TOMORROW

skepticism or by opinions acquired through the political socialization processes discussed in Chapter 6. But media influence may be more subtle than simply changing certain opinions or actions. With the decline of political parties, trade unions, and public associations, ordinary citizens have few alternatives but to get their information from the mass media.[14]

Although the media may not shape our *particular* opinions, they play a large role in determining *what* we think about. Almost by default, the power of the mass media is great in establishing what is and isn't debated in the public arena. By concentrating on one issue and not another over time, the media effectively set the agenda of political discussion. The media don't tell us what to think and do, but rather what to think *about* and what is worth doing. When the media omit or underplay a topic, it's not likely to get much attention unless powerful members of Congress or the president want to publicize it. But even powerful politicians may be reluctant to confront the media's agendas and concerns. People who have been exposed to a steady stream of information about a particular issue are more likely to rate that issue as important. Stories that are neglected tend to disappear from the political agenda.[15]

Setting the agenda in certain ways is what the media do best—or worst. By deciding *what* to report, the media not only report the debate, but shape and limit it. Determining what influences the media as they set the agenda is of prime political importance and the most significant measure of their increasing power. When the media set the agenda, whose voice is reflected and whose ignored?

CORPORATE INFLUENCE AND THE MEDIA

Excluding important exceptions like National Public Radio and the Public Broadcasting System, the American mass media have long been owned by private individuals and institutions and not by government. There is no "Ministry of Propaganda" that controls what we read, see, and hear. Moreover, the press is afforded special protection under the Constitution's First Amendment (see Chapter 16).

Ownership by the Few

Government may not print newspapers or run TV stations, but neither do crusading journalists or partisans. Just as McDonald's grew from a single hamburger stand into a giant fast-food chain, the diffuse and decentralized ownership of American media became concentrated in corporations with great power and particular interests to push before government. The present-day press is an enormous concentration of private power, accountable only to the people who hold its stock, not the public.

In the merger mania of the 1980s, the news media already owned by a few became even more concentrated. The concentration has not been limited to any one medium: Today's megacorporations own diversified holdings from TV networks through newspapers to production studios, cable channels, and book publishers. In 1982, perhaps fifty corporations controlled most of the American news media and book publishing. By 1990, the number was down to twenty-six. In 1993, hi-tech cable companies like QVC Network Inc. hoped to build new empires by acquiring entertainment companies like Paramount. The co-chair of Time-Warner Inc., one of the newest corporate leviathans, predicted that by the turn of the century a half-dozen or so giants would dominate not only the U.S. media, but worldwide TV, book publishing, newsmagazines, the information superhighway, and cinema production as well.[16]

The merger mania of the 1980s certainly did not bypass the media corporations. NBC was swallowed by General Electric, ABC by CapCities Communication, and CBS became one of the holdings of tobacco and hotel tycoon Lawrence Tisch. All three networks and their parent corporations maintained significant investments in cable TV, the supposed rival of the established networks. In newspaperland, Gannett Inc. expanded its holdings to include *USA Today* and numerous suburban papers. The Gannett empire included ten TV and sixteen radio stations, a news wire service, and the polling firm of Louis Harris. Dozens of independent local newspapers either died, or were bought by chains like Knight-Ridder or, like the *Boston Globe* and many other papers, by the New York Times Company.[17]

Increasingly, major U.S. news organizations are not only owned by large corporations, but directed by people with connections to the major banks, investment brokers, insurance companies, electric utilities, and oil companies of the world. Time-Warner, the largest, has directors from Mobil Oil and ARCO, as well as from major military contractors like General Dynamics, AT&T, and IBM. On the board of the "liberal" New York Times Company is George Munro, retired head of Phelps-Dodge, a company known for its virulent attacks on unions. The Times board also contains bankers who helped support LILCO, a Long Island, New York, utility that faced massive citizen opposition to its Shoreham nuclear power plant.[18]

Do the ties between the news media and corporate giants affect the definition and substance of the news? Executives and news reporters assert their independence, but it might be asked if freedom of the press is endangered by the fact that only a few corporations actually own our mass media outlets.

General Electric. Through advertisements asserting that it "brings good things to life," the General Electric Company has become one of the most visible American corporations. With over $50 billion in annual sales, GE makes more than lightbulbs and dishwashers. As America's second largest military contractor, GE produces, among other weapon parts, detonators for nuclear devices. GE also supplies equipment for nuclear power plants both here and abroad.

GE's criminal record is not good. In 1985, the company was found guilty of defrauding the U.S. government. In 1988, it was named in a 321-count indictment on similar grounds. GE is responsible for 47 toxic waste dumps around the country, targeted by the U.S. Environmental Protection Agency for cleanup. In 1986, the company admitted dumping 400,000 pounds of carcinogenic PCBs into New York's Hudson River. As a result, commercial and recreational fishing were banned from a large section of the river. GE chairman, "Neutron" Jack Welch, whose nickname stems from his propensity to fire people while keeping GE's buildings and investments intact, has boosted profits, but at what costs?

In the 1980s, GE bought NBC, and Jack Welch chairs both companies' boards of directors. Does this fact influence what NBC News reports? In the late 1980s, NBC News dutifully reported one of the indictments against its corporate parent in a ten-second blurb on the half-hour long "Nightly News." Yet, in 1990, on a "Today" segment about consumer boycotts, the sizable boycott against GE was not mentioned. In 1987, NBC News aired a documentary called "The French Lesson." Chief correspondent Steve Delaney reported admiringly on the supposed safety and popularity of the French nuclear power industry, comparing French acceptance of nuclear power with the "difficulty . . . of rational dialogue" in the United States. The documentary was awarded a prize by the Westinghouse Foundation, itself the producer of nuclear technology and the second largest radio network owner in the United States. Nowhere did NBC News mention that its owner was the largest American seller of nuclear power plants.[19]

As dramatic as NBC's treatment of French nuclear power plants may be in demonstrating the power of corporations to affect news coverage, it is not atypical. Most corporate influence, however, is more subtle, and is usually not a question of executives advocating favorable stories or squashing exposes they don't like. Corporate influence usually consists of self-censorship. No sane news staff is likely to generate a proposal for a documentary that may offend the corporate parent, so no direct censorship is needed. Tom Brokaw doesn't praise GE, Westinghouse, or even nuclear power; NBC News just doesn't show us the often tragic and costly consequences of corporate behavior.

One notable exception seems to support the general rule. In November 1992 NBC's program "Dateline" aired footage of a General Motors pickup truck that appeared to burst into flames when broadsided by another car. The report seemed to confirm a Georgia court's judgment against GM for causing the death of a seventeen-year-old in a similar accident. GM's pickups were already under investigation by the National Highway Traffic Safety Administration (NHTSA) for defective gas tanks.

GM's response to the NBC broadcast indicates what happens when corporate power is challenged, even by another corporation. It filed a lawsuit against NBC News, claiming that "Dateline"'s' footage had been faked, and demanded an on-air apology from Jane Pauley, the program's host. Pauley and co-host Stone Phillips soon admitted on the air that the fire had indeed been staged. NBC agreed to pay $2 million in out-of-court money to the automaker and to discipline the journalists responsible for the story. Even after the settlement and apology, GM pulled its ads for a time from NBC. Ironically, in April of 1993 NHTSA found that GM pickups' gas tanks were defective and should be recalled.

The lesson of this case is not only that reporters must be absolutely professional. When the story involves a major corporation like GM, reporters and news executives must proceed with caution, lest they cause court battles and declining advertising incomes. Perhaps for this reason, investigative reporting seen on "60 Minutes," "Prime Time Live," or "Dateline" usually avoids corporate wrongdoing stories, concentrating instead on less influential people like dishonest car dealers and doctors, small-time stock swindlers, and others with fewer defenses.[20]

Advertising for the Affluent

As the GM-NBC brouhaha indicates, big corporations need not own a network to influence one. Advertising is another powerful influence on media programming in general and TV news in particular. Procter & Gamble, one of the networks' largest advertising clients, declared in a policy memo that it would refuse to advertise on programs that "will give offense, either directly or indirectly, to any commercial organization of any sort."[21] Network executives regularly review their programming with advertisers to ensure that program content is not offensive to the company and to potential customers. In the late 1980s, for example, ABC's censors scrapped a political discussion on the networks' highly rated "thirtysomething" when the script had one of the major characters commenting unfavorably on the safety standards of U.S. cars.[22] In perhaps the most famous instance of the 1980s, ABC dropped its highly respected "Lou Grant" series following accusations that its star, Edward Asner, was sympathetic to the armed insurrection against El Salvador's American-financed rightist government. ABC and one "Lou Grant" sponsor had received letters objecting both to the show and to Asner. Ironically, Asner had played a hard-hitting editor, absolutely committed to journalism's independence and integrity.[23]

The influence of advertising is often not so direct. Because advertisers want to attract people with lots of money, they gravitate toward shows with **upscale demographics**—shows that are watched by those with the most buying power. Network producers, in turn, gear their programming toward such shows.

The effort to attract affluent consumers applies significantly to public affairs programming, and even more to newsmagazines and elite newspapers like the *New York Times* and *Washington Post*. An affluent and well-educated TV audience is interested in international affairs, business news, stock market quotations, real estate deals, and details of the Federal Reserve Board's recent doings. They are *not* likely to be interested in news programs on ethnic politics, unemployment, social movements, trade union issues, or the nutritional content of federally financed school lunches. Thus, while the supposedly "liberal" *Post* and *New York Times* run twenty pages of business news every day (replete with ads for stockbrokers, "connoisseur class" airplane service, and Chivas Regal scotch), neither has "labor" or "consumer" correspondents. Public affairs TV is no different; corporate sponsors of PBS broadcasts use their contributions to polish their corporate images before a highly educated audience.

The Popular Democratic Alternative

Corporate-owned news outlets are the loudest channel of America's corporate voice. However, that voice is not always solo. Even the established media sometimes live up to their democratic promise. Official and corporate misdeeds from Watergate to Abscam to Iran–*contra* eventually sparked press attention. Spinning the radio dial, you can still find a talk show whose guests include a neighborhood organizer from the South Bronx squaring off against a city official. Some city papers in large urban markets, such as *Newsday* in New York, the *San Jose Mercury*, and the *Dallas Morning News*, still remain lively forums for important local issues.

A small but vibrant critical press remains alive on the margins of the corporate-dominated media. From *Mother Jones*, *In These Times*, and *Ms.* on the left to the right's *American Spectator*, and Rush Limbaugh's syndicated radio talk show, investigative reporting and older political traditions remain alive (see Table 7.2). Although cable TV has become nearly monopolized by corporate giants, local cable channels and the information superhighway have great democratic possibilities because they provide new means of person-to-person communications. In Chapter 6, we noted that the movement to curb nuclear power began as a fringe group that has become a powerful source, along with other environmental publications, of alternative journalism. Changes in the media's treatment of women, African Americans, and Latinos were shaped by the increased political organization of these groups. The most important role of alternative media is

---

TABLE 7.2		
Alternative Print Media and Their Circulations, 1992 (by subscription and newstand sales)	**Name**	**Circulation**
	Mother Jones	200,000
	Nation	100,000
	Progressive	50.000
	Tikkun	40,000
	In These Times	32,000
	UTNE Reader	30,000
	Z Magazine	19,000

Source: Gale Directory of Publications and Broadcast Media (Detroit: Gale Research, Inc. 125th edition), 1993.

to break stories and pioneer cultural and political trends that corporate media are unwilling to examine. Although late in coming, major media coverage of the savings and loan scandal, CIA misdeeds abroad, and corporate shenanigans at home eventually achieved prominence, but only after the investigative groundwork provided by the alternative press.

Without important alternative news sources, there would be few reasons to speak of a Democratic debate. Nevertheless, the alternative press has a difficult time making headway among the corporate-dominated mass media. A fuller democracy would incorporate alternative ideas into its mass media.

GOVERNMENTAL INFLUENCE ON THE MEDIA

Private ownership of the news media avoids the greater evil of government ownership. Yet private media ownership is hardly a guarantee against governmental manipulation. Although the news is full of critical stories about particular "bad apples" in government, rarely are its critical capacities used to oppose the basic political assumptions and goals of governmental institutions. As with corporate control of news organizations, the effect of government on the media is both blatant and subtle.

Regulation of Broadcasting

Since 1934 and the passage of the Federal Communications Act, the licensing and regulation of radio (and later, TV) by the Federal Communications Commission (FCC) have given government and sometimes the public a degree of power over the airwaves. One of the early goals of the FCC was to promote competition and prevent monopolies in broadcasting, under the assumption that the public airwaves should present the broadest possible spectrum of views.

The federal courts interpret the validity and scope of the FCC's provisions in particular cases. Until recent years, the FCC's seven commissioners and chair, appointed by the president and approved by Congress, implemented four basic principles in its regulatory functions. The first was the **5–5–10 rule,** whereby TV stations were required to reserve percentages of their programs for local news, public affairs, and nonentertainment programming. The **one-to-a-customer** rule limited ownership of radio stations in the same city where a company owned other media. Third, the **Equal Time Provision** required that stations selling commercial time to one political candidate sell time to others. If political candidates of one party received free time, their opponents would as well. The much vaguer **Fairness Rule** required broadcasters to provide "reasonable" time for the expression of opposing views on the airwaves.[24]

Since the inception of these rules, they have been opposed by the networks and the local radio and TV stations. Their motives have been both "sacred"—the defense of free speech—and "profane"—the defense of profit. Until recently the FCC and the federal courts charged with interpreting its provisions have withstood pressures to abolish the provisions completely. A modicum of news and public affairs programming on radio and TV was preserved, a total monopolization of TV and radio stations in specific localities prevented, and some degree of public access and diversity maintained.

Over time and with increasing frequency, the courts and the FCC have succumbed to pressures from stations and networks that weaken and even eliminate public accountability of the broadcast media. In the 1960s, the FCC dealt an initial blow to the fairness doctrine by allowing local TV and radio stations to count national network news as local news broadcasting. As a result, the diversity supposedly encouraged by local ownership of TV stations has eroded. To fulfill their obligations to public affairs programming, local stations have often simply purchased more national news programming from the networks. In 1973, the Supreme Court ruled that broadcasters had the right to refuse paid political advertising, even if they had accepted advertising from another candidate. In the 1980s, the onslaught became much more intense, supported by FCC commissioners opposed to regulation and by courts with pro-business judges appointed by the Reagan and Bush administrations. The 5–5–10 regulation was gutted when the FCC dropped the requirement that stations submit programming logs to be monitored for compliance. The equal time provision was reinterpreted to mean that stations no longer had to provide equal time to all candidates but only ones of their own choosing. The fairness doctrine's already weak teeth were removed; it now applies mostly to responses to station editorials and not to news or other programming. The FCC's one-to-a-customer ruling was eroded in the name of free enterprise. In all these cases, an already minimal regulation of the press by government in the name of the public interest lost to the corporate onslaught. So too did the ability for citizen groups to challenge the renewal of station licenses.[25]

From Disinformation to Intimidation

If government has generally withdrawn from regulating broadcasting in the public interest, certain parts of government have attempted to control the media in their own interests. Throughout the Cold War, the CIA organized "disinformation" campaigns to plant fabricated or trumped up stories that confused and discredited alleged opponents of U.S. interests. In the 1980s, for example, CIA director William Casey successfully disseminated false information about the supposed connections between Nicaragua's Sandinistas and the drug trade, leaked untrue information about Soviet missile strength, and even organized an association of newspaper owners friendly to the cause of overthrowing the Sandinista regime. During the 1989 invasion of Panama, the Agency successfully disguised its longtime relationship with Panamanian dictator Manuel Noriega.[26]

J. Edgar Hoover ran the FBI for nearly sixty years, and part of his longevity rested on his ability to buy, intimidate, and manipulate reporters. Hoover's FBI agents spied on many reporters deemed unfriendly. They blackmailed some by threatening to reveal aberrant sexual behavior or alleged affiliations with "pinko" organizations. In the 1960s, the FBI leaked negative stories about Martin Luther King, Jr., to the then-young reporter Patrick Buchanan, who later became an aide to Richard Nixon and a 1992 presidential candidate. After Hoover died, the Bureau's activities continued in the Nixon counterintelligence program, infiltrating left and antiwar newspapers and leaking stories designed to discredit antiwar leaders to friendly newspapers like the *San Diego Union*.[27]

The Revolving Door

In most cases, governmental influence over the news is not direct. A subtler example of its influence is the **revolving door.** Quite often, independent journalists are picked to be government officials, and retiring government officials find new and distinguished careers in journalism. When government insiders become working journalists and vice versa, the wall between media and political authority may be weakened and incentives for reporters to file controversial stories lessened.

"Celebrity" journalists are particularly prone to be beneficiaries of the revolving door. George Will soared to journalistic fame with ABC and through a widely syndicated column, but in 1980 coached Ronald Reagan for his debate with Jimmy Carter. Employed by ABC at the time, Will later praised Reagan's debate performance in front of the TV cameras. (After his dual role as coach and commentator was revealed, Will apologized.) Leslie Gelb, a State Department official in the Carter Administration, helps edit the *New York Time*'s editorial page, which also contains William Safire's columns. Safire served as Nixon's special White House assistant. Ted Koppel touts his friendship with Henry Kissinger, who once offered him a job as press spokesperson for the Nixon State Department.

The revolving door champion may, however, be David Gergen. Gergen served as communications director first under Gerald Ford and then Ronald Reagan. During his time with Republican Reagan, Gergen effectively complained to the media that they were "unfairly" dumping on Reagan's economic policies. In the mid-1980s, Gergen retired from public service. He then became editor of the independent newsmagazine *U.S. News & World Report* and a journalist for the *MacNeil–Lehrer News Hour*. In early 1993, Gergen jumped back into government service, this time serving Democratic President Clinton as communications director; he still serves as a guest on *MacNeil–Lehrer*.

TV journalists strive for objectivity, but bias is often revealed in the experts chosen as commentators. Most TV experts tend to be fellow insiders, former government officials, academics associated with Washington think tanks, or officials themselves. *Chicago Tribune* columnist Clarence Page has labelled this phenomenon "the Rolodex syndrome." When a particularly dramatic story appears, the networks, including CNN, seem to possess a similar guest list of former government officials recast as either journalists or neutral experts. In this context, the revolving door spins rapidly. A study of Ted Koppel's "Nightline" reveals that over 80 percent of his guests were professionals, government officials,

A British soldier tells press photographers to leave the scene of an Iraqi SCUD missile attack on an army barracks in Saudi Arabia. The U.S. government and its allies imposed unprecedented press censorship during the 1991 Gulf War.

or corporate representatives, with Kissinger, former Secretary of State Al Haig, and Carter National Security Adviser Zbgniew Brzezinski leading the list.[28]

The Persian Gulf War of 1991 most reveals the implications of the decaying wall between government and media. During the war, the Pentagon enacted the toughest news media restrictions in U.S. history. The Pentagon controlled the movement of all journalists in Saudi Arabia, Kuwait, and Iraq, and supplied all of their combat images. Because much of the action was in the air, the Pentagon fed the media news video, usually of laser-guided "smart" bombs hitting their targets. Reporters were grouped into "pools", and the Pentagon reserved the right to censor news stories, deleting such information as the fact that Stealth bomber pilots sometimes watched X-rated movies before bombing runs.

At home, however, the revolving door and Rolodex syndrome seemed to quell potential press criticism of the Pentagon's restrictions. Anthony Cordesman, a former Pentagon and National Security Council official, frequently appeared as an analyst on ABC. General James Blackwell delivered military commentary on CNN, praising weapons he had helped to develop as a consultant for Lockheed Corporation. CBS hired General Michael Dugan, who had been fired by George Bush for asserting that the United States should have assassinated Sadaam Hussein's family. NBC hired Edward Peck, a former U.S. ambassador to Iraq. Not surprisingly, out of the 878 on-air sources studied during the Gulf War, only one represented a national peace organization. Hodding Carter, who served as State Department spokesperson in the Carter Administration, said on C-SPAN, "If I were the government, I'd be paying for the kind of press coverage (the war) is getting right now."[29] To top it all off, in 1992 ABC News rewarded the director of the Pentagon's media-muzzling program by hiring him as one of its major Washington correspondents.

Media Bias: Which Way Does It Go?

One common response to the charge of overzealous governmental influence on the media has been to deny its existence. Another has been to claim that the media are overwhelmingly liberal, prone to grinding ideological axes against government, big business, and "family values." In recent years, Senator Jesse Helms has led a spirited attack on all three networks precisely for alleged "liberal" biases. Helms has been joined by other senators (especially the "moderate" Bob Dole, Senate minority leader) in the attempt to cut off federal support for the Corporation for Public Broadcasting, the major source of funding for PBS news shows.[30] Organizations such as Accuracy in Media (AIM) and the Media Research Center have concluded that the media are unduly influenced by the supposed liberalism of most journalists.[31]

Such charges rest on very slim and partial evidence. For one thing, they virtually ignore the effects of corporate ownership and governmental influence. Surveys of journalists do indicate that they are somewhat more likely than the public at large to vote for Democrats for president and that they are slightly more liberal than the public as a whole. The tilt toward liberalism is particularly pronounced among women, African-American, and Latino journalists.[32]

Yet the numbers are not overwhelmingly tilted, as only 23 percent of journalists call themselves liberal, 19 percent are avowed conservatives, and the rest are "middle of the roaders." Moreover, the journalists who label themselves liberal have a far from radical, or even politicized, definition of the term. Journalists tend to define liberalism as "not bound by doctrines or committed to a point of view in advance." Contrary to the idea that reporters are at odds with major economic and political institutions, only 14 percent think being an adversary of business is important, and only 21 percent think "being an adversary of government" is. Providing analyses of complex problems and getting news to the public quickly rank as higher priorities for the average journalist.[33]

Overall, the social profile of average American journalists mirrors that of other professionals, except that most working journalists are generally paid less than even college professors. While women, African Americans, Latinos, and Asian Americans have made employment gains in journalism over the last twenty years, the majority are white males who hold college degrees and come from upper-income Protestant homes. None of these characteristics supports the notion that journalists are serious threats to the established aides.[34]

M AKING (AND CREATING) THE NEWS

We have detailed some possible effects of corporate ownership and government influence on the mass media. Yet it is another thing to say *how* journalists are affected by such influences.

Most reporters do not have the connections, status, or seven-figure salaries of Dan Rather, Diane Sawyer, or Peter Jennings, who are Washington power centers in themselves. For the average reporter, *making the news* is about the much less colorful daily business of gathering facts, attending press conferences, and interviewing sources. For news editors who supervise reporters, making the news is about assigning reporters to fast-breaking stories, ensuring that reporters' stories live up to certain professional standards, and making daily decisions about which news will appear where. From inside any news organization, blatant pressures from advertisers, the parent corporation, or the CIA or FBI may seem remote. News media professionals can point to stories exposing corporate and governmental shenanigans—like Wall Street insider training—that were unearthed through adherence to the high-minded standards of American journalism, including independence.

Thus, journalistic standards may be a significant check on bias in the news media. If reporters are *objective*, they remove their own ideological points of view from their stories and let the facts speak for themselves. As they seek *balance*, they report the diverse views of different spokespersons when a dispute arises. Moreover, as news organizations compete to better inform the American public, they create the marketplace of ideas that is supposed to be the major justification for their competition.

These standards are professed by most reporters, producers, and editors, including the celebrities. But reporters and editors encounter problems when they try to uphold these standards in day-to-day news operations.

The Problem of Sources

Issues, facts, and events become news only when reporters report them. To report them, journalists must be present where they happen. Thus, reporters' locations often determine the subjects selected for attention by the news media. The vast majority of American political reporting comes from Washington, D.C. The White House, the Congress, the Justice Department, the Pentagon, and other government agencies are the major "beats" of political reporters. Government agencies and institutions, as well as interest groups that can afford it, have become not only the major objects of political reporting, but also the sources for most political news. Government and corporate press relations personnel abound to "inform" the press. In Washington alone, an army of 13,000 federal employees generate publicity for several thousand correspondents. In the early years of the Reagan administration, the Pentagon spent $100 million on press relations and the Air Force generated over 600,000 press releases.[35]

It is understandable that Washington activities make news. But Washington journalists report mostly what they hear in Washington. The only balance sought is within the restricted realm of Washington think tanks, government agencies, and monied interests. Almost all the sources on which journalists rely for information have direct, often personal, stakes in what is reported. Moreover, press relations bureaucracies influence the press, and journalists rely on their staffs to provide access to interviews, background information, and inside scoops. The result, Robert Entman has claimed, is that "the news largely consists of information supplied by sources who support democracy in the abstract, but must in specific encounters with the press subordinate that ideal to the protection of their own political interests."[36]

It is difficult to see how objectivity and balance can operate in Washington. Some Washington beats—especially the White House, State Department, and offices of the major congressional leaders—serve as the chief sources for hundreds of reporters. The press releases, interviews, and press conferences emanating from these sources make news by themselves. Even if false, what is said by the presidential press secretary must be reported. For "balance" or a response, another government official is quoted. Less likely to be quoted are groups without extensive clout or without Washington press officers. Thus, media reporting often reflects reality as construed by different representatives of the status quo. Robert Entman has further observed that the "reports [of journalists], while not ideologically biased, typically provide partial accounts that assist some causes while damaging others. . . . An unacknowledged . . . function of objectivity is to make it easier to . . . make journalism safe for the elite news managers who populate the political market."[37]

McNews

The concentration on similar sources does not mean that all news is reported in the same way. TV news focuses on the dramatic and the immediate, and is more likely to cover one-time events and the doings of interesting people. In contrast, the print media report on institutions, issues, and policies, in most cases providing more information and facts than TV. The media marketplace is also competitive: Reporters and their news organizations compete to achieve better access to news sources.

Despite these important contrasts, "news products" are remarkably similar. Many newspapers rely on the wire services of Associated Press, United Press International, or Reuters for their stories. The New York Times Company and other media giants supply articles to smaller newspapers, while local news stations often depend on their networks for important national stories. TV places a premium on the predictability of where news will happen. Camera crews and reporters must be prepared in advance to cover speeches, hearings, floods, or politicians' junkets. Events that can be preplanned for the TV cameras have an advantage over spontaneous events. Besides Washington, D.C., news beats include, in order of importance, New York City, Los Angeles, and Chicago, and lately Atlanta or Houston. News happening outside the reach of the national news bureaus in these cities is likely to get much less attention.[38]

Although print and TV reporters compete for stories, they also cooperate in a phenomenon known as **pack journalism.** Most of the time, reporters covering political campaigns and presidential trips travel together, receive the same press kits, attend the same press conferences, and face the same requirements to file a story by the deadline. In these interactions, they acquire a collective sense of where the story does and doesn't lie. As Timothy Crouse said in his study of the 1972 presidential race, reporters "arrive at their answers just as independently as a class of honest seventh graders using the same geometry text."[39]

The result is a remarkably similar *spin* on a story and a strong consensus, forged by what the pack sees and hears. What they see and hear is extremely limited by the nature of the beat and often by the public relations talents employed by the persons being covered. When the pack travels with political candidates, the after-effects and pre-preparation of a candidate's visit are often missed, and the press can seriously misread the candidate's strength or weakness. Such was the case with the rise of Jimmy Carter in 1976, or the failure of John Connally in 1980 and John Glenn in 1984 to get substantial support. Reporters covering a war, like that in the Persian Gulf, saw only a minute, carefully prescribed portion of the conflict's effects.

Conversely, if the pack doesn't see something, it simply isn't covered. Nuclear waste disposal sites in eastern Washington State and the Angolan civil war generally don't appear on the news because reporters aren't stationed there to cover these potentially important stories. The big stories are often missed by hundreds of journalists assigned to cover conventional institutions and politicians. The exposure of major scandals like Watergate or Iran–*contra* was hardly due to the huge numbers of reporters stationed at the Nixon or Reagan White House. The pack remained ignorant of both stories until well after the events had occurred.

The pack is not an association of equals. Among reporters, the *New York Times*, *Wall Street Journal*, and *Washington Post* possess influence far beyond that of other news sources, including the networks. Stories that appear in these newspapers may work their way into other news media because, if the *Times* or *Post* reported it, it is almost by definition news. Although some reporters knew about government lies regarding the Vietnam War, it took the *New York Times'* coverage of the 1968 Tet offensive and its release of the Pentagon Papers (a secret history of the war) in 1970 that burst the dam of media silence on the government's war policies. Many news outlets are reluctant to run news stories about major national institutional figures and events if they have not been covered first by one of the "Big Three."[40]

Campaign Journalism: Night of the Living Deadline

So far, we've stressed that the news media are profoundly affected by outside influences like government, corporations, sources, and beats. Each raises some doubt about whether journalistic objectivity can be realized in practice, because the world of corporations, government, and Washington interest groups is limited. To some degree, each influence makes bias toward the support of existing institutions almost inevitable.

However, it would be a mistake to envision news organizations as membranes through which the views of elites pass unfiltered. If this were so, it would be difficult to explain why most elites complain about the press coverage they receive and often even attack the media, as vice presidents Spiro Agnew and Dan Quayle did.

Media coverage of political campaigns shows that the press is independent as well as concerned to accentuate its role as interpreter and arbiter. Most scholarship suggests that campaign journalism does not brainwash the public to favor a particular political ideology or party. Although positive and negative stories are sometimes run about particular candidates, and on some occasions the media seems to tilt toward a particular platform, the coverage has been found to be generally balanced in partisan terms. Some scholars even argue that the media pay little attention to political parties because the media have almost replaced them as opinion leaders during election campaigns.[41]

Balance between the political parties is one thing. Campaign journalism is not balanced, however, when it comes to defining what political campaigns are really about. Campaign journalism tends to define elections in terms of the personal, the dramatic, and the immediate—as big-stakes combat between driven individuals and their egos. The key factor in this portrayal is the attention given to campaign strategy and the insider games of consultants, advertisers, and pollsters. By concentrating on private and often covert wheelings and dealings, journalists seem to say that money and expertise are the only political resources that count. The sources for information therefore become biased toward the experts and a narrow range of participants. As if to empower itself, campaign journalism often becomes a contest in which consultants, pundits, pollsters, and other journalistic experts become the key interpreters of candidates.

Hidden bias in news coverage can best be seen in the kinds of stories reporters are most likely to cover. Topping the most reported list are stories about campaigns as "games" in which the candidates are the players and the goal is election day victory. Campaign events and speeches are seen entirely in terms of whether they contribute or detract from the presumed goal of winning. Most campaign journalism concentrates on the "horserace." Each primary is seen as a test of each candidate's tactics and strategy, ultimately leading to the Kentucky Derby in November.[42]

In covering the horserace, campaign journalists spend very little time examining the truth or falsity of candidates' statements, their policy positions, or the overall historical, political, and international context in which an election takes place. Instead, the intention and effectiveness of campaign strategies are given endless commentary. In 1988, for example, there was very little reporting on whether George Bush's charges that Dukakis had "done nothing" about a "polluted Boston Harbor" were true, but there was sizable commentary about the intentions of Lee Atwater, Bush's media "wizard," who had run the ad, and whether voters believed it. Even debates between candidates—the only occasions when they actually are in face-to-face conversation—are analyzed in terms of images, one-liners, predebate strategies, and scripts. Much of the commentary focuses on how well the candidate has been prepared by his or her handlers, followed by commentary about who "won" the debate by performing according to predebate strategies and media expectations.[43]

Given all the attention to the stage management of a campaign, it is natural for the press to report anything unrehearsed as a dramatic revelation. The gaffes and personal transgressions of candidates thus often become defining moments for campaign journalism. In 1988, Gary Hart's campaign ended when the press discovered he had had a mistress—and misled the press about it. Assertions by Gennifer Flowers that she had had a long affair with Bill Clinton dominated the political campaign before the New Hampshire primary of 1992, boosting Clinton's name recognition—and high negative ratings in polls—by over twenty points in several weeks.

Table 7.3 reflects the extent to which the horserace and personal character stories dominate campaign news.[44] The dominance of both is driven by a search for drama. The news media magnify the meanings of isolated events such as the outcome of the New Hampshire primary, an off-the-cuff remark, or a withering one-liner. In 1976, Jimmy Carter confessed to *Playboy* that he sometimes had "lust in his heart." In the resulting uproar, another, more important, comment in the interview was ignored: "The traveling press," Carter observed, "have zero interest in any issue unless it's a matter of my making a mistake. What they're looking for is a forty-seven-second argument between me and another candidate." Succeeding campaigns were to prove Carter wrong about the forty-seven seconds. In 1988, it took Lloyd Bentsen considerably less time to deliver his potent prescribed line to his opponent, Dan Quayle: "I knew Jack Kennedy. Jack Kennedy was a friend of mine. And Senator, you're no Jack Kennedy."[45]

Supporters of the media justify horserace journalism as a concession to the popular desire for sensation and entertainment. Yet both public opinion polls and TV ratings indicate that the media rendition of politics as a game alienates many citizens. James Boylan, one of the founding editors of the *Columbia Journalism Review*, argues that nonvoters "fail to see in current politics, as presented by the media, any connection between their vote and their political interests." Part of the justification for horserace journalism is a rationale for the media's

TABLE 7.3 **Focus of TV News Coverage, 1992 Presidential Election**	Period	Policy Issues	Horserace/Character
	Primary Season	36%	64%
	General Election	40%	60%
	Total	38%	62%

Source: Adapted from Center for Media and Public Affairs, Washington, D.C. Content analysis of ABC, CBS, and NBC, January 1, 1991, to November 2, 1992.

role as interpreter of the campaign. Boylan goes on to say that campaign "information, the raw material of news, turns out to be the peculiar property of those in power and their attendant experts and publicists."[46]

Cynicism and indifference toward both the electoral process and the candidates have increased with modern campaign coverage, as knowledge about the candidates and their positions has decreased. This reality hardly pleases the candidates, who are forced to run a press "gantlet" during the average campaign.[47]

The Media in the 1992 Campaign

Was 1992 any different? Writing early in the primary season, columnist Russell Baker said no:

> The modern Presidential campaign seems as depressingly inevitable as a Sunday afternoon in February. . . . There are the usual candidates with the usual charisma making the usual sounds in response to the usual polls while being subjected to the usual analysis from the usual media oracles who, having consulted the usual engineers, come to the usual conclusion that the most usual candidate in the pack will prevail, as usual.[48]

Many observers, however, did see innovations. The most significant novelty of 1992 was the growth of "unconventional" media, the so-called *new news* that partially bypassed the pack and the established press corps. New news reflected the desire of candidates to get their messages to voters without the commentary of reporters and pundits. Ross Perot was the first to see the advantages of

Independent 1992 presidential candidate Ross Perot appears on his own paid "infomercial" to press the case for balancing the federal budget. The 1992 presidential campaign featured many innovative attempts by the candidates to get their messages past press scrutiny.

bypassing press conferences and press scrutiny and instead appeared on talk shows like *Larry King Live* and in his own expensive "infomercials." Clinton, sensing his advantage in face-to-face interactions with audiences and guests, followed suit with appearances on *Arsenio Hall* and dozens of electronic town meetings.

The fall campaign also saw the rise of new technology to influence media coverage. Clinton's campaign developed a computerized bank of possible responses to the Bush campaign's charges. Within hours of a Bush attack, the Clinton forces faxed responses to news organizations around the country. Clinton also spoke on live hookups to local news stations broadcasting in states where he thought he might win. His campaign established its own camera coverage of Clinton speeches in an effort to feed local and independent stations free, and favorable, news footage.[49]

The established media also made some changes in response to criticism of **sound bites,** those five- to ten-second excerpts from the candidates' speeches. CBS nearly eliminated the shortest sound bites, but as the network showed the candidates less, the commentary of campaign reporters and designated experts expanded. ABC News reviewed the commercials run by the candidates for their truth value. In general, the established media devoted slightly more time to the coverage of policy issues, even as horserace journalism still thrived.[50]

If polls are a reliable measure, voters were less critical of 1992 press coverage than they had been of 1988 coverage. Favorable evaluations rose, especially among Democratic, populist, and previously disaffected voters. Although Republican, libertarian, and new conservative voters believed that the press had been too hard on President Bush, their evaluations didn't decline from 1988. Most of the new media formats that bypassed the established press corps—from talk shows to electronic town halls to presidential debates in which ordinary citizens asked the questions—were overwhelmingly approved. Nevertheless, the majority of voters still graded press performance as only fair or poor.[51]

How much really did change in the media's 1992 campaign coverage? Many changes were less the result of voter disenchantment as they were candidates' efforts to avoid press scrutiny and reach the voters directly. Most campaign coverage, however, remained monopolized by journalist insiders who interpreted candidate strategies, blunders, and personal attacks. Campaigns were still covered as if voters were passive consumers in a media market rather than active citizens with the ability to converse and debate. Although talk shows and phone-in programs appeared to give voters an independent voice, both formats remained managed by the hosts, their producers, and the candidates' staffs. As Wilson Carey McWilliams observes, "The media audience cannot hold its studio 'representatives' accountable, nor can the individuals who make up the 'community' of questioners speak to one another without the assistance of the media themselves."[52]

What's missing from campaign journalism and therefore from campaigns? Chapter 9 deals with this question more completely. But the exceptions of 1992 seem to prove the rule: In the unusual moments when voters and citizens talk face to face about their concerns and agendas, the cycle of citizen indifference is broken. At times in 1992, voters did seem to force both the candidates and the media to respond to uncomfortable questions.

It remains to be seen if popular hostility to press control of campaigns will be substantially changed by new formats like the talk show, infomercial, and MTV campaign coverage. Ironically, the media seem to be hearing the famous line from the film *Network:* "[We're] as mad as hell and won't take it anymore!" The media may know much more than the public about the internal workings of political campaigns. Yet they seem to fail at their central democratic task. Rather than widening public discussion to include diverse voices, the media's false objectivity often hinders the democratic debate.[53]

THE PRESIDENCY AND THE MEDIA: BITTERSWEET RELATIONSHIP

As the epicenter of political activity, the White House seems tailored to attract media attention. Unlike Congress, with its 535 members and complicated procedures, the presidency fits the media's requirements for speed, clarity, and marketability. The media cast the president as a larger-than-life figure, prone to spectacular successes and failures. Indeed, presidential and media power seem to have grown together in American life (see Chapter 13 for further analysis of how presidents influence the media).

In part, the presidency's centrality in media coverage is the product of this century's most aggressive chief executives. Theodore Roosevelt was the first to use the White House press corps as a direct line to the people. Franklin Roosevelt pioneered the use of radio in communicating to citizens, and John Kennedy used frequent televised press conferences to build popular support for his policies. In dealing with the press, the White House has certain advantages. As the most important political actor on the American scene, the president is both a particular individual and a symbol of the nation. In practical terms, the White House can reward cooperative journalists and punish unfriendly ones by granting and denying access to interviews with the president and key members of the administration.

Desirous of media attention, presidents have become both more dependent on and vulnerable to it in recent years. As the press has become larger and more professional, its investigative ambitions have increased. Spectacular scandals have taught the press that adversarial reporting can improve its reputation, serve the public interest, and increase reporters' statuses.

Especially since the 1960s, media scrutiny has both promoted presidential power and destroyed it. To some political scientists, the president–press relationship is by nature adversarial. Austin Ranney has observed, "no television correspondent . . . has ever won an Emmy, or even a promotion . . . for focusing on what a marvelous job . . . a President is doing."[54] But to others, the relationship is fundamentally cooperative or even symbiotic: "Presidents and news people depend on each other in their efforts to do the job for which they are responsible."[55]

Actually, surveys of media coverage of recent presidents show that favorable stories outnumber unfavorable ones by a 2 to 1 ratio.[56] Yet the unfavorable stories and the complaints of presidents about them make it appear that the White House is "under siege" from the press corps. Actually, there are very particular circumstances when the president, his agenda, his policies, and his character come under intensive press scrutiny. These moments of cooperation and conflict between press and president seem to have little to do with the president's objective performance in office. What factors determine the relationship?

The news media's treatment of a President seems to rely on two factors. The first is the president's perceived popularity in public opinion surveys and his reputation among key Washington elites. The second is the White House press office's ability to "handle" the press by getting its version of the facts out consistently.[57]

The press often eases negative stories about a president when he is able to sustain a positive image by muting criticism from other Washington politicians. Material potentially useful to criticize the president—Larry Sabato calls it "feeding frenzies that weren't"—is either not covered or buried in the back pages. Conversely, the media "pile on" when the president is perceived to falter in either public or insider-Washington support. Under such conditions, Washington gossip about the president increases, as does the president's vulnerability to accusations of scandal and personal misconduct. The big White House scandals from Watergate to Iran–*contra* were "discovered" by the press only long after they had occurred. In both, the degree of press scrutiny seemed to have little to do with the president's record.[58] In Chapter 13, we discuss Presidents Reagan and Clinton and their changing rapport with the press.

CONCLUSION: THE MEDIA AND THE DEMOCRATIC DEBATE

From CNN to MTV through the more conventional networks, present-day American mass media are more diverse than ever. In an era when hundreds of channels and custom-designed periodicals suit every taste, political media have the opportunity to be as varied as the public they serve.

Although diversity reigns in many media areas, political news seems to be an exception. The media are not sharply partisan. But they remain part of big business and as such tend to ignore stories potentially dangerous to the status quo. Conformity in defining and reporting the news is the usual result. While journalists may strive for objectivity, they do so in a newsmaking world dominated by official sources. Generally excluded are the views of non-newsmakers like participants in social movements, "extremists," and experts from organizations with little clout in Washington. Moreover, journalists are compelled to choose stories that entertain, but do not inspire citizen action and participation. Politics tends to appear as power games between elite personalities and ambitions that often attract, repel, or enrage us. Ultimately, the news media seem to be "saying that ordinary people cannot manage politics and should not try, that politics is for and about elites, not for or about the viewer."[59]

Despite these tendencies, epitaphs for the democratic character of the mass media are not entirely appropriate. The media can still reflect and enrich our democratic debate. Yet, for popular democrats, prompting the media to live up to their full democratic potential remains an uphill battle.

KEY TERMS

yellow journalism
information superhighway
upscale demographics
5–5–10 rule
Equal Time Provision

Fairness Rule
revolving door
pack journalism
sound bites

SUGGESTED READINGS

Ronald Berkman and Laura Kitch, *The Politics of the Mass Media* (New York: St. Martin's Press, 1990). A hard-hitting text that makes a critical case against current standards of reporting, media ownership, and conservative bias.

Noam Chomsky and Edward Herman, *Manufacturing Consent: The Political Economy of the Mass Media* (New York: Pantheon, 1988). A damning indictment of the ties between media, corporate America, and the repressive Gulf War policies of the U.S. government.

Michael Baruch Grossman and Martha Joynt Kumar, *Portraying the President: The White House and the News Media* (Baltimore: Johns Hopkins University Press, 1981). An analysis of the huge White House press operation and the press corps.

Shanto Iyengar and Donald Kinder, *News that Matters* (Chicago: University of Chicago Press, 1987). How the media set the political agenda through their choice of news stories.

Thomas Patterson, *Out of Order* (New York: Alfred Knopf, 1993). A noted political scientist takes a critical look at the relationship between the press and political candidates.

Larry Sabato, *Feeding Frenzy: How Attack Journalism Has Transformed American Politics* (New York: Free Press, 1991). A well-documented set of case studies showing why news organizations "pile on" vulnerable politicians and officeholders.

CHAPTER

8

Where's the Party?

Dateline: Washington, Kansas, 1892

The People's Party rally began with a long procession from town to the grove. Each Alliance and Peoples' Party club member carried an appropriate banner. For two days, over a thousand people heard speeches, listened to band music, and sang songs. Nearly everybody, men, women and children, wore the same kind of badge. "Equal rights to all, special privileges to none" was the favorite.

Dateline: Michigan, Fall, 1988

Michael Dukakis . . . put on a flak suit and a helmet with his name written on it and climbed into a camouflage painted M1 tank. As he held onto a 30mm machine gun, the driver wheeled the tank around. "So what do you think? Do I look like I belong up here?" he shouted to reporters as the theme from the movie "Patton" blared over the loudspeakers.[1]

Although almost one hundred years apart, these two campaign reports show that American electoral politics has always had an important element of theater. Free elections have existed for two centuries, and they've almost always been times for hoopla and passion. Whether in Kansas in 1892, Michigan in 1988, or on the road with the Clinton–Gore bus caravan of 1992, those who would govern have to grab the people's attention to get votes. Yet despite their similarities, these accounts also signify enormous changes that have transformed our political parties and the meaning of elections.

Return for a moment to 1892. Kansas farmers rallied under the banner of a political party, the "people's party," or Populists. Their loyalty to the Populist Party went beyond just voting for it. Their massive, open-air rally was not only support for a political candidate but also a community festival. A thousand farmers, most probably with little schooling, put up with two days of political speechmaking. The banners they brought testified to a great political cause— economic equality. The party's 1892 presidential candidate was James B. Weaver, but he wasn't even present. Nevertheless, the Populist faithful made the election a serious and entertaining collective effort.[2]

For these Populists or even for their Democratic and Republican counterparts in 1892, Michael Dukakis's tank ride would have seemed strange. The event didn't even occur at a campaign rally, but was staged for reporters gathered to record the event for millions of TV viewers. The candidate himself was at center stage, not the Democratic party's supporters. Dukakis spoke only to advertise himself. Designed by his campaign consultants, the tank ride was supposed to be a persuasive symbol for large numbers of undecided voters who neither cared that he was a Democrat nor knew his policy positions.

These two events capture the themes of this chapter. Does the strength or weakness of our political parties affect American electoral democracy? Parties have long balanced elite and popular democracy, both now and in the past. Along with elections, they are the most visible testaments to the existence of democracy in America. Yet political parties are much weaker than they should be in one key area: They fall short of inspiring activism or even consistent

The 1988 Democratic presidential candidate, Michael Dukakis, rides in a tank to demonstrate his defense policy. Such theatrics have become important events in modern election campaigns.

loyalty among average Americans. At the grassroots, our political parties are not very strong, and their weaknesses bolster elite democracy.

This chapter explains these statements by looking at the activities of political parties in democratic countries. It then assesses the peculiarities of American parties and their historical record. We discuss why and how our parties have declined, and evaluate how their decline affects electoral democracy and the current democratic debate.

WHAT POLITICAL PARTIES DO

Throughout American history, political parties have competed for votes in elections. What makes them different from other political organizations like social movements, interest groups, debating societies, or groups loyal to leaders? American political parties aren't always distinguishable from such organizations, but at their strongest and most democratic they are unique.

The most important democratic functions of political parties are organizing and mobilizing individual citizens around elections and voting. Parties combine isolated individuals into coherent blocs of voters. They provide a forum for citizens to converse, come to common agreement, and magnify the power of citizenship through voting. By bringing people together, parties also educate voters in the ways of political life, while representing the interests of active voters. By organizing, mobilizing, and educating voters, parties make elections more important than other, more elitist ways of achieving political influence.

While interest groups usually win concessions from government through lobbying and personal connections, voters are the central resource of political parties (see Chapter 10).

Parties naturally want to win as many votes as they can, if only because more votes means more elected officials for them. Parties thus spend much time getting their supporters to the polls. Mobilizing maximum support usually requires parties to build *coalitions* among religions, regions, classes, races, and other social divisions in American public opinion. Good coalitions slowly alter the narrow claims of groups and individuals through compromise and cohesion. They become the larger, more comprehensive claims of a successful political party. This *party philosophy* becomes important as a way of holding different kinds of voters together and forming an identity that lasts.[3]

American parties also recruit and nominate candidates, and help them campaign for public office. When they are strong, our parties have ensured that there is some minimal similarity between individuals who claim to be Republicans or Democrats. Thus, parties can present choices to voters. As they compete, parties clarify these choices to voters by accentuating ideological and policy differences. Because political parties want to get their candidates elected, they stimulate debate with the competition, highlighting important differences for the electorate to judge.

Strong political parties also organize and discipline their elected officials. American parties were born in the late 1790s from the realization that chaos would result if each senator or House member represented only the interests of his or her district or state. Where the Federalists saw many factions, political parties have bridged the differences among such interests. By bringing representatives together, parties can make our political institutions accountable for their performance. At their best, parties bridge institutions like the Congress and presidency as well, thereby partly reducing the checks and balances, separation of powers, and fragmentation built into the American Constitution. When the same party controls the executive and legislative branches, voters have at least some capacity to praise—or blame—the party in power for its performance. When parties are weak, Congress or the president can blame each other for "gridlock," denying their responsibility.[4]

WHY AMERICAN PARTIES ARE UNIQUE

Listing everything cohesive parties can do is abstract. Scholars of American politics, who have coined the phrase *responsible party system* to stress these potential democratic virtues of parties, have also found a gap between party functions and political reality. For most of American political history, our parties haven't performed these functions very well.

Listing party activities is useful, however, because it provides standards to assess their real, less dramatic roles. Whom do they organize and mobilize, and who is left out? Compared to the media, do they really educate people, or do they just manipulate voters? Are the philosophical differences between our parties clear? If parties organize elected officials, why is it so difficult to get anything done in Washington? Today's citizens ask such questions. The marks they give in response are not very high: Parties are often seen as corrupt anachronisms or as vehicles for ambitious individuals.

American political parties have at times lived up to their democratic functions and at other times denied them. Their histories are complex. Next, we trace their uniqueness compared to political parties elsewhere in the democratic world.

Age and the Weight of Tradition

America is a relatively young nation, but our Republican and Democratic parties are extremely old. Born with Thomas Jefferson and already mature when Andrew Jackson assumed the presidency in 1828, the Democratic party is one of the oldest institutions in the democratic world. The Republicans are younger, but can still trace their origins to the 1840s and 1850s and the battle to prohibit slavery from expanding into the North and West.

It matters that our parties are old. Democrats and Republicans were already quite well organized before the Industrial Revolution and the movement of America from a rural to an urban nation. Both parties were already mature before the rise of the modern corporation and the division of American society into modern social classes. Both parties were active before large numbers of eastern and southern European immigrants transformed the face of America and when most African Americans were still slaves. Our parties predate the enfranchisement of women (1920). They were very powerful organizations before America had a strong and expansive federal government and a predominant role in world affairs.[5]

As a result of their age, Samuel Huntington has commented that "our parties resemble a massive geological formation composed of different strata, each representing a constituency or group added to the party in one political era and then subordinated to new strata produced in subsequent political eras." Many citizens remain loyal to parties out of habit and tradition, not because of their stances on public policy issues, their vision of the future, or their responses to current events.[6]

Our parties therefore persist not only because of what they now are, but because of the many and often contradictory identities they have accumulated over time. Both major parties can be conservative and tradition-bound institutions. Although party elites, leaders, and philosophies often change, their appeals to party loyalists often remain vivid recollections of the past. In this way, parties see voting much less as an opportunity for democratic participation than as a way to maintain the status quo.[7]

For example, white northern Protestants became an important part of the Republican Party as early as the 1850s. Although Republican party policies and philosophy have changed since then, as have white northern Protestants, the GOP still receives a very large share of its voter support from this group, especially in local elections. The same is true for white southerners. Although many of them have become Republicans or independents, most white southerners maintain their loyalty to the Democrats, the party of their great-grandparents, especially in local and state elections.

Political Parties as Local Organizations

American parties count on more than tradition. Reflecting their nineteenth-century beginnings, they're still organized and oriented toward particular states, regions, and locales and not toward the national and international concerns that have often come to dominate the political debate. At the national level, both parties have often been loose coalitions of groups that have had little in common but their desire to nominate a winning presidential candidate.

Take as an example the social groups that supported the Republicans and Democrats of 1920. In the Republican bastion of upstate New York, the GOP was defined as the party of anti-immigration, Protestantism, agriculture, and Lincoln. Yet in New York City and Boston, Republicanism meant the party of big business and of the up-and-coming professional middle class. Southern Republicans were mostly descendants of freed slaves who saw the GOP as the party of Lincoln and Reconstruction. In their local complexity, Democrats were even more bewildering: What possible link could exist between Irish and Italian immigrants in New York and Boston, largely Catholic and poor, and Southern plantation owners who were Protestant and rich? For very different reasons, all were Democrats.[8]

The local origins of American parties have often caused weak national organization and vagueness about their roles in relationship to national problems. A visitor to Berlin, London, or Rome would find the headquarters of the major political parties each occupying an entire large, multistoried office building. Yet when the headquarters of the Democratic National Committee was burglarized in 1972 by employees of President Richard Nixon's campaign, they found only a few rented offices in Washington's Watergate complex. The center of the nation's largest political party was far smaller than the Safeway Supermarket downstairs and the luxury co-op apartments above.

Ideological Fuzziness

Particularly in the nineteenth century, tradition and localism were not the only features of American parties. Because our parties comprise disparate, even conflicting social groups, they are far different from the newer political parties in western Europe. Generally, Western European political parties originally organized strong national identities and comprehensive political ideologies. They were usually highly organized, complete with national offices for propaganda; the party press; and sections for women, labor, youth, and others. The first European mass political parties—Social Democrats in Germany, Socialists in France and Italy, and the Labor party in Great Britain—were born out of the class tensions accompanying the Industrial Revolution. Their opponents were forced to compete for votes and tried to form mass political parties as well. Compared to American parties, European parties historically have been better organized for political combat and clearer about their philosophies and constituents. They've depended on consistent ideology and on loyal membership to organize their national electorates.[9]

In contrast, American parties have rarely made ideological appeals, nor can they be distinguished from one another on the basis of their philosophies on the role of national government, the nature of democracy, the role of big business, or any such national concerns. While the British Conservative party or its opponent, the Labor party, has a distinct set of principles that can be traced back through time, our major parties have often contained factions with varying principles. Our parties tend to blur social differences and national concerns, rather than accenting them—one reason that no strong socialist or social democratic party has developed in the United States. People with strong ideological beliefs often are absorbed as factions within the major parties, as the parties attempt to catch all the voters they can.[10]

Patronage

For a long time U.S. parties held their factions together through concrete material benefits—jobs, contracts, or special laws—awarded to their key supporters. Long ago, the German sociologist Max Weber saw American parties as the inventors of democratic **patronage,** or the idea that winning parties "paid off" their supporters with the spoils of office.

The most highly developed form of patronage in American history was the urban **political machine.** In midwestern and eastern cities after the Civil War and well into the twentieth century, party machines thrived by building connections between city halls and highly developed ward (neighborhood) party organizations. In return for votes, party organizations gave aid to the poorest, rewarded some with city contracts, and provided government jobs to thousands of recent immigrants and other potential voters.

Political machines shunned broad-based programs; to maintain power, they concentrated on individual benefits in return for votes. Often ruthless with opponents, they were, in retrospect, the epitome of corruption. But for millions of immigrants to America's cities, they sometimes served as buffers for integration into an often brutal American political economy. The most famous political machine, New York's Tammany Hall, made hundreds of Irish Americans into city policemen and firemen. But political machines were also hierarchical and repressive. Even as late as the 1950s, 1960s, and 1970s, Chicago's Democratic machine, led by Mayor Richard J. Daley, rewarded Chicago's white population with the bulk of city services while depriving black neighborhoods of their due proportion. Although party machines are a thing of the past, they help explain how American parties survived without clear ideologies and principles (see Chapter 5).[11]

Three's a Crowd: Why Only Two Parties?

Finally, decentralization, tradition, patronage, and ideological fuzziness may not be enough to explain an obvious fact about our parties. For the most part, only two have dominated. A two-party system is a rarity in the rest of the world. Some argue that America has two parties because Americans don't have many political differences. A more complete explanation lies in our electoral laws and our entrenched system of campaign finance, created by the two parties to keep them dominant. In most states, getting a new party on the ballot is so difficult that it exhausts the time and resources of third-party activists.

Although third parties like the Populists, Socialists, and Progressives on the left and George Wallace's American Independent party on the right have often had important effects on the Democrats and Republicans, our electoral system makes it nearly impossible to elect their candidates to office. A plurality of the votes in a state or legislative district is necessary to get any representation at all. The **single-member district system** and plurality voting virtually assure a two-party system by preventing new third, fourth, and fifth parties from winning representation without beating both major parties. Many third parties flounder, although they garner many votes, because they cannot win a plurality.[12]

The Constitution also created a system whereby the president is not directly elected by the people, but chosen by an electoral college. Like single-member district systems, this is a "winner take all" method. Presidential candidates receiving one vote less than a plurality in a particular state receive no electoral votes from that state at all (with one exception, Maine, which apportions electoral votes by congressional district). The very existence of the electoral college makes presidential bids by small parties or individual candidates unlikely to succeed. For example, Ross Perot received no electoral votes, even though he garnered 19 percent of the popular vote. Many voters are deterred from voting for challengers to the two parties because they believe their votes are wasted.

The historical features of American parties indicate that they sometimes channel political conflict away from the issues created by the modern economic and political status quo. Sometimes our parties have stifled a popular democratic political agenda, especially questions about class inequality and business influence. Whether by accident or by design, our parties often reenforce elite democracy by organizing the population to bolster, not challenge, the status quo. One supporter of the elite democratic roles of political parties looks favorably on American parties precisely for this ability to "control society." A more telling comment could not be made about most American political party history.[13]

Nevertheless, our political parties have served popular democracy in crucial moments, particularly during crises. That they are not ideological or highly organized can mean that they are open to outsiders, challengers, and even radical swings in direction under certain circumstances.

REALIGNING ELECTIONS

The features that make American parties unique also make them effective instruments of elite democracy. Yet our two parties have survived, and in the process they have undergone dramatic changes. Long struggles have occurred within, between, and outside the parties to strengthen, weaken, change, and even abolish them. The resulting looseness and openness have sometimes made American parties the instruments for popular democratic political movements.[14]

The democratic debate within and about our political parties has been most heated before, after, and during what political scientists call **realigning elections.** Table 8.1 lists these important electoral moments. In the last two hundred years, we've had only five—a few say six—such events. During realigning periods, our parties have tried to shape the electorate and respond to new political pressures, conflicts, and tensions among the citizenry. In some cases, new parties were born or achieved power for the first time through realigning elections, as did the Republicans in 1860. In others, like 1896 and 1932, the parties kept their names but changed their philosophies, prompting realignments in the social coalitions that supported them; large increases in voter participation in elections; and enormous policy changes in national, state, and local governments. Although rare, realigning elections are important because their effects last long after the election. They create new **party systems.** Usually, one dominant party emerges to shape the national political agenda, and new voters retain their new party loyalties in succeeding elections, even passing such loyalties on to future generations.[15]

By giving birth to new political eras and party systems, realigning elections have been called by Walter Dean Burnham "America's surrogate for revolution." In one dramatic sense, they are. Realigning elections feature significant increases in voter turnout amongst previous nonvoters, caused by an electorate clearly divided about the nation's future. Many voters change their party allegiances, others vote to defend the status quo, but in realigning elections voters identify candidates with their parties, and parties present a distinctive view of politics.

Realigning elections are powerful revelations of what happens when democracy is not a spectator sport. They bring the divisions between the parties into rough alignment with divisions between citizen groups, and thus temporarily fulfill the hopes of popular democrats.[16]

Most political scientists agree that we haven't had a realigning election in sixty years and that the prospects for having one soon are not bright. If this is true, then the weakness of present-day parties can be partly explained by the fact that they are the remote descendants of previous realignments. The next section probes the 1896 and 1932 realigning elections to better understand the nature of our current parties.

The Earthquake of 1896

Held in the aftermath of a severe economic depression, during rapid urbanization and emerging corporate capitalism, the 1896 election featured two contrasting visions of the nation's future. The first vision recalled the Anti-federalists and protested the new inequalities of wealth and power that were growing in industrializing America. These sentiments were crystallized in the candidacy of the "Great Commoner" William Jennings Bryan, nominated by Populists and Democrats in 1896. The second vision promised corporate-led prosperity, social stability, and increased American international power, brought about by a new Republican party under William McKinley.

TABLE 8.1	Election	Party System	Big Issues	Partisan Consequences
Realigning Elections and Their Consequences	1800 (Jefferson)	*First:* Democratic-Republicans over Federalists	"Privilege;" agrarian vs. urban interests; power of national government	Repudiation of Federalist Party
	1828 (Jackson)	*Second:* Democrats over Whigs	Democracy of common man; state vs. federal power	First mass party system; introduction of patronage; Democratic predominance
	1860 (Lincoln)	*Third:* Republicans over Democrats	Slavery; states' rights; North vs. South	Republicans as party of Union; growth of urban machines; the Solid South
	1896 (McKinley)	*Fourth:* Republicans over Democrats and Populists	National depression; industrialized North vs. agrarian South and West; monopolies vs. "the People"	Republicans as party of modern business prosperity; decline of party competition; Jim Crow in South
	1932 (Roosevelt)	*Fifth:* Democrats over Republicans	Depression; social rights; government responsibility for economy	Democrats as party of equality and prosperity; mobilization in North; Solid South persists
	1980 (Reagan)	*Sixth:* Partisan dealignment and "split-level" rule	Race, economic decline; American strength as world power	Party decomposition at grassroots; breakup of Democratic South; candidate-centered campaigns

The election split the nation's regions, and to some extent the nation's rich and poor. Bryan's stronghold was among the farmers in the underdeveloped agricultural South and West (in places like Kansas). The Republicans were strong among the middle and upper classes of the urban Midwest and Northeast. The real battle in 1896 was for the swing votes of Catholics and industrial workers; Bryan's Protestant fundamentalism and his concentration on farmers helped the

Republicans. McKinley's $3.5 million campaign war chest, an overwhelming sum in those days, also helped. Amidst charges that the Democrats were "anarchists" and the Republicans "plutocrats," eight in ten American voters went to the polls. Never since has a higher percentage of eligible voters gone to the polls in a national election. The result: McKinley and the Republicans carried the populous Northeast and Midwest, Bryan the agricultural South and West.[17]

The System of 1896

Like all realigning elections, the 1896 election was important for its long-term consequences. It created a new way of doing politics, a *system of 1896* that featured thirty-six years of more or less uninterrupted Republican national control and corporate domination of an expanding national state. The Democrats were eventually left with only the solid support of a diminished electorate in the old Confederate states.

The system had its ironies and unforeseen consequences. Born in an election that crystallized all the passions and arguments of elite and popular democracy, the new party system went on to squelch nearly all participatory energies. In their midwestern and northeastern strongholds, the now dominant Republicans moved to consolidate their control over the politics and voters of those states. In the cities, industrial workers and immigrants were a special target because their loyalty to the new Republicanism was far from secure. Many of the Republican-dominated states established ways to make voting difficult for immigrants and industrial workers.[18]

A second irony of the system of 1896 is that it gave birth to a powerful if varied movement among new middle-class teachers, scholars, lawyers, doctors, and other newly educated professionals. Under the banner of **Progressivism,** many different kinds of reformers rose to challenge what they saw as the un-relieved greed, mindless inefficiency, and rampant corruption of machine-dominated local and state governments. Progressives not only objected to Republicans and Democrats, but also attacked parties as a principle of democratic government. They called for nonpartisan elections free from party control, government laws regulating parties and their procedures, and a civil service and bureaucracy free from party patronage. A special Progressive target was the urban political machine and its ethnic politicians and voters. In the name of democracy, Progressives joined others to ensure that the electoral rolls were purified of their supposed corruption. The kind of difficult registration requirements outlined in Chapter 5 were pioneered by many Progressives as a way of ensuring efficient government and good citizenship.[19] Thus, although they appealed to the people to take control of government, they made citizen participation difficult. According to historian Samuel Hays, many Progressives "distrust[ed] greater political participation in making decisions about complicated and technical questions."[20]

In the North, the combination of Republican domination, Democratic weakness, and Progressive reforms weakened party competition in society and party power in government. The system of 1896's legacy was steady declines in voter turnout and a gap between ordinary people and elections. By 1924, twenty-eight years after McKinley's election, only 30 percent of the working-class voters of industrial Pittsburgh, Chicago, and Philadelphia were showing up at the polls.

In their remaining southern stronghold, the Democrats were achieving similar ends by more blatant means. Here, the electorate to be controlled was not ethnic industrial workers, but populist blacks and potentially rebellious poor whites. Left free to organize, both could be opponents of the "New South's" plantation and factory owners. Although efforts had been made to disenfranchise freed blacks before 1896, in the early part of the century these efforts intensified. The means were Ku Klux Klan terror and the implementation of official racial segregation and discrimination through *Jim Crow laws*. "White primaries" excluded blacks from voting in the Democrats' nomination contests. Poll taxes, literacy tests, and other devices provided further weapons by which blacks—and many poor whites—were excluded from political life.

Writing more than a half century after the 1896 election, V. O. Key in his classic *Southern Politics* found that one party control of the South turned campaigns into "debates over personalities" and that "voters had no real way of telling the difference between the candidates." For a southern Democratic politician to get elected, he had to promise personal favors to and governmental protection for the economic elites in his state. These "gentlemen" tended to fund the

The Ku Klux Klan conducts a cross-burning in Monroe, Georgia, in 1982. Up until the 1960s, the "Invisible Empire" helped maintain racism, segregation, and white control of Southern political structures through a campaign of murder, terror, and intimidation.

campaigns and owned the major newspapers crucial to success among the white electorate. Once in power, governors and legislators served their personal cliques of supporters, neglecting ordinary people and their needs or silencing them with false promises and empty clichés. Key concluded that "the haves, rather than the have nots," were the sole beneficiaries of the southern one-party system.[21]

Overall, the ultimate effect of the system of 1896 was to produce a party system in which the dominant southern economic and political elites were all Democrats and most of the dominant economic elites of the North were predominantly Republican or distrustful of parties altogether. In each region, the parties almost stopped performing their democratic functions. Without much democratic debate or competition, voter turnout fell to 43 percent in 1924, when "Silent" Cal Coolidge assumed the presidency.

1932: Rise of the New Deal Democrats

If the system of 1896 was still with us, we would have little reason to talk about parties as instruments of popular democracy. The system allowed business elites free rein in politics. One consequence of business dominance, some argue, was the Great Depression of 1929. In the elections of 1932 and 1936, the system of 1896 collapsed outside the South. Nationally, the election and reelection of Franklin Roosevelt were catalysts for an attempted renewal of both parties, this time with the Democrats as the dominant national party.

By the mid-1930s, new Democratic majorities in Congress and the northern states were built on militant organizations of steel workers, coal miners, auto workers, and the high number of unemployed. Among ethnic industrial workers, especially Catholics and Jews, the Democrats mobilized and organized the strongest party bonds. Senators and House members from the highly industrialized states provided the impetus for new measures and new participants in activist government. New Deal legislation created jobs, encouraged the growth of the union movement, and established a minimum wage and the Social Security system. At least in the North, the Jewish, Catholic, and worker votes cascading to the Democrats met an unequal but opposite reaction: Republican strength in middle- and upper-class Protestant neighborhoods increased by 1940 to unprecedented levels. In contrast to the system of 1896, turnout spurred through party competition and grassroots activism surged in the North. Despite the revival of the Democrats, fears of the Republicans, and political polarization in U.S. society, however, nationwide turnout did not reach the levels of 1896.

One of the reasons was that the now dominant Democratic party was really two different regional parties. With its northern working-class support, the Democratic party came close to resembling the British Labor party or social democratic parties in Germany and elsewhere. Activists were often able to organize new Democratic voters by appealing to economic justice for the rights of citizens to a job, to join unions, and bargain with employers.

Southern revival of the Democratic party, when it happened at all, was much more muted. There, the system of 1896's effects largely persisted, especially Democrats' identity as the party of racial segregation and white domination.

Although some southern Democrats tried to ignore or underplay racial questions and concentrated on issues of economic inequality (people like Hugo Black, "Big" Jim Folsom, and Lister Hill of Alabama; Claude Pepper of Florida; and Huey Long of Louisiana), southern Democrats at their most radical never challenged racial segregation. While Roosevelt himself began to gain votes among the few southern blacks who could vote, most southern Democrats still tried to exclude them from the polling booth. As a result, many of the most equalitarian of New Deal programs, such as a national system of economic planning and farm legislation that rewarded sharecroppers and tenant farmers rather than large plantation owners, were stymied in Congress by the opposition of conservative southern Democrats. In addition, coalitions of southern Democrats and Republicans in Congress compromised many of the equalitarian features of the New Deal's job and Social Security programs.

From its beginning, the potentially radical thrust of the New Deal coalition was blunted by the Democrats' elite southern wing. With substantial congressional power, they preserved "white man's democracy" in the South and slowed the progress of popular democracy so evident in the northern Democratic party. Although the New Deal coalition in the North extended popular democracy by building a much stronger Democratic party at the grassroots, the character of the southern Democratic party still more closely resembled the system of 1896 than it did the "system of 1932." The importance of the Solid South in the Democratic coalition affected the party and its identity for decades afterwards.[22]

Realigning elections and their aftermaths suggest that American parties can sometimes be effective instruments of popular democracy because they mobilize and organize voters and because they provide meaningful choices and accountability. But American parties in "normal" elections often lose or ignore democratic energies. In the South of an earlier era, the Democratic party didn't organize voters as much as it excluded them. In the North before 1932, Republican domination was based on excluding the opposition from effective roles. Republicans organized their voters not for effective participation, but to encourage stability and apathy.

The different roles our parties have played can thus spark contrasting evaluations. In the late E. E. Schattschneider's words: "If democracy means anything at all, it means that the majority has the right to organize for the purpose of taking over the government. Party government is strong because it has behind it the great moral authority of the majority and the force of a strong traditional belief in majority rule." Yet another student of American politics, Clinton Rossiter, was probably also right, if for different reasons, when he said that American parties are "one of the truly conservative arrangements in the world of politics."[23]

PRESENT-DAY PARTIES: REPUBLICAN ASCENDANCY, DEMOCRATIC COMEBACKS, OR DEALIGNMENT?

Democrats and Republicans, products of their pasts, still dominate almost all national and state political offices. In the 1960s and 1980s, again in the midst of enormous political, social, and economic tensions, some observers predicted another realigning election. After Ronald Reagan's 1980 and 1984 victories and the GOP's capture of a Senate majority for six years, hopeful Republicans heralded a new Republican era. Yet the Democrats regained the Senate in 1986, held on to a large majority in the House of Representatives, and elected Bill Clinton as president in 1992.

American society has changed since the last real realignment sixty years ago. How have our parties changed, and how have they remained the same? Are they acting to control society as elite democrats hope or "mobilize" it as popular democrats want? Although our parties still do many of the same things, they are also in trouble at the grassroots, where they seem to be losing the ability to control voters, to be controlled by them, or to mobilize and educate them.[24]

Crisis of the Parties

Americans generally aren't members of political parties—we don't pay dues, buy a party newspaper, or carry a party membership card. Either party's strength can be measured only by asking people about their attitudes towards them. This is called **party identification.** How many people think of themselves as Democrats, Republicans, or independents? How strongly do people feel about their identification? The answers to these questions are not encouraging for either party.

The Democrats

As Table 8.2 shows, the Democrats have lost many of their loyalists over the past three or four decades. Although a third of the electorate still identify themselves with the party, there are fewer strong Democrats, many more weak identifiers, and a sizable voter shift toward independence from both parties.

The core Democratic supporters are African Americans, Jews, Latinos (with the exception of Cuban Americans) and the poorest and least educated voters of all races, in that order. Yet even among these loyal Democrats, party identification has slipped, especially among younger people.

Among Catholics, union members, and blue-collar workers, once also part of the foundation of the New Deal Democratic party, Democratic membership also has been slipping since the 1960s. Many Catholics have abandoned the party, and in the late 1980s Republican identifiers were almost even with Democrats, only to fall back again in 1992. While all of these voters gave a plurality to President Clinton during the 1992 election, the Democrats can't count on their consistent support.[25]

As Figure 8.1 shows, the steepest declines in Democratic support have been among southern whites. Since the 1964 election, wide majorities of them have rejected Democratic presidential candidates. Currently their identification with the GOP surpasses that of white northern Protestants, forty years ago the

TABLE 8.2

Changing Party Identification, 1952–92, in Percent

Category	1952	1960	1968	1980	1988	1992
Strong Democrats	22	21	20	18	17	18
Weak Democrats	25	23	25	23	18	17
Total	47	44	45	41	35	35
Independents (includes "leaners" to either party)	22	24	30	34	36	38
Weak Republicans	14	13	14	14	14	14
Strong Republicans	13	14	10	9	14	11
Total	27	27	24	23	28	25

Source: Survey Research Center, Center for Political Studies, University of Michigan, compiled from election study surveys.

Republican's core supporters. In the rest of the nation, the Democrats have also lost white support, but to a much lesser extent.[26]

The Democrats retain some of their New Deal identity. As for depth of party loyalty, however, they are weak. Perhaps the most ominous portent for the Democrats is that their core loyalists are in the middle-aged to elderly segments of the electorate. Who will sustain the party once those with strong loyalties have passed from the scene?

FIGURE 8.1

Shifts Toward GOP Among Southern Whites

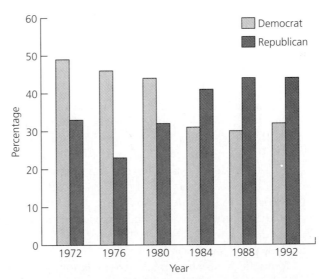

Sources: Data drawn from CBS/*NY Times* Polls, 1972–88; Voter Research and Surveys poll, 1992.

The Republicans

If our parties were stronger at the grassroots, Democratic losses would mean decisive Republican gains. But despite some jumps in the early 1980s, levels of GOP identification have not changed dramatically. The Republicans have elected many of their presidential candidates but have built only a few new political loyalties at the Democrats' expense. They remain a minority party.

As noted earlier, the Republicans *have* made dramatic gains among southern whites. The shift began as early as 1948 when many white southerners abandoned the Democrats' national presidential candidates. By 1964, Republican Barry Goldwater won many states of the old Confederacy. By 1968, Alabama Governor and third-party candidate George Wallace and Richard Nixon split the southern states. By 1972 Richard Nixon won all the southern states. The shift in partisan identification has occurred more slowly, but by the 1980s southern white voters (especially the young) gave the GOP a 6 percent advantage over the Democrats. High-income southern men nearly delivered a bloc vote to the Republican presidential candidates of the 1980s. In 1988, George Bush received about 80 percent of their votes.[27]

The Republicans have also picked up loyalists among white "born-again" Protestants and Catholics, approximately 15 percent of the electorate. Nearly eight in ten supported Ronald Reagan and George Bush in the elections of the 1980s, and most translated their support to the Republicans for lesser offices. In 1992, Baptist Bill Clinton and Texan Ross Perot drew some born-again support away, but that still gave Bush a twenty-four-point lead over the combined totals of both. Over half of white born-again Christians identify themselves as Republicans, with Democrats and independents dividing the remainder.[28]

Republicans used to get their largest majorities among white northern Protestants at all levels of wealth and education. By the 1980s, their lead among this group had diminished—the lower-income segments became increasingly independent or Democratic, or simply dropped out of the electorate. Middle-income Protestants moved away from Republican loyalty as well, while upper-income northern white Protestants increased their already high support for the GOP.

Throughout the 1980s, observers spoke of a gender gap, by which they usually meant that women were more Democratic than men. Conversely, men became more Republican than women, providing the GOP with a 7 percent lead. In the 1980s, men's margin of support for the Republicans outweighed women's slight tilt in identification toward the Democrats. But both genders supplied majorities to Reagan and Bush in 1984 and 1988. By 1992, though, the gender gap worked to hurt the Republicans. Men gave Bill Clinton only a 1 percent plurality, while women provided large majorities for Clinton and women Democrats running for the Senate.[29] Figure 8.2 demonstrates the changing gender basis of party identification.

Republicans also have made inroads among younger voters, once a key Democratic group. In the early 1980s, eighteen- to twenty-nine-year-olds identified

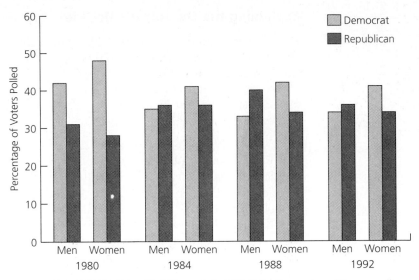

FIGURE 8.2

The Gender Gap Since 1980

Source: 1980–1988/CBS New York Times Poll; 1992 Voter Research and Survey polls.

with the GOP by a margin of 8 percent over the Democrats. GOP support among the young, however, isn't that intense, as Bill Clinton and Ross Perot did quite well among young people.

Independents and a Fluid Electorate

Should the Republicans be pleased with their gains? In the early 1980s, Democratic losses appeared to be the beginning of a realignment toward the Republicans. In retrospect, though, the amount of Republican conversions is not all that significant. Many people were merely voting for Republican presidential candidates without becoming Republicans.

The most noteworthy feature of politics in the last twenty-five years is the rise of independents and those whose party identification is weak. The parties still have strongholds, but they are diminishing. Among the bulk of the electorate—voters under fifty—the largest group is neither Democrats or Republicans, but independents. Much of the current electorate is thus "fluid" and chooses candidates of both parties.

THE PARTIES IN RECENT PRESIDENTIAL ELECTIONS

The facts just mentioned raise more questions than they answer. What happened to the Democrats? Why were the Republicans unable to take full advantage of Democratic decay? Did the 1992 election represent a Democratic revival?

Explaining the Democrats' Decline

Will Rogers said in the 1930s: "I belong to no organized party. I'm a Democrat." The modern Democratic party survives as a weaker, more divided, and somewhat changed descendant of its 1930s New Deal parent. The sources of its weakness and the changes it has undergone are due to racial tension, the Vietnam War and its aftermath, culture wars, and middle-class economic stagnation.

Politics of Race. To placate the Solid South, the self-proclaimed party of the people long denied the most basic rights to African Americans. For many northern New Deal Democrats, their party's equivocation had always been an uncomfortable compromise assuring party majorities in Congress and a Democratic President. By the early 1960s and the arrival of the civil rights movement and massive white southern resistance to it, the race question could no longer be smothered. After some foot dragging, both John Kennedy and Lyndon Johnson removed the system of legal segregation in the South with the full force of new Federal laws.

The national Democratic party paid for its conversion to the civil rights cause. It had to confront its own segregationist wing. As the Democrats gained votes among new African American voters, they gradually lost about two-thirds of Southern whites. Posing as a less extreme alternative to discredited segregationists, in 1968 Republican Richard Nixon formulated a southern strategy to lure conservative former Democrats into the Republican party. Since 1968, only southern Democrats Clinton and Carter have won any southern states.[30]

To the dismay of Johnson, the civil rights struggles led to new tensions between white and black Democrats in northern cities, the chief bastion of the party outside the South. In cities with increasingly large black populations, city halls were run mostly by white Democrats resistant to new black demands for social services and political representation. In response to widespread rioting and peaceful political protest in black neighborhoods, Johnson launched the Great Society. This complex set of federal programs was designed to eliminate the worst poverty from affluent America. But the political logic of the Great Society was equally important. Johnson's programs provided money for the construction companies and downtown interests of white-dominated city governments, but also substantial aid for new programs directed at inner-city minorities. The Great Society did bring many people out of abject poverty. But it split the Democrats' core support among the poor from the middle-class and working-class whites who lived in the cities or suburbs.

In 1968, George Wallace and Richard Nixon appealed to the fears, and pocketbooks, of working-class whites. Both blamed Great Society programs and liberal Democrats for increased tax bills, declining property values, crime, job insecurity, and busing to achieve racial integration of the schools. White ethnic neighborhoods in the urban core were becoming disillusioned with Democratic liberalism's supposed favoritism toward blacks.[31]

The Democrats Change the Rules: Who Benefits?

Democracy and the Democratic party were put on trial in the turbulent year of 1968. With antiwar protest and the Vietnam War at fevered pitches, Democratic President Lyndon Johnson dropped out of the election race. In April, Martin Luther King, Jr., was killed, unleashing mourning and rage in the inner cities. Minnesota Senator Eugene McCarthy and Senator Robert F. Kennedy challenged Johnson and his designated heir, Vice President Hubert Humphrey, the candidate of the "regulars" for the Democratic nomination. McCarthy and Kennedy both promised an end to the war; their followers included young people, minorities, and women. Yet at his very moment of triumph in the California primary, Kennedy was assassinated, Humphrey went on to win the party's nomination in the most tumultuous convention in the Democrats' history.

Humphrey won the nomination, even though he hadn't run in a single primary. Most of his delegates had been appointed by party leaders and were predominantly white, male, and over forty. After Humphrey lost the general election to Richard Nixon, party dissenters struck back with proposals to transform the party's rules. They won a major victory when the McGovern–Fraser Commission implemented reforms. By 1972, party primaries and caucuses began to replace smoke-filled rooms and party "bosses" as the means of choosing delegates. At the party's 1972 national convention, state delegations were required to broaden the representation of women, minorities, and the young. In succeeding years, the party eliminated winner-take-all primaries, a practice that denied any delegates to candidates who received less than a plurality of the votes. Instead, presidential candidates now receive a proportion of delegates roughly equal to their percentage of the caucus and primary totals (proportional representation).

The impact of these and other changes has been immense. Most present-day delegates are chosen in party primaries and some through caucuses of interested citizens. At least in theory, both encourage extensive citizen participation. On gender, racial, and age criteria, Democratic delegates look more like the party grassroots than they did in 1968.

Reform hasn't come without critics, however. Some scholars believe party organizations have been weakened by depriving party leaders of the right to review presidential candidates. Others complain that more primaries have furthered the powers of leftist activists, represented by the nomination and subsequent defeat of George McGovern in 1972. In the late 1970s and 1980s, the antireformers struck back, reestablishing some appointed delegates ("superdelegates"), reducing some quotas, and nibbling away at proportional representation. Yet the presidential preferences of those who resist reforms have often fared poorly. Walter Mondale and Michael Dukakis were the choices of the regulars (as was Humphrey), but their defeats were almost as large as McGovern's.

For the democratic debate, the real question is if Democratic party reforms have strengthened or weakened the role of ordinary citizens. On the positive side, many more voters have participated in the nomination process since 1968. On the negative side, democratic participation needs strengthening. The battle over party rules isn't over yet.

Sources: See William Crotty and John S. Jackson, *Presidential Primaries and Nominations* (Washington, D.C.: Congressional Quarterly, 1985); Austin Ranney, *Curing the Mischiefs of Faction* (Berkeley: University of California Press, 1975); Norman Mailer, *Miami and the Siege of Chicago* (New York: Pantheon, 1969).

Vietnam. The Democrats (and the nation) also split over the Vietnam War, a conflict begun and expanded by Democrats Kennedy and Johnson. Although the leadership of U.S. trade unions generally supported it, many liberal and civil rights activists, including Martin Luther King, Jr., did not. The party's intellectuals, always an important part of its status, were sharply divided. In 1968, university students and others demonstrated for withdrawal from Vietnam and campaigned for antiwar Senators Eugene McCarthy and Robert Kennedy. Other Democrats, despite growing misgivings about the war, scorned antiwar protest as unpatriotic.

In 1968, the tensions peaked at the party's Chicago convention. While the nation watched on TV, the Democrats literally tore themselves apart as the Chicago police beat both antiwar demonstrators and convention delegates outside the convention hall. The spectacle didn't help in November. Only four years after Lyndon Johnson had defeated Barry Goldwater by a huge landslide, the Democratic standard-bearer Hubert Humphrey lost to Richard Nixon.[32]

Culture Wars. From feminists to environmental activists, the social movements spawned in the 1960s questioned political and economic power and conventional attitudes toward sexuality, the family, and nature. Always a diverse coalition of outsiders, the Democrats were far more open to the claims of these movements than the Republicans. Since the 1970s, these movement organizations have gained influence in the Democratic party. Along with labor and people of color, groups like the National Organization of Women and the Sierra Club are often powerful in the Democratic party's reform wing.

Each battle over new cultural issues also had its costs. The party became vulnerable to what Republicans began to call **wedge issues**—questions that divide older, generally working-class Democrats from the newer groups who became active in the 1960s. Wedge issues include the party's support for a ban on public school prayer, its concern that law and order not intrude on personal and civil rights, its support for freedom of choice on abortion, and its relatively tolerant policies regarding homosexuality. From Nixon to George Bush in 1988, Republican presidential victories have rested on splitting off discontented Democratic constituencies.[33]

Economic Stagnation. Finally, all Democratic divisions were worsened by the economic decline or stagnation suffered by most low- and middle-income groups since the early 1970s. Even though much of the decline occurred during Republican administrations, the secret of GOP success was its ability to blame "big government" and Democratic party policies for it. With the Democratic party already torn by other conflicts, Republican claims succeeded to some degree.

Republican Revolution from Above

Writing in 1968, Kevin Phillips, a young adviser to Richard Nixon, urged Republicans to become the new, populist, "silent majority" party, made up of the unpoor, the unrich, the unblack, the uncool—those who worked every day,

Hundreds of Democratic party delegates and anti–Vietnam War protestors were injured by the Chicago police and National Guard during the 1968 Democratic Convention. Democratic Party splits over the Vietnam War helped Republican Richard Nixon win the presidency in 1968 and 1972.

paid their taxes, went to war, and didn't protest or demonstrate. By making the most of the social and economic divisions of the 1960s, the Republicans sailed to victory in five of the six presidential elections between 1968 and 1988. Has the strategy developed by the young Phillips been a success, the 1992 reversal notwithstanding?[34]

In the 1970s the GOP did partly rebuild itself as the party of resurgent patriotism, optimism, and the promise of prosperity. Through **supply-side economics,** the Republicans promised tax cuts for everyone, fewer regulations on business, and a reduction of governmental programs designed to serve poor Americans. At the same time, Republicans called for a new military buildup to counter what they saw as the military and political threat of the Soviet Union.

The Republicans advertised their economic reforms as cost-free, and rode to victory in 1980 on the promise that a new surge in corporate investment would create more jobs, raise the standard of living for everybody, and eventually even increase tax revenues as people got wealthier. But their real key to success was less the policies they proposed than the failed administration of Democrat Jimmy Carter. High inflation, big tax bills and the threat of unemployment allowed GOP candidate Ronald Reagan to make the 1980 election a referendum on the Carter Administration. Since many normally Democratic voters were worse off economically than they had been when Carter took office, they cast their votes in 1980 for the Republican candidate.[35]

Republicans since Nixon had used wedge issues to attract some Democrats uneasy about the spectre of social and cultural change symbolized by feminnists, gays, and alternative lifestyles. But it took the rise of Christian Right organizations in the 1970s to focus these attacks on vulnerable Democrats. In the 1970s, TV ministers such as Jerry Falwell and Pat Robertson organized and developed powerful organizations that were thrown into partisan politics on behalf of the GOP. Through new organizations like the National Conservative Political Action Committee, the religious right raised substantial sums of money. They used it to defeat liberal Democratic senators in Western states, gaining the GOP a Senate majority in 1980.

Under Ronald Reagan's leadership, the Republican Party in 1980 consummated a new marriage between pro-business economics and Protestant fundamentalists. The vastly more focused influence and money of America's top corporations helped Republican economic proposals and ideas gain plausibility as alternatives to the Democrats' policies. Associations like the U.S. Chamber of Commerce and Business Roundtable served as pipelines for corporate donations to new think tanks like the American Enterprise Institute, the Hoover Institution, and the Heritage Foundation. Each of these research and policy foundations produced reports, studies, and expert media commentators confirming the intellectual validity of the new conservative agenda.[36]

Even from the beginning, there were reasons to doubt that voter anger against Democratic presidents was directed at all Democrats. For most of the twenty years of Republican presidents, the voters had returned Democratic majorities to Congress. During the entire period, Democrats held on to a majority of the nation's governorships and state legislatures. Contrary to the pattern of past realignments that created new dominant parties, voter turnout continued to drop.

Three GOP presidential victories in the 1980s and their six-year control of the Senate thus led many to think that the American electorate had indeed realigned. Yet even in the midst of GOP gains, there were reasons to doubt that the electorate had made a decisive shift. Voters elected Republican presidents, but they continued to return Democratic majorities to the House of Representatives. Since 1968 and through the 1980s, Democrats held on to a majority of the nation's governorships and state legislatures. In 1986, the GOP lost its narrow Senate majority. Nor did the Republicans make many inroads among the vast pool of non-voters; the GOP surge was accompanied by continued decline in voter turnout.

Perhaps the GOP's Achilles heel was its elitism—the party had really not succeeded in moving working- and middle-class former Democrats firmly into its ranks. **Reagan Democrats** had provided votes to Ronald Reagan and George Bush in the expectation of increasing incomes and better jobs, but hadn't converted many voters to Republicanism. When economic growth led to economic recession by 1990, the grassroots weakness of the GOP was revealed. More than two decades after the young Kevin Phillips had called for an "emerging Republican majority," he pronounced it stillborn. Phillips described the top ranks of the Republican party to be "a collection of well-paid counselors and lobbyists for domestic and foreign interests ranging from the Tobacco Institute to South Africa and Toyota, an elite as distant from the Iowa and Idaho grass roots as their Democratic predecessors."[37]

The Election of 1992: Revival of the Democrats?

Among the many changes and continuities in the 1992 election, one fact stood out. Bill Clinton's victory and Ross Perot's strong showing made it impossible to argue the case for voter realignment toward the Republican party. Ronald Reagan's understudy, George Bush, got only 37.4 percent of the popular vote, defeated in a campaign in which both Clinton and Perot attacked the GOP's policy agenda.

But was the 1992 election more a defeat for the Republicans than a victory for a new Democratic party? One election does not make a revival. Still, Clinton's victory was in some ways impressive.

Democrat Clinton broke what many thought was a permanent Republican lock on the electoral votes of many states. Since 1968, Republicans had gained the consistent support of twenty-one southern and western states, including the biggest prize, California. In the three elections of the 1980s, the GOP seemed to have added another seventeen states. Yet as Figure 8.3 shows, Clinton broke the lock by winning formerly Republican California, Colorado, Louisiana, and Kentucky.

More telling are shifts in the support of social groups that were supposed to be the core of the Republicans' grassroots revival. Table 8.3 presents the breakdown of group support for the 1992 candidates and comparisons with 1988. Clinton retained the Democrats' core strengths among the nonwhite, the poor, the elderly, Jews, and people with less than a college education. He also built a solid lead among women, especially single women. But Clinton also won pluralities among voters who were supposedly Republican converts. The Republicans lost a sizable proportion of Reagan Democrats, the potential new backbone of a revived Republicanism. For the first time since the 1960s, the Democratic candidate virtually tied the Republican nominee among all white voters and won pluralities among white voters in all regions but the South. (The 1992 and 1994 congressional elections are examined below and in Chapter 9.)

A year after Clinton's inauguration, the numbers looked even better for the Democrats. For the first time since 1984, the Democrats led the GOP in party identification among eighteen- to twenty-nine-year-olds, and their lead among all voters had grown to 8 percent, thanks to new recruits among independents and Republicans. On almost all important issues, including crime and welfare reform, the public rated the Democrats higher than the GOP in their ability to achieve positive results.[38]

After so many years out of the White House, Democrats had every reason to be pleased with Clinton's victory. The 1992 Democratic coalition could represent a reversal of the party's decline since the 1960s. In Jesse Jackson's words, Democrats demonstrated that those "who never left the party and those who did leave must pull together in order to win." Cemented by the economic fallout of the Reagan–Bush years, the Democratic coalition's victory could end the Republican ability to exploit Democratic weakness.[39]

It is possible, however, that the 1992 election was less a victory for the revived Democratic party than simply the Republican party's turn to experience decline.

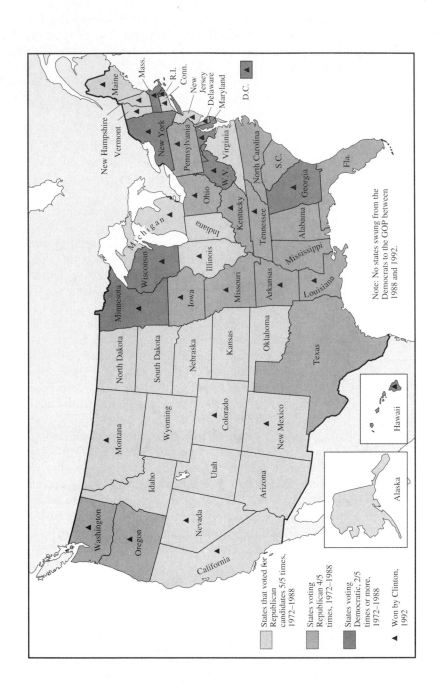

FIGURE 8.3   Breaking the Republican Lock on the White House

Note: No states swung from the Democrats to the GOP between 1988 and 1992.

States that voted for Republican candidates, 5/5 times, 1972–1988

States voting Republican 4/5 times, 1972–1988

States voting Democratic, 2/5 times or more, 1972–1988

▲ Won by Clinton, 1992

TABLE 8.3

Portrait of the
American Electorate
in the Presidential
Elections of 1988
and 1992

% 1992 Total	1988			1992	
	Bush	Duka.	Clinton	Bush	Perot
100	53	45	43	38	19
Race					
87 White	59	40	39	41	20
8 Black	12	86	82	11	7
3 Hispanic	30	69	62	25	14
1 Asian origin	N/A	N/A	29	55	16
Age					
22 18–29	52	47	44	34	22
38 30–44	54	45	42	38	20
24 45–59	57	42	41	40	19
16 60 & over	50	49	50	38	12
Education					
6 no h.s.	43	56	55	28	17
25 h.s. grad	50	49	43	36	20
29 some coll.	57	42	42	37	21
24 col. grad	62	37	40	41	19
16 adv. degree	50	48	49	36	15
Income					
14 <15K	37	62	59	23	18
24 15–30K	49	50	45	35	20
30 30–50K	56	44	41	38	21
20 50–75K	56	42	40	42	18
13 >75K	62	37	36	48	16
Employment status					
68 employed	56	43	42	38	20
5 f.t. student	44	54	50	35	15
6 unemployed	37	62	56	24	20
8 homemaker	58	41	36	45	19
13 retired	50	49	51	36	13
Religion					
49 Wh. Prot.	66	33	33	46	21
27 Catholic	52	47	44	36	20
4 Jewish	35	64	78	12	10
17 born again	81	18	23	61	15
Voting history					
11 first time voters	51	47	48	30	22
Marital status					
65 married	57	42	40	40	20
35 single	46	53	49	33	18
35 married men	60	39	38	40	21
19 single women	42	57	51	34	15
Partisanship					
35 GOP	91	8	10	73	17
27 Ind	55	43	38	32	20
38 Dem	17	82	77	10	13

Source: "Portrait of the Electorate", *New York Times,* Nov. 5, 1992. "N/A" means statistics not available. Copyright © 1992 by the New York Times Company. Reprinted by Permission.

In this sense, the 1992 election may only underscore the weakness of *both* parties at the grassroots.

The primary evidence for mutual party weakness is the success of Ross Perot. Perot, with his 19 percent of the vote, amassed the largest vote total by a candidate hailing from *neither* major party since Theodore Roosevelt's "Bull Moose" party candidacy in 1912. Perot's level of support makes Clinton's victory less decisive and Bush's defeat even more complete. With but 43 percent of the popular vote, Clinton's victory percentage was the third smallest in U.S. history, and *less* than Michael Dukakis garnered in his 1988 *loss.* The rejection of Republican Bush was even greater than it first seemed. Due to Perot's showing and Clinton's inroads, Republicans retained only 60 percent of their 1988 proportion of the vote.

Second, although core Republican and Democratic groups remained loyal in 1992, such voters are becoming rarer. In 1988, only one out of three voters said they made their choices based on their party affiliation. By 1992, less than one in five Bush supporters favored him just because he was a Republican, and only one in four voters supported Clinton because he was a Democrat. Both parties, in short, mattered less than they had even in 1988. In 1992, large majorities of both Clinton and Perot supporters said simply that they were voting for "change."[40]

The 1994 Congressional Elections

In the 1980s, Republicans learned that apparent electoral mandates in presidential years weaken quickly, for the party in the White House almost always loses some seats in Congress in the next election. The 1994 off-year election was a much bigger and apparently more disastrous lesson of the same kind for the Democrats. Long-simmering voter anger and cynicism that had worked for the Democrats in 1992 turned against all Washington politicians in early 1994 and then was effectively harnessed against Congressional Democrats in the fall. President Clinton and a Democratic Congress became lightning rods for voter grievances aganst Washington. The Democrats lost their Senate majority and 9 seats as well as their House majority and a whopping 52 seats. Democratic House losses were particularly acute in the South and among freshmen members—the "anti-Washington" outsiders who two years before had been elected to "change" government. For the first time since 1954, Republicans held both houses, and jubilant leaders like Newt Gingrich were quick to christen the 1994 election as a revolution for Republican conservatism and a rejection of Clinton liberalism.

Is there any reason to believe that massive voter support for the Republicans will be translated into a historic new voter allegiance to the GOP in the future? Perhaps, but there are reasons to caution against such interpretations. Exit polls suggest that party identification had hardly changed since 1992—Democrats still held a slight lead over the GOP and the number of independent voters remained larger than that of either party. The GOP's energetic Christian Right base was especially active in 1994, while Democratic core voters stayed away from the polls in droves. Overall turnout remained low, and crucial independent and Perot voters supported the GOP less to show approval of their policies than to express frustration with the governing Democrats. Republican challengers, moreover, were able to outspend Democrats in almost all the contests for open seats.

Conservative commentator Kevin Phillips called GOP gains only the "pretense" of vitality on top of an "electoral volcano" that will continue to rumble in the party system. One 1994 survey concluded that "each party has failed in adding . . . to its base" and that "neither has a clear advantage on . . . key dimensions" of concern to voters. Even as they elected large numbers of Republicans, a majority of the electorate expressed support for the formation of a third party.[41]

THE POLITICS OF DEALIGNMENT

With such a volatile and restive electorate, the future of both our parties is far from clear or certain. What is clear is that both parties seem unable to realign the electorate, and that the electorate is less likely to look to them for direction. Scholars use the term *party dealignment* to describe the processes that are eroding our party system. As they weaken, our parties become less able to initiate democratic change or electoral realignments. What are the symptoms of party dealignment?[42]

Generals Without Armies: Current Party Organization

At their liveliest, American parties possessed strong local party organizations and provided for two-way communication between voters and officeholders. At the grassroots, party organizations were forums for citizens to meet, debate, and hold elected officials accountable for their actions and policies.

Figure 8.4 presents a pyramid of present-day party organization. On paper, the pyramid seems to represent a viable democratic structure linking millions of voters to local party activists who operate the party "machinery" in neighborhoods and precincts. The parties at the grassroots send representatives to more important county and congressional district committees, who in turn elect a state central (or executive) committee. Each state party then sends representatives to either the Democratic National Committee (DNC) or the Republican National Committee (RNC). From the ranks of the national committees come the national chairpersons, who plan the national convention, raise funds, and coordinate state races. At the national convention, a platform is drafted and developed, and presidential and vice-presidential candidates are nominated.

This formal work of party organizations still is important to American political life. Over seventy million voters form the base of the pyramid. At the top, the national committees and so-called affiliated committees, along with the national chairpersons, perform crucial functions. For example, national Democratic chairpersons Paul Kirk and Ron Brown are credited with rebuilding the Democrats' bank accounts and technical campaign expertise during the 1980s and early 1990s. In the 1970s, GOP chairman Bill Brock revitalized the party after the Watergate scandal and prepared the way for the 1980 Reagan victory.

FIGURE 8.4

Pyramid of American Party Organization

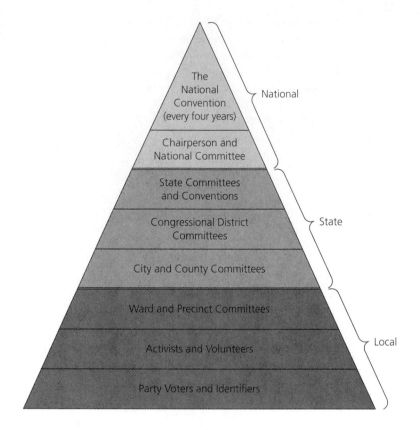

The National Convention (every four years) — National

Chairperson and National Committee

State Committees and Conventions

Congressional District Committees — State

City and County Committees

Ward and Precinct Committees

Activists and Volunteers — Local

Party Voters and Identifiers

Yet at the state and local levels, the roles and power of party organizations vary radically. Some local party groups actively recruit, fund, and coordinate diverse campaigns for public office. A few launch voter registration drives. In counties, towns and city neighborhoods, party organizations sometimes find candidates to run for lesser offices like tax assessor, city councilperson and county supervisor, while helping the campaigns of all candidates on the party "line."

Nevertheless, something is missing from Figure 8.4. There is very little going on at the base of the pyramid. For one thing, party organizations have lost much control of the nominating processes for the most important offices. Virtually anyone with campaign dollars who claims to be a Democrat or Republican can run for either party's nomination for any office. In presidential years, four-fifths of the states now conduct *primary elections* to select national convention delegates pledged to individual candidates for president. In most cases, the task of nominating candidates is left to the party's registered voters through *closed primaries*. Some states have *open primaries*, in which voters registered in any party (or no party at all) may cast votes to nominate candidates. Others, such as Iowa, conduct *caucuses* in which candidates' supporters meet to select delegates. Whatever the merits of these processes, they render party organizations powerless to control their own nominees.[43]

Moreover, the national party conventions have largely lost their character as forums for debate and conflict. Instead, their formats are carefully controlled to best showcase the presidential and vice presidential nominees. Delegates, reduced to spectators and cheerleaders, make few decisions.

Where the pyramid makes least sense is where it should count most in the democratic debate. With some exceptions, grassroots party organizations have few members and little influence. Consider as an example the Democratic party's plans for a bicentennial birthday party in 1992. The DNC wanted to invite all its officeholders to a grand Washington celebration. But they also asked their staff to invite the party activists and regulars responsible for running the party machinery, walking the precincts, and holding the meetings. Staffers at the DNC searched their computer files for the names. To everyone's surprise, there weren't any. The largest and oldest political party in the United States hadn't found time to collect the names of its activists, even though it had extensive lists of contributors. Consulting the state party committees, the DNC staff had some-what better results. But many of the countywide party organizations had few activists or none at all.

This symptom of dealignment is hard to measure. To be sure, many Americans belong to groups that support the parties—labor unions, environmentalists, and feminists often help Democrats; right-to-life and business groups, the Republi-

cans. A 1986 study reveals that grassroots parties in some cities are active during some campaigns, and in recent years Christian groups have made a comeback at the GOP's grassroots. The numbers of activists, though, are not impressive. Do you know anyone who attends meetings of the local Republican or Democratic town committees? Consult the Yellow Pages to see whether the parties have offices or even phone numbers. Ask your grandparents whether the parties currently are more organized than they were in the 1930s, 1940s, or 1950s. The answers you get tend to cast doubts on the democratic future of our parties.[44]

Survey data reflect the fact that involvement is low at the base of the pyramid. Even in 1980, when the Reagan Revolution began, overwhelming numbers of voters agreed that parties seemed to be only interested in people's votes, but not in their opinions. Only 18 percent of the electorate thought that parties help government pay attention to what people think. Almost as many thought joining a protest march would be as effective as being a party activist. A majority ranked other kinds of political action (like writing letters or giving money) as more effective. Although Americans may not always be hostile to political parties, mass indifference appears to be the norm.[45]

Candidates Instead of Parties. In Chapter 7, we saw how media campaign coverage neglected parties in favor of individual candidates. Our elections have become contests between individuals regardless of their party labels. Although most people who identify with one party still vote for most candidates of that party, when people vote for Reagan, Bush, Clinton, or their House member, they tell pollsters they are voting for the person and not a party.

At first glance, voting for the person may seem to be an expression of thoughtful independence. But most voters can't evaluate the candidates in terms of even the most elementary political philosophies. (See Chapter 9 for ways candidates worsen the confusion.) Candidates may be avid members of political parties and have strong political philosophies. Those political philosophies and party affiliations will matter when they are in office. Yet when parties dealign in the electorate, all the voters see are candidates' personalities, which have little relevance to later policy decisions they make in office. In this way, party dealignment makes it difficult for voters to hold politicians accountable, and for politicians to lead knowledgeable citizens in new policy directions.

The 1980 electoral victory of Ronald Reagan over Jimmy Carter is a perfect example of this phenomenon. Reagan had long been a conservative Republican activist and was arguably the most extreme right-winger to have gained the presidency in this century. Yet his victory over Jimmy Carter in 1980 had little to do with his party affiliation. Polls indicated that the 1980 election was about the political leadership qualities of Reagan and Carter. Voters focused on Reagan as an alternative to Carter, not Republicans as an alternative to Democrats. In a contest over performance, leadership, and personality, the affable yet strong Reagan won easily. In the high moments of his presidency, Reagan won high marks for leadership. Ironically, the majority of voters disapproved of his actual economic and social policies. When the electorate is dealigning, such gaps between opinions about policies and people become common.[46]

Dealignment and Retrospective Voting. Judging between competing personalities is one symptom of party dealignment and decline. Another is the voter tendency to judge candidates on their perceived recent performance in office, rather than on their ideas, party philosophies, or future plans. When the nation is in bad shape, voters abandon their already weak party affiliations and vote against *whoever* is in power. Political scientists label this phenomenon **retrospective voting**. Its rise helped Ronald Reagan and, more recently, Bill Clinton. The problem with retrospective voting is that it supplies no guide from voters about future policies. All voters know is that the incumbent has presided over bad times and should be thrown out of office.[47]

Split-ticket Voting and Dealignment. A final symptom of dealignment is a rise in **split-ticket voting**. In the 1970s and 1980s, from half to two-thirds of the electorate did not vote consistently for candidates of the same party. Instead, they chose among candidates of different parties or, more recently, voted for an independent candidate like Ross Perot.

Split-ticket voting may promote the kind of **governmental gridlock** that in turn angers the very same voters. For most of the period from 1968 until the 1992 election, the result of split-ticket voting was a Democratic Congress and a Republican president. Republican presidents and Democratic Congresses couldn't agree on taxation, the budget, social programs, foreign policy, and other matters. Each claimed a mandate from the voters, but the mandate was contradictory. Members of Congress blamed each other and the president for gridlock, and the president regularly blamed Congress. To govern at all, Republican and Democratic leaders concluded backroom deals, only to deny them publicly. Presidents Reagan and Bush resorted to frequent vetoes of congressional legislation.[48]

Is Decay Reversible?

Some measure of the difficulties the Democrats face became apparent in the first years of Clinton's presidency. The President quickly discovered that the voter mandate for "change" didn't easily translate into consistent support for his policies even in the Democratic Party. Besieged by Congressional Republicans and Ross Perot, Clinton also found that some Democratic officeholders were ready to abandon the party's agenda in the midst of a fury of lobbying and attacks. Clinton's victory, it seems, only restates the essential problem. Like the Republicans, the Democrats lacked broad-based grassroots ties that could serve as a counterweight to opposition attacks. Deprived of strong grassroots, the first Democratic administration in 15 years seemed unsupported and anchorless.

CONCLUSION: THE PARTY ISN'T OVER

Is it too late for the major parties to be revived as popular democratic instruments? Historically, times like ours have parented new parties and transformed old ones. For present-day Democrats and Republicans, the challenge is to entice millions of politically isolated citizens into public places where they can speak and act together. For the critics of our two parties gathered around Ross Perot, the challenge is to turn loyalty to a man who has never won an election into lively democratic conversation and focused action for political reform.

These are substantial challenges in the current political climate. To address them, we need to examine the developments that have weakened grassroots party politics. From Perot's teledemocracy to the women's movement, modern political campaigns are crucial tests for interests, movements, money, and candidates. In the next chapter, we probe their substance and meaning.

KEY TERMS

patronage
political machine
single-member district system
realigning elections
party systems
Progressivism
party identification

wedge issues
supply-side economics
Reagan Democrats
retrospective voting
split-ticket voting
governmental gridlock

SUGGESTED READINGS

Walter Dean Burnham, *The Current Crisis in American Politics* (New York: Oxford University Press, 1983). A collection of pathbreaking essays by a noted scholar of American elections.

E. J. Dionne, *Why Americans Hate Politics* (New York: Simon and Schuster, 1991). A journalist argues that liberals and conservatives of both parties are out of touch with the concerns of a restive citizenry.

Thomas Edsall and Mary Edsall, *Chain Reaction: The Impact of Race, Rights and Taxes on American Politics* (New York: Norton and Company, 1992). A compelling and controversial account

of the Democrats' decline and GOP's rise in the 1970s and 1980s.

Frank Sorauf and Paul Allen Beck, *Party Politics in America* (Glenview, Ill.: Scott Foresman, 1988). A rigorous and comprehensive account of contemporary party organization at the level of power and at the grassroots.

Martin Wattenberg, *The Decline of American Political Parties, 1952–1988* (Cambridge, Mass.: Harvard University Press, 1990). A political scientist traces the erosion of partisan identification and suggests many consequences.

CHAPTER·

9

The Best Campaigning
Money Can Buy

If loyalties to American political parties have become weaker at the grass-roots, campaigns have become ever more important. Electoral campaigns put American democracy to the test, for they're the moments when the potential power of democracy is most visible. If through elections American political destiny momentarily rests directly on the people's shoulders, the political campaign becomes the prime setting where political choices are formed.

Thus, political campaigns could be models of popular democracy. Political elites are directly challenged, and both elites and popular democrats must struggle for voter support. Candidates must respond to public opinion, meet voters, and withstand media and opponents' scrutiny. For voters, campaigns can be occasions for intensive debate and participation in political activities. With the focus on ordinary voters' concerns, otherwise insulated political elites have potentially much to lose during campaigns.

Present-day campaigns retain much of this popular democratic character. They can expand public debate, but also limit it. Although sometimes stimulating citizenship, campaigns also make citizens into perplexed and cynical spectators. They can draw voter attention to important political questions, or can they create and then exploit momentary passions irrelevant to long-lasting public concerns. Politicians can be held accountable for public actions and policies, or judged on their private behavior and personalities. While they can bolster popular democratic citizenship, campaigns can also reenforce elite democracy.

American political campaigns have always presented this mix of possibilities. Generally, however, as political parties at the grassroots have decayed, modern political campaigns have increasingly limited popular democracy. Our campaigns are now more personalized, money driven, and professionalized than they used to be. This chapter probes the effects of these developments on candidates, voters, and parties. It examines different campaigns for the ways they frame essential political questions, and suggests how to bring political campaigns back to their popular democratic roots.

PERSONALIZED CAMPAIGNS

From Ross Perot and his one-liners, through Clinton and his saxophone, and George Bush's exultant Desert Storm speeches, modern political contests are what political scientists call **candidate-centered campaigns.** Candidates are judged primarily by their planned dramatic actions, use of symbols, and TV performances. Issues matter only insofar as they underscore the candidates' personal qualities. Modern campaigns are mostly contests between candidates struggling for center stage.

In modern campaigns, presidential candidates can emerge from relative political obscurity and rise to national prominence within only weeks or months. A year before Jimmy Carter and Bill Clinton were elected president, fewer than one in five Americans knew who they were. Ross Perot achieved nearly instant status through highly visible performances on the *Larry King Live* show. The candidate-centered campaign forms (and for opponents, destroys) shifting emotional and political attachments among voters.[1]

Similarly, House and Senate campaigns are becoming miniature versions of the presidential "sweepstakes"—although party allegiances matter in these less visible races, they are increasingly candidate-centered as well. Candidates must first achieve personal fame and notoriety (**name recognition**). Turning that fame into the domination of the campaign debate is the second task. Winning on election day is the third. Once elected, politicians must protect their positive images from media revelations and future opponents.

Today's campaigns can be extraordinarily volatile. Voter opinions about individuals can shift according to charges, countercharges, and revelations during the campaign. Left to judge among constantly changing candidate reputations, voters come to distrust the truth value of all the images that politicians try to create.

The Nomination Process: Planning and Maintaining Momentum

The road to nomination and election as president is a struggle of endurance and planning. Presidential bids start long before election year and the fifty separate primaries and caucuses potential candidates must face to win their party's nomination (see Chapter 8). Incumbent presidents often have the chief advantage of recognition by the electorate before the election year begins.

For less well known presidential hopefuls, the hurdles of the campaign process are much more daunting and unpredictable. Major features of the process are summarized in Table 9.1. To win requires personal organization, money, perception, image, and luck. Take President Clinton's long voyage to the Democratic nomination and White House in 1992. Becoming the Democratic nominee meant establishing early credibility as a serious contender. Long before the voters even knew who he was, Clinton had raised substantial amounts of cash. He had impressed the "great mentioners"—newspaper columnists, network news anchors, and key Washington insiders whose attention makes or breaks a candidate's early chances. By the time Clinton declared his candidacy in October

---

TABLE 9.1

Campaigning for President: Essential Steps

Two years before the election

Goal: Become a viable candidate.
1. Form an electoral base and a distinctive theme.
2. Visit key states, like New Hampshire and Iowa, where convention delegates are first selected. Visit key politicians and potential contributors. Campaign for members of Congress in these states.
3. Establish contacts with news media by appearing before key interest groups and TV programs such as *Face the Nation* and *This Week with David Brinkley.*

One year before the election

Goals: Build a competent campaign team, achieve name recognition, raise enough money to hire a permanent campaign staff.
1. Register an official campaign organization with the Federal Elections Commission.
2. Fundraise in at least twenty states to qualify for federal assistance. Fundraise in other states to acquire the maximum allowed amount of money.
3. Assemble a campaign team that includes campaign managers, lawyers, and political consultants specializing in press relations, media, fundraising, polling, speechwriting, and issue development.
4. Campaign in Iowa and New Hampshire, but include key states like New York and Super Tuesday states that hold primaries the following March.
5. Announce candidacy.

TABLE 9.1

(continued)

~~~~~~~~~~

Primary season, January–June, election year

Goal: Assembling a majority of delegates to your party's national convention in the summer.

1. Win or take a close second in Iowa caucuses and New Hampshire primary in late January and February.
2. Sustain momentum by winning key states in early March's Super Tuesday primaries.
3. Continue to develop fundraising and staff for April and May primaries and caucuses, especially New York, Pennsylvania, Illinois, and Michigan.
4. Establish a lead over nearest contenders by late April, causing them to drop out. Pick up their supporters.
5. Begin to act like your party's nominee by unifying your party against the opposition.
6. Win last primaries by convincing margins.
7. Dominate rules, procedures, and platform deliberations preceding national convention. Interview and investigate vice-presidential candidates.
8. In your acceptance speech, unite your party while addressing the broader nation.

General election: Convention to November's first Tuesday

Goal: Amass 271 electoral votes and win the presidency.

1. Develop target states where campaign and media spending will be concentrated.
2. Develop a theme that dominates your campaign.
3. Develop a coalition for electoral victory and possible later governing. Enlist members of Congress and prominent local politicians.
4. Develop a common line of attack against your opponent(s).
5. Expand your organization, especially "soft money" fundraising. (See Key Terms.)
6. Establish system for transition to presidency.

1991, he had compiled a long list of financial backers and contacts in both journalism and academia.

The biggest boost to Clinton's candidacy, however, came from events beyond his control. The party's best known leaders—Mario Cuomo, Lloyd Bentsen, and Jesse Jackson—decided not to run. Instead, Clinton faced five even more obscure opponents, freeing up money that would otherwise have been donated to better known Democrats and garnering more media attention.

Clinton and his then small campaign staff had to win the party's early primaries and caucuses, whose participants were the most loyal Democratic voters. Clinton pitched his campaign to the middle of the Democratic party but amended his stance by saying he was a "new" kind of Democrat willing to moderate but not jettison the party's traditional liberalism. Clinton posed as the candidate of a new generation, as a competent coalition builder, and as the only candidate who could regain lost Democratic Southerners. At the same time, Clinton hoped to win over the party's traditional supporters by attacking the economic policies of Reagan and Bush.

As a relatively conservative Southern Democrat, Clinton in late 1991 might have seemed a long shot for the Democratic nomination. But the important early Democratic primaries are in New Hampshire and the Southern states, where Clinton's moderation was an advantage. Consequently, Clinton threw most of his campaign activities and money into New Hampshire and the Super Tuesday contests of early March. Winning or coming close in these contests created a sense of "momentum" and "inevitability" about his candidacy, resulting in increased media attention and campaign contributions, and promoting later primary victories in states with stronger liberal traditions like New York, Illinois, and Michigan. By the time "big" states like Ohio and California cast their votes in June, Clinton would be the only real choice, as other candidates fell victim to lack of money, resources, and momentum. He could then unite the party by the Democratic convention in July, confidently attacking the GOP in the Fall campaign.[2]

The Clinton strategy eventually succeeded. Yet, typical of candidate-centered campaigns, much of Clinton's success was based on the drama of scandal and his successful struggle to overcome it. Clinton became a household name, not through his politics or ideas but through allegations of personal misconduct. His supposed affairs and draft-dodging, and his mostly successful struggles to rebut these charges, put his family, morals, and character on center stage. Before voters knew much about him, Clinton and his wife Hillary, appeared on "60 Minutes" to rebut charges of immorality. A personalized campaign may not have

Bill Clinton never faced charges as serious as this in 1992, but he did withstand numerous character assaults.

been Clinton's wish, but that is what he and most other candidates face. A measure of his success came from transforming initially negative images of his character into respect for his competence and later guarded admiration for his rise from humble and troubled circumstances. After his second-place finish in New Hampshire, he dubbed himself the "Comeback Kid," and by the time he was nominated in July 1992, everyone knew the personal stories of his alcoholic father, persevering mother, troubled brother, and rise from difficult circumstances. Candidate-centered contests are less battles between differing ideologies than referenda on the performances of candidates.[3]

If candidates are so important in campaigns, it is important to ask about their personality characteristics required for success in the heavily mined and shifting electoral battlefield. First, potential winners like Clinton must have "fire in the belly" a superextraordinary personal ambition to succeed and to dedicate one's entire life to what it takes to endure and win in an election. Second, candidates must be thick-skinned. With the entire process centered on you, your personality, your character, your past, your record and your campaign performance, the modern candidates must be able to withstand blows to the ego that would fell lesser mortals. Third, modern candidates cannot be particularly circumspect; they must put their noses to the grindstone, strategizing long in advance. Bill Clinton was thinking about his quest for the presidency even when he was a student at Oxford University. Ambition, thick skin, and type A personality are not new to politics in America. Because today's campaigns feature personalities in conflict, however, successful candidates can never be certain about the public's loyalties. In sharp contrast to the stabilities in public opinion noted in Chapter 6, Figure 9.1 reveals how candidate popularity can shift during campaigns. For candidates, modern campaigns are often unpredictable roller coasters.

THE PERMANENT CAMPAIGN GAME

To protect themselves against risk, elected officials engage in what Sidney Blumenthal has called the "permanent campaign." With little but their fragile images and personal backers on which to rely, politicians must constantly look over their shoulders, defending themselves. Like entrepreneurs, they must establish "product loyalty." Although politicians may not like the permanent campaign, it's an understandable reaction to the tumult they perceive on the electoral battleground.[4]

Like any game, the permanent campaign has stated and unstated rules, tried and true strategies, and techniques that successful candidates learn quickly. In recent years, most voters and some politicians have become disillusioned with the campaign game. But in the absence of new rules, the campaign game often exists by default, with enormous consequences for the democratic debate. The following sections examine the strategies of the permanent campaign game. The

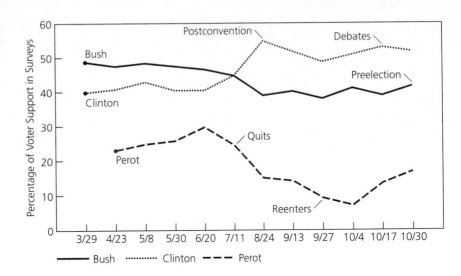

FIGURE 9.1

1992 Swings in Popularity

object of the game is to win votes. Yet, what role do ordinary voters play in the campaign game? Are they pawns, spectators, or players?

Money

The essential pieces of the campaign game are the chips—the money needed to even contemplate a race for the House, Senate, or presidency. How much is necessary? Where does it come from?

Dimensions of the Cash Pile. Like college tuition, congressional campaign costs have risen more rapidly than inflation. The average House winner spent about $550,000 in 1992, while the average Senate victor spent over $4 million. Stated in another way, the average Senator had to raise about $2,000 every day of his or her six-year term to stay in office, while an average House Member needed only $750 daily. Two decades ago, electoral victory cost only a fifth as much.[5]

In 1992, the presidential primaries of both parties cost about $200 million. Clinton and Bush received over $117 million in public funds to run their fall campaigns, over two and a half times the 1976 figure. That figure does not include the far greater amounts of money from so-called "soft" sources that would raise the total to close to $350 million. (See section on "soft money" below). Adding Perot's $69 million and considering inflation, the contest was the most costly in American history. Yet, despite the rise in 1992 to over $2.5 billion for all federal offices, electing the American government still costs less than the combined advertising budgets of the Big Three automakers, or of Procter & Gamble and Dow Chemical.[6]

Who Money Favors. The size of the cash pile is a concern. But equally important is the distribution of campaign cash among incumbents and challengers and Democrats and Republicans in Congress. In the last several decades, congressional incumbents of both parties have had an overwhelming advantage in campaign money. Those who occupied influential committee and subcommittee posts in the House and Senate received an even larger cut. In fact, some Congressional leaders have so much campaign cash that they are able to form their own organizations devoted to funding—and influencing—needy candidates and colleagues who are less fortunate. Senate Minority Leader Bob Dole raised an astounding $7.1 million to defend his safe Kansas seat from 1989 to 1993; Dole gave almost $1 million of it to more vulnerable colleagues. Democratic House Speaker Tom Foley and Majority Leader Richard Gephardt dispensed over $.5 million to selected Democratic colleagues during the same period.[7]

Table 9.2 shows the massive incumbency advantage. By 1992, incumbents raised twelve times more money than did challenges from political action committees, or PACs. (See more on these below). Of approximately $374 million coming to House candidates from all sources in 1992, incumbents received $249 million. Meanwhile, 1992 Senate incumbents outspent their challengers by 3 to 1. In the 1980s and 1990s, incumbents' money advantage actually rose.[8]

Until the 1992 and 1994 elections, being a House and Senate incumbent almost guaranteed reelection. In 1988, only 7 incumbents were defeated in House races, and in 1990 only 15 were. Senate races were similar: In 1988 4 incumbents lost their seats and in 1990 only 1 did. In the 1980s, 95 percent of incumbents retained their House seats—a lower turnover than in the former Soviet Union's Politburo. Because they draw better known challengers, Senate seats are sometimes more competitive. Still, 83 percent of their incumbents were reelected in the last decade.

With all these money advantages, what did it take for an incumbent to lose? Ross Baker has written that most defeated incumbents have to be either "unlucky, inept or venal."[9] Former Nevada Republican Senator Chic Hecht was inept. Hecht was defeated in 1988 after a string of gaffes that would have made even Dan Quayle blush. The Senator, who had not been able to prevent the siting of nuclear waste dumps in his home state of Nevada, continually referred to them

TABLE 9.2	**House Races**	**$ Spent (millions)**
Incumbency Money Advantage, 1992	Incumbents	203
	Challengers	63
	Senate Races	**$ Spent (millions)**
	Incumbents	65
	Challengers	25

Source: Federal Election Commission, press release, March 4, 1993, p. 7.

as "nuclear suppositories." A former Army intelligence officer, he continually said "overt" operations when he really meant "covert." During a debate, Hecht had to ask a reporter to refresh his memory about the content of the Constitution's First Amendment.

The incumbents' money advantage has not always meant electoral victory, but most of the time it has. Moreover, it has established the central rule of the campaign game: to win, challengers must match or surpass incumbent money piles. In most elections in which incumbents have been defeated, challengers have raised at least 80 percent as much money as their incumbent opponents. Most challengers, however, simply cannot raise that kind of cash. In House races, the median amount challengers spent in the late 1980s was $48,000, and virtually all that spent that amount were defeated. The successful challengers, on the other hand, had over $540,000 at their disposal. Thus, the permanent campaign game does not always favor incumbents. Still, the serious challenges to incumbents also rest on big money.[10]

1992 and 1994: The More Things Change, the More They Stay the Same.
Because campaign cash had become an issue, the 1992 elections were supposed to be different. Congressional scandal and gridlock led to a general indictment of Congress by angry citizens and potential challengers alike. In March 1992, only 17 percent of Americans thought that Congress was doing a good job. To retain their seats, incumbents tried to distance themselves from the legislative body in which they served. House incumbents were on the defensive for an additional reason. After the 1990 census, congressional seats were reapportioned and district lines redrawn by the states to reflect shifts in the American population. Many incumbents, especially in the Northeast and Midwest, were forced to run in new districts where they were little known. Taken together, these factors led over 52 House members into retirement and another 13 to run for other offices. Nineteen additional House members were defeated in the spring primaries, at the height of public concern about the House banking scandal (see Chapter 12). Another 24 incumbents lost in the November election.

In November, 110 new House members and 13 new Senators were elected, the biggest turnover in Congress since 1948. With many new women and nonwhite members, the Senate and House looked slightly more representative of the American population than it had been. Moreover, many of the victorious challengers in both parties won precisely because they had campaigned against corruption and gridlock in Congress. Both newly elected and incumbent members of Congress promised to work to reform Congress if elected.

The new 1992 members may or may not enact changes; Chapter 12 discusses that subject. This chapter's focus is the 1992 campaign game. Money remained the chief ingredient of electoral success. Some senior, well-funded, and powerful members of the House, like Democrat Mary Rose Oakar and Republican Guy Van der Jagt, were heavily implicated in the House banking scandal. They lost, despite outspending their opponents. But most of the 325 House members involved in the scandal and who nonetheless stood for reelection in November still won. Among House incumbents running for re–election, 90 percent were returned to office, and in the Senate the figure was 85 percent.

The reason was that 1992 incumbents greatly increased their cash piles to fend off challengers. Senate incumbents compiled a record 9 to 1 money advantage over their opponents from PACs and a 3 to 1 margin in overall campaign spending. Although House challengers increased their spending dramatically, incumbents increased theirs even more.[11] Thereby, rising voter distrust of Congress did not result in much of a revolution, at least regarding campaign money. At best, popular anger made incumbent members of Congress insecure about their reelection prospects. Some were defeated, and others won against challengers by lesser victory margins. Yet in general, the winners staved off defeat by raising still more money. With some notable exceptions, money strategies still worked.

Moreover, although almost all challengers attacked Congress in 1992, the victorious ones played the money game as well as and sometimes better than the incumbents they defeated. As a group they were committed to change Congress and the money game, but Beth Donovan has observed that upon arrival in Washington, "the freshmen cancelled plans to torch Congress."[12]

The 1994 Congressional elections handed the GOP majorities in both House and Senate for the first time since 1954 and defied the trends of the last two decades. Notable incumbents went down to defeat, including former Speaker Tom Foley. Among the most rancorous, negative, and expensive in American electoral history, the 1994 campaign addressed an electorate suspicious of both parties and hostile to all Washington "insiders." But on Election Day, independent voters and Perot supporters vented their rage solely on the governing Democrats and President Clinton. Survey data showed that swing voters had moved to the GOP not because of its ideology, but because they were frustrated with government and willing to give Republican "outsiders" a chance at Congressional control; the GOP didn't lose a single incumbent in the Senate or the House.

The 1994 GOP surge partly defied the "incumbency advantage" norm, especially in the South. But money also helped the GOP, and there were other consistencies with the usual campaign game. Incumbent senators amassed a 3 to 1 money advantage over challengers. Only two Democratic incumbent senators were defeated, and both ran only even in the money race with their GOP challengers. It was in their victories in "open seats" that the GOP gained most of their new senators, and here the GOP had equal or better financing.

In their many House victories, Republican candidates in most cases either matched or outspent losing Democratic incumbents. In the open seats won by the GOP, the Republicans had an overall money advantage. GOP House incumbents all returned partly because they had a 5 to 1 money advantage. And even in the huge GOP tide, over 80 percent of Democratic House incumbents survived. Ironically, it was House Democratic freshmen—yesterday's anti-incumbent "outsiders"—that were the most vulnerable to GOP challengers. Perhaps in 1996 or 1998, anti-incumbency fever will turn its force against 1994's Republican freshmen "outsiders," who played the insider money game to perfection.

Still, there is evidence that members of Congress want to break their addiction to the money game, if only because the entire process has become a burden not only for the voters but also for the candidates. In the words of defeated Pennsylvania Democrat Peter Kostmayer, who raised $1.2 million but still lost his House seat in 1992: "Fundraising became the dominant part of my campaigns—and campaigning came to dominate my life. . . . Members of Congress despise the process but are addicted to it, terrified that change means defeat."[13]

Campaign Rules

Where do people like Kostmayer go for their cash? The cynical and simple view is that candidates sell themselves to special interests or to the rich in a frank exchange of money for favors.

There are some people in Congress who do sell influences in return for campaign cash. California's former Democratic Senator Alan Cranston was censured for trading cash for special favors to savings and loan mogul Charles Keating. Others, like New York's Al D'Amato, nicknamed "Senator Sleaze," have come close to the same fate. Generally, though, outright bribery is ruled out by astute players of the permanent campaign game. To most members of Congress it is inappropriate and unethical. To the merely cynical, bribery could backfire as it did for Cranston. But most of all, bribery is simply not necessary. Current campaign finance laws keep the money coming through more complex, and entirely legal, political channels.

The size and distribution of cash are strongly related to the sources permitted to contribute to campaigns under federal law. Current federal campaign financing laws are largely products of the revulsion following President Nixon's 1972 campaign, fueled by the revelations of the Watergate scandal. The Nixon campaign took in millions of unreported cash contributions. Often handed over in paper bags or in carry-on luggage, Nixon's money came from interests as diverse as dairy farmers, the ITT Corporation, and individuals like H. Ross Perot (who gave $200,000 to Nixon in 1972). Usually, the Nixon people returned the contributions in the currency of ambassadorships, tax loopholes, or lenient interpretations of federal regulations.

Nevertheless, the Federal Election Campaign Act of 1971 and its subsequent amendments were passed with a real intention to reform the process. Twenty or so years later, however, virtually no one is satisfied with its key provisions. The act's least controversial feature has been establishment of a Federal Elections Commission, mandated to judge violations of the law and to compile, for the first time, data about who is giving how much money to whom.

As Table 9.3 shows, federal campaign laws establish different procedures to regulate presidential and congressional elections. When written, presidential campaign finance laws were something of a model. Theoretically, they abolished the worst abuses of campaign fundraising and established spending caps and full disclosure in return for taxpayer support. Critics of these provisions initially claimed they excluded independent and third-party candidates. But the attacks

TABLE 9.3

Federal Regulations,
Funding of
Presidential
and Congressional
Campaigns, 1994

Disclosure

Campaigns must report all contributions over $100 and expenditures to the Federal Election Commission (FEC).

Campaigns may not

Accept contributions from foreigners.
Take cash contributions over $100.
Take contributions over the prescribed limits.

Individual contribution limits

$1,000 to each candidate or candidate committee for each election.
$25,000 limit to all federal candidates.
$20,000 limit to *national* party committees.
$5,000 limit to PAC or other political committee.
No federal limits on contributions to state parties (soft money).
No limits on contributions that are independent of a candidate's organization.

Political action committees (PACs): Congressional Elections

PACs must have at least 50 members, give to at least 5 federal candidates, and register six months before the first contribution.
$5,000 limit to any candidate in any one election.
$15,000 limit to any one national party committee in one year.
No regulation of PAC contributions at state party level.
No caps on absolute spending by any single PAC.
No limits on the amount of "independent" expenditures.

Presidential primary funding

Candidates running for their party's nomination may receive matching funds from the federal treasury if they raise at least $5,000 in contributions of $250 or less in 20 states.
In return, candidates must accept spending caps established by the FEC.

Presidential general election funding

The federal government pays the entire cost of the general election campaigns of the major presidential candidates. Those candidates representing smaller parties qualify for funding by receiving 5% or more of the vote in a presidential election. In return, presidential candidates accept absolute spending caps.
Money from so called "soft" sources is not counted as part of official campaign expenses.

lessened when independent John Anderson received 1980 matching funds, and have almost disappeared because Lenora Fulani, of the small New Alliance Party, received 1992 matching funds. In recent years, fewer taxpayers have checked the box that allocates $1 of their tax bills to the fund, but the fund will probably be broadened anyway. (See discussion of "soft money" below.)

Much more complex and controversial is regulation of spending for House and Senate races, also summarized in Table 9.3. To limit large contributions (as opposed to powerful contributors), federal law limits amounts contributed to the official campaign organization of any one candidate and also requires full disclosure of contributors' names to the FEC. But the 1976 U.S. Supreme Court case *Buckley* v. *Valeo* declared attempts to impose absolute campaign spending limits in congressional elections to be unconstitutional. The Court refused to limit the amounts of personal money candidates could contribute to their own campaigns and, most important, left unregulated the amount of spending "independent" of a candidate's organization. Through additional court rulings, members of Congress elected before 1979 were even allowed to keep unspent campaign monies for personal use, should they be defeated or retire from Congress.[14]

After these rulings, a prominent legal loophole turned out to be "independent" efforts on behalf of candidates. Individuals and groups could provide "in kind" services—everything from benefit rock concerts to free polling and consulting—to candidates without limitations. Volunteering isn't counted as a campaign contribution, nor are registration drives targeting people inclined to vote for one of the candidates. Tax exempt "foundations" have been established to funnel research services into campaigns. The wealthy can "lend" money to campaigns without regulation or disclosure.[15] (See more on "soft" money below).

PACs. The most important consequence of the new laws has been the formation of **political action committees** or **PACs,** "voluntary" organizations that channel money from members of corporations, trade associations, labor unions, and other groups into House and Senate campaigns. From a mere 608 in 1974, their numbers have grown to over 4,000 by 1994. Individual companies form *corporate* PACs and whole industries create *trade association* PACs. Labor unions and professional associations form PACS as well. Any medium size company or trade association peddling California prunes, beer, soda, jet fighters, or American wheat is likely to sponsor a PAC. The health insurance industry increased their PAC representations and campaign contributions when health care reforms were proposed in 1993. Dentists, realtors, teachers, lawyers, cheese producers, exporters, importers, and other claimants on legislation all have their PACs as well. Neither college professors nor college students have a PAC; nor do the homeless, welfare recipients, or poor children.

Ideological PACs usually have broader goals than increasing tariffs on Turkish figs or promoting the use of ethanol. For instance, in the late 1970s and early 1980s, the National Conservative Political Action Committee (NCPAC) became famous and feared for its ability to target money to defeat liberal Democratic senators. The National Rifle Association (NRA) contributed over $1.7 million to federal candidates in the 1992 election season. Ideological PACs crisscross the political spectrum. Although conservative ideological PACs are better funded, environmental and feminist PACs (especially Emily's List) have grown as well.

Since the 1970s, PAC money has constituted an increasing share of contributions to candidates, even though individual contributions are still greater. Despite calls for the regulation or even elimination of PACs (see below), especially corporate ones, they are likely to survive by a different name because of the powerful interests they represent.[16]

The sheer number and variety of PACs make them seem to be examples of democracy at work. Most are small and give money to only a selected group of incumbents and challengers. Moreover, the amounts of money most individual PACs give are unimpressive by Washington standards. Thus, the idea that PACs buy influence may seem extreme. Given the contribution limits, their effects could be seen as minimal.

Indeed, rules governing PACs appear to create a level playing field open to all. Among the richest PACs are the left-leaning Machinists Union and the conservative American Bankers Association. Any group of fifty people can form a PAC. Without giving to a PAC, individuals still have the ability to contribute directly to a candidate.[17]

Yet a closer look at PACs and their cumulative effects reveals a massive conservative ideological and pro-business bias in their operation. Corporate and trade association PACs—generally conservative groups—outspend labor union and other liberal PACs by nearly 2 to 1. Although the U.S. Chamber of Commerce's PAC, the NRA's PAC, and anti-abortion PACs have different legislative agendas, *Washington Post* correspondent Thomas Byrne Edsall's comment that "the financial elites of all these groups share a common conservative economic view" cannot be taken lightly.[18]

As we noted above, congressional incumbents are vastly more popular than challengers with PACs. PACs usually give the maximum to members of congressional committees that deal with legislation of direct bearing on the PAC's interest. As a result, the chairs and senior members of the major committees in Congress usually receive large amounts of PAC cash even though they usually face very limited challenges in their districts and states. Ten months before the 1990 election, PAC money helped Republican Senator Phil Gramm of Texas to accumulate over $6 million in contributions and New York Democratic Congressman Charles Schumer over $1.2 million.[19]

The money trail may have a special effect on individual Democrats in Congress. The liberalism of many Democratic incumbents is probably diluted by "split level" contributions. Democrats in Congress used to get the bulk of their money from unions and liberal PACs. But a greater current source of Democratic money is business and trade association PACs formed by realtors, oil producers, insurance companies, utilities, large law firms, and brokerage houses. Congressional Democrats now receive over three times more money from corporations than from unions. Jake Lewis, a long-time Senate committee aide, comments, "We've had a lot of liberals (on the Banking Committee) who were good on housing and would take care of the banks on the other side. As long as they take care of the banks, they could be as liberal as they wanted." Such comments account for part of the Democratic party's identity problems: In the late 1940s, more than 50 percent of voters described Democrats as the party "of average working people." Today, only 13 percent do.[20]

Republicans get their money from interests that are less contradictory. Almost all of it comes from conservative ideological, corporate, and trade association PACs. The pro-business "purity" of campaign contributions reenforces Republican conservatism, whereas the Democrats' variety weakens the party's once strong identity with economic liberalism.[21]

Are PACs really grassroots organizations? In theory, local church groups and neighborhood associations can fund PACs as much as business executives do. Yet in 1992, only 18 percent of American adults gave money either to PACs or directly to campaigns. Studies indicate a tremendous class skew in who gives. Only 1 percent of those with family incomes under $10,000 a year contribute to PACs or parties and candidates. Although only about one in thirty American families makes $125,000 a year or more, this group contributes over a quarter of all campaign dollars. As a form of political participation available to average citizens, giving money ranks well below voting or discussing politics.[22]

The class bias built into the money game is furthered by the fact that members of corporate hierarchies make the lion's share of political contributions. Corporations have ways of convincing employees to give campaign money. Take the case of Cherry Payment Systems, a Midwest marketing company. In February 1992, a regional manager, William Neiss, received a letter from Cherry's chairman recommending that he buy—for $15,000—a table at the "President's Dinner," a "gala" affair with President Bush, Vice President Quayle, and other Republican luminaries. The letter was accompanied by a memo from Neiss's boss, asking "who will be in attendance for this great opportunity to rub elbows with the most powerful people in the country?" A later memo warned: "The people who join us are going to display both their commitment to the company and their desire to get the most of the money they earn by supporting the Republican Party." Neiss refused to buy in, and the next day was fired. Although the Cherry Systems case may be extreme, and probably illegal under election law (Neiss is suing), executives in major corporations are often "asked" to make contributions to PACs and other organizations favored by management.[23]

Similarly, doctors, lawyers, real estate brokers, and others are very likely to be members of professional associations that form PACs. Less likely members are bank tellers, secretaries, hamburger flippers, hospital orderlies, and the other nonunionized job categories in what was called in Chapter 4 the "new service economy."

Like American corporations, the internal organization of most PACs is thus hardly a model of democracy. When PACs make decisions about how to spend their money, many members are generally left out of the discussion. In the words of Iowa Republican Congressman Jim Leach, "individuals who control other people's money become power brokers in an elitist society. Their views, not the small contributors to their associations, become the views that carry influence."[24]

In this way, PACs both create and sustain the congressional status quo. That status quo provides access points to corporate and trade associations intent on bending federal laws their way. The policy consequences of monied access to Congress—from the savings and loan collapse to watered-down health care reform, from tax cuts for the wealthy to the absence of strict regulations of toxic waste disposal—cannot, however, be blamed solely on PACs. But they are a part of it. In Senator Dale Bumpers's words: "If you're on Banking or on the Finance Committee, you don't even have to open your mouth. They'll throw money at you over the transom."[25]

Soft Money. Both the personal campaign and the campaign money game are direct outgrowths of the decline of political parties at the grassroots. Yet there is really nothing incompatible about either and a new type of top-heavy, money-loaded political party. Political scientists Barbara and Stephen Salmore have suggested that both Republicans and Democrats are becoming "parties of office-holders." With few soldiers and many generals, our political parties are still strong in Washington.[26]

Another new party function the Salmores could have included is the parties' roles as "mail drops for money," distributors of cash and advice to the personal campaigns of both incumbents and challengers. The Republican National Committee and the GOP's Senate and House campaign committees led the way in the mid-1970s. They began to provide Republican candidates with cash, consultants, pollsters, direct mail advice, media facilities, and quick courses in public speaking and press relations. By 1988, the Republican party spent over $250 million on such assistance. The Democratic National Committee and the party's House and Senate campaign committees were late getting into the game, but by 1988 raised $135 million. By 1992, the money gap between the two "mail-drop" parties had nearly closed.

Although the amount of money various party committees and member PACs can contribute to candidates remains limited by law, one gigantic loophole has strengthened the new top-heavy parties. Both parties have found a legal way to peel unlimited, uncapped, and even undisclosed **soft money** from contributors.

The loophole is promoted through the legal distinction between the state and national political parties (see Chapter 8). State party activity is not subject to federal law. Any contributor can, for example, donate unlimited cash to the Colorado State Republican Committee for ads, polls, and "get out the vote drives" for Colorado Republicans. Not so coincidentally, helping small-town Colorado Republicans also aids Republican congressional, senatorial, and presidential candidates. If desired, the Colorado GOP can even donate money to its poorer party colleagues in other states. The national committees of both parties can accept sizable contributions, and the money can be put into the states where its use is legal.

The soft-money loophole allowed Colorado brewer Joseph Coors to donate $150,000 to the Republican cause. *New Yorker* writer Elizabeth Drew reports its effects, quoting a deputy chairman of the Republican National Committee: "If Mobil Oil wanted to give you $20 million, I think they would give you $20 million bucks, and you don't have to show it."[27] Table 9.4 lists some of the

TABLE 9.4	Who They Are	What They Gave	What Happened
All-Stars of Team 100	William Lloyd Davis Developer Santa Monica, California	$176,540	FAA clears way for $35 million federal grant for Denver air terminal adjacent to industrial park sponsored by Davis's group.
	Heinz Prechter President, American Sunroof Corp. Southgate, Michigan	$183,100	Joins Bush's trip to Japan; lands lucrative deal for his company.
	Edgar Marston III General Counsel, Southdown, Inc. Houston	$125,000	At Southdown's behest, administration imposes first cement tariffs in twenty-six years.
	Lodwrick Cook CEO, Atlantic Richfield Los Angeles	$862,360	Provision for reformulated gas added to Bush's clean air proposal; White House push for Alaska oil drilling.
	T. Boone Pickens Oilman, corporate raider Amarillo, Texas	$302,660	Pressed by Pickens, administration inserts natural-gas proposal into national energy plan.
	J. W. Boswell Agribusinessman Los Angeles	$125,000	Bush releases water from federally controlled reservoirs, benefitting Boswell's agribusiness interests in California's Central Valley.
	Edward Addison President, Southern Company Services Atlanta	$105,000	Justice Department kills two-year, $50 million criminal tax probe of Southern, a major electric utility.

Source: "George Bush's Ruling Class," COMMON CAUSE MAGAZINE, April/May/June 1992, 2030 M Street, Washington, D.C., 20036, 202/833-1200. Used with permission.

contributors to Team 100, the name the GOP gives to its soft-money organization.

Before 1992, the GOP's soft-money efforts had yielded three times more cash than the Democrats were able to raise. But first the prospect, and then the reality, of Clinton in the White House turned out to be very good for the Democrats' bank accounts. Between July 1992 and June 1994, the Democrats collected over $40 million in soft-money contributions—more than the GOP had been able to raise in the first two years of the Bush administration. As with PAC contributions, Democratic soft-money donors are somewhat more diverse than the GOP's sources. Time-Warner, Inc. topped the list with $.5 million in contributions. Other corporate sources include the ever-generous Archer Daniels Midland Company, the Walt Disney Company, MCA, and the Bronfmans, who are owners of Seagram's and big investors in Time-Warner. But unions such as the American Federation of County, State and Municipal Employees (AFSCME) and the National Education Association (NEA) both donated over $200,000.[28]

With this much money under their control, both our political parties are very much alive. Increasingly, though, their identities are as loose alliances of wealthy contributors or conduits for both soft and hard money.

RISE OF HIGH-TECH POLITICS

Although money has always been important as a campaign resource, it has not necessarily been dominant. Why do political campaigns go to such great lengths to get it?

One way to answer this query is to look at what money buys. Money is necessary to buy the new high technology of politics—everything from elaborate and continuous polling, to expensive TV advertisements, to teams of experts and press handlers, to a multitude of modern ways to shape voter attitudes. In the personal campaign game, when a candidate's reputation can change overnight, political high technology and professionalization promise knowledge and therefore control of both the campaign and the voters. While money is the currency of the campaign game, equally important are the high-tech politics and enhanced professional strategies of candidates. Before we assess the impact of political high tech on the democratic debate, it must be defined more precisely.

Political Consultants

Political campaigns used to be run by party "bosses"—stereotypically fat, usually bald, untidy, cigar-smoking, and rough-talking men. These bosses have been replaced by new ones—well-coiffed, personable, and generally healthy-looking political consultants. Unlike party professionals of the past, modern consultants are accountable to no group of voters in wards and precincts, but only to the candidates who pay their salaries. Unlike the scorned party boss of history, the consultant doesn't employ disciplined party hacks, buy votes, or organize many volunteer efforts. The currency of political consultants is high technology as it applies to politics.

Professional political consultants have been around for about thirty years. Nowadays, they have become necessary and even dominant components in most political campaigns. Like many new things, the political consulting business began in California, where the firms of Spencer Roberts and Whitaker and Baxter pioneered the new profession. Ronald Reagan's 1966 rise to the California governorship was one of Stu Spencer's major achievements and one of the first for campaign handlers. Almost no present-day candidate can do without consultants, if only because all the other candidates have them.[29]

What do consultants offer? Candidates have choices about whether they hire a "full service firm" or form their own "campaign team" from the expert pool. In the past, most political consultants worked for conservatives, liberals, or moderates, depending on the consultants' own ideological preferences. But campaign professionalization is now so advanced that increasing numbers of firms and individuals hire themselves to the highest bidder, especially in House races. Campaign consultants have even generated their own monthly magazine.[30]

Some political consultants have become powerful and famous in their own right. Jimmy Carter's pollster, Patrick Caddell, George Bush's Robert Teeter, and Bill Clinton's James Carville and Paul Begala not only ran their patrons' campaigns, but also served as important presidential advisers after the election victories they helped bring about. More typical, however, are specialists of lesser fame who concentrate on polling, TV and radio advertising, direct-mail fundraising, and press relations.

Polling

Polling is the basis for all other modern campaign activities. Surveys plumb both name recognition and voter attitudes about candidates, their opponents, and the issues of most and least concern to voters. In well-funded campaigns, polling provides constant, even daily tracking of voter opinion, allowing experts to monitor the campaign's success in reaching groups targeted for selective appeals. In recent years, polling has been supplemented by the use of **focus groups.** A small number of people selected by the pollsters are invited to view videos of the candidate's recent public appearances and TV performances. Sometimes they are asked to push "hot" and "cold" buttons as they watch, indicating degrees of positive or negative reactions to what they see and hear. Through both polling and focus groups, campaign specialists test and refine changing campaign themes and strategies.[31]

Media Advertising

Polling is useful only insofar as the candidate's weaknesses are dimmed and strengths accented in subsequent TV and radio advertising. Media advertising currently is the most expensive part of Senate, gubernatorial, and presidential races. The importance of campaign media specialists has grown accordingly. They've got to make quick choices about the themes of commercials. (Which "issues" should be presented? Should the candidate talk in the ads? When should positives be reinforced? When should opponents be attacked?) Media consultants also decide where and when to purchase TV and radio time, how to pace the commercials during the course of a campaign, and how to respond to an opponent's attacks. In the early days of TV advertising, consultants usually developed ad themes well in advance of campaigns. But in recent years, and especially in the 1988 and 1992 presidential races, TV advertising strategies have become "interactive." Media specialists must sometimes create new ads overnight to respond to an opponent's attack or shift campaign strategy to reflect the latest focus group and tracking poll findings.

Media consultants for presidential candidates cannot simply manufacture images out of thin air, because the major candidates usually have established records. But in the much more numerous congressional and state races, where candidates are often unknown, the potential for creativity is enormous. The consultant's dream is a pliable candidate who allows the experts to work unhindered. For example, consultant Robert Goodman did a marvelous job creating Malcolm Wallop as a retired Wyoming senator back in 1978. Wallop, a New Yorker by birth, a Yale graduate, and a polo-playing relative of Queen Elizabeth, was effectively cast as an average Western cowboy. Here's a transcript of one Goodman ad.

> VISUAL: (Wallop, dressed as a cowboy, is saddling and mounting his horse.)
>
> ANNOUNCER: Everywhere you look these days, the federal government is there, telling you what they think, telling you what they think you ought to think. Telling you how to do things, setting up rules you can't follow. I think the federal government is going too far. Now they say if you don't take a portable facility along with you on a roundup, you can't go.
>
> VISUALS: (Wallop appears angry and disgusted, matching the announcer's sarcastic tone, as the camera pans a porta-potty strapped to a donkey tied to Wallop's horse.)
>
> ANNOUNCER: We need someone to tell 'em about Wyoming. Malcolm Wallop will.
>
> POSTER: Malcolm Wallop for US Senate.[32]

Goodman's version of this cowboy senator "walloped" his Democratic opponent in the fall election.

Direct-Mail and Media Fundraising

Political advertising and polling are expensive. To help pay for advertising and polling consultants, modern campaigns need fundraising consultants. In congressional races, maintaining contacts with PACs and with the national and state parties who dispense money requires trained specialists. Presidential primaries now often couples advertisements with fundraising appeals through toll-free 800 numbers. Computer direct-mail experts handle the funding of most campaigns, however. Consultants in direct mail compile names from friendly political organizations, magazine subscription lists, the professions, and interest groups such as the American Medical Association or the National Association of Realtors. They tailor the text of computer-generated letters to accent themes of interest to the addressees.

Like polling and advertising, direct mail features virtually no two-way conversations between the candidates' staff and the voters. Approval or disapproval is measured solely in terms of money gained versus the fundraising costs. A bad direct-mail expert, for instance, might neglect to mention a candidate's pro-gun policy to readers of *Field and Stream* or might write a letter with false claims that could be leaked to the candidate's opponents and later used to discredit its creator. Good direct-mail experts are more sensitive to the limits of the possible. They may not even have contacts with the candidate's organization and may work for PACs or entirely separately from official campaign organizations. In 1980, NCPAC, a pioneer in direct mail, took credit for defeating four liberal Democratic senators. Direct mail funded "attack ads" but did not urge a vote for the liberals' opponents. Direct mail has had enormous effects on campaigns. In 1986 alone, the Republican party used it to raise $256 million.[33]

Press and Media Relations

The general relationship between campaigns and the news media is discussed in Chapter 7. Here we note some new departures. "Press relations" no longer means just handing out press kits and making the candidate available for chats with the national press.

Today's press relations techniques are much more complex than in the past. In the 1992 presidential elections, press relations specialists helped all the candidates to avoid traditional reporters and established forums. Consultants tried to find novel ways for candidates to communicate directly with voters, thereby avoiding the insider "hard-ball" questions often posed by national reporters. With direct satellite hookups to local TV stations, the campaign strategist decides where and when the candidate's valuable time can be best used in targeted media markets. Press relations can also be expressed through duelling fax machines. In 1992, the Little Rock, Arkansas, headquarters of the Clinton campaign successfully countered the daily Bush faxes impugning Clinton's record by choreographing "rapid responses" to every news outlet in the country.[34]

Effects of High-Tech Political Consultants on Election Results

Campaigning involves a large bureaucracy and the money to fuel it. One view of the political consulting business is that it is not worth much concern. Since hundreds of would-be image makers have failed, the consulting business, like any other, is checked by the "marketplace"—in this case, of voters. Another view is that consultants represent the ultimate corruption of U.S. political campaigns. Candidates become mere commodities to be packaged and repackaged to a gullible electorate.[35]

Closer to the truth, perhaps, is that the rise of high-tech politics has helped individual candidates win the campaign game, but with some ironic costs to the credibility and reputation of all politicians. As political consulting becomes a specialized business, it helps to discredit the political process by boosting voter cynicism about all politicians and political claims. Voters watch political advertising, and studies show that they are affected by specific commercials. They watch insider accounts of strategy shifts and attempts to repackage candidates. They march to the polls and choose between the competing images that have been presented. Yet the whole process leaves many voters (or potential voters) feeling abused. As professionalization increases, campaigns seem to turn off voters, although they still elect candidates to office.[36]

Negative Campaigning. The growth and sophistication of negative campaigning provide some support for this view. In the early days of high-tech politics, it was more important for each campaign to define its candidate mostly in positive terms. But in the new political warfare, importance is placed on defining opponents in negative terms so that valuable time and money are spent by opponents on defense rather than offense. The stakes here are high; victory often goes to the candidate best able to besmirch the record and reputation of any opponent.

The 1988 presidential campaign was the best example of negative campaigning. In August of 1988, Governor Michael Dukakis led then Vice President George Bush in the polls. Using focus groups, the Bush campaign discovered that positive feelings about Dukakis were not firm. On questions of race, crime, patriotism, and other "wedge" issues, he was vulnerable. The commercials created by Bush's team—led by Lee Atwater—changed the election by turning voter uncertainty into profound voter doubts about Dukakis. In the most famous ad, Dukakis was blamed for granting a prison furlough to Willie Horton, a black convict who later raped a woman. Though the ad was often criticized for its racism, it was apparently effective.[37]

Through repetition and the media attention this ad and others created, the Republican consultants successfully defined Dukakis and the 1988 campaign agenda. By Labor Day of 1988, Bush had passed Dukakis in the polls. Dukakis had put himself on the wrong side of what some call a **valence issue**—an "issue" like patriotism or crime about which there is no real disagreement. The Dukakis campaign's failure to respond to the attacks is cited as one of the greatest blunders in high-tech campaign history. Dukakis and his consultants mistakenly believed that voters wouldn't take the Bush ads seriously. Yet in a world of personal campaigns in which voters do not know the candidates, negative campaigning can be effective.

George Bush won throug such efforts in 1988, but the electorate's view of the campaign process suffered. According to Times-Mirror polls, only 59 percent of 1988 voters thought they had learned enough to make a valid judgment about the candidates during the campaign season. Voters gave political consultants, TV ads, and pollsters low marks for their performances.[38]

The 1992 presidential campaign was different for three reasons. The first is that negative campaigning itself had become an issue, and therefore had to be used by all three contenders with more caution than in 1988. Second, Bill Clinton's political consultants vowed not to repeat Dukakis's mistakes. Each time the Bush forces raised questions about Clinton's draft record, honesty, or trustworthiness, Clinton's consultants immediately counterattacked. Clinton's advertising consultant, Frank Greer, even obtained scripts of Bush's negative ads before they appeared, so that a televised response could appear immediately after they were broadcast. The third change was Perot's innovation, the infomercial. Negative advertising is difficult to sustain if the candidate, in this case Perot, appears personally and talks for a long time. In such formats, too many attacks on opponents appear to be mean spirited.

The 1992 election campaign did not eliminate negative campaigning, yet it was an improvement over 1988. Ironically, voters in polls gave the 1992 commercials a more positive rating than they had in 1988 but deemed commercials as a whole, less important for their eventual decision. Although voters don't like negative advertising, it is effective in contemporary elections, with their weak parties and candidate domination. Voter loyalty to candidates is thin because there are few ways to learn about political claims besides the charges and counter-charges engineered by consultants and broadcast by the media.

For the most part, modern campaigns miss the essence of popular democracy—citizen involvement. It's replaced by strategizing among experts and talk among the candidates alone. Ironic for campaigns consciously rooted in specific personalities is that their themes do not even come from the candidates themselves. Campaign themes are more often than not left to those who conduct the focus groups, sift the polls, and prepare the candidates' next attack ads. In this electoral climate, the media, along with competing teams of consultants, become the political agenda's creators.

Media Dependency. One common response to the rise of political consultants and negative campaigning has been that neither is new and that they are in any case intrinsic to democratic electoral politics. Jefferson, Jackson, Lincoln, and other great American presidents fended off personal attacks during their election campaigns and delivered attacks as well. Grover Cleveland's wife had to swear that he hadn't abused her.[39]

Indeed, mudslinging isn't new, but it's more effective and more sophisticated than it used to be. The real difference is in the central importance of image making and destroying. In Wilson Carey McWilliams's words, people like Cleveland and his opponent James Blaine campaigned in an America "dense with associations," in "a traditional politics that drew citizens into public places" and in a setting where "the vast majority of the press was local" and "judged the propriety and authenticity" of such slurs. In contrast, present-day campaign management occurs in "a context where the people are more exposed to and dependent on the mass media," where the "private, individualistic, self-protective side of American culture" is emphasized over "citizenship and public life."[40] Infomercials and Willie Horton–type ads presume few conversations between voters and between voters and candidates. Voters judge the validity of each charge and countercharge alone and at home, and they can find little independent confirmation or denial of the truth or falsity of the mudslinging. In the money-driven, high-tech campaign game, focus groups and polling matter not because they make the campaign democratic, but because they empower campaign bureaucracies to manipulate public opinion by reshaping and posturing the candidate at will.

Ultimately, the high-tech campaign may even be self-defeating. Voters, sensing manipulation, lose interest in campaign politics. "We keep pushing the button, but the public's response is no longer there" complained Democratic consultant Carter Eskew in 1992. A solution could be a new generation of ads contrived to look less slick and manipulative, ads that look "all natural." Another consultant says "Ads won't work if they look like political ads. That's why I want to do stuff that hasn't been done, like hand-held shots." If these consultants get their way, the false alternative to high-tech politics will be more sophisticated illusions, not changes in the campaign game itself.[41]

CAMPAIGNING AND POPULAR DEMOCRACY

If the personalized, monied, and high-tech strategies were the total political campaign package, there would be little democratic debate. Campaigns in which citizens are seen as focus groups registering hot or cold responses more closely resemble a psychology laboratory than democracy. That the "subjects" get to vote on the success of the experiment is of little value. Left unchecked, the campaign game is a prime example of elite democracy. Citizens turn from participants into spectators; politicians, from democratic leaders to image merchants.

The modern campaign game is under fire from a host of critics, including ordinary voters and politicians themselves. Although eliminating money and high technology from political campaigns altogether is unlikely, redirecting campaign rules toward popular democracy is possible.

1992: Voters Take Command?

At its worst, the campaign game feeds off of voter cynicism. Insofar as voters accept the game as the only one in town, politicians can play it without pressure to change the rules. But voters can change the campaign game. When they expect and demand more, candidates are forced to respond. Sometimes this response improves the campaign game by bringing it closer to popular democratic politics.

The 1992 presidential election is a case in point. Voters began the campaign of 1992 in a cynical mood, skeptical about the candidates and their claims as they were about the meaning of their own participation. But by the fall campaign and November election, most voters felt more positive about the process, the candidates, and themselves than they had either in 1988 or at the beginning of the campaign year. A majority felt that the 1992 presidential campaign had taught them something, and that they had taught the candidates something as well. Levels of interest in and knowledge about the candidates were higher than they had been in the 1980s, and voter turnout reversed its downward slide. What had affected voter attitudes? Had voters changed the nature of the campaign or had the campaigns changed them?

To begin with, voters took control by demanding from the candidates specific policies and proposals. Although questions of character still mattered to some voters, their views of the nation's past and future mattered more. Democratic presidential candidate Paul Tsongas was perhaps the first to realize what the new mood meant. In the early Democratic primaries, he made unexpected headway by writing and distributing long pamphlets about his policy stances. The other Democratic candidates, including Bill Clinton, followed his lead. In dozens of debates, the rhetoric of the early campaign gave way to reasoned dialogue between the Democrats. Ross Perot's entry into the race helped, for his attacks concentrated attention on the follies of Washington party politics and the absence of "straight talk" in the political debate.

As the campaign progressed through the summer conventions, the restiveness and attention of the voters prevented a replay of the 1988 race. As the economy began to dominate the campaign dialogue, it became more difficult for the candidates to trade personal attacks. All three of the candidates, with George Bush in the lead, were forced to give diagnoses of what had gone wrong in the 1980s. The declining quality of life of the American middle class became the lightning rod for detailed discussions of the health-care crisis, the deficit, taxes, and the state of American schools and other public institutions.

In the fall campaign, George Bush's team attempted to repeat their successful 1988 attack ads. The ads fell flat. The election became a referendum less on character than on change versus the status quo. Although voters consistently ranked Bush's character ahead of Clinton's and Perot's, the candidate best able to articulate a vision of change was the eventual winner.

Seeking change, the voters demanded and to a certain extent succeeded in forcing the candidates to appear in settings where the agenda wasn't controlled entirely by campaign managers or reporters. In the second presidential debate, a citizen questioner insisted that all three candidates declare a moratorium on personal attacks. Sources of information about the candidates broadened beyond the evening news and candidate commercials. First with Perot and his appearances on *Larry King Live* and later through numerous candidate appearances in open settings, the candidates were forced to answer hard questions and address voter concerns. Generally, the more the candidates appeared on talk shows, on call-in programs, and in debates, the less character was an important factor and the less campaign advertising became the central battleground of the campaign. The 1992 presidential debates, with various new "interactive" formats, were ranked as "very helpful" by most voters.

As the campaign shifted from advertisements and negative campaigning to issues and discussion, voters began to feel more informed about the process and more involved in it. From the summer to election day in November, more Americans than in the three previous elections were paying attention to the electoral contest. Each time a candidate appeared on a national phone-in program, over a million attempted phone calls were registered. Participation in such formats was particularly popular among the youngest voters, those least attached to the political parties.[42]

Can we therefore say the voters were in control in the 1992 election? In part, yes. Candidates were forced to share the stage and the agenda with voters and adversaries. Reasons to be hesitant nevertheless exist. Talk shows like *Phil Donahue* or *Oprah Winfrey* seem democratic, but neither the TV nor studio audiences can talk to each other without the technology and conditions of the fast-moving entertainment format. Forums like Ross Perot's electronic town hall appearance to be democratic town meetings, but the camera control and the program agenda—not to mention the money to pay for them—remain in the hands of the candidate. Many of Perot's volunteers complained that their real role was only to support his candidacy and not participate in forming its agenda. Electronic democracy may be no substitute for genuine dialogue among voters. Still, the 1992 presidential campaign gives reason for cautious optimism, if only because voters became more aware of the game's limitations.[43]

Grassroots Campaigns

Are there ever campaigns in which voters are powerful from the start? Such efforts might be called **grassroots campaigns.** Grassroots campaigns value volunteer efforts and organization; downplay the role of advertising and money; and make the candidate reliant for direction, support, and advice on organized voters. They change the campaign game by making "organized people" just as important as "organized money" and consultants. Voters' activities become as important as the candidates'.

The victory of Paul Wellstone in the 1990 Minnesota Senate race is an excellent case study of such a campaign. Wellstone bucked the incumbency advantage, defeating a popular and personally wealthy Republican senator. The feature box on this page details how Wellstone beat the odds, building and maintaining a powerful volunteer organization and a set of commitments to a new politics.

Senate candidate Paul Wellstone left his breakfast unfinished to greet voters at Mike's Cafe in the Minnesota Iron Range community of Hibbing. Wellstone's 1990 victory surprised many who believe that grassroots campaigns can't be won in today's money-rich campaign environment.

A CLOSER LOOK

Grassroots Campaigns Change the Campaign Game

Paul Wellstone, a short, bald, disheveled college professor in rural Northfield, Minnesota, was hardly a political consultant's dream of the ideal Senate candidate. Moreover, in overwhelmingly white and Protestant Minnesota, he was Jewish and had led Jesse Jackson's losing effort to win the 1988 Minnesota primary. In 1990, Wellstone faced well-known Republican incumbent Senator Rudy Boschwitz. With a $7 million campaign treasury and one of the best political consulting teams, Boschwitz spent more on TV advertising in the campaign's last weekend than Wellstone spent in 18 months. Yet in 1990, Paul Wellstone beat Boschwitz to become Minnesota's junior Democratic senator. How Wellstone turned conventional "liabilities" into strengths reveals that there are popular democratic alternatives to the high-tech money campaign game.

Wellstone began his campaign in 1989 with a long list of Minnesota activists and an old schoolbus customized to serve as a mobile campaign headquarters. Visiting mining towns, Indian reservations, farm hamlets, college campuses, and minority neighborhoods in Minneapolis, Wellstone left volunteers behind to contact neighbors and colleagues. To save money on billboards, Wellstone volunteers stood at major intersections with their posters. To economize on TV advertising, Wellstone appeared on local radio and cable TV stations and challenged his opponent to numerous debates. Instead of hiring a full-service consulting firm, Wellstone recruited his ablest supporters as paid workers in Minnesota's small towns and urban precincts. With the help of labor and environmental groups, Wellstone phone banks contacted 300,000 voters. Spontaneous and informal, he refused to utter sound bites.

Wellstone's message was simple: Boschwitz, he claimed, was part of the inside-the-Beltway politics that had succumbed to pro-corporate policies. He'd lost contact with ordinary working families' insecurity about their jobs, their health, and their kids' education. Without mincing words, Wellstone promised to be a different kind of senator. He proposed large cuts in the military budget, sizable increases in corporate taxation, and new measures from health insurance to nutritional programs to help ordinary people raise and care for their children. Refusing corporate money, Wellstone promised to be a people's representative in Washington. But his wasn't a lone crusade: Wellstone talked about how to rebuild grassroots organizations and the Minnesota Democratic party to make candidates like him accountable to ordinary people, not monied interests. As his campaign caught fire, Wellstone's bus became a symbol for a new amateur politics that united Democratic officeholders with a powerful coalition of grassroots groups. Outspent 7 to 1 and given little chance of winning by the experts, Wellstone was the only challenger to defeat an incumbent senator in 1990. He's up for reelection in 1996.

Sources: Dennis McGrath, "Running Uphill: Eight Weeks Inside the Wellstone Campaign," *Minneapolis Star-Tribune,* November 11, 1990, pp. A16–20; Dirk Johnson, "The 1990 Elections: Minnesota Professor's Everyman Appeal Wins a Senate Seat," *New York Times,* November 11, 1990, p. 26; Richard Berke, "Several Won Big by Spending Less," *New York Times,* November 2, 1990, p. A9.

Changing the Rules of the Campaign Game

Widespread voter anger and disenchantment with the political process can lead in many directions. One way of bucking the trends is to run a campaign like Paul Wellstone's; another is to advocate *term limits*, a subject we discuss in Chapter 12. But the most effective way to address the imbalance in favor of elite democracy is campaign finance reform.

Reforming the campaign game by changing the sources and role of money in campaigns is difficult for the simple reason that most of the people who write the campaign rules benefit from the existing ones. In addition, the campaign game is part of a much larger system of elite democracy involving the power of PACs, corporate contributors, and top-heavy party organizations. In the current political climate, everybody favors campaign reform, but not everybody means it.

For these reasons, it is a testimony to the power of the democratic debate that meaningful campaign reform has been put on the agenda at all. Meaningful campaign reform may be defined as new laws that weaken the connection between organized money, political parties, and candidates, all part of the unlevel playing field favoring elite democracy. At the very least, campaign reforms could be aimed at making money less dominant and thereby enabling candidates with grassroots connections to run for public office.

With his inaugural call "to give the capital back to the people," President Clinton in early 1993 proposed dramatic changes in the federal government's campaign rulebook. The new president proposed to limit the size of particular PAC contributions and ban "leadership PACs controlled by powerful members of congress." Clinton also called for limits and regulations on soft money and for public funding for incumbents and opponents who upheld new campaign spending caps. Common Cause director Fred Wertheimer, a long-time advocate of extensive campaign reform, labelled the proposals "a door to fundamental change."

The political obstacles facing campaign finance reform can be traced by looking at what happened to the proposals during the next eighteen months. In late 1993, the Democratic-controlled House and Senate each passed distinct and watered-down versions of Clinton's proposals. Democratic House members, more dependent on PACs, passed a bill calling for public funding of campaigns while keeping PACs in place. The Senate passed a bill with no public funding requirement at all, but that did eliminate PACs and applied restrictions on overall campaign spending. Both bills did, however, apply new and tougher legislation to regulate the use of soft money. GOP members of Congress, whose campaign money derives more from individual donors, opposed both bills.

For nearly a year, House and Senate Democrats let their competing reform proposals languish. President Clinton, whose attention had shifted to a bruising and losing battle for health-care reform, did little to insist on a compromise bill. Moreover, Clinton had been busy raising a massive amount of soft money in the effort to stave off huge Democratic losses in the 1994 Congressional elections. Finally, on the day before Congress adjourned for the 1994 campaign, House and Senate Democrats developed a compromise proposal calling for partial public funding of campaigns, some limits on expenditures, and reductions in the amount of allowable PAC contributions. It was too late, however. Eager to deprive Clinton and the Democrats of any victories before an election, the GOP conducted a successful filibuster of the bill in the waning hours of the 1994 session. Despite overwhelming popular distrust of Congress, campaign finance reform fell victim to partisan wrangling, a weak and disinterested White House, and the naked self-interest of members of Congress.[44]

CONCLUSION: WHO WINS THE CAMPAIGN GAME?

The campaign game is often an impenetrable and vicious circle of big money, high-tech consultants, and manufactured images. When the game is played to perfection, it reinforces elite power by depriving citizens of the wherewithal to participate in and shape campaigns. Without this crucial element of citizen participation, campaigns become less popular control of government than political control of the population by existing elites. Deprived of the means to converse and debate among themselves and with politicians, citizens have two choices: to withdraw from their already limited roles in the game or to fight to re-shape it.

Eventually, however, citizens reject the cramped roles assigned to them as spectators, money sources, and laboratory subjects. When they do, the campaign game cannot sustain even elite democratic power, for elections confer neither mandates to govern nor real security to officeholders. In recent years, the campaign game is showing signs of decay. Tales of scandal, special privileges, and gridlock have led many to question the game, its rules, and its policy results. The game itself has become a campaign issue, and playing it with impunity now involves risks as well as benefits.

"The people who are running things," Williams Greider tells us, "are especially prone to error when they are isolated from the shared ideas and instincts of the larger community." The quest for campaign reform, for grassroots campaigns, and for new ways of bringing politicians into dialogue with voters are healthy signs that the democratic debate may be reviving. Such a revival will depend much more on the organization of citizens than on the goodwill of elites. Our next chapter focuses on the interest groups and political movements that dot the landscape of American politics, for they help organize citizen politics.[45]

KEY TERMS

candidate-centered campaigns
name recognition
political action committees (PACs)
soft money

focus group
valence issue
grassroots campaigns

SUGGESTED READINGS

Kathleen Hall Jamieson, *Dirty Politics* (New York: Oxford University Press, 1992). An esteemed political scientist looks at the long history of political mud-slinging.

David Moore, *The Superpollsters: How They Measure and Manipulate Public Opinion in America* (New York: Four Walls Eight Windows, 1992). An historical and critical account of the growth and biases built into the industry of public-opinion polling.

Gerald Pomper, ed., *The Election of 1992* (Chatham, N.J.: Chatham House Publishers, 1993). A stimulating collection of essays tracing changes and continuities in the 1992 presidential and congressional campaigns.

Frank Sorauf, *Money in American Elections* (Glenview, Ill.: Scott Foresman, 1988). An exhaustive and balanced look at the rules and practices governing contemporary campaigns, with an interesting point of view on what money does—and doesn't—buy.

Martin Wattenberg, *The Rise of Candidate-Centered Politics* (Cambridge: Harvard University Press, 1991). A careful yet provocative look at what happens to the electoral and governing processes when both are ruled by personalities rather than party organizations.

CHAPTER 10

Interest-Group Politics

Until now this text has focused on elections as the main method for holding government officials democratically accountable. Elections, however, are crude devices for communicating citizens' rich and varied political desires. Elections enable us to vote for or against an individual, but they do not allow us to express more refined political views, and they do not measure the intensity of our preferences. Between elections, at least in theory, elected officials have complete discretion (with the exception that some state and local officials are subject to recall elections). As we saw in previous chapters, American elections are further flawed in practice: Less than half the electorate turns out for most elections, poor and working-class citizens are underrepresented, and the wealthy wield undue influence through campaign contributions. What happened to a proposed tax on energy illustrates the importance of the politics that takes place *between* elections.

Early in 1993, President Clinton, newly elected on a promise to address the huge budget deficit, proposed a broad-based energy tax as part of the deficit reduction package he submitted to Congress. The tax was based on the total amount of energy consumed in British thermal units, or BTUs. Clinton maintained that the BTU tax would be fair to all regions of the country and sectors of industry, promote energy conservation and reduce pollution, and raise $72 billion over five years to reduce the deficit.

Powerful lobbyists from energy-producing states and energy-intensive export industries, like petrochemicals, came out against the BTU tax in the House of Representatives, where it was first introduced. To win passage of his economic plan in the House, Clinton negotiated a series of exemptions to the BTU tax. According to the *New York Times*, "What resulted, some experts say, is one of the most exemption-loaded, head-scratchingly complicated, brow furrowing revenue raisers in history." To apply different rates, for example, diesel fuel would have been "dyed in enough distinguishing colors to make Crayola green with envy." Exemptions were granted "not just to certain molecules but to one subatomic particle, the electron."[1]

By the time the BTU tax got to the Senate, it was viewed by many as overly complex and unworkable. So many exemptions had been granted that the energy tax began to resemble Swiss cheese, and those who where still taxed called the whole plan unfair. Under heavy pressure, the Senate rejected a broad-based energy tax and substituted a tax on gasoline and diesel fuel, exempting aircraft fuel, that would take in only about $22 billion over five years.

Pressure groups continued to lobby against energy taxes as Congress worked to patch together a bill acceptable to both houses. The final bill that passed the House and the Senate in August 1993 contained a 4.3-cent-per-gallon tax on gasoline that would raise only about $5 billion per year. (The United States has the lowest tax on gasoline of all the major advanced industrial countries.)

The fate of Clinton's BTU tax illustrates the limits of electoral politics and the power of interest groups in American politics. Much of the action in our political system takes place after the election, when the voters recede into their daily routines and the elected officials travel to the capital city to make policy. After the election, citizens can talk to their representatives (or they can send a **lobbyist** to talk for them). They can send a message to elected officials indirectly through publicized events, like mass demonstrations. This chapter and the next examine two examples of extra-electoral politics: interest group politics and mass movement politics. Both types are necessary for a democracy, and both raise troubling issues for elite and popular democrats.

INTEREST-GROUP POLITICS AND THE DEMOCRATIC DEBATE

Interest-group politics can be defined as any attempt by an organized group to influence public policies through normal extra-electoral channels such as lobbying, letter writing, testifying before legislative committees, or advertising.

Interest-group politics cannot be separated from electoral politics because interest groups often try to persuade officials that supporting interest-group policies will enhance their chances for reelection. Also, interest groups often contribute money to campaigns through political action committees (PACs). Nevertheless, interest-group politics can be distinguished from electoral politics because interest groups, unlike parties, do not seek to win political office. They attempt to influence policy through other means.

Interest groups are held together by the shared goals or interests of their members. The goals of interest groups are varied, stretching from economic goals (limits on foreign car imports) to social goals (the right to family leave) to political goals (campaign finance reform) to humanitarian goals (shelter for the homeless). The interests that hold groups together can be as broad as clean air or as narrow as allowing heavier trucks to ride on interstate highways. Generally, however, narrow economic interests are better represented in the interest-group system than broad political or moral concerns.

Although both elite and popular democrats consider interest groups necessary in a democracy, their evaluations of interest-group politics differ. Interest-group politics fits the elite democratic conception of democracy and human nature: Most people are not interested in politics and view politics as a way of protecting private interests. Most people have neither the time nor the inclination to participate directly in politics. In the interest-group system, people's desires are represented by political specialists, called lobbyists, who moderate their views to be effective in the give and take of the pressure-group system. Moreover, because policy choices are often highly technical, interest groups hire experts who communicate complex information to decision makers.

According to one variant of elite democratic theory called pluralism (examined later), the U.S. interest-group system is open and accessible. Not every group has equal access, but every group can make itself heard at some point in the system.

Finally, we should note that many elite democrats criticize the U.S. interest-group system. Since the 1960s, they argue, the system has become "overheated," with special interests bombarding the system and steering the policy process to benefit narrow groups at public expense. Later in the chapter we examine the criticism that interest-group politics has become too accessible or participatory, overwhelming the system with emotional demands.

Popular democrats have always been more critical of interest-group politics than elite democrats. By relying on representatives and hired experts, interest-group politics asks too little of ordinary citizens who are given few opportunities to participate. Interest-group politics suppresses passionate political participation by requiring that every issue be passed through an elaborate system of political representation, bargaining, and compromise. Moreover, by narrowing the scope of conflict to small groups in Washington, D.C., interest-group politics gives an advantage to elites. By giving power to those who control information, popular democrats believe, interest-group politics excludes the masses of ordinary citizens. In short, interest-group politics is easily manipulated by elites—

technical experts and political insiders who know how to play the game "inside the Beltway" in Washington.

Unlike elite democrats, popular democrats view the influx of new citizens' groups into the interest-group system beginning in the 1960s as a healthy development. Despite the opening up of interest-group politics to new groups, however, popular democrats charge that the system is still biased in favor of elites with political connections or the money to purchase them. The solution is to mobilize people at the grassroots to demand that their interests be represented. The problem with the interest-group system is not too much democracy, as elite democrats maintain, but too little.

As we examine the competing claims of elite and popular democrats about interest-group politics, the reader should keep the democratic debate in mind: Is the playing field of interest-group politics level, giving every interest a fair chance to win, or is it tilted in favor of well-connected elites and those who have the money to hire them?

INTEREST-GROUP POLITICS IN THE UNITED STATES

Before the New Deal of the 1930s, Washington, D.C., was a sleepy town with few diversions other than politics. Since then, Washington has become a vibrant cosmopolitan city, the center of one of the fastest-growing metropolitan areas in the country, with high-paid white collar workers spilling over the boundaries of the District of Columbia to occupy wealthy suburbs in Maryland and Virginia. The metropolitan area surrounding our nation's capital now boasts the best-educated and highest-paid work force in the nation. This prosperity did not stem solely from the growth in the number of government workers, but also from a tremendous expansion in the number of people who make a living trying to influence public policy.

Interest-group politics is big business in Washington. Legally, to work the halls of Congress, you must register with the U.S. House of Representatives and Senate. In 1992, 6,104 lobbyists were registered with the House, but this is an underestimate.[2] The best source of information on interest groups is called *Washington Representatives*, a directory of "persons working to influence politics and actions to advance their own or their client's interest." By 1991, more than 14,500 interest representatives were listed.[3] The number of people who work to influence government is much greater. Scholars estimate that there are another 50,000 or 60,000 more lobbyists and employees of law firms and trade associations. Interest groups do not just try to influence legislation. They also try to influence the implementation of laws through federal regulations and decisions by executive agencies. Including the lawyers, lobbyists, public relations specialists, trade association and corporate representatives who keep track of and attempt to change federal regulations, the number exceeds 100,000.

The Washington interest-group community is large and diverse. It includes powerful business associations such as the U.S. Chamber of Commerce and trade associations representing specific industries such as the U.S. Hide, Skin and Leather Association. It includes organizations with millions of members such as the AFL-CIO coalition of unions, and organizations with only one member, in particular the Washington offices of national corporations such as IBM and GM. It includes public as well as private associations such as the National Governors Association and the National League of Cities. It also includes lobbyists hired by foreign governments to represent their interests in Washington, a feature of our interest-group system that has increasingly come under attack. Two of the best represented foreign governments are Japan and Israel. Table 10.1 lists some of the major interest groups in Washington, D.C.

Interest groups play a more powerful role in American politics than in most other Western democracies. There are two main reasons for this. First, American political institutions stimulate interest-group politics. As we know from Chapter

TABLE 10.1 — Some Major Interest Groups	Members	Staff	Budget
Economic Interest Groups			
National Association of Manufacturers	12,500	180	$14,000,000
Business Roundtable	213	18	Not Listed
United States Chamber of Commerce	Not Listed	1100	$65,000,000
Trade Associations			
American Petroleum Institute	250	400	Not Listed
Association of Bank Holding Companies	110	8	Not Listed
Labor Groups			
American Federation of Labor-Congress of Industrial Organizations (AFL-CIO)	14,100,000	400	Not Listed
American Federation of State, County and Municipal Employees (AFSCME)	1,300,000	Not Listed	Not Listed
International Brotherhood of Teamsters	2,000,000	Not Listed	Not Listed
United Automobile Workers (UAW)	1,400,000	Not Listed	Triennial
Farm Groups			
American Farm Bureau Federation	3,983,870	102	Not Listed
National Farm Workers Association	100,000	Not Listed	$5,000,000
Professionally Motivated Groups			
American Bar Association (ABA)	375,000	800	$65,000,000
American Medical Association (AMA)	271,000	Not Listed	Not Listed
Association of Trial Lawyers of America (ATLA)	56,000	175	Not Listed
Educational Quasi-union Groups			
American Association of University Professors (AAUP)	42,000	34	$3,073,000
American Federation of Teachers (AFT)	790,000	Not Listed	$40,000,000
National Education Association (NEA)	2,000,800	600	$147,500,000

TABLE 10.1		Members	Staff	Budget
Continued	**Public Interest Groups**			
	American Civil Liberties Union (ACLU)	375,000	125	Not Listed
	Common Cause	265,000	136	$11,218,300
	National Rifle Association (NRA)	2,524,000	460	$66,000,000
	National Taxpayers Union	200,000	21	$3,200,000
	Public Citizen	100,000	Not Listed	$7,000,000
	Sierra Club	650,000	294	$35,000,000
	American Association of Retired Persons (AARP)	32,000,000	1,200	Not Listed
	National Association for the Advancement of Colored People (NAACP)	400,000	132	Not Listed
	National Organization of Women (NOW)	280,000	30	Not Listed
	Salvation Army	446,403	36,484	$6,128,260
	Southern Poverty Law Center	Not Listed	Not Listed	$2,000,000
	Public Agency Groups			
	National Governors Association	55	106	$11,000,000
	National Conference of State Legislators	Not Listed	145	$8,000,000
	National Association of Counties	1,900	65	Not Listed
	National League of Cities	1450	75	$8,500,000
	U.S. Conference of Mayors	600	50	$3,800,000
	International City Management Association	7,836	100	Not Listed

Source: Peggy Kneffel Daniels and Carol A. Schwartz, eds., *The Enclyopedia of Associations* (Detroit: Gale Research Inc., 1993).

2, fearing tyranny of the majority in a democratic government, the Federalists wrote a Constitution that fragmented policymaking authority—including the separation of powers into three branches; the bicameral Congress (now with decision making further fragmented into committees and subcommittees); the power of the courts to intervene in administrative decisions; and the division of power among federal, state, and local governments. In this way, the Constitution created a government having many access points for interest groups. In addition, U.S. interest groups are able to intervene on the administrative side of government, influencing the implementation of a law after it is passed. Critics of the interest-group system charge that in striving to protect the country against tyranny by majorities, the founders created a system that stimulates too much interest-group activity, making it prone to tyranny by minorities.

The second reason for the exceptional strength of interest-group politics in the United States is the weakness of political parties, discussed in Chapter 8. In European countries interest groups usually operate through the powerful political parties, which aggregate interests and devise legislative programs. In the United States, some interest groups, such as labor unions and business organizations, work through the Democratic or Republican parties, but for the most part they operate as independent political entrepreneurs. The thesis that strong parties inhibit interest-group politics is confirmed by research at the local level showing that cities with strong parties, such as Chicago with its political machine, have less powerful interest groups than cities with weak parties, such as New York.[4]

Traditional Lobbying: The Insider Strategy

Interest groups are often referred to as lobbies, as in "gun lobby" or "steel lobby." (The term *lobbyist* stems from the mid-seventeenth century, when people would plead their cases with members of the British Parliament in a large lobby outside the House of Commons.) Interest groups are also referred to as pressure groups. Both terms have taken on negative connotations, evoking images of pot-bellied, cigar-smoking influence peddlers prowling the halls of Congress with bags of money to corrupt legislators. In fact, lobbying is an essential function in a democracy. Interest-group politics is protected by the First Amendment, which guarantees freedom of association, "or the right of the people peaceably to assemble, and to petition the Government for a redress of grievances." Can you imagine a democracy in which the government prohibited people from joining together and pressuring the government?

Of course, corruption is a problem in interest-group politics. Perhaps the most notorious recent example is the California savings and loan that contributed $1.3 million to the campaigns of five U.S. senators in exchange for their intervention with federal regulators. As federal regulators looked the other way, the savings and loan went bankrupt in 1989. The bailout cost the federal taxpayers $2.5 billion. Some perfectly legal practices verge on corruption. Lobbyists frequently purchase large numbers of tickets to congressional fundraisers or pay fat fees for short appearances at association gatherings. Although a certain amount of corruption and bribery occur, the image of money-toting lobbyists buying votes misrepresents the normal operation of interest-group politics in the United States. Corruption of the democratic process is more subtle (and pervasive) than the conventional image suggests.

In discussing interest-group politics it is important to distinguish between an **insider strategy** and an **outsider strategy.** The insider strategy is what we normally think of as interest-group politics. It involves direct access to decision makers in Washington, relying on one-on-one persuasion to convince powerful people that the interest group's position makes sense. The insider strategy depends on access to what used to be called the "old-boy" network. The outsider strategy, on the other hand, relies on mobilizing forces outside Washington to pressure decision makers. The insider and outsider strategies are often coordinated with each other, but traditional interest-group politics is usually associated with the insider strategy. Use of the outsider strategy expanded in the 1960s. (We examine that strategy later in the chapter.)

The insider strategy takes place largely behind closed doors and is most effective when applied to issues sufficiently narrow in scope not to have caught the public's attention. Speaking about lobbying around the 1986 Tax Reform Act, Representative Pete Stark, Democrat of California, observed, "The fewer the number of taxpayers affected, and the more dull and arcane the subject matter, the longer the line of lobbyists."[5]

The effectiveness of the insider strategy stems from the fact that legislation has become so complex that neither legislators nor their staffs are able to keep up with pertinent information. As we show in Chapter 12, most of the work of Congress takes place in specialized committees and subcommittees, but even the specialized staffs attached to these committees cannot keep up with the staggering growth of information relevant to policymaking. Lobbyists therefore perform an important function in a modern democracy: They provide decision makers with detailed information on the effects of policies.

The insider lobbying strategy applies to the executive branch as well as Congress. Political issues are almost never completely settled when a bill is passed. Congress usually formulates broad policies that leave a great deal of discretion to executive branch employees. Thus, for example, the Environmental Protection Agency (EPA) has the power to set standards for particular pollutants. Agencies formulating policies usually issue draft regulations in the *Federal Register,* a publication of all administrative regulations issued by the federal government. During the comment period, interest groups can try to influence the regulations before they are issued in final form. They can also testify at hearings held by an agency to consider regulatory actions.

Whether dealing with Congress or the executive branch, a successful lobbyist must develop relations of trust with key decision makers. One piece of false information that embarrasses the decision maker could result in a lobbyist's loss of access. Lobbyists, however, are not completely objective. They specialize in information that favors their client's cause, but they must not bias the facts too much. Members of Congress are especially interested in how a bill will affect their home districts. Thus, for example, for a bill that would require businesses to provide health insurance for their employees, legislators would want to know how businesses in their district would be affected and whether any would be forced out of business.

From morning phone calls to afternoon golf dates to evening cocktail parties, lobbyists spend most of their time keeping up personal contacts and seeking out the latest information. Access is the key. A survey of interest groups found that 98 percent contacted government officials directly to express their views and 95 percent engaged in informal contacts with officials at conventions, over lunch, and so forth.[6] Eventually, skilled lobbyists make decision makers dependent on them. Policy makers begin to call on them. It is almost like the lobbyists are working for the decision makers. They become sources of hard-to-obtain information for overworked government officials and their staffs. As one legislative aide observed:

> My boss demands a speech and a statement for the *Congressional Record* for every bill we introduce or co-sponsor—and we have a lot of bills. I just can't do it all myself. The better lobbyists, when they have a proposal they are pushing, bring it to me along with a couple of speeches, a *Record* insert, and a fact sheet.[7]

A troubling aspect of lobbying is the so-called revolving door. Most lobbyists gained their knowledge and contacts in government working either for Congress or for an executive agency. When they leave governmental service, they get a job with a lobbying firm or interest group, usually at much higher pay, exploiting their access and knowledge to the benefit of their clients. James Watt, former Secretary of the Interior under Ronald Reagan, reportedly received $250,000 from a client for a single phone call to a high-level official in the Department of Housing and Urban Development (HUD).

In 1978, Congress passed the Ethics in Government Act to deal with abuses of the revolving door. The act forbids former executive branch employees from lobbying their former agencies on any issue for one year and forbids lobbying at all, with no time limit, on issues in which they were "personally and substantially involved."[8] Lyn Nofziger, former Reagan White House aide, was convicted of illegally using his contacts with the White House on behalf of various business interests and labor unions. Former members of Congress are also heavily involved in lobbying, even though the 1989 Ethics in Government Act barred former elected officials from lobbying anywhere on Capitol Hill for one year.

Growth of Interest-Group Politics

Interest-group politics has always been more prominent in the United States than in other countries, but since the 1960s interest-group activity has exploded in Washington. As Figure 10.1 shows, between 1977 and 1991 the number of people representing groups in Washington more than tripled, increasing from 4,000 in 1977 to more than 14,500 in 1991. Lobbyists in Washington now have their own lobbies, including the American League of Lobbyists and the American Society of Association Executives.

Part of the reason for the proliferation of interest groups is the decline of political parties and the fragmentation of power in Congress, especially following congressional reforms that opened up the seniority system in the mid-1970s. The continued growth of the federal presence in the economy and the proliferation of federal regulations have also stimulated interest-group activity. Interest-group politics appears to be growing at the expense of electoral politics. Citing declining electoral participation rates, party decay, and institutional deadlock in the federal government, some scholars have labelled the present period the "postelectoral" era in American politics.[9]

The increase in interest-group activity is also attributed to the tremendous upsurge of participation in the 1960s and 1970s that created new interest groups representing broad citizens' groups and the poor. Of interest groups that existed in 1981, 76 percent of the citizens' groups and 79 percent of the social welfare and poor people's organizations had been formed since 1960.[10] In response, corporations countermobilized: The number of corporations with offices in Washington increased tenfold between 1961 and 1982.[11]

The tremendous growth of interest-group activity in American national government raises disturbing questions. Have we created an interest-group society

Growth of Washington Interest Representatives, 1977–1991

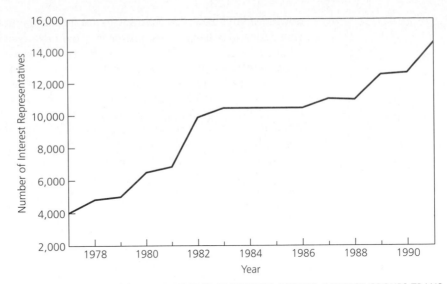

Source: Data reprinted from THE POLITICS OF INTEREST GROUPS: INTEREST GROUPS TRANS-FORMED by Mark Petracca, ed., copyright © 1992 by permission of Westview Press, Boulder, Colorado.

in which every group feels entitled to have its problems solved by government? Are the new interest groups autonomous expressions of citizens or have they been spawned by governmental programs and regulations? Have some interest groups become so entrenched in government that we can no longer distinguish between public government and private interests? Answers to these questions depend on our understanding of who is represented by the expanded interest-group system.

HOW REPRESENTATIVE IS THE PRESSURE-GROUP SYSTEM?

If the U.S. interest-group system truly represents the many diverse interests of the citizenry, then it might be one of the most democratic features of our political system. This argument is the cornerstone of a variant of elite democratic theory called **pluralism.**[12] Pluralist theory views the interest-group system as a political marketplace with the following characteristics:

1. Free Competition. Most people do not participate directly in decision making but, like consumers in the economy, they are represented by leaders, or political entrepreneurs, who compete for their support. Competition ensures that all major interests are heard.

2. Dispersed Power. Money is an important source of power, but other resources are equally important, including motivation, leadership, organizational skills, knowledge, and expertise. Elites who are influential in one issue arena tend not to be active in others. Thus, power is widely dispersed.

3. Bargaining. Success in the interest-group system requires bargaining and compromise with other interests. Pluralist politics thus discourages rigid moralistic or ideological politics that threatens democratic stability.

4. Balance. Mobilization on one side of an issue produces mobilization on the other side; public policies thus reflect a balance of competing interests that approximates the interest of society as a whole.

An examination of the interest groups in the American political system indicates that pluralist theory is deeply flawed. Although no one is prevented from organizing an interest group, some groups and issues are easier than others to organize and gain greatest access to power.

Table 10.2 shows the composition of the pressure-group community in 1981. Corporations constituted 20.6 percent of those having their own Washington offices but 45.7 percent of all organizations having a Washington presence. The difference in the two columns reflects the fact that most corporations do not

	Organizations Having Their Own Washington Offices	All Organizations Having Washington Representation
Corporations	20.6%	45.7%
Trade and other business associations	30.6	17.9
Foreign commerce and corporations	.5	6.5
Professional associations	14.8	6.9
Unions	3.3	1.7
Citizens' groups	8.7	4.1
Civil rights groups/Minority organizations	1.7	1.3
Social welfare and the poor	1.3	.6
New Entrants (elderly, women, handicapped)	2.5	1.1
Governmental units—U.S.	1.4	4.2
Other foreign	1.2	2.0
Other unknown	13.4	8.2
	100.0%	100.2%
	(N = 2810)	(N = 6601)

TABLE 10.2

The Washington Pressure Group Community

Source: Compiled by Kay Lehman Schlozman and John T. Tierney, *Organized Interests and American Democracy* (New York: Harper & Row, 1986), p. 67.

have their own offices in Washington but hire someone to represent them. Most citizens' groups, on the other hand, have their own Washington offices.

Table 10.2 shows the disproportionate influence of business in the pressure-group system. Whose interests are represented by corporations? As we saw in Chapter 4, corporations, especially the largest ones that are most overrepresented in Washington, are not held democratically accountable by consumers; they exert power over the marketplace. Corporate lobbies represent the interests of producers—the owners and managers of corporations—not the interests of consumers. Sometimes, as when automobile manufacturers lobby for limits on imports, corporate lobbies represent the interests of workers in the corporation, but mostly they lobby to increase the power of management to be free of governmental regulations and to achieve maximum profits free of taxation. A separate set of lobbies have grown up to represent the interests of consumers, which we will discuss later.

The overrepresentation of wealthy corporate interests is further exposed by comparing the representation of different groups in the economy. Of the interest groups in Washington that represent people in their *economic* roles, 88 percent represent corporations or professional associations, even though only 16 percent of American adults were managers or white-collar professionals in 1980.[13] Contrary to pluralist theory, the pressure-group system does not represent a balance of the various interests in society but is heavily biased in favor of corporations and the wealthy.

Individual membership in interest groups is also class biased. A 1981 Gallup poll found that about 20 million Americans were members of special-interest organizations and another 20 million had given money to such groups during the past year. This means that large numbers of people participate in the interest-group system, but many others are not represented at all. Overall, the survey found that only about 13 percent of the adult population were members of special-interest groups.[14] As Figure 10.2 shows, membership in special-interest organizations is skewed by income, with high-income individuals participating at over twice the rate of low-income individuals. Poor people are rarely in a position to invest their scarce resources, whether time or money, in the achievement of remote political goals.

Whether we look at interest groups themselves or at their members, the system is biased in favor of large corporations and the wealthy. All interests are free to organize but, contrary to pluralist theory, power is not widely dispersed. As E. E. Schattschneider concluded in a well-known critique of pluralist theory: "The flaw in the pluralist heaven is that the heavenly chorus sings with a strong upper-class accent."[15]

COLLECTIVE ACTION AND THE RISE OF PUBLIC INTEREST GROUPS

Narrow economic interests tend to dominate the interest-group system not just because they have greater resources, but because they find it easier to overcome

FIGURE 10.2

Participation in Interest Groups by Income Class

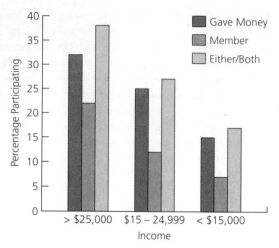

Source: The Gallup Poll: Public Opinion 1981 (Wilmington, Delaware: Scholarly Resources Inc., 1982), p. 178.

what political scientists call the **collective action problem.**[16] The collective action problem arises when we assume that each member of a group pursues his or her individual interest. Everyone in the group will benefit from governmental action. To provide the common benefit, however, an interest group needs to be formed to pressure the government. The problem is that everyone in the group will benefit regardless of their contributions to the collective action (and one individual's contribution rarely makes a difference in the outcome). Thus, most people will try to take a "free ride" and the interest group will never get off the ground.

Collective action is less of a problem for large corporations, however, when one or a few companies dominate an industry. With fewer members in the interest group, each recognizes that his or her contribution is necessary for success. Analysis of the problem of collective action helps explain why producer groups dominated by a handful of corporations are relatively successful in organizing interest groups and obtaining collective benefits, whereas consumer groups, trying to represent the interests of millions of dispersed consumers, are so difficult to organize.

In the 1960s and early 1970s, a different species of organized interest, the public-interest group, flowered. A **public-interest group** can be defined as any group seeking governmental action that will not principally benefit the members of the group. Most interest groups seek benefits for their members; a steel producers lobby, for example, seeks limits on imported steel to shut out foreign competition. A public-interest group, on the other hand, seeks policies that, at least in the minds of the members, will benefit society as a whole. The League of Women Voters, which seeks a better informed electorate, is a classic example of a public-interest group. Consumer groups that seek safer and more reliable consumer goods are public-interest groups because everybody benefits from their efforts, not just the leaders and members of the group.

Public-interest groups would appear to have a difficult time overcoming the collective action problem because their benefits are so widespread. Nevertheless, they proliferated in the 1960s and 1970s, with 76 percent of the citizens' groups in existence in 1980 having formed in the previous twenty years.[17] The rise of public-interest groups shows that people join groups not only to benefit from them materially but also because they believe in the purposes of the group, whether it be safer cars, cleaner air, or fairer elections. Environmental groups such as the Sierra Club (450,000 members) and the Environmental Defense Fund (60,000 members) have successfully attracted members, even though the benefits of the collective action are widely distributed. (We should note that nearly all public interest groups provide their members with specific benefits for joining—all the way from bumper stickers to magazine subscriptions.) People are also attracted to citizens' groups by the companionship that arises from participating with like-minded people in a political cause. Compared to special-interest groups, public-interest groups are more consistent with the popular democratic view of human nature, which sees people as naturally inclined to participate in politics and capable of transcending their own parochial interests in favor of a broader public good.

Cultivating the Outsider Strategy

The public-interest groups that emerged in the 1960s did not rely primarily on an insider strategy. Instead, public-interest groups cultivated an outsider strategy in which they appealed to citizens outside Washington to put pressure on Congress and the executive branch to address their issues. Instead of trying to persuade individual politicians and officials behind closed doors, they took their issues to the public, dramatizing the effects of inaction and skillfully using the media to communicate their message to the American people. By carefully documenting facts and then exposing problems, often through emotional congressional hearings and published exposés, the public-interest groups swayed public opinion. Politicians were forced to respond.

In short, the rise of public-interest groups opened the elite-dominated interest-group system in Washington to an upsurge in popular democratic participation. Although the outsider strategy succeeded in democratizing the system for a time, it had weaknesses that contributed to a reassertion of elite democratic power. Nevertheless, the rise of public-interest groups shows that the American political system is not impervious to popular democratic pressure. One person, even someone lacking wealth and political connections, can make a difference.

Ralph Nader: Expanding Democratic Citizenship

Little in Ralph Nader's background suggested that he would become the scourge of corporate America.[18] The son of Lebanese immigrant parents, Nader was something of a nerd, often carrying a briefcase to school and reading late into the night. Ironically, his high school yearbook predicted he would become a

At a news conference on July 5, 1977, Ralph Nader watches three-year-old Lynn Sutcliffe sit calmly as an air bag "explodes" in her face. Nader was an advocate of air bags long before U.S. automakers offered them as a standard safety option.

corporate executive. After graduating with honors from Princeton University, Nader attended Harvard Law School. Disappointed with the vocational orientation of Harvard, which he called a "high-priced tool factory," Nader got mediocre grades, often skipping required classes to concentrate on issues that interested him. After graduating from law school, he practiced law for a number of years in a rather undistinguished fashion.

What set Nader apart from other lawyers was his interest—some called it an obsession—with automobile safety. Cars of the early 1960s were not designed with safety foremost in mind. They had lethal protruding fins, unsafe steering mechanisms, dangerous dashboards, and no seatbelts. Nader's concern with automobile safety stemmed from an incident in 1956 when he "saw a little girl almost decapitated in an accident when the glove compartment door flew open and became a guillotine for the child as she was thrown forward in a 15-mile-an-hour collision."[19] Nader focused on the "second collision"—the collision between the human body and the car. He felt strongly that cars could be designed more safely and that American car companies irresponsibly designed them with the singular goal of increasing sales.

In 1964 Nader moved to Washington, D.C., as a consultant to the U.S. Labor Department to write a report on what the federal government could do to improve automobile safety. The final report, a 234-page tome with 99 pages of footnotes, indicted Detroit automakers in careful technical language. Like most government reports, Nader's would have probably gathered dust on a shelf if not for other developments that demonstrated Nader's ability to dramatize social problems.

First, in 1965 Nader published a book entitled *Unsafe at Any Speed*.[20] Eschewing the dry technical language of the report, the book was an emotional indictment of the auto industry, with vivid accounts of the mayhem caused by unsafe auto design. Nader singled out GM and the Corvair, with its strong oversteering tendency and vulnerability to "one-car accidents." Nader called the Corvair "one of the greatest acts of industrial irresponsibility in the present century." *Unsafe at Any Speed* quickly became a best-seller.

Meanwhile, with over a hundred lawsuits pending against the Corvair, GM began an exhaustive investigation of Nader. The detective hired to do the job was instructed that "They (GM) want to get something, somewhere, on this guy to get him out of their hair, and to shut him up." This was not a typical background check, as further directions to the detective indicated: "Apparently he's in his early thirties and unmarried. . . . Interesting angle there. . . . They said 'Who is he laying? If it's girls, who are they? If not girls, maybe boys, who?' They want to know this."[21] The exhaustive investigation turned up nothing to use against Nader, who led a spartan lifestyle.

When word of the investigation became public, GM first denied it. At this time, however, Senator Abraham Ribicoff of Connecticut began hearings on auto safety, and Ralph Nader became a star witness. The senators became concerned that GM was trying to intimidate a congressional witness, and the president of GM, John Roche, was called to testify. Unable to deny knowledge of the investigation any longer, Roche was forced to make a public apology to Nader. The image of one of the world's most powerful corporations trying to crush a lone reformer captured the public's imagination. The publicity generated public pressure that resulted in one of the first comprehensive pieces of consumer legislation, the 1966 Traffic and Motor Vehicle Safety Act.

The safety features that we take for granted today—seatbelts and shoulder harnesses, head rests, collapsible steering columns, padded dashboards—grew out of the automobile safety debate that Nader triggered. The government-mandated and "voluntary" safety devices that were introduced in the 1960s have saved thousands of lives. Even though Americans drive many more miles than they used to, automobile deaths have declined since the 1960s.

Nader sued GM for violation of privacy and after a four-year legal battle settled out of court for $425,000. He used the profits from the lawsuit, the royalties from his book, and fees for his many speeches to provide initial funding for a series of public-interest groups that represented consumer interests. As Figure 10.3 shows, Nader has constructed a formidable network of citizens' groups.

Nader's groups rely on idealistic young people who are willing to work long hours at low pay in a public-interest cause. Las Vegas nightclub singer Connie Smith, for example, quit her job to work for Nader so she could "do something worthwhile."[22] Law students come to Washington for the summer to work on task forces investigating such issues as water pollution, bank lending practices, and food additives. Nader began public interest research groups (PIRGs) on college campuses. Supported by student fees, PIRGs lobby and do research on behalf of students and consumers. In 1994 there were PIRGs in twenty-two states, with chapters on ninety college campuses (see Table 10.3).

Nader and his associates are credited with the enactment of key consumer laws, including the Wholesome Meat Act of 1967, the Natural Gas Pipeline Safety Act of 1968, the Radiation Control for Health and Safety Act of 1969, and the Comprehensive Occupational Safety and Health Act of 1970. Nader has continued his frenetic work schedule on behalf of consumer issues, even mounting a write-in campaign for the 1992 Democratic presidential primary in New Hampshire, billing himself the "none-of-the-above candidate."

Nader and his citizens' consumer movements draw from the American tradition of popular democracy. Although sometimes accused of being a communist, Nader is a strong believer in competitive capitalism in which corporations are held accountable by competition, governmental regulation, and consumer- and worker-owned businesses. Above all, Nader believes in an active citizenry, based on what he has called "the average American's natural inclination to want more democracy, not less, and to instinctively distrust power that is concentrated in few hands."[23]

At the same time, Nader's vision of citizen action, of how to democratize interest-group politics, is flawed. Thanks to Nader and his "raiders," the policy-

---

TABLE 10.3

States with Public Interest Research Groups (PIRGs) and Numbers of College Campuses with Chapters, 1994

AKPIRG (Alaska)—0	MPIRG (Minnesota)—6
AZPIRG—0	NJPIRG—6
CALPIRG—4	NMPIRG—1
CONNPIRG—2	NYPIRG—20
COPIRG (Colorado)—5	Ohio PIRG—1
Florida PIRG—4	OSPIRG (Oregon State PIRG)—5
Illinois PIRG—1	PennPIRG—0
MaryPIRG—1	PIRGIM (PIRG in Michigan)—1
MassPIRG—28	VPIRG (Vermont)—1
MontPIRG—1	WASHPIRG—2
MOPIRG (Missouri)—2	WISPIRG (Wisconsin)—1

Source: New York Public Interest Research Group.

FIGURE 10.3

The Nader Network

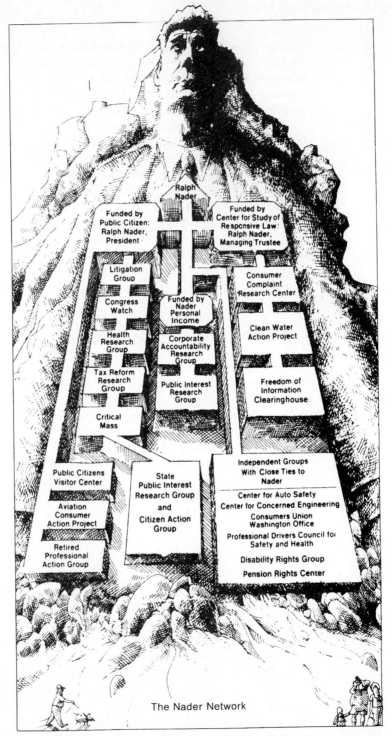

The Nader Network

Source: Wilson, James Q., AMERICAN GOVERNMENT: BRIEF VERSION, Second Edition. Copyright © 1990 by D.C. Heath and Company, Inc. Used with permission.

making process has opened to information and analysis. Information is not equally available to everyone, however. The entry barriers to influencing the interest-group system as Nader did are high; few citizens have Harvard law degrees. In addition, the consumer issues Nader has emphasized benefit the middle class more than the working class and the poor.

Finally, Nader's example of democratic citizenship has an ironic elitist twist to it. Most of the early citizens' groups emerged out of grassroots organizing. Over the years, however, many of the public-interest groups with offices in Washington have become staff dominated, surviving on grants from wealthy patrons or foundations. Groups in which the staff communicates with the membership only through direct-mail fundraising techniques are more consistent with the values of elite democracy. One study found that almost one-third of all public-interest groups had no members at all. Moreover, more than half of those with members had no way for them to affect the policy stands of the group. On the other hand, about one-third of all public-interest groups have local chapters with active members.[24] These groups function as building blocks of popular democracy.

THE NEW LOBBYING: ELITE COUNTERMOBILIZATION

The public-interest movement hoped to pioneer an outsider strategy that would democratize the interest-group system. What had previously been a closed pressure-group system dominated by white males representing dominant producer interests was suddenly thrown open to new groups concerned about consumer product safety and quality, worker health and safety, women's issues, corporate governance, and environmental degradation. The rise of public-interest groups generated the impression that the system had become more balanced between producers and consumers, rich and poor.

In the mid-1970s, however, corporate elites countermobilized and by the 1980s they once again dominated the interest-group system. In 1970, only a small number of Fortune 500 companies had public relations offices in Washington; ten years later 80 percent did.[25] Between 1960 and 1980, business's share of organizations having representation in Washington increased from 57 percent to 72 percent. Citizens' groups, as a proportion of all groups having representation in Washington, fell from 9 percent to 5 percent, and the labor union proportion of the total plummeted from 11 percent to 2 percent. Only 2 percent of all interest groups in Washington represented issues concerning civil rights, social welfare, or the poor.[26] According to a Senate study, public-interest groups were stretched so thin that they did not even attend half of the formal proceedings on regulatory issues; when they did appear, they often were outnumbered 10 to 1 by industry representatives. Corporations invested 50 to 100 times more resources than public-interest groups on many important matters.[27]

In the 1960s, corporate elites had been taken off guard by the outsider strategies pioneered by citizens' groups and became alarmed by their success in imposing federal regulations on business. Corporations staged a remarkable political comeback beginning in the mid-1970s, however, gathering information

The Battle Over Snuff: Corporate Clout

Although cigarette smoking has declined in recent years, sales of another tobacco product potentially just as dangerous, oral snuff, have soared. This occurrence is a case study in how corporate elites have regained control of the interest-group system through powerful combinations of insider and outsider lobbying strategies.

Unlike the plugs bulging from the cheeks of professional baseball players, oral snuff is simply wedged in the mouth. Delivering a huge jolt of nicotine, oral snuff is highly addictive. Although touted in advertisements as a harmless alternative to cigarettes, in fact, users are fifty times more likely to develop throat cancer and four times more likely to develop mouth cancer than nonusers.

In 1986, health advocates succeeded in passing a smokeless tobacco law that required warning labels on cans and in advertisements, banned broadcast ads, and called for a federal antisnuff educational campaign. The snuff industry, however, has undermined the law and killed all efforts to enact stronger legislation. To represent their interests in Washington, the tobacco companies created the Smokeless Tobacco Council. Retaining some of Washington's best-known lobbyists and public relations firms, including Bonner & Associates, they developed a grassroots campaign that could bombard lawmakers with letters and phone calls from ordinary citizens.

The snuff producers also distributed large amounts of money to ensure political access. PACs associated with the Smokeless Tobacco Council and the largest producer, U.S. Tobacco (UST), contributed almost $1 million to congressional candidates between 1987 and 1992. UST gave $576,000 to the Republican party in 1988, together with another $100,000 from the presi-

dent of UST, Louis Bantle. In addition, Bantle raised $350,000 for the 1992 Bush campaign. Hedging its bets, UST spread nearly $150,000 around Democratic party accounts between 1988 and 1992. To enhance its corporate image, UST also gave millions of dollars to various charities, ironically including the American Cancer Society and the national Alcohol and Drug Abuse Council.

The political campaign to fend off attacks on snuff has been remarkably effective. Even though the tax on a can of snuff is only one-eighth that on a pack of cigarettes, efforts to increase the excise tax on snuff have failed. Administration enforcement of the 1986 law has been lax. After the Federal Trade Commission (FTC) ruled that the health warning did not have to be carried on promotional items like T-shirts, Public Citizen, a watchdog group founded by Ralph Nader, sued and a U.S. Appeals Court ordered the FTC to enforce the law fully.

Even though a 1986 report to the Surgeon General found strong evidence that snuff causes cancer, snuff sales have soared. Snuff producers have successfully aimed the product at young males using professional athletes like former Dallas Cowboy running back Walt Garrison and handing out free samples at rodeos and fairs. According to a government survey, close to one-fifth of all high school boys have used snuff, beginning at an average age of nine. Commenting on the rising use of snuff, U.S. Surgeon General Antonia Novello predicted: "If we don't reverse this trend now, we could be looking at an epidemic of oral cancer 20–30 years from now."

Source: Jeffrey Denny, "The King of Snuff," *Common Cause Magazine,* Summer 1993, pp. 20–27.

on the costs of regulation, effectively using the media to communicate their message, and forging broad coalitions with related interests. Above all, corporate elites learned to use the same outsider strategies that had been used so effectively against them by the consumer movement.

Corporate elites were not simply engaging in a power grab. They believed that public-interest politics and government regulation of business were harming the nation. In making their case they recalled the elite democratic idea that elites should filter the passionate demands of the people. Too much democracy, they said, would overload the system with too many demands.[28] The masses were being manipulated into supporting governmental regulations by emotional appeals from liberal activists who would benefit from the new jobs in the expanded regulatory state. In the long run, elite democrats argued, regulatory burdens would stifle growth, hurting all Americans' standards of living.

Corporate elites portrayed their views not as private interests but as a new version of the public interest: Freeing business from regulatory and tax burdens would ultimately benefit all Americans; a rising tide would lift all boats. During difficult economic times, beginning in the early 1970s, ordinary citizens were receptive to the message that excessive regulations and high taxes were hurting the economy. Using the outsider strategies pioneered by citizen groups, corporate elites mobilized grassroots pressure on Congress, greatly enhancing the power of their insider lobbyists in Washington. Moreover, the development of new communication technologies enabled corporate elites to play the game even more effectively than public-interest advocates.

Corporate Image Advertising

Realizing that they could no longer rely on insider deals, corporation elites began a sustained effort to shape public opinion. Spending on corporate image advertising soared. **Corporate image advertising** does not promote the company's products but rather attempts to shape public opinion about business in general or the positive contribution of a particular industry, such as the chemical industry, to American life. In 1978 a congressional committee estimated that corporations spent $1 billion per year on this type of advertising.[29]

Perhaps the best known example of corporate image advertising is Mobil Oil's ads that appear regularly in business publications and prominent newspapers like the *New York Times*. Essentially paid editorials extolling big business and warning against the dangers of big government, the Mobil ads use popular democratic language to support elite democratic positions. Commenting on the environmental movement, for example, one ad stated: "We feel the need to express, from time to time, our belief that those who object to economic development on ecological grounds may often be expressing mere rhetoric and couching their real elitist motives in terms they see as popular and effective."[30]

Think Tanks

Another widely used method for shaping public opinion is corporate funding of think tanks. **Think tanks** are nonprofit institutions that conduct public policy

Corporate image advertising is an effective way of creating a positive image with the public in order to stop or reduce government regulation of business.

research. Although they sometimes do research for governments or private companies, think tanks are funded primarily by foundation and corporate grants. This enables them to hire senior scholars who are given substantial leeway to research public policy issues. Like Nader's Raiders, they then disseminate the results in technical reports, as well as popular books and articles.

Think tanks shape public policy debates in Washington by setting the policy agenda and framing policy alternatives. The production of ideas is crucial to the policy process. Conservative think tanks associated with the corporate agenda became influential in the 1980s by developing ideas like supply-side economics, privatization, and deregulation. The costs of private enterprise, exposed by consumer groups, were countered by studies that examined the costs of governmental regulation.

Since 1970, corporate-funded conservative think tanks have become highly influential. One of the best known is the American Enterprise Institute (AEI), whose budget increased more than tenfold between 1970 and 1980. Contributors to AEI in 1987 read like a Who's Who of corporate America: Chase Manhattan Bank ($171,000); Procter & Gamble ($165,000); Exxon ($130,000); GM ($100,000);—to name only a few.[31] AEI employs the top social scientists in the country, and there is no evidence that corporate money has corrupted their scholarship. Nevertheless, AEI sets a broad research agenda that promotes conservative, free-market thinking.

The Heritage Foundation is a conservative think tank that promotes specific corporate agendas. Founded in 1973, the Heritage Foundation saw its budget grow from $1.0 million in fiscal year 1976–77 to $7.1 million in 1981–82. Joseph Coors, right-wing president of the Coors Brewing Company, is a major supporter of the Heritage Foundation, along with Richard Mellon Scaife, heir to the Mellon banking, oil, and industrial fortune. Corporate donors include Mobil Oil, Dow Chemical, Gulf Oil, and the Reader's Digest Association.[32] Other conservative think tanks that helped shift the policy debate to the right include the National Bureau of Economic Research, the Hoover Institution, the Center for the Study of American Business, and the American Council for Capital Formation.

There are liberal think tanks in Washington as well, like the influential Brookings Institution and the Urban Institute. However, they also rely on corporate funding, and in the 1980s their policy prescriptions drifted to the right. Labor and public interest think tanks like the Economic Policy Institute and the Institute for Policy Studies have minimal resources compared to the corporate think tanks.

Direct Marketing

A third method used successfully by corporate elites to seize the agenda from citizens' groups is direct marketing. **Direct marketing** is the targeted solicitation of individuals for political support, sometimes by phone but more often by mail. The advantage of direct marketing is that, much more than with radio or TV, the political appeal can be adapted to specialized audiences. Pioneered by public interest groups, which often relied on individual membership dues for funding, direct marketing has been greatly enhanced over the years by high-speed computers that maintain huge mailing lists broken down into segments for specialized appeals. By the 1983–84 election cycle, direct marketing of politics had induced 14 million people to contribute almost $1 billion to various political candidates and causes and had generated 20 million letters to Congress.[33]

Direct-mail marketing begins by prospecting a large mailing list. This is expensive, and usually only 1 or 2 percent reply to the appeal. Respondents comprise the "house list," which can be solicited again and again for support, typically with a 10 percent to 20 percent response rate. Mailing lists are traded and sold between organizations. One enterprising researcher enrolled her four-month-old son in six organizations to trace direct-mail fundraising. Over the next year and a half the infant received 18 pounds of mail—185 solicitations from the original six organizations and 63 from 32 other organizations that bought or rented mailing lists.[34]

Direct-mail solicitations are cleverly designed so they are not thrown in the wastebasket unopened. They are often addressed directly to the individual ("Dear Mr. Malone") and contain emotional appeals that evoke an exaggerated threat to the individual. A letter from Common Cause talks about "the threat posed by the torrents of special interest campaign cash," which it calls "Alarming. Outrageous. Downright dangerous." A solicitation from the Christian family right begins: "Just When You Thought Your Children Were Safe From Homosexual Advances, Congress Introduces House Resolution #427: The 'Gay Bill of Rights.' "[35]

Computers break mailing lists into niches for specialized appeals. By a simple command, the computer can produce letters for those on the mailing list who live, for example, in the districts of representatives who serve on the House Banking, Finance, and Urban Affairs Committee. Lobbyists increasingly see direct mail as a way to supplement their insider strategy with an outsider strategy that carefully orchestrates "grassroots" pressure on Congress. In 1976 Richard Viguerie, the remarkably successful direct-mail fundraiser for the New Right, mobilized 720,000 letters to President Gerald Ford to veto labor's common situs picketing bill.[36]

Direct-mail and other technologies have spawned a new generation of public relations firms in Washington, D.C., that can, for the right amount of money, generate a grassroots movement for just about anybody. They are so sophisticated that recognizing the difference between manufactured public opinion and genuine expressions of public sentiment is often difficult; or, as they say in the lobbying industry, you cannot tell if it is "grass roots or Astro Turf."[37]

A good example of the new breed of lobbyists is Bonner & Associates, a small but sophisticated public relations firm located on K Street near the Capitol. Jack Bonner emphasizes that corporate grassroots politics was borrowed from the public-interest groups that perfected the technique of using factual accusations to generate emotional public responses. "Politics turns on emotion," Bonner says. "That's why industry has lost in the past and that's why we win. We bring emotion to the table."[38]

Bonner takes pride in being able to find ordinary citizens who have no financial interest in the policy but are willing to support his corporate clients' positions; he calls them "white hat" citizens. The offices of Bonner & Associates have a boiler room with three hundred phone lines and a sophisticated computer system. Young people sit in little booths every day dialing around the country in search of "white hat" citizens who are willing to endorse corporate political objectives. To speak out against the 1990 clean air legislation, Bonner was able to find senior citizens, disabled Americans, and farmers willing to testify against the law on the basis of questionable corporate claims that tougher fuel economy standards would make profitably manufacturing vans, station wagons, and small trucks impossible.

THE NEW INTEREST-GROUP POLITICS: DEMOCRACY FOR HIRE

The new style lobbying developed by the public-interest movement in the 1960s and 1970s has tilted the playing field for interest-group activity. Instead of insider lobbyists and congressional leaders striking policy deals behind closed doors, the process is now more decentralized and public, with information and policy analysis playing more prominent roles. Congressional hearings are more important, as well, with expert witnesses amassing mountains of information on each issue. The emphasis on information in the complex policymaking process gives the advantage to those who control information. The new regulatory laws have created more complex policy environments controlled by "issue networks" of specialists.[39] Elected representatives, even presidents, are forced to defer to the issue networks, as democratic control passes from elected leaders to unelected

technocrats. Few citizens possess the expertise or the time to track complex regulations on new drugs or the latest scientific knowledge on carcinogens, whereas corporations do.

In a large country like the United States the increasing sophistication of the mass media and direct marketing has given an advantage to interests with substantial resources. American politics is approaching "democracy for hire." The Natural Gas Supply Association spent $1 million on a "grassroots" campaign for decontrol of gas prices. One organizer of the campaign observed: ". . . even for $1 million, it can't be a nationwide effort. None of these grass-roots efforts comes cheaply. When you start mailing letters in any quantity, you run into a bundle."[40] Not surprisingly, citizens' groups report less access to public relations experts and their sophisticated technologies than business groups.[41]

It is clear who has the financial resources to use the new technologies. Interviewing interest representatives in Washington, researchers found that few corporations expressed a need for more money—only 9 percent. On the other hand, 58 percent of unions and citizens' groups said they needed more money.[42] A chemical company can deduct the cost of flying its executives into Washington to testify against the Clean Air Act; ordinary citizens must pay their own ways. Corporations use tax-exempt contributions to support supposedly nonpartisan foundations that shape public opinion. Most taxpayers do not itemize deductions on their tax returns and therefore are not eligible for a tax deduction.

In short, corporate elites have adapted well to the new environment of interest-group politics. By controlling information and taking advantage of new technologies for identifying and communicating with political supporters, corporations have been able to develop effective grassroots strategies of their own.

CONCLUSION: HOW DEMOCRATIC IS THE INTEREST-GROUP SYSTEM?

Interest-group politics in America is both highly accessible and highly unequal. The rapid rise to power in the 1960s of Ralph Nader and his network of public-interest organizations demonstrates that determined citizens, even those lacking money, political insider status, and an institutional base, can penetrate the system. The interest-group system provides an important safety valve in American politics that promotes democratic stability. Government elites cannot simply ignore groups of citizens; ordinary citizens have a chance to be heard, and if they are smart and well organized they can usually attain influence in the interest-group system. By providing access, interest-group politics promotes loyalty to the system. The ability of interest group politics to co-opt many groups into the system by giving them a piece of the action is in many ways the genius of American politics. By contrast, in authoritarian systems, people know that they cannot participate and they are forced to either withdraw from politics or turn to violence to achieve their ends.

Although the American interest-group system is highly accessible, overall, power is distributed highly unequally in the system. Large corporations and the wealthy have much greater access to power than other groups. Large amounts of money enable them to amplify their voices by exploiting the new political technologies. On the other hand, many groups are not adequately represented. The unemployed and homemakers, for example, have no groups to represent them in Washington. Other interests, like those of the poor, minorities, and consumers, are severely underrepresented.

If elites are ordinarily able to use their financial resources to control the policy process, how do we account for the period in the late 1960s and early 1970s when the system was relatively open to popular democratic influences? The answer lies in the relationship between interest-group politics and the topic of our next chapter, mass-movement politics. Public-interest groups were able to pass landmark legislation like the Clean Air Act not just because of tenacious and talented leaders like Ralph Nader. During this period, mass movements like the civil rights, feminist, and environmental movements took to the streets to demand democratic rights and social justice. These movements threatened political elites, who, sensing that the alternative was radical change, suddenly became more open to reformers like Nader. We now turn to see how protest politics, the ultimate outsider strategy, periodically overcomes the inertia of American politics by giving popular democrats a weapon that money cannot buy.

KEY TERMS

interest-group politics
insider strategy
outsider strategy
Federal Register
pluralism

collective action problem
public-interest group
corporate image advertising
think tanks
direct marketing

SUGGESTED READINGS

Jeffrey H. Birnbaum and Alan S. Murray, *Showdown at Gucci Gulch: Lawmakers, Lobbyists, and the Unlikely Triumph of Tax Reform* (New York: Random House, 1987). An insider's account of the 1986 tax reform by two journalists from the *Wall Street Journal* showing the limits of interest-group politics.

William Greider, *Who Will Tell the People? The Betrayal of American Democracy* (New York: Simon & Schuster, 1992). Shows how the corporate elites were able to reassert their power over the interest group system after the rise of public interest groups.

Mancur Olson, Jr., *The Logic of Collective Action: Public Goods and the Theory*

of Groups (New York: Schocken Books, 1968). A leading statement of rational actor theory that explains why broad public interest groups have trouble organizing themselves.

E. E. Schattschneider, *Semisovereign People: A Realist's View of Democracy in America* (New York: Holt, Rinehart & Winston, 1960). A brief but penetrating analysis of the elitist bias in interest group politics.

Kay Lehman Schlozman and John T. Tierney, *Organized Interests and American Democracy* (New York: Harper & Row, 1986). The best overall treatment of interest groups in American national politics.

Mass Movements

In the mid-1950s, Montgomery, Alabama, like most southern cities, had laws requiring segregation of nearly all public functions, including public transportation.[1] Blacks were required to sit in the backs of buses. Blacks could not pass through the white section at the front of a bus, which meant that after they had bought a ticket they had to get off and reenter through the back door. The ordinance in Montgomery had a special twist: Bus drivers, all of whom were white, were empowered to enforce a floating line between the races. As more whites got on, bus drivers would order a whole row of blacks to get up and move to the back of the bus to make room. A number of black women thus could be forced to stand to make room for one white man.

On December 1, 1955, Rosa Parks, a middle-aged black woman, boarded a bus in downtown Montgomery. The thirty-six seats on the bus were soon filled with twenty-two blacks and fourteen whites. Seeing a white man standing in the front of the bus, the driver turned around and told the four blacks sitting in the row just behind the whites to get up and move to the back. Rosa Parks refused. The driver threatened to arrest her, but Parks again refused to move. Summoned to the scene, police officers arrested Parks, took her to the police station, booked her, fingerprinted her, and put her in jail.

Word of Parks's arrest swept quickly through the activists in Montgomery's black community. The local NAACP chapter had been searching for a good case to challenge the segregation laws through the courts. Parks's commitment to the cause and unquestioned character made her an ideal test case. Despite the potential for white recriminations, Parks agreed to go forward with the case. At the same time, the Women's Political Council, a group of black professional women, decided to call for a one-day boycott of the buses to protest the arrest. They distributed 35,000 copies of a simple leaflet that called for all blacks to boycott the city buses on Monday, December 5. A group of ministers agreed to spread word of the boycott in their Sunday sermons and to hold a mass meeting on Monday night to decide if the boycott should continue.

On Monday, Rosa Parks was found guilty of violating Alabama's segregation laws. Given a suspended sentence, she was fined $10 and forced to pay $4 in court costs. The boycott was a stunning success; few, if any, blacks rode the buses that day. Since blacks made up about 75 percent of the bus riders, many buses were almost empty. Monday afternoon black leaders and preachers met to plan the mass meeting that night. They formed a new organization called the Montgomery Improvement Association. As president, the group elected the new minister in town, Martin Luther King, Jr. Only twenty-six years old, King was articulate and intelligent, having just received a doctorate from Boston University. But according to some participants, he was chosen because, having been in town only a few months, he was completely independent—the white establishment had not yet "put their hand" on him.

King rushed home after the meeting and had barely twenty minutes to prepare his speech. That night the church was jammed. Loudspeakers amplified the speeches to the crowd that spread over several acres outside. King began slowly, carefully describing the circumstances of the boycott, including the arrest of Rosa Parks and praising her integrity and "Christian commitment." Then King paused and intoned in his resonant voice, "And you know, my friends, there comes a time when people get tired of being trampled over by the iron feet of oppression." As if releasing years of frustration, the crowd broke instantly into a flood of yeses, cheers, and applause.

After electrifying the crowd King stepped back to examine the pitfalls of the boycott. Stressing that "we are not here advocating violence," he said: "The only weapon we have in our hands this evening is the weapon of protest." King placed their protest firmly within the American democratic tradition. "If we were trapped in the dungeon of a totalitarian regime—we couldn't do this. But the great glory of American democracy is the right to protest for right."

Getting to the heart of the matter—the justice of their cause—King continued: "If we are wrong, the Supreme Court of this nation is wrong. If we are wrong— God Almighty is wrong! And we are determined here in Montgomery," King

Martin Luther King, Jr., is seized by the police outside the Montgomery, Alabama, courthouse in September 1958.

went on quoting the words of an Old Testament prophet, "to work and fight until justice runs down like water, and righteousness like a mighty stream!" The crowd erupted in a release of pent-up emotion.

King's rhetoric seemed to lift the crowd onto a higher level of unity and resolve. The crowd grew silent as Ralph Abernathy recited the three cautious demands the Montgomery Improvement Association had chosen for the boycott: (1) courteous treatment on the buses; (2) seating on a first-come, first-serve basis, with whites in the front and blacks in the back; (3) hiring of black drivers for black bus routes. When Abernathy asked for the vote, people in the church slowly began standing, at first in ones and twos, until everyone in the Holt Street Baptist Church was standing in affirmation. Cheers erupted from those standing outside.

The Montgomery bus boycott lasted thirteen months. It was a remarkable feat of mass mobilization; 50,000 blacks walked to work every day, attended mass meetings, and remained true to the principles of nonviolent resistance even in the face of hostility and provocation from the white establishment. The bus company was denied 40,000 fares a day. Overcoming deep class divisions within the black community, the movement organized carpools in which middle-class blacks lent their cars with little compensation so that poor blacks could get to work. Soon police began to ticket carpoolers on trumped-up charges, but the carpools continued. King's house was bombed, as were the houses of other boycott leaders.

Refusing to compromise, the white leadership in Montgomery made every effort to repress the movement, but they failed to see how these actions would play to a national audience. Eighty-nine leaders of the movement, including King and twenty-four other ministers, were indicted on charges of conspiring to boycott. The national media immediately picked up the story, creating sympathy for King and his followers by portraying them as martyrs to a just cause. The movement could not have begun to pay for the favorable news coverage that followed. The Montgomery Improvement Association began to receive contributions from all over the country and the world. King became a national celebrity, later appearing on the cover of *Time* magazine.

Finally, a special three-judge federal district court ruled that Montgomery's system of bus segregation violated the U.S. Constitution. Montgomery's city government appealed the case to the Supreme Court, but lost. Thirteen months after the boycott began, Montgomery's blacks were able to get on buses and sit anywhere they wanted. They had triumphed in the face of incredible odds.

The "Montgomery model" of nonviolent resistance soon spread to other cities across the South. Black preachers formed the Southern Christian Leadership Conference (SCLC), which led the civil rights movement in the years ahead. Protests erupted in more than nine hundred communities, battering down the walls of segregation brick by brick. Using boycotts, sit-ins at lunch counters, marches, and massive demonstrations, the civil rights movement built national momentum, culminating in the 1963 March on Washington where King delivered his famous "I Have a Dream" speech. Feeling the pressure, Congress passed the 1964 Civil Rights Act, which prohibited segregation in public accommodations and discrimination in hiring, and the 1965 Voting Rights Act, which put the weight of the federal government behind giving blacks the right to vote.

This chapter examines the American tradition of protest politics exemplified by the civil rights movement. **Protest politics** can be defined as political actions such as boycotts and demonstrations designed to broaden conflicts and activate third parties to pressure the bargaining situation in ways favorable to the protestors.[2] When protest politics mobilizes large numbers of previously passive bystanders to become active participants, it reaches the stature of a **mass movement.**

Periodically, throughout American history, mass movements have enabled poor people and minorities, previously shut out of the system, to make themselves heard. After examining the goals and tactics that distinguish protest politics from electoral and interest-group politics, we explore the dilemmas that leaders of mass movements face in keeping protests alive and achieving their objectives. We also examine the viewpoint of elite democrats, who view mass movements as threats to democratic order and stability. Finally, focusing on the modern mass movements that emerged in the 1960s, we present a popular democratic defense of protest movements showing how they level the playing field and fulfill the participatory promise of American democracy.

MASS MOVEMENTS: THE POWER OF PROTEST

The civil rights movement is only one example of the power of protest in American politics. Like interest groups, mass movements are a form of extra-electoral politics; they try to influence government outside of elections. Interest-group politics and mass politics often blend into each other. Interest groups sometimes organize demonstrations or pickets, and it is common for mass movements to lobby Congress. Over time, mass movements often spawn interest groups that become part of the pressure-group system in Washington. Nevertheless, interest-group politics and protest politics are distinct phenomena, whose primary differences have to do with (1) their goals and (2) the means used to achieve those goals.

Goals of Mass Movements

Whereas interest groups usually focus on specific material goals, such as lower taxes or more governmental benefits, mass movements seek broad moral and ideological goals that affect the whole society, such as the "right to life" of the anti-abortion movement or ending the war in Vietnam. As a result, mass-movement goals are not easily subject to bargaining and compromise. The abolitionist movement, for example, refused to compromise on its goal of abolishing slavery. For mass movements, it is not a matter of more or less, but right or wrong. Table 11.1 lists the most important mass movements in American history, together with their main goals.

The Montgomery bus boycott movement started out as an interest group, asking for three reforms that would not end segregation but simply make it more humane. The refusal of whites to compromise on these issues, King later wrote, caused a shift in people's thinking.

> (T)he experience taught me a lesson. . . . even when we asked for justice within the segregation laws, the "powers that be" were not willing to grant it. Justice and equality, I saw, would never come while segregation remained, because the basic purpose of segregation was to perpetuate injustice and inequality.[3]

At that moment, the goals of the Montgomery boycott shifted from better treatment for blacks within segregation to an end to segregation, or equal rights for all, a goal that could not be compromised. At that point, Montgomery's blacks made the transition from an interest group to a mass movement that could appeal to all Americans on the basis of human dignity, equality, and fairness.

Tactics of Mass Movements: Protest as a Political Resource

Mass movements are differentiated from interest groups not only by their goals but also by the different political means they use to achieve their goals. Mass

TABLE 11.1

Mass Movements in American History

Movement	Primary Period of Activism	Major Goal(s)
Abolitionist	Three decades before Civil War (1830–1860)	Abolition of Slavery
Nativist	1850s and 1890s–1920s	Restrict immigration
Populist	1880s and 1890s	Democratic control over railroads, banks, and nation's money supply
Labor	Reached peaks in the 1880s, 1890s, and 1930s	Enhance power of workers to achieve decent wages and benefits, protect jobs, and guarantee safe working environments.
Women's suffrage	Late nineteenth and early twentieth centuries	Voting rights for women
Temperance	Late nineteenth and early twentieth centuries	Prohibition of alcohol
Nuclear disarmament	Late 1950s and early 1960s	End nuclear testing
	Late 1970s and early 1980s	Ban the bomb
Civil rights	1950s and 1960s	Equal rights for black Americans
Anti-Vietnam War	Late 1960s and early 1970s	U.S. out of Vietnam
Student	1960s and 1970s	Student rights and democratic governance of universities
Neighborhood organizing	1960s–present	Community control
Women's liberation or feminist	1970s–present	Equality for women in all aspects of life
Antinuclear	1970s and 1980s	Stop the construction of nuclear power plants
Environmental	1970s–present	Stop environmental destruction
Pro-life (anti-abortion)	1970s–present	Outlaw abortion
Native American rights	1970s–present	Tribal autonomy
Gay rights	1970s–present	Equal rights for homosexuals

movements have a broad array of what we might call "protest tactics" to choose from, including petitions, demonstrations, boycotts, strikes, civil disobedience, confrontations and disruptions, riots, and even violent revolution (see Figure 11.1). Unlike interest groups, mass movements do not target their efforts directly on decision makers; they aim, instead, to educate and mobilize broader publics who in turn put pressure on decision makers. Mass-movement politics attempts to broaden the scope of conflict in the hope that battles that would be lost in the narrow lobbies of Congress can be won in the streets or in the broad arena of public opinion. Mass-movement politics, therefore, has much more participatory potential than interest-group politics. By relying on mass mobilization and the moral appeal of their cause, people with few political resources can use protest tactics to gain power in the political system.

Mass-movement tactics vary all the way from the legal to the clearly illegal, with a large gray area in the middle. Where to draw the line between legal and illegal tactics is hotly debated. In choosing tactics, protesters must go far enough to dramatize their cause but not so far as to alienate potential supporters. Most tactics used by mass movements are legal and protected by the First Amendment guarantees of freedom of speech, press, and "the right of the people peaceably to assemble, and to petition the Government for a redress of grievances." Driven by frustration with normal politics, protest movements sometimes resort to illegal methods, including violence, to dramatize their causes.

Mass movements are necessary because no democracy is perfect; and even if a democracy guaranteed majority rule, it would still need some devices to enable minorities to make themselves heard. Blacks in Montgomery, for example, could not turn to electoral politics to achieve their objectives. Representing only 37 percent of the city's population, blacks lacked the votes to take over city government through elections. More important, blacks were prevented from registering to vote by legal obstacles and outright intimidation. In 1952 only about one in five eligible blacks in the South was registered to vote.[4] Interest-group politics was also not a viable option, because whites in Montgomery were unwilling to bargain or compromise; for them, segregation was an all or nothing matter.

Following normal political channels, therefore, Montgomery blacks had no chance of success. The boycott, however, was a weapon they could use: By withdrawing their fares from the bus company, they could inflict fiscal pain. But it is unlikely that the boycott alone would have brought significant change. The only chance the blacks had was to appeal to a broader audience to put pressure on the entrenched white elite in Montgomery to alter the system of racial

FIGURE 11.1   **Tactical Options of Protest Movements**

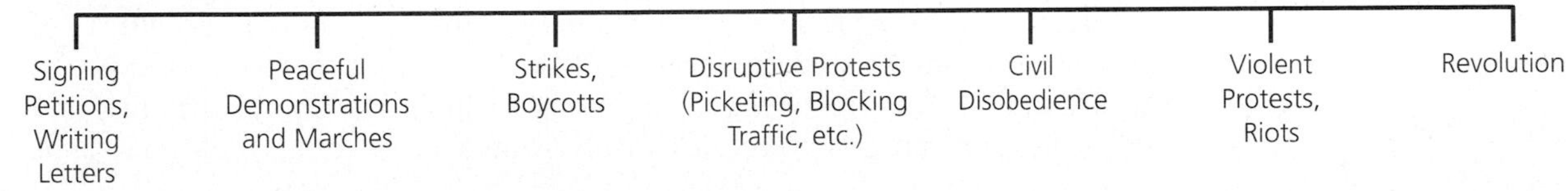

| Signing Petitions, Writing Letters | Peaceful Demonstrations and Marches | Strikes, Boycotts | Disruptive Protests (Picketing, Blocking Traffic, etc.) | Civil Disobedience | Violent Protests, Riots | Revolution |

segregation. As King said in his speech, the only weapon they had was "the weapon of protest."

MASS MOVEMENTS IN AMERICAN HISTORY

As Figure 11.1 shows, American politics has been shaken repeatedly by mass movements. About once in a generation, waves of democratic participation, with strong levelling tendencies, sweep the country: The original revolutionary thrust of the 1770s; the Jacksonian era of the 1830s; the culmination of the antislavery movement in the 1850s; the Populist movement of the 1890s; the economic movements, including the labor movement, that rose out of the Great Depression of the 1930s; and the social movements that began in the 1960s. Mass movements have probably played a greater role in American politics than in any other Western democracy.

Some mass movements in the United States, such as the nativist movement and one of its offshoots, the Ku Klux Klan, have had antidemocratic goals of excluding certain groups from full democratic citizenship. Most mass movements, however, have been popular democratic in character, striving to include previously excluded groups (e.g., blacks, Latinos, women, workers, students, gays, and American Indians) in the full benefits of democratic citizenship. In appealing to the American people, popular democratic mass movements have called on two deeply held sets of beliefs—one rooted in politics and the other in religion—that counter Americans' well-known individualism.

First, Americans share a set of core political beliefs in liberty, equality, democracy, and the rule of law. These beliefs are embodied in certain sacred political texts, including the Declaration of Independence ("all men are created equal") and Lincoln's Gettysburg Address ("government of the people, by the people and for the people"). The American political creed is by its nature inclusive and has frequently been cited by protesting groups to legitimate their causes. Thus, the women's suffrage movement asserted that liberty and equality should apply to all people and not just men. Martin Luther King, Jr., repeatedly used the language of equality and rights to legitimatize the black cause to a broader white audience. Ideologically speaking, popular democrats have always had an advantage over elite democrats, being able to tap into a wellspring of egalitarian political beliefs.

Popular democratic mass movements have also been nurtured by American religious traditions stressing that everyone is equal in the eyes of God, that even the least of us should be treated with dignity and respect, and that morality is a force in the world. Martin Luther King's frequent use of the language of the Old Testament, comparing the liberation struggles of blacks to the efforts of the tribes of Israel to escape from exile in Egypt, is a brilliant example of the political relevance of religion in American politics. The abolitionist and temperance movements were also firmly rooted in religious traditions, as is the modern pro-life anti-abortion movement, which has adopted many of the direct action tactics of the civil rights movement.

MASS MOVEMENTS AND THE DEMOCRATIC DEBATE

As the name suggests, mass movements involve large numbers of ordinary citizens in direct political actions. The protest tactics used by mass movements are disruptive and confrontational. It is not surprising, therefore, that mass movements and their protest tactics have been the subjects of heated controversy between elite and popular democrats.

From the time of Shay's Rebellion, before the Constitution was written, to the violent demonstrations against the Vietnam War, elite democrats have always been suspicious of mass movements. Their attitude is reflected in Alexander Hamilton's statement: "The People! The People is a great beast!"[5] The direct involvement of the masses in political action is dangerous, according to elite democrats. Mass movements can quickly degenerate into lawless mobs that threaten stable democracy. It is safer for political passions to be filtered through representative institutions where elites can deliberate on the long-term interest of the country as a whole.[6]

Elite democrats maintain that the goals of mass movements in American history have often been utopian and impractical. Elites criticize mass movements for being against economic growth and progress. The Populist movement at the turn of the century, for example, was attacked as an emotional reaction against progress and industrialization, an ill-fated attempt to hold on to a doomed agrarian way of life. (The contemporary environmental movement has been attacked on similar grounds.) According to elite democrats, mass movements lack concrete programs for reform that can benefit the people involved; instead they seek moral or ideological goals that are unrealizable and threaten to overwhelm democratic institutions. Lacking practical reforms, mass movements traffic in moral absolutes.[7]

Elite democrats criticize not only the goals of mass movements but also their tactics. In stable democracies participation is channeled through representative institutions and interest-group bargaining. Protest politics brings masses of people into direct participation through confrontational tactics that threaten to divide society into warring camps, elite democrats warn, undermining the norms of tolerance and civility essential to a healthy democracy. Mass movements are not expressions of people's natural desire to participate in politics. Instead, people are drawn into mass movements by clever leaders, or demagogues, who manipulate people's emotions, whipping up resentment against the wealthy and the privileged.

Protest tactics can easily get out of hand, elite democrats charge. People in large crowds, or mobs, are incapable of thinking rationally and often do things that, upon reflection, they would never do. Elite democrats favor orderly interest-group politics over mass-movement politics. One scholar summed up the elite democratic position this way: "Mass politics involve irrationality and chaos; group politics produce sensible and orderly conflict."[8] In short, mass movements are dangerous to democracy.

The attitude of popular democrats toward mass movements is reflected in a quote by Thomas Jefferson. Remarking on Shay's Rebellion, which Federalists viewed as a sign of impending anarchy, Jefferson wrote to James Madison: "I hold it that a little rebellion now and then is a good thing, and as necessary in the political world as storms in the physical."[9] After all, popular democrats point out, the country was born in protest. The Boston Tea Party was an illegal destruction of property intended to dramatize the colonists' opposition to British rule, in particular "taxation without representation."

According to popular democrats, periodic elections and interest-group bargaining are inadequate to fulfill the participatory promise of American democracy. Popular democrats see mass movements as ways for the people to communicate directly with the government, unimpeded by experts or elites. Protest tactics enable people to engage their full personality and most deeply held beliefs in the democratic process.

Popular democrats maintain that protest politics is necessary for greater equality in the American political system. Mass-movement politics is one arena that is not biased in favor of wealthy elites. Throughout American history significant reforms have always come about because of pressure from below by mass movements. Protest politics is not only a way to vent emotions but also a way to overcome the inertia of the American system of checks and balances, to bring about much needed change. Far from threatening democracy, mass movements fulfill it by including more and more groups in the benefits of democratic citizenship. The primary threat to democracy comes not from mass movements but from elites who use repression to block change and hang on to their powers and privileges.

MASS MOVEMENTS: THE NECESSARY INGREDIENTS

Protest is a political resource that can be used by disadvantaged groups lacking traditional sources of political power, such as money or connections, to influence the system. Protest, however, cannot be used by any disadvantaged group at any time to level the playing field of democratic politics. Only rarely do the necessary ingredients of successful protest movements come together. About half of the eligible voters don't even get to the polls for a presidential election every four years. Protest movements require much deeper levels of commitment than voting, such as the willingness of blacks in Montgomery to walk to work for thirteen months instead of taking the bus. Protest movements must engage the whole personalities of participants to transcend normal politics. Even when participants are engaged, remarkable leadership is necessary for movements to stay alive and achieve their goals.

For protest movements to even get off the ground, five ingredients are necessary:

1. *Rising Expectations.* History has shown that people will endure oppressive conditions for a long time without rebelling. It is not when conditions are at their worst that people rebel, but when conditions have begun to improve and people begin to perceive a gap between the way things are and the way they could be. According to one theory, it is not deprivation itself that drives people to rebel, but the feeling that one's group is being deprived of resources and opportunities available to other groups in the society. This is known as the theory of **relative deprivation.**[10]

In the civil rights movement, blacks had suffered under Jim Crow segregation laws since the nineteenth century, but resistance had been limited. One event that raised black expectations was World War II. Many black men died fighting fascism. Those who returned were less willing to accept second-class citizenship, especially after President Truman integrated the armed forces. Urbanization of blacks following the mechanization of southern agriculture also brought many blacks into contact with new ideas and new opportunities that raised expectations. Most importantly, the 1954 Supreme Court decision in *Brown* v. *Board of Topeka* put the power and prestige of the Supreme Court behind the cause of integration. Black people felt they were not alone. As King put it in his Montgomery speech, "If we are wrong, the Supreme Court of this nation is wrong."

2. *Social Resources.* Isolated individuals cannot build social movements. Social movements require networks that can spread the word and involve people in the movement.[11] Social movements require what Sara Evans and Harry Boyte call "free spaces"—organizations between private families and large public organizations in which people can learn self-respect, cooperation, group identity, and the leadership skills necessary for democratic participation.[12] Black churches provided spaces for the civil rights movement that were free from white domination, where blacks could express their true feelings and develop confidence in their abilities. Most of the leadership of the civil rights movement came out of the black churches, where traditions of commitment to the congregation and skills in sermonizing nurtured effective leaders. The national organizations of black Baptist churches formed networks that helped the SCLC spread the Montgomery model throughout the South.

All protest movements in American history have been nurtured in free spaces. Building on earlier organizations like the Grange, the Populist movement of the late nineteenth century built a vast network of Farmers Alliances that within a few years involved two million families. The purpose of the Alliances was to cooperatively market crops and purchase supplies, but they also created free spaces where people could learn the skills of democracy.[13]

The feminist movement grew out of the free spaces created by the civil rights movement in the South and the new left organized mainly on college campuses. Ironically, it was discrimination in these supposedly egalitarian movements that drove women to form their own movement. In the civil rights movement, women, who performed much of the crucial behind-the-scenes work, developed confidence in their abilities and learned the skills of political organizing. At the same time, they were excluded from decision making and public leadership roles. When women in the Student Nonviolent Coordinating Committee (SNCC— known as "snick"), the radical student wing of the civil rights movement, raised the issue of sex roles, one of the leaders, Stokely Carmichael, is reported to have said: "The only position for women in SNCC is prone."[14] Such remarks caused many black women to examine gender, along with race, as a cause of discrimination.

Shortly thereafter, the rise of black nationalism forced many white women out of the civil rights movement and into the new left, organizing against the Vietnam War. There they found that their concerns about sex roles were ignored, even ridiculed, by white men as well. The clash between the egalitarian ideas of the movement and the unequal sex roles within it were too much to bear. Women began meeting separately in small "consciousness-raising groups," where they could articulate their concerns in a supportive atmosphere. Spreading across the country, consciousness-raising groups became free spaces where women could recognize their common problems and develop the confidence to bring about change.

3. An Appealing Moral Cause. Mass movements in the United States fail unless they can appeal to fundamental American values. Animal rights activists, for example, have a moral cause, but they have been unable to make the transition to a mass movement. Most Americans do not believe that animals deserve the same rights as human beings. The civil rights movement, on the other hand, had an appealing moral cause because the demand for equal rights resonated with all Americans. By wrapping itself in Christian values and rhetoric, the movement was nearly impossible to criticize as un-American. Later, when parts of the civil rights movement shifted from a rhetoric of equal rights to a rhetoric of black nationalism and black power, appealing more to African and Muslim traditions, public sympathy for the movement rapidly eroded.

4. Transformational Leadership. The leaders of parties and interest groups are usually **transactional leaders**—they broker mutually beneficial exchanges with followers, such as patronage jobs for votes or tax breaks for campaign contributions. Mass movements, however, require **transforming leaders** who engage the full personalities of followers, teaching them to go beyond self-interest and express their commitments in direct political action.[15] Martin Luther King, Jr., was such a leader, who challenged his followers to live up to their highest moral beliefs. Elizabeth Cady Stanton, the early leader of the women's suffrage movement, was also a transforming leader. In 1848 Stanton adapted the language of the Declaration of Independence to the cause of women's rights by writing the Declaration of Sentiments, a kind of bill of rights for women. By word and by example Stanton encouraged women to step out of their assigned sphere of family and home and become actors in the public sphere of democratic politics. For more than fifty years she lectured, petitioned, organized, and wrote to encourage women to find their public voices.[16]

5. Consciousness Raising. When the necessary ingredients are present for a mass movement, a sudden change of political consciousness happens. People look at political facts differently. Reflecting on the moment at the Holt Street Baptist Church after King's electrifying speech, when Montgomery's black community voted to continue the boycott, Ralph Abernathy described just such a change in consciousness. "The fear that had shackled us across the years—all left suddenly when we were in that church together."[17]

The 1960s were full of such moments of consciousness raising. The environmental movement talked about the "greening of America"—the development of an ecological consciousness. People began to look at economic activity not in terms of its contributions to the gross national product (GNP) but in terms of its contributions to a sustainable environment.

Perhaps the best example of changed consciousness is the women's movement. Before the feminist movement, women had accepted a sharp distinction between the private sphere of home and family, where women spent most of their lives, and the public sphere of work and political action, dominated by men. Participation in the feminist movement encouraged women not only to enter the public world of work and politics on an equal basis with men, but also to challenge the overall distinction between the public world of politics and the personal world of the family. Women began to expand their definition of politics and challenge unequal power relations with men in all spheres.

PROTEST TACTICS: WALKING A FINE LINE

Protest politics, by its very nature, is confrontational and tension-producing. Protestors deliberately provoke those in power to get a reaction from them. Saul Alinsky was a skilled practitioner and theoretician of protest politics. In the 1930s, he organized the Back of the Yards area of Chicago, an area made famous by Upton Sinclair's exposé of the meat-packing industry in *The Jungle*. Alinsky understood the necessity of conflict if disadvantaged people were to gain power. "A PEOPLE'S ORGANIZATION is a conflict group," Alinsky wrote.[18] Conflict has two positive effects for the protest movement. First, it mobilizes the people. A good fight against a common enemy unifies an organization, heightens morale, and mobilizes energies.

Second, conflict has the effect, especially if the protesters are viewed as underdogs, of drawing third parties into the fray who pressure elites to negotiate. Protest is a form of political ju jitsu; a movement with few political resources can use the power of the opponent to its own advantage. In Montgomery the indictment of eighty-nine blacks, including twenty-five ministers, on trumped-up charges of conspiring to boycott brought national attention to the cause.

The protesters celebrated the arrests because they knew the media would paint the white establishment as the aggressors and themselves as the underdogs. Later, SCLC orchestrated Project C—for "confrontation"—in Birmingham, Alabama. "Bull" Connor, Birmingham's commissioner of public safety, played his assigned role perfectly, using powerful fire hoses and vicious police dogs against defenseless children. As the media sent out pictures of the brutality, sympathy for the civil rights movement soared.

The tactical problem for protest movements is to promote confrontation without appearing as the aggressors. Although protest tactics are powerful, like dynamite, if not properly handled they can explode in the faces of those they are designed to help. Protest leaders often face a tactical dilemma: They must push confrontation far enough to sustain the movement and satisfy the needs of the protestors for direct action; if they go too far, however, they can alienate potential supporters or even create a backlash that strengthens their opponents.

One method for coping with this tactical dilemma is **civil disobedience,** which can be defined as the deliberate violation of the law to dramatize a cause by persons who are willing to accept the punishment of the law. Civil disobedience provides a middle ground between peaceful demonstrations (which are often ignored) and violent confrontations (which can cause a backlash). Civil disobedience is not an attempt to evade the law. An act of civil disobedience, such as being arrested while blocking the shipment of arms during the Vietnam War, is done completely in the open, without any violence, and with a sense of moral seriousness.

The American tradition of civil disobedience can be traced back to Henry David Thoreau (1817–1862). Passionately opposed to slavery and to the Mexican War, which he saw as a fight for the slave masters, Thoreau refused to pay his poll taxes. As a result, he was thrown in prison. In 1849 Thoreau wrote a powerful essay, later entitled "Civil Disobedience," in which he argued that unjust laws should not be obeyed. "The only obligation which I have a right to assume is to do at any time what I think right," Thoreau argued.[19] Thoreau acted as an individual; he was not part of a mass movement. His writings, however, inspired many leaders to incorporate civil disobedience into their movements.

Mohandas K. Gandhi (1869–1948) read Thoreau and incorporated his ideas about civil disobedience into his successful movement to free India from British rule. Gandhi believed that a careful campaign of civil disobedience could mobilize **satyagraha,** or "truth force," to persuade opponents of the justice of a cause. Gandhi stressed that movements of civil disobedience must be willing to negotiate at all times, so long as basic principles are not sacrificed.

Martin Luther King, Jr., read Thoreau as a college student and later adapted the ideas of Gandhi to American conditions. King did not begin the Montgomery campaign with a preplanned strategy of nonviolent resistance. Drawn to nonviolence by his religious training, King reflected on the experiences of the civil rights movement and gradually developed a sophisticated philosophy of nonviolent resistance. King was able to adapt to new conditions and learn from the experiences of

The problem for protest movements is how to promote confrontation without appearing as the aggressor. This photograph of National Guardsmen raising bayonets to block protestors in Memphis, Tennessee, effectively portrays the marchers as underdogs fighting for human dignity (March 29, 1968).

others. Dissatisfied with the slow progress being made under the leadership of King and the other ministers in SCLC, college students formed SNCC to push a more aggressive grassroots approach to the struggle. King later praised the student sit-ins at lunch counters across the South for having sought nonviolent confrontations with the segregation laws. His "Letter from a Birmingham Jail," originally written in the margins of a newspaper and on scraps of toilet paper, has become a classic defense of nonviolent protest that is read the world over.

Mass-movement leaders like King often find it difficult to balance the needs of protestors, who demand more and more radical action to express their moral outrage, with the need to appeal for outside support, which usually requires moderation and patience. In the civil rights movement, young blacks became frustrated as their brothers and sisters were beaten by racist police. In the mid-1960s, the civil rights movement split, with more radical blacks joining the "black power" movement under the leadership of the Black Panther Party for Self-Defense and the Black Muslims, led by the charismatic Malcolm X. The movement never recovered from the split. The issue of integration versus black separatism divides the black community to this day.

THE ELITE DEMOCRATIC RESPONSE TO MASS MOVEMENTS

Notwithstanding repeated elite democratic warnings that mass movements threaten political order, elites have many resources for controlling mass movements. It takes as much leadership skill to deflate a mass movement, however, as it does to build one. Political elites have two basic strategies: repression (forcibly attacking the movement) or co-optation (giving in to some of the demands). Political elites face a strategic dilemma that is similar to that faced by mass movements: If they give in too readily, they risk encouraging more militancy and more demands; on the other hand, if they refuse to give in at all and try to repress the movement with force, they risk creating public sympathy for the protesters. Essentially, political elites engage in a complex game of chess with mass movements and their leaders.

The accessibility of American political institutions to interest groups has enabled the demands of mass movements to be incorporated into the system. In this way mass movements are converted into interest groups. Meeting only certain demands of a mass movement deflates the moral indignation of the movement and splits reformers from the radicals. If the white leadership in Montgomery had given in to the initial demands of the boycott movement to humanize the system of segregation on the buses, the effect would have been to deflate, or at the very least divide, the movement. By refusing to give an inch, the white leadership in Montgomery made a serious tactical error. Their intransigence fueled the movement and caused the protestors to shift their goal from reforming segregation to ending segregation altogether.

Skillfully devised reforms, on the other hand, can not only divide the movement but also draw parts of the leadership into the system to administer the new reforms. A good example is President Lyndon Johnson's War on Poverty, which was partly a response to the civil rights movement and the urban riots of the 1960s. The War on Poverty gave black activists jobs in federal antipoverty programs, deflecting their energies away from organizing the movement. Militant black leaders were literally co-opted by federal money.[20] Democracies are supposed to operate this way—making concessions in the face of popular pressure. As we discussed in the previous chapter, mass movements provided the pressure that enabled public-interest groups to pass reform legislation in the 1960s and 1970s, including new laws on environmental protection and worker safety. Interest-group politics, then, is a safety valve that can deflate mass movements.

In choosing a strategy of concessions or co-optation, those defending the status quo have an advantage: Time is on their side; mass movements cannot maintain a fever pitch of activism for long. Delay is one of the best weapons in the hands of elites. When a problem is brought to public awareness by a mass movement, those in power commonly appoint a commission to find a solution. This strategy gives the impression that something is being done without commitment to specific actions. By the time the commission's report comes out, the mass movement will have lost its momentum. Even if the report recommends significant reforms, there is no guarantee that they will be enacted. A good example is President Johnson's appointment of the Kerner Commission in 1967 to study the causes of the urban riots. The Kerner Commission recommended significant reforms, but very few were ever enacted.[21]

Tokenism is another response: Insignificant reforms or symbolic gestures create the impression that serious action is being taken to solve the problem.

These symbolic gestures quiet the protestors, but few tangible benefits are delivered. Political scientist Murray Edelman calls this "symbolic reassurance."[22] Appointing members of the aggrieved group—blacks, women, or gays, for example—to commissions or highly visible governmental posts is often used to create the impression of change. Tokenism, it is called. The leaders of student movements demanding radical changes in college curriculums in the 1960s were often appointed to committees to study the problems and come up with solutions. The opportunity to serve on committees with professors and top administrators was flattering to student leaders, but the effect was often to separate the leadership from the movement and involve them in a long process of negotiation. The key to the success of co-optation is calming the confrontational atmosphere that feeds mass movements long enough for protestors to lose interest. Once they stall, mass movements are very difficult to restart.

When mass movements reach a certain momentum, the tactic of concessions loses its effectiveness and elites often turn to repression.[23] Just as protesters feel justified in using confrontation and sometimes even violence to promote their causes, elites sometimes feel justified in using repression when mass movements threaten their power or violate the law. The United States has a proud tradition of upholding the civil rights of dissenters, but as Chapter 16 shows, when elites have felt threatened by mass movements they often have resorted to repression. American labor history is especially violent. Before passage of the Wagner Act in 1935 (which guaranteed workers the right to organize a union), workers turned to strikes and picket lines that often became violent in order to gain recognition. Governments frequently intervened on the side of owners. In the Pullman strike of 1894, for example, President Grover Cleveland, at the request of the railroads, called in federal troops who, along with municipal police, put down the strike by railroad workers at a cost of thirty-four deaths and millions of dollars of property damage.

Ironically, the civil rights movement, which was committed to nonviolence and democratic rights, had its civil liberties repeatedly violated by the government in an attempt to discredit it, and especially its charismatic leader, Martin Luther King, Jr. The Federal Bureau of Investigation (FBI) secretly planted newspaper articles alleging that the movement was manipulated by communists. Convincing evidence on this charge has never been made public. Under the direction of FBI Chief J. Edgar Hoover, the FBI treated King as an enemy, employing a campaign of character assassination using wiretaps of King's phone conversations. The FBI fed information on King's sex life and the plans of the civil rights movement to the Kennedy administration that helped it resist pressures for racial change.[24]

SIXTIES' PROTEST MOVEMENTS: THE ELITE DEMOCRATIC CRITIQUE

The democratic debate over the place of protest politics in American democracy became especially heated following the rapid rise of social protest movements in the 1960s. Many of these movements are still active, in various forms, in the

1990s. According to elite democrats, radical protest movements threaten to divide American society into hostile factions and overwhelm political and economic institutions with demands for change. People are losing faith in our institutions, according to this view, and elites are losing the ability to govern effectively in the public interest. Sixties-style protest movements are not expressions of grassroots democracy, elite democrats charge, but vehicles used by new counterelites to acquire power. After all the conflict and tension, few significant reforms have resulted.

Elite democrats criticize both the goals and the tactics of the protest movements. The goals, they maintain, are irrational and utopian. Business elites, for example, criticize the environmental movement for putting environmental goals above everything else. Instead of compromising, opponents charge, environmentalists demand an end to all ecological damage, even at tremendous cost to the American standard of living. According to elite democrats, environmental activists with secure white-collar professional jobs demand sacrifice from lower-class workers in the name of environmental purity. Like earlier mass movements, the environmental movement is charged with being against progress, of wanting to turn the clock back to a simpler age. In general, social movements encourage every group—from blacks to women, from Native Americans to gays, from students to the disabled—to demand their "rights" with little concern for the general welfare of society.

Elite democrats also criticize the tactics developed by the protest movements beginning in the 1960s. The tactics of protest, elite democrats charge, began to be used by any group that wanted to "shake more benefits from the government money tree." In a biting essay satirizing the sixties, entitled "Mau-Mauing the Flak Catchers," Tom Wolfe described how protest tactics had gotten out of hand:

> Going downtown to mau-mau the bureaucrats got to be routine practice in San Francisco. . . . They sat back and waited for you to come rolling in with your certified angry militants, your guaranteed frustrated ghetto youth, looking like a bunch of wild men. Then you had your test confrontation. If you were outrageous enough, if you could shake up the bureaucrats so bad that their eyes froze into iceballs and their mouths twisted up into smiles of sheer physical panic, into shit-eating grins, so to speak—then they knew you were the real goods. They knew you were the right studs to give the poverty grants and community organizing jobs to.[25]

According to an editorial in the *Wall Street Journal*, the murder of abortion doctor David Gunn in Pensacola, Florida, on March 10, 1993, by an anti-abortion protestor is evidence that confrontation politics is still out of control. Protest movements have created a new political culture, the elite business publication charged, that encourages every group to express its needs without concern for the overall welfare of society:

> What in the past had been simply illegal became "civil disobedience." If you could claim, and it was never too hard to claim, that your group was engaged

in an act of civil disobedience—taking over a building, preventing a government official from speaking, bursting onto the grounds of a nuclear cooling station, destroying animal research, desecrating communion hosts—the shapers of opinion would blow right past the broken rules to seek an understanding of the "dissidents" (in the '60s and '70s) and "activists" (in the '80s and now).[26]

According to elite democratic critics, by encouraging people to assert their needs by pressuring government, protest movements weaken the authority of government at the same time that the demands on government are multiplying. Political scientist Samuel Huntington termed this phenomenon the "democratic distemper."[27] According to Huntington, the problem was caused by an "excess of democracy." In the 1960s and 1970s, as people made more and more demands on government to solve their problems, government responded with massive social programs, "overloading" the system."[28] The result was increasing fiscal deficits and a governmental tendency to pay attention to minority interests, aided by protest tactics, at the expense of the public interest.

At the same time that citizens demanded more from government, however, they were unwilling to sanction governmental authority and thus contradictorily rendered government less able to satisfy their demands. The result was a decline in public trust and confidence in government. As Huntington warned: "The surge of participatory democracy and egalitarianism gravely weakened, where it did not demolish, the likelihood that anyone in any institution could give an order to someone else and have it promptly obeyed."[29] In short, as the politics of protest spread, society became ungovernable.

The Popular Democratic Response: Elite Distemper

Although popular democrats acknowledge excesses in social protest movements, they argue that, overall, the participatory upsurge of protest movements beginning in the 1960s strengthened American democracy rather than weakened it. Whenever long suppressed issues are finally addressed by a political system, conflict is bound to result. Conflict is inevitable in a democracy—and healthy. Popular democrats maintain that elite democrats criticize protest movements not because they threaten democracy, but because they threaten the powers and privileges of elites. The main threat to democracy comes not from a "democratic distemper"—ordinary people demanding their rights—but from an "elite distemper"—fearful elites refusing to change and reacting to protestors with repression and violence.[30]

A good example of elite repression is the campaign of the government under presidents Johnson and Nixon against the anti–Vietnam War movement. Viewing opposition to the war almost as an act of treason, the government harassed antiwar leaders, violated civil liberties, and infiltrated antiwar organizations to spread dissension. In 1968, antiwar protestors organized a demonstration at the Democratic National Convention in Chicago. Denied permission to hold a rally

A Kent State University student tosses a tear-gas bomb back at the National Guardsmen, who fired on the demonstrating crowd, killing four. The Kent State incident became a symbol of government repression of the antiwar movement.

near the convention, the protestors were infiltrated by FBI and Chicago police agents who spread disinformation and encouraged protestors to violate the law. When demonstrators tried to march on the convention, police attacked, clubbing not just demonstrators but journalists and bystanders as well. As outraged demonstrators chanted "The whole world is watching!" news cameras recorded the ugly scene for a shocked TV audience.[31] The commission appointed to study the causes of the conflict put most of the blame on the city administration and concluded that the police had rioted.[32]

The Chicago riots polarized public opinion about the war. Some people, especially blacks and younger college-educated whites, sympathized with the demonstrators and felt that the police had used excessive force. Most Americans, however, were repulsed by what they saw as mobs of long-haired radicals, hurling curses at the police and waving communist flags.[33] Gradually, public opinion shifted against the war. Nevertheless, the war continued, frustrating antiwar protestors and shaking their faith in American democracy. In the so-called Days of Rage, antiwar activists launched indiscriminate acts of violence and destruction in American cities to "bring the war home." The cycle of repression and violence precipitated by the Vietnam War divided the country deeply, stretching the fabric of American democracy to the breaking point. According to popular democrats the fault lies more with the elites responsible for the war and for repressing legitimate dissent than with the protestors.

Achievements of Mass Movements

Popular democrats maintain that protest movements have not been mere expressions of emotion; they have brought concrete reforms that helped make this country more egalitarian and democratic. Pursuing normal channels of electoral and interest-group politics, many groups find it difficult to even get their issues onto the agenda for discussion. Protest movements succeeded in putting previously ignored issues, like equal rights for black Americans, onto the political agenda. As we pointed out in the previous chapter, new issues represented by public-interest groups would never have made it onto the agenda of interest group politics without the threat of protest movements to goad the system into action.

In the controversy over protest politics we often lose sight of the wide range of reforms enacted by mass movements. A few of their accomplishments follow.

1. Civil Rights Movement. The civil rights movement began the long process of integrating African Americans into the democratic process. Largely as a result of changes in voting laws, the number of black elected officials in the United States increased from 1,469 in 1970 to 7,370 in 1990.[34] Critics often point out that U.S. race relations are still highly problematic. Consider, however, where race relations would be if African Americans were still being denied basic civil rights like the right to vote.

2. Environmental Movement. As a result of the environmental movement, large construction projects must now issue environmental impact statements (EISs), giving the public a chance to comment; substantial progress has been made cleaning up the nation's polluted waters, with aquatic life returning to many bodies of water; and in communities across the nation recycling programs are saving energy and reducing the volume of solid waste.

Members of a church in Gabriel, Louisiana, protest the construction of a hazardous waste recycling plant in their community (Summer 1993).

The Environmental Justice Movement

According to conventional wisdom, the mass movements of the 1960s and 1970s died in the 1980s and 1990s. Although fewer mass demonstrations in Washington capture media attention, mass-movement politics did not die, it simply shifted its focus. A good example is the environmental justice movement, a unique combination of the civil rights and environmental movements.

From its inception, the environmental movement was dominated by white middle-class activists. In September 1982, five hundred predominantly black residents of Warren County, North Carolina, were arrested for blocking the path of trucks carrying toxic PCBs to a hazardous landfill in their community. Among those arrested was the Reverend Benjamin Chavis. Suspicious as to why North Carolina would dump its poisons in a black community, Chavis began a nationwide study, entitled *Toxic Wastes and Race in the United States.* The study concluded that "race was consistently a more prominent factor in the location of commercial hazardous waste facilities than any other factor examined." Chavis coined the term *environmental racism* to describe the phenomenon. (In April 1993 Chavis was appointed executive director of the NAACP; he was removed from the post in August 1994.)

Subsequent studies by the federal government and independent researchers have confirmed that African Americans, even after controlling for income, are exposed to more environmental hazards. According to the data, poor blacks are exposed to neurologically damaging levels of lead at almost twice the rate of the poorest whites; blacks are twice as likely as whites to live in counties with the highest levels of industrial toxins; and blacks are 50 percent more likely to die from acute exposure to hazardous materials outside the home.

A loose coalition of church, civil rights, labor, environmental, and community groups, the environmental justice movement has been led by blacks. Like the early civil rights movement, however, it has not pursued an exclusively black strategy but has articulated goals that appeal to whites as well. As Chavis expressed it: "We're not saying take the incinerators and toxic-waste dumps out of our communities and put them in white communities—we're saying they should not be in anybody's community. You can't get justice by doing an injustice on somebody else."

In fighting environmental racism, the movement has raised basic issues of popular democracy. In Kettleman City, California, residents organized themselves into "People for Clean Air and Water" in opposition to a hazardous waste incinerator. They sued the company building the incinerator, charging that it violated their civil rights by failing to provide notices about the plant in Spanish (40 percent of the residents are monolingual Spanish speakers). A California court ruled in their favor, setting a precedent that communities must be informed and participate meaningfully in environmental decisions that affect them.

Although active mostly at the local level, the environmental justice movement won an important national victory in 1994 when President Clinton signed an executive order giving federal agencies one year to address the disproportionate environmental hazards that their policies have imposed on low-income and minority populations.

Sources: "A Place at the Table: A Sierra Club Roundtable on Race, Justice, and the Environment," *Sierra* 78, May/June 1993, pp. 51–58, 90–91; Benjamin A. Goldman, "Polluting the Poor," *Nation,* October 5, 1992, pp. 348–49; The White House, Office of the Press Secretary, press briefing by EPA Administrator Carol Browner and Attorney General Janet Reno, February 11, 1994.

3. Antinuclear Movement. The antinuclear movement succeeded in pushing the regulatory agencies to fully consider the dangers of nuclear power plants. As a result, few new nuclear power plants are constructed in the United States anymore. The chances of a Chernobyl-type disaster are low and alternatives to nuclear energy are being pursued more vigorously, including solar energy and conservation.

4. Antiwar Movement. Besides helping to bring the Vietnam War to a close, the antiwar movement exposed the unchecked war-making powers of the president. In 1973, Congress passed the War Powers Act, limiting the ability of future presidents to wage wars without the approval of Congress.

5. Neighborhood Organizing Movement. Neighborhood protests, including lying down in front of bulldozers, have stopped highway engineers and urban renewal planners from ramming their projects through low-income and minority neighborhoods without taking into account the costs to local residents.

The preceding examples illustrate that mass movements have changed American politics since the 1960s. The movement that has had the most profound effect on American politics, however, is the feminist movement, for it has influenced not only particular political practices, but also the very way we think about politics.

The Feminist Movement: The Personal Is Political

A major goal of the feminist movement was to help women enter the public worlds of work and politics that had previously been dominated by men. The movement has made progress in many fields. Interestingly, the word *sex* was added to Title VII of the 1964 Civil Rights Act, prohibiting discrimination in employment, not by feminists but by a southern congressman who wanted to subject the bill to ridicule.[35] Once the bill had passed, women began lobbying to ensure implementation. In 1965 President Johnson signed Order 11246, which required that all employers holding federal contracts—covering about one-third of the work force—to agree not to discriminate in employment practices and to undertake affirmative action programs to rectify past discrimination.

The women's movement did not peak until 1970, when it began seriously influencing legislation. Whereas only ten women's rights bills passed Congress in the 1960s, in the 1970s seventy-one such bills passed.[36] One of the most important was Title IX of the 1972 Higher Education Act, which opened collegiate sports to women, among other things.

The effect of this legislation, along with private lawsuits against sex discrimination, has been to open opportunities for women in work and politics. The numbers of women doctors and lawyers have increased significantly, as have those of mail carriers, construction workers, movie directors, and news anchors. Women's earnings have increased as well. The median salary of full-time women employees increased from 59 percent of men's salaries in 1970 to 70 percent in 1991. Moreover, women have become more active in politics. The number of women in Congress increased from 11 in 1969 (10 members of the House and 1 senator) to 53 in 1993 (47 members of the House and 6 senators).[37]

The effect of the women's movement has gone well beyond increasing women's rights to participate in previously male-dominated arenas. The movement has expanded the definition of politics to include relations that were previously considered cultural or even personal, especially family relations. This side of the feminist movement is captured by the slogan: "The personal is political." The effect of subjecting a range of previously unquestioned activities to political analysis has been profound. Feminism has even altered our language, with new terms like *Ms.* and *chairperson*. Both women and men have begun to question gender roles in the family and have pressed for more male involvement in childrearing. Various forms of sexual harassment, previously tolerated, are now being challenged by women. Women have questioned the rigid ideal of beauty held over them and have demanded control over their bodies, including the right to choose an abortion. Women have challenged the power of male doctors, especially over childbirth, and midwives have organized for more authority to deliver babies. The crimes of rape and wife beating have been exposed, and women have demanded protection from police and the courts. Thousands of battered women's shelters and rape crisis shelters have opened.

The politicization of male–female relations has caused a backlash in the form of a movement to defend traditional family values. In the mid-1970s, Phyllis Schlafly started a Stop ERA (Equal Rights Amendment) campaign. ERA was

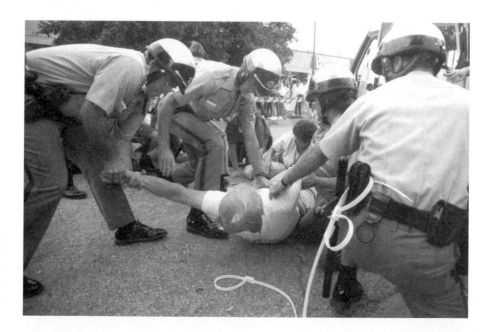

Wichita, Nebraska, police officers wrestle with an antiabortion protestor as he tries to block access to a Women's Health Care Services Clinic.

an amendment to the Constitution that would have outlawed discrimination on the basis of sex. Stop ERA warned that equal rights would mean drafting women into the army, men no longer supporting their wives, and unisex toilets. After passing Congress in 1972, the ERA fell three short of the required number of states to become a part of the Constitution. Opponents of feminism claimed a victory. Led by the Christian right, the anti-abortion movement applied the confrontational methods of the civil rights movement to stop abortions. Operation Rescue trained people in the practice of civil disobedience. Blocking entrances to abortion clinics, large numbers of protestors were arrested, giving valuable publicity to the movement.

The issue of family values entered the 1992 presidential campaign in an unusual way when Vice President Dan Quayle criticized an episode of the TV series "Murphy Brown" for glamorizing, he said, the decision of its lead character to have a baby out of wedlock. The Bush campaign attacked Clinton as an opponent of family values. Clinton made every effort to defend traditional family values, but his positions on issues like daycare and family leave identified him more closely with feminism. Also, in contrast to the traditional image portrayed by Barbara Bush, Hillary Rodham Clinton symbolized, for many, feminist values. Not surprisingly, Clinton did better among women voters than among men.[38]

In short, no matter where you stand on the feminist movement, you cannot deny that it has had a profound effect on American society and politics. The movement succeeded in placing a range of new issues on the political agenda—a feat that no political party or interest group could have accomplished.

CONCLUSION: THE NECESSITY OF MASS MOVEMENTS

American democracy has always struggled with the question of where to draw the line in protest politics. To give protestors complete freedom to disrupt people's lives and to engage in civil disobedience without punishment would enable minorities to dictate terms to society. On the other hand, to prohibit boycotts, strikes, pickets, and marches and to severely punish civil disobedience would stifle protest politics altogether. If we err in any direction, we should err in the direction of tolerating protest movements, because they are crucial for the healthy functioning of American democracy.

First, when the proper ingredients come together, mass movements level the playing field of American politics, offering a way for minorities and the politically disenfranchised to be heard in the system. As we saw in previous chapters, electoral politics and interest-group politics are normally biased in favor of the wealthy, the highly educated, and the politically connected.

Second, mass movements provide a way to overcome the inertia created by the American system of checks and balances. Our fragmented system of government, established by the Constitution, gives narrow constituencies seeking material benefits good access to policymaking. Broader groups, especially those with political or moral concerns, find it difficult to be heard in the system of electoral politics and interest-group bargaining. Mass movements provide a way for groups with broader goals, such as basic rights for blacks or Native Americans, to force the system into action.

Finally, in an era of distant government and impersonal bureaucracies, mass movements provide a way for people to express their deepest feelings about politics in direct actions with like-minded citizens. Mass movements help keep the participatory promise of American democracy alive.

KEY TERMS

protest politics
mass movement
relative deprivation
transactional leader

transforming leader
civil disobedience
satyagraha

SUGGESTED READINGS

Saul D. Alinsky, *Reveille for Radicals* (New York: Vintage Books, 1969). A classic statement by one of the great theoreticians and practitioners of protest politics in the United States.

Barbara Sinclair Deckard, *The Women's Movement: Political, Socioeconomic, and Psychological Issues* (New York: Harper & Row, 1983). A comprehensive study of the women's movement covering its goals and organization.

Samuel Huntington, *American Politics: The Promise of Disharmony* (Cambridge, Mass.: Harvard University Press, 1981). A critique of mass movement politics from an elite democratic viewpoint.

Francis Fox Piven and Richard A. Cloward, *Poor People's Movements: Why They Succeed, How They Fail* (New York: Pantheon, 1977). Argues that when poor people's movements turn into interest groups, they become co-opted and cease to represent the interests of the poor.

Juan, Williams, *Eyes on the Prize: America's Civil Rights Years 1954–1965* (New York: Penguin Books, 1988). A vivid account of the civil rights movement, produced in conjunction with a riveting television documentary that is available on videotape.

PART

·THREE·

INSTITUTIONS

From the beginning of the American political system, one of the core issues in the democratic debate has been the character of American national institutions. As we saw in Part One, the founders set up an elite democratic system in which only the House of Representatives would be directly elected by the people; the other national institutions would be indirectly selected and thus partially insulated from popular passions and pressures. Yet the logic of democracy in America has compelled all national institutions to become more responsive to the popular will. How do American national institutions today reflect the ongoing struggle between elite democracy and popular democracy?

Chapter 12 considers Congress, the branch of government most open to public input. Congress contains both popular democratic and elite democratic elements, and the chapter examines how this combination is the source of both the legislature's distinctive strengths and its disturbing weaknesses.

Chapter 13 covers the presidency. Modern presidents claim to be champions of popular democracy, leaders in the pursuit of the public good. We show how the presidential

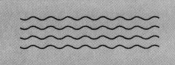

rhetoric of popular democracy often disguises the methods and objectives of elite democracy.

Bureaucracy appears to most Americans as a frustrating bastion of elitism. Chapter 14 explodes some common myths about bureaucracy in America, showing how elite democrats largely built bureaucracy in America but now often fear it, and how popular democrats largely opposed bureaucracy but now often need it.

The judiciary remains the most overtly elitist branch of national government. Yet Chapter 15 suggests a democratic paradox: Preservation of the fundamental rules and values of popular democracy sometimes depends on the conscience and commitments of a judicial elite. This chapter focuses on how this elite crafts its decisions and shapes them to be acceptable to others in the political system.

Congress: Between Elite and Popular Democracy

At first glance, Congress appears to be the most democratic of the three branches of American national government. Its members spend more time with ordinary citizens than do presidents and federal judges. Its operations are more open to the public. If popular democracy retains an important place in the national government, Congress would seem to be its home.

If we think back to the original debate (described in Chapter 2) over the national legislature, however, we see that the democratic character of Congress is a matter of controversy. The Federalists designed the House to be more democratic and the Senate more elitist, but hoped that representatives in both bodies would be superior men who would filter out the people's selfish passions and promote their true welfare. The Anti-federalists worried that legislators of this elite stripe would become arrogant and corrupt, and argued for representatives who would closely resemble ordinary people. Some of the Federalists' and Anti-federalists' hopes have been realized—and some of their fears as well. Present-day Congress is a volatile mixture of elite democracy and popular democracy.

Reacting to the popular democratic state legislatures of the revolutionary period, James Madison argued that the new national legislature should have a more stable and knowledgeable membership. Longer terms of office and a more selective electoral process would produce legislators who would act in "a cool and deliberate" fashion and craft laws of lasting national value.[1] The contemporary Congress has, in many respects, fulfilled Madison's hopes. Members of Congress tend to be well educated and often affluent political professionals whose electoral advantages as incumbents make lengthy congressional careers likely. Specializing in the subject matters of the committees and subcommittees to which they have been assigned (often at their own requests), members develop substantial expertise in the various fields of public policy. Thus, in terms of stability and knowledge, Congress meets the requirements of elite democracy.

Yet the modern Congress also reveals some pitfalls of elite democracy against which the Anti-federalists warned. Rather than rising above the narrow interests of factions, Congress often serves the most well-connected and financed of those factions. Special interests, with their bountiful campaign contributions, technical information, and threats of electoral punishment, constantly pressure members of Congress to define public policy in a manner favorable to them. Members also tend to become privileged political insiders who enjoy aristocratic "perks" of high office, just as Anti-federalist writers dreaded.

Elements of popular democracy are as evident in the contemporary Congress as are elements of elite democracy. With members of the House facing reelection every two years, and senators facing the voters every six years (as a result of the 17th Amendment, adopted in 1913), representatives need to stay in close touch with their constituents if they hope to enjoy a career in Congress. The closeness of representatives to constituents sometimes takes the narrow and locally oriented forms that the Federalists denounced in the behavior of the revolutionary state legislatures. When members of Congress curry favor with the voters back home with "pork-barrel" (projects such as dams or office buildings that bring jobs and money into a district) or spend inordinate amounts of their time and staff resources on "casework" (assistance to individual constituents), Congress is diverted from its responsibility to draft laws that serve a national interest.

Although this chapter is frequently critical of the failings of Congress, behind the criticism lies the conviction that a strong and effective Congress is crucial to the fate of popular democracy in America. Elite democrats argue that in a complex, dangerous, and technological world, Congress, with its inefficient methods of decision making, has become outdated. They point out that in most other political systems legislative power has receded and strong executives become dominant. Popular democrats respond that unless legislative power balances executive power, democracy is in trouble. Only a vital Congress can ensure that government will be sensitive to the concerns of ordinary citizens and forge genuine compromises between their diverse viewpoints. Above all, whereas the executive branch makes decisions behind closed doors, in the halls of Congress citizens can hear public arguments about the public good.

We begin our examination of Congress with a brief discussion of representation, the key concept in legislative politics. Next, we turn to look at our representatives—who they are, how they are elected and stay elected, and how they relate to their constituents between elections. From the individual we turn to the institutional, considering differences between the House and Senate, committees and subcommittees, party leadership, floor action, and influences on voting. Examining executive–legislative relations shows Congress grappling with its sometime partner and more frequent adversary. At the end of the chapter, we return to the subject of Congress and the two forms of democracy, focusing on increasing public unhappiness with Congress as reflected in the movement for term limits on congressional members.

REPRESENTATION

When we say that Congress is our most representative branch of government, what do we mean by the word *representative?* There are three distinct concepts of representation in common use.

The first considers a representative a **delegate.** In this view, a representative comes from a particular district or state and has the responsibility of reflecting the opinions, feelings, and interests of the voters in that district or state. As a delegate, the representative "re-presents" what the folks back home are saying. Advocates of the delegate concept suggest that in a large and complex nation ordinary people can affect national government only when their representatives follow their wishes.

Those who believe that a representative should be a **trustee** insist that the voters choose on the basis of integrity and good judgment rather than strict adherence to district sentiments. Rather than re-presenting the views of constituents, the representative as trustee does what he or she thinks is best. What is best, in the eyes of the trustee, is the national interest, even if it conflicts with the interests of constituents.

A third concept suggests that a legislator must be a **member of a responsible party.** Belonging to a party that is united on the basis of its program for governance, the representative promises to follow this program once in office. The emphasis is neither on the local district nor on individual judgment; rather, it is on responsibility to a program that voters across the nation have chosen. The party responsibility model of representation allows majority sentiment at the polls to be translated into majority rule in the legislature.

Strong arguments can be made for and against each of these concepts of representation. How do they relate to the conflict between elite democracy and popular democracy? The delegate idea of representation has much in common with popular democracy and most closely resembles the Anti-federalist view of representation. Representatives deeply rooted in the culture and values of their constituents, closely attuned to what they are experiencing and thinking, and determined to fight for what is best for them are absolutely vital to a democratic political order. On the other hand, delegates can take this idea of representation too far, catering to the most narrow of district interests, forgetting larger responsibilities to the common good, and fragmenting the legislature so badly that it becomes incapable of responding to problems of a national scope.

The trustee notion is more elitist and closer to what the Federalists proposed. Representatives entrusted to follow their own convictions may produce legislation that is wiser, more expertly crafted, and in the national interest. Yet they may also get out of touch with ordinary citizens, form partnerships with the economic elites who lobby them, and focus on their own perpetuation as political elites. Ordinarily a figure of elite democracy, the trustee can draw closer to popular democracy by educating constituents about common interests.

The party responsibility idea of representation has, perhaps, the greatest potential for popular democracy, allowing ordinary people to send a signal of what they want and transforming that signal into governmental action. Yet this idea of representation is least applicable to American legislative politics. Compared to political parties in other democracies, American political parties at the national level have historically been weak. American legislators have been delegates and trustees more often than they have been members of responsible parties. Nonetheless, the party responsibility concept is not without significance. Party cohesiveness in Congress has been growing, for reasons we note later in the chapter. Legislators who operate as strong partisans may be essential figures in the furtherance of popular democracy at the national level.

WHO ARE AMERICA'S REPRESENTATIVES?

The Constitution excludes few adult Americans from Congress. Members of the House of Representatives must be at least 25 years of age and have held U.S. citizenship for seven years. For the Senate, the comparable requirements are 30 years of age and nine years of citizenship. But this inclusiveness of the Constitution has became exclusive by factors of class, race, and sex. Rather than closely reflecting the demographic characteristics of the American people, Congress has been dominated by well-educated and affluent white males. There are, however, encouraging signs of growing diversity in Congress, as individuals from previously underrepresented groups are elected in larger numbers.

To observe both the enduring social biases and the growing social equality in Congress, consider the social composition of the 103rd Congress (1993–1994).[2] For this Congress, as for its predecessors, the membership by no means reflects a cross-section of the American people. Most members of Congress are local elites, with levels of education and income well above the averages for their districts or states. The largest single occupational category for members of Congress is the law; 239 of the 535 members of the 103rd Congress are lawyers (yet less than 1% of Americans belong to the legal profession). The second ranking occupation is business, with 155 individuals. Third and fourth are public service and education, with 97 and 77 individuals, respectively. Few members of Congress come from the working class or from labor unions; the 103rd Congress contains only two individuals who previously served as officials of labor unions. That membership in Congress is so highly skewed on the basis of class reflects in part the advantages of an upper- or at least middle-class education and occupational skills. It also reflects financial advantages: Individuals from the working class lack the personal funds and access to monied supporters that individuals from local economic elites, such as lawyers and businesspeople, enjoy.

Women and racial minorities have also been underrepresented in Congress. Reflecting traditional assumptions about gender and entrenched practices of occupational and political discrimination, women hold only 11 percent of House seats and 7 percent of Senate seats. Historical patterns of racial discrimination and prejudice are reflected in the Senate; African Americans make up 9 percent of the House and Hispanics make up 4 percent, whereas the Senate contains only one African American and no Hispanics.

Although the numbers seem to indicate that Congress remains a bastion of privileged white males, they actually represent an improvement over the 102nd Congress. In the 1992 elections, the women's movement and growing political sophistication of women produced an increase in the numbers of women from 28 to 47 in the House and from 2 to 6 in the Senate. (A special Senate election in Texas in the spring of 1993 added a seventh woman, Republican Kay Bailey Hutchison.) Benefitting from congressional redistricting designed to enhance minority representation, African-American membership in the House rose from 25 to 38, and Hispanic representation rose from 10 to 17. A fitting symbol for the new prominence of previously underrepresented groups was the election in 1992 of an African-American woman, Carol Mosely Braun, as a senator from Illinois. Also notable was the election of Ben Nighthorse Campbell, a Native American, as senator from Colorado. The 103rd Congress does not reflect the diversity of America, but it looks more like America (to borrow a phrase from President Clinton) than Congress ever has.

The Senate remains less diverse than the House: Running for the Senate requires much more money, advantaging those with access to economic elites. Personal wealth often comes into play in campaigns, and the Senate is sometimes called, with only slight exaggeration, a "millionaire's club." Statewide elections make it difficult for racial minorities to win. The barriers to minority representation in the Senate are obvious when we consider that Carol Mosely Braun is only the second African American elected to the Senate in the twentieth century.

While the trend toward greater diversity in Congress should encourage supporters of popular democracy, the continuing dominance by upper-middle- and

Ben Nighthorse Campbell (D-CO) and Carol Mosely Braun (D-IL) were elected to the Senate in 1992. Campbell is the first Native American and Braun is the first African-American woman ever elected to the Senate.

upper-class white males suggests the power of elite democracy. But demographics do not tell the whole story. Whichever class, race, or sex representatives are, they must be elected by the voters. Defending the proposed House of Representatives against charges that it would be the home of an aristocracy, James Madison argued that the electoral connection would override any elite biases and make legislators faithful servants of their constituents. "Duty, gratitude, interest, ambition itself," he wrote, "are the cords by which [representatives] will be bound to fidelity and sympathy with the great mass of the people."[3]

REPRESENTATIVES AND THEIR CONSTITUENTS

Congressional elections are the linchpin of the connection between representatives and their constituents. In the electoral process the voters are supposed to determine what kind of representation they will have. Yet electoral competition for Congress is often stacked in favor of those already in power; possessing superior resources, especially money, incumbents win most congressional races.

In earlier eras of American politics, the parties played a major role in recruiting congressional candidates, financing their campaigns, and mobilizing voters on their behalf. But in an era of party decline the typical congressional candidate is self-selected. Successful candidates usually share certain characteristics. First, they are experienced public officials, having gained visibility and stature in such offices as mayors, district attorneys, or state legislators. Second, they are ambitious—running for Congress requires an ego strong enough to overcome attacks and insults, and to compensate for loss of privacy, family time, and more lucrative career opportunities. Third, they are willing to work hard—a congressional race requires physical and emotional energy. Amazing feats of campaigning are not uncommon. In a successful 1974 bid for a House seat in South Dakota, Larry Pressler shook an estimated 300 to 500 hands a day for 80 days. In an unsuccessful 1986 try for a House seat in Ohio, Gary Suhadolnik rang more than 40,000 doorbells.[4]

Experience, ambition, and willingness to work hard mean little unless a candidate for Congress also can raise large sums of money for the campaign. Congressional contests, as Chapter 9 showed, have become very expensive.

Getting Elected

Anyone contemplating a run for Congress must confront one reality: Incumbents are reelected almost always in House elections, whereas in Senate elections challengers have a slightly better chance. Unless there is an open seat (the incumbent has retired or died), the odds against the aspiring candidate winning a congressional race would scare off all but the hardiest political gamblers. In the House, incumbents regularly win over 90 percent of the contests. Sometimes, as in 1986 and 1988, incumbent reelection rates run as high as 98 percent. Senate incumbents are often nearly as successful; in 1984, for example, 90 percent were reelected, while in 1990 an extraordinary 97 percent of incumbents won (only one incumbent senator was defeated). The aspiring candidate has the greatest chance to win at a moment of political turmoil, when incumbents are more vulnerable. In 1986, for instance, amid growing public unhappiness with the Reagan administration, Republicans lost majority control of the Senate as only 75 percent of incumbents were victorious. In 1992, the House banking scandal and other embarrassments led to the election of 110 new members (only 24 incumbents were defeated in the general election, but many others retired or were defeated in their party's primaries).[5]

Why do incumbents do so well and challengers so poorly? Many factors favor the incumbent, but at the top of the list is money. With years in office to stockpile campaign funds, the incumbent generally has an enormous head start in fundraising. As discussed in Chapter 10, special interests and business PACs, seeking access to legislators (and assuming that those in office are good bets to be reelected), contribute primarily to incumbents. As a result, the typical incumbent has a huge advantage over the typical challenger in campaign funds.

Incumbency bestows advantages beyond fundraising. Incumbents generally enjoy greater name recognition than challengers. Voters entering the voting booth are more likely to recognize the names of incumbents. And these names generally evoke favorable feelings. Table 12.1 shows that when voters are surveyed on various dimensions of legislative performance, incumbents are evaluated favorably by 80 percent to 90 percent of the respondents.

Name recognition, accompanied by favorable feelings, is an outcome members of Congress have given themselves extensive resources to achieve. Through the **franking privilege,** they send mass mailings to constituents without having to pay postage. Newsletters, for example, publicize their accomplishments and often ask constituents to express their views on major national issues, portraying incumbents skilled in the ways of Washington yet open to the sentiments of the folks back home. (Figure 12.1 shows the scope of congressional mailings. Note that recent mailings have gone up each election year.) Through generous travel allowances, members return to their districts often, attending group meetings, mingling at ceremonial events, and making their faces as familiar as possible. Due to the growth of personal staff, members can deploy personal assistants to work in district offices to help constituents, a practice known as **casework.** Casework earns the gratitude of individual voters and enhances the incumbents' reputations among their family and friends.

Incumbents' advantages scare off the kind of politically experienced challengers who might give them a difficult race. As Gary Jacobson has written,

FIGURE 12.1

Incoming and Outgoing Congressional Mail, 1972–1993

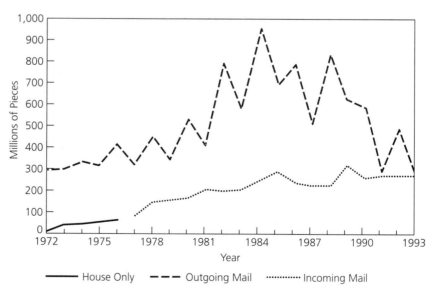

Source: Davidson, Roger H., and Walter J. Oleszek, CONGRESS AND ITS MEMBERS, Fourth Edition. Copyright © 1994 by CQ Press. Used with permission.

TABLE 12.1

Evaluations of
the Incumbent's
Performance and
the Vote in the 1988
House Elections
(in percentages:
N = 758)

Relevant Responses	Evaluation of Performance	Distribution of Responses	Voting for Incumbent
86 General job performance	Approve	92	88
	Disapprove	8	17
District Services			
92 How good a job of keeping in touch with people?	Very good	34	89
	Fairly good	51	81
	Fairly poor	10	66
	Very poor	6	49
92 Expectations about incumbent's helpfulness in solving voter's problem	Very helpful	38	90
	Somewhat helpful	51	78
	Not very helpful	8	44
	It depends	4	81
17 Level of satisfaction with response to voter-initiated contact	Very satisfied	62	93
	Somewhat satisfied	31	75
	Not very satisfied	5	50
	Not at all satisfied	3	50
18 Level of friend's satisfaction with response	Very satisfied	68	92
	Somewhat satisfied	24	75
	Not very satisfied	7	30
	Not at all satisfied	1	0
24 Could voter recall anything special incumbent did for the district?	Yes	24	87
	No	76	76
Voting and Policy			
46 General agreement or disagreement with incumbent's votes	Agreed	55	96
	Agreed, disagreed about equally	36	79
	Disagreed	9	16
16 Agreed or disagreed with vote on a particular bill	Agreed	77	91
	Disagreed	23	43
24 Which candidate would do a better job on most important problem?	Incumbent	93	97
	Challenger	7	3

Source: From THE POLITICS OF CONGRESSIONAL ELECTIONS, Third Edition by Gary C. Jacobson. Copyright © 1992 by HarperCollins Publishers, Inc. Reprinted by permission.

"Most incumbent House members face obscure, politically inexperienced opponents whose resources fall far short of what it takes to mount a serious campaign."[6] That the power of incumbency rests partly on the weakness of most challengers is illustrated by the case of Congressman Robert Leggett from California's Fourth District. Leggett's challenger in 1976 was a little known retired civil servant. Before election day, the press revealed that the incumbent had fathered two children by one of his staff assistants, was supporting two different households, and had forged his wife's name to obtain a deed. Yet Leggett won reelection.[7]

Why is incumbency less powerful in the Senate than in the House? As a more prestigious institution (and with only two positions per state), the Senate draws more prominent individuals into challenges to incumbents. Such individuals have a better chance of raising the funds to conduct a serious campaign. Statewide constituencies reduce incumbents' opportunities to mingle with them while necessitating more reliance on mass media, through which well-financed challengers can hope to match incumbents in name recognition. Finally, senators' positions on controversial national issues are more visible to constituents than those of House members, leading to greater vulnerability should the incumbent have taken unpopular stands.

The Permanent Campaign

Incumbents would not win reelection at such imposing rates if they did not devote so much of their time, energy, and resources to it between electoral campaigns. Political scientists who study Congress have found that the pursuit of reelection shapes the relationships between representatives and their constituents.

In his book *Congress: The Electoral Connection*, David Mayhew argues that the principal objective of members of Congress is reelection, and that most of their behavior can be understood as means to this end. He highlights three kinds of activity that serve the **reelection motive:** (1) advertising, (2) credit claiming, and (3) position taking. Through advertising—newsletters, trips to the district, interviews with local TV—legislators make themselves familiar "brand names." Through credit claiming, members lead voters to understand that federal projects for their districts, such as highways, office buildings, or military bases, result from their influence in Washington. Through position taking, representatives enunciate positions on national and international issues that please the voters back home, whether or not the representatives are doing anything about these issues.[8]

A second political scientist, Morris Fiorina, argues in *Congress: Keystone of the Washington Establishment* that a particular relationship between representatives and constituents is important to the electoral success of incumbents. The growth of casework best explains the increases in incumbency advantage in the last several decades. Fiorina presents a cynical scenario through which incumbents promote their own electoral interests. First, members of Congress establish new programs that expand the federal bureaucracy. Second, the bureaucrats take actions that aggravate or frustrate citizens, who turn to their representatives for assistance. Finally, as Fiorina describes it, "the cycle closes when the congressman lends a sympathetic ear, piously denounces the evils of bureaucracy, intervenes in the latter's decisions, and rides a grateful electorate to ever more impressive electoral showings. Congressmen take credit coming and going."[9]

Perhaps the most impressive attempt to explain how representatives relate to constituents is Richard Fenno's book, *Home Style*. After observing members of the House in their home districts, Fenno noticed that each developed a certain "presentation of self." Each representative portrayed herself or himself in a way that was personally appealing to constituents. Thus, one rural congressman had a person-to-person style, driving from town to town, getting out and shaking hands, even recalling names and family details of supporters. In contrast, a second representative from a more urban/suburban district stressed his skill as an articulator of issues. In these and other cases Fenno observed, the "presentation of self" was part natural (what felt comfortable to the representative) and part calculated (what the voters wanted).

If representatives develop an effective "presentation of self," they signal that they are well qualified, that they identify with the people of their districts, and that they empathize with their constituents' problems. If voters become convinced of all three, they come to trust their representatives. Having won the trust of constituents, representatives can vote as they see fit on most legislative matters. Moreover, trusted incumbents are likely reelected incumbents. Fenno's analysis of trust helps to explain a seeming paradox about Congress—that most voters have a negative view of Congress as a whole but a highly positive view of their own representatives.[10]

Mayhew, Fiorina, and Fenno suggest that representatives devote much of their time and thought to pleasing constituents. Preoccupied with reelection, the contemporary representative is, as Madison predicted, bound to the voters; an aloof legislator with an aristocratic style, in the classic vein of elite democracy, would not stand a chance today. Yet adherents of popular democracy cannot take much pleasure from these three theorists' views. All three suggest that legislators curry favor with voters through mostly superficial imagery and narrowly directed benefits. None of the three depicts legislators who approach their constituents as an intelligent public, capable of learning about issues and developing a concern for a larger common good. If popular democracy characterizes the contemporary connection between representatives and their constituents, it is the popular democracy of the permanent campaign.

The permanent campaign exacts a toll from representatives as well as citizens. Weary of endless campaigning and fundraising, and frustrated by partisan bickering and public backbiting, an unusually large number of House and Senate members chose not to run for reelection in 1992 and 1994. The effectiveness of the permanent campaign also seemed to be waning in 1994, at least for House Democrats. Although only two Democratic incumbents in the Senate were unseated in 1994, more than thirty Democratic incumbents in the House (about

15 percent) were swept away by a Republican tide (see Chapters 8 and 9 on the 1994 congressional elections).

As permanent campaigners, representatives spend a great deal of time in their districts, advertising themselves and attending to the narrower interests of their constituents. Yet their success at winning reelection in this fashion ironically encourages elite democracy in one of its most negative forms: the elite democracy of the privileged Washington insider. The Anti-federalist writer Brutus predicted that "in so extensive a republic, the great officers of government would soon become above the control of the people, and abuse their power to the purpose of aggrandizing themselves. . . ." Contemporary members of the House of Representatives are hardly the tyrants against which Brutus warned, but their nearly permanent status as incumbents promotes petty self-aggrandizement. (See the box on the House banking scandal of 1992.)

CONGRESS AS AN INSTITUTION

Some political scientists who study Congress believe that we can understand the institution by examining the behavior of the 435 individuals in the House and 100 individuals in the Senate. Congress, according to this view, produces the laws and policies it enacts due to the motives of its members. To understand the representatives is thus to understand Congress.

Other political scientists, although not denying the importance of individual motives, suggest that institutions themselves have an independent effect. When complicated rules and procedures link individuals together in a common effort, the outcomes that an institution like Congress produces are likely to reflect more than individual motives. Institutional forms and rules matter. To understand Congress, we must understand not only the representatives, but also the institution within which they work.[11]

Different institutional features tug Congress in different directions. The committee system fragments decision making into small arenas where powerful special interests dominate and strengthens elite democratic tendencies in Congress. Parties and their leadership offer opportunity for popular democratic tendencies to prevail. And the recent increase in floor activity, while making Congress somewhat more unruly and unpredictable, has enhanced the vitality of public debate, a central concern for popular democrats.

House and Senate

Congress is composed of two institutions, the House and the Senate. As we saw in Chapter 2, the founders designed these two institutions to be distinct and to serve as checks on one another. The two institutions are still distinct, although not always in the ways the founders anticipated. What are the current differences between the House and the Senate?

The most obvious and important difference is membership size. An institution with 435 members is likely to be organized and run differently from an institution with 100 members. The greater size of House membership has led to a greater reliance on formal rules to structure behavior and avoid chaos. It also encourages greater issue specialization for members. With an equal number of issues and fewer members, senators focus on a broad range of policy questions.[12]

One of the principal differences that the founders established between the House and Senate—that representatives were elected directly by the people and senators selected by state legislatures—was eliminated by the 17th Amendment, which provided for the direct election of senators. Nonetheless, constitutional differences between the two institutions continue. The Senate's special constitutional role in international matters, through its votes on treaties and diplomatic personnel, has given it a more prominent place than the House in the making of American foreign policy. Its responsibility to "advise and consent" to presidential nominees has given it an important role in executive and judicial selection. The Senate's constitutional design as a deliberative forum for discussing measures of national importance, as compared to the greater responsiveness of the House to local concerns, has also shaped senators' roles.

Less bound by rules, with a broader focus on issues, and with a larger constitutional mandate, senators see themselves as special individuals more than House members. (Perhaps by way of compensation, House members argue that they are closer to the people.) The superior self-image of senators is evident in the contrast drawn by Hugh Scott, former minority leader in the Senate: "The House is a massive creature. . . . It's more lethargic, more like a hippopotamus. . . . [Senators are] like antelope or deer who leap with some grace from subject to subject, issue to issue. There is a great deal more grace of movement in a herd of antelope than in a group of hippopotamuses."[13] The Senate's sense of superiority—and the resulting resentments of House members—have been furthered by the modern media, which concentrate on senators as colorful newsmakers.

The House is a more structured institution, more heavily influenced by local pressures on the one hand and more susceptible to centralized party leadership on the other. The Senate is a more fluid institution in which each of the members has greater individual latitude. The House allows less debate but is better organized to reach decisions; the Senate produces a more vigorous dialogue but has a harder time coming to conclusions. Some observers see this difference as healthy for the democratic vitality of Congress.

Congressional Committees

Although differences between House and Senate exist, certain institutional forms and practices are common to both. Foremost is the **committee system**—the system whereby most of the work of Congress is done by smaller groups. That Congress does most of its work through its committees creates problems, but this division of labor is necessary and inescapable. Lacking committees, Roger Davidson and Walter Oleszek observe, Congress "could not handle 12,000 bills and nearly 100,000 nominations biennially, a national budget of more than $1.5 trillion, and a limitless array of controversial issues. Although floor actions often refine legislative products, committees are the means by which Congress sifts through an otherwise impossible jumble of bills, proposals, and issues."[14]

There are several kinds of committees in the House and the Senate. *Standing committees,* the most important, are permanent bodies that perform the bulk of the work. They gather information through investigations and hearings, draft legislation, and report it to their parent chambers for a potential vote. The majority of bills proposed by individual members of Congress never get past the standing committee that considers them; these committees thus have great negative power. *Select committees* are designed for short-term investigations and lack the power to draft legislation. A recent example of a select committee investigated the Iran–*Contra* scandal during the Reagan presidency. *Joint committees* include members from both houses and are designed to produce information rather than legislation; examples are the Joint Economic Committee, which studies the economy, and the Joint Taxation Committee. *Conference committees* meet to reconcile differences when the House and Senate pass alternative versions of the same law. Composed of the members from each chamber of Congress who have been the central actors on the bill in question, they produce the final language of the law.

Because much of an individual member's legislative life is spent in committee work, obtaining an assignment to a standing committee is a matter of great importance. Party committees in each house attempt to place members in accordance with their wishes. In the Senate, with its smaller numbers, every member is assured a spot on one of the most prestigious committees. In the House, however, there is often intense competition for places on Rules, Appropriations, Ways and Means, and Budget committees. Some legislators are less concerned about winning a spot on one of these powerful committees than on joining a committee that deals with a subject crucial to their constituents. Representatives and senators from farm states, for example, gravitate toward the agriculture committees.

Once a member has joined a committee, the usual pattern is to remain there, developing expertise and, even more important, **seniority.** Seniority is crucial to gaining a leadership position. Under the congressional seniority system, the member from the majority party who has the most years of continuous service on a committee becomes its chair. Until the 1970s the seniority system was automatically followed, even when a chair held positions at odds with the rest of the committee's majority. The House Democrats, as the majority party, re- formed this system in the early 1970s, giving power over the selection of chairs to the party's caucus. Although seniority has continued to determine most chairs, a few have been unseated in subsequent votes. Along with other reforms relating to committees (to be discussed later in this section), the demise of an automatic

Rep. Charles Schumer (D-NY) fires a semiautomatic assault pistol at a police firing range. This "photo opportunity" allows Schumer to dramatize legislation he has introduced in 1994 to ban such weapons.

seniority system diminished the nearly autocratic power that committee chairs had once wielded. Now, the power of committee chairs depends largely on how much political skill and policy expertise they possess.

Committees engage in a number of activities. Senate committees examine and vote on presidential nominations to the executive and judicial branches. Committees in both houses engage in oversight of the federal bureaucracy. Most important, committees prepare legislation for their parent chambers. The preparation of legislation contains three distinct stages: hearings, markups, and reports. **Hearings** allow witnesses for and against a proposed bill to make statements and answer questions. They build a supportive public climate for a bill that the committee majority wishes to advance, and they may gain valuable personal publicity for the committee's leadership. The actual drafting of legislation is called the **markup.** In writing a bill, the committee majority must be concerned about how it will be received by the parent chamber, the other house of Congress, the president, the public, and often the interest groups directly affected. If the committee majority favors a bill, a report is prepared for the parent chamber, explaining its purposes and provisions. Because many bills are lengthy and complex, the persuasiveness of the report may be crucial if the committee's work is to be upheld by the parent chamber.

That the House and Senate so often go along with the recommendations of their standing committees is a testimony to the expertise of committee members. Many committee and subcommittee chairs in the House and Senate dominate legislative debates because their colleagues respect their expertise. Sam Nunn, a Georgia Democrat, exerts great influence over defense policy as chair of the Senate Armed Services Committee, and Henry Waxman is a powerful force in health-care policy through his position as chair of the House Commerce Committee's subcommittee on Health and the Environment. Committee expertise is critical in legislative–executive relations as well; without it Congress would not stand much of a chance in conflicts with policy experts working for the president. The expertise found among long-time members of committees is important evidence for the elite democratic claim that elites bring greater expertise to the art of governance.

While the committee system divides the congressional workload and fosters expertise, it also creates some of Congress's most enduring problems. One is a classic problem of elite democracy: Greater expertise is fostered, but this expertise is self-serving. Legislators often join a particular committee because they wish to serve interest groups that are important in their home districts or states. These legislators form alliances with the major interest groups and executive agencies with which their committees interact.

In the *iron triangles* that result, interest groups testify before the committee in favor of existing and potential programs that benefit them. Committee members support such programs in the bills they draft—and gain political support and campaign contributions from the interest groups. The agencies, with their missions and budgets supported by interest group and committee, implement the programs in a way that pleases the interest group and the committee (see Figure 12.2). In recent years, many iron triangles have become less rigid, with outside policy experts, public-interest groups, and the press having more input. Some scholars believe that looser "issue networks" with shifting participants are now more common than the old triangular alliances. Yet the narrowly focused expertise that shapes the work of congressional committees and subcommittees remains for the most part the expertise of those whose interests are at stake.

The committee system, critics have long charged, promotes special interests instead of the general interest. Although the public is unaware of most specialized committee deliberations, special interests, by effectively targeting their campaign contributions and lobbying efforts at key committee members, develop considerable influence.

The committee system tends to promote the particular over the general in another sense. Congress has few mechanisms to relate or compare the bills produced by its various committees. Inconsistencies are likely to result in its legislation. To take a notorious example, its agriculture committees support

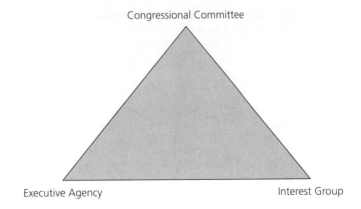

FIGURE 12.2

The Iron Triangle

subsidies for tobacco growers while its health committees support measures to protect the public from the dangers of smoking.

Although the committee system has long been central to the organization and functioning of Congress, its character has changed considerably in recent decades. One important trend affecting the system has been the growth in committee staff. As the regular workload of committees increased—and as committee leaders sought to gain media attention by initiating new and innovative legislation—large numbers of staff aides were hired. These aides have come to perform many of the functions that we associate with committee leaders: developing ideas for legislation, planning hearings to promote them, lining up support for the resulting bills, and negotiating the details they contain. Legislators have turned over so much of their work to their staffs that one congressional scholar, Michael Malbin, has dubbed these staffs our "unelected representatives."[15] The expertise on congressional committees has been enhanced by the growth of large committee staffs, but it is not necessarily the expertise of the committee's members.

A second trend affecting committees has involved subcommittees—smaller and more specialized units of the parent committee. Although greater reliance on subcommittees, like greater reliance on staff, reflects Congress's expanded workload, the real impetus to the rise of subcommittees came during a wave of congressional reform in the early 1970s. The Democrats in the House strengthened subcommittees at the expense of committees for two reasons: to diminish the power of committee chairs and to allow newer representatives to claim a piece of the legislative "pie."

After these reforms, subcommittees took over much of the work of committees, and some observers began to herald the era of "subcommittee government." But the new era was short-lived, due to the enormous budget deficits of the Reagan presidency. As Lawrence Dodd and Bruce Oppenheimer observe, "Seemingly overnight, the rationale for subcommittee government was gone: Without money to spend, there was less need for a highly specialized system of subcommittees."[16]

On the whole, present-day committees are not as powerful as those in the past. Subcommittees have taken over much of the detailed bill drafting from their parent committees. Deficits have reduced the opportunities for most committees to push new programs. Committees have also lost influence to party leaders, and their work is now more susceptible to alteration and rejection once it reaches the floor of the House or Senate. Still, as Steven Smith and Christopher Deering write, "committees remain the principal, if not always fully autonomous, players in nearly all policy decisions."[17]

Parties in Congress

The committee system divides the work of Congress to keep it manageable. But what has been divided has to be reassembled. The most important mechanisms Congress possesses for coordinating its members and their work are its parties and their leaders. Strong party leadership and substantial party unity sharpen legislative debate and enhance the prospect that Congress will be an effective vehicle for the goals of popular democracy.

Independents are occasionally elected to Congress (one independent socialist, Bernard Sanders of Vermont, sits in the 103rd Congress), but almost all members belong to one of the two major parties. Party is the vehicle through which the House and Senate are organized. Seats on committees and committee leadership are determined on the basis of party. Party gatherings—called *caucuses* by the House Democrats, *conferences* by the House Republicans and by both parties in the Senate—choose leaders to run their institutions and sometimes set broad policy directions as well. The party's leaders play important roles in supplying unity to otherwise individualized and fragmented legislative bodies.

Traditionally, congressional parties have been weak, at least when compared to the strong, disciplined parties found in most parliamentary democracies around the world. If legislators gain and retain their offices through their own efforts rather than through their parties, they are going to place the task of pleasing their constituents ahead of the task of cooperating with fellow partisans. Party weakness has also stemmed from the ideological diversity characteristic of America's major parties. A Republican party divided between moderates, pragmatic conservatives, and "hard-right" conservatives, and a Democratic party split between northern liberals and southern conservatives, have had a hard time finding common party ground.

Recently, however, the parties in Congress have been growing more cohesive and unified. Measures of party unity in voting show increases in both parties and both chambers. The House provides the most clear-cut example. In 1972, party unity scores (which show how frequently party members vote together) were 70 percent among House Democrats and 76 percent among House Republicans. By 1992, party unity scores were 86 percent among House Democrats and 84 percent among House Republicans. The most dramatic change came in the partisan behavior of southern Democrats, who often voted with Republicans in the past. In 1972, the party unity score for southern Democrats in the House was 44 percent; by 1992 this score had risen to 79 percent.[18]

Why did partisan unity increase if parties had traditionally been weak and were generally on the decline? Several factors came together to spark a resurgence of parties in Congress. Among the Democrats, a key factor was the shrinking ideological difference between northern and southern members. Thanks to the Voting Rights Act of 1965, southern Democrats gained large numbers of African-American supporters while losing many conservatives to the Republicans; as their electoral base came to resemble that of northern Democrats, so did their voting behavior. Among the Republicans, the electoral successes of Ronald Reagan made the party more conservative; ideological diversity within the party waned. President Reagan's effect on partisanship within Congress was not restricted to his own party. Pursuing a strong conservative legislative agenda, often in a confrontational manner, Reagan forced the Democrats to pull together as a more united opposition party.

The lines of partisan conflict sharpened by Reagan have continued in Congress during the Bush and Clinton presidencies. The Republicans, in particular, exhibited remarkable party unity in opposition to Clinton's deficit-reduction plan in 1993. Not a single Republican in either the House or the Senate crossed party lines to vote for the Clinton budget.

Stronger congressional parties require strong congressional leadership. As the next section shows, the capacity of Congress to coordinate its efforts and achieve effective results rests heavily on the powers and skills of its party leaders.

Congressional Leadership

Among the leadership positions in Congress, only one—**Speaker of the House of Representatives**—is specifically mentioned in the U.S. Constitution. The Speaker of the House is the most visible and prestigious congressional leader (and stands second, after the vice president, in the line of presidential succession). Technically chosen by the whole House but in practice selected by a vote of the majority party in that chamber, the Speaker exercises a combination of procedural, policy, and partisan leadership. As a procedural leader, the Speaker presides over the House, scheduling floor business and determining which members are recognized (allowed to speak on the floor). As a policy leader, the Speaker may promote a substantive agenda that clashes with the agenda of a president from the other party, or may coordinate efforts on policy with a president from the same party. As a party leader, the Speaker can aid fellow partisans through influence over their committee assignments and assistance in their campaign fundraising.

The Speaker is the top figure in a complex leadership structure in the House. Beneath the Speaker, on the majority party side, is the **majority leader.** While the Speaker presides over the House, the majority leader runs party operations on the floor. Along with the Speaker, the majority leader shapes the legislative schedule, confers with members of the party, consults with the president (when he or she is from the same party), and promotes a party perspective through the national media. Underneath the majority leader are *whips*, who assist the party's top leaders by gathering information and "counting noses" on forthcoming votes, and by encouraging partisan loyalty through persuasion and personal attention. The minority party has a similar leadership structure. The **minority leader** runs party operations on the floor of the House, and is also assisted by an elaborate whip system.

There is no equivalent figure to the Speaker in the Senate. Constitutionally, the vice president presides over the Senate, and when he or she is absent the presiding officer is the *president pro tempore*—usually the most senior senator from the majority party. The highest elected leader in the Senate is the majority leader, whose leadership roles resemble those of the House counterpart: determining the scheduling of legislative business, shaping the party's policy agenda, consulting with the president, and speaking for the Senate's position in the national media. Assisting the majority leader in rallying party support for legislation, as in the House, are whips who keep in close touch with the party's contingent. The minority leader is the other major leadership figure in the Senate. Minority leaders are expected to criticize the policies advanced by the majority party and to present their own party's alternatives. Minority whips assist the minority leader in mounting unified opposition to the majority party's aspirations.

Congressional leadership demands a high level of interpersonal, political, and intellectual skills. Because members win their seats on their own, their "bosses" are their constituents and not their party leaders. Further, congressional leaders do not have a large number of favors to bestow on legislators who provide them support. Unable to issue orders, congressional leaders must be talented at persuasion—at finding the right mix of political and ideological arguments to craft a majority for their party's positions. Coalition builders rather than commanders, they may occasionally twist arms to achieve results but rely mostly on the arts of negotiation, conciliation, and compromise.

Occasionally, a congressional leader of great ambition plays a more dominant role in the House or Senate. The most legendary Senate majority leader in this century was Lyndon Johnson during the 1950s. Extracting every ounce of influence he could from his limited position, Johnson achieved nearly unprecedented power in the Senate. More recently in the House, Jim Wright became a forceful and controversial Speaker. Yet leadership of this type is usually short-lived in a Congress whose members pride themselves on their autonomy. Thus, it was no accident that the men who succeeded Johnson as majority leader in the Senate and Wright as Speaker of the House had leadership styles that emphasized conciliation rather than domination.

Although congressional leadership varies with the leadership style of the individuals involved, there has been a recent trend toward stronger congressional leadership, most evident in the House. The greater party unity in Congress has been both a cause and a consequence of strengthened party leadership. Special features of the politics of the 1980s also benefitted party leadership. The more Presidents Reagan and Bush pushed a conservative Republican agenda, the more the majority Democrats turned to the Speaker of the House to combat it with a liberal Democratic agenda. As budget deficits mounted, legislative action shifted from debates over new spending programs to debates over the budget itself—an area where party leaders rather than rank-and-file members took the principal roles. The climate in the House grew more partisan during the 1980s, and party leaders took center stage more often.[19]

Senators, with their greater sense of individual responsibility, tend to resist strong leadership more than representatives. Yet in the 1980s and 1990s leadership became more important to the Senate as well as to the House. The Senate Republican leader after 1984, Robert Dole of Kansas, has been a major force both in advancing the programs of Republican presidents and in retarding those of a Democrat in the White House. When the Democrats selected a new majority leader in 1989, they picked George Mitchell of Maine, largely because he would be an articulate voice, especially in the national media, in opposition to President Bush. Mitchell quickly proved in 1989 that he was a match for Bush when he blocked the president's favorite legislative program, a tax cut on capital gains.[20]

Past congressional leadership has sometimes been hierarchical and elitist. Yet strong leadership may be a requirement for greater popular democracy in the contemporary Congress. Strong congressional leaders, as long as they respond to the views of their party's contingent, make an indispensable contribution to more cohesive parties in Congress. More cohesive parties, in turn, generate a more organized, coherent, and engaging national debate over the issues before Congress. They enable majority sentiment in the nation, informed by such debate, to be transformed into majority action in the legislative process. By frustrating majority action, a fragmented and disorganized Congress usually serves elite interests. Organized by strong party leadership, Congress is more likely to serve popular democracy.

Floor Activity

Committees do the detailed preparatory work on bills, and party leadership shapes the strategies to advance or defeat them. But much depends on what happens to a bill when it reaches the floor of the House or Senate. (For the stages by which a bill becomes or fails to become a law, see Figure 12.3.) In considering congressional floor activity, we look at both rules and procedures and recent increases in floor action.

As large institutions, the House and Senate require elaborate rules and procedures to conduct business. Those hoping to pass or defeat specific legislation must work within these rules. Knowledge about congressional rules often develops with experience and seniority, and may allow a particularly skilled parliamentarian to gain an advantage in floor maneuvering over a bill.

As we mentioned earlier, the House is a more rule-bound institution than the Senate. Ordinarily, a bill cannot be considered by the House as a whole

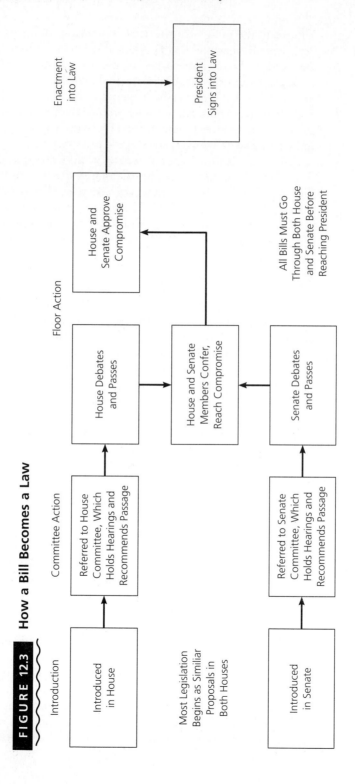

FIGURE 12.3   How a Bill Becomes a Law

until it has obtained a **rule** from the Rules Committee. This rule will determine how much time is devoted to floor debate of the bill and what kind of amendments can be offered on the floor. Under an *open rule*, any germane, or relevant, amendment can be presented. Under a *closed rule*, no amendments can be introduced.

The Senate, less than one-quarter the size of the House, operates with looser rules, allowing greater freedom of action to individual members. The differences between House and Senate rules are most dramatic with respect to amendments and debates. Where proposed amendments in the House must be germane to the subject of a bill, Ross Baker observes, "senators can introduce floor amendments that have nothing at all to do with the bill as it comes to the floor from a committee."[21] The Senate's lack of a germaneness rule enhances the ability of senators to play complex strategic games on the floor. For example, a senator who favors a measure that has been bottled up in committee can attach it as an amendment to an unrelated bill; a senator opposed to a bill may load it with amendments to draw a presidential veto.

Senators are unrestricted as well in the time they can talk about a bill. Senate debate can go on as long as senators insist. The practice of trying to talk a bill to death is known as the **filibuster.** Filibusters were most commonly employed by southern opponents of civil rights legislation in the 1950s and 1960s. But in recent decades, filibusters have been used to block different kinds of legislation. For example, a Republican filibuster killed President Clinton's economic stimulus program in 1993. The Senate does have a procedure, known as **cloture,** whereby debate can be terminated by a vote of three-fifths of the membership. Yet such a large majority is hard to obtain.

Decades ago, when Congress was more hierarchical, with committee chairs ruling the roost and junior members functioning as apprentices, what happened on the floor was mostly a ratification of decisions already made in committees. But starting in the 1970s, a new generation of congressmen and -women, skilled at winning office through campaigning and media use, and impatient with the dominance of a committee oligarchy, transformed the House and Senate into more egalitarian institutions. With committees and their chairs becoming less powerful, and individual members insisting on a greater say, more began to happen on the floor.[22]

In the House, the bills introduced on the floor by committee chairs are now more likely to be amended or challenged. Whereas in the past bills that enjoyed overwhelming committee support ordinarily had smooth sailing, in the contemporary House the fate of legislation on the floor is uncertain. A dramatic increase in floor activity is even more evident in the Senate. Between the 1950s and the 1980s, senators increased the number of amendments they offered fourfold. According to political scientist Barbara Sinclair, "Almost all senators, regardless of party, region, seniority, or ideology, are now floor activists."[23]

A Congress in which action takes place on the floor may be a more chaotic and less efficient legislature. Yet the decline of dominant committee chairs and the growth of floor activity by younger members has also made Congress a more open, innovative, and democratic institution. It used to be said that tourists observing the House or Senate from the galleries were misled into believing that they were seeing Congress in action; the real business was taking place in closed committee sessions. Today, citizens who visit the galleries or watch congressional proceedings on C-Span are more likely to see something real.

Deciding How to Vote

Once legislation has been drafted in committee, pushed by party leaders, debated and perhaps amended on the floor, it comes to the vote of the members. In theory, each legislator should vote on a bill only after giving it thorough consideration. Faced with hundreds of votes on myriad issues, however, the legislator has to make quick decisions.

Political scientist John Kingdon found that a number of factors affect voting decisions.[24] Because reelection is a priority for every member of Congress, the reactions of constituents are one of the most powerful influences on voting decisions. Casting a vote, a representative or senator is likely to ponder whether that vote can be explained back home. For many bills, however, the constituency will signal a legislator little. In these cases, the legislator is likely to turn to colleagues for cues. Fellow members are available for consultation and they make the same political calculations.

Interest groups are another influential factor in shaping voting decisions. In Kingdon's study, interest groups ranked third in importance behind constituents and colleagues. Interest groups deploy lobbyists to provide legislators with information and analysis on bills—couched in terms that support the groups' objectives. They also influence members of Congress through campaign contributions. The most effective approach for an interest group often is to mobilize its members to contact their own representatives or senators. The president and his administration are another factor in voting decisions. Through party legislative leadership and the congressional liaison staff, a president tries to sway members of Congress to back the administration's legislative program (see Chapter 13).

When totalling the factors that influence voting decisions, it is easy to overlook the person who votes. Members of Congress are not passive targets; they have their own policy preferences. They are not, however, completely free to follow their consciences; they don't want to anger constituents. Yet most of the time the personal element can enter the voting decision.

Do the factors affecting voting decisions lead members to support narrow, parochial goals or to promote a larger public good? According to congressional scholar R. Douglas Arnold, whether members vote for narrow or general benefits depends largely on their constituencies. When attentive elites in the district or important interest groups nationwide are the only ones paying attention, the legislator is likely to vote for the particular benefits they desire. But when this same legislator believes that the normally inattentive majority is aroused about an issue, such as auto safety or water pollution, he or she is likely to vote for broader democratic interests. What alters the legislator's voting calculation often is the effort of what Arnold calls an "instigator." A president, a legislative leader, or public educators outside of the government can change the context of the voting decision in favor of popular democracy.[25]

CONGRESS AND THE EXECUTIVE

The Constitution placed Congress first among the three branches of the federal government, devoting Article 1 to the selection, organization, and powers of the legislature. During the nineteenth century, Congress was the preeminent branch, except for brief periods under strong presidents. But the twentieth century has witnessed the rise of "presidential government," with the executive seizing the lead and Congress following.

Although the overall balance of power has shifted from Capitol Hill to the White House, the dynamic of power between the two branches never remains static. From the New Deal of Franklin Roosevelt to the Great Society of Lyndon Johnson, Congress acquiesced in the rise of a strong presidency, particularly in foreign and defense policy. But the Vietnam War prodded Congress to challenge the presidency on international affairs and war making. The sweeping power plays of President Nixon compelled Congress to reassert itself in budget making and domestic policy as well. During the "divided government" of the 1980s and early 1990s, with the Republicans entrenched in the White House and the Democrats controlling Congress, warfare between the two branches was frequent.[26]

Budgetary Politics

One of the primary elements in the rise of presidential government during the middle decades of the twentieth century was presidential capture of a preponderant share of the power of the purse. A legislature dominated by scattered committee power could not produce a coherent budget; a unitary executive, aided by a Bureau of the Budget (renamed the Office of Management and Budget in 1970) could. Congress found itself reduced to snipping budgets framed by the executive. Two developments in the early 1970s, however, propelled Congress to recapture some budgetary power. First, a fragmented congressional budgetary process generated excessive spending. Second (and probably more important), President Nixon usurped Congress's budgetary authority so cavalierly that he forced legislators to develop new defensive weapons.

The vehicle Congress chose to reassert its budget-making authority was the **Budget and Impoundment Control Act of 1974.** This act established new budget committees in the House and Senate. It also created a Congressional Budget Office (CBO), a staff of budgetary and economic experts that provided members with information and analysis comparable to those supplied to the president by the Office of Management and Budget. With the assistance of the

CBO, House and Senate budget committees were to draft two concurrent budget resolutions. The first, due in May each year, was to set targets for federal spending, thereby constraining other, authorizing committees. The second resolution, due in September, was to set final, binding budgetary totals for Congress. Through this new process, Congress hoped to subject the budget to a more coherent review and establish its own priorities against those of the president.

The new budget process did enhance congressional power, but it also intensified conflict between Congress and the executive. It was the presidency of Ronald Reagan that turned the budget into the annual battlefield of national politics. In 1981, Reagan dominated Congress, achieving massive tax cuts and increases in defense spending. He did not, however, persuade Congress to cut domestic spending as deeply as he wished. The result was mounting federal deficits that loomed over all congressional deliberations.

After Reagan's first-year success, conflicts over the budget consumed much of Congress's time; it had to junk one of the two budget resolutions provided in the 1974 law. Even so, during the 1980s more than 50 percent of congressional roll-call votes concerned budgetary matters.[27] Few new programs that called for spending federal dollars received serious consideration; the size of the deficit was invoked to rule them out.

Unable to bring huge deficits under control, Congress resorted to a desperate measure in 1985. The Gramm–Rudman–Hollings bill, named for its Senate sponsors, sought to establish an automatic mechanism for eliminating the deficit. The bill set target figures under which the deficit would decline each year until 1993, when it was supposed to disappear. If Congress and the president could not agree on a budget that hit these figures, the executive would have to reach them through across-the-board spending cuts divided evenly between defense and domestic programs. Advocates of this approach suggested that the prospect of automatic spending cuts would be so unpleasant that Congress and the president would be compelled to reach budget agreements to avert them. But the Gramm–Rudman–Hollings approach was a failure: Congress and the president found ways to circumvent it, and federal deficits grew larger by the early 1990s.

The new budgetary system that Congress created in the 1970s (and modified in the 1980s) has made the two branches more equal in budgetary power. Unfortunately, the two branches have also grown more equal in shirking responsibility for unprecedented federal deficits. Neither has been willing to risk the displeasure of voters by supporting the level of tax increases and spending cuts that would bring the deficit under control.

Foreign Policy

Foreign policy has been the preferred field of action for most presidents in the twentieth century. Presidents have substantial authority and resources in this policy arena. Preference, authority, and resources have sometimes led presidents and their supporters to claim foreign policy as almost exclusively executive in character. Yet the Constitution bestows authority and entrusts responsibility to

Congress as well as the executive in shaping the relationship of the United States to the rest of the world. Through its appropriations authority, Congress funds American activities abroad. It has the sole power to declare war, and is responsible for raising and maintaining military forces. The power "to regulate commerce with foreign nations" draws it into matters of international trade. Moreover, the Senate has the responsibility to deliberate on treaties with other countries.

Despite these constitutional powers, Congress accepted presidential dominance over foreign policy from World War II to the Vietnam War, the era of the "Cold War consensus." It was the disaster of Vietnam—a presidential war—that shook Congress out of its compliant stance. Starting in the early 1970s, Congress began to reassert its role in foreign policy issues: war making, covert actions by the CIA, arms sales to foreign nations, and trade strategy. When it engaged in battles with the White House, the presidency still usually enjoyed the upper hand. Yet Congress won some notable victories—for example, instituting economic sanctions, over a veto by President Reagan, against the apartheid government of South Africa in 1986.

Unhappy with this renewed assertiveness, critics charge that Congress should not interfere with presidential conduct of foreign policy. Congress, they allege, moves too slowly, acts too indecisively, deliberates in too much ignorance, and is too obsessed with reelection pressures to handle the dilemmas of diplomacy and war. But its inadequacies in foreign policy, congressional scholar Eileen Burgin observes, are exaggerated. Congress can act swiftly if necessary, employing expedited procedures; besides, most foreign policy matters require careful consideration. Although most of its members are inexpert on matters of foreign policy, its foreign affairs and armed services committees boast many impressive students of international affairs. If Congress approaches global events with one eye on the reactions of constituents, the same is often true of the president.[28]

That Congress can be both more responsive to constituents and more prudent than the president in foreign policy is evident in the struggle between the two branches over Nicaragua during the 1980s. President Reagan and his staff developed an obsession with the radical Sandanista regime that had taken power in Nicaragua in the 1979 revolution. In the view of the White House, a Marxist government in a Central American nation with a population of only two million people posed a sinister threat not only to its neighbors but also to the United States. Reagan built up an army of *contra* guerrillas—many of them former troops of Nicaragua's deposed dictator—and began a secret war to overthrow the Sandanista government.

As this secret war escalated, attracting public attention, many members of Congress became disturbed. Debates over Nicaragua became a fixture in Congress. By slim majorities, aid to the *contra* guerrillas was cut off on several occasions. Although disapproving of the Sandanista regime, the congressional majority preferred a diplomatic solution, to be worked out by its Latin American neighbors. Congress never stopped the president's war against the Nicaraguan government. Denied funds for the *contras*, the White House resorted to covert and illegal measures that later came to light in the Iran–*contra* scandal. But the actions of Congress set limits to the *contra* war, and headed off the prospect that the United States would intervene with its own troops.

Throughout the debates over Nicaragua, the congressional view reflected public sentiments, whereas the presidential view opposed them. Polls repeatedly indicated that Americans were against aid to the *contras* by margins of greater than 2 to 1. Foreign policy should not be made simply by public opinion polls. But in this case, neither the public nor the majority in Congress favored an extremist policy. It was the president and his supporters who preferred a brutal war to a diplomatic settlement.[29]

Congress is not always prudent about international affairs. But its voice is welcome in foreign policy because the alternative is a presidential monologue. When presidents have dominated foreign policy, they have been inclined to secret deliberations, covert actions, and manipulative rhetoric. Congressional participation in foreign policy opens this arena, generating debate, increasing options, and allowing public input. Elite democrats admire a president who is the sole master of foreign policy. Popular democrats turn to Congress to ensure the public's voice in foreign affairs.

Congressional Oversight of the Executive Branch

The most extensive relationship between Congress and the executive involves legislative oversight of the bureaucracy. **Oversight** is the review by congressional committees of the operations of executive branch agencies. In one sense, oversight is simply a logical process—Congress must review what the bureaucracy does to see if laws are being properly implemented. In another sense, oversight is a highly political process—Congress's chief means for contesting the president over guidance of the federal bureaucracy.

Oversight can take many forms. The most visible is the congressional hearing. In an oversight hearing, top agency administrators appear before a congressional committee to report on their implementation of programs and to answer questions. Members of Congress not only elicit useful information but also remind the administrators who controls their statutory authority and budget resources. Informal methods of oversight are even more common, and usually less conflictive. Committees may request written reports from agencies, or committee staffers may engage in extensive communications with their agency counterparts.

Most legislators used to give oversight short shrift because it was routine and brought few personal payoffs in electoral terms. But oversight activities have increased during the last two decades. According to Joel Aberbach, the rise in congressional oversight stemmed from converging factors. Voters grew unhappy with the size and cost of the federal bureaucracy, making congressional inquiries into poor bureaucratic performance more politically attractive. Deficits made new federal programs more difficult to enact, enhancing the attractiveness as an alternative of greater oversight of existing programs. Aggressive presidents laid claim to monopolistic control of the bureaucracy, making oversight a prime congressional weapon of self-defense. Moreover, increased staff resources provided Congress with the personnel and expertise to perform oversight effectively.[30]

Although the term *oversight* implies a watchful Congress, alert to poor performance in the executive branch, many committees and subcommittees approach the agencies they examine less as skeptics than as advocates. They take a proprietary interest in the agency and its programs, and use oversight hearings to portray them favorably. The position of advocate is understandable when members gravitate to committees and subcommittees that work with programs they care deeply about; an environmentally minded member, for example, will be an advocate for the programs of the Environmental Protection Agency. But advocacy can also become a tool in the iron triangles discussed earlier.

As oversight activities have increased over the last two decades, critics have complained that Congress is interfering excessively with the executive branch and trying to "micromanage" its operations. This complaint has been justified in some instances. Yet the increase in congressional oversight has been, on balance, a welcome development, at least from the standpoint of popular democracy. Oversight is one of the chief means that Congress possesses to hold the presidency and the civil service accountable. Vigorous oversight activities prevent the bureaucracy from becoming a closed world of inaccessible experts. Some oversight is technical and dull; some is narrowly self-serving advocacy. But many oversight hearings have alerted the public to matters that otherwise would have been known only to a small circle of elites.

REPAIRING CONGRESS

If Congress is the "people's branch" of the national government, the people are not very happy with their institution. Every indicator of public opinion shows a high level of public displeasure with Congress. Congressional failures to bring the deficit under control have been only part of the problem. Even worse, attempts by members of Congress to raise their own salaries have brought storms of protest. Ethical abuses by a few prominent congressmen (such as House Speaker Jim Wright, House Ways and Means Chair Dan Rostenkowski, and Senator Robert Packwood), along with the widespread ethical laxity disclosed in the House banking scandal, have outraged the public.

Beginning in the 1980s and accelerating in the 1990s, a movement for **legislative term limits** has claimed to have a democratic remedy for the ills of Congress (and state legislatures as well). Although term limit proposals are varied, their defining characteristic is to set mandatory limits on the consecutive terms legislators can serve. If careerist politicians, entrenched in office with the power of incumbency, have become an unaccountable elite, the solution, proponents of

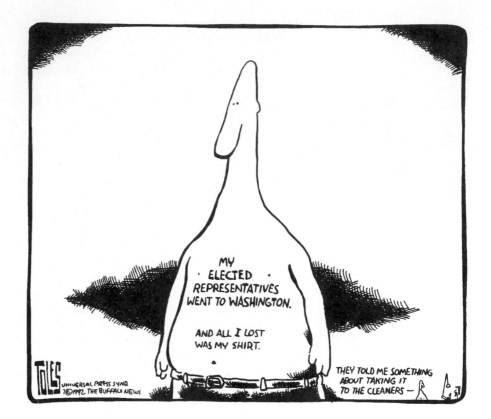

Popular disenchantment with Congress has been running high. Representatives are often viewed as living like aristocrats at the people's expense.

term limits argue, is simple: eliminate the possibility of a long-term legislative career. Term limit proposals have struck a responsive chord with the public. In 1990, voters in three states adopted them; in 1992, they were passed, often by overwhelming majorities, in all fourteen states that had placed them on the ballot.[31]

At first glance, term limits appears to be a popular democratic idea. The goal of the movement for term limits echoes the Anti-federalist objective that legislators not grow remote from the people they represent. But what served popular democracy two hundred years ago may not do so today, under vastly different political circumstances. The consequences of installing term limits are not yet clear. But term limits are likely to weaken the legislature, the most democratic branch of government, and to strengthen its competitors for power. For instance, legislators who have only a brief time in office may become even more dependent on interest groups than they are at present—for information, campaign funds, and even jobs when their legislative careers expire. Short-term legislators, lacking expertise and stature, may also become more dependent on the presidency.

The House Banking Scandal

At the core of public disenchantment with Congress is the perception that its long-time incumbents have become political insiders who grant themselves privileges unavailable to their constituents. Elected to be direct representatives of the people, many members of Congress seem to think of themselves as political elites. To many Americans, prime evidence for this kind of corruption is the House banking scandal of 1992.

The House bank deposited House members' paychecks and cashed checks for them. When a member wrote a check for more than his or her balance (an "overdraft"), the bank paid the check, providing, in effect, an interest-free loan. As *Newsweek* commented, "Any ordinary American who bounced two or three sizable checks would risk felony charges. But members of the House have long occupied a surreal feudal kingdom with perks, privileges, and protection unknown beyond the Hill."

When the House banking scandal erupted into the news in the spring of 1992, it was revealed that hundreds of representatives had taken advantage of the special overdraft privilege. Some members were flagrant abusers; by one count, 66 of them had written about 20,000 bad checks worth over $10 million. The public was understandably irate. According to a *Newsweek* survey, 78 percent disapproved of the way Congress was doing its job and 75 percent believed that members of Congress did not understand the problems of ordinary citizens.

Caught in the glare of this publicity, members of the House hastened to confess their sins in the hope that the voters would forgive—and re-elect—them. Some of the smaller offenders plausibly argued that the House bank was so poorly run that they had never been made aware of their overdrafts. Others groped for

explanations that might engage the sympathy of their constituents. Perhaps the most imaginative was offered by Robert Dornan (R—Calif.), a fiery activist from the religious right. Dornan told the House that a check he had bounced had gone to pay for a backyard shrine to the Virgin Mary.

The scandal left voters feeling bitter, and many large-scale offenders lost in the 1992 elections. Of the 269 sitting members with overdrafts, 77 retired or were defeated in primaries and the general election. The larger the number of overdrafts, the more likely it was that the offender retired or was defeated.

The House banking scandal should be kept in perspective. Even after going to prison and paying a six-hundred-million-dollar fine, Wall Street stock manipulator Michael Milken retained the bulk of his fortune. Compared to Wall Street predators like Milken, the legislators tarred by the House banking scandal were small potatoes. Yet voters were right to be angry. Incumbents—permanent campaigners—had won constituents' trust; the House banking system violated that trust.

Many members of Congress are admirable people and effective legislators. But as popular democrats since the Anti-federalists have warned, the temptations of political privilege are hard to resist. Popular democratic reforms aimed at Congress, such as public financing of campaigns and bans on gifts from lobbyists, attempt to remove these temptations without undermining the effectiveness of the legislative branch.

Sources: Eloise Salholz, "Caught in the Act," *Newsweek*, March 23, 1992; *CQ Guide to Current American Government, Spring 1993* (Washington, D.C.: CQ Press, 1993).

CONCLUSION: THE DEMOCRATIC REVITALIZATION OF CONGRESS

The public correctly senses that the contemporary Congress is in need of democratic revitalization. However, citizens need to recognize that they are also part of the problem. So long as they reelect members of Congress on the basis of pork barrel projects and casework, they will not obtain a legislature concerned with the common good.

Another element in democratic revitalization is campaign finance reform. Public financing of candidates will lessen the advantages of incumbency, restore greater electoral competition, and save members of Congress from the endless and demeaning task of raising funds from well-heeled interest groups. Also crucial for democratic revitalization is public pressure on Congress. An unhappy public can send a message to Congress with its votes. Citizens' groups and mass movements can dramatize issues, lobby Congress, and change the political environment so that democratic reform becomes an electoral imperative.

Popular democrats have a great stake in the democratic revitalization of Congress. Rejecting the idea that Congress is an antiquated body that should play second fiddle to the more efficient presidency, they believe that in an increasingly diverse society such as ours, an open and broadly representative legislature is more necessary than ever. Yet Congress remains poised between elite and popular democracy. Its strength, its creativity, and its legitimacy benefit from reforms that enhance its popular democratic side.

KEY TERMS

delegate
trustee
member of a responsible party
franking privilege
casework
reelection motive
committee system
seniority system
hearings
markup
Speaker of the House of Representatives

majority leader
minority leader
rule
filibuster
cloture
Budget and Impoundment Control Act of 1974
oversight
legislative term limits

SUGGESTED READINGS

Roger H. Davidson and Walter J. Oleszek, *Congress and Its Members*, Fourth Edition (Washington, D.C.: CQ Press, 1994). A comprehensive text focusing on the tension between the representative and the lawmaking roles of Congress.

Lawrence C. Dodd and Bruce I. Oppenheimer, eds., *Congress Reconsidered*, Fifth Edition (Washington, D.C.: CQ Press, 1993). An anthology of original, thought-provoking articles on the contemporary Congress.

Richard E. Fenno, Jr., *Home Style: House Members in Their Districts* (Boston: Little, Brown and Company, 1978). The classic study of how legislators present themselves to their constituents in order to win their trust and their votes.

Morris P. Fiorina, *Congress: Keystone of the Washington Establishment*, Second Edition (New Haven: Yale University Press, 1989). A skeptical view of Congress that depicts members creating bureaucratic messes and then attacking those messes for electoral effect.

Gary C. Jacobson, *The Politics of Congressional Elections*, Third Edition (New York: HarperCollins, 1992). The leading text on how members of Congress convert their biennial exposure to popular democracy into elite longevity in office.

Presidential Leadership and the Democratic Debate

Americans focus many of their hopes and fears on the White House. The president is not only the most visible person in the American political system, but also the person to whom most Americans turn for leadership. In a political system marked by a multiplicity of interest groups, a decentralized Congress, and relatively weak political parties, only the president, it is commonly believed, can unify the nation. Americans associate leadership with "great" presidents, especially in great crises: Abraham Lincoln during the Civil War, Franklin Delano Roosevelt during the Great Depression, John F. Kennedy in the Cuban missile crisis. Each new president is evaluated on leadership ability.

The need for presidential leadership is easy to see. Less easy to see are its dangers. In the original debate over the presidential office, both the need and the dangers were forcefully presented by the Federalists and Anti-federalists, speaking in opposing voices that we have come to identify with elite democracy and popular democracy. Their arguments continue to echo today, as we grapple with whether a democracy can concentrate great power in the hands of a single individual.

The most brilliant advocate of strong presidential leadership in the original debate was Alexander Hamilton. Hamilton believed that the American Revolution had gone too far in placing government directly in the hands of the people and of legislators immediately responsive to the people. A strong executive of uncommon talent and experience was needed to guide public affairs. As Hamilton put it, "Energy in the executive is a leading character in the definition of good government."[1]

Anti-federalists saw the new presidency in a different light. With painful memories of royal governors and the British king, they worried that Hamilton's lofty executive office was a potential breeding ground for monarchical and aristocratic tendencies. Patrick Henry lamented that "there is to be a great and mighty President, with very extensive powers: the powers of a King. He is to be supported in extravagant magnificence."[2] George Mason insisted that executive strength was not necessary when the republic could call on the strength of committed citizens. A better principle than executive power, he said, was the "invincible principle . . . to be found in the love, the affection, the attachment of the citizens to their laws, to their freedom, and to their country."[3]

In modern American politics, Hamilton's case for presidential leadership has been dominant.[4] If an active national government is to address the problems of a complex society and economy in a dangerous international environment, it requires energy and direction. In a political system prone to stalemate, such energy and direction can, it seems, come only from the White House. The ideas and initiatives that presidents put forward may originate elsewhere, but if they are to generate the political support needed for adoption, they must have effective presidential backing.

National emergencies, as much as national direction, require presidential leadership. When a crisis emerges, a swift response is more likely to come from the executive than from the other branches of government. The words of Hamilton still ring true in such moments: "Decision, activity, secrecy, and dispatch will generally characterize the proceedings of one man in a much more eminent degree than the proceedings of any greater number. . . ."[5]

But for a more balanced view of presidential leadership, we also need to listen to the Anti-federalist voices. When Patrick Henry warned that presidents would live like kings in "extravagant magnificence," he would be wrong about nineteenth-century presidents like Andrew Jackson and Abraham Lincoln, but right about Lyndon Johnson, Richard Nixon, Ronald Reagan, and George Bush. It would not have surprised Henry that even a populist like Bill Clinton would indulge himself in luxuries like a $200 haircut.

A modern president has a staff of 400 to 500 people, as many as a royal court. While many of these staff aides concentrate on matters of policy and politics, a president's personal comforts are well attended. George Reedy has written that the president lives more like a monarch than an ordinary American citizen: "Every conceivable facility is made available, from the very latest and most luxurious jet aircraft to a masseur constantly in attendance to soothe raw presidential nerves."[6] This lavish lifestyle may seem a fair reward for the extraordinary burdens a president must bear. Yet it sets a president apart from the experiences and problems of ordinary people. Modern presidents like to present themselves as representatives of American aspirations, yet their style of living removes them from the people for whom they claim to speak.

In voicing his fear that the president would possess royal powers, Patrick Henry underestimated the effectiveness of the checks and balances that the framers of the Constitution built into the fabric of the political system. Yet the arbitrary tendencies Henry dreaded can be detected in the modern presidency. Presidents have found in the vaguely defined concept of executive power the capacity to make war on their own initiatives, to mask some of their actions in the deepest secrecy, and to employ the agencies under their authority to repress opponents. What historian Arthur Schlesinger, Jr., labeled "the imperial presidency" of the Vietnam War and Watergate bears a close resemblance to Henry's monarchical executive.[7]

In an age of low electoral turnout and widespread cynicism, George Mason's assertion that the commitment of citizens was a greater source of strength to the nation than executive power sounds even more outdated than Henry's fears. Yet Mason's words can be read as a warning about the cost to popular democracy of too great a dependence on presidential leadership. Citizens who look to the White House to take care of their problems are inclined to forget the potential—and the democratic value—of their own political activities.

This chapter views presidential leadership in its creative and its dangerous forms. It is important to recognize both the requirements for presidential leadership and the risks of such leadership for a democratic political order. To understand leadership as powerful and paradoxical as the American presidency, a sober appreciation is needed, as well as a healthy dose of skepticism and critical thought.

WHO ARE OUR PRESIDENTS?

What kinds of men have Americans turned to for presidential leadership? (We speak of men here because, until now, no women have been seriously considered by a major party as presidential nominees.) The Constitution sets only minimal qualifications: the president must be "a natural born citizen," must be at least thirty-five years old, and must have resided in the United States for at least fourteen years. The majority of American adults are eligible to be president.

In practice, however, presidents tend to be drawn from a limited pool. According to historian Edward Pessen, they have disproportionately come from privileged backgrounds.[8] Approximately half of our presidents can be categorized as upper class, although an upper-class origin has been less common in the twentieth century than before. Class advantages can give a presidential aspirant uncommon opportunities for education, status, and connections. They do not, however, necessarily predict the policies a president may favor. Franklin D. Roosevelt and John F. Kennedy were born to wealth, but pursued presidential policies attacked by most of the wealthy. In contrast, Richard Nixon and Ronald Reagan came from lower-middle-class backgrounds, but both were applauded by the wealthy for their policies toward business.

We find even less diversity when we turn from class background to ethnic and religious backgrounds. Of the forty-one presidents, the ancestors of thirty-six came from the British Isles; of the other five, three were of Dutch origins (Van Buren and the two Roosevelts), and two (Hoover and Eisenhower) were of Germanic origins.[9] All presidents except one (Kennedy) have been Protestants. To come from eastern or southern Europe, or to be born female, Jewish, black,

President George Bush joins movie star Arnold Schwarzenegger on stationary bikes to promote physical fitness. Posing with action-hero Schwarzenegger helped Bush to shed the image of an upper-class "wimp."

or Hispanic, has ruled out of consideration for the presidency many able and talented Americans.

Twenty-five of our presidents were practicing lawyers at some point in their careers. Recently, however, former lawyers have been less likely to monopolize the White House; since World War II, only Richard Nixon, Gerald Ford, and Bill Clinton began their careers as attorneys. For most of those who have made it to the presidency, attainment of the nation's highest office has capped a long career in politics. The best launching pads for a presidential bid have been the positions of governor, U.S. senator, and (especially in recent years) vice president.[10]

For much of American history, presidential candidates have been men with support from key leaders and factions of their political parties. But as major parties have undergone a decline, the quest for the presidency has become personalized. Candidates now build their own campaign organizations and seek to win enough delegates in primaries and caucuses to gain the nomination, in effect, even before the party's national convention begins. This type of presidential politics places a great emphasis on the candidate's personality. It also leaves the successful candidate with personal supporters but an uncertain base of support among constituent groups that compose his or her party.[11]

The political system shows signs of drawing its presidents from a wider range of Americans in the future. Spiro Agnew, a Greek American, was Richard Nixon's vice president and a leading contender for the 1976 Republican nomination until evidence of corruption forced him to resign his office. Michael Dukakis, another Greek American, became the Democrats' presidential nominee in 1988. Geraldine Ferraro was the first woman (and first Italian American) to run on a major party ticket as a vice-presidential candidate when she was selected as Democrat Walter Mondale's running mate in 1984. Jesse Jackson attracted growing attention in 1984 and 1988 as an African-American candidate for the presidency.

Presidents present themselves as representatives of all the American people. But until now, we cannot say that presidents have actually been, at least in terms of their class, ethnicity, religion, gender, and occupational paths, the most representative Americans. Presidential origins are marked by characteristics we associate with elite democracy.

THE PRESIDENCY AS AN INSTITUTION

In our concern for strong presidential leadership, we focus on the individual who occupies the White House. How an administration performs is vitally affected by a president's personal characteristics and actions. Yet most media commentators and ordinary citizens overemphasize the personal side. The presidency—as distinct from the president—is an institution, and we need to understand its institutional features.

White House Staff

The part of the institutionalized presidency that most directly surrounds the individual president is the **White House staff** (known officially as the White House Office). The White House staff comprises the president's personal aides and advisers, along with their numerous assistants. It has undergone dramatic growth over the last sixty years. Before Franklin D. Roosevelt, presidents had only a handful of personal aides. Abraham Lincoln had to cope with the Civil War with the help of only two personal secretaries. When a telephone was first installed in the White House, Grover Cleveland answered it himself. As late as World War I, Woodrow Wilson typed many of his own speeches.

During the Great Depression of the 1930s, as new responsibilities flooded the White House, Franklin Roosevelt recognized, in the words of the Brownlow Committee that he appointed, "the president needs help." It was Roosevelt who initiated the dramatic expansion of White House staff. But later presidents would oversee a staff far larger than Roosevelt had imagined. At its height, FDR's staff numbered around 50 people. By Richard Nixon's second term, the staff had grown to over 550 individuals. Nixon's successors, responding to charges that the presidential staff had become dangerously bloated, cut it back, but only a little (see Table 13.1).

The White House staff not only has expanded since the 1930s, but also has taken on important new functions. Before Franklin Roosevelt, presidents tended to turn for advice to cabinet members. Although presidents still consider their cabinet selections important, since the 1930s they have downgraded most cabinet heads, relying instead on their staff for assistance in decision making and even in managing federal policies. Staff members have done more than serve as the president's extra eyes, ears, and hands. Some of them—such as H. R. Haldeman

TABLE 13.1 Size of White House Staff	President	White House Staff: Average Number of Full-time Employees per Administration
	Truman	243
	Eisenhower	361
	Kennedy	384
	Johnson	284
	Nixon	514
	Ford	530
	Carter	403
	Reagan	370
	Bush	378

Source: Harold W. Stanley and Richard G. Niemi, VITAL STATISTICS ON AMERICAN POLITICS. Fourth Edition. Copyright © 1993 by CQ Press. Used with permission.

under Nixon, Hamilton Jordan under Carter, Edwin Meese under Reagan, and John Sununu under Bush—have become key decision-makers in their own right.[12]

Why have recent presidents turned to White House staff rather than cabinet members for advice? To understand this phenomenon, we must consider the differences between cabinet members and White House staffers.

A president may have had little personal contact with most members of the cabinet before assuming office. The cabinet is selected with several criteria in mind: public prestige, managerial ability, interest-group or geographic representativeness (e.g., the secretary of the treasury usually is drawn from the business or financial communities, while the secretary of the interior is traditionally a westerner). Potential cabinet heads must pass Senate scrutiny and receive senatorial confirmation. Further, cabinet secretaries can be summoned to appear before congressional committees, where they may be pressed to reveal information the president would rather keep confidential.

In contrast, top White House staff do not usually come to their jobs from power positions. Rather, they are individuals personally attached to the president—men or women who have worked for the president in the past and whose loyalty is long standing. Top staff members often reflect the president's roots and political base. Bill Clinton has drawn many of his key aides, including his first chief of staff, from Arkansas. White House staff do not need Senate confirmation. Unlike cabinet heads, they cannot ordinarily be questioned by Congress, due to claims of separation of powers and executive privilege.

Considering the differences between cabinet and staff presents clues as to why presidents prefer to work with staff. A president has greater flexibility with staff: he or she can hire anyone, move staff members from task to task, replace ineffective or incompatible staff members with less public notice than when dismissing a cabinet member. A president also can assume greater loyalty from staff. Cabinet members must answer to many forces besides the president who appointed them: congressional committees that control the budget and statutory authority for their departments, the interest groups that are important clienteles for their departments, the civil servants who work in their departments. But White House staffers answer only to the president. Their loyalty is undivided.[13]

Offering a president greater flexibility and loyalty than the cabinet, a large and powerful White House staff seems to increase the president's reach and power. But growth of this kind of White House staff has been a mixed blessing for presidents. Members of their staffs have several potential weaknesses. Staff members lack the authority and departmental resources that come with holding a cabinet post. Their influence is completely dependent on the president. Staff members also pay a price for their undivided loyalty. They are not exposed to as wide an array of political forces as heads of executive departments.

Highly dependent and overly loyal advisers are not necessarily the best advisers. Desiring to curry favor with a president, staff members have sometimes presented their bosses with distorted pictures of the reality outside the White House.[14] Rather than enhancing presidential power, they have produced a peculiar presidential blindness, evident in the presidencies of Johnson, Nixon, and Reagan.

A contemporary president requires an extensive White House staff. But the tendency of that staff to enhance the illusion of presidential power and wisdom must be avoided.

Executive Office of the President

The White House Office is part of the **Executive Office of the President (EOP),** established under Franklin Roosevelt in 1939. The other most important components of the EOP are the Office of Management and Budget (OMB), Council of Economic Advisers (CEA), and National Security Council (NSC). Whereas the White House staff was designed to provide the president with personal and political assistance, the other EOP units were to provide institutional—i.e., objective and expert—advice to the president as a policymaker (see Figure 13.1).

The largest and most important institutional unit in the EOP is the **Office of Management and Budget (OMB).** OMB prepares the annual presidential budget. It scrutinizes legislative proposals originating in the agencies of the executive branch to ensure that they accord with the program of the president. It recommends signing or vetoing legislation. In addition, it oversees the management methods of the entire executive establishment.

FIGURE 13.1

Executive Office of the President

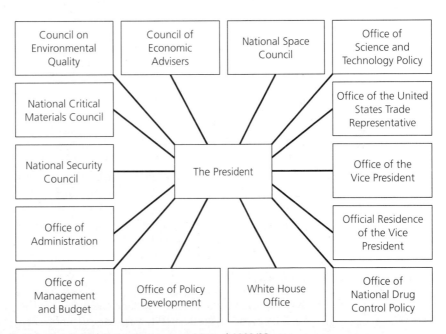

Source: The United States Government Manual 1992/93.

The **Council of Economic Advisers (CEA)** was established in 1946 to provide regular assistance of professional economists. The CEA has a chair and two other members, along with their staffs. It analyzes economic conditions, projects economic trends, and drafts the president's annual economic report.

The **National Security Council (NSC)** was established in 1947 to coordinate the military and diplomatic aspects of foreign policy in an age of American global involvement. Officially, it brings together the top national-security decision makers: the president, vice president, secretary of state, secretary of defense, director of the Central Intelligence Agency, and chair of the Joint Chiefs of Staff. More important than formal meetings of the NSC, however, is the work of its staff, headed by the president's assistant for national security. (See Chapter 19 for a more detailed discussion of the NSC.)

Although the original idea for the EOP was to provide a president with expert institutional advice to balance the more personal and partisan advice of staff, the distinction has diminished in recent years. The White House has made the institutional components of the EOP more political, more directly responsive to the president's personal views and political needs.[15]

Recent presidents have placed trusted aides at the helm of OMB. OMB head Richard Darman was a prominent adviser to President Bush, and Leon Panetta performed a similar role for President Clinton before becoming White House Chief of Staff in 1994. The NSC was used by President Reagan to implement secret presidential policies involving arms sales to Iran and control of the *contra* forces in Nicaragua. The Reagan aide in charge of these projects, Lt. Colonel Oliver North, did not fit the profile of an objective, neutral, institutional aide. The CEA had a different fate in the Reagan presidency. When a Harvard professor appointed by Reagan as chair, Martin Feldstein, did not concur with the White House position on the economy and raised public doubts about the huge budget deficits, he was frozen out of decision making and ridiculed by the president's press spokesman. After Feldstein resigned, the Reagan White House did not fill his position for many months.

As has been the case with White House staff, the EOP has been turned into a central instrument of presidential views and politics. This extension of personal power, from the president's oval office outward, has been justified as an indispensable tool of leadership. But the enhancement of presidential power has not always meant the enhancement of presidential wisdom. A highly politicized OMB under David Stockman manipulated budget numbers to conceal how Reagan's tax cut of 1981 would generate a massive deficit. A highly politicized NSC helped Reagan stumble into the disaster of the Iran–*contra* affair. Some scholars believe that the EOP might serve the presidency better if it was not so politicized.

Cabinet

Beyond the White House staff and the EOP lies the cabinet and the vast expanse of the executive branch. The **president's cabinet** is composed of the appointed heads of the fourteen principal executive agencies, plus a few others, such as the U.S. ambassador to the United Nations. Americans use the term *cabinet* in two ways. In the first, the cabinet is simply the collection of individuals appointed by the president to head the principal executive agencies. In the second, the cabinet is a collegial body, meeting together with the president to supply their collective advice.

Most presidents talk of using the cabinet as a collective forum. Meetings of the cabinet make excellent TV and photo opportunities, showing off the president surrounded by prestigious and weighty advisers. In actuality, cabinet meetings are routine affairs, useful for little more than symbolism. Not surprisingly, most cabinet members come to meetings to pursue the interests of their own departments. Presidents learn not to expect much from a meeting of the cabinet, and instead solicit advice from the individuals directly engaged in policy matters.

The cabinet is more accurately described, therefore, as the collection of individual department heads. In this collection, not all heads are equal. As Thomas E. Cronin has shown, presidents turn most often to their "inner cabinet," composed of the secretaries of state, defense, and treasury, along with the attorney general.[16] These cabinet secretaries handle the subjects most important to the president. Until President Clinton appointed Janet Reno as attorney general, all "inner cabinet" members had been white males.

The "outer cabinet" contains the remainder of the departments, such as agriculture, education, and veterans affairs. The business of these departments is not ordinarily central to a president's program. When presidents have selected women or minorities for their cabinets, it has, until Reno, been for outer cabinet posts. Members of the outer cabinet often find that the prestige of their title is

President Bill Clinton announces the appointment of Janet Reno as attorney general. Reno is the first woman ever to join a president's "inner cabinet."

not matched by their proximity to the president. For example, when President Nixon's secretary of the interior, Walter Hickel, unhappily resigned in 1970, he observed that he had seen the president in private only twice in fifteen months.

Managing the Bureaucracy

If presidents are to control the vast federal bureaucracy, they need the assistance of a strong cabinet. But cabinet members are subject to tugs besides the directives of the White House—pressures from Congress, from interest groups, from the staffs of their own agencies. Presidents and their White House staffers have complained about members of the outer cabinet, who have been accused of "going native" (taking on the perspectives of the departments they were appointed to head) or of building personal empires.

Whatever help they receive from their cabinet appointees, presidents find the management of the federal bureaucracy arduous. Prescribed by the Constitution, it is a task that requires a president to "take Care that the Laws be faithfully executed. . . ." In traditional management theory, the executive branch should be a pyramid, with the president on top, and bureaucrats underneath carrying out decisions. But the modern administrative state diverges from this theory.

A number of factors limit a president's control over the bureaucracy. The vast size of the modern administrative state is itself a limitation, because no president, even with the help of a large White House staff, can keep track of more than a fraction of what is taking place in the bureaucracy. The historical shift from patronage to civil service also has limited presidential control. Civil servants, unlike White House staffers, do not depend on the president for their jobs, and are likely to be less concerned about the success of the president than about the mission, budget, and growth of their own agencies. (The perspective of civil servants may seem narrow compared to that of the White House, but civil servants often have more experience and knowledge in their fields than White House staff.) In addition, executive agencies may be part of iron triangles (discussed in Chapter 12), resistant to control from the White House.

The capacity of executive agencies to resist directives has frustrated presidents. As President Truman prepared to hand over his office to the newly elected General Eisenhower, he predicted: "He will sit here and he'll say, 'Do this! Do that!' And nothing will happen. Poor Ike—it won't be a bit like the Army!"[17] Frustration with managing the bureaucracy has led presidents to try to shift functions from that bureaucracy into the White House itself. More recently, it has led to determined campaigns to recast the bureaucracy in the president's ideological mold.

Reagan and the Bureaucracy

No modern president was as successful in recasting the bureaucracy as Ronald Reagan. Reagan came into office with a strong conservative agenda. His White House deployed several strategies of executive control. Most important was a personnel strategy. Presidential appointees to the bureaucracy were tightly screened by a personnel office in the White House; loyalty to Reagan and his conservative philosophy was a more important criterion for appointment than past experience or professional expertise. Another strategic weapon was the budget. In a period of large deficits, the budget was used as a tool of administrative discipline. Agencies that the Reagan White House saw as unfriendly to its agenda saw their budgets cut and their staffs reduced. Agencies whose behavior the Reagan White House hoped to change knew that they would be fiscally hurt if they did not satisfy the White House.

Reagan's gaining the upper hand over the bureaucracy has impressed many observers. If presidents are to fulfill the public's expectations of leadership, these observers contend, they must use all available bureaucratic resources. In the view of political scientist Richard Nathan, Reagan's administrative strategy shows the way for both conservative and liberal presidents of the future. Regardless of ideology or partisanship, presidents should be sure that "politics penetrates operations," that the president controls the bureaucracy.[18]

If we examine presidential leadership from a more critical perspective, however, this domination of the bureaucracy appears more problematic. Too much presidential domination may not be good for the civil service. During the Reagan presidency, many expert civil servants were demoralized (some effectively terminated) by political appointees whose main interest was undermining their agencies' missions.

Presidential domination sometimes can oppose democratic values. Many of the agencies that the Reagan White House tried to undermine or transform were carrying out laws passed by Congress and favored by most Americans. The Reagan White House undercut laws it did not like through bureaucratic methods that drew little press or public notice. For example, the Occupational Safety and Health Administration (OSHA) was created by Congress to protect Americans against unsafe conditions and toxic substances in the workplace. But the Reagan administration looked on OSHA as harassing businesspeople. Under the administrative strategy of the Reagan White House, OSHA's practices were quietly changed. Safety and health regulations were postponed or cancelled, while budget cuts meant fewer safety and health inspections of factories by OSHA civil servants.[19]

The weakening of OSHA was successful presidential leadership, if leadership is measured by the executives achieving their objectives. But was it good public policy and good democratic procedure? Skillful leadership is needed to prevent the bureaucracy from impeding a president's legitimate objectives. But political and ideological domination may place too high a premium on presidential leadership by slighting other values—public preferences, legislative intent, a skilled civil service—that carry weight in a democratic political order.

THE PRESIDENCY AND THE CONGRESS

Exercising presidential leadership over the executive branch is a formidable task. Equally formidable is winning congressional support for legislation. The relationship between the president and Congress is seldom smooth. Conflict is more common than cooperation—as the framers of the Constitution intended. In the *Federalist Papers*, James Madison set down the theory of checks and balances: "Ambition must be made to counteract ambition."[20] The clash of presidential and congressional ambitions is constitutional theory in action.

This clash is often presented as a competition between the national viewpoint of the presidency and the localistic viewpoint of members of Congress. The idea that the presidency is a better servant of the public interest than Congress is another facet of the case for presidential leadership as the key to the health of our political system. But the idea is not well founded. Sometimes, presidents take a national standpoint, while Congress responds with parochial objections. Generally, however, it is more accurate to say that while presidents speak for a broader coalition of interests than *individual* members of Congress, Congress *as a whole* may speak for an equally broad, or broader coalition.

Before accepting the claim that Congress is locally oriented and the president alone speaks for the national interest, we should remember that neither branch has a monopoly on the representation of public ends. Some public ends have been represented better by the White House at one point in time, and by the majority in Congress at another. Social welfare and civil rights legislation drew greater support from Presidents Kennedy and Johnson than from Congress between 1961 and 1969, but from 1969 to 1977 the same kind of legislation had more backing in Congress than in the administrations of Presidents Nixon and Ford. In this case, insisting that what the presidency favors is more in the national interest than what Congress favors would require us to believe that social welfare and civil rights programs ceased to be in the national interest as soon as the White House changed hands.

Congressional Roadblocks

Why does Congress so often oppose the president? Perhaps the most important source of conflict is the way they are elected. Elected in districts or states, members of Congress have a different constituency than the president. To keep their jobs, they must satisfy voters who are not necessarily backers of the president. Moreover, members of Congress build their own campaign organizations and raise their own campaign funds. With different constituencies and independent political bases, they must "chart their own course."

Presidential efforts to push legislation through Congress may also be frustrated by congressional structure. Power in Congress is fragmented and decentralized, with a shifting cast of characters holding positions of influence on each new legislative proposal. The congressional reforms of the 1970s, although successful in many respects, had the effect of making this fragmentation worse. A decentralized legislative process presents the White House with successive barriers, tripping over any of which loses the legislative race.

Presidents are hardly helpless. Which factors determine success with Congress? A leading student of this question, George C. Edwards, has argued that a president's success in securing passage of legislation depends on the partisan composition of Congress and the president's standing with the American public. Examining the years 1953 to 1986, Edwards found that the level of support for a president's program from members of his own party ranged from 22 to 41 percentage points greater than the level of support from members of the other party.[21] A president enjoying a large partisan majority in Congress is thus primed for a successful legislative record, whereas a president facing a majority from the other party has dubious legislative prospects.

But a favorable partisan balance in Congress does not guarantee legislative success, as Bill Clinton has painfully learned. A president's public popularity is another important factor. A popular president is likely to have favorable ratings among constituents. Congresspeople will not want to appear at odds with a popular president. On the other hand, a president whose popularity is sinking can be opposed by members of Congress with little fear of electoral retribution. To be successful with Congress, a president usually needs both a favorable partisan balance and a favorable standing in the public opinion polls. Lacking the latter, President Clinton barely got his deficit-reduction plan through Congress in 1993.[22]

Presidential Resources

The president has resources to improve the prospects that he or she gets congressional approval. The legislative program sets the congressional agenda. By establishing a strong, well-timed agenda, a president can shape the terms in which subsequent congressional debate is conducted. Working for that agenda on the president's behalf is the **legislative liaison staff,** a portion of the White House staff that spends its time on Capitol Hill. Members of the liaison staff keep the president informed of the political maneuvering for important bills and provide favors to members of Congress in the hopes that they will later return these favors to the White House with their votes.

The favors that the White House offers are valuable but limited. To win a few swing voters in a tight legislative contest, presidents can promise federal judgeships or positions as U.S. attorneys. Federal grants or contracts can be steered to the district or state of a crucial legislator. Minor provisions of a bill can be altered to favor interest groups. In his uphill 1993 battle to win House approval of the North American Free Trade Agreement (NAFTA), President Clinton successfully wooed several pivotal southern legislators with concessions on citrus and peanut butter imports.[23]

A resource that the White House possesses in somewhat greater abundance is the mystique of the presidency. To be photographed with the president or called to meet with the president at the White House can boost a representative's standing with constituents. Apart from political gain, few members of Congress are immune to the mystique of presidential authority. Ronald Reagan thus bestowed presidential cufflinks on numerous members of Congress and invited legislators to use the presidential box at the Kennedy Center in Washington.

George Bush took members of Congress and their families on personally guided tours of the White House, highlighted by a souvenir snapshot of the visitors in the Lincoln bedroom.

If all else fails, a president retains the constitutional weapon of the **veto.** When Congress presents the president with a bill, ten days (Sundays excepted) are given to sign it into law, veto (disapprove) it and return it with a message explaining objections, or do nothing, in which case it becomes law without a signature. Should the president exercise the second option, a two-thirds vote in each legislative branch is necessary to override the veto. If Congress adjourns during the ten-day period and the president does not sign the bill, it is blocked with a "pocket veto."

Overrides of presidential vetoes are infrequent. For example, Jimmy Carter's vetoes were upheld 93.5 percent of the time, whereas George Bush had only one veto overridden during his entire presidency (see Table 13.2). Numerous vetoes are, however, a sign of presidential weakness. They are more common in administrations in which the opposition party controls Congress and is pursuing its own legislative agenda. Gerald Ford vetoed more bills in two and a half years than Kennedy and Johnson did in eight. The threat—as opposed to the actual use—of a veto may be handy for any president. It can force Congress to make a bill more acceptable to the White House.

Although the public expects presidents to demonstrate leadership by establishing a strong record of congressional successes, the constitutional system of checks and balances ensures a difficult time with Congress. A case in point is social policy, which comprises education, health care, housing, welfare, and the environment. Presidents with liberal social policy agendas have often been frustrated by Congress. Medical care for the aged under Social Security was first proposed by President Truman and later by President Kennedy but was only passed under President Johnson. For fifteen years, the American Medical Association lobbied successfully in Congress to block Medicare. (Although the bill was finally passed, it left medical fees to be determined by physicians, opening the door to huge profits for doctors.)

Presidents with conservative social policy agendas may similarly be stalled by congressional opposition. President Reagan spoke in favor of anti-abortion and school-prayer legislation, but he made little progress. Opposition in Congress and among mobilized groups was formidable, so the Reagan White House backed away from a legislative fight, saving its scarce political capital for tax and budget legislation. The changes that Reagan and his conservative supporters hoped to see in social policy were ultimately pursued through conservative appointments to the federal judiciary.

We can point to occasions where presidents have been the masters of Congress. But the famous instances where presidents pushed a sweeping and innovative program through Congress—Roosevelt's "first hundred days" of 1933, Johnson's Great Society of 1965, Reagan's tax and budget cuts of 1981—stand out in large part because they have been so rare. Much of the time, the presidency and the Congress squabble, mired in stalemates, or vieing for credit.

TABLE 13.2

Presidential Vetoes (1789–1992)

President	Regular Vetoes	Pocket Vetoes	Total Vetoes	Vetoes Overridden
George Washington	2		2	
John Adams			0	
Thomas Jefferson			0	
James Madison	5	2	7	
James Monroe	1		1	
John Q. Adams			0	
Andrew Jackson	5	7	12	
Martin Van Buren		1	1	
W. H. Harrison			0	
John Tyler	6	4	10	1
James K. Polk	2	1	3	
Zachary Taylor			0	
Millard Fillmore			0	
Franklin Pierce	9		9	5
James Buchanan	4	3	7	
Abraham Lincoln	2	5	7	
Andrew Jackson	21	8	29	15
Ulysses S. Grant	45	48	93	4
Rutherford B. Hayes	12	1	13	1
James A. Garfield			0	
Chester A. Arthur	4	8	12	1
Grover Cleveland	304	110	414	2
Benjamin Harrison	19	25	44	1
Grover Cleveland	42	128	170	5
William McKinley	6	36	42	
Theodore Roosevelt	42	40	82	1
William H. Taft	30	9	39	1
Woodrow Wilson	33	11	44	6
Warren G. Harding	5	1	6	
Calvin Coolidge	20	30	50	4
Herbert Hoover	21	16	37	3
Franklin D. Roosevelt	372	263	635	9
Harry S. Truman	180	70	250	12
Dwight D. Eisenhower	73	108	181	2
John F. Kennedy	12	9	21	
Lyndon B. Johnson	16	14	30	
Richard M. Nixon	26	17	43	7
Gerald R. Ford	48	18	66	12
Jimmy Carter	13	18	31	2
Ronald Reagan	39	39	78	9
George Bush	29	16	45	1
Total	1448	1066	2514	104

Source: Presidential Vetoes. 1789–1991, Office of the Secretary of the Senate (U.S. Government Printing Office, 1992). Update by Gregory Harness, Head Reference Librarian, 1993.

That presidents cannot ordinarily dominate Congress has been frustrating to champions of presidential leadership. But wisdom and democratic purpose are not always on the president's side. Congressional checks on the president fulfill the original constitutional concern to avert a dangerous concentration of power. That Congress represents political constituencies which may not gain a sympathetic hearing from the presidency can produce legislation that may support narrow special interests, but also legislation that may benefit weak or threatened groups, such as the poor. Rather than expecting presidents to triumph over Congress, we should accept the normality of conflict between the two branches and judge each branch on whether it finds common ground with the other on the most important matters affecting the public interest.

THE PRESIDENCY AND ECONOMIC POWER

Congress is not the only powerful and independent institution with which a president must come to terms. Numerous centers of private power possess resources that presidents want and resources to constrain them. Clashes between the White House and Capitol Hill are familiar dramas in American politics. Less visible are the connections between the presidency and the reigning powers of the political economy.

The modern American economy, dominated by multinational corporations and financial enterprises, requires direction to ensure predictability. The presidency, with its Hamiltonian potential for unified will, decisiveness, and swiftness, has long been seen as the only national institution capable of such centralized direction. Presidential responsibility has thus grown with the rise of the corporate economy.

Before the New Deal, the federal government seldom tried to affect overall economic conditions. But once the Great Depression revealed the disastrous consequences of an uncontrolled economy, President Franklin Roosevelt asserted presidential responsibility. His role became a legal responsibility of every president after him, thanks to the **Employment Act of 1946.** It gave the federal government—and especially the president—the duty "to foster and promote free competitive enterprise, to avoid economic fluctuations or to diminish the effects thereof, and to maintain employment, production, and purchasing power." The act also established the Council of Economic Advisers to assist the president and required an annual economic report to Congress.

What can presidents do to promote a healthy economy? Three policy tools are available to the president as an economic manager: fiscal policy, monetary policy, and incomes policy. Fiscal policy involves federal taxation and spending to affect economic conditions. The president can, for example, propose a tax cut; such a cut will, predictably, increase economic activity. Monetary policy involves the money supply and the level of interest rates. For example, the president can, with the cooperation of the Federal Reserve, slow down inflationary pressures in the economy through higher interest rates that make borrowing money more expensive. Incomes policy is an effort to deal directly with rising prices. A president can, for instance, ask the CEA to develop wage–price guideposts and ask business and labor to adhere to them.

All these actions require the president to obtain the agreement of other powerful actors and institutions. A president can propose changes in federal taxation or spending, but Congress has the final authority over them. Presidents can suggest monetary policy, but the Federal Reserve Board has the final say. They can ask business and labor to avoid price and wage decisions that fuel inflation, but short of mandatory wage–price controls (a rarity in peacetime), little can be done.

Presidential power over the economy is limited by the structural power of the corporate sector, which, as we saw in Chapter 4, plays a decisive role in determining the level of private investment in America. This investment is critical to the health of the economy. Although investment decisions are made largely on economic grounds, spokespeople for big business like to attribute lagging investment to the lack of "business confidence" in a president with whom they differ. No president wants to be viewed as undermining business confidence.

Some presidents have smooth sailing with the corporate sector. Presidents Eisenhower, Nixon, Reagan, and Bush ran administrations that pleased the corporate sector. Other presidents have had a rockier relationship. Elected in the face of corporate opposition, Presidents Kennedy and Carter struggled against charges that they were ruining business confidence and jeopardizing the health of the American economy.

Kennedy's Courtship of the Corporate Sector

The relationship between President Kennedy and the corporate sector provides an excellent illustration of how the politics of business confidence affects the presidency. From the start of his administration, big business looked at Kennedy, elected with labor and minority support, with suspicion. Despite friendly rhetoric and policies, Kennedy could not convince corporate executives that he was not a threat. Then, in 1962, Kennedy had to move against the leading corporations in the steel industry to force them to withdraw a price increase that would have wrecked the president's anti-inflation policy. Unhappy business leaders blamed Kennedy when, a month later, the stock market suffered a huge drop. They predicted a new recession as the fruit of Kennedy's destruction of business confidence.

In the face of a brewing crisis between the corporate sector and the White House, Kennedy retreated. He and his administration went to great lengths to show business leaders that he meant no harm. At Kennedy's request, one of his top aides, Theodore Sorensen, drew up "a long-range campaign designed to soften . . . business hostility." Because the Kennedy administration was already proposing tax breaks beneficial to corporate investment, some of this campaign was psychological. Corporate executives, Sorensen thought, had to be made to feel at home in the Kennedy White House, so he proposed, among other things, "a series of presidential luncheons or black-tie stag dinners for business leaders."[24]

The Kennedy administration wanted to avoid further offenses to the business community. In this light, Sorensen recommended the following:

> Can the President, or the Attorney General, or the Special Counsel, meet quietly and individually with the heads of the regulatory agencies, the anti-trust division, the wage-hour, Food-and-Drug, and other enforcement activities—to emphasize that there are times to steam ahead, to pursue, to be zealous, and there are times to be cooperative and understanding (and the latter is more appropriate now). [Also], to explore what they can do or refrain from doing. Can the SEC [Securities and Exchange Commission, which regulates the stock market], tone down its investigation? Are there broad new areas of investigation planned that can be postponed?[25]

President Kennedy had never wanted to challenge big business; he had wanted to pursue policies that promoted economic growth. But when push came to shove, he felt that he had to offer both substantive benefits and psychological gestures to woo the business community. As president, Kennedy represented all the people, but as economic manager, he gave priority to big business. Rather than furthering the egalitarian economic objectives of popular democracy, he had to further the objectives of an economic elite that constantly criticized him.

Kennedy's relation with business is not unique. No president since Franklin Roosevelt has been able to challenge the corporate sector. President Clinton has carefully avoided conflicts with the corporate and financial communities. From the outset of his administration, he has courted business leaders, not to mention teaming with business lobbyists to push NAFTA through Congress over the opposition of organized labor.

Whether Democrats or Republicans occupy the White House, corporate power is a major constraint on presidential action. The business community does not have to have one of its own in the White House to benefit from presidential policymaking. Its weapon of business confidence deters presidents from a popular democratic economic agenda.

THE PRESIDENCY AND NATIONAL SECURITY

Presidential freedom of action is more extensive in foreign and military policy. Presidents are not free of opposition in this area. Nonetheless, they have exceptional resources in conducting America's international relations—resources that cannot be matched by any other national institutions.

The Constitution is an important source of these resources. It entrusts the president with making treaties and appointing American ambassadors, although it requires the concurrence of two-thirds of the Senate for the first and a majority of the Senate for the second. The president also receives ambassadors from other governments, and although this may appear merely ceremonial, it has been interpreted as giving the president a unilateral power of U.S. recognition.

The presence of these powers in Article 2 suggests that the framers of the Constitution expected the president to bear principal responsibility for the ongoing conduct of America's international relations.

The Supreme Court has upheld a paramount role for the president in the conduct of American foreign policy. In *United States* v. *Curtiss-Wright Corporation* (1936), the Court gave presidents a wide latitude in foreign policy. Writing for the majority, Justice Sutherland proclaimed "the very delicate, plenary, and exclusive power of the president as the sole organ of the federal government in international relations—a power which does not require as a basis for its exercise an act of Congress."[26]

If the Constitution and the Supreme Court have bolstered the president's position in international affairs, so have the institutional resources of the executive branch. The president receives information from American diplomatic and military personnel stationed around the globe, besides secret information from the Central Intelligence Agency (CIA) and the military intelligence services. When foreign policy controversies arise, presidents claim to be the most knowledgeable actors on the scene.

Presidential Dominance in Foreign Affairs

Because the nation needs a coherent foreign policy, a strong case can be made for presidential leadership in this area. Some scholars believe that a weakness in American foreign policy making is that the president does not have enough control.[27] Congress frequently insists on an independent role in foreign policy. Even within the executive branch, different agencies—the State Department, Defense Department, Treasury Department, CIA, National Security Council staff—compete to shape foreign policy. With all the resources in this area, a president still may have a hard time ensuring that the United States speaks with one voice to other countries.

Presidential leadership is necessary in foreign policy, but is not without its dangers, as U.S. history since World War II has evidenced. During this era, the United States began to intervene in the affairs of other nations around the globe in the name of anti-communism and freedom. Employing the military machinery and covert capacities of a growing national-security state, presidents staked out claims of authority that were constitutionally, politically, and morally questionable. In the name of presidential leadership, there were disturbing abuses of power in the areas of war-making, secrecy, and repression.

Believing that placing the decision to go to war in the hands of a single individual was dangerous, the drafters of the Constitution entrusted that decision to the assembled representatives of the people. The president was to be the commander-in-chief of the armed forces once Congress determined the need for armed hostilities. Historically, however, it proved hard to keep presidents in this secondary role. Without any congressional declaration of war, presidents began to use American forces, for example, to repulse attacks on American property abroad, to suppress domestic turmoil, or to fight small-scale wars.

The capacity of a president to employ American armed forces became controversial during the Vietnam War. Presidents Johnson and Nixon were determined to carry out their Vietnam policies against rising antiwar protests from American citizens and within Congress. Once the legal authority for their war making was questioned, they asserted that the commander-in-chief clause in the Constitution gave them vast military powers. When Nixon extended the war into neighboring Cambodia in 1970, he justified his action on the grounds that, as commander-in-chief, he had the right to take any action necessary to protect American troops. With even less justification, he ordered the continued bombing of Cambodia in 1973, even after all American ground forces had been withdrawn. Nixon became precisely what both the framers of the Constitution and their Anti-federalist critics feared: the eighteenth-century British monarch who involved the nation in war on the basis of personal whim.

Congress Attempts to Rein the Executive

Congress attempted to reassert its constitutional role in war making by passing, over Nixon's veto, the **War Powers Resolution of 1973.** According to this resolution, the president must, if circumstances permit, consult with Congress before sending American forces into a situation where armed conflict is anticipated. The president must also provide Congress with a written report within forty-eight hours of dispatching American forces into combat. After sixty days, the president must withdraw these forces from combat unless Congress has declared war or otherwise authorized continued engagement. An additional thirty days is granted to remove them from combat if the president claims that this period is needed for their safe withdrawal.

Presidents since Nixon have complained that the War Powers Resolution ties their hands and undercuts American national security. The resolution actually has had little effect. Dramatic military actions since 1973, such as the invasion of Grenada or the war in the Persian Gulf, have not been hampered by the War Powers Resolution. Because the president has enjoyed a near monopoly on information in these situations and the public has supported presidential actions, Congress has been reluctant to insist on the requirements it established in 1973. The War Powers Resolution might have more of an impact in a protracted military conflict like the Vietnam War. It provides public and congressional opposition with a legal mechanism to call a heedless president to heel. Inadequate though it may be, the War Powers Resolution serves as a statement that we recognize the dangerous potential for abuse in the presidential power to make war.

Presidential Secrecy

There is similar potential for abuse in the **presidential power of secrecy.** Once the United States became involved in a worldwide cold war against communism, revolution, and nationalism, new powers of secrecy were assumed by the White

House. As we shall see in more detail in Chapter 19, the CIA, created in 1947, became a weapon of presidential policymaking in foreign affairs. Through the CIA, presidents could intervene covertly in the politics of other nations, bribing politicians, financing pro-American parties, or encouraging military coups against governments the president regarded as unfavorable to U.S. interests. Clouded evidence even suggests that the CIA offered presidents means to assassinate foreign leaders.

Many presidential decisions in foreign policy are secret. Journalist Eve Pell estimates that President Reagan produced approximately three hundred National Security Decision Directives (NSDD)—executive directives in foreign policy not revealed to any other branch of government. Although the contents remain secret, we do know that NSDDs ordered the arming and training of the Nicaraguan *contras*, the invasion of Grenada, and counterterrorist violence in the Middle East. In some cases, presidential secrecy was probably justified. "More often," Pell writes, "N.S.D.D.s appear to have been issued to evade congressional scrutiny and public debate."[28]

When presidents' dominant foreign policy role has been challenged, some have resorted to secret repressive tactics. The Nixon administration undertook a notorious covert campaign to destroy its critics. Journalists had their phones wiretapped. A secret White House unit, known as the Plumbers, engaged in illegal break-ins to gather damaging material on foes of Nixon's Vietnam policy. The White House compiled a large list of these critics—the Enemies List—and sought to use the auditing mechanisms of the Internal Revenue Service to harass them. Fundamental American liberties became insignificant when they stood in the way of presidential power.[29]

Secret action is enticing. It offers a president opportunity to advance foreign policy goals through methods that would raise ethical and constitutional questions if pursued openly. It allows a policy to persist even when it lacks support from majorities in Congress and the American people. Moreover, it is rationalized by the elite democratic argument that presidents have a superior vantage point and greater expertise than Congress and the public in international affairs. But secret action denies the people presidential accountability.

Americans are often asked to support presidential ventures in international affairs. We need to understand the requirements for presidential leadership in foreign policy. But we also need to recall the Anti-federalist fear of an executive who might move beyond the democratic reach of the people. Vietnam, Watergate, and Iran–*contra* stand as testaments to the potential for presidential abuses of democracy in the name of national security.

A New Era?

Will the formidable power over foreign policy amassed by presidents during the Cold War years be maintained now that the Cold War is over? President Bush's successful assertion of power in the Gulf War suggests that little has changed. With the United States as the only remaining superpower, the president may even be stronger than ever. On the other hand, the inability of either Bush or Clinton to counter Serbian aggression in Bosnia suggests a contrary lesson: Lacking the clear-cut structure of American–Soviet competition, post–Cold War conflicts may not lend themselves to management by American presidents. Furthermore, the American public appears less inclined to support presidential activism in foreign policy.

The end of the Cold War has opened a new democratic debate over American foreign policy (see Chapter 19). A key question in this debate—one that the Clinton administration has struggled to answer—is the role of presidential power in a dramatically transformed international environment.

THE PRESIDENT, THE MEDIA, AND THE AMERICAN PEOPLE

Rooted in the assumptions of elite democracy, the framers of the Constitution did not want a president to get too close to the American people. They placed the immediate choice of the chief executive in the hands of electors, who were supposed to be the most distinguished political elite in each state. The framers expected that the dignity of the president's office and the long duration of the president's term would provide insulation from mass passion or popular demand for economic change.[30]

Modern presidents, in contrast, claim a close bond with the American people. Cultivating public support has become a central activity of the White House.

President Clinton answers questions at a televised town meeting in Southfield, Michigan. Clinton's "populist" style of leadership features intimate contacts with ordinary citizens.

If popular democracy has a voice in national politics, it would seem, at first glance, to be the voice that originates from the White House.

Present-day presidents campaign for public support because it enhances their political influence. Congress reacts more favorably to a popular than an unpopular president; bureaucrats and interest-group leaders are similarly impressed by high presidential poll ratings. If the American political system possessed strong parties, a president could count on more stable support. In the absence of such parties, presidents are on their own.

To gain public support, presidents are increasingly, in the words of political scientist Samuel Kernell, "going public." A growing percentage of presidential time is spent on the road, selling presidential policy. Kernell suggests that "public speaking, political travel, and appearances before special constituencies outside Washington constitute the repertoire of modern leadership."[31]

Such presidential efforts do not necessarily succeed. As the presidency has grown in power, so have public expectations. Americans hold high and often contradictory expectations of presidents. They expect presidents to bring prosperity, peace, and prestige to the nation, while combining the qualities of a statesman and a politician.[32]

Most presidents have not been able to live up to these inflated expectations. Starting with high rates of public approval in the "honeymoon" period at the beginning of their administrations, they have not been able to prevent declines in popularity over the long term. Such declines are not inevitable, however. President Eisenhower's popularity consistently remained at high levels. President Reagan recovered from huge declines in public approval during the recession of 1981–82 and the Iran-*contra* affair to leave office as a popular figure.

The media play a major role in a modern president's relationship with the American people. If we listened only to presidents and their White House staffs, we might conclude that the media function as an impediment to presidential communication with the public. A huge corps of journalists is stationed at the White House to report on a president's every word and deed; when the president travels, the press corps follows. Presidential blunders or White House staff conflicts are often highlighted by the media, while the president's policy proposals are closely scrutinized by reporters and editorial columnists for hidden political motives. Some presidents' political standing has been badly damaged by negative media coverage.[33]

White House complaints about the media, however, tell only one side of the story. The media—especially TV—provide a vehicle through which a modern president can cultivate support. The White House staff includes a Press Office and an Office of Communications; if these units are skilled at public relations, the media provide opportunities for dramatic presidential appearances, colorful photo opportunities, and engrossing human interest stories about the "first family." If the president has an attractive personality and is a skilled public speaker, the media can amplify his or her charm, wit, or eloquence in a manner that presidents living before the age of television might well have envied.

The media are a two-edged sword, sometimes cutting a president, but at other times wielded by the White House as a potent weapon. Consider the difference between media coverage of Presidents Reagan and Clinton.

Reagan's Mastery of the Media

In recent years, the acknowledged White House master of media relations has been the Great Communicator, Ronald Reagan.[34] For the first six of his eight years in office (until the Iran–*contra* scandal), he and his expert team controlled most information about his administration. Reagan used free network airtime for highly successful public pronouncements from the Oval Office, speeches that the press could only watch and not question. Meanwhile, blunders potentially destructive to his popularity were either deflected to his subordinates or largely ignored by his press office and thus by the media. Although much went wrong in the Reagan administration, media trouble did not stick to its chief, who became known as the "Teflon" president.

How did Reagan and his team do it? The Reagan secret of success lay not so much in his policy accomplishments as in his ability to serve the media's need for drama, action, and excitement. His press team provided the media with premanufactured photo and TV opportunities. When Reagan visited the militarized border between North Korea and South Korea in 1985, his every move was choreographed to produce an image of the leader of the free world confronting the "evil empire." Later in his presidency, his press team engineered dramatic film footage of Reagan "ending" the Cold War through his friendly encounters with Soviet leader Mikhail Gorbachev.

Reagan and his team also knew how to avoid angering the press. Unlike Nixon and his media aides, who attempted to deal with a press they perceived as hostile by threatening and attacking it, Reagan and his media team fended off the press more subtly. The White House plugged leaks to the press by subjecting governmental employees to lie detector tests, and barred the press from covering major events like the 1983 invasion of Grenada on the grounds of national security. When the press protested, they were met with a warm smile and a friendly wave. Journalists could not probe the president's thinking, because his press handlers kept him away from impromptu press questions.

Reagan's mastery of the media deterred the press from the aggressive investigations that the Johnson, Nixon, and Carter White Houses had faced. By achieving an appealing image through the media, the Teflon president was able to make successes cling to his presidency while avoiding personal responsibility for failures and scandals. Artfully transforming debates about his policies into awed discussion of his communication skills, Reagan shaped the media agenda.

Clinton: The Media Strike Back

If Reagan was the Teflon president, perhaps Bill Clinton should be called the "Velcro" president. It took only a few days in office for Clinton's media image to change from inspiring leader of a new generation to politically inept waffler devoid of conviction. Just thirty hours after the inauguration, NBC's Lisa Meyers told the nightly news audience that the Clinton White House looked like "the Not-Ready-for-Primetime Players." A week after the inauguration, Eric Engberg of CBS said that the Clinton presidency had "come unstuck."[35]

Almost weekly, reporters stressed the president's falling popularity ratings and his administration's clumsiness at Washington power politics. From presidential haircuts to gays in the military, Clinton took media flak. Conservative commentators complained that he was too radical, and liberal commentators found him lacking passionate commitment. Toward the end of his first year in office, a frustrated Clinton lashed back at the liberal media, from whom he expected greater sympathy, in an interview with the editors of *Rolling Stone*. "I have fought more damn battles here for more things than any president has in 20 years, with the possible exception of Reagan's first budget, and not gotten one damn bit of credit from the knee-jerk liberal press, and I am sick and tired of it, and you can put that in the damn article."[36]

Clinton's problems with the media are a puzzle. After all, hadn't his campaign for the presidency been innovative in utilizing new media (e.g., cable TV interviews and electronic town hall meetings) for direct communications with citizens? One clue to Clinton's difficulties with the press is contained in this question. As Richard Berke of the *New York Times* observed, Clinton entered the presidency with an all-too-obvious strategy to "tightly control the information flow to reporters as the president speaks to the people."[37] In his first months as president, however, there were more efforts to control the press than to speak directly to the people. But Clinton learned that the press could still determine how much of his message reached the public.

Clinton's media team angered the White House press corps long before the White House had developed all the new means of influencing citizens. It closed staff offices from reporters, made it known that press conferences would be infrequent, and limited interviews with top administration officials. Feeling bypassed and manipulated, the White House press corps struck back in the first months of the Clinton presidency. In addition to negative coverage, the networks refused to provide live coverage for the president's first press conference. Clinton was forced to reorganize his media team and alter his media strategy after only four months in office. Bringing David Gergen into the White House as his media advisor (see chapter 7), the president managed to enhance his standing with the press. In 1994, however, as the Whitewater scandal bubbled, relations between Clinton and reporters again soured.

Developments in White House–media relations transcend personalities. With the end of the Cold War, presidents have a diminished capacity for foreign policy drama. Whereas Reagan could go to the Berlin Wall, Korea, and numerous summits with the Soviets, all of which provided heroic TV, Clinton had to face Bosnia, Somalia, and Haiti, hardly colorful "photo opportunities." The proliferation of cable channels also hurt Clinton. With the mass audience fragmented into multiple media markets, a president can no longer dominate the

Clinton's Town Meetings

Can a president escape the cocoonlike isolation of the White House and stay in touch with the people who elected him? Or are a president's contacts with ordinary Americans really designed to provide colorful television footage for the manipulative public-relations machine of the modern executive? Consider President Bill Clinton's televised town meetings, in which a cross-section of citizens can ask him about anything.

Clinton first employed the town meeting format during his 1992 campaign. As president, he traveled to Detroit for a meeting on his economic program and to Tampa for one on his health-care reform proposal. He even took the electronic town meeting to Russia during his January 1994 trip. Clinton claims that the principal purpose of the forums is to stay in close contact with the people. As he put it during the Detroit meeting, "I can see now . . . how easy it is for a president to get out of touch, to be caught up in the trappings of Washington."

A skeptical press, however, has been inclined to interpret the town meetings as slick salesmanship. Clinton, most journalists suggest, is engaging in an end run around the press and its sharp questioning and going directly to ordinary people, who will treat him with greater deference. His political purpose is apparent: to put pressure on Congress through televised images of a populist president winning the people over to his programs.

Careful White House attention to minute symbols of presidential populism supplies some evidence for this skeptical view. When the television station in Detroit that was hosting the meeting offered a comfortably upholstered stool for the president to perch on, Clinton's staffers instead requested a plain wooden stool. Rather than appearing privileged, the president would come across like the average Joe pulling up to the bar at the end of the workday. The station insisted on its stool—so Clinton stayed on his feet for almost the entire meeting, moving close to members of the audience and achieving an even greater appearance of intimacy.

But this skepticism can be carried too far. Clinton's encounters with the public in his town meetings have been too unscripted and open, too full of energy and feeling, to be dismissed as merely a publicity gimmick. The president appears to listen carefully to members of the audience, to be stimulated by their questions, and to be moved by their often painful personal stories. And the audience appears to respond with great interest to the president's messages.

President Clinton certainly takes advantage of popular democratic images in his town meetings to advance his own political ends. But there are enough moments of genuine interaction and dialogue between citizens and the president to regard these town meetings as an advance for popular democracy, too.

Sources: Elayne Rapping, "Television and Democracy," *The Progressive* (April 1993): 36–38; Sidney Blumenthal, "The Syndicated Presidency," *The New Yorker,* April 5, 1993: 42–47; *New York Times,* February 10, 1993, February 11, 1993, January 15, 1994; *Newsweek,* October 4, 1993: 36.

airwaves as Reagan did. Clinton's efforts to rivet the nation's attention have had to compete with dozens of other choices now available to television viewers.[38]

Clinton's rocky press relationship may be distinctive to his presidency or it may herald a new era in which presidents have a tougher time using the media to communicate. The latter would be unfortunate if a president wanted to educate the American people about new problems and policies. But it also may reduce White House manipulation of the public through the media. From the standpoint of popular democracy, the diminishing ability of a president to dominate the media is welcome. A vital democratic debate is not monopolized by the occupant of the White House.[39]

THE PRESIDENCY AND DEMOCRATIC MOVEMENTS

Presidents try to sway public opinion through the media. Can members of the public directly sway the president? What impact can popular democratic movements have on presidential policies?

Some of the finest presidential moments have come when the chief executive responded to citizens and moved the nation closer to fulfillment of its democratic values. When Abraham Lincoln responded to mounting abolitionist pressures by emancipating slaves, when Franklin Roosevelt supported mobilized labor for collective bargaining rights, when Lyndon Johnson endorsed the civil rights movement by voicing its slogan, "We shall overcome," the presidency became an instrument of popular democratic leadership. These presidents were moved in the direction of popular democracy by the force of popular pressures, which compelled them to rethink their previous political calculations. But their popular democratic leadership was not simply a matter of gaining new support or attracting new voters. Mass movements educated these presidents, giving them a new understanding of democratic responsibilities.

Earlier in the chapter, we saw how President Kennedy responded to pressure from big business. But big business was not the only group to influence him; the civil rights movement also changed where Kennedy stood.[40]

Kennedy was sympathetic to the movement for racial equality. But civil rights did not hold a high priority for him. He wished to concentrate on the Cold War struggle against communism. He worried that strong backing for black equality would cost him support among southern members of Congress and southern voters. So, he refused to push civil rights legislation or make statements about the immorality of racial discrimination, settling instead for quiet and gradual administrative actions.

The civil rights movement refused to settle for Kennedy's token gestures. The issue of racial equality was too central to democracy to permit the continuance of an unjust status quo. Movement organizations began dramatic campaigns of civil disobedience (see Chapter 11), designed not only to compel action from local white elites but also to pressure the president. In his first two years in office, Kennedy was able to resist this pressure. But in 1963, when civil rights demonstrators led by Martin Luther King, Jr., in Birmingham, Alabama, were savagely attacked with dogs and fire hoses, a horrified nation looked to the president.

Kennedy did respond, offering an example of popular democratic leadership. Having been educated himself by the Birmingham demonstrations about the depth of the racial crisis, he was ready to sweep aside his previous caution and take bold action. He proposed a major civil rights law (see Chapter 16). Equally important, he spoke to the nation with words that captured the moral urgency of the civil rights struggle: "We are confronted primarily with a moral issue. It is as old as the Scriptures and is as clear as the American Constitution. . . . This nation, for all of its hopes and all its boasts, will not be fully free until all its citizens are free."[41]

CONCLUSION: THE ELITE DEMOCRATIC PRESIDENCY

The story of Kennedy and the civil rights movement shows that presidents sometimes act as popular democratic leaders. It also suggests requirements of the role. If presidents are genuinely concerned to promote popular democracy, they should respect the capacities and intelligence of the people they claim to lead. Rather than manipulating public opinion, they should engage in a dialogue with citizens. Rather than aiming only to boost their own power, they should recognize their responsibility to empower ordinary citizens.

Presidents will not play the part of popular democratic leader very frequently. More often, the presidency is an instrument of elite democracy. Surrounded by a huge staff and living like monarchs, presidents tend to be cut off from ordinary Americans. Elitist attitudes and secrecy further distance the president, while making accountability difficult. Connections to and pressures from organized private interests, especially from the corporate sector, contradict the presidential claim to represent popular democracy. Presidents may cloak themselves in the symbols of popular democracy, but the modern presidential drama, featuring larger-than-life chief executives and passive citizens, is a far cry from the authentic American tradition of popular democracy.

KEY TERMS

White House staff
Executive Office of the President (EOP)
Office of Management and Budget (OMB)
Council of Economic Advisers (CEA)
National Security Council (NSC)
president's cabinet
legislative liaison staff
veto
Employment Act of 1946
War Powers Resolution of 1973
presidential power of secrecy

SUGGESTED READINGS

Terry Eastland, *Energy in the Executive: The Case for the Strong Presidency* (New York: Free Press, 1992). A Reagan conservative's forceful case for a contemporary version of Alexander Hamilton's strong presidency.

Bruce Miroff, *Icons of Democracy: American Leaders as Heroes, Aristocrats, Dissenters, and Democrats* (New York: Basic Books, 1993). Portraits of both elite democratic and popular democratic leadership.

Michael Nelson, ed., *The Presidency and the Political System*, Fourth Edition (Washington, D.C.: CQ Press, 1995).

A lively anthology of original articles on the presidency.

Richard E. Neustadt, *Presidential Power and the Modern Presidents* (New York: Free Press, 1990). The classic work on how presidents can gain—or lose—personal power in the White House.

Stephen Skowronek, *The Politics Presidents Make: Leadership from John Adams to George Bush* (Cambridge: Harvard University Press, 1993). An intriguing historical theory that relates presidential success or failure to the rise and fall of political regimes.

CHAPTER 14

Bureaucracy: Myth and Reality

Nobody much likes bureaucracy. To the individual citizen, bureaucracy means time-wasting activities performed by surly civil servants. To conservatives, bureaucracy represents the heavy, clumsy hand of government interfering with free enterprise and freedom of choice. To liberals and radicals, bureaucracy is the rule of remote, unaccountable elites focused on maintaining the status quo. It sometimes seems that the only champions of bureaucracy are the bureaucrats themselves.

Bureaucracy comprises the units of the executive branch organized in a hierarchical fashion, governed through formal rules, and distinguished by specialized functions. This chapter concentrates on bureaucracy at the national level. Although all federal bureaus have hierarchy, rule-bound behavior, and specialization, they vary considerably in how they are organized, who staffs them, and what work they do. The employee of the Social Security Administration in Washington processing checks for Social Security recipients and the forest ranger checking on wildlife in the remote reaches of a national park are both bureaucrats. Thus, bureaucracy is not the drab monolith that the stereotypes present.

Bureaucracy is indeed a problem for a democratic political order, but it is also a necessity. It is a problem because bureaucratic hierarchy, expertise, and insulation from direct accountability can produce government operations that ignore the concerns of ordinary citizens. It is a necessity because our modern complex society, including the programs and policies that a democratic majority wants, requires skilled public administration.

This chapter neither bashes nor praises bureaucracy. Rather, it explains the democratic debate over bureaucracy in American politics. Two sets of key questions characterize this debate. First, how much bureaucracy do we need? Can bureaucracy be drastically cut back—for example, by turning to the alternative of economic markets, as some elite democrats now propose? Second, where bureaucracy is necessary, whose influence shapes its behavior? Are bureaucratic agencies predominantly influenced by elites? Or are these agencies responsive to popular democratic forces?

The chapter begins with a short history of the democratic debate over bureaucracy and then examines the size and scope of the modern administrative state in America, clearing away in the process some common myths about bureaucracy. Bureaucracies are inevitably entangled in politics, and the next two sections look at the internal and external political worlds of bureaucracy. Regulation of the economy by government—the principal preoccupation of conservative critics of bureaucracy—is the subject of the fifth section of the chapter. Finally, the chapter discusses competing proposals for reforming bureaucracy: technocratic, market oriented, and popular democratic.

THE DEMOCRATIC DEBATE OVER BUREAUCRACY: A SHORT HISTORY

Bureaucracy has been one of the principal battlegrounds between elite democrats and popular democrats, both of whom have approached the issue with mixed emotions. Elite democrats have usually been the ones building up bureaucratic capacity in the federal government, but sometimes they have feared that what they have built might be transformed into an instrument of popular democratic control. (This fear is central to the contemporary elite reaction against bureaucracy.) Popular democrats have usually resisted the growth of bureaucracy, but sometimes they have needed it to turn popular democratic objectives into reality.

The Beginnings of American Administration

The Constitution says very little about how the president, as chief executive, will delegate the actual enforcement of the laws. When the first administration was formed under George Washington, there was not much of a bureaucracy. Befitting the aristocratic perspective of the Federalists, national administrators were recruited from the class of "gentlemen," and it was assumed that their personal character and reputation would ensure their good conduct without the need for impersonal rules and institutional checks.

However, Alexander Hamilton saw that a more systematic, impersonal, *bureaucratic* organization of government could achieve some of the central goals of elite democracy. In *The Federalist Papers*, he wrote that the people's "confidence in and obedience to a government will commonly be proportioned to the goodness or badness of its administration."[1] Associating popular democratic politics with disorder, Hamilton thought that efficient administration would pacify the people, turning them from active citizens into satisfied recipients of government services. As secretary of the Treasury, he made his own department into a model of bureaucratic organization and efficiency.[2]

The first major challenge to the rule of gentleman administrators came from Jacksonian Democracy. Speaking the language of popular democracy, President Jackson proclaimed, "The duties of all public officers are, or at least admit of being made so plain and simple that men of intelligence may readily qualify themselves for their performance."[3] Although Jackson seemed to be saying that ordinary citizens should fill most of the federal posts, in practice he removed only about 10 percent of the civil servants who had labored under his predecessors and replaced them mostly with well-connected lawyers. Jackson's presidency was notable, however, for relying less on trust in the personal character of administrators and more on formal rules and procedures to supervise their behavior. In this regard, Matthew Crenson writes, "the chief administrative legacy of the Jacksonians was bureaucracy."[4]

The Spoils System and Civil Service Reform

Jackson's successors followed his rhetoric more than his practice, turning out large numbers of officeholders and replacing them with supporters. Under this **spoils system,** the victor in each presidential election considered federal employment mostly as an opportunity for political patronage. In one sense, the nineteenth-century spoils system was democratic: It allowed ordinary people, through their work in a political party, to achieve government positions previously reserved for elites. But the periodic shuffling of civil servants made for inefficient administration, and the close ties of civil servants to local party machines opened the door to corruption.

The system's defects sparked a reform movement after the Civil War that aimed to institute a different basis for selecting national administrators. Reformers demanded that federal employment be based not on party service but on competitive examinations and other measures of competence. Their cause was given a boost when a disappointed office seeker, crazed by his failure to get a patronage position, assassinated President James A. Garfield in 1881. With public attention now fixed on the evils of the spoils system, Congress passed the Pendleton Act in 1883, establishing a civil service commission to administer a "merit" system for federal employment. Civil service reform, although an important step toward a more efficient and honest federal bureaucracy, was also a victory for elite democrats: Reformers were mainly from the upper class and expected that their class would regain its once-dominant role in administration through examinations that favored the highly educated.

As industrialization transformed American life in the closing decades of the nineteenth century, the problem of regulating the giant business corporations that were emerging gave a further impetus to builders of bureaucracy. Allied with upper-class civil service reformers seeking to expand the administrative capacities of the federal government was a new class of professionals, especially lawyers and social scientists. These state builders were largely elite democrats whose goal was a more rational, expert-dominated administrative order insulated from the partisan strife of popular politics. They were stalemated, however, by foes of a federal bureaucracy. Some were genuine popular democrats afraid of new institutions beyond the people's reach. Others, however, were concerned mainly with preserving local party machines and their pork-barrel prizes.[5]

It was in the first decades of the twentieth century—the Progressive era—that the bureaucratic state in America first assumed its modern form. The Progressives hoped to combine popular democracy and elite democracy. They sponsored reforms, such as the initiative, referendum, and recall (which allow citizens to vote on legislation and to remove elected officials), that aimed to take power away from party bosses and return it directly to the people. They also proposed to staff an expanded administrative order with scientifically trained and politically neutral experts. As James Morone has written, "At the heart of the Progressive agenda lay a political paradox: government would simultaneously be returned to the people and placed beyond them, in the hands of the experts."[6] But the Progressives succeeded neither in restoring power to the people nor in achieving scientific administration. The agencies of government they created to regulate an industrial economy generally found it impossible to devise truly scientific standards that furthered the public interest. Even worse, the elite economic interests that were supposed to be the subjects of regulation generally became the most powerful influence on the regulators.

The New Deal and Bureaucracy

The Great Depression led to an expansion of the federal bureaucracy beyond even the hopes of the Progressive reformers, and the New Deal changed the attitudes of popular democrats toward bureaucracy. Just as in the case of federalism (Chapter 3), the need to achieve control over the corporations compelled popular democrats to accept a more powerful and bureaucratic federal government. Yet elite democrats still retained considerable influence within this government. The hastily built administrative apparatus of Franklin Roosevelt contained both popular democratic and elite democratic elements.

Harry Hopkins, a leading administrator, was one example of the New Deal's success in reconciling popular democracy and bureaucracy. President Roosevelt placed Hopkins in charge of federal efforts to aid the unemployed. Hopkins took charge of these efforts in a fashion that led biographer George McJimsey to dub him "democracy's bureaucrat."[7] Putting a public works program for the unemployed into operation with remarkable speed, Hopkins proclaimed, "The only thing that counts is action . . . and we are going to surround [the program] with as few regulations as possible."[8] Determined to avoid bureaucratic red tape, Hopkins was equally determined to avoid the bureaucrat's reliance on a formal hierarchy of superiors and subordinates. He ran his Washington office through group discussion and kept in close touch with administrators in the field who were working with the unemployed.

Hopkins's values, as much as his methods, made him a popular democrat as bureaucrat. When critics complained of waste and confusion in the public works programs that Hopkins headed, he conceded that he had made mistakes. But he would not apologize for them because they had been made "in the interests of the people that were broke."[9] To Hopkins, administration was not primarily a matter of scientific expertise but an opportunity to practice civic virtue. "One of the proudest and finest things that ever happened and ever can happen to me," he said, "is the opportunity to work for this government of ours and the people who make it up. . . . I wouldn't give this last two years of my life for a life work done in another type of endeavor. I have learned, as I never knew before, what it means to love your country."[10]

Unfortunately, much of the bureaucratic machinery created by the New Deal did not reflect either Hopkins's methods or his values. To cope with the emergency conditions of the Depression, the New Deal tied many of the new administrative agencies to the industrial and agricultural interests with which they dealt. Allowing private interests to play a powerful role in public agencies was supposed to be a temporary measure. But when the Depression passed, the tight bonds between private interests and public agencies remained. The bureaucratic state became, to a disturbing degree, a special-interest state in which administrative expertise was placed in the service of economic elites.

The next major expansion of American bureaucracy came during the 1960s and early 1970s, with new administrative units established to carry out popular democratic goals such as environmental protection, consumer safety, and the elimination of poverty. Yet while the bureaucracy was becoming a more complicated mixture of elite and popular democratic elements, its image was becoming more simplistic and negative. Bureaucracy—with a capital *B*—became a bogeyman for critics of every political persuasion. Conservatives saw a swollen and monstrous Bureaucracy as the chief threat to individual freedom. Liberals and radicals saw an arrogant and stifling Bureaucracy as the chief barrier to social change. It was the conservatives, with the election of Ronald Reagan in 1980, who had the chance to act on their ideological hostility to bureaucracy.

From Reagan to Clinton: Attack or Reinvent Bureaucracy?

President Reagan entered office as an avowed enemy of bureaucracy, and during his eight years as chief executive he presided over an unprecedented assault on federal administration. Because Congress blunted many of his attacks, Reagan was not able to enact drastic cuts in the federal bureaucracy. But he did manage to heap scorn on bureaucracy and to broadcast negative stereotypes of it to the public.

Big government, the president told Americans, best served the public by "shriveling up and going away."[11] White House chief of staff Edwin Meese showed off a doll he named "The Bureaucrat"; he put the doll on a pile of papers and pointed out how it just sat there and did nothing.[12] In this hostile climate, many civil servants felt undermined and demoralized. The bureaucracy managed to survive Ronald Reagan. But a serious democratic debate over bureaucracy, based on a recognition of its true features, had been obscured by scornful stereotypes.

President Clinton has tackled the topic of bureaucratic reform. Even though Clinton hopes, like Reagan, to cut down the size of the bureaucracy, his goal is different: He wants the federal government to work better, not to shrivel up and go away. Developed by Vice President Al Gore, Clinton's plan speaks of "reinventing government." In practice, this means downsizing the civil service, turning some public functions over to private businesses, and cutting red tape by allowing government workers more freedom and initiative in how they perform their jobs. Whether Clinton proves more successful than previous presidents in remaking bureaucracy, however, will depend on a long political struggle over the administrative state.

THE MODERN ADMINISTRATIVE STATE IN AMERICA

The present-day federal government is largely an **administrative state.** It is involved in regulating or supporting almost every imaginable form of social activity by means of a large, complex, and diverse bureaucracy. In this section, we present a snapshot of the contemporary federal bureaucracy, depicting its most important features. We also set these features against some prevailing myths about bureaucracy.

The Civil Service

About 3 million Americans work as civil servants in the federal bureaucracy. (About 1.75 million more serve in the armed forces—a number that is declining with the end of the Cold War.) Approximately 90 percent of these federal employees work outside Washington, D.C., contrary to the image of a centralized bureaucratic machine. Most bureaucrats deliver services where the people are— whether as Social Security branch workers, air traffic controllers, or civilian employees at military installations. Although the federal bureaucracy draws the most attention from critics, it is actually smaller in terms of personnel than state and local governments. The states employ about 4 million workers, and local governments employ nearly 10 million.[13] When all levels of government are taken into account, 1 out of 6 employed people in the United States can be called a government bureaucrat![14] (See Table 14.1.)

A majority of federal bureaucrats hold their positions in accordance with the General Schedule, a merit-based personnel system in which there are eighteen pay grades. At the bottom of the General Schedule, GS-1, are the most menial tasks. At the top, GS-18, are executive positions of considerable responsibility and

TABLE 14.1

Governmental Employment, 1985

Government	Full-time and Part-time Employees (in thousands)
Federal Civilian	2,964[a]
State	3,984
Local	(9,685)
County	1,891
Municipalities	2,467
School Districts	4,416
Townships	392
Special Districts	519
Total	16,633

[a]This figure excludes some 55,000 federal employees who work for the legislative and judicial branches as well as the White House staff. Full time equivalent employment in the executive branch approximated 2,854,000 in the mid-1980s. See U.S. Office of Management and Budget, *Special Analyses: Budget of the United States Government, Fiscal Year 1988* (Washington, D.C. Government Printing Office, 1987), p. 2.

Source: U.S. Department of Commerce, *Statistical Abstract of the United States, 1987* (Washington, D.C.: Government Printing Office, 1986), pp. 280, 311.

high pay. Competitive examinations and formal education are the two principal determinants of merit in the General Schedule. But other factors may be taken into account, with preference given to armed forces veterans and affirmative action programs for minorities.

Most civil servants spend their entire career in the same agency. Congress attempted to change this situation with the passage of the Civil Service Reform Act of 1978, which created the Senior Executive Service (SES). The SES (which is above the General Schedule) was supposed to enable presidents to choose from a pool of the most talented career executives and shift them to whatever agencies required their particular skills. The SES would also make federal service more challenging to top bureaucrats. As B. Guy Peters observes, "The managers were supposed to have the opportunity for substantial bonuses, sabbaticals, and more important positions, but ran a greater risk of being fired for poor performance than if they had remained members of the General Schedule system."[15] Contrary to these objectives, President Reagan manipulated the SES to fulfill his ideological goals.

At the highest reaches of the bureaucracy are the president's political appointees. Their merits are not necessarily the same as those of career civil servants. Certainly, managerial competence is valued for political appointees, but so are loyalty to the president and agreement with his political program. Presidential appointees are sometimes called "in and outers" because their tenure in public service is usually short; most, in fact, do not last for the four years of a president's term.

Types of Federal Agencies

The administrative state in America is made up of a bewildering variety of bureaucracies (see Figure 14.1). Federal agencies differ from one another on many scores: form of organization, type of leadership, breadth or narrowness of function, political dependence on or independence from the president, financial dependence on or independence from Congress.

Cabinet departments are the bureaucratic agencies most familiar to Americans. When the federal government was formed, its first agencies were the Departments of State, Treasury, and War (along with the individual position of attorney general). Today, there are fourteen cabinet departments, each headed by a secretary appointed by the president: State, Treasury, Defense, Interior, Agriculture, Justice, Commerce, Labor, Health and Human Services, Housing and Urban Development, Transportation, Energy, Education, and Veterans Affairs. The fourteen departments vary enormously in size and complexity. But each is responsible for a broad area of governmental operations whose administration is divided up among specialized bureaus within the department.

Independent agencies stand outside the cabinet departments and generally handle more narrow areas of government operation. Examples are the Environmental Protection Agency (EPA), the National Aeronautics and Space

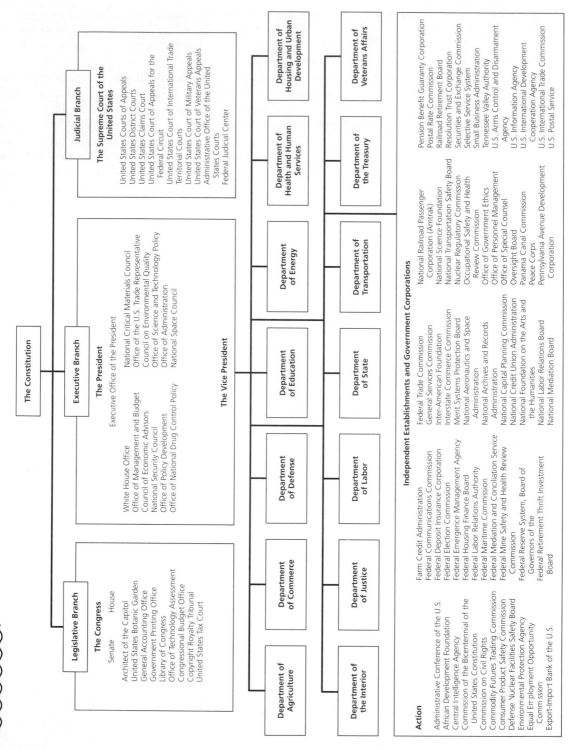

FIGURE 14.1 The Government of the United States

The Constitution

Legislative Branch

The Congress

Senate   House

Architect of the Capitol
United States Botanic Garden
General Accounting Office
Government Printing Office
Library of Congress
Office of Technology Assessment
Congressional Budget Office
Copyright Royalty Tribunal
United States Tax Court

Executive Branch

The President

Executive Office of the President

White House Office
Office of Management and Budget
Council of Economic Advisors
National Security Council
Office of Policy Development
Office of National Drug Control Policy

National Critical Materials Council
Office of the U.S. Trade Representative
Council on Environmental Quality
Office of Science and Technology Policy
Office of Administration
National Space Council

The Vice President

Judicial Branch

The Supreme Court of the United States

United States Courts of Appeals
United States District Courts
United States Claims Court
United States Court of Appeals for the Federal Circuit
United States Court of International Trade
Territorial Courts
United States Court of Military Appeals
United States Court of Veterans Appeals
Administrative Office of the United States Courts
Federal Judicial Center

Department of Agriculture

Department of Commerce

Department of Defense

Department of Education

Department of Energy

Department of Health and Human Services

Department of Housing and Urban Development

Department of the Interior

Department of Justice

Department of Labor

Department of State

Department of Transportation

Department of the Treasury

Department of Veterans Affairs

Independent Establishments and Government Corporations

Action
Administrative Conference of the U.S.
African Development Foundation
Central Intelligence Agency
Commission of the Bicentennial of the United States Constitution
Commission on Civil Rights
Commodity Futures Trading Commission
Consumer Product Safety Commission
Defense Nuclear Facilities Safety Board
Environmental Protection Agency
Equal Employment Opportunity Commission
Export-Import Bank of the U.S.

Farm Credit Administration
Federal Communications Commission
Federal Deposit Insurance Corporation
Federal Election Commission
Federal Emergence Management Agency
Federal Housing Finance Board
Federal Labor Relations Authority
Federal Maritime Commission
Federal Mediation and Conciliation Service
Federal Mine Safety and Health Review Commission
Federal Reserve System, Board of Governors of the
Federal Retirement Thrift Investment Board

Federal Trade Commission
General Services Commission
Inter-American Foundation
Interstate Commerce Commission
Merit Systems Protection Board
National Aeronautics and Space Administration
National Archives and Records Administration
National Capital Planning Commission
National Credit Union Administration
National Foundation on the Arts and the Humanities
National Labor Relations Board
National Mediation Board

National Railroad Passenger Corporation (Amtrak)
National Science Foundation
National Transportation Safety Board
Nuclear Regulatory Commission
Occupational Safety and Health Review Commission
Office of Government Ethics
Office of Personnel Management
Office of Special Counsel
Oversight Board
Panama Canal Commission
Peace Corps
Pennsylvania Avenue Development Corporation

Pension Benefit Guaranty Corporation
Postal Rate Commission
Railroad Retirement Board
Resolution Trust Corporation
Securities and Exchange Commission
Selective Service System
Small Business Administration
Tennessee Valley Authority
U.S. Arms Control and Disarmament Agency
U.S. Information Agency
U.S. International Development Cooperation Agency
U.S. International Trade Commission
U.S. Postal Service

Source: U.S. Government Manual, 1990.

Administration (NASA), and the Central Intelligence Agency (CIA). Like cabinet departments, most independent agencies are headed by a single individual appointed by the president. Some, however, like the Merit System Protection Board that governs federal employment, are multiheaded. Congress sometimes creates independent agencies, rather than simply establishing new bureaus within existing cabinet departments, in the hope that a new agency will be more innovative if it is free of the bureaucratic routines and intraorganizational conflicts that typify existing cabinet departments.

Independent regulatory commissions are designed to regulate various sectors of the economy. Examples are the Interstate Commerce Commission (ICC), which regulates ground transportation; the Nuclear Regulatory Commission, which regulates the nuclear power industry; and the Securities and Exchange Commission (SEC), which regulates the stock market. By creating multimember commissions drawn from both parties and by giving the commissioners long terms and exemption from presidential removal, Congress has tried to distance these agencies from political pressures and make them neutral and expert regulators. In practice, however, the independent regulatory commissions have not been able to separate administration from politics. Presidents are able to exert some influence by their choice of a chair for the commission. The regulated industry itself is a constant source of political pressure as it lobbies the commission for favorable decisions.

Public corporations are government agencies that engage in business activities. The most familiar of these is the Postal Service (until 1971, the Post Office was a cabinet department). Others are the Tennessee Valley Authority (TVA), which generates and sells electric power; Amtrak, which operates passenger railroads; and the Corporation for Public Broadcasting, which sponsors public television and radio. Public corporations have been created largely to carry out economic activities deemed unprofitable by private businesses. The organizational form of public corporations protects them from most political influences. Further, they enjoy far greater financial independence than other kinds of federal agencies, such as the ability to borrow money on their own rather than relying solely on appropriations from Congress.

Federal foundations and endowments allow the government to sponsor scientific and cultural activities that otherwise might languish for lack of funds. The National Science Foundation (NSF) is a major donor to scientific research in the United States. The National Institutes of Health (NIH) funds research on dangerous diseases, such as acquired immune deficiency syndrome (AIDS). The National Endowment for the Humanities (NEH) and the National Endowment for the Arts (NEA) support the creative projects of scholars, writers, and artists. Although these foundations and endowments ostensibly serve lofty ends, they are often embroiled in nasty political controversies. Many religious and cultural conservatives were outraged, for example, when the NEA funded photographic exhibitions by Robert Mapplethorpe, whose work included graphic scenes of gay sexuality, and they successfully pressured Congress to impose restrictions on NEA grants to artists.

Myth and Reality in the Administrative State

Probably the most powerful of the myths about the modern administrative state concerns the identity of the typical bureaucrat. The faceless bureaucrat of myth is inefficient and lazy, on the one hand, aggressive and hyperactive in meddling in people's lives, on the other. But in truth bureaucrats are ordinary people. Compared to presidents and members of Congress, bureaucrats as a group are more representative of the American population.

Indeed, in the hiring and promotion of women and minorities, the federal bureaucracy compares well to businesses in the private sector. In 1985, women held 47 percent of the positions, and African Americans held 15 percent (greater than their percentage in the population). It is true that women and minorities tend to be clustered in the lower levels of the General Schedule in clerical and laboring jobs. But although white males hold most of the top-level positions, the share held by women and minorities has been increasing.[16]

Even if bureaucrats do resemble other Americans in these ways, proponents of the bureaucratic myth contend that the rigid rules of bureaucracy attract people with authoritarian personalities and that the tedious nature of bureaucratic work makes civil servants frustrated and irritable. In this view, bureaucrats, however average they may be, are afflicted with a "bureaucratic mentality." Yet empirical studies by social psychologists have found that public employees are at least as open-minded and flexible as those who work in private businesses. As for the image of the miserable and angry civil servant, Charles Goodsell notes that "in general, government bureaucrats are positive about their jobs, believe they can take initiatives and exert influence, and feel personally rewarded by the work they do."[17]

But if bureaucrats are ordinary people with regular personalities and a positive attitude toward their work, why do most citizens have a negative attitude toward bureaucracy? Actually, this view has more to do with bureaucracy in the abstract. It reflects constant bureaucracy bashing by politicians and the media. When questioned about contact with civil servants, a large majority report satisfactory experiences. For example, a national survey conducted by the University of Michigan asked respondents how satisfied they were in their request for assistance from a government agency: 69 percent said they were satisfied; 26 percent said they were not. When asked whether they had been treated fairly, 76 percent answered yes.[18]

The myth of bureaucracy rests not only on stereotypes of the individual bureaucrat but also on stereotypes of the organizations that make up the federal bureaucracy. According to these stereotypes, federal agencies are gigantic in size, aggressively growing larger all the time, and immensely powerful. In reality, federal agencies come in many sizes and shapes. The Department of Defense, with over one million civilian employees, supports the image of a gigantic bureaucracy. But most other cabinet departments and independent agencies are much smaller. The Department of Education, for instance, has fewer than five thousand employees (see Table 14.2).

TABLE 14.2		

Size of U.S. Government Executive Departments: Civilian Personnel and Budget

Department	Personnel	Budget ($ Billions)
Agriculture	109,261	48.7
Commerce	37,507	2.7
Defense	1,038,412	317.6
Education	4,735	23.7
Energy	16,762	13.4
Health and Human Services	118,094	464.2
Housing and Urban Development	13,978	23.0
Interior	73,400	5.7
Justice	87,541	9.0
Labor	18,507	26.3
State	25,821	4.1
Transportation	67,740	28.8
Treasury	163,929	254.9
Veterans Affairs	215,306	30.1

Source: *Budget of the U.S. Government, FY 1991.*

The mythical bureaucratic agency is power hungry, eagerly grasping for ever-larger functions, programs, and budgets. But real bureaucratic agencies are hesitant about growth if it threatens their identity. Most agencies have a **mission,** a central task to which its members are committed. They welcome more authority and money in pursuit of this mission. But they are not eager to take on divergent missions even when these would bring growth to the agency. Thus, the Department of Agriculture, which defines its mission as assisting America's farmers, has been unhappy with—and tried to get rid of—its role in the welfare area as administrator of the food stamp program. And the Army, whose mission is to mount large-scale infantry operations, has never been enthusiastic about small-scale antiguerrilla warfare.[19]

Most bureaucratic agencies are not as large or as imperialistic as believers in the bureaucratic myth presume. Neither are they as powerful. Subject to many constraining forces, federal agencies tend to be defensive rather than offensive, to placate other holders of power more than assert their own power.[20]

In criticizing the prevalent myth about bureaucracy, we do not mean to claim that all is well with the American administrative state. Many problems of rigidity, inefficiency, and promotion of bureaucratic goals over public needs deserve attention. The prevalent myth, however, focuses attention on bureaucracy simply to turn it into a scapegoat. Bureaucracy is a convenient scapegoat for elected politicians who wish to divert attention from their own inability to carry through on the promises they make to voters. It is a convenient scapegoat for citizens who resent both the taxes they pay and the social ills that never seem to get cured by federal spending.

BUREAUCRATS AS POLICYMAKERS

Understanding bureaucracy in a realistic way requires, above all, a recognition that it is a *political* institution. The scholars who founded the study of public administration in the United States (one of them a future president, Woodrow Wilson) sought to distinguish administration from politics. Bureaucracies existed, they claimed, only to provide the technical means for carrying out ends that political (i.e., elected) officials had decided.[21] Today, few believe in the politics/administration dichotomy. Administrators operate in an intensely political environment, and they must make key political decisions themselves. They are policymakers, not just technicians.

Administrators are politically influential because they possess **expertise.** Bureaucrats tend to know more than anyone else about their particular areas of responsibility. Expertise may come through a combination of specialization and experience. Compare the career civil servant, who has spent many years dealing with one particular policy area, to the elected official, who must tackle many different policy areas with a shorter base of experience. An even more formidable ground of expertise is professional training. "A variety of highly trained elites," writes Francis Rourke, "practice their trade in public organizations—physicists, economists, engineers."[22] The arguments of these elites carry special weight because they are presumed to draw from professional knowledge. Elected officials are the bosses of civil servants but often defer to their expertise.

Bureaucratic expertise is central to the democratic debate over bureaucracy. In the eighteenth and nineteenth centuries, it was elite democrats who were most enthused about bureaucratic expertise. Since the New Deal, however, many elite democrats have come to favor the market mechanisms of the private sector and have grown skeptical about expertise in government. Popular democrats are also troubled by the claims of expertise but recognize that their political agenda requires the help of experts. How, for example, can we clean up the environment without the efforts of environmental scientists?

Administrators are also politically influential because they exercise considerable **discretion.** Handed broad and vague policy guidelines by elected officials, administrators give policy substance through numerous, more concrete, decisions. For example, Congress directs the Occupational Safety and Health Administration (OSHA) to protect employees from cancer-causing chemicals in the workplace. It is up to OSHA to set allowable exposure levels for various carcinogens. In determining these levels, OSHA administrators make decisions about which companies and unions are likely to disagree; inevitably, the decisions will be political and not just technical.

Legislation can be so precise and detailed that it reduces bureaucratic discretion to a minimum. But for both political and technical reasons, such precision is usually not possible. In certain cases, a legislative majority can be constructed only through ambiguous language that leaves contending parties satisfied that their concerns have been heard. As a result, political conflict in Congress is displaced into the bureaucratic domain. In other cases, Congress may lack the time, expertise, or foreknowledge to write precise legislation and counts on bureaucratic discretion to fill in the blanks.

Expertise and discretion make administrators influential in policymaking. They employ that influence indirectly and directly. Administrators exercise *indirect influence* over policy in their capacity as advisers to elected officials. When a president, for example, faces a major policy decision, he or she turns to the pertinent bureaucratic agency for data, analysis, and recommendations. The agency cannot determine what the president will decide, but it may be able to shape how he or she thinks about the decision.

Bureaucratic advice may be couched in the language of technical expertise, but it is seldom neutral and purely technical. An agency is likely to tell the president to achieve a desired end by giving it, rather than another agency, the resources and the responsibility to do the job. If the president is considering the problem of a growing welfare population, for example, the Department of Labor is likely to recommend that the problem be approached through job training programs for which it will assume the lead role. In contrast, the Department of Health and Human Services is likely to propose welfare reform, for which it, not the Department of Labor, will be responsible.

Administrators exercise *direct influence* through the **rule-making authority** that Congress delegates to the bureaucracy. When agencies give specificity to vague congressional mandates by issuing rules, these rules carry the force of law. And since they are far more precise than the legislation under which they were drafted, they shape policy in important ways. Each year, the bureaucracy issues a far larger number of rules than Congress passes laws, and these rules are published in the *Federal Register*. Limits to arbitrary rule making are established in the Administrative Procedures Act of 1946, which all agencies must follow. Before a new rule can be put into effect, for instance, interested citizens and groups must receive advance notice and be permitted to comment on it.

Rule making by administrators is considered "quasi-legislative." The bureaucracy also possesses "quasi-judicial" authority in the form of **administrative adjudication.** Whereas rules govern a large number of parties and cover future behavior, adjudications affect only the individual parties in a case and cover past behavior. Adjudication is the province of administrative law judges. Cases in administrative law must follow the rules of due process, but the requirements of due process are not as strict as in the regular courts; thus, there is no right to a jury trial in administrative law. Administrative law judges handle far more cases than federal court judges do.

American citizens most often come into contact with federal authority through rules issued by administrators and decisions handed down by administrative law judges. Indeed, bureaucrats make many of the policy decisions that affect our lives. Much of this is inevitable, and some of it may even be desirable for the advancement of democratic goals. Yet these people are not elected or necessarily visible in their exercise of power. How to hold administrators, with their expertise and their discretion, their rule-making and adjudicatory authority, accountable to the people and their elected representatives is an enduring problem for a democratic society.

THE POLITICAL ENVIRONMENT OF BUREAUCRACY

Bureaucracy is a political institution not only because administrators possess political influence but also because they operate in a highly political environment. A formal, hierarchical, technically focused bureaucracy could wait passively for elected officials to order it into action. But real bureaucratic agencies exist in an environment where policies reflect political, rather than technical, values; where resources are scarce; and where rivals seek to encroach on cherished turf. Thus, agencies actively seek to mobilize political support from others—the public, interest groups, Congress, the White House—and these same political forces seek to shape what agencies do.

Seeking Political Support

Some administrative agencies, such as the Federal Maritime Commission, function largely out of sight of the general public. Other agencies, however, are highly visible to the public and take steps to ensure favorable citizens' impressions—the more favorable the public is, the better the agency is likely to be treated by Congress and the president. Agencies can inform the public about their work, while casting that work in a positive light through free booklets, public-service ads on television, and Washington headquarters tours. Agencies can attempt to wrap their activities in the mantle of mysterious expertise and glamorous risk-taking—these have been favorite tactics of both the armed forces and NASA. To be visible, however, is to be vulnerable should things go wrong. When the space shuttle *Challenger* exploded after takeoff in 1986, killing all seven crew members, including a schoolteacher, NASA suffered a public-relations disaster as well as a human tragedy.

The public is too inattentive, and its backing too fickle, to provide most agencies with all the political support they need. "Hence," Francis Rourke observes,

> it is essential to every agency's power position to have the support of attentive groups whose attachment is grounded on an enduring tie. The groups an agency provides tangible benefits to are the most natural basis of such political support, and it is with these interest groups that agencies ordinarily establish the firmest alliances.[23]

Those agencies and interest groups that lack powerful enough allies may actually go about *creating* what they need. An interest group may push to establish or upgrade a federal agency in order to advance its own agenda; thus, the National Education Association was the principal force behind the creation of the Department of Education. And an agency without adequate political support may help

---

set up an interest group to back it, as happened when the Department of Agriculture sponsored the formation of the American Farm Bureau Federation.

The immediate masters of bureaucratic agencies are Congress and the president, so their political support is indispensable. Congress determines the statutory authority of an agency and holds the purse strings for its annual appropriation. The leadership of an agency must therefore take care to cultivate goodwill on Capitol Hill. Political support is obtained from the key legislative and appropriations committees by respectful, even deferential treatment and by more tangible promises. As James Q. Wilson notes, "Whenever an agency sends up a budget request it makes certain that there will be projects in it that will serve the districts represented by the members of the appropriations subcommittees (as well as members of certain key legislative committees)."[24] The goodwill of the president is also a goal of bureaucratic chiefs, who do not want the White House staff or the Office of Management and Budget (OMB) frowning on their legislative and budget requests. Yet presidents, as we saw in Chapter 13, often complain that bureaucrats are insufficiently loyal and take steps to bring the bureaucracy under tighter White House control.

The more successful an agency is in gaining political support from the public, interest groups, Congress, and the president, the greater **autonomy** it will enjoy in the sense of freedom from control by external forces. Autonomy allows a bureaucracy to pursue its mission unhindered. Although this can be desirable, too much autonomy may also prove dangerous. Probably the extreme case of an autonomous federal agency was the Federal Bureau of Investigation (FBI) under J. Edgar Hoover.

Hoover's FBI

J. Edgar Hoover was a master at winning popular support through publicity. His FBI first captured the public's imagination during the Depression years with several highly publicized apprehensions (or killings) of notorious bank robbers, such as John Dillinger. Soon, magazines, radio, and the movies (and later TV) were filled with dramatic stories about the exploits of Hoover and his G-men (government men). Hoover even cultivated children, with toy companies pouring out G-men badges, guns, and other paraphernalia with the FBI's cooperation.[25]

While Hoover was awing the public, he was courting—or threatening—his bosses in the White House. For the president who sponsored his rise to preeminence, Franklin Roosevelt, Hoover was willing to overstep the laws. Biographer Richard Gid Powers writes that "Hoover passed along political gossip about Roosevelt's friends and enemies, information about the plans of possible election opponents, and background material that might spare the president involvement in embarrassing situations."[26] During later administrations, when Hoover's image and power were at their peak, he used fear as much as flattery to keep presidents at bay. Hoover's personal files held secrets, everyone in Washington believed, that would sully the reputation of any president (or other political figure) who dared to challenge Hoover's autonomous power at the FBI.

FBI Director J. Edgar Hoover (center) testifies before a Senate subcommittee on communist subversion. Hoover was a master of popular dramas that legitimized his autocratic power at the FBI.

In J. Edgar Hoover's case, autonomy led to autocratic power. Virtually unchecked by presidents or Congress and idolized by the public, Hoover was free to wield his power in an often ruthless fashion. During the early years of the Cold War, he was a fanatical anticommunist and employed the FBI to destroy the careers and lives of numerous individuals suspected of "subversive" activities. When the civil rights movement rose to its zenith in the 1960s, he developed a personal loathing for Martin Luther King, Jr. and set out to destroy him. Convinced that King was the friend of communists as well as sexually promiscuous, Hoover had the FBI bug King's hotel rooms and wiretap his telephones. When neither political leaders nor the press was willing to make use of Hoover's tapes, one of his aides sent a copy to King, accompanied by a bizarre note implying that King could escape public exposure only by committing suicide![27] Under Hoover, the FBI became a nightmare bureaucracy.

Constraints on Bureaucracy

Fortunately, the kind of autonomy that Hoover achieved at the FBI is rare. Agencies struggle to mobilize political support not only to increase their autonomy but also to fend off threats to already established autonomy. The political environment that most agencies face is filled with potentially constraining forces: other agencies, Congress, the president, the courts, interest groups, and the public. These checks and constraints are double-edged. On the one hand, they prevent most agencies from becoming the arbitrary and oppressive bureaucracies that prevailing myths depict (and that occasionally exist, as with Hoover's FBI). On the other hand, the existence of such "potent centrifugal forces," Charles Levine, B. Guy Peters, and Frank Thompson write, "frequently makes it difficult for officials to design and implement coherent public policies."[28] As is also the case for Congress and the president, checks and balances in the bureaucracy yield greater safety but lesser effectiveness.

An agency seeking to carry out its core mission may be threatened by another agency promoting *its* core mission. A classic illustration of such conflict between agencies, which scholars call **bureaucratic politics,** is the feud between the Air Force and the Navy over bombing. Since the end of World War II, there has been a belief among Navy officers that the Air Force seeks to control all aviation and a conflicting belief among Air Force officers that the Navy, with its aircraft carriers, tries to encroach on the Air Force speciality of strategic bombing. The services have competed to promote their core missions. As Morton Halperin describes the conflict:

> In Korea and especially in Vietnam the Navy sought as large a role as possible for carrier-based aircraft in an effort to demonstrate that carriers could operate as effectively, if not more effectively, than land-based air power. The Air Force, on the other hand, sought to restrict the role of the Navy. . . . This controversy probably led each service to exaggerate the effectiveness of its bombing in order to outshine the other.[29]

In the competitive world of bureaucracy, agencies look for allies on Capitol Hill and in the White House. But friends in high places can sometimes turn into bosses, interested less in supporting the agency's agenda than in advancing their own. Both Congress and the president have in recent years intensified their efforts to shape bureaucratic behavior. Congressional oversight of the bureaucracy has increased, with legislators using formal hearings and informal contacts to signal how they want programs implemented. Presidential efforts to control the bureaucracy through personnel and budgetary strategies have been even more notable, especially during the Reagan presidency. The struggle between Congress and the presidency over the bureaucracy has become more visible, but it is an old struggle rooted in the Constitution. As James Q. Wilson comments, "That document makes the president and Congress rivals for control of the American administrative system. The rivalry leads to struggle and the struggle breeds frustration."[30] This frustration grows out of the requirement that federal agencies serve two different—and often opposed—masters.

A third master has entered the picture in recent decades: the federal courts. For most of American history, judges did not intervene in the actions of bureaucrats, believing that administrative discretion was not subject to the same judicial scrutiny as legislation. But since the New Deal, the federal courts have been more willing to take up cases of agency decision-making. The courts have enabled citizens to bring suits against agencies and have required agencies to justify their discretionary actions. Judges have even ordered federal agencies to

The HUD Scandal

The political forces at play in the life of a bureaucratic agency can serve as healthy checks on its search for autonomy. But political forces also may manipulate bureaucracy in an unhealthy manner. Consider the scandal at the Department of Housing and Urban Development (HUD) that erupted into the headlines in 1989. Many Americans regarded the HUD scandal as another demonstration of wasteful and ineffective bureaucracy. The problem in this instance, however, was not too much bureaucracy but too little: HUD lacked the impersonal rules and political neutrality to prevent corruption. The HUD scandal is an illustration of what can happen when bureaucracy is corrupted by political and economic elites.

Although the HUD scandal came to light during George Bush's presidency, the events in question happened during Ronald Reagan's. It was Reagan's political appointees and their aides, not career civil servants, who wasted an estimated $4–8 billion through mismanagement and graft. What made this ripoff of the taxpayers even more outrageous was that the money was largely diverted from a program (Moderate Rehabilitation) designed to renovate housing for people with low incomes into the pockets of prominent Republicans and politically connected real estate developers.

The scandal was marked by a combination of neglect and sleaze. The man whom Reagan had chosen to head HUD, Samuel Pierce, exercised slack control over the department. His executive assistant, Deborah Gore Dean, stepped into the void and directed awards for the Moderate Rehabilitation housing program mostly to her political cronies and to developers who had made large campaign contributions to Republicans. Some political appointees at HUD itself cashed in, quitting their jobs and then turning to their friends still at the agency to steer them toward large contracts. Lobbyists with friends at HUD also made a bundle. James Watt, Reagan's former secretary of the interior, earned $420,000 from lobbying at HUD, reportedly for eight phone calls and a half-hour talk with Secretary Pierce.

The worst offenders in the HUD scandal were eventually prosecuted. In October 1993, a jury convicted Deborah Gore Dean of twelve felony counts of defrauding the government, accepting a bribe, and lying to Congress. She was the eleventh person found guilty of corruption in this affair.

In a democracy, politics should steer bureaucracy. But what kind of politics? Elite democrats trust the executive to oversee the bureaucracy and direct it to the fulfillment of the public good. Popular democrats can point to events like the HUD scandal to suggest that executive direction of the bureaucracy, largely hidden from public view, may favor elite interests instead. They propose to open the closed-door world of the bureaucracy as much as possible to a politics of greater citizen awareness and input.

Sources: Steven Waldman, "The HUD Ripoff," *Newsweek,* August 7, 1989: 16–22; Stephen Labaton, "Ex-Official Is Convicted in H.U.D. Scandal in 80s," *New York Times,* October 27, 1993.

change how they implement policy. Administrators now must worry not only about how a congressional committee or a White House staff member may respond to their behavior but also about how a district court judge may rule on its legality.

BUREAUCRACY AND THE POLITICAL ECONOMY

How much bureaucracy do Americans need? The initial answer of a popular democrat would be "far less." Many citizens complain that the administrative state stifles individual freedom with excessive forms, rules, and personnel. Yet the most influential advocates of bureaucratic downsizing have been not ordinary citizens but members of the business community, and their unhappiness with bureaucracy has less to do with freedom than with profits. In the face of business assaults on bureaucracy since the 1970s, popular democrats have found themselves in the unexpected position of having to defend it.

Popular democrats historically opposed the bureaucratization of American politics and remain worried about the reign of unaccountable elites in the administrative state. Nevertheless, they have also had to acknowledge that their past victories in extending protections to ordinary people against the abuses of private power can be preserved only with the help of administrative agencies. Hence, the historical roles of elite democrats and popular democrats have been reversed: Elite democrats largely built the administrative state but now want to shrink it, while popular democrats defend an administrative state they once feared.

The contemporary debate over bureaucracy has focused primarily on those agencies that regulate the economy. **Regulation** is "a process or activity in which government requires or proscribes certain activities or behavior on the part of individuals and institutions . . . and does so through a continuing administrative process, generally through specially designated regulatory agencies."[31] Understanding the contemporary struggle over regulation means distinguishing two different types. **Economic regulation** is usually conducted by an independent regulatory commission, covers a specific industry, and focuses on matters of prices, quality of services, and ability to enter or leave the industry. **Social regulation** is usually conducted by a single-headed agency answerable to the president, covers all industries, and focuses on such matters as environmental protection, safety, health, and nondiscrimination. It is the latter type that has generated the most controversy.

Economic Regulation

Economic regulation has the longer history in American politics. As industrialization strained the capacities of a weak national state, Congress created independent regulatory commissions to bring the changing economy under some measure of control. The prototype of the new regulatory agency was the Interstate

Commerce Commission (ICC), formed in 1887 to regulate the railroad industry. Industrial abuses paved the way for the development of economic regulation, which has often been portrayed as a victory for popular democracy over economic elites. Revisionist historians, however, have shown that industrialists themselves sometimes pushed for federal regulation, hoping to limit competition or to avert public ownership.[32]

Regardless of whether independent regulatory commissions sprang into existence to serve popular or elite interests, many of them entered into a cozy relationship with the industries they were supposed to oversee. According to the "capture thesis," once a regulatory commission was established and the public and its elected officials turned their attention elsewhere, the only political force exercising constant leverage on the commission was the regulated industry, which captured the commission and made it an ally rather than a check. Although this thesis still has some validity, recent scholarship has pointed out its flaws. In the past few decades, Congress and the presidency have exercised greater influence over the independent regulatory commissions. And public-interest groups have turned their attention to the commissions, bringing pressure to bear as a counterveiling force against the regulated industries.[33]

In this changed political climate, economic regulation has sometimes regained its character as protection of the public against the abuses of private economic power. Yet private economic power has formidable resources with which to fight back. In the 1970s, the Federal Trade Commission (FTC), acting on a mandate from Congress, began to issue new rules for the protection of consumers. A proposed code for the funeral industry would have required an item-by-item accounting of funeral costs instead of a lump-sum charge that grieving clients would be unlikely to question. Another code for the used-car industry would have required that the results of a detailed inspection be posted on the windshield. But undertakers and used-car dealers mobilized and brought political pressure on Congress, and the FTC was forced to withdraw these codes.

Although most economic regulation has not been very burdensome to business, there has been a movement in recent years, promoted by economists and backed by business elites, to scale down the role of the government in the economy. Advocates of such **deregulation** argue that market forces will promote the interests of producers and consumers alike far more efficiently than the intrusive hand of government. Deregulation began during the presidencies of Gerald Ford and Jimmy Carter and accelerated during the presidency of Ronald Reagan, with the most notable changes in the fields of transportation, communications, and banking. Existing regulatory controls were relaxed, and private economic forces were trusted to serve the public interest by engaging in market competition.

How well has deregulation worked? In the case of the airline industry, the positive effects of deregulation (air fares in general have declined, and the number of passengers has increased) have outweighed the negative. The situation is different, however, in the case of savings and loans (S&Ls). When Congress and the president took controls off this industry in the early 1980s, savings and loan operators went wild. Poorly conceived real estate loans, financial gimmicks that bilked small investors, and outright looting by operators sent many S&Ls into massive debt. Thanks to government insurance of deposits up to $100,000, the federal government and ultimately the taxpayers have had to pick up the tab, estimated by some analysts eventually to run as high as $500 billion (about $2,000 for every man, woman, and child in the United States). In this case, the assumption that the market automatically promotes the public good has been shown to be mistaken.

Social Regulation

Debates over economic regulation versus deregulation center on which approach has a more beneficial effect on people's pocketbooks. Debates over social regulation versus deregulation tend to pit the physical, moral, and aesthetic well-being of the American people against considerations of economics. Whereas economic regulation goes back to the late nineteenth century, social regulation has largely been a product of the 1960s and 1970s. Examples of social regulation include:

Consumer safety (e.g., strict rules on sleepwear and cribs for babies, seat belts and air bags for automobiles)

Worker safety and health (e.g., OSHA rules on exposure to asbestos in the workplace)

Environmental protection (e.g., EPA rules on factory emissions under the Clean Air Act)

Wildlife protection (e.g., the Endangered Species Act)

Antidiscrimination protection (e.g., rules of the Equal Opportunity Employment Commission prohibiting job discrimination against racial minorities)[34]

When contemporary foes of bureaucracy rail against "overregulation," it is principally social regulation that they have in mind. Businesses have learned to live comfortably with economic regulation, but they are adamant about the ill effects of social regulation. Social regulation draws so much fire from the business community in part because in such areas as worker health and safety, clean air and water, and nondiscrimination, it touches almost all businesses, unlike the more narrowly targeted approach in economic regulation. Social regulation also imposes costs on businesses that cut into profits.

The origins of social regulation hold another clue to business hostility. The social regulation measures of the 1960s and 1970s were supported by Congress and the president in response to the civil rights movement, the environmental movement, and the consumer safety movement. Social regulation, in other words, has been a potent political vehicle for popular democrats in their struggle against economic elites.

A major assault on social regulation was launched during the presidency of Ronald Reagan. The intellectual justification for this assault was the damage

Scientists from the Environmental Protection Agency take samples of the toxic chemical Dioxin from Times Beach, Missouri. Regulation of environmental pollution and toxic waste was a major source of the bureaucratic expansion of the 1970s.

regulation was supposedly doing to the American economy. Overregulation, opponents charged, was imposing such massive costs on American businesses as to prevent them from investing in productive new technologies, a crippling practice in an era where they faced mounting international competition. Intellectual critics of social regulation were sincere in these arguments, but many of the business backers of this critique were concerned less about the health of the U.S. economy than about their corporations' profits.

To cut back on social regulation, the Reagan administration adopted a variety of tactics. Budgets for the social regulatory agencies were slashed. Political appointees were selected who were known to be hostile to the missions of the agencies they were to head; Anne Gorsuch Burford, a vehement opponent of environmental regulation, thus became Reagan's first head of the Environmental

Protection Agency. New social regulation had to clear the hurdle of a mode of analysis with a built-in bias against such regulation. The Reagan administration claimed that it was using **cost-benefit analysis** as a neutral tool, determining if the dollar benefits of proposed regulation were greater than the dollar costs. The problem was that no clear dollar value could be placed on such intangible benefits as the worth of a human life or the beauty of a natural setting, whereas the costs incurred by an industry were readily quantifiable. Consequently, many new regulations were bound to fail the test of cost-benefit analysis.

The success of the Reagan administration's attack on social regulation was limited, however, by the countermobilization of friends of social regulation. They fought with increasing success to preserve their earlier victories. Supporters of social regulation turned to the courts and to Congress to blunt the Reagan administration's efforts. In the past, gains won by loosely organized popular democratic forces had been eroded by well-organized elites. But this time, the popular democratic forces, organized in public-interest groups, had an impressive staying power.

The issue of how much bureaucracy Americans need is also a matter of what citizens want from government. Certainly, bureaucratic agencies can be too big, inefficient, or wasteful. And agency accountability remains a pressing issue. But much of the present-day administrative state is necessary to protect the public and provide it with services. As we saw at the end of Chapter 4, popular democrats seek to democratize private, corporate bureaucracies, making them more accountable to consumers, workers, and communities. If powerful corporations were limited in these ways, much regulatory bureaucracy would not be needed. Short of such fundamental reforms, however, modern government cannot be "de-bureaucratized" without major costs to the public.

Bureaucracy, with all of its flaws, is part and parcel of modern American democracy. Thus, the question of whose influence shapes bureaucracy's behavior becomes all the more important. That question lies at the heart of the contemporary debate over bureaucratic reform.

THE DEMOCRATIC DEBATE OVER REFORMING THE BUREAUCRACY

Bureaucratic inefficiency, irrationality, and arrogance are perennial targets for reform. But reformers of bureaucracy do not all necessarily share the same assumptions or seek the same ends. Elite democrats struggle against popular democrats over who will influence the workings of the administrative state. There are three major prescriptions for reform in this struggle: an elite democratic quest for technocratic solutions, an elite democratic turn to markets, and a popular democratic push for citizen controls.

Technocratic Reforms

The technocratic perspective on reform aims to find some rational, comprehensive, technical device for overcoming bureaucratic self-seeking and inefficiency.

Developed by academic experts and sponsored by chief executives, technocratic schemes try to control bureaucracy from the top down. They resemble Alexander Hamilton's vision of a wise executive creating a more systematic administrative machine to serve his ends. Their rise and fall under a succession of presidents suggest that modern executives have been less successful than Hamilton in imposing their preferred order on the administrative state.

Zero-based budgeting (ZBB), President Carter's pet project, illustrates the promise and disappointments in technocratic, top-down reform. Most bureaucratic agencies start with their current budget and seek incremental improvements for the following year. Consequently, existing programs are refunded with little attention paid to how well they are working. The aim of ZBB was to force each agency to begin with a zero appropriation and justify funding for each program. But this well-intentioned scheme to weed out poor programs quickly petered out. Bureaucratic agencies naturally had little desire to justify their existence every year. And neither the agencies nor a politically harried chief executive like Carter had the time or energy to engage in the comprehensive review that ZBB necessitated.

Market Reforms

The market reform approach proposes to measure bureaucratic performance by the yardstick of economic efficiency and to turn to nonbureaucratic alternatives when they can do better than government agencies. For example, is assisting low-income citizens in obtaining decent housing an important governmental objective? Rather than government building and running housing projects for low-income families, it could issue such families vouchers to pay part of their rent in privately owned apartment buildings. And where private companies can perform functions more cheaply than government agencies, shouldn't government contract out these functions—an idea known as **privatization?** Proponents of market reform believe that markets are generally superior to governments in securing both individual freedom and economic efficiency.[35]

In the desire to enhance individual freedom of choice, the market approach is compatible with popular democracy. Yet popular democrats are suspicious of claims that markets are the panacea for the problems of bureaucracy. As we have seen, competition in the American marketplace is imperfect, with large and wealthy corporations often in a dominant position. To substitute private businesses for government agencies is to trust too much in such imperfect markets and to rely for the fulfillment of public needs on those interested only in profit.

What ultimately places advocates of market reforms in the elite democratic camp is the same assumption that guided the Federalists: that self-interest and the acquisition of property are the people's overriding concerns and that the good society results from a proper channelling of self-seeking motives. With this assumption, market forces deserve a larger scope. But popular democrats since the Anti-federalists also have valued equality and active citizenship, and these are not fostered by markets. Private businesses may be more efficient (i.e., cost less) than government agencies in many areas. But this is true in part because government agencies, far more than private businesses, are expected to reflect democratic values of openness, universal service, and equity. Popular democrats are not indifferent to measures of efficiency in evaluating bureaucracy, but they do not make efficiency the sole and sovereign test.

Popular Democratic Reforms

The popular democratic approach to reforming bureaucracy focuses on greater citizen understanding and influence—control from the bottom up. Popular democrats seek to make bureaucratic decisions more open to public scrutiny. Just as the Anti-federalists sought a government that would mirror the people's concerns, so contemporary popular democrats seek a bureaucracy that is in touch with ordinary citizens. The popular democratic approach assumes that ordinary citizens are individual consumers of government services who also can deliberate intelligently about the public interest. Taking inspiration from the

President Bill Clinton and Vice President Al Gore pose with stacks of bureaucratic regulations to publicize their plan for "reinventing government." Clinton and Gore have joined a long line of bureaucratic reformers—most of whom have had limited success.

popular democratic movements of the 1960s, this approach has already had an impact on the American administrative state.

Government agencies can evade accountability by using secrecy. Therefore, the first requirement for greater citizen influence is greater openness in the bureaucracy. The most positive step in this direction has been the Freedom of Information Act of 1966, amended (and improved) by further legislation in 1974. This act requires government agencies to make available their records (exempting certain sensitive materials) when citizens and citizen groups request them. Thanks to the Freedom of Information Act, citizens have been alerted to such bureaucratic secrets as inspection reports from the Department of Agriculture on the sale of unhealthy meat, Nuclear Regulatory Commission reports on inadequate security at nuclear power plants, and widespread injuries and deaths caused by defective automobiles that the government had refused to recall.[36] Another step toward a more open bureaucracy is the Government in the Sunshine Act of 1976, which requires regulatory commissions to open their meetings to the public.

Once citizens are better informed about federal agency activities, the second requirement for popular influence is greater public input into bureaucratic decision-making. In the past two decades, Congress has frequently mandated that administrative agencies hold public hearings before taking action. Lobbyists have always been able to register their views with agencies; public hearings give citizens and citizen groups a chance to do the same. Some critics disparage hearings as symbolic gestures that appease the public but have little real effect. Yet in some areas—especially environmental protection—hearings have had a significant impact on policy.

Popular democratic reforms of bureaucracy have not been a cure-all, but they have made significant strides. As William Gormley, Jr. comments, "By broadening and improving public intervention in administrative proceedings, reformers helped to create a more humane, more responsive, and more innovative bureaucracy. This was no small accomplishment."[37]

Greater popular control of bureaucracy also requires involving citizens in policy implementation. Rather than trust bureaucratic experts to carry out policies alone, citizens directly affected should cooperate in enforcement. The case of safety and health codes for the workplace illustrates what happens when ordinary people are shut out of the implementation process.

When Congress established OSHA, Charles Noble points out, the legislation "did not require employers to establish in-plant health and safety committees that might require worker participation."[38] Thus, workers had no part in the implementation of safety and health rules, which was left to factory inspectors from OSHA. The inspectors were far too few in number to provide vigorous enforcement, so the chance that a firm would be inspected in a year was approximately 1 in 100.[39] Matters worsened when President Reagan, hostile to OSHA's mission, further reduced the agency's efforts. As a result, hostile businesses and an unfriendly administration gravely weakened the workplace protection promised by the legislation.

Although bureaucracy can be reformed from the bottom up, ordinary citizens are limited in the time and resources they can devote to influencing bureaucratic behavior. Furthermore, the narrow, technical nature of many agency decisions shuts out all but the affected interest groups and the bureaucratic experts.

Popular democratic influence can, however, be furthered without requiring direct, sustained citizen involvement. Much depends, for example, on the bureaucracy's prevalent attitudes toward citizens. An agency with an image of itself as professional, expert, and elite is likely to look down on the constituency it serves. In contrast, an agency with the spirit of Harry Hopkins shows respect to its constituency. It is up to those who train and select civil servants, from teachers of public administration all the way up to the president, to instill in future bureaucrats the egalitarian values of popular democracy.

Popular democratic influence over bureaucracy also depends on the effort of elected representatives, particularly in the legislature. When citizens and citizen groups are inattentive, legislators enter into mutually rewarding alliances with agencies and interest groups. When citizens and citizen groups are watching legislators, Congress often prods bureaucratic agencies to be more responsive to the public. The pressures that push Congress toward popular democracy lead it to push the bureaucracy in the same direction.

Because popular discontent with big government remains high, all three perspectives on bureaucratic reform continue to press their cases. President Clinton's "reinvention of government" plan is a synthesis of the technocratic, the market, and the popular democratic approaches. In believing that a sweeping new approach guided by the White House can remake bureaucracy, Clinton's plan smacks of the technocratic. In emphasizing cutbacks to the federal work force and privatization of some government functions, his plan has a strong market element. But Clinton's belief that ordinary government workers should be freed from red tape and "empowered" to operate in a more responsible manner draws on the popular democratic understanding of human nature and civic virtue.

CONCLUSION: BEYOND MONSTER BUREAUCRACY

In contemporary American political discourse, Bureaucracy—with a capital *B*—is a monster. This Bureaucracy is composed of massive and ponderous organizations staffed by authoritarian drones. It smothers individual freedom under a blanket of unnecessary rules. And it grows more powerful all the time, not in the interest of the American people but in the service of its own voracious appetites. What is wrong with American government today, most people think, is mostly the consequence of Bureaucracy.

Monster Bureaucracy is a mythical creature—a hobbyhorse for irate citizens and a scapegoat for calculating politicians. When we look at real American bureaucracies, we see their diversity: They come in different organizational forms and sizes and pursue an enormous variety of missions. The people who staff them are not a perverse bureaucratic breed but rather a cross-section of the American people. And the interests that bureaucrats further range from the most narrow and selfish to the most lofty and communal. Some agencies are entangled with economic elites in cozy, mutually rewarding alliances. Others try to put into practice the most important legislative victories that popular democrats have won against such elites.

Bureaucracy is one of the most important arenas for political struggle in modern America. The political character of bureaucracy stems in part from the expertise and discretion that administrators possess, which make them key policymakers in their own right. It results from the attempts of federal agencies to mobilize external political support in their search for greater autonomy. And it is underscored by the efforts of every other political force—interest groups, public-interest groups, Congress, the president, the courts—to direct these agencies in accordance with their preferred course of action. These political forces recognize that bureaucratic agencies, operating at the point where government directly touches the lives of the American people, are worth fighting over.

Monster Bureaucracy has to be hit with a bludgeon. Real bureaucracies may need reform. But how we approach such reform depends on where we stand in the democratic debate. If we follow the tradition of elite democracy initiated by Alexander Hamilton, we should place our trust in new forms of expertise, deployed by a wise chief executive, that will coordinate and reshape bureaucracy from the top down. If we follow the newer school of elite democracy, which claims the superiority of private markets to public agencies, we should make efficiency our standard and let business do much of what government is accustomed to doing. And if we follow the popular democratic tradition, with its commitments to citizen action, civic virtue, and an egalitarian society, we should open up the world of bureaucracy wherever possible to the grievances, opinions, and democratic hopes of ordinary people.

KEY TERMS

bureaucracy	rule-making authority
spoils system	administrative adjudication
administrative state	autonomy
cabinet departments	bureaucratic politics
independent agencies	regulation
independent regulatory commissions	economic regulation
public corporations	social regulation
federal foundations and endowments	deregulation
mission	cost-benefit analysis
expertise	privatization
discretion	

SUGGESTED READINGS

Charles T. Goodsell, *The Case for Bureaucracy: A Public Administration Polemic*, 3rd ed. (Chatham, N.J.: Chatham House, 1994). A lively polemic that takes on the prevailing myths about a Monster Bureaucracy.

William T. Gormley, Jr., *Taming the Bureaucracy: Muscles, Prayers, and Other Strategies* (Princeton, N.J.: Princeton University Press, 1989). A thoughtful account of the varied strategies that have been adopted to reform bureaucracy.

Eugene Lewis, *Public Entrepreneurship: Toward a Theory of Bureaucratic Political Power* (Bloomington: Indiana University Press, 1980). A study of three bureaucrats—Hyman Rickover, J. Edgar Hoover, and Robert Moses—who obtained exceptional power and autonomy in their bureaucratic fiefdoms.

James A. Morone, *The Democratic Wish: Popular Participation and the Limits of American Government* (New York: Basic Books, 1990). An ironic argument about how the democratic desire to bring government back to the people results instead in more bureaucracy.

James Q. Wilson, *Bureaucracy: What Government Agencies Do and Why They Do It* (New York: Basic Books, 1989). A wide-ranging, insightful treatise on bureaucracy in the United States.

CHAPTER 15

The Judiciary and the Democratic Paradox

As a contribution to combatting the violence in "drug wars" between cocaine lords, Congress passed a law requiring a mandatory thirty-year sentence for anyone using a machine gun fitted with a silencer during drug trafficking. Under this law, John Angus Smith was charged, convicted, and sentenced in a federal court in Florida for trading just such a weapon to an undercover agent for two ounces of cocaine. Smith appealed his stiff sentence all the way to the United States Supreme Court, arguing that the law had been aimed at the violent use of weapons and not at their place in an economic exchange.

The decision in *Smith* v. *United States*, handed down in 1993, upheld the sentence by a vote of 6–3. Writing for the Court, Justice Sandra Day O'Connor observed that Congress had not stipulated in the law that firearms had to be used *as weapons* to require the mandatory sentence. It was not the job of the Supreme Court, she said, to restrict the meaning of the congressional language in this case.

Writing for the three dissenters, Justice Antonin Scalia was incredulous at O'Connor's reasoning. "The court," he wrote, "does not appear to grasp the distinction between how a word can be used and how it ordinarily is used." Scalia offered a colorful illustration of his point: "When someone asks, 'Do you use a cane?' he is not inquiring whether you have your grandfather's silver-handled walking stick on display in the hall; he wants to know whether you walk with a cane." O'Connor fired back at Scalia's lecture about ordinary language with a historical rejoinder: A cane had been used as a weapon by a southern congressman to fell Senator Charles Sumner, an ardent antislavery advocate, shortly before the Civil War.[1]

This minor but intriguing case demonstrates that the business of the U.S. Supreme Court is largely to determine the meaning of the words in federal laws and the Constitution. Justices of the Court, far more than legislators and executives, are engaged in acts of *interpretation*.

The case also reveals that judicial interpretation involves *debate and conflict*. The sparring between O'Connor and Scalia is typical of many Court decisions. Behind the facade of neutral justice handed down by grave and learned elders of the law, we find arguments among nine human beings with forceful personalities and passionate convictions.

As a nation with a tradition of transforming myriad issues into legal matters, the United States has an extensive judiciary at both the federal and state levels. The federal courts are organized in a three-tier system, which we describe later in the chapter. But our primary focus is on the highest tier, the Supreme Court of the United States.

The nine justices of the Supreme Court form a unique elite. Appointed rather than elected, for tenures that run on "good behavior" until retirement or death, the justices have carved out for themselves the formidable role of serving as final arbiters of the Constitution. Their authority is strengthened by powerful symbolism, as they hand down decisions wearing their black robes in their marble temple, and protected by the cloak of expertise, as they pronounce their judgments in the esoteric language of the law. In all these ways, the judiciary is the least democratic branch of the federal government. Indeed, it can be said, as David O'Brien writes, that "the Court wields an antidemocratic power."[2]

Yet the Court's relationship to elite democracy and popular democracy is not this simple. The Supreme Court may be (and has been in its history) a pillar of elite democracy, upholding the interests of the powerful and privileged in the name of authority, expertise, or private property. But the Court also may be (and has been in its history) a champion of the fundamental rules of democratic politics in the face of intolerant and repressive majorities. And the Court may be (and has been in its history) the last hope for the weakest citizens—racial minorities, the poor, persons accused of crimes. Elitist in form and character, the Supreme Court is nonetheless a vital and sometimes surprising participant in the democratic debate.

This chapter begins with a consideration of contemporary debates over the proper role of the judiciary and assesses the Court's paradoxical position with respect to democracy. Next, the chapter looks back at the history of the Supreme Court, noting how the Court's relationship to democracy has changed from one era to the next. Subsequent sections cover judicial selection, the lower federal courts, the processes through which the Supreme Court functions, and the politics that divides it. Finally, the chapter examines the place of the Supreme Court in the broader political system and sums up its role in the democratic debate.

JUDICIAL POWER AND THE DEMOCRATIC PARADOX

What is the place of an unelected judiciary in a democratic republic? Answers to this question begin with a recognition of the Supreme Court's fundamental power: **judicial review.** This is the power of courts to invalidate the actions of legislatures and executives on the grounds that these actions conflict with the Constitution. This power was first asserted by the Supreme Court in the landmark case of *Marbury* v. *Madison* (1803). Although the *power* of judicial review remained controversial for much of the nineteenth century, almost no one today would question it. But questions do arise about the proper *extent* of judicial review. How far should the Court go in overturning the actions of the other federal branches or the state governments? In setting these actions against the language of the Constitution, how should the Court interpret the Constitution?

The Debate over Interpreting the Constitution

The most recent debate over the Court's role and its reading of the Constitution took place during Reagan's presidency. On one side was Reagan's attorney general, Edwin Meese. On the other was an associate justice of the Supreme Court (and one of its most influential members in recent decades), William Brennan. Meese argued for a more restricted role and for stricter interpretation. Brennan defended a broader province and method of interpretation. Their arguments are worth considering, for they introduce us to the contemporary democratic debate over the judiciary.

Meese, unhappy with the Supreme Court's "liberal" decisions of the preceding decades, argued that it was meddling with the affairs of the other federal branches and especially the state governments. This overreaching, he charged, arose not from constitutional duty but from an exaggerated sense of the Court's own powers and a loose reading of the Constitution. Meese believed that the Court conveniently construed the Constitution "as an empty vessel into which each generation may pour its passion and prejudice."[3] As a result, the Court's decisions represented "more policy choices than articulations of constitutional principle."[4] Yet nobody had authorized the justices of the Supreme Court to make policy choices and impose them on elected officials.

According to Meese, the Court could return to its legitimate—and more restrained—role through a **jurisprudence of original intention.**[5] By this, he meant that "the text of the document and the original intention of those who framed it would be the judicial standard in giving effect to the Constitution."[6] The standard of original intention, Meese argued, would make judges into faithful servants of the Constitution. "Any other standard," he warned, "suffers the defect of pouring new meaning into old words, thus creating new powers and new rights totally at odds with the logic of our Constitution and its commitment to the rule of law."[7]

Brennan, an influential force in crafting many of the Supreme Court decisions that Meese was attacking, presented a dramatically different understanding of the Court's proper role. To Brennan, a jurisprudence of original intention was "arrogance cloaked as humility."[8] It was, he argued, impossible to recover the founders' precise intent for each phrase of the Constitution. The records of their era are incomplete and ambiguous, and what they do reveal are disagreement, rather than consensus, over meaning. Brennan detected a political motive beneath the claim of fidelity to the intentions of the founders: The jurisprudence of original intention was a conservative philosophy that required the Supreme Court to "turn a blind eye to social progress."[9]

Brennan's alternative to original intention gave the judiciary a far broader role in reading the Constitution—and in affecting American life.

> We current Justices read the Constitution in the only way that we can: as Twentieth Century Americans. We look to the history of the time of framing and to the intervening history of interpretation. But the ultimate question must be, what do the words of the text mean in our time? For the genius of the Constitution rests not in any static meaning it might have had in a world that is dead and gone, but in the adaptability of its great principles to cope with current problems and current needs.[10]

The lines between Meese and Brennan were sharply drawn. Meese wanted the judiciary to play a cautious role, restricting itself to the views of the framers

Angered by controversial Warren Court decisions on race, crime, and school prayer, conservatives called for the impeachment of the Chief Justice. The Warren Court represents the high point of judicial activism on behalf of libertarian and egalitarian values.

of the Constitution and subsequent amendments; Brennan wanted it to play an active role, adapting constitutional language to changing times. Yet each insisted that his *jurisprudence* (judicial philosophy) was the democratic one. A "Jurisprudence of Original Intention," Meese wrote, "reflects a deeply rooted commitment to democracy" because it adheres to the Constitution as "the fundamental will of the people."[11] Brennan replied that the Constitution as he interpreted it "embodies the aspiration to social justice, brotherhood, and human dignity that brought this nation into being."[12]

Whose claim to be the defender of democracy—Meese's or Brennan's—is more valid? Before we can decide between them, we must look more closely at the relationship between judicial power and democracy. Once we have examined this relationship, we can return to their debate.

The Judiciary and Democracy

There are several ways in which the Supreme Court is *not* a democratic institution. First, members of the judiciary are not elected; they are nominated by the president and confirmed by the Senate. Second, federal judges serve during good behavior—that is, until they retire, die, or are impeached by the House and convicted by the Senate. No justice of the Supreme Court has ever been removed through impeachment and conviction. (The Jeffersonians impeached Federalist Justice Samuel Chase but failed to win conviction in the Senate.) Consequently, members of the Court are held accountable only indirectly—by Congress through its power over jurisdiction, by presidents through their appointment power, and by members of the public through their decisions on complying with judicial rulings.

Third, justices wield their power of judicial review by striking down actions taken by elected officials at the federal or state level. The exercise of judicial review is thus *countermajoritarian*, meaning that majority rule has to give way if the Court believes that the actions of the majority conflict with the Constitution.

Fourth, the federal judiciary historically has been even less representative demographically than Congress and the executive branch. Almost all justices have been white, male, and affluent. (Women and African Americans have finally won some representation on the federal bench in the past three decades.) Equally important, they have all been lawyers, which means that one of the most powerful branches of the national government is the exclusive domain of the legal profession.

That nonlawyers are effectively excluded from the judicial branch may be inevitable, but it has some important consequences for American democracy. The Constitution, ostensibly an expression of the will of the people, has become a lawyers' document. As John Brigham observes, "Doctrines announced by [the] Court on the Constitution have all but supplanted the text itself."[13] Debate over the Constitution, which in the nineteenth century was not uncommon among ordinary citizens, is now an expert enterprise reserved mostly for the Court and its supporters and critics in the legal community.

There is, it seems, a potent democratic case to be made against a strong and active judiciary. Yet the paradox is that this nondemocratic power may be essential for preserving democratic values and rules. Nowhere is this more apparent than in the areas of individual and minority rights. Majority rule can be used to impose unwelcome beliefs on individuals and to prohibit the expression of unconventional views. Majorities can repress and exploit minorities, whether of race, creed, or color. A democracy with unrestrained majority rule would eventually undermine the very conditions of personal and political freedom that gave it life. It would be like a sports league in which the team that won the first game was able to set the rules for all succeeding games. A countermajoritarian judiciary therefore stands as a guardian for the abiding values and conditions that democracy requires.[14]

The Court serves democracy not only when it protects individual and minority rights from infringement by majorities but also when it publicly explains its actions. The Court's impact on public thinking may be limited by its legal language, yet no other branch of government offers such extensive and reasoned accounts of its decisions or elaborates on so many fundamental democratic principles. It was the Supreme Court, for example, that explained to Americans why segregated schools denied African Americans the equal protection of the laws and why coerced confessions denied criminal defendants the right to a fair trial.

Ironically, the mystique of the Supreme Court, which shields it from democratic control, may help preserve its role as upholder of democracy. A public that thinks of the black-robed justices as priestly devotees of the Constitution is more likely to accept countermajoritarian decisions than is a public that views the justices as partisan policymakers. Democratic citizens should be skeptical and questioning, rather than reverent, toward authority, but in the case of the Supreme Court a little reverence may have its place.

The Meese-Brennan Debate Briefly Revisited

We are now in a better position to return to the Meese-Brennan debate and consider their rival claims to have democracy on their side. In seeking to restrict the role of the federal judiciary, Meese's case emphasizes the Court's nondemocratic aspects. His critique of the judiciary echoes the complaints of popular democrats in the past. One of Meese's allies in the debate, Robert Bork, spells out this argument succinctly: "We are increasingly governed not by law or elected representatives but by an unelected, unrepresentative, unaccountable committee of lawyers applying no will but their own."[15] In Meese's version of democracy, judges should not impede other officials unless their acts clearly violate the original intention of the framers.

Brennan's jurisprudence uses the means of elite democracy to advance the ends of popular democracy. Judges—indisputably an elite in terms of occupation and expertise—should advance the goals of social justice and human dignity by serving as forceful advocates for a democracy of inclusion, equality, and fairness. Reading the Constitution as a charter for such popular democratic values, they cannot be bound by the fuzzy notion of original intention—especially since the original intenders, the Federalists, were elite democrats! Although popular democrats may naturally mistrust the judicial elite, Brennan wants them to recognize how this elite may sometimes be their ally.

THE SUPREME COURT IN HISTORY

For an institution that derives much of its authority from its role as sacred guardian of a timeless text, the Supreme Court has been profoundly shaped by its history. The Court's relationship to history is, however, double edged. On the one hand, the Court treats history with reverence, claiming to follow past decisions as **precedents** and apply them to new circumstances. On the other hand, the Court has engaged in some dramatic historical shifts. For most of its history, the Supreme Court was a pillar of elite democracy, a champion of national authority and private property against the popular democratic forces struggling for greater equality. Since the 1930s, however, the Court has largely abandoned its stance as the protector of economic elites, adopting instead a new focus on civil liberties and civil rights.

John Marshall and Judicial Power

The Supreme Court did not become a major force in the American political system immediately on ratification of the Constitution. ARTICLE III of the Constitution, establishing the judicial branch, was brief and vague, leaving the role of the Court an open question. During its first decade under the Constitution, the Court was relatively weak. Nonetheless, popular democrats feared its potential as a home for a judicial aristocracy. During the ratification debates, Alexander Hamilton, the arch elite democrat, had championed a judicial branch that could invalidate the actions of the other branches or the states as contrary to the Constitution. Anti-federalist writers, such as Brutus, had warned that this judiciary might promote the powers of a remote federal government while diminishing the powers of state governments closer to the people. With the triumph of Jeffersonian democracy over the elitism of the Federalists in 1800, the more radical Jeffersonians hoped that the power of the federal judiciary could be severely curtailed. Legal historian Kermit Hall observes, "Radicals distrusted lawyers and believed that local democracy in an agrarian society based on 'common sense and common honesty between man and men . . .' offered the surest road to justice."[16]

But it was the fears, not the hopes, of the more radical popular democrats that were to be realized. For as Jefferson was assuming the presidency, John Marshall was taking over as chief justice of the Supreme Court. Appointed by President Adams in the waning days of his administration, Marshall, a Federalist, was gifted with great intellectual force, rhetorical grace, and political shrewdness. And he had a vision for the Court: to establish it coequally with the other branches and turn it into a sponsor of national authority and economic development (a vision that he shared with Alexander Hamilton). Marshall dominated the Supreme Court for thirty-four years, serving from 1801 until his death in 1835. The Marshall Court, more than the words of ART. III, established the judicial branch as the powerful political force that later generations of Americans came to regard as a key part of the constitutional design.

Marshall's agenda for the Court depended on establishing the power of judicial review. But he wanted to avoid a head-on collision with the Jeffersonian majority that controlled the executive and legislative branches. In a stroke of judicial genius, he found the perfect vehicle for judicial review in the case of *Marbury* v. *Madison* (1803). William Marbury had been appointed by President Adams to a position as justice of the peace for the District of Columbia, but the papers for his commission had not been delivered by the time Jefferson supplanted Adams in the White House. Jefferson's secretary of state, James Madison, refused to hand over the papers. Marbury asked the Supreme Court to order Madison, through a writ of mandamus, to give him his commission.

Marshall's opinion in *Marbury* v. *Madison* held that the secretary of state had wrongfully withheld the commission. But the Supreme Court, he went on, could do nothing to rectify this injustice because the authority to issue writs of mandamus, mandated by the Judiciary Act of 1789, was unconstitutional—it expanded the original jurisdiction of the Court beyond what was specified in ART. III. In bold rhetorical strokes, he crafted the doctrine of judicial review. It was evident, he argued, that "a law repugnant to the constitution is void" and that "it is emphatically the province and duty of the judicial department to say what the law is."[17] Notice how shrewdly Marshall bolstered the power of the Supreme Court. He avoided a confrontation with the Jefferson administration by ruling that the Supreme Court was powerless to reverse the action toward Marbury. But he advanced the Supreme Court's power in the long term by making it, and not the other branches, the final arbiter of constitutionality.

Once Marshall had established the Court's power of judicial review, he moved gradually to further his vision of a powerful national government promoting capitalist economic development. Striking down Maryland's attempt to tax the Bank of the United States in *McCulloch* v. *Maryland* (1819), he emphasized the constitutional supremacy of the federal government over the states (see Chapter 3). And then in *Gibbons* v. *Ogden* (1824), the Marshall Court ruled that the Interstate Commerce Clause, under which Gibbons held a federal coasting license for his steamboat line, was superior to the steamboat monopoly granted to Ogden by the state of New York.

As the *Gibbons* case indicates, Marshall was able to advance his goal of economic development in conjunction with his goal of national authority. He read the Constitution, Robert McCloskey writes, "so as to provide maximum protection to property rights and maximum support for the idea of nationalism."[18] Marshall's decision in *Dartmouth College* v. *Woodward* (1819) blocked the effort of New Hampshire Jeffersonians to oust the Federalist trustees of Dartmouth College. The college's royal charter, he ruled, was a contract, and the Constitution forbade the states from interfering with contractual obligations, such as that to Dartmouth's existing trustees. Thanks to Marshall's decision, the Contract Clause of the Constitution became a major barrier to state regulation of private businesses.

The Taney Court

When John Marshall died, and Andrew Jackson, a frequent foe of Marshall's, appointed Roger Taney as chief justice, supporters of the Court as the champion of nationalism and capitalism shuddered. Surely, they thought, the Court would now become a supporter of states' rights and egalitarian attacks on property. But Marshall had set the Court on a course that was not easily altered. Historians now find more continuity than change between the Marshall and the Taney Courts. Although Taney was more sympathetic to state governments, he upheld national authority and capitalist development. The Taney Court's most important economic decision came in *Charles River Bridge* v. *Warren Bridge* (1837). In ruling that the Massachusetts legislature could charter a new bridge even when it undercut the profitability of a previously chartered bridge, whose owners claimed that their monopoly rights had been violated, the Taney Court fostered a more competitive capitalist system.

Taney's most notorious decision, however, came in *Dred Scott* v. *Sandford* (1857). The *Dred Scott* decision is universally regarded as the worst in the history of the Supreme Court. In a remarkable bit of political miscalculation, Taney thought that the Court could solve with one decision the brewing crisis between North and South over slavery. His solution took the southern side on every burning question of the day: Slaves were held to be a form of property protected by the Constitution, and Congress was told it had no power to forbid or abolish slavery in the western territories. Taney went even further, almost taunting northern champions of the antislavery cause with his vicious racist remark that blacks were regarded by the founders "as beings of an inferior order" who "had no rights which the white man was bound to respect."[19] Taney's ruling and rhetoric incensed the North and increased sectional tensions, helping to lead to a civil war that would obliterate his fateful misuse of judicial power.

From the Civil War to the Roosevelt Revolution

The Civil War confirmed on the battlefield what John Marshall had claimed on the bench: the supremacy of the federal government over the states. After the Civil War, the Supreme Court became preoccupied with Marshall's other major concern: the rights of property. For seventy years, the Court played a critical, activist role in the development of corporate capitalism in America. The Court reread the Constitution, turning the eighteenth-century founders into proponents of the free-market capitalism worshipped by business elites of the late nineteenth century. Legal expertise and judicial authority were weapons that elite democrats fired repeatedly—and successfully—to shoot down the cause of popular democracy.

The industrial capitalist order that was growing rapidly in the years after the Civil War imposed heavy costs on workers, farmers, and owners of small businesses. Popular democratic forces, such as the agrarian Granger movement and the Populist movement, gained power in some states and passed legislation to protect ordinary people against capitalist exploitation, especially by the railroads. As the popular democratic forces mobilized, Michael Benedict writes, "the justices became convinced that the Court must serve as the bulwark of property rights against threatened radical legislation."[20] The Court set up a roadblock against state efforts to regulate the railroads in *Wabash, St. Louis & Pacific Railway Co.* v. *Illinois* (1886). Striking down Illinois's popular democratic legislation, the Court ruled in *Wabash* that states had no power to regulate rail rates for shipments that crossed their borders. The Court said in effect that only the federal government could regulate commerce.

A Court dominated by the doctrine of laissez faire (i.e., government should not interfere in the free market) was not, however, favorably disposed toward federal regulation either. When the government attempted to use the new Sherman Antitrust Act to break up the monopolistic "sugar trust," the Court overturned that action through a narrow interpretation of the Commerce Clause. In *United States* v. *E. C. Knight Co.* (1895), the Court ruled that manufacturing was a local activity and thus not covered under the Commerce Clause, even when the goods produced were destined for shipment across state lines.

The Court stretched the doctrine of laissez faire the farthest in redefining the meaning of "due process of law." The drafters of the Fourteenth Amendment had included this phrase to protect newly freed African Americans from arbitrary actions by state governments in the South. But the Supreme Court ignored the plight of blacks and turned the Fourteenth Amendment instead into a protective shield for corporations. It was a violation of due process, the Court often ruled, when a state interfered with the contractual freedom of employers and employees to make whatever "bargains" they wished. Thus, in *Lochner* v. *New York* (1905), the Court struck down a New York law setting maximum hours for bakery workers. "Freedom of contract" was the watchword of the Court, and popular democratic legislation to protect working people from oppressive conditions was declared unconstitutional.

In the face of popular democratic criticism during the Progressive era, the Supreme Court pragmatically allowed some federal and state regulation of the economy. But as Progressivism faded and a new conservative era set in after World War I, the majority of the Court hardened in its laissez-faire dogma. It was this majority that fought the most bitter battle in the history of the Court—against Franklin Roosevelt and the New Deal. Once Roosevelt and his Democratic majority in Congress passed far-reaching measures to revive an economy mired in the worst depression in its history, the question of power over the economy was joined by the Court . In *Schecter* v. *United States* (1935), the Court invalidated the National Industrial Recovery Act, the principal New Deal vehicle for managing the industrial sector. In *United States* v. *Butler* (1936), it knocked down the Agricultural Administration Act, Roosevelt's effort to restore the agricultural sector. The 1936 election gave Roosevelt the largest mandate in presidential history, but the Supreme Court now seemed an impassable barrier to his efforts to improve the economy and reform it in popular democratic fashion.

Early in 1937, Roosevelt unveiled a program to smash through this barrier. He claimed (in deceptive fashion) that he was acting only to enhance the efficiency of a Court dominated by elderly judges. His proposal was that the president be given the authority to add an additional justice each time a sitting justice over the age of seventy refused to retire. (The size of the Supreme Court is not set by the Constitution.) Popular though Roosevelt was, his **court-packing plan** was a political fiasco. Public opinion sided with the Court, and Roosevelt suffered a major defeat in Congress. He lost because the public revered the Supreme Court, despite its unpopular recent decisions. He also lost because his plan was viewed as a vehicle to advance his own executive power.

Yet Roosevelt won the larger battle with the Court in the end. While the debate raged over the court-packing plan, the Court narrowly approved two key New Deal measures—the National Labor Relations Act and the Social Security Act—during the spring of 1937. And in the next few years, deaths and resignations of the conservatives who had stymied the president permitted him to name a New Deal majority to the Court. Roosevelt's appointees ended seventy years of laissez-faire doctrine. In one of the most important shifts in the history of the Supreme Court—a "Roosevelt revolution"—they took the Court largely out of the business of economic policy.

A signpost of the Roosevelt revolution was the case of *Wickard* v. *Filburn* (1942), in which a unanimous Court said that the federal government could extend the Interstate Commerce Clause even to regulate wheat consumed on the same farm on which it was grown. A Supreme Court that read federal authority this broadly was a Court that no longer wished to question the economic judgments of the elected branches. It would no longer champion property rights and elite democracy. But what would its new role be?

The Modern Court

Since the Roosevelt revolution, the Court's role has centered on civil liberties and civil rights (see Chapter 16). This constant preoccupation with questions of civil liberties and civil rights has not meant a consistent pattern of rulings, however. Responding to changing issues and public moods, and profoundly affected by changing personnel, the Court has gone through several distinct eras in its treatment of civil liberties and civil rights.

Several of the key Court decisions in the fifteen years after 1937 sided with governmental authority over civil liberties and civil rights. Thus, the Court upheld the wartime incarceration of Japanese Americans and the early Cold War conviction of leading American communists. It was only with the emergence of the Warren Court (1953–1969) that it blazed a strong path in support of individual liberties and the rights of racial minorities. But its activism on behalf of the rights of dissenters, criminal defendants, and African Americans won it many vocal enemies, including successful presidential candidate Richard Nixon in 1968.

Nixon had the opportunity to name four new justices, among them Warren Burger as replacement for the retiring Earl Warren. The Burger Court (1969–1986), however, did not carry out the conservative counterrevolution that Nixon had advocated. Holdovers from the Warren Court and Nixon appointees who proved more moderate than expected made the Burger Court a transitional body, cutting back on some of the Warren Court landmarks, especially in matters of criminal procedure, but also announcing a fundamental new right in the area of abortion. It is only in the current era of the Rehnquist Court (1986–present) that a new conservative jurisprudence, shaped by the appointees of Presidents Reagan and Bush, is crystallizing. (For membership changes on the Supreme Court since 1960, see Figure 15.1.)

JUDICIAL SELECTION

ARTICLE II, SECTION 2 of the Constitution states that the president "shall nominate, and by and with the advice and consent of the Senate, shall appoint . . . judges of the supreme court." The same clause applies to judges in the lower federal courts, which were created by acts of Congress. These few words did not specify the processes by which a president would pick judicial nominees and the Senate consider them or what advice and consent comprised. Should the Senate defer to the president's judgment, rejecting a nominee only when that individual was found lacking in judicial competence or personal integrity? Or should the Senate's judgment be equal to the president's, allowing the Senate to reject a nominee of unquestioned competence and character on political or ideological grounds? With so little settled by the language of the Constitution, judicial selection has become, for presidents and senators alike, an intensely political affair.

Lower Federal Court Nominations

The politics of judicial selection operates differently for the lower federal courts than for the Supreme Court. Judges of the district courts (described in the next section) serve only in a district within one state, and the senators from that state are closely involved in their selection. According to the tradition of **senatorial courtesy,** if the senior senator from the president's party objects to a district court nominee for his or her state, the Senate as a whole will withhold consent. As a consequence, presidents consult closely with senators on district court nominations and may turn the choice over to them in exchange for future political support on other matters. Senatorial courtesy was somewhat weakened recently when the White House, particularly under Reagan and Bush, insisted on having more of a say on district court appointments. Individual senators have always had less power—and presidents have had more leeway—in appointing judges to the U.S. courts of appeals (also described in the next section), whose jurisdiction extends over several states.

Although presidents have to share power over lower federal court nominations, they have much to gain by taking a strong interest in judicial selection at this level. Since the Supreme Court hears only a handful of cases, the vast majority of federal court decisions are rendered by the district courts and courts of appeals. Since retirement rates are higher on the lower courts than on the Supreme Court, and since Congress periodically creates new judicial positions to keep up with the expanding workload of a litigious society, a president can exercise more influence through lower court nominations than through Supreme

FIGURE 15.1 Membership of the Supreme Court (1960s to 1994)

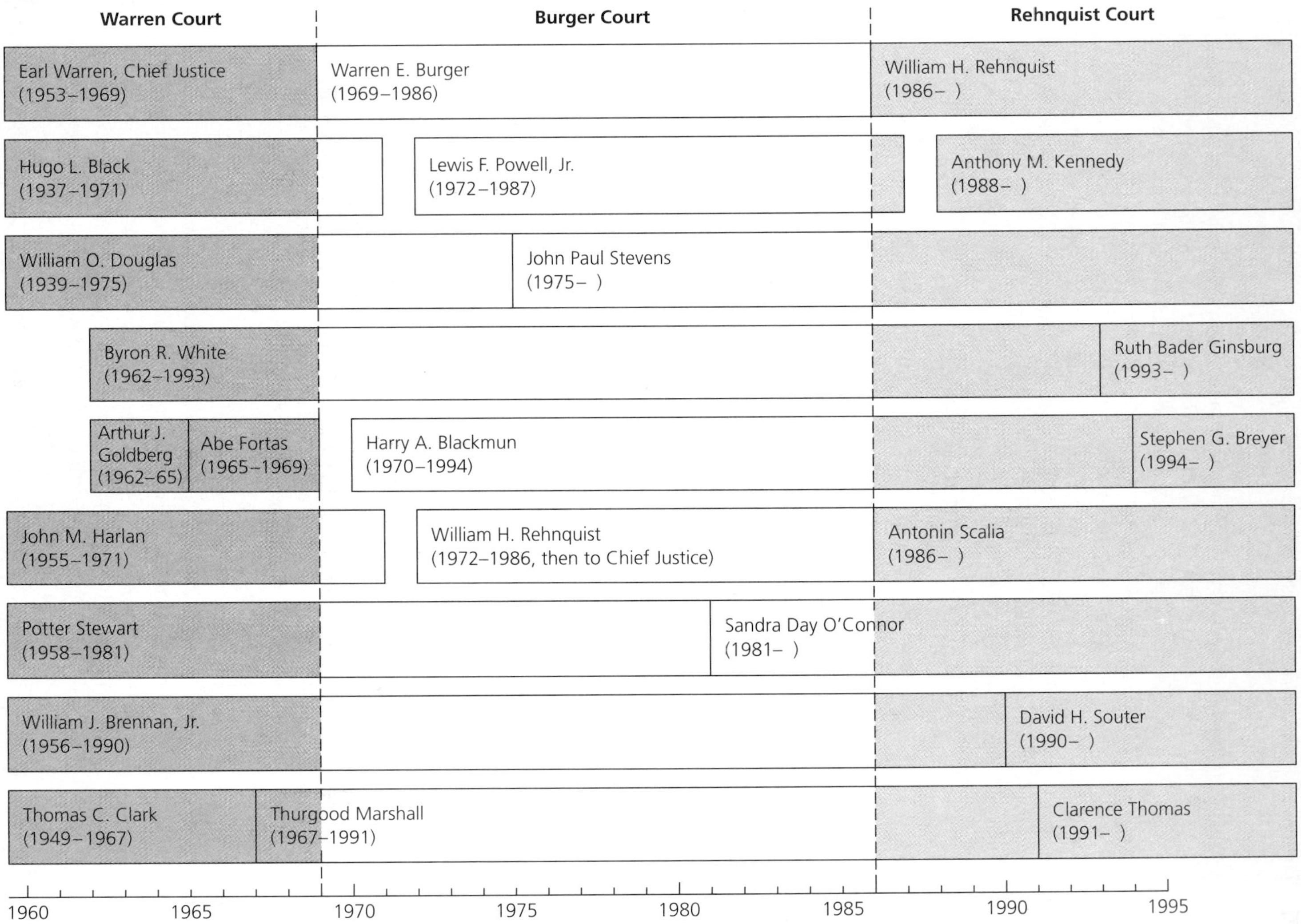

Warren Court

Earl Warren, Chief Justice (1953–1969)

Hugo L. Black (1937–1971)

William O. Douglas (1939–1975)

Byron R. White (1962–1993)

Arthur J. Goldberg (1962–65)

Abe Fortas (1965–1969)

John M. Harlan (1955–1971)

Potter Stewart (1958–1981)

William J. Brennan, Jr. (1956–1990)

Thomas C. Clark (1949–1967)

Thurgood Marshall (1967–1991)

Burger Court

Warren E. Burger (1969–1986)

Lewis F. Powell, Jr. (1972–1987)

John Paul Stevens (1975–)

Harry A. Blackmun (1970–1994)

William H. Rehnquist (1972–1986, then to Chief Justice)

Sandra Day O'Connor (1981–)

Rehnquist Court

William H. Rehnquist (1986–)

Anthony M. Kennedy (1988–)

Ruth Bader Ginsburg (1993–)

Stephen G. Breyer (1994–)

Antonin Scalia (1986–)

David H. Souter (1990–)

Clarence Thomas (1991–)

1960 1965 1970 1975 1980 1985 1990 1995

Source: Based on Stephen L. Wasby, *The Supreme Court in the Federal Judicial System*, 4th ed. Chicago: Nelson Hall Publishers, 1993.

Court nominations. During Reagan's eight years as president, he appointed approximately half of all lower court judges (372 out of 736), giving the lower federal courts a more conservative slant.[21] But Bill Clinton has the opportunity to shift the lower courts in another direction. Coming into office with 115 federal judgeships vacant, retirements by existing judges averaging 10 per month, and a Congress likely to create new positions, Clinton, according to some estimates, will appoint half the judges on the lower federal courts in only four years![22]

Supreme Court Nominations

Most presidents have less of an opportunity in the course of a four-year term to reshape the Supreme Court than the lower federal courts. Nonetheless, any presidential nomination to the Supreme Court today is likely to initiate a high-stakes political drama, for every new member may make a major difference in determining what the Constitution and the laws mean. Some of the Court's landmark decisions have come in 5–4 votes; a replacement of only one justice would have produced a different outcome. And some new appointees influence the Court with more than just their votes. They may prove to be a catalyst for the formation of a firm voting bloc, as was the case with the liberal Justice William Brennan. Or they may bring to the Court a forceful ideological perspective, as is the case with current conservative Justice Antonin Scalia.[23]

The appointment process for a new justice of the Supreme Court begins when an existing justice retires or dies. In deliberating over a replacement, contemporary presidents tend to rely heavily on the Justice Department and legal counselors on the White House staff for advice on prospective nominees. The elite of the legal profession also plays a regular role in the selection process. The American Bar Association's Standing Committee on Federal Judiciary rates candidates as "well qualified," "qualified," or "not qualified," and a president is likely to back away from a prospective nominee who has not obtained the highest rating. (More informally, prominent law professors tend to line up for or against nominees.) Viewing Supreme Court decisions as critical to the constituencies they represent, many interest groups also are involved in the politics of judicial selection. Thus, several of the nominees of Presidents Reagan and Bush were vigorously opposed by civil rights and women's groups, which feared that these nominees would roll back the egalitarian gains of recent decades.

The drama of Supreme Court nominations reaches its apex in the hearing room of the Senate Judiciary Committee. In this televised forum, senators are able to question nominees directly about their legal experience and judicial philosophy. Although questions about controversial issues currently before the Court, such as abortion, are supposed to be off limits, senators usually find means to probe these matters. Some recent nominees, such as Robert Bork, have entertained these questions. Others, such as David Souter, perhaps learning from Bork's rejection, have fended them off with bland generalities.

In announcing the nomination of a new justice, the president is likely to highlight the legal expertise of the nominee. Less will be said about the real criterion that governs most selections: politics. As David O'Brien observes, "The presidential impulse to pack the Court with politically compatible justices is irresistible."[24]

Presidential nominations are influenced by important political forces in the nation. In the past, geographic considerations were significant, as presidents tried to ensure that each region of the country was represented on the Court. Geographic considerations have faded in the face of issues of gender, race, and religion. Thus, when Thurgood Marshall, the only African-American justice in the history of the Supreme Court, retired in 1991, President Bush found an African-American conservative, Clarence Thomas, to replace him. When given a first opportunity to appoint a Supreme Court justice, President Clinton chose a woman, Ruth Bader Ginsburg. An even more important political factor is ideology. Presidents' impacts on public policy depend not only on the legislation they sponsor or the executive actions they take but also on the decisions of the Court that reflect the ideological difference that their nominees have made.

Do presidents get what they want from their appointments to the Supreme Court? Do justices, with the independence of a lifetime tenure, continue to hold to the ideological path that the presidents who appointed them anticipated at the time of nomination? Legal scholar Laurence Tribe says yes. Tribe debunks what he calls "the myth of the surprised president." Presidents who have set out deliberately to alter the ideological direction of the Court, he shows, have generally succeeded in their strategies.[25] Nevertheless, counterexamples suggest that presidents don't always predict the future correctly. For instance, President Nixon's second appointee, Harry Blackmun, surprised everyone by becoming one of the Court's most liberal members.

Given the political basis of Court nominations, presidents are sometimes unsuccessful with them in the Senate. About 20 percent of nominees have failed to win confirmation, with rejection rates running particularly high in the mid-nineteenth century and the past twenty-five years (both periods of intense partisan conflict). Four factors seem to explain these defeats. First, the partisan composition of the Senate is crucial: A president is more likely to be defeated if the opposition party has a majority in the Senate. Second, timing is important: A president is less likely to succeed if a vacancy on the Supreme Court occurs during the fourth year of the term, as senators hold off to see what the new election will bring. Third, ideology has become central: Nominees face tougher sledding in the Senate if they are perceived as ideologically extreme or likely to tip a precarious ideological balance on the present Court. Fourth, presidential management is significant: A president can seriously harm the chances of a nominee through political blunders during the selection process.[26]

Even though the process of judicial selection has always been political, politicization recently has intensified as the stakes in controlling the Supreme Court on issues like abortion, affirmative action, and criminal procedure have grown. When President Reagan proposed Robert Bork for the High Court in 1987, political forces on both the left and right mobilized to do battle over the

Clarence Thomas and the Politics of Judicial Selection

Although the judiciary is the most elite branch of the federal government, the contemporary politics of judicial selection exposes it to a large dose of popular democracy. Opening up a democratic debate over issues of law, ideology, race, and gender, President George Bush's 1991 nomination of Clarence Thomas to the Supreme Court produced an extraordinary political drama.

The retirement of Justice Thurgood Marshall, the venerable champion of civil rights and the first African American to serve on the Court, provided Bush with an opportunity to solidify the Court's emerging conservative majority. His replacement for Marshall was an oddity among African Americans. Clarence Thomas was born in poverty in Georgia, raised as a Catholic, attended Holy Cross College and Yale Law School under affirmative action programs, and then became a vocal critic of affirmative action. In the 1980s, Thomas was one of the few African Americans to hold prominent administrative positions in the Reagan administration. As a reward for his services to the conservative cause, Thomas was appointed to the federal appellate bench in 1989.

The Senate Judiciary Committee's hearings on the Supreme Court nomination in September 1991 focused on Thomas's ideology. Democratic senators tried repeatedly to prod him to reveal the right-wing views they presumed he held. Saying he did not want to jeopardize his impartiality in future cases, Thomas avoided answering most of the specific questions posed to him. He even claimed that he had never discussed the Court's decision on abortion in *Roe* v. *Wade* in the eighteen years since it was announced.

Before the Senate could vote on Thomas, an even more remarkable drama began to unfold. University of Oklahoma law professor Anita Hill, a former assistant to Thomas at the Department of Education and the Equal Employment Opportunity Commission, claimed that he had sexually harassed her in the early 1980s. In nationally tele-vised hearings of the Judiciary Committee, she recounted that Thomas continually pressured her to date him while she worked at the Department of Education and that after she repeatedly refused, he talked to her about pornographic films he had seen and boasted about the size of his sexual organ.

Appearing after Hill, Thomas forcefully denied all of her charges. He blasted the televised hearings themselves as "a high-tech lynching for uppity blacks who deign to think for themselves." Television viewers were transfixed by the dramatic charges and counter-charges. They struggled to answer the question of who was telling the truth.

Public opinion polls showed that the majority ultimately believed Thomas—perhaps because Republican senators on the Judiciary Committee aggressively attacked Hill's character and mental stability. Thomas was narrowly confirmed by the Senate, 52–48. During his first full term on the Supreme Court, he quickly aligned himself with its most conservative justice, Antonin Scalia. Thomas's appointment had won conservatives a reliable vote on the Supreme Court.

Yet the controversy over his nomination—especially the Anita Hill affair—also breathed new vigor into the women's movement. Female candidates for Congress, furious at the all-male Judiciary Committee for its treatment of Hill, successfully turned the 1992 elections into "the year of the woman" (see Chapter 12). And public awareness of the problem of sexual harassment reached new heights.

The debate over the nomination of Clarence Thomas was heated and sometimes nasty. But it did stimulate greater popular awareness of the forces struggling to shape the Supreme Court today.

Sources: Timothy M. Phelps and Helen Winternitz, *Capitol Games: Clarence Thomas, Anita Hill, and the Story of a Supreme Court Nomination* (New York: Hyperion, 1992); Christopher E. Smith and Scott Patrick Johnson, "The First-Term Performance of Justice Clarence Thomas," *Judicature* 76 (January 1993): 172–74.

nomination. But it was Bork himself who was the star of the drama. A prominent conservative jurist and an adherent of the same original intent school of constitutional interpretation as Attorney General Meese, Bork tried to paint himself as more of a moderate during the Senate Judiciary Committee hearings. But a majority of the committee deemed this an unconvincing "confirmation conversion," and Bork was rejected by both the committee and the full Senate. Clarence Thomas narrowly avoided Bork's fate after President Bush nominated him in 1991.

Some recent nominations have drawn little opposition. President Clinton's moderate nominees, Ruth Bader Ginsburg and Stephen G. Breyer, easily won Senate approval. But the acrimonious politics that swirled around the Bork and Thomas nominations has led to widespread complaints that the selection process has become a political circus. Yet would it be better to go back to the quiet elite proceedings of the past, in which political and legal insiders chose justices of the Supreme Court while the public remained in ignorance until the final outcome? The American people have much at stake in the matter of who will be sitting on the Court for decades to come. From the standpoint of popular democracy, they should welcome a process that, despite its occasional excesses, opens up judicial selection to their scrutiny.

THE FEDERAL COURT SYSTEM

Presidential appointees to the judicial branch serve in a three-tier federal court system: district courts, courts of appeals, and Supreme Court. (In addition, there are a number of specialized federal courts, such as bankruptcy and tax courts.) The Constitution only specified "one Supreme Court," leaving it to Congress to create "inferior courts" as it deemed necessary. The first Congress passed the Judiciary Act of 1789, establishing district courts and circuit courts underneath the Supreme Court. The circuit courts did not have their own personnel; instead, one district judge and two Supreme Court justices had to "ride circuit" to hear appeals throughout a large region. The combination of primitive transportation and lodging and elderly justices made riding circuit a painful contradiction to the prestigious life of the Supreme Court. After repeated protests from the justices, Congress finally created new circuit courts, the courts of appeals, with their own judges, in 1891. Although the basic structure of the federal court system has been set since that date, Congress periodically passes legislation that alters important facets of the judicial branch. Figure 15.2 outlines the current structure of the federal court system.

U.S. District Courts

On the bottom level of the three-tier federal court system are the U.S. district courts. The district courts are courts of **original jurisdiction,** meaning the courts where almost all federal cases begin. And they are the trial courts for the

FIGURE 15.2   Basic Structure of the Federal Court System

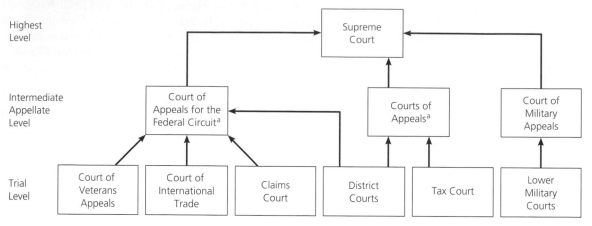

Note: Arrows indicate most common routes of appeals. Some specialized courts of minor importance are excluded.
ªThese courts also hear appeals from administrative agencies

federal system, resolving both criminal and civil cases, sometimes with judge and jury and sometimes with judge only. There are currently 94 U.S. district courts; each state has at least one, and the larger states have as many as four. As of 1993, there were 649 district court judgeships.

The caseload of the district courts is large and rapidly expanding—one reason that Congress periodically enlarges the number of judgeships. Around 250,000 cases a year are filed with the district courts, 80 percent of which are civil cases (lawsuits between two parties). In the great majority of these cases, the district courts have the final say: Decisions are not appealed, are settled before any higher court rulings occur, or are affirmed by the courts of appeals.

Although the Supreme Court attracts most of the public attention, the district courts have been central to the contemporary democratic debate over judicial power in two major areas. One involves the historic domination of the judiciary by affluent white males. With the rise of the civil rights and women's movements, this domination was called into question. But recent presidents have responded differently to calls to open the judicial branch to previously excluded groups. Jimmy Carter was the first chief executive to make a concerted effort to increase the number of female and minority judges; of Carter's appointments to the district courts, 14.4 percent were female, and 13.9 percent were African American. Ronald Reagan preferred white males; of his district court appointments, 8.3 percent were female, and only 2.1 percent were African American. Trying to recast the Republican image in more moderate terms, George Bush acted more like Carter than Reagan; of Bush's district court appointments, 19.6 percent went to women (more than Carter) and 6.8 percent to African Americans.[27]

District court judges have also been central to the democratic debate over the proper extent of judicial power. In the past several decades, they have issued controversial judicial orders that school districts bus children to desegregate, that communities provide racially integrated housing, and that state officials improve deplorable conditions in prisons and mental hospitals. Critics, using many of the same arguments that Attorney General Meese employed against Supreme Court decisions, have contended that an "imperial judiciary" now dictates public policy to the local and state officials elected by the people. A close study by political scientist Phillip Cooper of some of the most controversial district court orders shows, however, that judges do not intervene in local and state affairs because they are eager to stretch their power. Rather, he writes, "they simply are not in a position to refuse to respond to proper cases instituted by appropriate parties under provisions of statutory or constitutional law."[28] District courts have been on the firing line because they are where the politically weakest citizens can go to assert their legal rights.

U.S. Courts of Appeals

The U.S. courts of appeals, the middle tier of the federal court system, hear appeals of decisions rendered by the district courts, specialized courts, and federal regulatory agencies. As **appellate courts,** the courts of appeals bear some resemblance to the Supreme Court and have sometimes been called "mini–Supreme Courts." Yet there are some major differences in the appellate role of the two. Whereas the Supreme Court can choose the cases it hears, courts of appeals must hear every case brought to them. Whereas the Supreme Court is interested in large questions of constitutional and statutory interpretation rather than the fate of the particular parties to a case, courts of appeals seek to correct errors in lower court decisions to ensure that justice is done to the individuals involved. Because the Supreme Court is too busy to consider many types of federal cases, however, the courts of appeals do effectively decide policy in a number of areas of law.

There are twelve courts of appeals with general appellate jurisdiction—one in the District of Columbia and eleven numbered circuits that cover several contiguous states plus associated territories. The circuits vary in size; the First Circuit (Maine, New Hampshire, Massachusetts, Rhode Island, and Puerto Rico) has only 6 judges, whereas the Ninth Circuit (nine western states plus the territories of Guam and the Northern Marianas) has 28 judges. There are a total of 167 appeals court judges to handle a huge caseload. Over thirty thousand cases are filed with the courts of appeals each year, of which about five thousand reach a formal hearing.

Courts of appeals hearings do not retry cases; new factual evidence is not introduced, and no witnesses appear. Lawyers for the two sides in a case make oral arguments and present written briefs to the judges. Ordinarily, a three-judge panel will hear a case (and decisions are sometimes made by 2–1 vote).

In especially important cases, a court of appeals may sit *en banc*, with all of its members participating. What makes the courts of appeals so significant a force in the federal court system is that few of their decisions are ever overturned. As Stephen Wasby observes, "Because very few cases are appealed from there to the Supreme Court, which denies most petitions for review, appeals court rulings are left as the final judicial statement in the great bulk of cases."[29]

U.S. Supreme Court

The highest tier of the federal court system is the Supreme Court of the United States. Not only does it take cases that originate in the lower federal courts; it also hears cases that originate in state courts if these cases raise constitutional issues (see Figure 15.3). That the Supreme Court is "the highest court in the land" invests it with great authority. Justice Robert Jackson once wryly observed of the Court, "We are not final because we are infallible, we are infallible only because we are final."[30]

The Supreme Court has both original jurisdiction and appellate jurisdiction. The Constitution limits original jurisdiction to "all cases affecting ambassadors, other public ministers and counsels, and those in which a State shall be party." Few cases arise that qualify under these terms. Almost all of what the Supreme Court does falls under its second constitutional role as an appellate court. Congress has the power to define such appellate jurisdiction. At times in the past, it has curtailed this jurisdiction for political reasons, but the modern norm has been to leave the Court free to choose its cases.

Supreme Court decisions are powerful not only because they are the final judicial rulings in a case but also because they establish precedents that bind the lower federal courts and the state courts. Once the Supreme Court has spoken, judges at lower levels are supposed to bring their decisions into line with its interpretation of the Constitution and the laws. But guidance to lower courts is imperfect when the language of Supreme Court decisions is vague or when new circumstances arise that differ from those of the case used to establish a precedent. Consequently, decision-making in a complex area such as criminal procedure or affirmative action may shuttle back and forth for years between the lower courts and the Supreme Court.

THE SUPREME COURT: PROCESS

We turn now to a more thorough examination of the Supreme Court as an institution. First, we look at the processes through which the Court hears cases and arrives at its decisions. Second, we look at the politics of those decisions. As shall be seen, the Court is an institution in which the logic and rules of the law genuinely matter, as do the personalities and political beliefs of the human beings who pronounce the law.

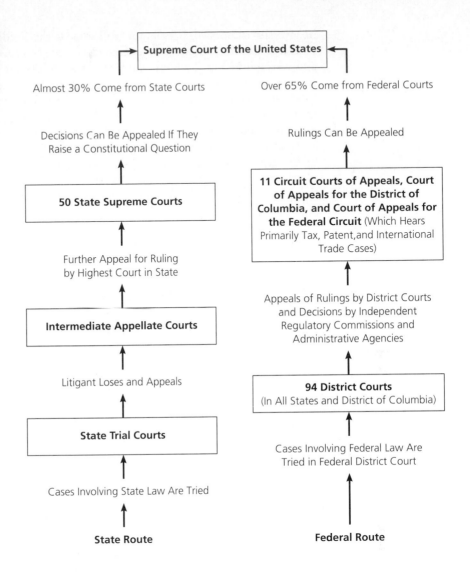

FIGURE 15.3

**Avenues of Appeal:
The Two Main
Routes to the
Supreme Court**

Supreme Court of the United States

Almost 30% Come from State Courts

Over 65% Come from Federal Courts

Decisions Can Be Appealed If They
Raise a Constitutional Question

Rulings Can Be Appealed

50 State Supreme Courts

**11 Circuit Courts of Appeals, Court
of Appeals for the District of
Columbia, and Court of Appeals for
the Federal Circuit** (Which Hears
Primarily Tax, Patent, and International
Trade Cases)

Further Appeal for Ruling
by Highest Court in State

Intermediate Appellate Courts

Appeals of Rulings by District Courts
and Decisions by Independent
Regulatory Commissions and
Administrative Agencies

Litigant Loses and Appeals

94 District Courts
(In All States and District of Columbia)

State Trial Courts

Cases Involving Federal Law Are
Tried in Federal District Court

Cases Involving State Law Are Tried

State Route

Federal Route

Note: In addition, some cases come directly to the Supreme Court from trial courts when
they involve reapportionment or civil rights disputes. Appeals from the Court of Military
Appeals also go directly to the Supreme Court. A few cases come on "original jurisdiction"
and involve disputes between state governments.

Choosing Cases

Each session of the Supreme Court begins on the first Monday in October and
concludes in late June or early July of the following year. Between five thousand
and six thousand cases are filed per year; of these, the Supreme Court will grant
a review and produce a written opinion in about 2 percent! Disgruntled parties

in lawsuits often swear that they will appeal the verdict "all the way to the Supreme Court." Obviously, the chance that the Supreme Court will hear their appeal is minuscule. The only party that has a high rate of success in having its appeals heard before the Supreme Court is the federal government itself. The solicitor general, the third-ranking official in the Department of Justice, determines which cases involving the federal government should be appealed to the Supreme Court, and the Court regards petitions from the solicitor general with a favorable disposition, accepting approximately 80 percent of them.

In the past, several categories of cases had to be reviewed by the Supreme Court. Facing a mounting caseload, the justices pressed Congress to relieve them of the burden of mandatory jurisdiction. The 1988 Act to Improve the Administration of Justice left the Court free in all but a few areas to choose the cases it wishes to hear. Today, about 99 percent of the Court's cases arrive through a *writ of certiorari*. The losing party in a lower court proceeding petitions the Supreme Court for this writ; should the Court choose to "grant cert" (shorthand for certiorari), it orders the lower court to send the records of the case.

The mountain of cert petitions that arrives at the Supreme Court by the beginning of its fall term has to be sifted to find the few worthy of the Court's full attention. Because the number of petitions has risen, justices have turned over the work of screening them to their law clerks, recent graduates of the nation's elite law schools. Armed with memos from clerks, the justices meet to decide which cases to hear. According to the informal **rule of four,** at least four justices must agree that a case deserves consideration.

Since almost all cases reach the Court through writs of certiorari, the justices have considerable latitude in setting their own agenda. In each year's session, they can accept cases that allow them to grapple with a constitutional or statutory issue that they deem ripe for determination and reject cases if they wish to sidestep some other controversial issue. The traditional view of the Court as being unable to do anything until a case comes before it understates the Court's power to select a few cases as vehicles for its deliberate reshaping of the law.[31]

Even when the Court agrees to take a case, it may choose to decide it without full consideration, a process known as *summary disposition*. In these instances, the Court produces only a one-or-two sentence ruling, which may affirm or reverse a lower court decision or send the case back to the lower court for a further hearing. These opinions are announced *per curiam* (by the Court) and are not signed by an individual justice. After denying the vast majority of petitions for certiorari, and handling some of the remainder through summary dispositions, the Supreme Court leaves itself fewer than 150 cases each year for full consideration.

Deciding Cases

When a case is granted full treatment, attorneys for the two sides are given several months to prepare *briefs*—written statements that argue their respective legal positions to the justices. Additional briefs may be filed by individuals or groups that are not parties in a lawsuit but have an interest in the issues it raises; these are known as *amicus curiae* (friend of the court) briefs. Having read these briefs, the justices allow attorneys for the contending litigants to appear in **oral argument.** Each side has only half an hour to present its strongest arguments to the Court. Oral argument often proves to be a battle for the attorney—but less with opposing counsel than with the justices themselves. Lawyers are not allowed to read from prepared texts, and some justices have a habit of asking barbed questions during oral arguments.

The justices meet in conference twice a week (Wednesdays and Fridays) to discuss the cases they have just heard in oral argument. The chief justice begins the discussion by presenting his or her views on how the case should be resolved. The other eight justices follow with their comments in order of their seniority on the High Court. Formal votes ordinarily are not taken since the positions of the justices have been made clear in their comments. After all nine justices have spoken, one is selected to write a majority opinion for the Court. If the chief justice is in the majority, he or she assigns the opinion. If the chief justice is in the minority, the senior justice on the majority side makes the assignment. The voting alignment at this stage is tentative. Justices may still switch their votes—which makes the next stage, the writing of opinions, all the more crucial.

Most opinions fall considerably short of the literary standard associated with such great judicial writers of the past as Oliver Wendell Holmes, Jr. One reason is that today's justices, harried by their huge caseload, have turned over the composition of the first draft of their opinions to their law clerks. "Drafted by clerks who are former law-review editors," law professor Bryan Garner complains, "the opinions partake of most of the negative traits of law-review articles."[32]

There is a second, and more important, reason that most contemporary opinions do not make great reading: They are often the product of multiple authors. The justice authoring an opinion circulates a draft to colleagues on the Court, and the others in the majority propose changes in language as well as argument, which are incorporated into subsequent drafts. Opinions for the Court, David O'Brien points out, are "negotiated documents": The process of finding common ground among at least five justices takes precedence over the personal style and preferences of an individual author.[33]

The real test of a majority opinion is not whether it sparkles in style but whether it wins the necessary votes. The justice assigned to write the opinion for the Court must hold on to the votes that constituted the initial majority and, if he or she is persuasive enough, perhaps pick up additional votes. The risk is that an opinion may lose votes along the way; in a closely divided Court, a majority opinion may thus become a minority one as a justice or two switches sides. This happened, for example, in *Bowers* v. *Hardwick* (1986), the most important case so far regarding homosexual rights (see Chapter 16).

The majority opinion announces the position of the Court. Justices who do not want to add their names to this opinion have two options. If they agree with the result announced in the majority opinion but not with the reasoning that justifies this result (or if they simply want to make additional points not found in the majority opinion), they can write a **concurring opinion** that sets out their alternative course of argument. If they disagree with the result, they can write a **dissenting opinion** that challenges the majority's view of what the law should be. Other justices may then sign these concurrences or dissents.

Heated ideological differences and a growing penchant for individual expression over institutional loyalty have led to a marked increase in concurrences and dissents. This can be viewed as a favorable trend, particularly by those with a fondness for dissents as healthy expressions of disagreement or even as signs of a future (and presumably better) understanding of the law. Or it can be regarded as an unfortunate development because it makes the Court's message to the rest of the political system uncertain and even confusing.

Once all opinions have been drafted, the justices make their final decisions as to whether they will "join" the majority opinion, concurring opinions, or dissents. The Court is now ready for a public announcement of its holding in a case.

THE SUPREME COURT: POLITICS

Throughout the process of decision, from screening cases to announcing opinions, the procedures and precedents of the law are central to the work of the

Justices of the Supreme Court, 1994–95 term. From left: Clarence Thomas, Antonin Scalia, Sandra Day O'Connor, Anthony Kennedy, David Souter, Stephen Breyer, John Paul Stevens, William Rehnquist, and Ruth Bader Ginsburg.

Supreme Court. But the process is political as well as legal. Three political factors influence the Court in this regard: the leadership of the chief justice, the strategic action of other justices, and the central role of ideology in shaping judicial results.

The Chief Justice and Leadership

The chief justice has certain special prerogatives during the decision process, such as speaking first in conference and assigning opinions for the Court when in the majority. The chief justice also has unique administrative responsibilities, both over the Court's own building and personnel and over the federal judicial system as a whole. Nevertheless, the chief justice is only "first among equals"; when it comes to votes, he or she has only one. Whether a chief justice is a leader depends on intellectual talent, interpersonal skills, and ability to manage the business of the Court. A comparison of the three most recent chief justices shows how widely varying their leadership styles and impact can be.

The most influential chief justice in modern times was Earl Warren, who held the position from 1953 to 1969. Appointed by President Eisenhower, Warren was a former governor of California, and he brought his exceptional political talent to the role of chief justice. Although not a legal scholar, he developed a clear vision of the Court as a champion of individual liberties and equal rights and was increasingly effective in marshalling a majority to advance that vision. Warren's personal warmth and moral conviction won him the love and respect of most of his colleagues. Perhaps his greatest feat of leadership came early in his tenure, when he convinced several wavering justices that the Court should speak to the nation with unanimity when it took the historic step of declaring racial segregation to be unconstitutional.

It was one of Warren's sharpest critics, President Nixon, who appointed his successor, Warren Burger. Burger served as chief justice from 1969 to 1986. With a rugged face under a full mane of white hair, he looked every inch the part of a chief justice as a Hollywood movie would portray him. To his fellow justices, however, Burger was distinguished only in appearance. Most found him pompous in personal relations, poorly prepared for cases before the Court, and deficient in legal analysis. Burger had a passion and a talent for the administrative duties of the chief justice, but when it came to influencing the opinions handed down by the Court, he was a weak leader.[34]

When Burger retired in 1986, President Reagan elevated Associate Justice William Rehnquist to the position of chief justice. Since his appointment by President Nixon in 1971, Rehnquist had been the most conservative member of the Court. Although his views mark him as more extreme than Burger in ideological terms, he has proven to be a more effective leader. He has more intellectual firepower, winning him grudging respect even from his liberal adversaries. In personal style, he is unpretentious and good-humored, and he runs conferences efficiently. Rehnquist also has a critical advantage in leadership that Burger lacked: A majority on the current Court shares his conservative judicial philosophy. The Rehnquist Court is emerging in the 1990s as a powerful force for a conservative realignment of American law.

Strategic Action

The chief justice is not the only member of the Court who can exercise leadership. Any of the other eight justices can use *strategic action* to win a majority for a legal doctrine they favor. Justices who engage in strategic action calculate the mix of tactics that will likely win over enough votes to their preferred position. Such tactics may include (1) persuasion on the merits—intellectual arguments to change minds; (2) ingratiation—using personal warmth to woo potential supporters; (3) sanctions—threats to write a stinging concurrence or dissent; and (4) bargaining—negotiation over the argument and language of a decision. That justices of the Supreme Court act politically clashes with the myth that they are impartial guardians of the law. But as Walter Murphy, the foremost student of judicial strategy, has written, "By giving judges the responsibilities of statesmen we have also imposed on them the burdens of politicians."[35]

Ideology

Although the leadership abilities of a chief justice or the strategic action of other justices may significantly affect the work of the Court, the most powerful political factor is ideology. In deciding how to cast votes and frame opinions, justices are profoundly influenced by their own convictions about society. Changes in the doctrines announced by the Supreme Court stem less from developments internal to the law than from the arrival of new justices with differing ideological perspectives.[36]

The most common ideological distinction among justices is that between liberals and conservatives. Liberal justices tend to favor individual rights (e.g., of political dissenters and criminal defendants) when they clash with governmental authority, to support measures toward greater equality for such previously excluded groups as African Americans and women, and to validate government regulation of the economy. Conservative justices are more inclined to cherish the peace of the existing social order and the authority of the officials (executives, bureaucrats, police, prosecutors) who maintain it and to look with greater reverence at the rights of property owners. Some justices fall midway between these ideological poles; in a closely divided Court, these "centrists" may hold the balance of power.[37]

Students of the Supreme Court look not only at the ideology of individual justices but also at the formation of **ideological blocs.** An ideological bloc is a group of two or more justices who vote the same way with a high degree of regularity. Thus, we can speak of liberal blocs, conservative blocs, or moderate blocs, such as the bloc of four conservatives who frustrated Roosevelt's New Deal or the bloc of five liberals who spearheaded the expansion of civil liberties in the later years of the Warren Court. Members of an ideological bloc may directly coordinate their actions or may simply vote the same way out of shared beliefs even in the absence of close personal relations.

Identifying a bloc is a tricky business, though, performed more easily in hindsight. What may appear to be a cohesive ideological bloc on the Court one year may prove to be a fragmented collection of individuals the next. At the conclusion of the 1991–92 term, Court watchers thought they detected the formation of a new moderate conservative bloc, composed of Justices Kennedy, O'Connor, and Souter, that would hold the future balance of power. By the end of the 1992–93 term, the three supposed confederates in this bloc were heading in different directions—Kennedy to the right, O'Connor (less predictably) to the right, and Souter to the center.[38] The perils of bloc analysis are a reminder that, even though ideology plays a powerful role on the Court, it is the ideology of independent jurists and not of party regulars.

THE SUPREME COURT AND THE POLITICAL SYSTEM

Ideology is the single most potent force shaping the decisions of the Supreme Court. But other factors enter in, among them concern for how decisions will be received by other political actors. A Supreme Court decision must take into account multiple audiences: the lower courts that must apply the decision to other cases, the government officials who must enforce the decision, and the segment of the public that must abide by the decision. Lacking the power of the purse (financial power) and the power of the sword (executive power, including the use of force if necessary), the Supreme Court is dependent for its power on the reaction to its decisions. As Stephen Wasby remarks, "The Supreme Court may make law, or the law may be what the Supreme Court says it is, but *only after all others have had their say.*"[39] During the process of implementing the Court's decisions, it may be checked or held accountable by other institutions or political forces.

The Supreme Court's power also is greater in some policy areas than in others. In the area of foreign policy, the Supreme Court has seldom challenged the dominant role of the president. In economic policy, the Court used to be a major force, but since the Roosevelt revolution it has generally deferred to Congress and the executive. In these two areas, so crucial to the debate between elite democrats and popular democrats, the present-day Court is a relatively minor player. Where the Court *is* a major force is in the definition of individual rights and social practices. The rulings of the Court often touch on the conditions (sex, race, religion, education, crime) that most intimately affect how we lead our lives. It is this fact that has drawn the contemporary Court into so many controversies and set the stage for potential conflicts with other institutions and with public opinion.

When Supreme Court decisions require federal action, the response of the president is most important. Usually, presidents back up the Court's actions, regarding the enforcement of its decisions as a requirement of their oath of office. Sometimes, though, they drag their feet on implementation or repudiate a decision altogether. Believing that the decision in *Brown* v. *Board of Education* (1954) was forcing racial desegregation too rapidly on the South, President Eisenhower refused, despite repeated requests from others, to encourage southern compliance by placing his enormous prestige behind the Court's ruling. President Bush sharply criticized the Supreme Court's decision in *Texas* v. *Johnson* (1989), which upheld the right of a protester to burn an American flag as a form of symbolic speech protected under the First Amendment. He proposed a constitutional amendment to ban flag-burning—implying that he, and not the Court, stood for patriotism. But Bush failed to get the amendment through Congress. (Congress did pass a law against flag-burning—and the Court struck it down as well.)

Congress has power to chastise or discipline the Supreme Court since the legislative branch determines the appellate jurisdiction and even the size of the High Court. Congress sometimes altered the size of the Court during the nineteenth century. Since Roosevelt's court-packing fiasco, however, it has been politically unwise to propose adding or subtracting members, and the figure of nine justices seemingly has become sacrosanct. Supreme Court decisions based on the Constitution can be overturned only through the difficult process of constitutional amendment, so the ability of members of Congress to reverse specific decisions is far greater when the Court has been engaged in statutory interpretation. Thus, the Civil Rights Act of 1991, placing the burden of proof on employers in job discrimination lawsuits, overturned a dozen recent Supreme Court holdings.

Even though the justices don't face the public in elections, they know that compliance with their decisions depends ultimately on public opinion. Public views on the judicial branch tend, however, to be less clear than views on the other two branches. General public support for the Supreme Court is higher than for Congress or the presidency. On the other hand, public knowledge about the Court is lower. For example, surveys indicate that a majority cannot name even one sitting justice. The public is more attuned to controversial Court rulings than to the Court as an institution. Public support for the Court thus fell in response to decisions that favored the rights of criminal defendants. But it rose during the Watergate era, when the Court ordered President Nixon to hand over the tapes that revealed his participation in a criminal coverup, thereby forcing him to resign.[40]

Respect for law and the Supreme Court inclines most Americans to abide by judicial decisions, even those they disagree with. When the Court treads in the most sensitive areas, however, it may face major problems of evasion or resistance. Its ruling in *Engel* v. *Vitale* (1962) forbade prayer in the public schools as a violation of the First Amendment, yet decades later many public schools still conduct various forms of religious observance. Massive resistance greeted the Court's order for school desegregation throughout the South, and it was a decade and a half before desegregation occurred on a large scale.

What can the Supreme Court do to increase the prospects that government

Right-to-life signs deposited by demonstrators outside the Supreme Court. Americans' customary reverence for the Court does not preclude protest on an issue as controversial as abortion.

officials will enforce and ordinary citizens will comply with its rulings? Greater clarity and consensus increase the likelihood that decisions will be implemented; ambiguous decisions open avenues for evasion, and the multiple opinions rendered by a divided Court lead to confusion over just what the Court has said. Compliance may be fostered when the Court brings about change gradually, through a series of decisions, offering an affected population time to adjust to a new state of affairs. Above all, a Supreme Court concerned with compliance can take care not to get too far ahead of public opinion.

Indeed, because the Court is dependent on others for the implementation of its decisions, it cannot help but take heed of the political environment. If the Court goes too far in imposing its views, it is likely to discredit its own decisions and undermine its own authority, as the infamous *Dred Scott* case suggests. Yet a Court too preoccupied with public reaction to its decisions could never take a strong stand on behalf of the rights of persons accused of crimes, racial minorities, or radical dissenters. There is, it seems, a fine line between the political prudence of a Supreme Court justice and the political calculation of an elected official. The paradox of judicial power in a democracy is that it is the Supreme Court justice who, not having to face the electorate, may have the greater freedom—and responsibility—to protect the basic values and rules of a democratic society.

CONCLUSION: LAW, POLITICS, AND THE DEMOCRATIC DEBATE

In our examination of the federal judicial system, and especially in our treatment of the Supreme Court, law and politics are separate, yet intertwined. The judicial branch is fundamentally different from the other branches in that it is a legal order. Its business is resolving lawsuits or criminal cases. It follows legal procedures and rules for determining how cases are brought to and then handled by the High Court and gives considerable weight to past decisions as precedents on the grounds that law should be, as much as possible, settled and known. The impressive symbolic power of the Supreme Court—the black robes, the marble temple, and the confidential deliberations—rests on the mystique of the rule of law as something that transcends politics.

Yet politics shapes appointments to the Supreme Court, as presidents try to fill the Court with justices who will carry out the presidents' political and ideological agendas. Politics is found within the internal processes of the Court, as chief justices attempt to exercise leadership and other justices engage in strategic action. Political values influence the Court, with ideology the paramount factor in determining how different justices will vote on cases. Political sensitivity to other institutions and to public opinion characterizes a judicial branch aware of its dependence on others to carry out its decisions. Finally, the Court is political because its decisions set national policy on some of the issues that matter most to Americans.

It is because the judiciary is political, and indeed so important a policymaker, that there has been an intense democratic debate in recent years over its proper role in American life. Popular democrats of the past generally mistrusted the Court as a nondemocratic defender of elite privileges. Their arguments have been taken over by conservatives such as Edwin Meese, whose very different policy agenda also requires a Court that practices self-restraint and does not interfere much with other institutions. The position of a William Brennan represents a new departure for those who adhere to the values of popular democracy. In Brennan's argument, only an activist Court that adapts and modernizes the Constitution can bring out its fundamental democratic character and turn the law into a vehicle for the advancement of liberty and equality.

Liberty and equality are hallowed American values, but their meaning is contested by the opposing sides in the contemporary democratic debate over the judiciary. Should we, for example, permit revered American symbols, such as the flag, to be desecrated in the name of free speech? Should pornography be constitutionally protected as a form of free expression? Should evidence that incriminates defendants be excluded from court unless the police follow certain prescribed procedures? Should minorities or women be given special consideration by schools or employers in the name of affirmative action? Should a woman's decision to have an abortion come under the protection of the Bill of Rights? In the next chapter, we will see what the Supreme Court has said on these, and other, controversial questions. Our focus will be on what has been the Court's principal focus since the Roosevelt revolution: civil liberties and civil rights.

KEY TERMS

judicial review
jurisprudence of original intention
precedents
Marbury v. *Madison*
Gibbons v. *Ogden*
Dred Scott v. *Sandford*
court-packing plan
senatorial courtesy

original jurisdiction
appellate courts
rule of four
oral argument
concurring opinion
dissenting opinion
ideological bloc

SUGGESTED READINGS

Robert H. Bork, *The Tempting of America: The Political Seduction of the Law* (New York: Free Press, 1990). A rejected Supreme Court nominee's conservative attack on the judicial selection process and on liberal jurisprudence.

Kermit L. Hall et al., eds., *The Oxford Companion to the Supreme Court of the United States* (New York: Oxford University Press, 1992). Everything you want to know about the Supreme Court is presented in superb detail.

David M. O'Brien, *Storm Center: The Supreme Court in American Politics*, Third Edition (New York: W. W. Nor-

ton, 1993). A leading text on the Supreme Court that makes engaging use of historical anecdotes.

Laurence H. Tribe, *God Save This Honorable Court* (New York: New American Library, 1986). A Harvard Law professor's account of the history and politics of judicial selection, written in a popular style.

Bob Woodward and Scott Armstrong, *The Brethren: Inside the Supreme Court* (New York: Avon Books, 1981). Two investigative reporters provide a unique look at life inside the Supreme Court's "marble temple."

PART ·FOUR·

POLICY

For popular democrats, democracy requires more than majority rule; it also requires policies that protect basic rights and guarantee the conditions for a full and productive life. Part IV examines public policies—the outputs by government after the processes of political participation have worked their way through the political institutions.

Chapter 16 covers civil liberties and civil rights. Although Americans can justifiably take pride in the rights that they enjoy, recognition by the courts of many of these rights is quite recent. Civil liberties and civil rights can be protected and enlarged only by struggles that educate people about the importance of both in a democracy.

Economic policy is the subject of Chapter 17. Such policy has often been captured by elites which claim that only experts are qualified to make decisions for a complex modern economy. According to popular democrats, however, economic policy has profound political implications—especially for the distribution of wealth and income—and therefore should be made democratically accountable.

Chapter 18 investigates social policies, beginning with the debate over welfare and ending with the struggle over whether the United States should provide universal health

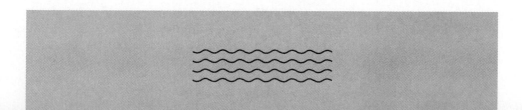

care. That American social policies leave many people with inadequate protection and others with none at all has clear political implications: People who have to struggle for the basic necessities of life cannot be full participants in the democratic process.

Chapter 19 examines U.S. policies toward the rest of the world. For decades the Cold War against communism was used to justify elite domination in national security policy. The end of the Cold War presents an opportunity to open up foreign policy to a debate over how to promote democracy at home and abroad.

Civil Liberties and Civil Rights

Some of the most stirring words in the history of American democracy have been penned by judges in support of the civil liberties and civil rights of unpopular individuals and groups. "If there is any fixed star in our constitutional constellation," wrote Supreme Court Justice Robert Jackson, upholding the right of young Jehovah's Witnesses not to salute the American flag in school, "it is that no official, high or petty, can prescribe what shall be orthodox in politics, nationalism, religion, or other matters of opinion or force citizens to confess by word or act their faith therein."[1] "If there is a bedrock principle underlying the First Amendment," wrote Justice William Brennan, upholding the right of a citizen to express political dissent by burning an American flag, "it is that Government may not prohibit the expression of any idea simply because society finds the idea itself offensive or disagreeable."[2] Against the grim background of intolerance and repression that has characterized most political systems around the globe, such affirmations of fundamental liberties and rights stand as one of the proudest accomplishments of democracy in the United States.

However, civil liberties and rights have been a focus of bitter conflict, not a subject of comfortable consensus, throughout American history. What strong supporters of civil liberties consider to be basic freedoms have appeared to many other Americans to be threats to order, morality, or community. The right of persons accused of crimes to the multiple protections of due process of law strikes many Americans as favoritism toward criminals at the expense of their victims. The right of authors, photographers, or filmmakers to portray sexual activity with only minimal restrictions strikes many as the protection of filth that corrupts society in general and degrades women in particular. The right of revolutionaries to call for the overthrow of our constitutional order strikes many as a denial of society's right of self-defense against its worst enemies. Struggles over civil liberties and civil rights often pit unpopular minorities or individuals against the popular majority and its elected representatives.

Civil liberties refer to the freedoms that individuals enjoy and that governments cannot invade. **Civil rights** refer to the powers and privileges that belong to us by virtue of our status as citizens. Freedom of speech and the free exercise of religion are liberties that need protection *from* government; voting and nondiscriminatory treatment in education and employment are rights that need protection *by* government. Such familiar civil liberties and civil rights are in fact a recent accomplishment. Despite the grand words of the Bill of Rights, despite the historic breakthrough of the Civil War amendments, for most of American history free speech was repressed, individual privacy invaded, and African Americans and women treated as second-class citizens. The flowering of civil liberties and civil rights has taken a long time and required a fierce struggle. And some of the advances that have been made remain precarious, with forces both outside and inside the current Supreme Court striving to roll them back. Civil liberties and civil rights remain one of the central arenas for the continuing democratic debate in America.

The ultimate voice in this debate has been that of the courts. Many social, political, and intellectual forces have battled over the definition of American liberties and rights. Since these liberties and rights are rooted in the Constitution, however, it has largely been the province of the federal judiciary to have the decisive say on their meaning and scope. Consequently, our focus in this chapter is mainly, though not exclusively, on Supreme Court cases.

The chapter begins with a perplexing issue in the democratic debate: how elites and ordinary citizens respond to controversial questions of civil liberties and civil rights. Next, the discussion turns to the historical bases for liberties and rights in America: the Bill of Rights, the Civil War amendments, and the constitutional revolution of the 1930s. The remainder of the chapter examines the major areas of civil liberties and civil rights: the First Amendment rights of expression, a free press, and religion; the rights of persons accused of crimes; the right of privacy; and the right of racial minorities and women to equality in every aspect of American life.

CIVIL LIBERTIES AND CIVIL RIGHTS: FOES AND FRIENDS

It has often been argued that elite democrats are supportive of civil liberties and civil rights, whereas the ordinary citizens in whom popular democrats trust are intolerant and repressive. Chapter 6 cited social science surveys indicating that support for civil liberties increases with education and political status. The conclusion frequently drawn from these studies is that civil liberties and civil rights have to be safeguarded from the authoritarian masses by democratically spirited elites.

Unfortunately, elite support for civil liberties and civil rights is less impressive in practice than in theory. The major attacks on civil liberties in recent times were spearheaded by decidedly elite figures: Senator Joseph McCarthy, Director of the FBI J. Edgar Hoover, President Richard Nixon. Therefore, when it comes to opposition to civil liberties and civil rights, the blame must be shared by elite democrats and popular democrats alike.

Where, then, are the friends of civil liberties and civil rights to be found? Focusing on court cases, as this chapter does, may give the impression that it has been justices of the Supreme Court who have singlehandedly advanced liberties and rights out of the depths of their own conscience and democratic faith. This is not the case: Ordinary citizens and democratic social movements also have played a key part in the struggle. Landmark advances in this area have been produced by a collaboration between elites and popular democratic forces. Thus, the credit for progress in civil liberties and civil rights, like the blame for hostility to them, must be shared by elite democrats and popular democrats.

Certainly, any account of progress in civil liberties and civil rights must highlight the beliefs, decisions, and arguments of their judicial champions. An honor roll for civil libertarians on the Supreme Court would include such great figures as Oliver Wendell Holmes, Louis Brandeis, Hugo Black, William O. Douglas, and Earl Warren. Probably the greatest civil libertarian on the High Court in recent years was William Brennan, who retired in 1990.

The son of Irish immigrants, Brennan grew up in a struggling middle-class family in New Jersey. He absorbed from his father, a labor leader and local reformer, a commitment to activism on behalf of the have-nots, a stance he was to maintain even as he ascended into the higher reaches of the judicial elite. Appointed to the Supreme Court by President Eisenhower in 1956 (an appointment that Eisenhower later regretted), he quickly became one of the leading architects of the civil liberties and civil rights advances of the Warren Court era. As the Court grew more conservative after the election of Richard Nixon, Brennan fought effectively to maintain the Warren Court precedents and even to expand them in such areas as equal rights for women. Skilled in crafting majorities among his fellow justices, he was eloquent when he found himself in dissent, especially as the Court began to affirm what he considered the inherent cruelty of the death penalty. If judicial elites have played an indispensable role in furthering American liberties and rights, it is because they have included individuals with the democratic commitments and conscience of a William Brennan.[3]

Whereas the justices who have championed civil liberties and civil rights in landmark cases are famous, the petitioners who brought these cases to the Supreme Court are obscure. Yet these ordinary citizens have made significant contributions to the struggle for civil liberties and civil rights.

Justice William Brennan was a champion of civil liberties and civil rights during his thirty-four years (1956–1990) on the Supreme Court. A leading figure in the Warren Court majority, Brennan fought a dogged rearguard battle for civil liberties on the Burger and Rehnquist Courts.

Consider J. D. and Ethel Shelley, the plaintiffs in *Shelley* v. *Kraemer* (1948). Working-class African Americans from rural Mississippi, they left the South after witnessing the beating of a black neighbor by white police. Settling in St. Louis, they saved for years so that they could move their six children from a crowded ghetto into a tree-lined middle-class neighborhood. Soon after they bought their house, however, they were served with eviction papers; the house was covered by a restrictive racial covenant that forbade its sale to "people of the Negro or Mongolian race." The Shelleys fought to keep their house—all the way to the Supreme Court. The Court ruled that a restrictive racial covenant as a private agreement was not in itself illegal. But any enforcement of such a covenant by a court *was* forbidden by the Fourteenth Amendment since this would involve the state government in supporting racial discrimination. The Shelleys won a victory that began to break down the legal barriers to the integration of American housing (although many more of these barriers remained to be surmounted).[4]

Another battler for civil liberties was Daniel Seeger, plaintiff in *Seeger* v. *United States* (1965). Seeger, the son of devout Catholic parents, drifted away from a traditional religious faith while retaining a passionate moral opposition to participation in warfare. Yet when he was drafted into military service and sought to claim conscientious objector (CO) status, he was stymied by a government form that read, "Do you believe in a Supreme Being? Check box yes, check box no." Since he refused to check either box, his application for CO status was turned down, and when he then refused to enter military service, he was sentenced to a year and a day in federal prison. The Supreme Court took Seeger's case and spared him from prison, establishing the principle that if the beliefs of a religiously unconventional CO play a similar role in his life that the belief in a Supreme Being plays in the life of the conventionally religious CO, the former should be exempted from military service.[5]

In addition to courageous individuals, popular democratic movements have been a source of key cases that reached the Supreme Court. The Legal Defense Fund of the National Association for the Advancement of Colored People (NAACP), the pioneer civil rights organization, represented the Shelleys in their struggle against racial covenants. The NAACP was the leading force behind the long campaign for desegregated schools. The contemporary women's movement, which sprung up in the 1960s, also played a pivotal role in reshaping the Court's agenda. As women pressed their case for equality with new vigor, the Court responded by considering the issues of abortion and gender discrimination.

The **American Civil Liberties Union (ACLU),** formed to defend free speech against government repression of dissenters during World War I, has taken the Bill of Rights as its cause ever since. The ACLU has fought for civil liberties and civil rights in many different areas, arguing more cases before the Supreme Court than any other organization save the federal government. The ACLU prides itself on upholding the liberties of the most unpopular and obnoxious groups. Its clients have included not only communists but also Nazis and Ku Klux Klan members.[6]

CIVIL LIBERTIES AND CIVIL RIGHTS: HISTORICAL BASES

Americans regard civil liberties and civil rights as their birthright. After all, the great charter of our freedom, the Bill of Rights, is almost as old as the nation itself. Yet the ringing words of the Bill of Rights took on a powerful meaning *in practice* only through a long struggle waged mainly by popular democratic forces. This section concentrates on three critical moments in this struggle: (1) the establishment of the Bill of Rights, (2) the Civil War amendments to the Constitution, and (3) the constitutional revolution of the 1930s.

The Bill of Rights

The Constitution drafted at Philadelphia in 1787 gave only limited recognition to civil liberties and civil rights. Provisions were incorporated to guarantee individuals the right of *habeas corpus* (persons placed under arrest must be promptly brought before a judge), except under dangerous circumstances of insurrection or invasion, and to prohibit the federal government from passing *bills of attainder* (laws that inflict punishment on individuals without trials) or *ex post facto laws* (laws that make an act committed in the past a punishable offense). But the Constitution left out most of the fundamental rights that had been incorporated in the bills of rights of the revolutionary state constitutions. The Federalist argument was that the Constitution was the charter of a limited government, so written restrictions on nonexistent powers to invade the people's liberty were unnecessary.

Anti-federalists were unpersuaded by this argument. Correctly observing the potential for an enormous concentration of power in the federal government, they insisted that the Constitution be amended to guarantee in express terms the basic liberties and rights of the people. Heeding this protest, the first Congress, sparked by the leadership of James Madison, drafted and passed ten amendments to the Constitution, collectively known as the Bill of Rights.[7] This monumental victory for the popular democrats of the founding era was, however, restricted to white males. The Bill of Rights did not address the issue of equality for racial minorities or women.

Civil liberties in America in the decades after passage of the Bill of Rights were much more precarious than its words would suggest. The impact of the Bill of Rights was limited by two factors. First, the meaning of its words would be determined only as specific cases reached the Supreme Court—whose members would not necessarily be civil libertarians. Second, the Supreme Court ruled, in the case of *Barron* v. *Baltimore* (1833), that the Bill of Rights applied only to the federal government and did not impose any restraints on state governments. Because political activity in nineteenth-century America was mostly at the state and local levels, the Bill of Rights lacked much practical impact in this era.

The Civil War Amendments

Civil liberties and civil rights in America had a second founding: the three constitutional amendments passed during the Civil War and Reconstruction era.

The Thirteenth Amendment abolished the institution of slavery. The Fourteenth Amendment protected the freed slaves against discrimination or repression by their former masters. Its key provision stated, "No state shall make or enforce any law which shall abridge the privileges or immunities of citizens of the United States; nor shall any state deprive any person of life, liberty, or property, without due process of law; nor deny to any person within its jurisdiction the equal protection of the laws." The Fifteenth Amendment extended the right of suffrage to the freed slaves—but only if they were male.

The **Civil War amendments,** an accomplishment of popular democratic struggle by abolitionists, radical Republicans, and African Americans, extended the Bill of Rights in two respects. First, to the emphasis of the first ten amendments on liberty, they added a new emphasis on equality. At least one previously excluded group—African Americans—was now promised equality under the Constitution. Second, they aimed to prohibit invasions of rights by state governments rather than by the federal government. Contrary to the decision in *Barron*, the Civil War amendments seemed to safeguard liberty against infringement by government at any level.

But the promises of the Civil War amendments were not kept for several generations. As the passions of the Civil War cooled, and as the northern industrial elite made its peace with the southern agricultural elite, the protection of the former slaves ceased to be of importance to persons in positions of power. The Supreme Court validated this change, ruling—in a painful historical irony—that the Fourteenth Amendment protected corporations, but not African Americans, from hostile state actions. Nevertheless, the Civil War amendments remained part of the text of the Constitution, available for a later generation that would reclaim their words and redeem their promises. Indeed, the modern flowering of liberties and rights has been based in large part on the just-quoted words of the Fourteenth Amendment.

The Constitutional Revolution of the 1930s

For most of the Supreme Court's history, it was more concerned with questions of property rights than with issues of civil liberties and civil rights. Yet when the Court backed down from further confrontation with President Franklin Roosevelt in 1937, and when Roosevelt had the subsequent opportunity to name a majority of justices, the Court was poised for a profound historical shift. The constitutional revolution of the 1930s, an expression of the popular democratic spirit of the New Deal, made civil liberties and civil rights for the first time the principal business of the Supreme Court.

This constitutional revolution was clearly enunciated in the case of *United States* v. *Carolene Products Co.* (1938). Writing for the Court, Justice Harlan Fiske Stone upheld congressional authority over commerce in this seemingly routine lawsuit. But Stone added a footnote to his opinion that pointed out how differently the Court might view governmental authority if civil liberties or civil rights, rather than commerce, were at issue.

Probably the most famous footnote in Court history, Stone's **footnote four** set out three conditions under which the Court would not grant government actions the "presumption of constitutionality." First, government actions would be questioned by the Court if they fell within the prohibitions of the Bill of Rights or the Fourteenth Amendment. Second, they would be questioned if they restricted "those political processes which can ordinarily be expected to bring about repeal of undesirable legislation" (e.g., free elections). Third, they would be questioned if they were directed at "particular religions, or national or racial minorities."[8] With footnote four, Stone signalled that the Court would now have as its priority the safeguarding of the Bill of Rights, of political freedoms, and of the rights of religious or racial minorities subjected to discriminatory treatment by an intolerant majority.

Footnote four articulated what scholars call the "double standard" of the modern Supreme Court. Legislation aimed at regulating the economy is subject only to "ordinary scrutiny" by the Court; the Court presumes that such legislation is constitutional so long as the government can show that the legislation has a "reasonable" basis. In contrast, legislation that might impinge on civil liberties and civil rights must meet the test of **strict scrutiny,** meaning the Court will strike the law down unless the government can demonstrate that a "compelling interest" necessitates such a law. This double standard has been justified on three grounds: that the freedoms protected by strict scrutiny are the basis of all other freedoms, that civil liberties and civil rights are explicitly guaranteed by the Bill of Rights and the Civil War amendments, and that courts themselves are ill-equipped to determine economic policy but well-equipped to handle the definition of fundamental liberties and rights.[9]

Footnote four did not make clear whether the Court intended to apply strict scrutiny to actions by state governments as well as by the federal government. In 1925, the Court had announced, in the case of *Gitlow* v. *New York*, that the right of free speech limited state governments as well as the federal government since free speech was part of the liberty protected from state invasion by the Due Process Clause of the Fourteenth Amendment. In 1937, the Court went further, stating in *Palko* v. *Connecticut* that several parts of the Bill of Rights applied to the states, through the mechanism of the Fourteenth Amendment, because these rights "represented the very essence of a scheme of ordered liberty."[10]

Since the constitutional revolution of the 1930s, the Supreme Court often has been divided about how much of the Bill of Rights is incorporated in the Fourteenth Amendment and therefore applies to state governments. Some strongly civil libertarian justices have argued for total **incorporation**—that is, every clause in the Bill of Rights applies to the states as well as to the federal government. But the dominant position has been selective incorporation, with the Court deciding one case at a time whether to apply each provision of the Bill of Rights to the states. The practical difference between total incorporation and selective incorporation diminished in the 1960s, however, as the Warren Court separately incorporated almost all of the provisions of the Bill of Rights. Today, the combination of the Bill of Rights and the Fourteenth Amendment protects civil liberties and civil rights from both the federal and state governments.

THE FIRST AMENDMENT

The words of the First Amendment, though few in number, establish the foundation of constitutional liberty in the United States: "Congress shall make no law respecting an establishment of religion, or prohibiting the free exercise thereof; or abridging the freedom of speech, or of the press; or the right of the people peaceably to assemble, and to petition the government for a redress of grievances."

This promise of liberty was more easily set down on paper than fulfilled in practice. For much of American history, the First Amendment was a frail barrier to repression. Consider the guarantee of freedom of speech. Less than a decade after the adoption of the Bill of Rights, the ruling Federalists passed a sedition act and dispatched several of their Jeffersonian opponents to jail for criticizing the administration in power. Later, when socialists and anarchists denounced the new capitalist elite, their meetings were frequently broken up and their publications suppressed. The right of free speech has been violated especially in times of war. During World War I, for example, many radical critics of American military involvement went to prison under a sedition act, including one of the greatest popular democrats in American history, Eugene V. Debs. The free speech of which we are so proud is a very recent phenomenon.[11]

Free Speech

The original proponents of a constitutional guarantee of free expression were most concerned with protecting *political speech*, such as criticism of the government or its officials. The prohibition on government interference was thus set down in absolute terms: "Congress shall make *no law* . . ." (emphasis added). But no Supreme Court majority has ever regarded the First Amendment as conferring an absolute protection for speech. The Court has had to grapple repeatedly with where to draw the boundary line dividing free speech from unprotected, and therefore punishable, speech.

The Supreme Court was first moved to draw such a boundary line in response to prosecutions of dissenters to World War I. Charles Schenck, a socialist, was prosecuted under the wartime Espionage Act for a pamphlet that urged young men to resist the draft. In *Schenck* v. *United States* (1919), the Court upheld the constitutionality of the Espionage Act and thus of Schenck's conviction. In the decision for the Court, Justice Oliver Wendell Holmes explained, in words that became famous, that speech was subject to the **clear and present danger test.**

The most stringent protection of free speech would not protect a man in falsely shouting fire in a theater and causing a panic. . . . The question in every case is whether the words used are used in such circumstances and are of such a nature as to create a clear and present danger that they will bring about the substantive evils that Congress has a right to prevent.[12]

Later, when a majority of the Court began to find every defendant guilty by this test, no matter what the circumstances, Justice Holmes, along with Justice Louis Brandeis, issued a series of eloquent dissents insisting that speech should be punishable only if it posed the threat of producing an *immediate* evil.

Fear of political radicalism lay at the heart of the repression of free speech during World War I and its aftermath. This same fear fostered a new repressive climate after World War II, as Americans became obsessed with an external threat from the Soviet Union and an internal threat from domestic communists. Fueling anticommunist hysteria during the early years of the Cold War were demagogic politicians, preeminent among them Senator Joseph McCarthy of Wisconsin. The senator gave his name to the phenomenon of **McCarthyism** by his tactics: waving phony lists of supposed communists in the government before the press, hauling individuals before his congressional committee and tarring their reputation for no other end than publicity, labelling any who opposed him conspirators against American freedom.

Influenced by the sour climate of McCarthyism, the Supreme Court went along with the effort of the executive branch to put the leaders of the American Communist party in prison. In *Dennis* v. *United States* (1951), the Court upheld the convictions of eleven top officials of the Communist party for violating the Smith Act, which made it a crime to advocate the violent overthrow of government in the United States, even though the puny American Communist party scarcely posed a present danger to the government. It was only after McCarthy and his methods came into disrepute and Cold War hysteria began to ease that the Supreme Court backed away from this repressive stance. The case of *Yates* v. *United States* (1957) also involved Smith Act prosecution of communist officials, but this time the defendants' convictions were reversed. Abstract advocacy of Communist party doctrine about revolution, the Court ruled, was protected speech. Only advocacy of immediate action to overthrow the government could be punished.

During the 1960s, radical political dissent was not restricted to communists. Many Americans began to engage in vocal political protests, especially against the war in Vietnam. It was at the end of this turbulent decade that the Warren Court, in *Brandenburg* v. *Ohio* (1969), finally gave a broad interpretation to the right of free speech. Clarence Brandenburg, a Ku Klux Klan leader, was convicted under an Ohio law for advocating racial conflict at a televised Klan rally. Overturning Brandenburg's conviction, the Court stated that government could punish an individual for advocating an illegal act only if "such advocacy is directed to inciting or producing imminent lawless action, and is likely to incite or produce such action."[13] Under such a test, only a few utterances—such as a speech that called for a riot and actually helped begin it—were still punishable. Political speech in the United States was at last given broad protection—nearly 180 years after the adoption of the Bill of Rights!

Gregory (Joey) Johnson, whose Texas conviction for burning an American flag was overturned by the Supreme Court in 1989. Representatives of unpopular causes have often been at the center of free speech controversies.

In recent decades, the Court has brought **symbolic speech**—political expression that communicates with visual symbols instead of words—under the protection of the First Amendment. Several high school and junior high school students in Des Moines, Iowa, were suspended after they wore black armbands to school as a way of protesting the war in Vietnam. Voiding the suspensions, the Court stated in *Tinker* v. *Des Moines Independent Community School District* (1969) that wearing an armband as a silent form of protest was "akin to pure speech."[14] More controversial than the *Tinker* decision was the Court's defense of symbolic speech in *Texas* v. *Johnson* (1989). Johnson had burned an American flag outside the 1984 Republican convention in Dallas, Texas, to protest Reagan's policies. Five justices—an unusual coalition of liberals Brennan, Marshall, and Blackmun and conservatives Scalia and Kennedy—voted to overturn Johnson's conviction on the grounds that the Texas statute against flag-burning violated the First Amendment by punishing the communication of a political message.

Unprotected Speech

Not all speech has been granted broad protection by the Supreme Court. Some kinds of expression are considered by the Court to be **unprotected speech**—speech unworthy of full First Amendment protection either because its social value is insignificant or because it verges on conduct that is harmful to others. Commercial speech, unlike political speech, can thus be regulated, as in bans on false advertising. *Fighting words*, such as derogatory names shouted at a police officer, can be punished on the grounds that they do not express any ideas or contribute to any search for truth (*Chaplinsky* v. *New Hampshire* [1942]). And *libel*—written communication that exposes the person written about to public shame, contempt, or ridicule—is subject to lawsuits for monetary damages. However, the Court ruled in *New York Times Co.* v. *Sullivan* (1964) that for a public official to win a judgment against a writer, the official must prove not only that the charge in question was false but also that it had been made with malice.

Drawing the line between protected and unprotected speech has been hardest for the Supreme Court in the area of **obscenity.** Probably no other term has been as difficult for the Court to define. The Court first entered the thicket of sexual expression in *Roth* v. *United States* (1957). In this case, Justice Brennan, declaring obscenity to be unprotected by the First Amendment, defined it as sexual material that appealed to "prurient interest"—that is, excited lust. Confronted by a book, magazine, or film about sex, the Court would decide "whether to the average person, applying contemporary community standards, the dominant theme of the material taken as a whole appeals to the prurient interest." Attempting to protect the free expression of ideas, even about sex, Brennan added that a work should be judged obscene only when it was "utterly without redeeming social importance."[15]

Despite Brennan's valiant effort to define obscenity, observe how many ambiguous terms dot his opinion: "prurient interest," "average person," "contemporary community standards," "redeeming social importance." After the *Roth* decision, obscenity cases became a headache for the Supreme Court. Perhaps their most ludicrous feature was that to study the evidence in a particular obscenity conviction, the mostly elderly justices had to sift through the pages of a sex magazine or sit through the screening of a porno film. It was little wonder that they lost the stomach for these cases and began to allow almost any sexual material to pass the minimal social value test unless it involved a sale of pornography to minors or particularly salacious advertising. Consequently, sexually explicit material became a booming market for enterprising pornographers.

Faced with this boom in pornography, the more conservative justices appointed by Richard Nixon tried to tighten the definition of obscenity in *Miller*

v. *California* (1973). Chief Justice Burger's opinion made two significant changes in obscenity doctrine. First, a sexually explicit work could no longer simply claim minimal social importance (for example, by including a brief scene on some social or political theme); now, the work had to possess "serious literary, artistic, political, or scientific value."[16] Second, prurient interest could be measured by local, rather than national, standards, which permitted a bookseller in a small town, for example, to be prosecuted for selling a work that could be legally sold in a more cosmopolitan city. But the *Miller* decision did little to stem the tide of pornography. And the Court soon had to back away from granting local communities a wide latitude to define obscenity after a Georgia town attempted to prosecute *Carnal Knowledge*, a popular Hollywood film, because it contained a simulated sexual act.

Conservative moralists have long decried the scope that the Supreme Court has given to the production of sexually explicit materials. In recent years, they have been joined by some feminists who regard pornography not only as degrading to women but also as contributing to their social subordination. This unusual alliance of conservatives and feminists prodded city councils in Minneapolis and Indianapolis to pass antipornography ordinances that banned any sexual materials deemed to buttress discrimination against women. But the Indianapolis ordinance was struck down by a federal judge on First Amendment grounds. The feminist challenge to pornography nonetheless remains a troubling issue, forcing us to weigh the rival claims of liberty and equality, of free expression and women's dignity.

Freedom of the Press

If the right of free speech promotes an open debate about political matters, the right of a free press provides democratic citizens with the information and analysis they need to enter intelligently into that debate. In authoritarian political systems, the government openly owns or covertly controls the press. In a democracy, the government is expected to keep its hands off the press. (Yet as we saw in Chapter 7, both governmental and economic elites in America possess special influence over the media.)

The landmark case defining freedom of the press was *Near* v. *Minnesota* (1931). J. M. Near was the publisher of the *Saturday Press*, a Minneapolis weekly that denounced a wide array of targets: corrupt officials, racketeers, Catholics, Jews, blacks, and labor unions. Minneapolis officials obtained a court injunction to close down Near's paper under a Minnesota law that allowed the banning of scandal sheets. The Supreme Court struck down the Minnesota law as a violation of freedom of the press because the law imposed **prior restraint.** A publisher like Near could still be sued for libel, but he could not be blocked from printing whatever he chose in the first place. The Court recognized that prior restraint, by allowing government officials to determine what information could be kept from publication, would effectively destroy freedom of the press.

Prior restraint was also at issue in a case involving the *New York Times;* this time the issue was government secrecy and deception during the Vietnam War. When a disillusioned Defense Department official, Daniel Ellsberg, leaked a copy of a classified department study of the war's history, known as the Pentagon Papers, to the *New York Times*, the Nixon administration obtained a lower court order temporarily halting the paper's publication of excerpts from the study. The Supreme Court's decision in *New York Times Co.* v. *United States* (1971) voided the order and permitted publication of the Pentagon Papers. But the six justices in the majority were divided in their reasoning. Justices Black, Brennan, and Douglas were opposed to prior restraint under any circumstances. Justices White, Marshall, and Stewart voted to allow publication because the Nixon administration had failed to make a convincing case for the disastrous consequences it claimed would follow once the Pentagon Papers became public. Freedom of the press again won a victory—but a majority of the Court seemed willing to accept prior restraint if the government could make a better case on possible harm to national security.

Even though broadcast media (radio and television) enjoy much the same freedom as print media (newspapers and magazines), they are subject to certain special constraints. Because broadcast frequencies are limited, the federal government regulates broadcast media through the Federal Communications Commission (FCC). And since messages broadcast through the media, unlike messages set in print, often reach audiences for which they were never intended, the FCC may ban words over the air that could not be kept out of print. In *F.C.C.* v. *Pacifica Foundation* (1978), the Court upheld a ban on further radio broadcasts of a hilarious monologue by comic George Carlin about Americans' obsession with "seven dirty words"—which Carlin used freely as part of his routine.[17] The issue here was not obscenity—Carlin's monologue did not excite lust and clearly had artistic value—but the harm done to children who might accidently hear the seven offensive words.

Separation of Church and State

The opening words of the First Amendment bar Congress from passing any law "respecting an establishment of religion." At the time the Bill of Rights was adopted, these words were aimed mainly at preventing the federal government from bestowing on any religious denomination the special privileges enjoyed by the official Anglican Church in England. But in modern times, the Supreme Court has given a far broader meaning to the **Establishment Clause,** reading it as requiring an almost complete separation of church and state. Religion and government are kept apart—even though America is one of the most religious nations in the world. Public opinion surveys, notes Garry Wills, show that "eight Americans in ten say they believe they will be called before God on Judgment Day to answer for their sins" and that the same percentage "believe God still works miracles."[18] This religious majority sometimes has difficulty understanding why the Supreme Court believes that government is not supposed to be in the business of supporting God.

School prayer cases illustrate how the Supreme Court, flying in the face of majority sentiments, has insisted that government stay out of religion. The Court has struck down the daily reading of a nondenominational prayer in New York public schools (*Engel* v. *Vitale* [1962]), Bible reading in Pennsylvania public schools (*Abington School District* v. *Schempp* [1963]), and even a moment of silence for meditation or prayer in Alabama public schools (*Wallace* v. *Jaffree* [1985]). School prayer, the Court has reasoned, represents a government endorsement of religion that inflicts psychological injury on students (and their parents) who are not religious believers. The Establishment Clause of the First Amendment mandates government neutrality toward religion.

The Court has not been quite as strict about government approval for religious symbols where school-age children are not involved. For example, in *Lynch* v. *Donnelly* (1984), the Court approved of a nativity scene erected by the city of Pawtucket, Rhode Island, during the Christmas season—but only because it was accompanied by a Santa's house, a Christmas tree, and colored lights that indicated the city's secular purpose (attracting shoppers to downtown stores). Such breaches in the "wall" separating church and state have so far been small. But some observers believe that larger ones may be likely from a court majority appointed by Presidents Reagan and Bush, both of whom had close ties with religious conservatives.

The Establishment Clause also has been central to the issue of government financial aid to religious schools. The Supreme Court's decisions in this area have not been as unpopular, however, as in the area of school prayer because Protestants and Jews do not favor aid that would go mostly to Catholic schools. Beginning in the 1940s, a long series of cases established the principle that government could not financially support religious schools, even in the name of secular educational purposes, although it could provide direct aid to their students (e.g., bus transportation). Chief Justice Burger summed up the Court's approach in *Lemon* v. *Kurtzman* (1971)—a ruling invalidating state payments for the teaching of secular subjects in parochial schools. According to the **Lemon test,** government aid to religious schools would be constitutional only if (1) it had a secular purpose, (2) its effect was neither to advance nor to inhibit religion, and (3) it did not entangle government and religious institutions in each other's affairs. Few forms of government aid to religious schools can survive the Lemon test.

Free Exercise of Religion

The Establishment Clause in the First Amendment is followed by the **Free Exercise Clause**—the right to believe in whatever religion one chooses. The Free Exercise Clause is a legacy of America's colonial past, as many of the original white settlers had fled religious oppression and persecution in England and other parts of Europe. It is also a practical necessity in a nation where the diversity of religious faiths is staggering.

The landmark free exercise case is *West Virginia State Board of Education* v.

Religious Freedom and Animal Sacrifice

A new wave of immigration from Latin America, Africa, and Asia is making the United States into an increasingly diverse, multicultural society. In 1993, the Supreme Court decided a case that raised profound questions about how much diversity Americans will tolerate. *Santería*, an Afro-Cuban religion, uses animal sacrifice in its religious rituals. When a Florida community sought to prevent a *santería* church from practicing its faith by enacting laws restricting animal sacrifice, a painful dilemma arose. Even though most Americans support constitutional protection for religious freedom, how far does that freedom extend? Are we willing to allow religious practices that are deeply offensive to the majority? What happens when a local government desperately seeks to stop the offensive practice through the law?

Originating in Cuba among African slaves in the nineteenth century, *santería* combines traditional African religion with elements of Catholicism. The faithful profess their devotion to spirits, called *orishas* (who resemble Catholic saints), primarily through animal sacrifice. Sacrifices are performed during birth, marriage, and death rites; healing ceremonies; and initiation of new members and priests. In *santería* chickens, pigeons, doves, ducks, guinea pigs, goats, sheep, and turtles are sacrificed by cutting the carotid artery in the neck. With the exception of healing and death rituals, the sacrificed animal is cooked and eaten.

Exiles from Cuba, where *santería* is outlawed, brought the religion to south Florida. They established the Church of the Lukumi Babalu Aye in the city of Hialeah. When it became known that the church intended to practice animal sacrifices, residents of Hialeah were outraged. An emergency meeting of the city council passed several ordinances making it illegal for anyone unnecessarily or cruelly to kill any animal and prohibiting the ritual sacrifice of animals unless its primary purpose was food consumption. Exemptions to these ordinances permitted the killing of animals in licensed slaughterhouses and kosher slaughter. The only conduct subject to Hialeah's restriction was the religious exercise of *santería* church members.

The Church of the Lukumi Babalu Aye challenged the ordinances as a violation of the First Amendment. A unanimous Supreme Court agreed. Writing for the Court, Justice Anthony Kennedy argued that Hialeah's laws did not meet the Court's test for justifiable restrictions of freedom of religion. The city's actions were neither neutral toward different religious groups nor of general applicability. Its ordinances were blatant attempts to restrict freedom of religion for followers of *santería*. Although *santería* practices may be offensive to the majority, the Court said, that majority cannot prohibit them without running roughshod over the First Amendment.

Does the Court's protection of *santería* animal sacrifice square with the values of popular democracy? Trusting the people, popular democrats are generally champions of majority rule. But popular democracy cannot be reduced to simple majoritarianism. It also involves other democratic values—among them tolerance for the beliefs and practices of unorthodox minorities. In this regard, popular democrats agree with the Court's ruling in the *santería* case.

Source: Church of the Lukumi Babalu Aye v. *City of Hialeah,* 113 S. Ct. 2217 (1993).

Barnette (1943). At stake was the right of schoolchildren to refuse to salute an American flag because their religious faith—Jehovah's Witnesses—forbade it. Three years earlier, in *Minersville School District* v. *Gobitis*, the Court had approved of expelling Witness children from school for refusal to salute the flag. But that decision led to brutal physical assaults on the Witnesses in many towns and also became an embarrassment as the United States entered a war against Nazi tyranny in the name of democratic freedom. With the powerful words of Justice Jackson (quoted at the beginning of this chapter), the Court changed its mind and gave a firm endorsement to the free exercise of religion even when it offended the most cherished sentiments of the majority.

Although the Free Exercise Clause protects any form of religious belief, the matter of religious conduct is more complicated. What happens when a religious order prescribes practices for its adherents that violate local, state, or federal laws having nothing to do with religion? The Court first struggled with this dilemma in *Reynolds* v. *United States* (1879), when it approved the outlawing of polygamy (where a man takes several wives), a key practice of the Mormon faith. A recent case, *Employment Division* v. *Smith* (1990), upheld the same distinction between belief and conduct. The Court denied the claim by two followers of the Native American Church that smoking the drug peyote, for which they had been fired from their job, was a religious sacrament protected by the Free Exercise Clause. The position of the Court was different, however, in *Church of Lukumi Babalu Aye* v. *City of Hialeah* (1993)—an intriguing case described in this chapter's box.

THE RIGHTS OF PERSONS ACCUSED OF CRIMES

Antonio Richard Rochin was a smalltime drug dealer with a record of run-ins with the Los Angeles police. Entering Rochin's house without a search or arrest warrant in June 1949, Los Angeles County deputy sheriffs found their suspect in his bedroom and spotted two morphine capsules on his night table. Rochin grabbed the capsules and put them in his mouth—at which point the officers kicked and beat him in the hope he would spit them out. He swallowed the capsules instead—and they beat him further in the vain hope that he would vomit them up. Finally, they bound and gagged Rochin and took him to a hospital, where a doctor pumped his stomach and provided the police with the evidence that was used to convict him in a California courtroom. When Rochin's appeal reached the U.S. Supreme Court, the unanimous justices threw out his conviction. Justice Felix Frankfurter, usually reluctant to intervene in state criminal justice proceedings, found the behavior of the Los Angeles deputies entirely unacceptable. "This is conduct that shocks the conscience," he wrote.[19]

This unpleasant story illustrates a point that many Americans do not like to acknowledge. Understandably fearful of the increasing levels of criminal behavior in American society, many view the constitutional protections bestowed on criminal suspects and defendants as a barrier to effective law enforcement and a threat to public safety. They complain that citizens, not just criminals, have rights. The *Rochin* case reminds us that before the Warren Court of the 1960s set down constitutional limits on the conduct of police and prosecutors, there was little to deter the authorities from using the most brutal and coercive practices in the name of combatting lawlessness. (Indeed, the much-publicized Rodney King beating case in Los Angeles in 1991 indicates that police brutality is still a problem.)

The constitutional bases for the rights of persons accused of crimes are Amendments Four, Five, Six, and Eight, applied to the states through incorporation in the Fourteenth Amendment. Application of these amendments to the criminal justice system at the state and local levels, where the vast majority of criminal proceedings takes place, is a recent phenomenon. The Warren Court of the 1960s set down most of the critical precedents in the area of criminal procedure. The Burger (1969–1986) and Rehnquist (1986–present) Courts, appointed by "law-and-order" presidents and responsive to the public outcry about crime, carved out numerous exceptions to these precedents.

Criminal Procedure: The Warren Court

Clarence Earl Gideon, a penniless drifter with a criminal record, was convicted for the felony offense of breaking and entering a poolroom and sentenced in a Florida court to five years in prison. Unable to afford an attorney, Gideon had had to defend himself after the judge refused to appoint professional counsel for him. The Supreme Court accepted Gideon's petition (appointing a prominent lawyer to argue his case before it) and ruled in *Gideon* v. *Wainwright* (1963) that the Sixth Amendment right of counsel is so essential to a fair trial that the state must pay for a lawyer for indigent defendants charged with a felony. Gideon won the chance for a second trial, at which he was acquitted after his court-appointed counsel convincingly demonstrated that the prosecution's star witness, who had fingered Gideon for the break-in, was probably the culprit.[20]

Cleveland police officers forced their way into the home of Dolree Mapp without a search warrant in the belief that she was hiding a man wanted for a recent bombing as well as illegal gambling paraphernalia. Their search of the house turned up neither a fugitive nor gambling materials—but they did discover sexual books and pictures. On the basis of this evidence, Mapp was sent to jail for possession of obscene literature. In *Mapp* v. *Ohio* (1961), the Warren Court reversed her conviction, holding that material seized in an illegal search could not be introduced as evidence in a state court, a doctrine known as the **exclusionary rule.** This rule, based on the Fourth Amendment, had been applied since 1914 to defendants in federal prosecutions. But its extension from the tax evaders and other white-collar defendants typically tried in federal courts to the wider range of defendants, including violent criminals, tried in state courts made the *Mapp* decision controversial.

Ernesto Miranda was arrested by Phoenix police on suspicion of rape and kidnapping. At first, Miranda maintained his innocence, but after two hours of police interrogation he signed a written confession to the crime. At no point had the police advised Miranda that he had a right to have an attorney present during the interrogation. In *Miranda* v. *Arizona* (1966), the Warren Court ruled the confession to be inadmissible as evidence in court, a violation of Miranda's Fifth Amendment right not to incriminate himself. The Court's majority, in this 5–4 decision, argued that police custody and interrogation tended to create such an intimidating atmosphere that individuals felt pressured to incriminate themselves in the absence of a lawyer's counsel. With the confession thrown out, Arizona retried Miranda for the same crime and convicted him on the basis of other evidence.

The effect of the decision was that police had to change their behavior and provide suspects with what came to be known as the **Miranda warnings.** Criminal suspects must be advised that (1) they have the right to remain silent, (2) anything they say can be used against them, (3) they have the right to speak to an attorney before police questioning and to have him or her present during interrogation, and, (4) if they cannot afford to hire an attorney, one will be provided at state expense before any questioning can take place.

The *Mapp* decision and even more the *Miranda* decision fueled widespread attacks on the Warren Court for crippling law enforcement at a time of rampant crime. Actually, these Warren Court decisions did not free many criminals. A prominent study of the exclusionary rule later estimated that less than 2.5 percent of felony arrests were undermined by the operation of this rule.[21] After initial grumbling, the police adapted to the requirement of providing *Miranda* warnings. Numerous studies found that criminal confessions continued to be made in large numbers even after suspects were informed of their rights.[22] Nonetheless, critics of the Warren Court convinced many Americans that the justices had in effect taken the handcuffs off criminal suspects and put them on the police.

Presidential candidate Richard Nixon seized on crime as a campaign issue in 1968, lambasting the Warren Court for coddling criminals and promising that his administration would appoint only law-and-order judges. Nixon's success with the issue encouraged other candidates, including his Republican successors in the White House. Supreme Court justices appointed by Nixon, Reagan, and Bush thus have been less likely than were justices of the Warren Court era to emphasize the constitutional rights of criminal suspects or defendants and more likely to emphasize the practical needs of police and prosecutors.

Criminal Procedure: The Burger and Rehnquist Courts

Of the three landmark Warren Court decisions on criminal justice just described, only the *Gideon* decision was received without controversy. No one seemed to doubt the proposition that there could not be a fair trial where the state was represented by a professionally trained prosecutor and the defendant had to represent himself or herself. So it is not surprising that the Burger Court went beyond the *Gideon* ruling in *Argersinger* v. *Hamlin* (1972), holding that the right of court-appointed counsel for the indigent should be extended from felony defendants to defendants facing misdemeanor charges that carried a jail sentence.

In the more controversial areas of the exclusionary rule and the *Miranda* warnings, however, the Burger and Rehnquist Courts have trimmed back the Warren Court precedents—without, up to now, explicitly disavowing them. Thus, in *United States* v. *Calandra* (1974), Justice Lewis Powell's majority opinion argued that illegally obtained evidence, although still barred from a trial because of the exclusionary rule, could be admitted before a grand jury considering whether to indict a suspect and thus bring him or her to trial. And in *United States* v. *Leon* (1984), Justice Byron White wrote that if police use a search warrant that later proves to have been invalid, the evidence seized is still admissible during the trial. So many exceptions have been approved by the Burger and Rehnquist Courts that legal scholar Thomas Davies calls the exclusionary rule a "shadow" of its former self.[23]

The Burger and Rehnquist Courts also have made it easier for police to obtain confessions by loosening up the requirements for *Miranda* warnings. For example, in emergency situations such as a threat to the safety of the arresting officer, the warnings are not required (*New York* v. *Quarles* [1984]). Nor do arresting officers have to notify suspects as to the specific offense with which they are charged (*Colorado* v. *Spring* [1987]).

The ultimate issue in a criminal justice system—imposition of the death sentence—was not tackled by the Supreme Court until 1972 in the case of *Furman* v. *Georgia*. With all four of President Nixon's appointees in dissent, the Court struck down existing death penalty laws in every state because the random and arbitrary fashion in which juries decided on capital punishment violated the Cruel And Unusual Punishment Clause of the Eighth Amendment. In response to this decision, state legislatures and the federal government revised their criminal laws to provide juries with explicit sentencing guidelines. The Court ratified this approach in *Gregg* v. *Georgia* (1976), and prison "death rows" reopened for a new cohort of the condemned.

Condemned prisoners find little support from the Rehnquist Court when they raise claims of constitutional rights. Warren McClesky, a black, had been sentenced to death for killing a white police officer in Atlanta. His lawyers introduced an extensive study showing that in Georgia homicide trials, a defendant who had murdered a white was 4.3 times more likely to be sentenced to death than a defendant who had murdered a black. They argued that McClesky's death sentence was a form of racial discrimination and thus a violation of the Fourteenth Amendment guarantee of equal protection of the laws. But a five-member majority rejected this argument in *McClesky* v. *Kemp* (1987), holding that the statistical evidence did not demonstrate discrimination in McClesky's particular case. After further appeals were rejected, McClesky was executed in 1991.

The criminal procedure decisions of the Burger and Rehnquist Courts have been more congenial to public opinion than those of the Warren Court. Critics of these decisions point out, however, that constitutional rights—even for the most despicable citizens—should not be decided by a popularity test. They argue that the Bill of Rights does not prevent us from putting criminal offenders behind bars, but it does require that we do so in a fair manner. This philosophy is well-expressed by Justice Brennan: "The interest of . . . [the government] is not that it shall win a case, but that justice shall be done."[24]

THE RIGHT OF PRIVACY

The controversy surrounding constitutional rights spelled out in the Bill of Rights has been extended to the issue of whether other rights can be legitimately derived from the text of the Constitution even if they are not spelled out there. A **right of privacy** is at the center of this debate. Civil libertarians have long contended for this right. In a 1928 dissent, Justice Louis Brandeis wrote, "The makers of our Constitution conferred, as against the government, the right to be let alone—the most comprehensive of rights and the right most valued by civilized men."[25] But what words in the Bill of Rights established the right to be let alone—the right of privacy?

The Supreme Court finally answered this question in 1965 in *Griswold* v. *Connecticut*. At issue was a Connecticut law that made it a crime for any person to use a drug or device for birth control. The Court invalidated this law as an invasion of the constitutionally protected right of privacy of married persons. Writing for the majority, Justice William O. Douglas argued that the enumerated guarantees of constitutional rights in the First, Third, Fourth, Fifth, and Ninth Amendments had "penumbras" (shadows) that extended beyond their specific words. These penumbras suggested the existence of "zones of privacy" that the government could not invade. In an important concurring opinion, Justice Arthur Goldberg took a different tack. He based a right of privacy on the words of the Ninth Amendment, which reads, "The enumeration in the Constitution, of certain rights, shall not be construed to deny or disparage others retained by the people." To the dissenters in *Griswold*, Justices Hugo Black and Potter Stewart, the right of privacy, whether found among penumbras or read into the Ninth Amendment, was a concoction of the justices lacking any basis in the Constitution.[26]

The *Griswold* case generated a heated controversy on the Court over the idea of a constitutional right of privacy. But few outside the Court paid attention to a decision striking down an antiquated law that even the dissenters in the case considered to be "silly." The right of privacy generated a major public controversy only when it was extended from a couple's freedom to choose contraception and avoid pregnancy to a woman's freedom to choose an abortion and terminate an unwanted pregnancy.

Abortion

The abortion issue was brought before the Supreme Court by two young lawyers, Sarah Weddington and Linda Coffee, who were inspired by the new feminist movement that had emerged in the 1960s. Their client in ***Roe v. Wade*** (1973) was

Norma McCorvey, a twenty-one-year-old woman who had carried an unwanted pregnancy to term because Texas, like most other states at that time, forbade abortions except to save the life of the mother. (McCorvey's identity was protected from publicity by the pseudonym "Jane Roe.") By a 7–2 vote, the Court struck down anti-abortion statutes in Texas and all other states on the grounds that they violated a woman's right of privacy, located in the Due Process Clause of the Fourteenth Amendment.

Authored by Justice Harry Blackmun, the decision for the Court divided pregnancy into three trimesters. During the first trimester, a state cannot interfere with a woman's right to choose an abortion in consultation with her doctor. During the second trimester, when abortions pose more of a medical risk, states can regulate them to safeguard maternal health. Only during the final trimester, when a fetus may be capable of surviving outside the womb, can a state impose severe restrictions or prohibitions on abortion. To the dissenters in the case, Justices Byron White and William Rehnquist, this trimester scheme was an arbitrary invention of the Court. They argued that the Court was enforcing on the states a right that had neither been enumerated in the Bill of Rights nor envisioned by the drafters of the Fourteenth Amendment.

Hailing the decision on abortion as a great victory for women's rights, the women's movement shifted its attention to other issues. But as supporters of *Roe* grew complacent, opponents of the decision mobilized to fight its results. The initial "right-to-life" movement was spearheaded by Catholic organizations. Later, they were joined by fundamentalist Protestant groups, such as the Reverend Jerry Falwell's Moral Majority. The religious fervor of right-to-life supporters was captured for political purposes by the conservatives of the New Right, whose candidate and hero was Ronald Reagan. Once in the White House, Reagan made abortion a litmus test for his nominees to the federal judiciary. By the end of his two terms, he had named three new justices to the Supreme Court, and *Roe* was at risk of reversal.[27]

Awakening to the peril to *Roe*, the "pro-choice" forces mobilized their supporters at last. After the Court announced early in 1989 that it would consider the restrictive laws on abortion passed by Missouri, a massive Washington rally attempted to show the justices that a majority of Americans wanted to preserve a woman's right to choose. Right-to-life forces girded for battle as well. The Court's decision in *Webster* v. *Reproductive Health Services* (1989) favored the right-to-life side. Missouri's restrictions on abortion, such as a ban on the use of public hospitals or employees to perform abortions except when the woman's life was in danger, were upheld by a 5–4 majority. But the Court stopped short of overturning *Roe* itself. One member of the majority, Sandra Day O'Connor, the only woman on the Supreme Court, was not willing to go that far.

Closely allied with the right-to-life movement, President Bush replaced two retiring supporters of the original *Roe* decision, Justices William Brennan and Thurgood Marshall, with David Souter and Clarence Thomas. The stage seemed set for the demise of *Roe* when the Court heard the case of *Planned Parenthood of Southeastern Pennsylvania* v. *Casey* (1992). But in a surprise twist to the historical

After right-to-life supporters mounted large demonstrations to pressure the Supreme Court, pro-choice backers of the *Roe* v. *Wade* decision mobilized in response. Here, a massive 1989 demonstration in Washington, D.C., precedes the Court's hearing of the Webster case.

drama of abortion rights, *Roe* survived. Most of Pennsylvania's restrictions were sustained by the Court, imposing new obstacles to women seeking an abortion. Yet even though four justices wanted to overturn *Roe*, restoring to the states the power to prohibit abortions, the critical fifth vote was still lacking. Justice O'Connor was now joined by Justice Anthony Kennedy (a Reagan appointee) and Justice Souter in a moderate conservative bloc willing to uphold restrictions on abortion but not willing to disclaim the constitutional right of a woman to choose an abortion. In an unusual joint opinion, the three argued that *Roe* was an important precedent deserving of respect and that overturning it would diminish both the legitimacy of the Supreme Court and the public's belief in the rule of law.

For right-to-life supporters, legal disappointment in the *Casey* decision was followed by political disappointment as the first pro-choice president in twelve years, Bill Clinton, was elected in 1992. When Justice Byron White, one of the two original dissenters in *Roe*, retired in 1993, Clinton replaced him with one of the pioneer legal advocates for women's rights, Ruth Bader Ginsburg. The landmark *Roe* decision, even though partially weakened in the *Webster* and *Casey* decisions, is thus likely to remain the law on abortion for the immediate future. Nevertheless, abortion engages deep passions on both sides, and it is not likely to disappear any time soon as one of the most heated and divisive issues in American public life.

Sexual Orientation

Is the right of privacy equally enjoyed by all Americans? In *Bowers* v. *Hardwick* (1986), the Supreme Court said no. Michael Hardwick was arrested after an Atlanta policeman, entering his bedroom to serve an arrest warrant for not paying a fine, found Hardwick engaged in homosexual conduct. Charges against Hardwick under Georgia's sodomy law were not prosecuted, but he brought a civil suit in federal court challenging the law as an invasion of his constitutionally protected right of privacy. A 5–4 majority rejected his challenge and upheld the sodomy law.

What distinguished Hardwick's claim to privacy from those in the *Griswold* or *Roe* decisions? Justice Byron White, writing for the majority, stated that those decisions involved "family, marriage, or procreation."[28] In other words, the right of privacy belongs to heterosexuals but not to homosexuals. Throughout this chapter we have witnessed occasions where the Supreme Court advanced civil liberties in the face of majority prejudice or hostility. The decision in *Bowers* should remind us that the Court may also side with conventional morality and ignore the cost to individual liberty.

CIVIL RIGHTS

Although this chapter highlights legal and legislative victories in the struggle for civil rights, primary credit for progress in the struggle belongs to the civil rights movement. The decades-long struggle by African Americans and their allies for civil rights not only prodded the white majority to act but also inspired similar movements for equality among Hispanic Americans, Native Americans, Americans with disabilities, and women. These groups' victories, such as the Americans with Disabilities Act of 1990, have redeemed a basic promise of popular democracy: respect for the dignity of every citizen.

Civil rights achievements of the 1950s and 1960s, establishing the objective of a racially just and equal society, are now applauded even by those who originally opposed them. The methods devised to attain that objective, however, have generated intense controversy since the end of the 1960s. As we shall see when we consider the practices of busing and affirmative action, many have come to argue that measures taken in the name of civil rights for racial minorities discriminate against the white majority. To the story of the heroic past of the struggle for civil rights must be appended the story of its painful present.

Fighting Segregation: From *Plessy* to *Brown*

Despite the constitutional amendments drafted during the Civil War and Reconstruction to protect blacks, they soon found themselves in a position of economic, political, and legal subordination. The commitment of the Fourteenth Amendment to equal protection of the laws for former slaves was mocked by a series of Supreme Court decisions refusing to enforce the amendment in the face of the southern states' new system of "Jim Crow" segregation. The last of these decisions, *Plessy* v. *Ferguson* (1896), established a legal justification for racial segregation that African Americans would have to combat for more than half a century.

The Supreme Court had to consider in the *Plessy* case whether a Louisiana law requiring railroads to provide **separate but equal** facilities for whites and blacks violated the equal protection of the laws. All but one of the justices found the practice legal, arguing that separation of the races did not imply that either race was unequal. If there was a stigma of black inferiority in segregation, the majority said, it was only because blacks viewed it that way. Repudiating this reasoning, the lone dissenter in the case, Justice John Marshall Harlan, offered a powerful and prophetic alternative: "The Constitution is color-blind, and neither knows nor tolerates classes among citizens."[29]

A little more than a decade later, in 1909, the **National Association for the Advancement of Colored People** was founded to take up the battle against racial segregation and discrimination. In the 1930s, its legal arm developed a careful, long-term strategy to demolish the separate but equal doctrine. Rather than a head-on assault on Jim Crow, which the Court was likely to rebuff, NAACP lawyers would chip away at segregation in the area of education, showing in case after case that separate facilities could not possibly be equal.

An illustration of the NAACP approach—and a case that underscores the indignities of segregation—was *McLaurin* v. *Oklahoma State Regents for Higher Education* (1950). When a federal district court ordered George McLaurin, an African American seeking a doctorate in education, admitted to the all-white University of Oklahoma, the school's regents insisted that his presence not violate state segregation laws. So McLaurin was initially forced to sit by himself in an anteroom outside the main classroom, to study by himself in the library at a desk hidden away from other students, and to eat by himself in a grimy alcove of the cafeteria. These restrictions were eased as the NAACP suit on McLaurin's behalf reached the Supreme Court, but the Court still struck down his separate treatment as a violation of his Fourteenth Amendment rights.[30]

The NAACP campaign finally reached fruition in ***Brown* v. *Board of Education of Topeka*** (1954), probably the most famous Supreme Court decision of the twentieth century. Thanks to skillful leadership by the new chief justice, Earl Warren, the Court was unanimous in rejecting the separate but equal

Admitted by court order to the all-white University of Oklahoma, George McLaurin is forced to sit apart from fellow students. The Supreme Court's 1950 decision requiring the university to treat McLaurin like other students was a key victory in the NAACP campaign against segregation.

doctrine in the field of education. The claim in the *Plessy* decision that segregation did not stamp blacks as inferior was repudiated in Warren's opinion for the Court: "Segregation of white and colored children in public schools has a detrimental effect upon the colored children. . . . A sense of inferiority affects the motivation to learn." The chief justice's concluding words marked a historic watershed for the Court and for the nation: "In the field of public education the doctrine of 'separate but equal' has no place. Separate educational facilities are inherently unequal."[31] Although the case dealt only with public schools, the *Brown* decision, reclaiming the original promise of the Fourteenth Amendment, inflicted a mortal wound on racial segregation in America.

But the death of segregation would not be swift. And the Supreme Court had to share a portion of the blame for its agonizingly slow demise. When the Court considered how to implement its decision in a second *Brown* case a year later, it was fearful of a hostile and potentially violent response by southern whites. So rather than setting a firm timetable for school desegregation, the Court returned the problem to the lower federal courts with the instruction that desegregation proceed "with all deliberate speed." These ambiguous words did not accomplish the goal of heading off southern white hostility and violence; instead, they only seemed to invite southern strategies of delay. The stage for the historic drama of civil rights now shifted from the Supreme Court to the cities and small towns of the South, where the civil rights movement, encouraged by *Brown*, would have to finish off a dying—but still powerful and violent—segregationist system.

Ending Segregation

Up to the *Brown* decision in 1954, the primary focus of the civil rights movement had been litigation, and its leading group had been the NAACP. After *Brown*, new civil rights groups emerged and intensified the pace of the struggle for equality by turning from litigation to direct action. Chapter 11 described the first great direct-action struggle, the Montgomery bus boycott. Subsequent direct-action struggles were risky, both in their use of civil disobedience to break unjust segregation laws and in the violence with which they were met by southern mobs and southern police. But these struggles were increasingly effective in riveting the attention of the North on the brutal injustices of southern segregation and in pressuring northern politicians to do something about them.

The legislative triumphs for civil rights in the mid-1960s can be traced directly to the movement campaigns that inspired them. In response to the direct-action campaign of Martin Luther King, Jr.'s Southern Christian Leadership Conference in Birmingham, Alabama, in 1963, President Kennedy proposed major civil rights legislation (see Chapter 13). Passed only after his death, the **Civil Rights Act of 1964** struck a powerful blow at segregation in many areas. Its most important provisions outlawed racial discrimination in public accommodations (such as hotels and restaurants) and in employment. In response to another direct-action campaign led by King and his organization in Selma, Alabama, early in 1965, President Johnson proposed landmark voting rights legislation. Responding more promptly this time, Congress passed the **Voting Rights Act of 1965.** This act, removing the barriers that southern officials had placed in the way of potential black registrants, finally gave effective enforcement to the Fifteenth Amendment.[32]

As the pace of the struggle against segregation picked up in other areas, school desegregation lagged behind. A decade after the *Brown* decision had mandated an end to segregated public schools, less than 2 percent of previously segregated school districts had changed their practices. By the end of the 1960s, the Supreme Court had had enough of all deliberate speed and was ready to order immediate desegregation. Given residential patterns that separated the races, however, significant desegregation could be accomplished only by busing schoolchildren. In the case of *Swann* v. *Charlotte-Mecklenburg Board of Education* (1971), a unanimous Court approved a massive busing plan for a sprawling urban/rural school district in North Carolina.

Ironically, court-ordered busing to end the perpetuation of all-white and all-black schools was more controversial in the North than in the South. Angry white parents in the North asked why their children should be bused to remedy patterns of discrimination for which they were not responsible. Despite widespread protests, federal judges ordered busing for such cities as Boston, Denver, and Los Angeles. But the limitations of busing as a remedy for racially separate schools became evident in a case from Detroit.

The phenomenon of "white flight" to the suburbs to escape an increasingly black city, combined with economic changes, left too few white children remaining in Detroit to achieve racial balance in the schools. So a federal judge ordered a busing plan that would have incorporated the city's suburbs as well as the city itself. In *Milliken* v. *Bradley* (1974), a 5–4 majority rejected the plan, arguing that suburban school districts that had not engaged in segregated practices could not be compelled to participate in a remedy for Detroit's segregation problem. Since only interdistrict desegregation plans like that in Detroit could ever achieve racial balance in the schools, the long-term result has been that African-American children are now more likely to attend an all-black school in a big city in the North than they are in the once-segregated South.

Affirmative Action

As the bitter controversy over busing receded in the late 1970s and 1980s, it was supplanted by an equally bitter debate over **affirmative action**—taking positive steps to award educational opportunities or jobs to racial minorities or women because these groups have been the victims of prior discrimination. Supporters of affirmative action argue that moving from past discrimination to a color- or gender-blind perspective is insufficient when white males already monopolize the good things in life. Only a deliberate policy of preferential treatment for groups victimized by discrimination, they insist, can overcome racial and gender inequities. Opponents of affirmative action argue that it goes beyond equal protection of the laws to promote equal results regardless of merit. Affirmative action, they say, is "reverse discrimination" against white males.

The Supreme Court has often seemed as divided and uncertain about affirmative action as the rest of American society. The first and most famous affirmative action case to reach the Court, *Regents of the University of California* v. *Bakke* (1978), had an inconclusive outcome. The University of California Medical School at Davis set aside 16 of the 100 slots in its entering class for members of racial minorities. Denied admission to the medical school, although his grades and test scores were higher than those of the minority students admitted, Alan Bakke sued, claiming a violation of his civil rights. A split Court rejected the idea of a fixed quota of positions for minorities and ordered Bakke's admission to the medical school. Yet the Court also ruled that taking race into consideration as part of a school's admission process was legitimate as a way of enhancing diversity in the student body.

Subsequent decisions sometimes advanced and sometimes cut back affirmative action. A year after the *Bakke* decision rejected quotas, the Court approved a numerical racial quota for a job training program in a Louisiana steel plant in *United Steelworkers of America* v. *Weber* (1979). What differentiated the Louisiana case was that the quota was a voluntary plan agreed to by the steel company and the union to rectify a traditional pattern of job discrimination and that

Weber had lost only temporarily the chance for a better job within the plant. If the *Weber* decision broadened the scope of affirmative action, the decision in *Firefighters Local Union No. 1794* v. *Stotts* (1984) narrowed it. Here the Court ruled that when economic hard times required a city to lay off workers, blacks hired under an affirmative action plan would lose their jobs before white workers with greater seniority.

Affirmative action for women was first considered by the Supreme Court in the 1987 case of *Johnson* v. *Santa Clara County*. Two employees of the Santa Clara County Transportation Agency, Diane Joyce and Paul Johnson, sought promotion to a better-paying craft position as a road dispatcher. Both passed an agency test, with Johnson achieving a slightly higher score. Since women held none of the agency's 238 craft positions, Johnson was passed over, and the promotion was given to Joyce on affirmative action grounds. The Court upheld the agency, establishing that voluntary affirmative action plans can operate to end the underrepresentation of women in job categories traditionally dominated by men.

Since the *Johnson* decision, affirmative action has been losing ground on the Supreme Court. In a series of 1989 decisions, the Rehnquist Court shifted the burden of proof in job discrimination suits from employer to employee. These decisions took away much of the incentive for employers to adopt affirmative action plans. More friendly to affirmative action, Congress passed the Civil Rights Act of 1991, amending Title VII of the 1964 law to place the burden of proof back on employers. But the conservative majority on the Court continues to signal its unhappiness with affirmative action. Decisions in 1993 on other civil rights questions—job bias and voting rights—indicate that this majority is now opposed to any social remedies that take race into account.

Equal Rights for Women

The struggle for equal rights for women has taken a different course than the civil rights struggle of African Americans. During Reconstruction, drafters of the Fifteenth Amendment excluded women on the grounds that there was not enough political support to enfranchise both black males and all females, an argument that infuriated pioneer feminist leaders Elizabeth Cady Stanton and Susan B. Anthony. It took several generations of struggle by the women's movement before women won the vote in 1920 with the Nineteenth Amendment. Having attained a goal denied for so long, the women's movement faded in strength for almost half a century.

Energized by the civil rights and New Left movements, a second women's movement sprang up in the 1960s. Modelling its strategy after the NAACP's historic campaign that led to the *Brown* decision, legal advocates from the new women's movement began to press test cases on women's rights on the Supreme Court in the early 1970s. They won some important victories. Yet there was no women's rights equivalent to *Brown*, no landmark case that established full-fledged equality for women. (The most important victory for women in the

Supreme Court—*Roe* v. *Wade*—was decided on the grounds of a right of privacy rather than equal rights for women.)

The first women's rights cases were the easiest. In *Reed* v. *Reed* (1971), argued before the Court by future justice Ruth Bader Ginsburg, the unanimous justices struck down an Idaho law favoring men over women as executors of estates. In *Frontiero* v. *Richardson* (1973), all but one justice voted to strike down a federal statute on military pay that discriminated against women. Blatant instances of discrimination against women, the Court was now saying, violated their right to equal protection.

But what test should the Court apply in cases of less blatant gender discrimination? Recall our earlier discussion of the double standard: most legislation is subject only to ordinary scrutiny, with government merely needing to present a reasonable basis for it, but legislation that infringes upon civil liberties and rights is subject to strict scrutiny, with the Court voiding it unless the government can prove a compelling interest. Women's rights advocates hoped that the Court would apply the same strict scrutiny in cases of discrimination against women that it used in cases of discrimination against racial minorities. But advocates were pressing this argument before the Burger Court, not the Warren Court.

In *Craig* v. *Boren* (1976), the women's movement fell short of its objective. At issue was an Oklahoma law that allowed women to buy beer at age eighteen but required men to wait until age twenty-one. The Court struck down the law as a violation of equal protection. But Justice Brennan could not get a majority of the Court to base this holding on strict scrutiny toward gender classifications. The best he could obtain was the creation of a new, intermediate category: *heightened scrutiny*. A statute that classified by gender would pass muster with the Court, according to this new form of scrutiny, only if it aimed at an important government objective and substantially furthered that objective. Women's rights now had more constitutional protection than before but less than the protection enjoyed by racial minorities.

Because the women's movement has shifted its resources to defend the *Roe* decision and abortion rights, fewer sex discrimination cases are now pressed on the Supreme Court. The Rehnquist Court has unanimously struck down a "fetal protection policy" through which a business excludes women from certain jobs on the grounds of hazards to pregnancy. But the conservative majority is not inclined to expand the scope of civil rights for women. Nevertheless, for the first time in history two women sit on the Supreme Court. It will take the combined efforts of an effective women's movement and supporters of women's rights on the Court itself for further gains to be made on behalf of equality for women.

CONCLUSION: THE STRUGGLE OVER LIBERTIES AND RIGHTS

Americans can legitimately take pride in the civil liberties and civil rights they enjoy today. Yet these liberties and rights are the result of long struggles and only recent landmark advances: free speech (1960s), rights of persons accused of crimes (1960s), right of privacy (1960s and 1970s), equal rights for blacks (1950s), and equal rights for women (1970s). The newness of the critical Supreme Court precedents and the political backlash that has trimmed back several and tried to overturn others indicate that the struggle over the definition of American liberties and rights is far from ended.

Both elite democrats and popular democrats have a checkered past in the area of civil liberties and civil rights. Elite democrats in positions of power, while mouthing rhetorical support for American liberties, have moved to limit them in times of crisis and challenge. Popular democrats have often backed and applauded the repressive measures that elites have instituted. Yet some elite democrats and some popular democrats have done better. Judicial champions of civil liberties and civil rights have understood how fundamental these freedoms and powers are to the creation and maintenance of a democratic society. Popular democratic forces (Anti-federalists, abolitionists, New Deal populists, blacks, feminists) have fought to establish civil liberties and civil rights in the first place, as well as to bring before the courts the cases that will broaden their definition and scope.

Given that a majority of ordinary Americans may not support civil liberties and civil rights when they protect unpopular individuals or groups, individuals committed to the values of popular democracy must recognize the responsibilities of democratic education. In the spirit of the tradition initiated by the Anti-federalists, they must remind others of the importance of an open and tolerant society, where new and unconventional ideas can circulate freely, where reigning elites can be challenged, where that spark of protest that launched the American revolutionary experiment can enlighten and revitalize American democracy. And with an emphasis on the importance of citizenship, popular democrats cannot rest content merely with the defense of American liberties and rights. They also must encourage other citizens to make active use of them.

KEY TERMS

civil liberties
civil rights
American Civil Liberties Union
  (ACLU)
Civil War amendments
footnote four
strict scrutiny
incorporation
clear and present danger test
McCarthyism
symbolic speech
unprotected speech
obscenity
prior restraint

Establishment Clause
Lemon test
Free Exercise Clause
exclusionary rule
Miranda warnings
right of privacy
Roe v. *Wade*
separate but equal
National Association for the Advance-
  ment of Colored People (NAACP)
Brown v. *Board of Education of Topeka*
Civil Rights Act of 1964
Voting Rights Act of 1965
affirmative action

SUGGESTED READINGS

James MacGregor Burns and Stewart Burns, *A People's Charter: The Pursuit of Rights in America* (New York: Vintage Books, 1993). A vivid chronicle of the struggles that have attempted to turn the words of the Bill of Rights into realities.

Barbara Hinkson Craig and David M. O'Brien, *Abortion and American Politics* (Chatham, N.J.: Chatham House Publishers, 1993). A thorough account of the political and legal battles over abortion that *Roe* v. *Wade* initiated.

Peter Irons, *The Courage of Their Convictions: Sixteen Americans Who Fought Their Way to the Supreme Court* (New York: Penguin Books, 1990). Portraits of ordinary Americans who tested the meaning of civil liberties and civil rights.

Richard Kluger, *Simple Justice* (New York: Alfred A. Knopf, 1976). A massive account of the NAACP's legal campaign against segregation, culminating in *Brown* v. *Board of Education*.

Anthony Lewis, *Gideon's Trumpet* (New York: Vintage Books, 1964). A classic story of how a penniless drifter won the right for all indigent defendants to have the courts appoint counsel for them.

Economic Policy:
Growth Versus Equality?

We often think of economics and politics as separate. "Free markets" supposedly operate independently of government. In fact, as we saw in Chapter 4, economics and politics are so closely linked in the United States that it is impossible to speak of a free market apart from government. Government has become a large and pervasive economic force that shapes the fates of individuals and whole communities. Consider the following example.

Located fifteen miles south of downtown Chicago, under the Skyway that takes motorists out of the city, southeast Chicago was once one of the world's premier steel-making centers. Tucked in among the huge steel mills covered with grime and belching smoke are row after row of square, neat bungalows housing steelworkers and their families from places like Serbia, Poland, and

Croatia. Viewed from the Skyway, the area looks depressed, but for decades it was a prosperous, tightly knit community.

Between 1979 and 1982, however, southeast Chicago was devastated by layoffs in the steel industry. The layoffs were not simply caused by the importation of heavily subsidized, and therefore cheaper, foreign steel. Huge federal deficits and a tight money policy at the Federal Reserve, the nation's central bank, caused interest rates to soar in the United States, making it expensive for American steelmakers to modernize. In addition, foreign investors were attracted to the high interest rates, causing the value of the American dollar to rise. Since each dollar was now worth more Japanese yen or German marks, U.S. steel became even more expensive abroad, and imported steel became even cheaper. Within a few years, more than half of the work force of southeast Chicago had been laid off, leaving a community devastated and demoralized.[1]

The economic forces that swept through southeast Chicago in the 1980s illustrate how government policies can affect lives. It is not surprising that voters view economic policies as important political issues. With the exception of periods of international crisis, Gallup polls have shown that Americans almost always identify an economic issue as "the most important problem facing the country." Voters hold incumbent presidents responsible for bad economic times. Just ask Jimmy Carter and George Bush.

There are many different ways to view economic policy, including conservative, libertarian, liberal, and Marxist. This chapter looks at economic policy through the lens of the democratic debate. Specifically, the chapter examines how elite and popular democrats have viewed the market system. Even though there is a broad consensus that the federal government has responsibility for the economy, there is deep disagreement between elite and popular democrats about how this responsibility should be carried out.

ECONOMIC POLICY AND THE DEMOCRATIC DEBATE

Elite democrats look at the economy through the lens of market economics, which views the economy as a mechanism, like a watch, in which all the gears operate in complex, yet predictable ways. Left alone, the market mechanism functions smoothly to maximize consumer satisfaction and corporate profits. The result is maximum expansion of wealth and the efficient allocation of goods and services.

The purpose, then, of government policies is not to intervene into the market mechanism but to ensure its smooth functioning. Policies that provide the conditions for smoothly functioning markets are called *macroeconomic* policies. These policies are designed to fine-tune the national economy as a whole but not to alter the distribution of economic activity across different sectors, classes, or places. Elite democrats, however, often disagree about macroeconomic policy. Some favor **fiscal policy,** using the government's taxing and spending policies to fine-tune the economy, while others favor **monetary policy,** controlling the money supply. But both sides agree that economic policy should confine itself to establishing the general conditions for markets to do their job.

The elite democratic view implies that primary responsibility for economic policy should be placed in the hands of economic experts, with only broad guidelines coming from ordinary citizens and their political representatives. Market economics claims to be, like physics, a value-free and objective science that understands how all the complex gears in the market mechanism are inter-related. Like expert watchmakers, economic experts know what needs to be done to insure that the mechanism runs smoothly. Economic policies do not involve political choices that determine winners and losers but simply attempt to set the general conditions that enable people and businesses to compete fairly in the marketplace.

The market view of the economy is consistent with the elite democratic view of human nature—that common people are basically motivated by material interests and are not well suited to engage in economic decision-making. According to this view, there is a built-in tradeoff between equality and efficiency. Too much equality lowers the incentive to work and invest, thereby damaging efficiency. Politicians, if too involved in economic policymaking, may use economic policies to redistribute wealth and thus promote their own re-election prospects. This ultimately will lower economic growth and hurt everyone, even the poor. Economic policymaking should therefore be left to the experts. Political representatives have a valid role to play, elite democrats admit, in choosing policies to address the inequalities and social problems created by a growing capitalist economy. But social policies should follow after economic policies and should interfere as little as possible with the operation of markets.

Instead of viewing the economy as a mechanism, popular democrats view it more as a plant with its roots deeply embedded in social and political relations. The mechanistic treatment of the economy, they say, ignores the human factor. Economies are not giant mechanisms that operate apart from political relations. The latter, in the form of tax policies, for example, greatly determine which investments are profitable and which are not. At the same time, economic trends shape the life chances of different groups in the population, the viability of whole communities, and, most important, the prospects for democratic participation and community control.

Popular democrats argue that people have a natural desire to participate in the decisions that affect their lives. Popular democrats do not believe that there is an unavoidable tradeoff between equality and growth. In fact, too much inequality can hurt growth by demoralizing those at the bottom and undermining the belief that anybody can get ahead through hard work. Too much inequality also causes social problems that ultimately all of us pay for.

The popular democratic view implies that power over economic policy should be largely taken away from so-called experts and given to ordinary citizens and their political representatives. The tradeoffs of economic policy should be debated in an open, democratic fashion—not hidden behind the veil of economic "science." Popular democrats do not believe that expanding democracy into economic policymaking will lead to incoherent policies that will undermine the economy. On the contrary, they argue, it is the isolation of economic policy in the hands of experts, who are removed from the pain caused by their policies, that results in destructive economic policies. More democratic economic policymaking would be better economic policymaking. Finally, popular democrats argue that economic policy should aim not only to maximize economic growth, but improve the quality of life for all citizens and enhance the prospects for a more democratic society.

In short, elite and popular democrats view economic policy very differently. The rest of the chapter examines elite and popular democratic policy prescriptions for the economy, focusing on the period since 1970, when the postwar prosperity came to an end and the American economy encountered new economic problems that sparked vigorous policy debates.

THE POSTWAR AMERICAN ECONOMY: FROM PROSPERITY TO STAGFLATION

The period from World War II until about 1970 was the golden age of American capitalism. The United States came out of the war with its productive capacity intact, while its competitors, especially Germany and Japan, were severely damaged. The United States maintained a trade surplus throughout this period, which contributed to the prosperity of American workers. As Figure 17.1 shows, the average weekly earnings of private production workers, controlled for infla-

FIGURE 17.1

Private-Production Workers' Average Weekly Earnings, 1947–1989 (in 1982 Dollars)

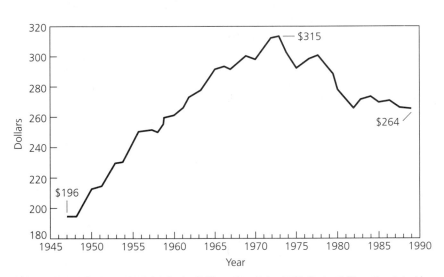

Source: From BOILING POINT by Kevin Phillips. Copyright 1991 Kevin Phillips. Reprinted by permission of Random House, Inc.

tion, increased steadily from 1947 until the early 1970s, when it began a long downward slide. Since 1970, most families have been able to maintain their incomes, but only by having two adult wage earners. Women, even those with young children, have entered the work force in increasing numbers.

In the 1970s, the United States also began to suffer from rising inflation and unemployment. Whereas both had remained low through the 1960s (see Figure 17.2), both began to soar in the 1970s. Inflation reached a peak of 13.5 percent in 1980, and unemployment reached 9.7 percent in 1982. Until the 1970s, however, economists had treated inflation and unemployment as tradeoffs: inflation, they believed, could be tamed by allowing unemployment to rise, and low unemployment would create inflationary pressures. But this belief proved untrue in the 1970s with the simultaneous increase in inflation and unemployment. Economists invented a new term for this unfortunate state of affairs: **stagflation.** Even though inflation appears to have been brought under control in the 1990s, the experience of double-digit inflation in the 1970s still haunts policymakers. Meanwhile, Americans have grown accustomed to such high levels

FIGURE 17.2

Inflation and Unemployment Rates, 1951–1992

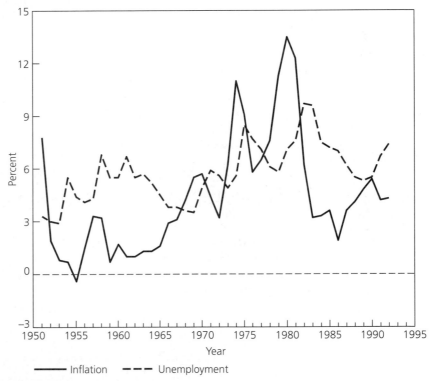

Based on Consumer Price Index for all items.

Source: Harold W. Stanley and Richard G. Niemi, *Vital Statistics on American Politics,* 4th ed. (Washington, D.C.: Congressional Quarterly, 1994), Tables 13-2 and 13-9.

of unemployment that economists have shifted their definition of "full employment" from 3 or 4 to 6 percent unemployment or even higher.

Another indicator of economic troubles is the emergence of a trade deficit. In 1971 the United States experienced its first merchandise trade deficit in this century. This meant that the United States bought more goods from other countries than it sold abroad (Figure 17.3). In industry after industry foreign imports penetrated American markets, causing rapid declines in U.S. industrial employment. Between 1970 and 1980, for example, the foreign share of the U.S. auto market jumped from 8 percent to 20 percent; in consumer electronics, from 10 to 50 percent.[2] Foreign brands such as Toyota, Nissan, and Sony have become well known to American consumers. After 1985, however, the U.S. share of world merchandise exports began to rise again, reaching almost 14 percent in 1993.[3] Also, the U.S. trade deficit is not as large as the figures suggest because they do not include trade in services, in which the United States has a large surplus.

To pay for rising foreign imports, the United States had to borrow heavily from abroad. As a result, in a few short years the United States went from being the world's largest creditor nation (foreigners owed us more than we owed them) to being the world's largest debtor nation. In 1981, U.S. net foreign investment (assets over debts) had reached a peak of $141 billion. Within four short years, sixty years of American overseas investment were undone. By 1985, foreign investment in the United States exceeded American investment abroad by $112 billion; by 1989, Americans as a whole were about $650 billion in the red.[4] In the short run, foreign investment in the U.S. economy is a good thing, boosting employment and production. In the long run, however, the United States will

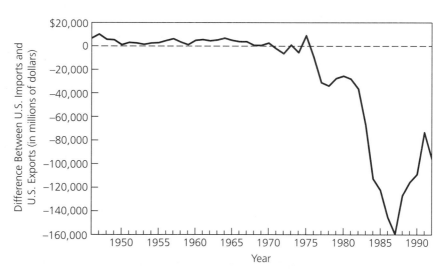

FIGURE 17.3

U.S. Balance of Trade, 1946–1992 (in Millions)

Source: Compiled by Harold W. Stanley and Richard G. Niemi, *Vital Statistics on American Politics,* 4th ed. (Washington, D.C.: Congressional Quarterly, 1994), p. 370.

be required to send abroad a stream of interest payments that will drain resources, potentially compromising national sovereignty.

Macroeconomic Policy: The Rise and Fall of Keynesianism

Capitalist economies have always been subject to ups and downs; periods of sustained growth and prosperity are invariably followed by periods of economic contraction and rising unemployment. What set apart the Great Depression from earlier economic downturns was its severity and its combination of an economic contraction and a financial panic, which was triggered by the stock market crash of 1929. Until then, most Americans assumed that there was little that could be done about the business cycle. The New Deal, however, tried to bring the country out of the Depression and reduce the human suffering caused by it. But in fact it was not until the government began borrowing and spending heavily to prepare for World War II that the unemployment rate fell to predepression levels and even lower.

The idea of using deficit spending (having the government spend more than it receives in tax revenues) to pull the economy out of a depression was promoted by English economist John Maynard Keynes (1883–1946). His classic work, *The General Theory of Employment, Interest, and Money* (1936), argued that capitalist economies do *not* have a natural tendency to employ all the nation's workers and achieve full productive capacity because consumers cannot buy all the products that a fully operating economy would produce. At a certain stage of the business cycle, Keynes argued, the savings rate is too high, and there is too little money left over for consumption. Keynes's solution is for the government to use fiscal policy, its control over taxing and spending, to make the economy perform at maximum capacity. When the economy begins to fall into a recession, the government stimulates consumer demand by spending more than it takes in through taxes. Deficit spending heats up the economy, putting people and productive capacity back to work. When demand is too high and an overheated economy begins to cause inflation, the government deliberately spends less than it takes in, cooling off the economy. Thus, Keynes did not endorse having a string of budget deficits, even in prosperous times, such as the United States has had in recent years.

Keynesianism dominated economic policymaking in the major industrial countries after World War II. Although Keynes's theory encouraged governments to take an active role in smoothing out the business cycle, it did not require any direct interventions in markets. Keynes argued that capitalist markets do a good job of allocating the resources they use; the problem is insufficient consumer demand, resulting in too much unemployment and unused productive capacity.

Keynes called for manipulating the overall level of consumer demand, but he said nothing about how that consumer demand should be distributed. Thus, Keynesianism was a theory that could be embraced at various times by both elite and popular democrats. European governments used Keynes to justify redistributing wealth through the welfare state and progressive taxes, a scheme based partly on the notion that giving more resources to those at the bottom would result in immediate increases in consumer demand because poor people save little. In the United States, Keynesianism was applied in a less egalitarian manner, justifying what has been called "military Keynesianism" and "business Keynesianism." Deficits were created by boosting military spending and by cutting taxes on business. The Kennedy tax cuts for investors, passed in 1964, were sold to the public, Congress, and the business community on explicitly Keynesian grounds. With the economy doing well in the 1960s, there was a broad consensus behind Keynesianism and an optimistic feeling that fiscal policy could be used to fine-tune the economy to prevent disastrous economic downturns. In a 1971 *Newsweek* cover story, President Nixon proclaimed, "We are all Keynesians now."

Reaganomics: The Supply-Side Experiment

With the economic troubles of the 1970s, the Keynesian consensus began to crumble. The problems of the U.S. economy did not appear to be the result of too much saving. Indeed, the savings rate was tumbling, and the soaring trade deficit seemed to be caused in part by inadequate savings and investment in the latest production technologies. For the first time, increases in the productivity of American workers lagged behind those of other countries. The problem seemed to lie not in underconsumption but in underinvestment.

Many economists began to move from a demand-side explanation of these economic troubles to a supply-side analysis. *Supply-side economics* argued that the cause of the economic problems was a capital shortage. We need to reduce consumption and put more of our resources into productive investment. Supply-siders especially stressed that we were consuming too much in the way of government services and that a bloated public sector was serving as a drag on economic growth. High levels of taxation reduced the incentive to work harder and to invest, and government regulations on the economy stifled private initiative. Ronald Reagan, a strong supporter of supply-side economics, was fond of telling the story that when the marginal income tax rate hit 94 percent during World War II, he stopped making movies.

Paradoxically, supply-siders stressed that the best way to reduce the federal deficit was to *reduce* taxes, not increase them. This idea was based on the **Laffer Curve,** which enterprising young economist Arthur B. Laffer first drew in 1974 on a cocktail napkin in a Washington restaurant (see Figure 17.4). Laffer argued that above a certain point increasing tax rates actually decreased total tax revenues because of the disincentive effects on productive effort. Tax rates were so high in the United States, Laffer argued, that by decreasing tax rates, the country could move down the Laffer Curve, unleashing an explosion of productive effort that would increase tax revenues. Laffer's ideas were popularized by Jude Wanniski, an editorial writer for the *Wall Street Journal.* Wanniski later remarked

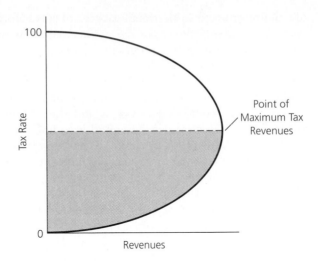

FIGURE 17.4

Laffer Curve

As the tax rate increases tax revenues eventually fall because of the disincentive effects of high taxes.

Source: Alfred L. Malabre, Jr., *Lost Prophets: An Insider's History of the Modern Economists* (Boston, Mass.: Harvard Business School Press, 1994), p. 181.

that, after seeing the Laffer Curve on the cocktail napkin, "it hit me as a wonderful propaganda device" for persuading policymakers to cut tax rates.[5]

As a candidate for president in 1980, Ronald Reagan enthusiastically embraced the tenets of supply-side economics. (One of his opponents in the Republican primaries, George Bush, ridiculed the supply-side approach as "voodoo economics.") Four weeks after his inauguration, Reagan presented Congress with *A Program for Economic Recovery*, which contained four key elements:

1. Cutting the growth of federal spending

2. Reducing personal income rates by 10 percent over three years and cutting the tax rate on capital investments in plant and equipment

3. Slashing government regulation of the economy

4. In cooperation with the Federal Reserve, limiting the growth of the money supply to control inflation and restore faith in the financial markets[6]

Inspired by supply-side economics, Reagan succeeded in enacting massive tax cuts in his **Economic Recovery Tax Act of 1981.** Individual tax rates were cut 23 percent over a three-year period, the marginal tax rate on the highest income group was cut from 70 percent to 50 percent, and a series of tax breaks for investors was written into law.

Reagan also enacted significant budget cuts during his first year in office. Following a shrewd political strategy, he succeeded in persuading each house of Congress to vote on an overall package of cuts before voting on the individual cuts. Since surveys show that the public wants less total federal spending but more spending on specific programs, by first requiring a vote on a total budget ceiling, Reagan succeeded in getting a favorable vote, thereby postponing the tough choices on where to cut until later. After 1981, however, the Reagan administration was not nearly so successful at enacting its program, as the Democratically controlled Congress and the administration bogged down in political trench warfare over taxes and spending.

How successful was Reaganomics? Its biggest success was in reducing the inflation rate, which tumbled from 13.5 percent in 1980 to 1.9 percent in 1986. Much of this is credited to the tight money policies of the Federal Reserve, which we examine later in the chapter.

The effort to decrease the federal budget deficit by reducing taxes clearly failed. Shortly after taking office, Reagan promised that his economic policies would balance the budget by 1984, but lower tax revenues combined with significant increases in defense spending resulted in the largest budget deficits in history. Ironically, the Reagan administration, which was officially opposed to Keynesianism, engaged in massive deficit spending that pulled the country out of the 1982 recession. When the economy heated up, however, the government did not generate budget surpluses, as Keynes had recommended, but continued massive deficit spending (Figure 17.5). Most economists believed that the United States was not so far out on the Laffer Curve that reducing tax rates would increase total revenue. (Indeed, as we saw in Chapter 4, in proportion

FIGURE 17.5

Federal Budget Surpluses and Deficits, 1950–1992 (in Billions)

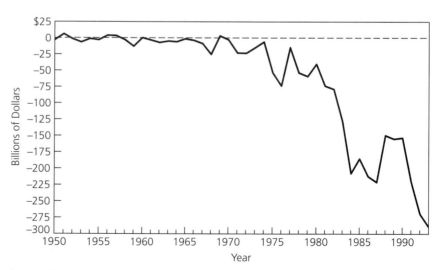

Source: Economic Report of the President (Transmitted to Congress February 1991) (Washington, D.C.: GPO, 1991); and U.S. Bureau of the Census, *Statistical Abstract of the United States 1993* (Washington, D.C.: GPO, 1993), p. 328.

A large crowd demonstrates in Washington, D.C., against the Reagan cuts (August 31, 1983).

to the overall economy, taxes in the United States are significantly lower than taxes in almost every other advanced industrial country.) The massive deficits of the 1980s helped sustain the second longest period of continuous peacetime expansion since World War II. But this prosperity was bought at a high price: a huge cumulative deficit ($3.3 trillion by 1990) that future generations of taxpayers will be required to pay back.

There is little evidence that the supply-side tax cuts significantly increased work effort, the savings rate, or investment.[7] In fact, the savings rate fell from an average of about 7 percent of income in the 1970s to only 2 percent in the 1980s.[8] Moreover, to finance the huge deficits, the federal government had to borrow hundreds of billions of dollars that otherwise could have gone into productive investment.

Defenders of supply-side economics argue that it was never given a fair chance. If the budget cuts Reagan asked for had been enacted by Congress, they argue, the deficit would have been much lower and productive investment higher. Certainly, Congress was partly to blame for the soaring budget deficits, but the amount of *discretionary spending* that Congress has the power to control is relatively small. About three-fourths of the budget is tied down by past commitments that politically and sometimes legally cannot be changed. Social Security payments, for example, are guaranteed by law. When Reagan cut taxes and increased the military budget, one of the few areas of discretionary spending, rising budget deficits were easy to predict.

Reagan did not succeed in cutting federal government spending, but he did succeed in cutting the rate of growth of spending. In the beginning, Director of the Budget David Stockman expressed the hope that "weak claims rather than weak clients" would be the targets of federal spending cuts. After the first-year budget was completed, Stockman admitted in private that the "claim of equity in shrinking the government was significantly compromised if not obliterated."[9] Middle-class entitlements were protected, while most of the cuts fell on low-income groups, especially the working poor. Funding for low-income housing programs, for example, fell from $30 billion in 1981 to $10 billion in 1986. Public-service jobs for the poor were eliminated, and federal grants to central cities, community development, schools serving low-income students, and social services for the poor were cut. By tightening eligibility standards for many social benefits, many working poor were excluded from government benefits. States and localities made up some, but by no means all, of these cuts. Even more than the spending cuts, however, it was the unequal impact of the tax changes that increased income inequalities in the 1980s.

THE DEMOCRATIC DEBATE OVER TAXES

The democratic debate over taxes pits the popular democratic belief in equality against the elite democratic faith in economic growth and investment. Popular democrats generally favor **progressive taxes,** defined as taxes that take a higher proportion of income as a person moves up the income ladder. (A **regressive tax,** then, is just the opposite: one where a wealthy person pays a smaller percentage of income than someone from the middle or poorer classes.) Elite democrats oppose using the tax system to redistribute wealth. By weakening incentives to work extra hard and to invest, elite democrats argue, progressive taxes choke off economic growth.

Until the twentieth century, the federal government was relatively small and was funded entirely through tariffs on imported goods and excise taxes on products like liquor and tobacco. Both sources of revenue were regressive, with the burden falling on ordinary consumers in the form of higher prices. In the late nineteenth century, the Populists called for a tax on incomes to curtail the great fortunes that had been accumulated by "Robber Barons" during the industrial period and to fund government on the basis of "ability to pay." The People's party platform for president in 1892 called for a graduated (progressive) income tax, a radical idea for its time. In 1895, however, the Supreme Court declared the income tax unconstitutional.[10] It was not until 1913 that the Sixteenth Amendment to the U.S. Constitution was approved, authorizing the imposition of a tax on incomes. Realizing its redistributive potential, elite democrats vigorously opposed an income tax, calling it on the Senate floor "socialism, communism, and devilism."[11] The income tax passed anyway. Over the years, it was gradually expanded until now it is the largest source of revenue for the federal government (Figure 17.6).

The fear of economic elites that the income tax would be used to redistribute wealth turned out to be exaggerated. Although no legal obstacle prevents low- and middle-income voters, who constitute a clear majority of the electorate, from using the income tax to radically redistribute wealth, in practice this has not happened. Public opinion on taxes is easily manipulated because the tax system has been made so technically complex. Most Americans do not understand concepts like accelerated depreciation or the oil depletion allowance. When they see high rates on the wealthy, they think the tax system is progressive.

The income tax rate on the wealthy has varied tremendously in the twentieth century (Figure 17.7). For many years, the top individual rate was quite high, reaching a maximum of 94 percent during World War II. The income tax appeared to be steeply progressive, making the rich pay higher rates. This was not true. Various deductions, exemptions, and exclusions enabled the wealthy to shelter large parts of their income from taxation so that the effective tax rate was much lower. Essentially, income tax politics in the twentieth century became

FIGURE 17.6   **Percentage Composition of Federal Government Receipts**

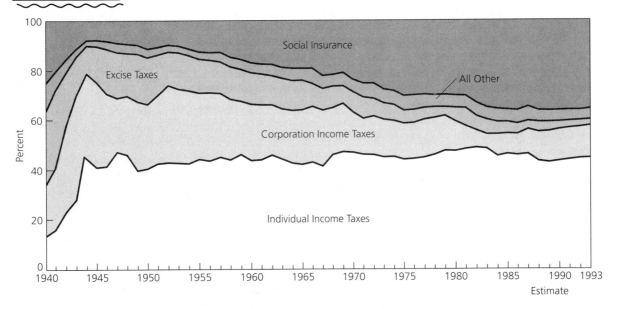

Source: Executive Office of the President, Office of Management and Budget, Historical Tables, *Budget of the United States Government, Fiscal Year 1989* (Washington, D.C.: U.S. Government Printing Office, 1989).

| FIGURE 17.7 | **Ups and Downs of Federal Taxes on Income** |

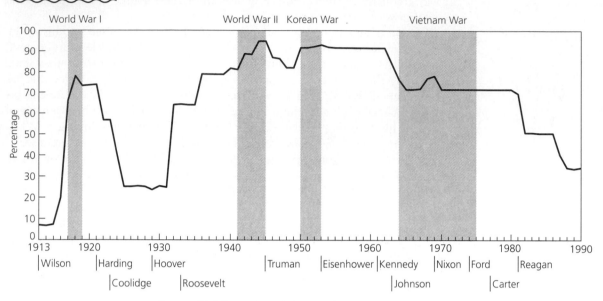

Source: Wall Street Journal, August 18, 1986.

a compromise between those who favored high marginal rates and those who favored generous exemptions.

Tax Expenditures: Hidden Inequalities

The technical complexity and low visibility of tax exemptions, or *tax expenditures,* have caused them to be misunderstood by most Americans. The tax expenditure concept highlights the fact that tax exemptions are essentially the same as spending programs. The government can either exempt certain income from taxes, or it can tax all income and write a check to the recipient for the value of the exemption. Either way the government is spending resources to subsidize certain taxpayers. Examples of tax expenditures are deductions on federal taxes for investing in new plants and equipment or for building low-income housing. In an effort to subject tax expenditures to public scrutiny, the Treasury Department in 1968 published the first budget for the United States that included tax expenditures. The Congressional Budget Act of 1974 made the concept of tax expenditures an integral part of the budget process.

The growth of tax expenditures has been astounding, far outpacing the growth of normal spending programs. Tax expenditures soared from $36.6 billion in 1967 to $253.5 billion in 1982, rising from 20.5 percent of federal outlays to 34.6 percent.[12] In 1994 tax expenditures totalled an estimated $478 billion.[13]

Tax expenditures go overwhelmingly to wealthy households. A Treasury Department study for 1977 found that the top 1.4 percent of taxpayers received 31.3 percent of the benefits delivered through tax expenditures. Those with incomes above $200,000 received an average tax subsidy of $535,653. At the same time that Congress debated the merits of the welfare state and cut most programs for the poor, tax expenditures for the middle class and upper classes, what one author called "fiscal welfare," soared. Between 1980 and 1986, for example, when federal spending on low-income housing fell, tax expenditures for the deductibility of mortgage interest on private homes increased from $16 billion to $30 billion.[14] In 1981, 85 percent of the homeowners making less than $15,000 received no benefits, while most wealthy homeowners took advantage of the tax expenditure at an average saving of about $4,500 per homeowner.[15]

Even though tax expenditures are expensive, they have distinct political advantages over conventional spending programs. First, they are buried in the tax code and therefore have low political visibility. Second, once enacted they do not need to be approved each year like conventional spending programs. Third, there are no congressional committees with oversight responsibilities for tax expenditures, and hearings are rarely held to scrutinize their effectiveness—as happens for spending programs.

Even when the top federal income tax rates were very high, overall the system was only mildly progressive, if at all, because of tax exemptions for the wealthy. Most scholars agree that state and local taxes are regressive because they are based not on income tax but on sales and property taxes. Needless to say, it is very difficult to calculate the overall effect of all taxes at all levels of government on the distribution of income. One major study concluded that through 1985, "the U.S. tax system [including all levels of government] is either moderately progressive or slightly regressive," depending on how the effects of corporate taxes are calculated.[16] (The question is whether companies pass on corporate taxes to consumers in the form of higher prices or whether the taxes are borne by the owners of the corporation.) If we assume that corporate taxes are regressive, then most Americans pay the same effective tax rate—with the exception of the poor, who pay *higher* rates, and the rich, who pay *lower* rates!

Taxes in the 1980s: Increased Regressivity

In the 1980s, the tax system became more regressive. There were three main causes of increased regressivity: (1) increases in payroll taxes, (2) a shift of government functions from the federal government to state and local governments, and (3) the effects of tax reform.

Payroll Taxes. Payroll taxes, like the Social Security tax, are highly regressive because they are levied at a fixed rate and then phased out for higher-income earners. Under the 1990 Social Security tax, earnings above $51,300 were not taxable. Regressive social insurance taxes as a proportion of federal taxes have grown significantly (see Figure 17.6), making the overall tax system more regressive.

A Shifting of Government Functions. In the 1980s, President Reagan shifted functions from the federal government to state and local governments. By cutting funding for federal programs, Reagan put pressure on state and local governments to fill the gaps. In 1982, regressive state and local tax revenues were less than the amount brought in by the weakly progressive federal income tax. By 1990, state and local tax revenues far exceeded revenue from the federal income tax. State and local governments, often facing determined tax revolts, became desperate for revenues to pay for their new responsibilities. The states instituted all sorts of new fundraising schemes, most of them regressive. (Wisconsin tried, unsuccessfully, to tax drinks on airplanes passing over the state!) State lotteries became a common way to raise revenues without raising taxes. By 1993, 37 states had lotteries, up from none in 1964.[17] The income from lotteries is notoriously regressive, coming mostly from lower-income families. Citizens are now charged user fees for such things as having garbage collected or using a park. As a percentage of income, user fees fall most heavily on low-income families.[18]

Tax Reform. Fueled by a public revulsion against tax expenditures, or loopholes, as they came to be known, the Tax Reform Act of 1986 was the most sweeping change of the income tax in America's history. Until then, the political logic of tax politics had been high marginal rates for the wealthy in exchange for large exemptions. In the 1980s, however, media exposure of the abuses of tax exemptions coupled with the feeling that tax rates were too high forced a reversal of the normal political logic. President Reagan and supply-siders like Jack Kemp supported reform as a way of reducing tax rates, while liberals like Senator Bill Bradley (D—New Jersey) supported reform as a way of closing tax loopholes for the wealthy. Industries with attractive loopholes lobbied furiously to protect their special treatment, but for once the idea of tax reform triumphed over narrow political interests in Congress.

The 1986 Tax Reform Act was hailed as a victory for progressive change (Table 17.1). On the positive side, it did cut many working poor off the tax rolls.

TABLE 17.1

Major Provisions of the 1986 Tax Reform Act

For individuals:
1. Replaced more than a dozen tax brackets with two basic brackets, 15 and 28 percent. (Previously, the highest bracket had been 50 percent.)
2. Eliminated tax exemptions for interest on consumer loans, sales taxes, and contributions to individual retirement accounts (IRAs) and the tax preferences for capital gains (increases in the value of property or stocks).

For corporations:
1. Cut the top tax rate from 46 percent to 34 percent.
2. Repealed the investment tax credit, stipulated that only 80 percent of business meals and entertainment could be deducted, and limited various other tax loopholes, such as such tax credits for research and development.

But although tax reform helped the working poor and did away with some unfair loopholes in the tax system, overall it did not make the federal income tax more progressive. Three years after tax reform, families making less than $10,000 saved an average of $37 on their taxes, while those making over $1 million saved on average $281,033 on their taxes.[19] This hardly represents progressive change.

In the 1990s, popular reaction against regressive taxes began to make itself heard in the political system. Bill Clinton and Ross Perot ran for president in 1992 partly on platforms of increasing taxes on the rich. In 1993, Clinton's Omnibus Budget Reconciliation Act squeaked through the House (218–216) and cleared the Senate by one vote (51–50), with Vice President Al Gore casting the tie-breaking vote. Designed mainly to cut the budget, the bill also took a step in the direction of a more progressive federal tax system by raising the federal income tax rate on the top 1.2 percent of American families. Overall, as a result of the budget deal, the Congressional Budget Office estimated that families making over $200,000 would see their federal taxes go up on average 17.4 percent, while families making less than $10,000 would enjoy an average tax cut of 14.9 percent.[20] The tax on the wealthy proved to be one of the least controversial parts of the 1993 budget deal.

THE DEMOCRATIC DEBATE OVER THE MONEY SUPPLY

The democratic debate over the money supply reached its greatest intensity in the late nineteenth century with the Populist movement. After the Civil War, the country experienced a long period of *deflation* (the opposite of inflation) in which prices fell. The wholesale price index dropped 65 percent between 1864 and 1890.[21] The main reason for the falling prices was that the money supply did not keep pace with the growth of the economy. With the same amount of dollars chasing more commodities, the dollar value of each commodity fell. Government policy was to have every dollar backed up by gold, and the supply of gold was limited.

Falling prices may sound good, but they are not good for everybody. Farmers especially found themselves squeezed between falling prices for their crops and rising interest rates for the money they had to borrow to buy land and to finance the spring planting. Most farmers were debtors, and deflation was like a tax forcing them to pay back their debts in more and more expensive dollars. Moreover, often there was simply not enough credit to go around. Creditors, on the other hand, benefitted from the deflation, because they were paid back in more and more valuable dollars. Those who make money by lending out or investing money naturally want to see the supply of money limited because this increases the price of money and they can charge higher interest rates for loans. To this day, the conflict between wealthy investors and the mass of debtors and business people needing credit remains at the heart of the democratic debate over the money supply.

In the late nineteenth century, the Populist mass movement arose in response to the crisis of small farmers and debtors. Eventually the Populist party joined with the Democratic party in 1896 to support William Jennings Bryan, who called for the minting of silver coins to expand the money supply. As we discussed in Chapter 8, William McKinley's victory over Bryan was a major defeat for popular democracy.

Ironically, shortly after Bryan's defeat, the discovery of gold in Alaska, Colorado, and South Africa increased the money supply and relieved the pressure of falling prices on farmers. The system was still beset by problems, however. Seasonal surges in the demand for agricultural credit sometimes strained the banking system, leading to financial panics, the worst coming in 1907. A congressional investigation exposed centralized control within the private banking system, and a call went out for reform. The result was the formation of the Federal Reserve in 1913. President Woodrow Wilson compromised with the bankers by creating a unique institution that combined the private powers of bankers with the public powers of government. In 1935, after criticism that contraction of the money supply had contributed to the Great Depression, the "Fed," as it is called, expanded its mission and took full charge of controlling the nation's money supply.

The *Federal Reserve* is run by a seven-member Board of Governors, including a chair, appointed by the president for fourteen-year terms with the advice and consent of the Senate. Because of the Fed chairman's (until now all have been men) leadership position setting monetary policy, which is crucial to the performance of the economy, he has been called "the second most powerful man in the United States." To carry out its policies, the Fed relies on twelve regional banks. The regional banks are private institutions owned by the approximately six thousand commercial banks that participate in the Federal Reserve system. The regional banks presidents are elected by each district's Board of Directors, which are chosen by the commercial "member banks" in each region (Figure 17.8).

The most important policymaking body at the Fed is the *Federal Open Market Committee* (FOMC), which basically determines the nation's money supply and powerfully influences interest rates. The FOMC is made up of the seven members of the Board of Governors and the presidents of five regional banks. These five seats rotate among the twelve regions, except for the New York bank, which, because of its importance, has a permanent seat. These five seats on the FOMC are not democratically accountable. The key decision-making body, then, is a mixture of private interests and public authority. As Representative Lee H. Hamilton, an Indiana Democrat, put the matter in 1991, "Nowhere else in the Government are private individuals permitted to participate in decisions which have such an enormous influence over the prosperity and well-being of millions of Americans."[22]

The Federal Reserve system appears to be technically sophisticated and complex, something only experts can understand. To ordinary citizens, it is a mystery how banks can "create" money. In fact, the basic mechanisms for controlling the money supply are quite simple. The American economy can be thought of

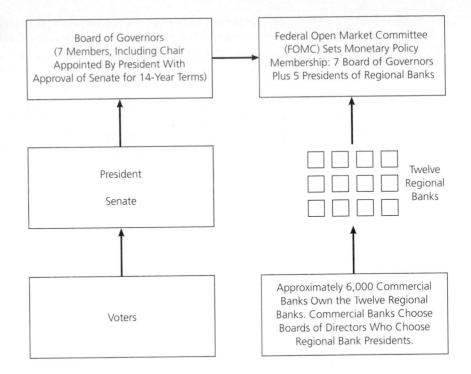

FIGURE 17.8

Governance of the Federal Reserve

as a gigantic plumbing system, with money circulating through the pipes at various rates and pressures. The Fed can be compared to a hydraulic engineer, who by turning various valves can either expand or contract the flow of money in the system.

The Fed has three basic valves for controlling the amount of money in circulation.

1. *Reserve requirements:* The Fed specifies what proportion of a bank's deposits must be held in reserve and cannot be loaned out. Increasing the reserve requirement restricts the ability of banks to make new loans, essentially reducing the money supply.

2. *The discount rate:* The banks that are members of the Federal Reserve system can borrow money from one of the twelve regional banks when they need additional reserves. The discount rate is the interest rate at which member banks can borrow. Raising the discount rate limits the expansion of reserves, thus limiting the ability of banks to make new loans. Lowering the discount rate makes it easier for banks to make new loans, thus increasing the money supply.

3. *Open-market transactions:* The Fed can buy or sell U.S. government securities, which are Treasury bonds originally sold by the U.S. government to

finance the budget deficit. When the Federal Reserve buys Treasury bonds, the money is simply credited to the accounts of the former owners of the bonds in one of the Federal Reserve banks. These funds are counted as additions to the reserves of the bank, which is now free to make more loans, increasing the money supply. Conversely, when the Fed sells Treasury bonds, it essentially shrinks the money supply. Because of their flexibility and immediate impact, open-market transactions are considered the Fed's most powerful instrument for controlling the money supply.

The democratic debate over the money supply revolves around who will control it and who will benefit and who will lose from monetary policy. The Federal Reserve system is basically run by elite democrats who argue that control over the money supply must be left in the hands of experts who understand how to protect the long-term interests of the American economy. If the money supply grows too rapidly, inflation will result, undermining the confidence of investors in the long-term value of their investments. Fearing that their returns will be eroded by inflation, potential investors turn to consumption, foreign investment, or speculation in gold or other commodities. In short, a too rapid growth in the money supply will undermine productive investment and slow the growth of the American economy, hurting everybody. If politicians controlled the money supply, elite democrats argue, they would be tempted to increase the money supply to stimulate the economy right before an election or to benefit the mass of debtors. The results would be disastrous.

According to critics like Wright Patman, a popular democratic representative from Texas from 1929 to the mid-1970s, the elites that run the Federal Reserve identify the interests of the American people with the interests of investors. But, popular democrats contend, the interests of Wall Street are different from the interests of Main Street. In fact, according to a study by the Federal Reserve itself, in 1983 the top 10 percent of American families owned 86 percent of the net financial assets. The majority of American families (55 percent) held no financial assets at all; overall, most Americans were debtors.[23] The Fed's tight money policies raise interest rates; with less money in circulation the cost of borrowing money goes up, hurting the majority of debtors. Tight money and deflation act like a regressive tax, shifting resources from debtors to creditors. The shortage of credit limits business expansion, especially hurting small businesses and farmers who depend on credit to see them through tough times. Finally, tight money damages sectors of the economy, like home and auto sales, that are dependent on the easy availability of credit.

Popular democrats do not simply recommend that the money supply and inflation be increased. Their point is that control over the money supply is a political question involving difficult tradeoffs among different interests. It should not be left in the hands of experts at the Federal Reserve, who are so remote from the pain caused by their tight money policies that they cannot make these tradeoffs intelligently. According to popular democrats, the Fed hides its political choices behind technical jargon and secret deliberations. A vice president of the

Boston regional bank once compared the Federal Reserve to a church whose priests control the mysterious workings of the money supply:

> The System is just like the Church. That's probably why I feel so comfortable with it. It's got a pope, the chairman; and a college of cardinals, the governors and bank presidents; and a curia, the senior staff. . . . We even have different orders of religious thought like Jesuits and Franciscans and Dominicans only we call them pragmatists and monetarists and neo-Keynesians.[24]

The democratic debate over the money supply was played out with special intensity in the conflicts over the shift in Federal Reserve policy beginning in the late 1970s.

The Experiment with Monetarism: Winners and Losers

In 1979, as the economy foundered, President Jimmy Carter saw his re-election chances dwindling. In July, Carter responded with a somber speech about the spiritual "malaise" of the country, which he followed with a reshuffling of his cabinet. G. William Miller left as chair of the Federal Reserve to become Treasury Secretary. Wall Street, shaken by double-digit inflation that was eroding investor confidence, watched Carter's appointment of a new chair closely, looking for signs that the Fed would get serious about fighting inflation. One of the top candidates was Paul Volcker, a fifty-one-year-old graduate of Harvard and Princeton who was well-known in Washington policy circles and Wall Street finance as a man of disciplined intellect and personal frugality. Bert Lance, a Georgia banker and personal friend of the president, warned Carter not to appoint Volcker, who, Lance predicted, would fight inflation by raising interest rates, thereby causing higher unemployment before the 1980 election. If Carter made this appointment, Lance warned, he would be "mortgaging his re-election to the Federal Reserve."[25]

Carter ignored Lance's warning and appointed Volcker. The reason was clear. As Stuart Eizenstat, the president's domestic policy adviser, put it, "Volcker was selected because he was the candidate of Wall Street. This was their price, in effect."[26]

During Volcker's tenure, the Federal Reserve came under the influence of an economic doctrine called **monetarism.** Led by Nobel Prize–winning economist Milton Friedman, monetarists argued that if the money supply grows only as fast as the productivity of the economy, the result will be steady growth and stable prices. A staunch defender of free markets, Friedman argued that government should interfere as little as possible in the economy.[27] Following an economic philosophy of small government, monetarists portrayed themselves as a conservative alternative to Keynesians, who, they charged, pushed an economic philosophy of big government.

In the fall of 1979, the Fed under Volcker's leadership officially adopted monetarism. This meant policymakers would look only at the money supply, attempting to achieve a moderate steady growth; interest rates would be allowed to fluctuate in response to the money supply targets. Using monetarist formulas, the Fed embarked on a series of swift policy shifts that sent the American economy on a roller-coaster ride. The Fed began by severely restricting the growth of the money supply, driving interest rates up to record levels, with the prime rate, the rate paid by the best commercial borrowers, peaking at 20 percent. The Fed lowered interest rates in the summer of 1980, but just before the 1980 election, the Fed drove interest rates up again.

These rising interest rates were an albatross around the neck of Jimmy Carter as he campaigned for re-election that fall. Lance's warning was coming true. In response, Carter engaged in the time-honored practice of "Fed bashing." At a town meeting in Pennsylvania, Carter expressed his frustration with the Fed:

> I don't have influence on it [the Federal Reserve], but that doesn't mean I have to sit mute. My own judgment is that the strictly monetary approach to the Fed's decision on the Discount rate and other banking policies is ill-advised. I think the Federal Reserve ought to look at other factors and balance them along with the supply of money.[28]

High interest rates were a major factor in Carter's defeat. Although the Fed abandoned monetarism a few years later, it continued its tight money policies through the 1980s, with devastating consequences for many Americans.

The Fed's policies succeeded in licking inflation. The increase in the Consumer Price Index fell from 13.5 percent in 1980 to 1.9 percent in 1986 and remained low into the 1990s. This victory was acquired at great cost, however; in the early 1980s the country suffered the worst recession since the Great Depression, with unemployment reaching 9.7 percent in 1982. Even though monetarists claimed that the costs of Fed policies were fairly distributed by free markets, in fact, the costs fell unequally on the American people.

Federal Reserve policies had a devastating effect on American industry. As foreign investors flocked to take advantage of the high interest rates in the United States, the value of the American dollar rose to new highs compared to foreign currencies. As a result, American manufactured products became more expensive for foreigners (it took more German marks or Japanese yen to buy one dollar's worth of goods), and foreign goods became cheaper in the United States. During a four-year period in the 1980s, U.S. exports declined by 16 percent, while imports surged by 66 percent.[29] The result was the soaring trade deficits and foreign debt noted earlier.

Most big businesses could generate funds internally from profits, but small businesses were much more vulnerable to high interest rates and the limited availability of credit. Bankruptcies soared. Farmers had been encouraged to go into debt by the high inflation rates before 1980. In 1979, for example, Kathy and Mike Bolin used their life savings to buy a 160-acre farm in Keokuk, Iowa. As interest rates soared and prices fell for their produce, the Bolins did everything they could to meet their loan payments, eliminating vacations and insurance, and even disconnecting the phone. There were no toys for the kids at Christmas. They failed, however, and their farm was put up for auction. "You can still pursue your dreams in America," said Kathy Bolin. "You just can't obtain them."[30] When a delegation of state legislators from thirteen distressed farm states visited Volcker in Washington, D.C., to plead for relief from high interest rates and price deflation, the Fed chair gave them a chilly response. "Look," Volcker said, "your constituents are unhappy, mine aren't."[31]

If Volcker's constituents were financial investors, they had every reason to be happy. According to Shearson Lehman, in the four years following 1981 returns on bonds averaged 18.5 percent, the most profitable era for bondholders in the twentieth century.[32] Income from capital (interest and dividends) increased dramatically compared to income from working (wages and salaries). In five short years, returns on capital nearly doubled as a proportion of total income, from 11 percent in 1979 to 20 percent in 1984.[33] Inequality soared. According to the Fed's own study, by 1989 the top 1 percent of American households possessed more wealth than the bottom 90 percent.[34]

The Issue of Fed Reform

The Federal Reserve is not a democratic institution. Although the majority of the FOMC, the committee that sets monetary policy, is appointed by the president, with fourteen-year terms, members of the Board of Governors are remarkably free from political pressure. Moreover, five of the twelve FOMC voting members represent private banks and have no democratic accountability. FOMC's deliberations are secret; only summaries of the meetings are released six weeks later. The independence and power of the Fed depend, in part, on effective political leadership by the chair of the Board of Governors.[35] But Congress and the president have always hesitated to put greater controls on the Fed for fear they will be accused of undermining the confidence of financial markets.

For fifty years prior to his death in the mid-1970s, Representative Wright Patman fought to make the Federal Reserve democratically accountable. The Fed, Patman charged, "was a dictatorship on money matters by a bankers' club."[36] In 1993, Representative Henry B. Gonzalez (D—Texas) took up Patman's cause and held hearings to bring democratic reforms to the Federal Reserve. He proposed a bill that would require the president to appoint the twelve regional bank presidents, force more timely and detailed records of the meetings, and expand opportunities for women, minorities, and nonbankers to serve as regional bank directors. Fed chair Alan Greenspan vehemently opposed the reforms, arguing that they would subject the Fed to undue political pressure.

Elite democrats argue that if Fed independence is undermined, the money supply will be manipulated by parochial political interests. Unwilling to impose the pain that is necessary to fight inflation, politicians will pressure the Fed to

boost the economy before an election, causing damaging inflation. The expert economists who run Fed policy do not have any political axes to grind; by analyzing economic trends, they can approximate monetary policies that maximize long-term economic stability.

Popular democrats respond that Fed policy involves value-laden tradeoffs that have no technical solutions. Fed policy must fairly balance different economic interests. Too often, the Fed has sacrificed unemployed workers on the altar of high interest rates. Studies show that the private bankers on the FOMC vote for tighter money more than do the presidential appointees.[37] Political representatives would listen more carefully to those hurt by tight money policies. Popular democrats point out that most countries subject their central bank to governmental control. Such control would enable coordination of monetary and fiscal policies and thereby avoid the destructiveness of the 1980s, when economic policymakers had their feet on the brake (tight money) and accelerator (massive deficit spending) at the same time.

With interest rates in 1993 at thirty-year lows, President Clinton had little reason to oppose the Fed and came out against Gonzalez's reforms, which died in committee. One thing is certain, however: The democratic debate over monetary policy will continue.

THE DEMOCRATIC DEBATE OVER INDUSTRIAL POLICY

On Friday, March 28, 1980, Steve Szumilyas went to work, as usual, at Wisconsin Steel's plant on Chicago's Southeast Side. His father had worked at the plant for forty years, and Szumilyas expected to do the same. It was a demanding, high-pressure job, but he liked the challenge. At 4:00 P.M., however, the foreman gave him the news that would shatter his life: At the end of the shift, the mill was closing; three thousand four hundred steelworkers would be out of a job.[38]

Steve Szumilyas's experience is common. An estimated thirty-two to thirty-eight million workers lost their jobs in the 1970s alone as a result of runaway shops and the closing of plants, stores, and offices.[39] The loss of industrial jobs became so widespread that a new term for it was coined: *deindustrialization*. The problem was not just that workers were losing jobs in manufacturing but also that the new jobs they found, usually in the service sector, paid much lower wages. After long stretches of unemployment, for example, Steve Szumilyas was only able to find a job driving a laundry truck at half his former wages. Deindustrialization became so widespread that it spawned a new school of popular music, "Heartland Rock." Bruce Springsteen's "Johnny 99," Bob Seeger's "Makin' Thunderbirds," and Billy Joel's "Allentown" all expressed the pain of deindustrialization. John Cougar Mellencamp's "Lonesome Jubilee" album is full of laid-off factory workers who take part-time jobs in drive-ins or write anguished "Dear Mr. President" letters.

Until now, this chapter has dealt solely with macroeconomic fiscal and monetary policies that address the general conditions that are necessary for markets to operate effectively. The problem of deindustrialization, however, raises the issue of *microeconomic* policies and industrial planning: Should the government intervene in markets to influence the allocation of resources among different industries, occupations, or regions of the country? For example, should the U.S. government have an industrial policy to revive the American steel industry?

Elite democrats are divided about industrial policy between what Kenneth Dolbeare calls "cowboy capitalists" and "Yankee capitalists."[40] Both agree that the basic source of the lackluster performance of the American economy since the 1970s is inadequate capital investment. The solution, then, is to cut consumption so that the country can invest more in productive capital. But cowboys and Yankee capitalists disagree on who should control the expanded sources of investment: private corporate elites or government elites?

Popular democrats disagree with both cowboy capitalists and Yankee capitalists. They argue that the basic problem is not a shortage of capital but waste in a corporate elite–dominated economy. Putting more power into the hands of workers, consumers, and communities, popular democrats maintain, would lead to solutions that do not require sacrifice by ordinary citizens. Far from being a threat to the economy, democratization is a key to economic revitalization.

The Case for Industrial Planning

According to free-market doctrine, deindustrialization is a painful but necessary process for adapting the American economy to the new global economy. Manufacturing jobs flee to places where it is cheaper to produce, especially Third World countries with low wages. In the meantime, however, more jobs are created in service industries in the United States. Overall, the process leads to greater productive efficiency and lower prices for American consumers. Any industrial policy that interferes with capital mobility will slow down this process of beneficial change and end up subsidizing economic dinosaurs that cannot compete in the new global economy.

In making the case for industrial policy, advocates stress that deindustrialization imposes tremendous economic and social costs. Whole cities, like Flint, Michigan, and Youngstown, Ohio, have been devastated by plant closures, resulting in a tragic waste of human resources. Displaced workers have a suicide rate thirty times greater than average and suffer from higher rates of divorce, violent crime, child and spouse abuse, mental illness, and deaths from cardiovascular disease and cirrhosis of the liver. The layoffs of fifteen thousand steelworkers from 1979 to 1983 cost governments $444 million in lost tax revenues and $163 million in unemployment insurance and food stamps.[41] By taking social costs into account (something private corporations do not do), industrial planning could make decisions that make more sense for society as a whole.

Advocates of industrial planning point out that the free market of cowboy capitalism is a myth. We already have industrial policies; we just don't call them that. Government policies have had a tremendous impact on deindustrialization. Many other federal policies in addition to the Fed's tight money policies have speeded up deindustrialization. Accelerated depreciation of industrial investments, providing a tax break on federal corporate taxes for new factories, rendered older factories less attractive and accelerated the flight of investment out of the Northeast to the Sunbelt and overseas. By enabling corporations to credit foreign taxes against domestic tax liabilities, the U.S. tax code subsidized the flight of industrial jobs overseas.

Advocates of industrial planning also point to the Pentagon as further evidence that the free market is a myth. By sheltering major sectors of industry from market competition, the Pentagon in effect has practiced industrial planning. The massive build-up of military spending in the 1980s led to the creation of sheltered industrial sectors. Firms in the so-called ACE industries (aerospace, communications, and electronics) enjoyed government subsidies for research and development of high technology and guaranteed buyers for their products. The aerospace industry, for example, received $15 billion in federal research and development contracts in 1989, compared to only $21 million for the steel industry.[42] Not surprisingly, the ACE industries showed significant trade surpluses at the same time that basic industries, like steel, starved of government support, lost out in the global marketplace. Advocates of industrial planning point to the end of the Cold War as a window of opportunity to shift resources to a more broad-based industrial policy that can revitalize American industry, generating more American jobs per dollar invested than money spent on the military.

In short, for advocates of industrial planning, the question is not whether the United States should have an industrial policy. It already has one. The question is whether it will be piecemeal or coordinated, run by elites or democratic. Even though advocates agree that the government must intervene more directly, they are divided between popular and elite democratic approaches.

Yankee Capitalism: Top-Down Planning

Elite democratic industrial planning goes all the way back to Alexander Hamilton's *Report on Manufactures* (1791), which called for subsidies and tariffs to support fledgling industries in the new country. Hamilton recognized the limits of the market: "Capital is wayward and timid in lending itself to new undertakings, and the State ought to excite the confidence of capitalists, who are ever cautious and sagacious, by aiding them to overcome the obstacles that lie in the way of all experiments."[43]

The basic idea behind elite democratic industrial planning is that government should not contradict the market but instead should help it operate smoothly and rapidly. In the present period, this means that government should promote the movement of capital and workers from "sunset" to "sunrise" industries.[44] The former are industries, like steel, where demand for the product is declining and automated systems of production limit job growth. The latter are industries, like computer software, that are on the cutting edge of technology and are enjoying rapid growth in demand for their product. Elite industrial planners emphasize the need to promote high-tech industries with substantial export potential. Those within the Democratic party who support high-tech industrial planning are often called Atari Democrats.

The big question for elite industrial planning is, Who should do it and in what institutional context? In response to the free-market criticism that industrial planning will be held hostage to special interests and pork-barrel politics, elite democrats recommend placing industrial policy in special institutions outside the political process, controlled by economic experts. Since the goal of industrial policy is to aid the market, not direct it, this is a job best done by technocratic planners, not politicians. Deciding which industries to subsidize is a matter best left to experts who understand changing technologies and consumer tastes. If members of Congress get involved in making industrial policy, elite democrats argue, they will tend to support declining industries in their districts instead of aiding sunrise industries.

Elite industrial planning calls for a partnership among business, government, and labor that will end their adversarial relationship. In most forms of top-down industrial planning, however, government and labor are clearly junior partners. A good example of elite democratic industrial planning is SEMATECH, a government-sponsored consortium of American chip makers, headquartered in Austin, Texas, that is designed to prevent Japan from taking over the markets for sophisticated computer chips.

During the 1992 campaign, Clinton campaigned vigorously for an industrial policy, calling for government support for high-speed trains, vertical liftoff aircraft, automated highways, and a new national information network linked by fiber optic cables. By appointing two strong advocates of industrial planning, Laura Tyson as chair of the Council of Economic Advisers and Robert Reich as Labor Secretary, Clinton seemed prepared to make a big push for industrial planning. Faced with a huge budget deficit, however, Clinton backed off and proposed only limited support for industrial planning. Instead of identifying sunrise industries and aggressively supporting them, Clinton called for modest increases in research and development funds for high-tech transportation infrastructure, information superhighways, and manufacturing technology.

The Popular Democratic Response: Bottom-Up Planning

Popular democrats reject the elite democratic approach to industrial policy, with its diagnosis that the cause of the problem is a capital shortage and that the purpose of planning should be to reinforce market mechanisms. Popular democratic economists argue that the social and political implications of economic policy must be taken into account.[45] The goal of industrial planning, therefore, should be not only greater economic growth but also the enhancement of democracy. The first principle of popular democratic industrial policy, thus, is to break down the wall between economics and politics and extend democratic decision-making into the economy.

Democratic decision-making is not just a luxury, popular democrats argue, but is also the key to solving our economic problems. The weaknesses of the American economy stem primarily not from a capital shortage but from the waste generated by corporate elites trying to hang onto power. American companies are top heavy with highly-paid executives who are unwilling to give up control—even to achieve greater efficiency. Labor-management conflict saps productive energy. Workers feel alienated from the corporation. Sensing that the corporation has no loyalty to them, as evidenced by plant closings and layoffs, workers reduce their work effort, steal from the company, and suffer from drug and alcohol problems. Consider what Steve Szumilya, the steelworker mentioned earlier, said shortly after he was laid off, "I'll never give another company what I gave them [Wisconsin Steel]. I try my darnedest, don't get me wrong, but then again, if I can get away with anything, I do it. I don't care about a company no more. They made me feel that way."[46] Management often responds to dissatisfied employees not by drawing workers into decision-making but by hiring more supervisory personnel in a wasteful effort to force greater work effort.

For popular democrats, the central problem of industrial planning is how to reduce the waste that is crippling the American economy. One popular democratic analysis of the economy estimated that in 1980 waste from such factors as unemployment, surplus supervisors, lower work commitment, and excessive spending in areas like the military, energy, and advertising cost the economy $1.2 trillion in useful output. To put it another way, eliminating that waste would have meant that everyone could have worked one-third fewer hours and still enjoyed the same standard of living.[47]

The industrial policy debate revolves to a great extent around a disagreement about human motivation. Elite democrats maintain that people are basically motivated by selfish material interests and that therefore inequalities are necessary to motivate people to work and invest. Workplace democracy, they say, is an unaffordable luxury in today's highly competitive global marketplace. Employees are simply not qualified to make highly technical and complex business decisions. Popular democrats argue, on the other hand, that beyond material interests people want to participate in the decisions that affect their lives. As a result, there is no hard-and-fast tradeoff between equality and growth. Too much inequality can hurt efficiency when those at the bottom become demoralized and lose faith in the belief that they can get ahead through hard work. Bringing employees into corporate decision-making, popular democrats maintain, will unleash creative energy and effort.

Popular democrats draw on two sources to substantiate their claim about human motivation. First, both cross-national and intranational data show no consistent relationship between inequality and better economic performance or growth.[48] Second, evidence is mounting on the positive effects of profit sharing and workplace democracy. Studies of enhanced worker participation in such tasks as job design have found that participation results in greater job satisfaction, commitment, and productivity and in a reduction in turnover and absenteeism. Summing up the evidence on worker-owned and -managed firms, one analysis conservatively estimated that they increase output per worker hour by about 15 percent.[49] In short, equality and growth are complementary.

In support of this program to extend democracy into the economy, popular democrats have called for an Economic Bill of Rights. This idea builds on Franklin D. Roosevelt's 1944 State of the Union message, in which he called for adding to the political Bill of Rights "a second Bill of Rights under which a new basis of security and prosperity can be established for all."[50] One union, the International Association of Machinists, proposed a "New Technology Bill of Rights" to deal with problems associated with a high-technology economy.[51] The most comprehensive statement of an Economic Bill of Rights is found in a book by economists Samuel Bowles, David Gordon, and Thomas Weisskopf entitled *Beyond the Wasteland.* The authors list four basic kinds of economic rights that should be guaranteed in a democratic society.[52]

1. *Right to economic security and equity:* This would comprise the right to a decent job, provided, if necessary, by the government.

2. *Right to a democratic workplace:* This would include public support for democratic trade unions and community-owned enterprises.

3. *Right to chart our economic futures:* This would include democratic control over the money supply.

4. *Right to a better way of life:* A more progressive tax system and dramatically reduced military spending would enhance the ability of the economic system to meet basic needs.

The authors go on to describe in detail (130 pages) how each of these rights could be guaranteed by specific national policies.

Popular democrats are not calling for socialism. They are not calling for government ownership of industry, and they are as opposed as cowboy capitalists to having bureaucrats in Washington, D.C., pick winners and losers. Popular democratic economic policy is an American hybrid calling for democratic internal control over corporations, which would still be subject to market competition. Specific reforms suggested by popular democrats, then, are designed to enhance democratic control over the economy.

1. *Plant-closing legislation:* Companies moving or closing down a factory would be required to give the workers advance notice as well as provide assistance to them and the community to deal with the social costs of change.[53] Workers would be helped to relocate when necessary, but the main goal would be to stabilize communities by bringing jobs to where people live.

2. *Workplace democracy:* By providing tax breaks to worker-owned factories, ensuring that workers control their own pension funds, and creating a national cooperative bank to loan money to cooperatively owned businesses, the government would not only extend democracy but also strengthen communities and increase productivity.

3. *Economic conversion:* The end of the Cold War makes it possible for the United States to cut Pentagon spending by half over the next ten years, resulting in annual savings reaching $140 billion. This would present a historic opportunity to convert productive facilities from military to civilian use. The federal government would provide funding to enable communities to make this transition in a democratic fashion, with as little disruption of the community fabric as possible.[54]

CONCLUSION: THE RELATIONSHIP BETWEEN ECONOMIC AND SOCIAL POLICY

The debate between popular democrats and elite democrats over economic policy is a debate not just over who should make economic policy but also over what should be included in it. For elite democrats, whether cowboy or Yankee capitalists, the purpose of economic policy is to reinforce the priorities of the

Worker Ownership: A Steel Town Fights for Its Life

One response to plant shutdowns has been for workers to buy the factory themselves. Worker ownership was given a big boost in 1974 when the federal government legislated tax breaks for worker buyouts in the form of *employee stock ownership plans (ESOPs)*. Many popular democrats view worker ownership not only as a way to save jobs but also as a way to expand democratic participation.

Located in Weirton, West Virginia, Weirton Steel was one of the world's leading producers of high-quality steel and tin. In the 1970s, however, profits stagnated as demand for steel and tin, which were increasingly being replaced by aluminum, declined. In 1982, Weirton's giant parent company, National Steel, announced that it would no longer invest in the plant and confronted the employees with a difficult choice: Either they buy the plant and invest large amounts of money to make it competitive, or National would turn it into a minor finishing plant with few jobs. Since Weirton employed seven thousand people in a town of only twenty-six thousand, the latter alternative would have had devastating effects for the community.

The workers responded by each kicking in $60 for a feasibility study, which showed that Weirton could succeed if the workers accepted a 32 percent pay cut. Many workers objected to pay cuts and were nervous about the deal. "It's scary," said Vince Bruno, an electrician at the plant. "No matter how you glorify it, it's still a gamble." With no alternative for saving their jobs, however, the workers decided to go forward. Uniting behind the workers, the community held bake sales, sock hops, and raffles to help raise the $2 million necessary to hire lawyers and investment bankers to make the complex deal a reality.

Because National needed to sell the plant (and not shut it down) to save money on pensions and severance pay, the employees were able to negotiate a purchase price of $66 million, only 22 percent of the asset value. The lower sale price enabled the cut in workers' pay to be lowered to 18 percent. The total cost of the deal was $386 million, with the employees going deeply into debt, mostly to pay for existing inventories of coal, iron ore, and unsold products.

With the closing of the deal in 1984, Weirton Steel became the largest worker-owned company in the United States. So far, it has been an economic success. In its first two years of operation, employment rose from seven thousand to eight thousand one hundred, and the company reported $122 million in profits, the highest profits per ton in the industry. Work teams were set up throughout the company, and workers were encouraged to participate in decision-making. After five years, workers acquired the right to elect the company's Board of Directors.

Although nationwide over eleven million people are now employed in worker-owned firms, the long-term effects of employee ownership on democracy are uncertain. One problem is that lower-paid workers will have incentives to sell their shares; control may therefore gravitate to the types of stockholders that usually control corporations. One great advantage of worker-owned factories, however, is that they reconnect firms with local communities, reducing the mobility of capital that has had devastating effects on the social and political life of so many American communities.

Sources: Warner Woodworth, Christopher Meek, and William Foote Whyte, eds., *Industrial Democracy: Strategies for Community Revitalization* (Beverly Hills, Calif.: Sage, 1985); Harry Anderson, "A Steel Town's Fight for Life," *Newsweek,* March 28, 1983, pp. 49–50; and James Megson and Michael O'Toole, "Employee Ownership: The Vehicle for Community Development and Local Economic Control" (Boston: ICA Group, April 1993).

marketplace, thus enhancing private consumption and wealth. Economic policy should strive to maximize the size of the economic pie; only afterward should social problems or the question of the distribution of the pie be taken up by political representatives.

For popular democrats, economic policy is simultaneously social policy, which is why such policymaking should not be left to economic experts. Economic policies have unequal effects on different sectors of the population and regions of the country and should therefore take into account social effects. The goal should be to choose economic policies that prevent social dislocations instead of waiting for social problems to arise and then devising social policies to clean up the mess.

The United States has one of the strongest economies in the world, which in recent years has shown surprising resilience, beating the Germans and the Japanese in many export markets. American workers are still the most productive in the world.[55] But economic policies should not be evaluated only by economic standards. Equally important is the standard of democracy. We will never realize our democratic potential if we spend over forty hours a week in hierarchical, undemocratic workplaces. Economic dislocations, like the sudden layoffs that devastated southeast Chicago, cause people to feel powerless and to withdraw from community life. Stable and secure communities are necessary for a well-functioning democracy. The goal of economic policy should be a democratic society and high quality of life, not just more private consumption and wealth.

KEY TERMS

fiscal policy
monetary policy
stagflation
Laffer Curve

Economic Recovery Tax Act of 1981
progressive tax
regressive tax
monetarism

SUGGESTED READINGS

Peter Bachrach and Aryeh Botwinick, *Power and Empowerment: A Radical Theory of Participatory Democracy* (Philadelphia: Temple University Press, 1992). A bold argument for workplace democracy as a way of creating more active citizens.

Donald L. Barlett and James B. Steele, *America: What Went Wrong?* (Kansas City, Missouri: Andrews and McMeel, 1992). A critique by two Pulitzer Prize-winning investigative reporters of how economic policy has benefitted the rich and the powerful—at the expense of everyone else.

Samuel Bowles, David M. Gordon, and Thomas E. Weiskopf, *After the Wasteland: A Democratic Economics for the Year 2000* (Armonk, N.Y.: M. E. Sharpe, 1990). Argues that the present elite-dominated economy creates tremendous waste, and that democratizing the economy can lead to both more equality and more efficiency.

William Greider, *Secrets of the Temple: How the Federal Reserve Runs the*

Country (New York: Simon and Schuster, 1987). Penetrates the veil of expertise that surrounds the Federal Reserve to expose the politics behind its decisions to regulate the money supply.

William A. Niskanen, *Reaganomics: An Insider's Account of the Policies and the* *People* (New York: Oxford University Press, 1988). A largely sympathetic account of the implementation of supply side economics, from a member of Reagan's Council of Economic Advisers.

CHAPTER.

18

Social Policy: The Reluctant Welfare State

After graduating from high school in Queens, New York, Gwen received a scholarship to the State University of New York at Stony Brook. After Gwen had been in college one and a half years, her mother became ill. Gwen dropped out of college and went home to take care of her mother. Within a month's time, the mother died. Married and with one child at the time, Gwen was devastated. She had what she later called a "nervous breakdown." She and her husband had purchased a three-family house in Queens. With Gwen unable to work, they fell behind on the payments and lost the house.

Forced onto welfare, Gwen ended up at the Martinique Hotel, an old hotel in Manhattan converted to emergency housing for the homeless. Her husband,

Bill, earned a small salary but not enough to support the family and pay prevailing rents in New York City. Bill lived with the family but was forced to sneak in and out of the Martinique. If welfare found out that they were living together, Gwen would lose her welfare check, food stamps, and government-funded health insurance.

Welfare regulations required Gwen to go out and look for housing on the private market. Carrying her two-year-old baby, Gwen took the subway every morning to Queens to look for an apartment. The welfare housing allowance was only $244, however, at least $100 below minimal rents in New York City. The author of a book on homelessness describes Gwen's condition as an exercise in futility: "Like a well-conditioned animal within a research lab, she pursues each channel of improbability that is presented. Every channel she explores returns her to the place where she began."[1] Gwen's frustration was only heightened by the fact that the depressing and dangerous room the government provided her at the Hotel Martinique cost $1,600 per month.

Gwen's story indicates why welfare is one of the most maligned (and least understood) public policies in the United States. The government spends large amounts of money on welfare, yet poverty is as big a problem as ever. Almost no one is happy with welfare—and for good reason. It is demeaning to the poor, encourages families to break up, and provides few incentives to work (every dollar earned generally results in a dollar reduction in welfare benefits).

Why has the United States persisted in a policy that is so unpopular and ineffective? That is one of the questions explored in this chapter. It begins by examining the contrasting approaches to social policy of elite and popular democrats. These differences reflect a deep split in opinions about the American welfare state. The chapter then examines the historical background of the welfare state—that is, the whole array of social policies in advanced industrial countries designed to redistribute wealth and help those who cannot support themselves in the private marketplace. After examining this history, the chapter explores several attempts to reform welfare and then concludes by examining the health care debate and the possibility of a major expansion of the welfare state in the United States.

THE DEMOCRATIC DEBATE OVER SOCIAL POLICY

Social policies depend on the answers to value-laden questions. When are people responsible for their own fate, and when should the government step in to help? Who deserves to be helped, and how much help should they receive? Should the government redistribute wealth? If so, how much?

The Elite Democratic Approach to Social Policy

For elite democrats, the purpose of social policies should be to provide a social safety net to catch those who fall between the cracks of the market economy.

Elite democrats distinguish between the **deserving poor** and the *undeserving poor*. The deserving poor are those who, through no fault of their own, cannot achieve a basic minimum standard of living by working. Single women with young children, persons too disabled to work, and the elderly are generally included in this category. Elite democrats assume that the market economy is fair and that any able-bodied person should be able to make a living. Able-bodied men and women without children are therefore the undeserving poor.

Since most elite democrats assume that the market economy allocates goods in the most efficient way, some explanation is needed for the stubborn persistence of poverty—especially the disproportionate poverty among minorities and women. In 1991, for example, the poverty rate for blacks (32.7 percent) was almost three times that for whites (11.3 percent); almost one-half the families headed by a single mother (46 percent) were living below the poverty level.[2]

Elite democrats blame poverty primarily on the characteristics of the poor themselves, not on society. Earlier in the century, elites often used the alleged genetic inferiority of the poor to explain persistent poverty.[3] Contemporary elite democrats generally adopt a cultural approach to explain poverty. According to the **culture of poverty** thesis, people are poor because they have certain values, passed on from generation to generation, that cause them to ignore opportunities to get ahead in the marketplace. Often applied to African Americans and Hispanics, the culture of poverty thesis views the poor as more impulsive and present oriented than the middle class. Instead of saving for the future and delaying gratification to get ahead, people raised in the culture of poverty seek immediate gratification. Lacking the work ethic, the chronically poor seek constant pleasure and are often sexually promiscuous.[4] The implication of this argument is that the poor are poor because they are different from the rest of society. Even if government offered them opportunities to get ahead, they would not take advantage of them. Short of taking babies out of the culture of poverty and raising them in middle-class values, we cannot cure poverty.

Elite democrats explain the fact that women are disproportionately represented among the poor not primarily by their low wage rates but by the dissolution of traditional families. Many elite democrats encourage women to work but acknowledge that since they often move in and out of the work force to have babies, they cannot earn as much as men. One of the best ways to alleviate poverty would be to reconstitute traditional families headed by a male breadwinner. As Vice President Dan Quayle said during the 1992 presidential campaign, "Marriage is probably the best anti-poverty program of all."[5]

The Popular Democratic Approach to Social Policy

According to popular democrats, the goal of social policy should not just be to provide a minimum standard of living but also to provide everyone with the resources necessary to become full and equal participants in society. For popular democrats, poverty is defined not just by an absolute standard (income below a certain amount) but also by a relative standard—the gap between the rich and the poor. Too much inequality threatens democracy because it gives the rich the resources to dominate and demoralize the poor, distorting democracy. Popular democrats do not distinguish between the deserving and the undeserving poor. Instead, popular democrats subscribe to the idea of basic **social rights.**[6] Just as there is a political Bill of Rights (Chapter 16) and should be an Economic Bill of Rights (Chapter 17), there also should be a Social Bill of Rights. All citizens should be entitled to basic educational and health services as well as minimum-income benefits. Basic social rights should be provided universally, without any stigma or necessity of going through an application process. According to popular democratic thought, social rights are necessary for full democratic participation. People who cannot read or write or who are worried about where their next meal is coming from are in no position to fully exercise their democratic political rights.[7]

Popular democrats tend to blame poverty on conditions in the environment, not on the characteristics of the poor. Popular democrats assume that given the proper circumstances, everyone wants to work and contribute to society. If some people are excluded from their fair share in the economy, it must be because of structural defects in the economic system. Poverty in the United States is disproportionately black and female because, popular democrats maintain, blacks and women are discriminated against. The goal of social policy should be to establish the foundations for equal participation in the economy. This means overcoming discrimination and helping discriminated-against minorities become economically self-sufficient. The goal of social policies should not be to buttress traditional families by making it more difficult for women to leave bad marriages. Instead, women should have the ability to command living wages so that they can afford to choose their family situation.

The debate between elite and popular democrats about social policy reflects the deep ambivalence that Americans have about the welfare state. On the one hand, Americans have a strong tradition of compassion for the poor, and many social policies have been enacted to help disadvantaged groups become full members of society. On the other hand, many ordinary citizens share elite democratic fears that redistributive social policies will overturn established power relations, including the power of whites over blacks, men over women, and owners over workers. These fears have limited the development of effective social policies and given rise to "the reluctant welfare state."[8] Americans' ambivalence also has resulted in a fundamental split in the modern American welfare state.

HISTORICAL ORIGINS OF THE AMERICAN WELFARE STATE

At the time of the founding, social policy never came up as a topic of debate between Federalists and Anti-federalists. It was assumed that almost everybody could become self-sufficient. The vast majority of people were farmers, and the abundance of land gave people the opportunity to support themselves. In fact, early American farmers met most of their own needs outside the marketplace, producing their own food and clothing and even building their own houses. Small farmers who owned their own land, popular democrats believed, had the independence and self-sufficiency to become active participants in the democratic process. The small number of people who could not take care of themselves—the severely disabled, the blind, and widows—were cared for by their families or by local charitable institutions.

The onset of industrialism changed all that. Technological advances, like the cotton gin and threshing machines, mechanized agriculture, forcing people off the land. Displaced agricultural workers were thrown together in crowded cities with immigrants from foreign lands speaking strange tongues. The social fabric was strained. Instead of working for themselves and owning the means of production, people now worked for capitalists in large factories. Increasingly, industrial workers and their families depended on the market to meet their needs. Industrialism meant increasing wealth and opportunity as well as increasing dependency on the money economy and misery for those at the bottom, who could find themselves suddenly thrown out of work by a recession or by technological change.

The welfare state developed in response to the vulnerability of people in rapidly changing capitalist economies. The United States lagged far behind European countries, however, in developing a welfare state. Until the 1930s, responsibility for those who could not take care of themselves was left almost completely in the hands of local governments and private charities. Programs for the disadvantaged varied greatly from one county to the next. The most common method of helping the poor was to place them in almshouses, where their behavior could be regulated and they could be forced to work. Such unfortunates were denied basic citizenship rights. Conditions in many almshouses were so oppressive that many poor preferred to suffer on their own.

All of this changed suddenly with the Great Depression. The inadequacy of local programs became obvious. The fact that millions of hard-working middle-class families were suddenly thrown into poverty dispelled any notion that they were to blame for their condition. Clearly, the Depression was a national problem, and the federal government had to deal with its consequences.

The modern American welfare state originated with the 1935 Social Security Act, probably the most important piece of domestic legislation in American history. The Social Security Act was made possible by popular democratic pressure driven by the misery of the Depression. For a short time, the power of elites to veto the expansion of federal social policies was suspended.

President Roosevelt especially felt the pressure from two popular political rivals. Shortly after Roosevelt took office, Dr. Francis E. Townsend, a former city health officer from California, floated a disarmingly simple proposal: Every American sixty or over should receive a monthly government pension of $200, with the provision that the money be spent within one month. Townsend was convinced that his proposal would not only relieve poverty among the elderly but also revive the economy. Many Americans agreed, and by 1935 there were Townsend clubs in almost every congressional district. Roosevelt also felt pressure from Senator Huey Long, former governor of Louisiana, who organized a national Share-Our-Wealth movement that called for, among other things, a limitation on fortunes and a guaranteed minimum income. A secret poll by the National Democratic Committee indicated that Long could tip the balance to the Republicans in the 1936 election.[9]

Roosevelt responded to this pressure by appointing a Committee on Economic Security to suggest sweeping changes in federal social policy. The committee proposed a two-tiered system, which was enacted in the 1935 Social Security Act: social insurance for the unemployed and the elderly and public assistance for the blind, the disabled, and single mothers with children (Table 18.1). The social insurance programs are called **entitlements** because everyone who pays into the system is entitled to the benefits. The public assistance programs are called **means-tested** because to obtain the benefits, a person must apply and prove that she or he lacks means of self-support. The split between entitlements and means-tested public assistance has decisively influenced the American welfare state ever since.

	Social Insurance Entitlements	Means-Tested Public Assistance
Basic Law (1935)	Social Security old-age insurance unemployment insurance	Aid to Dependent Children (ADC, later AFDC)
Eligibility	All who paid into the system are entitled to benefits.	Persons must apply and meet means tests; eligibility varies among states.
Administration	Social Security is administered entirely by the federal government. Unemployment insurance is administered by the states with federal controls.	Administered by the states; federal government provides matching grants and established minimum standards.
Major Changes	Widows included (1939) Disabled included (1956) Medicare added (1965) Social Security benefits indexed to inflation (1972) National health insurance???	Food stamps (1964) Medicaid added (1965) Family Support Act (FSA), Federal matching grants to states for programs to move welfare recipients into jobs (1988)

TABLE 18.1

The Two-Tiered American Welfare State

Entitlements

Social Security started out modestly, but over the years it has expanded tremendously, both in benefit levels and in number of people covered. Social Security was originally intended to be a mandatory insurance system in which retired persons would receive benefits according to how much they paid in. As people lived longer and longer, however, the benefits paid out far exceeded the taxes paid in. In addition, coverage was significantly expanded on three occasions: In 1939 widows were included, in 1956 the disabled were added, and in 1965 health insurance for the elderly was enacted. The system is paid for by a payroll tax known as FICA (Federal Insurance Contributions Act).

Although the Social Security tax is regressive because it is a flat rate up to a certain amount, above which people pay nothing, the benefits paid out for Social Security are quite progressive. They are based on the amount workers pay into the system. Therefore, high-income earners receive higher benefits. But formerly low-income workers are given proportionately higher benefits. More important, the benefits far exceed the amount each worker paid into the system. In fact, most people exhaust the funds they paid into the system within a few years. After that, their pension is essentially paid for by the present generation of workers.

With Social Security now including over 90 percent of the work force, it has become a classic case of *majoritarian* politics, where both the costs and the benefits are widely spread. Social Security is supported by a broad coalition uniting the poor and the middle class, blacks and whites, city dwellers and residents of small towns and suburbs. Politicians fall over each other trying to defend Social Security. Contemplating a run for the presidency in 1972, for example, Democrat Wilbur Mills, chair of the powerful House Ways and Means Committee, proposed a 20 percent increase as well as indexing payments to inflation—all without a tax increase! To obtain partial credit for the changes, President Nixon endorsed Mills's proposal, and it became the law in 1972. The result was soaring expenditures on Social Security and a crisis in the Social Security fund (Figure 18.1).

Social Security has become so politically popular that politicians refer to it as the "third rail" of American politics: Like the third rail on an electrified railway, if a person touches it, he or she is dead. Politicians are afraid to even talk about cutting Social Security benefits.

The evolution of Social Security has made it, in the words of a well-known scholar, "America's most effective antipoverty program."[10] As Figure 18.2 shows, the poverty rate among the elderly fell from 28 percent in the late 1960s to 12 percent in the mid-1980s. Increased Social Security retirement benefits were responsible for pulling many of the elderly out of poverty.

Means-Tested Public Assistance

The 1935 Social Security Act also set up a system of means-tested public assistance, primarily to help children in families without a male breadwinner—so-

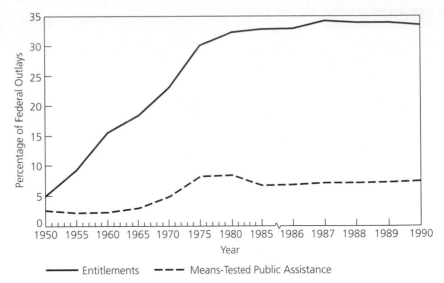

Source: Harold W. Stanley and Richard G. Niemi, *Vital Statistics in American Politics,* 4th ed. (Washington, D.C.: Congressional Quarterly, 1994), p. 384; U.S. Bureau of the Census, *Statistical Abstract of the United States 1993* (Washington, D.C.: GPO, 1993), p. 369.

called dependent children. Officially, the system is called Aid to Families with Dependent Children (AFDC), but commonly it is referred to (often pejoratively) as welfare. Welfare is now supplemented with other means-tested benefits, including food stamps and Medicaid (government health insurance for the poor).

Even though popular democratic pressure in the 1930s goaded the president and Congress into action, southern elites in Congress shaped how the political system responded to those pressures, exacting concessions that later crippled public assistance. Most important, although the legislation called for the federal government to pay for part of the cost of public assistance through matching grants, program benefits and eligibility were determined by the states (within broad guidelines set by the federal government). This was a concession to southern representatives, who did not want the South's economic system based on cheap, largely black labor disrupted by high welfare payments. Powerful southern representatives on the House Ways and Means Committee, for example, were able to eliminate the "decency and health" requirements of the original law, giving states more leeway in setting benefit levels.[11] As Table 18.2 shows, average benefit levels for public assistance vary tremendously, with southern states still lagging far behind.

The second tier of the American welfare state, then, has suffered from constant political attacks and dwindling benefits. Compared to other countries, U.S. social policies for the poor, especially children, are abysmal. Overall, public assistance benefits are not enough to pull most families out of poverty. At the same time that the poverty rate for the elderly dropped due to rising Social Security payments, the poverty rate for children soared (see Figure 18.2). Increas-

FIGURE 18.2

The Effects of Social Policies on Children and the Elderly, 1965–1986

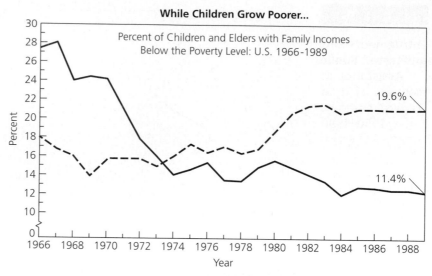

While Children Grow Poorer...

Percent of Children and Elders with Family Incomes Below the Poverty Level: U.S. 1966-1989

19.6%

11.4%

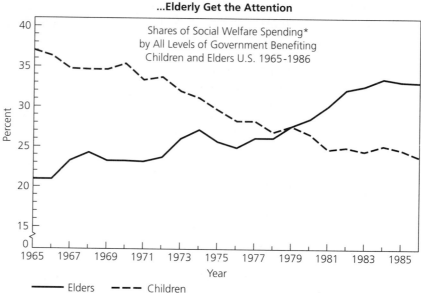

...Elderly Get the Attention

Shares of Social Welfare Spending* by All Levels of Government Benefiting Children and Elders U.S. 1965-1986

——— Elders   - - - Children

*Includes primary and secondary education, welfare, health programs, food stamps, Social Security, Medicare, and Medicaid.

Source: Washington Post Weekly Edition, March 4, 1991, p. 31. Copyright © 1991 The Washington Post. Reprinted with permission.

ingly, poverty among children is concentrated in single-parent households. In 1986 public policies succeeded in lifting fewer than 4 percent of poor children in single-parent families out of poverty.[12] Today, more than one out of five children lives below the poverty level.

TABLE 18.2	Eight Highest States		Eight Lowest States	
	Alaska	$691	Kentucky	$217
Average Monthly Public Assistance Payments, Eight Highest and Lowest States, 1991	California	632	South Carolina	203
	Hawaii	613	Arkansas	191
	Connecticut	565	Tennessee	187
	New York	550	Louisiana	170
	Massachusetts	532	Texas	166
	Vermont	524	Alabama	125
	Minnesota	524	Mississippi	122

Source: U.S. Bureau of the Census, *Statistical Abstract of the United States 1993* (Washington, D.C.: GPO, 1993), p. 382.

Moreover, welfare is not an entitlement; people must go through a demeaning application process and prove that they cannot support themselves. As a result, many people who need the programs do not receive benefits. In 1991, only 43.6 percent of the poor received any cash assistance; 27 percent received no assistance at all, including food stamps, Medicaid, or housing subsidies.[13]

Challenging the Stereotypes

Over the years, three stereotypes about welfare have formed that, for the most part, do not stand up to the facts. First, *welfare undermines the incentive to work.* Some critics of welfare argue not only that welfare does not solve the problem of poverty but also that welfare actually *causes* poverty. Charles Murray's influential book *Losing Ground* contends that high welfare benefits make it more attractive for people to be on welfare than to work.[14] As Milton and Rose Friedman put the matter, "Those on welfare have little incentive to earn income."[15]

In fact, welfare benefit levels are not generous. The official poverty line in the United States in 1991 was $6,932 for a single individual and $13,924 for a family of four.[16] Anyone who has tried to live on such low incomes, especially in areas with high housing costs, knows how difficult it is to make ends meet. Public assistance payments do not even raise incomes up to the poverty line. Even when noncash benefits, such as food stamps and Medicaid, are included, most families on welfare are still below the poverty line. And the situation has gotten worse in recent decades. Between 1972 and 1991, average benefit levels for public assistance and food stamps fell 27 percent in inflation-adjusted dollars.[17] No other group in American society has suffered such a painful drop in income. Notwithstanding media stereotypes of "welfare queens," welfare recipients do not live in the lap of luxury.

Researchers estimate that the effect of welfare on work force participation rates is small. One study of fifty welfare recipients in Chicago found that all were forced to supplement their incomes to make ends meet—many of them by working "off the books."[18] Another study found that if all public assistance programs for people under the age of sixty-five were completely eliminated, the number of hours worked by Americans would rise only by about 1 percent.[19] Finally, nearly all of the women who receive welfare already work taking care of children.

The second stereotype is that *generous welfare benefits encourage women to have babies outside of marriage and lead to family dissolution.* The argument here is that welfare encourages families to break up because a woman usually loses her welfare benefits if she lives with a man. Although welfare does discourage intact families, the correlation between welfare and single-parent families is weak.[20] The number of out-of-wedlock births increased in the 1970s and 1980s even as welfare benefits fell. States with lower benefit levels do not have lower rates of out-of-wedlock births. The incentive for having another baby on welfare is low; the per capita welfare grant falls with more children. In fact, between 1972 and 1992, the number of children in the average welfare family fell from three to two.[21]

Welfare is only a small part of the problem of out-of-wedlock births. Such births, divorce, and female-headed households have increased rapidly among middle-class whites as well, suggesting that there are broader cultural and economic forces behind these phenomena. Among the inner-city poor, a much more important cause of family dissolution, according to sociologist William Julius Wilson, is the inability of men to find jobs that can support a family.[22]

The third stereotype is that *welfare creates a permanent dependent class.* According to this argument, people become hooked on welfare, like a drug, staying on the dole for a long time and even raising the next generation to become welfare dependents. The research shows, however, that two-thirds of recipients get off welfare within three years or less.[23] There is, however, a minority of welfare recipients who stay on public assistance for a long time, absorbing a disproportionate share of the resources and thereby lending some truth to this stereotype.

Explaining America's Reluctant Welfare State

Overall, the United States spends less on social policies than any other developed nation, except Japan (Figure 18.3). (Large corporations in Japan are, of course, famous for providing generous benefits to their employees.) On the one hand, generous entitlement programs provide almost universal coverage for the elderly, with benefit levels comparable to those in other developed countries. On the other hand, means-tested welfare programs, which mostly benefit children, provide spotty coverage and inadequate benefits.

Most other developed countries have broad entitlement programs to address the needs of the nonelderly poor. The most important of these is health insurance. Other countries also have a system of child allowances in which every family, regardless of income, is entitled to a payment each year from the government for

FIGURE 18.3

Average Total Spending in Social Policies* as a Percentage of GNP/GDP, 1980–1986

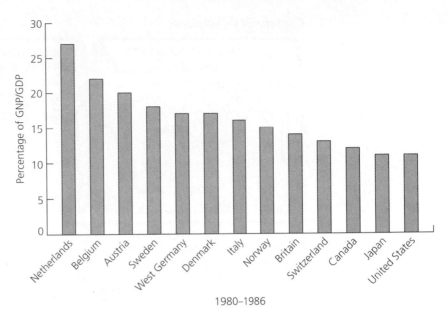

1980–1986

Source: Arnold J. Heidenheimer, Hugh Heclo, and Carolyn Teich Adams, *Comparative Public Policy: The Politics of Social Choice in America, Europe, and Japan,* 3rd ed. (New York: St. Martin's Press, 1990), p. 249.

each child. These allowances are politically popular and have played a major role in reducing poverty rate.[24]

The only exception to America's lagging behind is education. The United States provided universal public education well before Europe did and today enables more people to pursue higher education. The American tradition of public education played a major role in expanding popular democracy, giving citizens the skills necessary to participate in the democratic process and in the economy.

Our tradition of equal educational opportunity, however, is threatened today by unequal funding. Since funding for primary and secondary schools comes mostly out of local property taxes, children who happen to grow up in poor inner-city school districts suffer from inferior education.[25] With education being the key to good jobs in an information-based economy, inferior schools can doom children to a life of poverty and exclude them from full participation in the democratic process.[26]

Political scientists have long puzzled over why the American welfare state has lagged behind. One important reason is that means-tested welfare benefits evolved in such a way as to generate little popular support. Unlike Social Security, which is based on majoritarian politics, welfare is based on *client* politics, in which the benefits are targeted to a narrow constituency, while the costs are widely distributed over the public at large. In addition, unlike Social Security,

Cartoonist's Comment

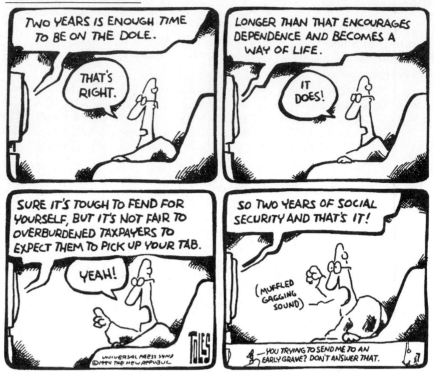

which is administered entirely by the federal government, responsibility for public assistance programs is divided between the federal government and state and local governments. This has weakened the ability of welfare to provide adequate benefits and has enabled powerful southern elites to restrict eligibility and benefits. Moreover, states hesitate to expand welfare benefits for fear of becoming "welfare magnets," attracting poor people from other states and creating a fiscal burden for state taxpayers.[27]

The main reason that welfare has fared so poorly, however, is that it violates deeply held American values. Americans believe in individual and family responsibility. All able-bodied persons should take care of themselves. Welfare has the reputation of rewarding lazy people who do not want to work and encouraging women to have babies without any means of supporting them, even though this reputation is not well substantiated by the facts. Most important, welfare violates the American belief that people should not be given "something for nothing."

The two-tiered American welfare state is based on the distinction between the deserving and undeserving poor. Welfare is reserved for the undeserving poor and therefore must be rendered an unattractive option to discourage people from seeking it. Social Security, on the other hand, goes to the deserving poor because it is based on contributory insurance in which people get out what they put in. As we have seen, however, this is not true: Social Security recipients exhaust their contributions within a few years and so, like welfare recipients, are getting something for nothing.

THE BACKLASH AGAINST WELFARE

During the 1960s, welfare expenditures grew rapidly, partly because of a militant welfare rights movement that encouraged people to apply for welfare.[28] As expenditures on welfare soared, taxes increased, and industrial jobs declined, a welfare "backlash" developed, especially among working-class white ethnics. A book on the flight of the Jews and Italians of Brooklyn from the Democratic to the Republican party quotes an enraged city worker: "These welfare people get as much as I do and I work my ass off and come home dead tired. They get up late and they can shack up all day long and watch the tube. With their welfare and food stamps, they come out better than me. . . . Let them tighten their belts like we have to."[29]

In the late 1960s, politicians began to exploit this resentment against welfare to mobilize votes. Former Alabama governor and segregationist George Wallace led the way in the 1968 presidential election, attracting a surprisingly large number of votes among northern white ethnics. Richard Nixon began to speak out for what he called the "silent majority" against government giveaways like welfare. Ronald Reagan built his political career partly by attacking welfare, saying that we could not solve problems by "throwing money" at them. In 1992, George Bush attacked welfare, promising to "make the able-bodied work." Not to be outdone, Bill Clinton put out an ad attacking welfare, stating, "For so long, Government has failed us, and one of its worst failures has been welfare. I have a plan to end welfare as we know it."[30]

Clearly, the resentment against welfare is not based only on economic factors; as we have seen, welfare is a relatively small part of federal and state budgets. This resentment is motivated partly by racism and sexism. Even though a majority of those on welfare are white, blacks represent a disproportionate share of recipients. In the public's mind, welfare is identified with blacks. Politicians have taken advantage of these sentiments. In 1991, for example, former Ku Klux Klan leader David Duke received a majority of the white vote in his race for governor of Louisiana by, among other things, mobilizing white resentments against black welfare recipients with statements like, "Middle-class families have difficulty affording children of their own right now and yet we are financing a very high illegitimate birth rate."[31] In fact, in 1991 in Louisiana each baby qualified the mother for only $11 extra per week—hardly a great incentive for having babies.

Another issue in the welfare debate concerns the role of women. When critics say that women on welfare do not work, they are ignoring the fact that raising children is work. The disapproving judgments of women on welfare seem to suggest that it is okay to stay home with children only if a woman is part of a traditional family with a male breadwinner. The reason for keeping welfare so unattractive, some feminists say, is to discourage women from leaving bad marriages, even if the husband is abusive.[32] In the public's mind, welfare is wrapped up in the cultural debates that began in the 1960s about permissiveness—promoting a lifestyle attuned to immediate gratification and sexual promiscuity. In fact, permissive values have spread throughout society in the past thirty years, driven by corporate advertising that uses immediate gratification to stimulate consumption. Hard-working Middle Americans raised with a strong work ethic find themselves bombarded by advertising that stresses pleasure-driven consumption. Fearing a loss of control, they project their own fears onto others, including blacks on welfare.[33]

Welfare is important for American politics, therefore, because it has become a powerful symbol of the failure of government, the failure of liberalism, and fears about shifting race, gender, and cultural relations. Perhaps the most damaging effect of welfare, however, has been on welfare recipients themselves, most of whom find the experience degrading and demeaning. Listen to the description of a former welfare mother: "Unlike social security, AFDC is distributed on a case-by-case basis, with enough strings to hang an elephant. It is meanly administered, hard to qualify for, hard to keep; it provides niggardly benefits and is tough to stomach with all its invasive attempts at behavior modification."[34] Welfare robs people of their pride and dignity, and it undermines popular democracy by stigmatizing the poor, placing them outside the mainstream of American society.

The Failure of a Guaranteed Annual Income

Linda Baldwin is the daughter of Mississippi migrants to Chicago's South Side. The first in her family to attend high school, she dropped out when she became pregnant at the age of seventeen. After ten years on welfare, Baldwin did what everyone said welfare recipients ought to do: She got a job. The only problem is her $6 an hour job as a youth counsellor leaves her with $169 less each month than welfare provided. "I had more money before I worked," said Baldwin in a wry tone. "Something is wrong with these laws. It's like they're telling you to stay home." Baldwin recognizes, however, that her decision to work is based on more than economics: "If you cease to struggle, you're not existent."[35]

Declining wages have created a growing group known as the "working poor," those who work full-time but find themselves still in poverty. The problem is that people who work lose welfare benefits and federal health insurance coverage. Going back to work also requires extra expenses, like daycare and transportation. Welfare recipients face a painful dilemma: inadequate welfare benefits or poverty-level wages.

Back in 1969, Richard Nixon, at the urging of his top urban affairs adviser, Daniel Patrick Moynihan, proposed a Family Assistance Plan (FAP) that would have addressed many welfare problems. Basically, it would have established a guaranteed minimum income for all Americans.

Nixon had a number of reasons for supporting welfare reform. At the time, welfare caseloads were soaring; between 1961 and 1969, the number of people on public assistance almost doubled.[36] Costs were skyrocketing. If Nixon could take credit for cleaning up the "welfare mess," it would enhance his prospects for re-election. Moreover, since a guaranteed income would be an entitlement for all Americans, FAP would eliminate the jobs of many social workers and administrators who vote overwhelmingly Democratic. Finally, Nixon, who had come from a poor family, was genuinely appalled at the welfare system. As he put it in a speech on FAP, "Our task is not only to lift people out of poverty, but from the standpoint of the child to erase the stigma of welfare and illegitimacy and apartness—to restore pride and dignity and self-respect."[37]

FAP was simple. The federal government would guarantee every American family of four an income of at least $1,600 (the equivalent of about $6,190 in 1992). The proposal would end the system of extremely low payments in some states, although states would be allowed to supplement the minimum federal income. Workers could keep the first $60 earned each month without reduction in benefits; beyond that benefits would be reduced by only fifty cents for each dollar earned. FAP would have eliminated in one fell swoop all of the demeaning regulations of means-tested public assistance. Everyone would have been eligible for the guaranteed income regardless of living arrangements.

Nixon knew, however, that there were problems with a guaranteed income. A Gallup poll showed that 62 percent of the American public opposed a guaranteed annual income. It smacked too much of getting something for nothing. Nixon therefore added a work requirement to his proposal: Everyone who received benefits would be required to accept work or training—the only exception being those physically unable to work or mothers of preschool children. Nixon called his proposal "workfare," not welfare.

The fate of FAP illustrates the difficulty of bringing about reform in the fragmented American political system, especially in an area freighted with so much ideological baggage. With the help of the powerful chair of the Ways and Means Committee, the bill passed easily in the House, 243–155. In the Senate, however, southern conservative Democrats and western Democrats, who dominated the crucial Finance Committee, attacked FAP because it would extend the contagion of welfare to millions more people. The proposal would have brought an estimated thirteen million more people into the system. (Advocates viewed this as a strength because the working poor would receive government help and the very poor would not be stigmatized by welfare.) The bill also came under attack by liberals who argued that the benefit levels were too low and the work incentives too severe. Liberal amendments to expand benefits, and therefore costs, helped kill the bill. FAP died in the Senate after being defeated by a 10–6 vote in the Finance Committee.

The failure of FAP shows the difficulty of devising a welfare reform that simultaneously keeps costs down and encourages people to enter the job market. The idea of a guaranteed annual income was revived, however, when a little-noticed provision in a 1975 tax law enabled working families with children to receive money from the government if their income fell below a certain level.

The *earned-income tax credit* was expanded significantly in the first year of the Clinton administration, providing a maximum refund of $3,370 to a minimum-wage worker supporting a family of four.[38] In the meantime, politicians continue to promise to get people off welfare and into jobs. While the political rhetoric has been easy to pronounce, achieving results has proven much more difficult.

The Debate over Workfare

President Nixon gave the term *workfare* national exposure in a 1969 televised speech announcing his welfare reform package.[39] Workfare was embraced by conservatives in the 1970s as a way of forcing people who refused to work off welfare. In the 1980s, liberals embraced workfare as a means of providing incentives for getting off welfare by funding services such as education, job training, and childcare. The 1981 Budget Act, supported by President Reagan, allowed states to experiment with programs that required welfare recipients to participate in job searches or community work experience to "earn" their welfare. Experiments in different states showed modest successes, building momentum for welfare reform.

In 1988, the welfare reform movement came together with the passage of the Family Support Act (FSA). FSA was supported by an unlikely coalition of liberals and conservatives, proving, once again, that "politics makes strange bedfellows." Everyone agreed on the need to strengthen systems for collecting child support payments from absent parents, and the final bill required states to collect payments from fathers who deserted their families by withholding money from their paychecks. A group of Republican and Democratic governors, including Governor Bill Clinton of Arkansas, pushed welfare reform based on experiments in their states moving welfare recipients into jobs. Conservatives, including President Reagan, supported the bill because it included mandatory work requirements; liberals supported the bill because it provided funding for additional services for welfare clients. Senator Moynihan, the old warhorse of welfare reform, shepherded the bill through Congress, seeing it as a way to inoculate welfare from political attack.

The key provision of the 1988 act was called JOBS (Job Opportunities and Basic Skills). The JOBS program provided $5.3 billion over five years for training, education, job search, and other supportive services. Under JOBS all states were required within five years to achieve a 20 percent participation rate for all eligible public assistance recipients, which included all welfare family heads with children over the age of three. Essentially, this meant that one out of every five welfare recipients would be required to get a job or go to school or a job training program.

Welfare reform was designed to implement a new social contract of mutual obligations between welfare recipients and government. The government was obligated to provide additional services to welfare recipients to help them become independent. Welfare recipients, in return, were obligated to participate in the programs and make every effort to become independent. The law was intended, in other words, to transform welfare from a program that promoted dependency into one that encouraged independence.

Initial evaluations of the program were mixed, suggesting that at best the results would be modest at present levels of funding. One study of six California counties found that a year after enrolling in the program, welfare recipients were earning 17 percent, or $1,902 more per year but that the percentage of single parents on welfare had declined only 3 percent.[40] Another study of JOBS in ten states found that implementation of the program was highly uneven; by 1992 over half of the federal money was unspent because states refused to come up with the relatively small matching funds. Most important, the report found that in none of the states did politicians champion the program and make a strong personal commitment to reforming welfare.[41]

The main problem with workfare is that it assumes that if welfare recipients have the right attitudes toward work and the right skills, they can become self-reliant, stable members of society. But there is increasing evidence that the problem of poverty lies not so much in the welfare recipients as in the job market. According to some estimates, more than half of the jobs created in the 1980s paid wages below the poverty level for a family of four.[42] Between 1973 and 1987, the average wage rates for male high school graduates fell 12 percent; for high school dropouts wages fell 18 percent.[43] Moreover, the unemployment rates among low-skilled, especially black, workers increased significantly. It makes no sense to push welfare mothers into a job market that has a declining capacity to absorb them.[44]

In June 1994 Clinton finally came out with his proposal to "end welfare as we know it" and limit welfare to no more than two years. Clinton's plan called for the expenditure of $9.3 billion over five years for expanded job training and child care, but that would only affect about one-third of welfare families. Estimates of the cost of guaranteeing every welfare recipient a job range as high as $20 billion.[45] Clearly, ending welfare is not a cheap or easy matter. It was clear that Clinton was marshalling his political resources for the battle over his proposed health-care reform—potentially the most significant piece of domestic legislation since the 1935 Social Security Act.

THE HEALTH-CARE POLICY DEBATE

Like welfare, health care is not a social entitlement in the United States. In fact, with the exception of South Africa, the United States is the only advanced industrial country that does not provide universal health insurance. To understand why this is so and why universal health care became an issue in the 1990s, we must examine the history of government involvement in health care and the serious problems that gradually accumulated to crisis proportions in the late twentieth century.

When Germany established the first system of compulsory medical insurance in 1883, the impetus came from conservative elites led by Chancellor Otto von

Bismarck, who, fearing the growth of the socialists, supported reforms to ensure workers' loyalty. Other nations soon followed suit: Austria in 1888, Hungary in 1891, Norway in 1909, Britain in 1911, and the Netherlands in 1913.[46]

In the United States, progressives proposed government-sponsored health insurance during World War I, during the Great Depression, and after World War II, but each time they were defeated. One important reason is the weakness of socialist parties in the United States, which were instrumental in goading elites into action in Europe. Also, the union movement in the United States was mostly opposed to government-mandated health care. Samuel Gompers, of the American Federation of Labor, opposed government-sponsored health insurance because it would weaken the ability of unions to provide such benefits to workers through labor negotiations. Business, of course, opposed mandatory health insurance because it would increase the cost of labor.

The main reason the United States failed to legislate health insurance, however, was the rise of a powerful medical profession that was essentially able to veto any attempt by government to intervene into the medical field.[47] In the early nineteenth century, doctors in the United States were divided and politically weak. In part this reflected the pre–Civil War popular democratic culture, which respected common sense over the claims of expert knowledge and scorned all efforts at professional monopolies. In the 1830s and 1840s, state legislatures did away with medical licensure; anyone, no matter how poorly educated, could put up a shingle and practice medicine, a highly competitive and low-salaried job. The weakness of the medical profession also reflected the lack of an agreed-on scientific model of medical practice.

Gradually, in the late nineteenth century, doctors united behind one model of medicine, supposedly based on science, and began to acquire powers of self-regulation. States began to license doctors, a practice that was upheld by the Supreme Court in 1882. In the first decade of the twentieth century, the American Medical Association (AMA) blossomed into a powerful organization, with membership soaring from eight thousand in 1900 to seventy thousand in 1910. The AMA led a movement to weed out substandard or unorthodox medical schools. The movement was remarkably successful, reducing the number of medical schools from 162 in 1906 to 95 in 1915. At the same time, the number of blacks and women practicing medicine declined. As the number of doctors licensed to practice medicine fell, salaries began to rise. If the goal of the AMA was to create a monopoly in the practice of medicine, it largely succeeded.

As a result of this newly created monopoly, medicine became one of the highest paid and most respected professions in the United States. The power of doctors was based on the ability of the medical profession to wrap itself in the aura of science, whose spectacular accomplishments were dazzling people. Increasingly, medical practice was viewed as being based on objective, scientific knowledge that laypersons could not understand. In classic elite fashion, doctors claimed control not only over doctor-patient relations but also over the whole field of health policy. Medicine became regulated by doctors, with little democratic input. In some states, doctors actually ran government policy, with medical societies trusted as the state Boards of Health.

The AMA played a pivotal role in defeating efforts to provide national health insurance. Franklin Roosevelt considered including health insurance as part of his 1935 Social Security Act but decided against it for fear that it would jeopardize the entire bill. Years later, in a revealing remark to a Senate committee chair, Roosevelt said of health insurance, "We can't go up against the State Medical Societies; we just can't do that."[48]

After World War II, President Harry Truman supported a national health insurance system for every American, with government paying the premiums of those too poor to pay themselves. In 1946, the Republicans won control of Congress and scuttled the plan, but Truman pushed it in the 1948 presidential election. The AMA led the attack on Truman's proposal, assessing each member an extra $25 just to fight national health insurance. The 1949 AMA campaign was the most expensive lobbying effort, up to that time, in American history. Playing on people's fears of communism, the AMA labelled Truman's proposal "socialized medicine." Asked one pamphlet, "Would socialized medicine lead to socialization of other phases of American life?" It answered by saying, "Lenin thought so. He declared: "Socialized medicine is the keystone to the arch of the Socialistic State."[49] The campaign was remarkably effective, with support for Truman's proposal falling from 58 percent to 36 percent in 1949. In 1950, the lobbying arm for national health insurance spent only $36,000; the AMA spent $2.5 million, placing ads decrying the threat to the American way of life in 1,033 newspapers, 1,600 radio stations, and 35 magazines. With key supporters defeated in the 1950 congressional election, and identified in the public's mind with communism, national health insurance was dead by the early 1950s.

In the 1960s, progressives were finally able to pass a limited form of national health insurance by identifying it with Social Security and targeting it to the elderly. Wilbur Mills the powerful chair of the House Ways and Means Committee, fashioned an ingenious compromise that facilitated passage of health insurance for the elderly in 1965. Democrats favored a mandatory program to provide hospital insurance for the elderly. Republicans supported a voluntary program in which the federal government would help elderly persons buy health insurance to pay for doctors' bills. Mills solved the problem by suddenly proposing to combine the two programs in one bill. Over the opposition of the AMA, the bill, which established **Medicare** (health insurance for the elderly), passed Congress. On July 30, 1965, President Johnson journeyed to Independence, Missouri, to sign the bill in the presence of Harry Truman.

As a result of this political compromise, Medicare, an entitlement program, has two parts. Part A is compulsory insurance for hospital services for people sixty-five and over. Workers pay a tax on wages, which is paid into a separate fund. In 1991, the program paid out $71.5 billion to over thirty-four million recipients. Part B is a voluntary program of medical insurance for people sixty-five and over. Enrollees pay a monthly premium for the insurance, which is subsidized by the government and covers the services of physicians and other qualified providers. In 1991, the federal government paid out $47.2 billion in Part B benefits.

A short time after passing Medicare, Congress passed the **Medicaid** program, means-tested health insurance for the poor. Whereas Medicare is run entirely by the federal government, Medicaid is a matching grant program to the states. With the exception of the requirement that all recipients of welfare receive Medicaid, states are free to set their own eligibility requirements and benefit levels. In 1991, 26.7 million people benefitted from Medicaid, more than half being children, costing the federal government over $77 billion.

Medicare and Medicaid preserved the two-tiered nature of the American welfare state. Both programs increased the access of the elderly and poor to medical services. In 1963, for example, almost 20 percent of Americans living beneath the poverty level had never visited a physician; by 1970, after enactment of Medicaid, the percentage had fallen to 8 percent.[50] The infant mortality rate of the poor, a prime indicator of general health, fell dramatically. Elderly people no longer had to worry that they would lose their life savings if they ended up in the hospital.

On the other hand, both programs were subjected to criticism. Medicaid was criticized because it paid only a standard low rate for medical services; thus poor people in low-income neighborhoods remained underserved by doctors. In addition, so-called Medicaid mills ripped off the taxpayers for unnecessary, and sometimes unperformed, medical services. At the insistence of the AMA, doctors were allowed to charge higher fees for Medicare services than the government would reimburse. As a result, the elderly had significant out-of-pocket expenses. Medicare contributed to medical inflation by reimbursing doctors at "prevailing rates," which meant that doctors had no incentive to decrease fees or curtail unnecessary surgeries or procedures. Little effort was put into preventive medicine.

As a result of Medicare and Medicaid, after 1965 public spending on health care soared in the United States, reaching 43.9 percent of total health-care spending in 1991.[51] The huge influx of government money contributed to soaring health-care costs and a gathering health-care crisis in the United States.

THE CURRENT HEALTH-CARE CRISIS

Two weaknesses of the American health-care system have fueled the widespread perception that the system is broken and needs to be fixed: the problem of the uninsured and rising costs.

The Problem of the Uninsured

By the early 1990s, thirty-seven million Americans were without any health insurance, and another twenty-five million were underinsured. Lack of health insurance or underinsurance means that a person is only a serious illness or an injury away from personal bankruptcy. In addition, one study showed that uninsured people were twice as likely to die over a fifteen-year period as people with health insurance.[52] The problem of the uninsured is not just a problem for the very poor, most of whom at least have minimal coverage under Medicaid. The problem also has spread to the working and middle classes. Among those who lack health insurance, 85 percent have a working adult in the family.[53] Over a two-year period, close to one-fourth of all Americans find themselves uninsured at some point. Insurance companies often reject applicants who have significant health risks (so-called pre-existing conditions). Many Americans are anxious about being able to afford decent health care at crucial points in their lives.

Rising Costs

Soaring health care costs give Americans good reason for anxiety. The United States now spends more per person on health care than any other nation in the world (Figure 18.4). By 1992, Americans were spending 14 percent (one-seventh) of their gross domestic product (GDP) on health care, up from 9 percent in 1980. In the long run, this trend will cripple the competitiveness of the United States in the global economy. Health-care costs already added about $1,100 to the cost of every car produced in the United States in 1992, about twice as much as Japan.[54]

FIGURE 18.4

Per Capita Spending on Health Care in Selected Countries, 1991

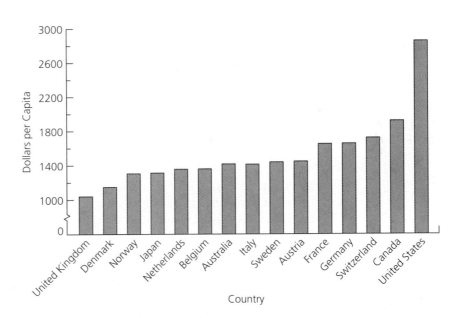

Source: U.S. Bureau of the Census, *Statistical Abstract of the United States 1993* (Washington, D.C.: GPO, 1993), p. 849.

There are many causes of rising health-care costs in the United States. Perhaps the main reason is that most fees are paid by third-party insurers, either private insurance companies or the government. Under third-party payments, neither patients nor medical providers have incentives to limit access to expensive services or keep cost per service down. Not surprisingly, American doctors are the highest paid in the world.[55] Their wealth has helped make them the object of expensive malpractice suits. Malpractice insurance now costs many doctors over $100,000 per year. As a result, doctors practice "defensive medicine," ordering additional tests even when they are of dubious value. Administrative costs are another problem. With over one thousand five hundred private health insurers offering different coverages and forms, health-care administrative costs have soared, eating up 25 percent of every health-care dollar.[56] Finally, the uninsured often wait to get help until a condition has worsened and is expensive to treat. Without regular access to a doctor, the uninsured often seek treatment in expensive emergency rooms at hospitals, which are required by the government to treat them. These added costs are shifted onto the insured in the form of higher hospital costs and higher insurance premiums.

Perhaps the high costs would be justifiable if Americans received the best health care in the world. They do not. Infant mortality rates, the number of babies who die at birth, is considered to be one of the best indicators of a nation's overall health. The United States has one of the worst infant mortality rates in the industrialized world. In fact, middle-class Americans with good health insurance receive among the best medical care in the world, and infant mortality rates are correspondingly low. The uninsured and the poor, however, receive poor medical care. A high proportion of poor women in inner-city neighborhoods have babies without having received any prenatal care. In 1988–1989, for example, the infant mortality rate for central Harlem was 23.4 per 1,000 births, about the same as Malaysia.[57] For the most part, we know what needs to be done to reduce infant mortality; what is lacking is the political will to do it.

THE FAILURE OF HEALTH-CARE REFORM

In 1991, Harris Wofford, former aid to President Kennedy, pulled a stunning upset in the Pennsylvania Senate race against his popular Republican opponent, Dick Thornburgh. Wofford made health care, especially the problem of the uninsured, the central theme of his campaign. The turning point in the campaign came when he aired a television commercial in which he said, "If criminals have the right to a lawyer, I think working Americans should have the right to a doctor."

Wofford's surprise victory signalled to politicians that health-care reform could be a political winner. In 1992, Bill Clinton ran for the presidency promising to provide health insurance for all Americans. In 1993, polls showed that almost two-thirds of Americans agreed that the federal government "should guarantee

Hillary Rodham Clinton: First Lady as Lightning Rod

At her 1969 commencement address at Wellesley College, Hillary Rodham observed, "We are, all of us, exploring a world that none of us understand." Twenty-five years later, Hillary Rodham Clinton is still exploring a difficult-to-understand world. As the most politically active First Lady to date, Hillary Clinton has become a lightning rod for society's conflicts about the expanding role of women in American society and politics.

The conflict over what she symbolizes began at the 1992 Republican National Convention, where Pat Buchanan labelled her a representative of "radical feminism," Marilyn Quayle criticized her as a career-oriented mother with overzealous ambitions, and First Lady Barbara Bush charged she was planning the first ever "co-presidency." When pollsters found that voters were fearful of an "empowered Nancy Reagan," Hillary Clinton toned down her image using a number of calculated actions, including the famous chocolate-chip-cookie-baking episode.

As First Lady, however, Hillary Clinton has reasserted an active political role. Cries of nepotism were heard after the president appointed her to head a 500-member task force to reform the nation's health-care system. But she came to the position with a powerful résumé. After earning a law degree at Yale, she worked with the Children's Defense Fund, chaired the board of the Legal Services Corporation in the late 1970s, and headed a committee that successfully raised educational standards in Arkansas in the 1980s.

Her work on health care earned grudging respect even from Republicans, who praised her mastery of policy detail and political skills. As Senator John H. Chafee (R—R.I.) remarked, "It's sort of condescending for so many people to say that they are surprised she is doing a good job. . . . She's a bright individual, and you give her any job and give her a little time, and she would do an outstanding job on it." According to a *Time*/CNN poll, 63 percent of the American people answered "yes" to the question "Is Hillary Clinton's prominent role in national policy appropriate?"

A portion of the population, however, responds negatively to Mrs. Clinton. In the same poll 91 percent thought she was "intelligent," but 41 percent felt she was "too pushy." The negative responses to Mrs. Clinton reflect the discomfort many Americans, women as well as men, still feel toward ambitious and powerful women occupying traditionally male turf. As *Time* surmised, "She is on a cultural seesaw held to a schizophrenic standard: everything she does that is soft is a calculated coverup of the careerist side; everything that isn't is a put-down of women who stay home and bake cookies."

The conflicts over Hillary Clinton's role as First Lady are a sign that even after the success of the women's suffrage movement and thirty years of the modern feminist movement (both discussed in Chapter 11), we have still not fully overcome the barriers to equal participation by women in democratic politics. A real sign that we have finally overcome these barriers will come when a woman finally wins the presidency and we begin to debate the proper role for the "First Man."

Sources: "Mrs. Clinton Conquers Hill, Sets Debate in Motion," *Congressional Quarterly,* October 2, 1993, pp. 2640–43; Margaret Carlson, "At the Center of Power," *Time,* May 10, 1993, pp. 29–36; and Gwen Ifill, "Clinton Assails G.O.P. Attack Aimed at Wife," *New York Times,* August 20, 1992.

First Lady Hillary Rodham Clinton signs Lucy Mangari's cast as she tours the St. Agnes Medical Center in Philadelphia on February 11, 1993.

medical care for all people who don't have health insurance."[58] Although a clear majority of Americans favored universal health care, by the end of the first two years of the Clinton administration health care reform was dead. The failure of health care reform illustrates key characteristics of American politics: the need for strong presidential leadership to achieve reform in a fragmented political system; the power of a partisan minority to block change through access to veto points in Congress; and the ability of elite-dominated interest-groups to use their access to money and the mass media to build "grassroots" opposition to legislation that challenges the status quo.

In the first few months of the Clinton administration, the momentum for health care reform seemed unstoppable. Soon after assuming office, Clinton appointed First Lady Hillary Rodham Clinton to head a massive task force to develop the administration's proposal on health care. Hearings were held around the country and over 500 experts were consulted in developing the legislation. Clinton introduced his National Health Security Act in a nationally televised speech on September 22, 1993. The Clinton plan would have required all employers to purchase health care insurance for their employees, paying, on average, 80 percent of the costs, while employees would pay the other 20 percent. Small businesses and the unemployed would be subsidized by the government, with universal coverage achieved by 1999. The Clinton plan proposed to control costs by organizing consumers into buying cooperatives and establishing a National Health Board to impose caps on the growth in health premiums.

Initially, the Clinton plan attracted wide public support, with one poll reporting 56 percent of the voters' approval and only 24 percent disapproval. By June 1994, however, public support had collapsed, with 53 percent expressing opposition to the President's plan.[59] By the fall of 1994 health care reform was dead in Congress and most of the voters did not seem to care. What happened to the apparent consensus on health care reform?

Clinton made a serious political miscalculation in developing his proposal outside of Congress. The dominance of policy experts over politicians in writing

Americans Are Calling For Health Care Reform.

Each day thousands of Americans call our 800 number looking for a better way to reform the health care system. They are getting a sweeping proposal developed by America's best insurance companies.

It will provide cradle to grave coverage for all Americans. Coverage you are sure to get even if you have an existing illness. Coverage you can afford and coverage you can keep even if you change jobs or lose your job. Best of all, you can chose to keep your present plan. This is the reform America wants.

A Better Way To Reform

We are committed to the health care reform America wants. Call toll free for your copy of the visionary proposal developed by the Health Insurance Association of America (HIAA) and endorsed by tens of thousands of farmers, seniors, businesses and individual consumers. Read the plan that will help make the President's plan better.

For A Better Way To Reform.
1-800-285-HEALTH

Coalition for Health
Insurance Choices

Sponsored by a coalition of thousands of businesses, individuals, consumers, farmers, seniors and insurers. Major funding by Health Insurance Assoc. of America.

The Harry and Louise ads were effective at stirring up doubts about President Clinton's health care proposal.

the legislation resulted in a 1,342-page bill that was complex and difficult for the public to understand. Republicans found it easy to attack the bill as another example of big government trying to intrude into people's lives. More importantly, once introduced into Congress the Clinton bill became a kind of political orphan. Lacking ownership of the Clinton bill, many in Congress, both Democrats and Republicans, found it more politically advantageous to champion their own bills, further dividing the forces of reform.

The most controversial component of the Clinton plan was the employer mandate, requiring that companies provide health insurance for all of their employees. Big business, which was otherwise sympathetic to health care reform, came out against the employer mandate and supported proposals in Congress that relied on market forces to keep health care costs down. Small businesses also came out against the plan, fearful that being forced to pay for their employees' health insurance would force many of them into bankruptcy.

In attempting to overhaul what amounted to one-seventh of the American economy, Clinton's health care proposal set in motion the biggest interest group lobbying effort in history. The various interests arrayed against reform raised an estimated $50 million, outspending supporters of the Clinton program by more than 4 to 1.[60] They used the money to fund an advertising campaign that skillfully raised doubts and fears about the Clinton plan. To pay for coverage for the 37 million uninsured, for example, the plan called for $100 billion in new taxes, mostly "sin taxes" on such items as liquor and cigarettes. The Anheuser-Busch Company outfitted its trucks with placards urging Bud drinkers to dial 1-800-BEER-TAX. Callers received a pamphlet describing how the Clinton health care plan would drain their pockets. The Health Insurance Association of America spent $10 million on slick ads in which a suburban couple, known as Harry and Louise, expressed doubts about people's ability to choose their own doctor under the Clinton plan. The President and the First Lady both blasted the ads as misleading but they turned out to be effective, generating 286,000 calls to a toll-free number.

The AMA also came out against major portions of Clinton's plan. In a letter to 670,000 doctors and 40,000 medical students, the AMA charged that the plan threatened to separate the heart from the soul of American medicine by "forcing a bureaucrat or an accountant to stand between patient and physician."[61] With a $7 million lobbying budget, the AMA was a formidable foe but it no longer possessed the veto power over health care reform that it once did. Only 43 percent of doctors were members in 1993, down from 70 percent in the early 1970s. Nevertheless, all the proposals left doctors as the primary gatekeepers determining what services would or would not be reimbursable.

Finally, health care reform was killed not just by political miscalculations by Clinton and powerful media attacks by special interests but also by partisanship within Congress. As the Clinton proposal began to wind its way through the congressional labyrinth, it came under attack from both the left and the right. On the left, critics charged that the Clinton plan compromised too much with the insurance industry. They proposed instead a single-payer plan, modelled on the Canadian system, in which the government would pay a standard fee for medical services for all citizens. On the right, Republicans played upon people's fears, heightened by the negative advertising campaign, that the Clinton plan would create a massive new federal bureaucracy and raise taxes. A series of weaker reform bills was introduced in the House and the Senate, draining support from the Clinton plan. Last-ditch efforts to stitch together bipartisan bills that would have moved slowly toward universal coverage without an employer mandate foundered on partisan bickering between the Republicans and the Democrats.

The failure of health care reform in 1994 illustrates that the system of government established by the Framers, with its many checks and balances, makes comprehensive reform difficult. The two earlier examples of successful social reform, Social Security in 1935 and Medicare and Medicaid in 1965, were made possible by huge Democratic majorities in both houses and the popularity of presidents Roosevelt and Johnson. Clinton lacked their popularity, and even though the Democrats controlled both houses of Congress, they were divided, with many conservative Democrats siding with the Republicans. Today there appears to be a new factor that makes comprehensive reform even more difficult: the power of the mass media. If interests defending the status quo can raise large amounts of money, it seems they can raise doubts and fears about any large-scale reforms. The result is political paralysis.

CONCLUSION: TOWARD A POPULAR DEMOCRATIC SOCIAL POLICY

Elite and popular democrats disagree on the goals of social policy. For elite democrats, the goal of social policy is to provide a basic minimum, or safety net, to take care of those who cannot take care of themselves in a competitive market economy. For popular democrats, the goal of social policy extends beyond a basic minimum living standard. The goal should be to provide all citizens with the basic social rights (education, health, minimum income) that are necessary for effective democratic participation. This means decreasing the gap between rich and poor so that the rich cannot buy the dependence of the poor. It also means guaranteeing these rights so as to avoid any dependence on the whim of government officials or the stigma that brands the recipients as different from the rest of society.

Has the United States succeeded in achieving the popular democratic goals of social policy? The answer is mixed. The top tier of the American welfare state, Social Security, has clearly been a success. People cannot be good citizens if they are anxious about how they will pay for essential medical services or food. Social Security and Medicare have helped elderly people cope with the vulnerabilities of old age without making them feel stigmatized or separated from the larger community. This has certainly contributed to the ability of the elderly to defend their interests and participate in politics.

The second tier of the American social policy, means-tested public assistance, on the other hand, has been a failure from the viewpoint of popular democracy. By forcing recipients to go through a demeaning application process, welfare stigmatizes the poor and makes them feel different from the rest of society. In particular, welfare makes outcasts of many single mothers and blacks, decreasing their ability for independent political action.

Democratic social policy challenges the myth of the self-made man. In our highly interdependent, complex society, no one is self-made anymore. All of us are dependent on government to achieve a high quality of life and to participate fully in democracy. The most successful social entitlement in the United States is the right to public education. Try to imagine what American democracy would be like without this massive system of public education that imparts the skills necessary to debate public policies and organize political associations to defend people's interests.

The most effective way of integrating the poor into society, however, would be to guarantee them a job. According to a 1992 poll, 70 percent of the public favors replacing "welfare with a system of guaranteed jobs."[62] The most important entitlement that popular democrats could enact would be the right of every American to a job at a salary that could support a family.

KEY TERMS

deserving poor
culture of poverty
social rights
entitlements

means-tested
Medicare
Medicaid

SUGGESTED READINGS

Theresa Funiciello, *Tyranny of Kindness: Dismantling the Welfare System to End Poverty in America* (New York: Atlantic Monthly Press, 1993). A hard-hitting critique of the welfare system by a former welfare mother, who argues for eliminating the current system and replacing it with a guaranteed income.

Christopher Jencks, *Rethinking Social Policy: Race, Poverty, and the Underclass* (New York: HarperCollins, 1992). A skillful synthesis of existing material on

which social policies work and which don't. Follows neither the liberal nor the conservative line.

Charles Murray, *Losing Ground: American Social Policy 1950–1980* (New York: Basic Books, 1984). Argues that welfare policies not only fail to cure poverty, they actually create poverty.

Paul Starr, *The Social Transformation of American Medicine: The Rise of a Sovereign Profession and the Making of a Vast Industry* (New York: Basic Books, 1982). The best historical account of the sources of the present health care crisis. Documents the rise of the American Medical Association (AMA) and the monopoly power of physicians.

William Julius Wilson, *The Truly Disadvantaged: The Inner City, the Underclass, and Public Policy* (Chicago: University of Chicago Press, 1987). An influential argument that the main cause of ghetto poverty is not the failure of government programs but the loss of industrial jobs, especially among black males.

CHAPTER

19

Foreign Policy in the National Security State

In the early 1960s, the Central Intelligence Agency (CIA), following the wishes of Presidents Eisenhower and Kennedy, was determined to get rid of Fidel Castro, the communist leader of revolutionary Cuba. Since coming to power in 1959, Castro had seized property in Cuba belonging to American corporations and had drawn his nation closer to the Soviet Union. An invasion force of Cuban exiles organized and trained by the CIA was smashed by Castro's forces at the

Bay of Pigs in 1961. But behind the scenes, the CIA was plotting an even more dire fate for Castro: assassination.[1]

The first undercover plot against Castro aimed merely to destroy his popularity. CIA officials were fearful that the charismatic Castro, most famous for his bushy black beard, would become a hero to the impoverished and the discontented throughout Latin America. So they cooked up a scheme to dust the Cuban leader's shoes with thallium salt, a powerful hair remover that would make his beard fall out. The plot was to be carried out when Castro was on a trip outside Cuba and would leave his shoes to be shined at the hotel in which he was staying. But Castro cancelled the trip.

Foiled in this prank, the CIA began to plot murder. It laced a box of Castro's favorite cigars with a botulism toxin, a poison so lethal that Castro would die just from putting the cigar in his mouth. The cigars were delivered to an unknown agent; it is not known what happened to him or to the cigars, but they never reached Castro.

Foiled again, the CIA became even more serious. To kill Castro, it hired experts: the Mafia. Castro had shut down Mafia gambling and prostitution operations in Cuba, so the mob had its own reasons for wanting Castro dead. The CIA paid three Mafia gangsters (two of whom were on the attorney general's list of most-wanted criminals) $150,000 in taxpayers' money for the attempt on Castro's life. Mafia agents in Cuba tried to slip poisoned pills, supplied by the CIA, into Castro's drink. But like the previous assassins, they could not get close enough to Castro to carry out the deed.

By now, CIA planners were desperate. They considered the possibility of depositing an exotic seashell rigged with explosives in an area where Castro liked to go skin diving. When this idea proved impractical, they tried to have an unwitting American diplomat offer Castro the gift of a diving suit. The suit was to be dusted with a fungus that would produce a chronic skin disease; its breathing apparatus was to be contaminated with tuberculosis germs. This idea, too, had to be discarded as impractical. Castro survived this—and several further—CIA plots.

What does this bizarre tale of CIA efforts to assassinate Castro, which sounds more like a bad made-for-TV-movie than a true story about an agency of the U.S. government, have to do with the democratic debate about American foreign policy? Elite democrats have long claimed that foreign policy, even more than domestic policy, requires the superior expertise and talent of elites. Ordinary citizens, they argue, are generally ignorant about events in other nations and are prone to emotional and fickle responses inconsistent with a realistic and stable foreign policy. Foreign policy therefore should largely be left in the hands of the president and the diplomatic and military experts who advise him. The tale of the CIA and Castro should lead us to question this conventional wisdom about wise elites and ignorant masses. When foreign policy decisions are made in secret chambers, with a handful of elite actors operating free of public scrutiny (and in the case of the CIA, public accountability), the result can be folly rather than wisdom. And the cost can be great, both to America's true national security and to its most cherished democratic values.

This chapter considers the democratic debate over foreign policy that has been waged since the nation's founding. The discussion begins with the original debate between Federalists and Anti-federalists, with elite democrats arguing for the necessity of expert guidance in a dangerous world of powerful adversaries and popular democrats warning of the threat to the maintenance of republican institutions posed by secret diplomacy and aggressive militarism. Briefly tracing the debate through American history, the chapter focuses on the era of the Cold War, when elite democrats succeeded in building a national security state to run the affairs of a global superpower. Next, the chapter describes the diplomatic, military, and intelligence agencies that conduct American relations with other nations and examines the impact that economic elites and public opinion have on foreign policy. The final section of the chapter considers the current democratic debate about what American foreign policy should be in a post–Cold War world.

BEGINNINGS OF THE DEMOCRATIC DEBATE OVER FOREIGN POLICY

Elite democrats and popular democrats of the founding generation differed not only on how Americans should govern themselves but also on how the American nation should relate to the rest of the world. The former favored executive control and promoted professional armies, while the latter sought public control and favored citizen militias.

The strongest proponent of the original elite position on foreign policy was Alexander Hamilton. In the *Federalist Papers*, Hamilton called on Americans to recognize that they lived in a dangerous world, where nations would fight regularly over power, territory, and commerce. Hamilton argued that the new United States needed professional armies and navies, like those of the great European powers, England and France. These forces would be required for defense and for the establishment of America as a great power, extending its influence throughout the Western Hemisphere.[2]

In Hamilton's conception of foreign and defense policy, the president was the dominant figure. Members of Congress lacked the information and experience to make wise decisions in foreign policy; furthermore, they could not act swiftly or keep diplomatic secrets. In contrast, the executive had the proper qualities for controlling foreign policy and using military might—in Hamilton's words, "decision, activity, secrecy, and dispatch."[3]

During the war between Great Britain and revolutionary France, Federalists boosted the primacy of the executive in foreign policy, using as their instrument President Washington's Proclamation of Neutrality of 1793. Later in that decade, they seized on the prospect of an American war against the French to create a professional army. It was Hamilton and his faction of Federalists who created the first American military establishment.[4]

The Anti-federalists feared just such an establishment. A standing army might overturn republican institutions and seize power for its commander (the example of Julius Caesar in ancient Rome was frequently cited). Or it might become a dangerous tool for the executive, tempting him to crush his domestic opponents or launch aggressive military adventures abroad. As an alternative to a professional military in times of peace, the Anti-federalists wanted to rely on state militias composed of armed citizens. (The Second Amendment reflects the importance the Anti-federalists gave to militias.) As Richard H. Kohn observes, popular democrats of the founding era associated "the militia with liberty, freedom, and colonial virtue—the standing army with European militarism, corruption, and tyranny."[5]

That citizen militias were capable only of defensive military operations reveals a great deal about the Anti-federalist view of foreign policy. The Anti-federalists did not want the new republic to become like the reigning great powers of the day. Rather than playing power politics, America should relate to the rest of the world as an example of how a people could flourish in freedom and self-government. A peaceful, commercial relationship with other nations could be governed as much by the people's representatives in Congress as by the executive. Foreign and defense policy of this kind would, the Anti-federalists believed, provide Americans with genuine security without threatening the republic's institutions and values.

In today's world of massive military forces and awesome technological destructiveness, some of the Anti-federalists' arguments sound old-fashioned. Yet the fundamental questions of the original democratic debate endure: Should American foreign and military policy be determined largely by a small elite acting often in secret and be directed toward the projection of American power abroad? Or should American foreign and defense policy be subject to greater popular democratic control and seek a form of national security that violates as little as possible the nation's professed values as a democratic society?

ISOLATION AND EXPANSION

For much of American history, elite democrats who shared Hamilton's vision of the United States as a great power were frustrated. **Isolationism,** not power politics, was the core principle of American foreign and defense policy. Apart from commercial relations, the United States sought to stay isolated from the political and military quarrels of the rest of the world. Protected by two vast oceans, the young republic concentrated on its internal development. Since military threats were remote, the standing army remained small. Only when the United States actually became engaged in a war did the military swell in size; once war was over, the citizen-soldiers who composed the bulk of the forces were rapidly demobilized.

Even though isolationism characterized American relations with other nations until well into the twentieth century, American foreign policy was neither as defensive nor as passive as the term seems to imply. The American republic from its inception was engaged in a process of **expansion,** first on a continental scale and later into Latin America and even Asia. American expansion drove the European powers from their remaining holdings on the continent. But it had a dark side: It also drove Native Americans from their ancestral lands, often in brutal fashion. And later it extended American power over Latin Americans and Filipinos, speaking the language of benevolence but employing the instrument of armed force. The responsibility for this dark side of American expansion belonged both to elite democrats and popular democrats.

Indian removal, the initial pillar of American expansion, was the work of popular democrats. The central figure in this removal was popular democratic hero Andrew Jackson. He understood that many ordinary Americans hungered for the fertile lands that the Indian tribes occupied—and he shared their incomprehension at Indians' refusal to give up their way of life and adopt the white

As assistant secretary of the navy, Theodore Roosevelt was one of the elite democrats pushing for a war with Spain. As leader of the Rough Riders cavalry in Cuba, Roosevelt turned the war into a popular adventure story.

man's economic and social practices. Under Jackson's leadership, Native Americans were driven from their homes in the southeastern states. As Richard Barnet notes, "In 1820, 125,000 Indians lived east of the Mississippi; by 1844 there were fewer than 30,000 left. Most had been forcibly relocated to the west. About a third had been wiped out."[6]

If popular democrats had their shameful moments in the history of American expansion, so, too, did elite democrats. Consider, for example, the clique of elite expansionists in the 1890s, led by such avowed admirers of Hamilton as Massachusetts Senator Henry Cabot Lodge and Assistant Secretary of the Navy Theodore Roosevelt. It was these elite expansionists, eager to project American power abroad, who prodded a wavering President William McKinley to fight a Spanish-American war and to extend the war from its ostensible focus, Cuba, halfway around the world to the Philippine Islands. The same men guided the subsequent American military campaign to crush Filipino nationalists, who wanted independence rather than American rule. A forerunner to the Vietnam conflict, the American war in the Philippines produced as many as two hundred thousand Filipino deaths.[7]

Although expansion drew support from both elites and masses, it always had its critics, who echoed the original Anti-federalist fear that America could become a great power only by violating its republican principles. America's role in the Mexican War, the war in the Philippines, and World War I was denounced by those who wanted the nation not to follow the path of European militarism and imperialism. These critics were especially outraged by claims that American expansion was motivated by a desire to spread liberty to other lands; they detected the real desire for wealth and power that such rhetoric disguised. Observe the satirical portrait of the American expansionist painted by a consistent critic of expansion, Abraham Lincoln:

> He is a great friend of humanity; and his desire for land is not selfish, but merely an impulse to extend the area of freedom. He is very anxious to fight for the liberation of enslaved nations and colonies, provided, always, they *have* land, and have *not* any liking for his interference. As to those who have no land, and would be glad of help from any quarter, he considers *they* can afford to wait a few hundred years longer.[8]

Even as the United States expanded across the continent (and into Latin America and the Philippines), even as it became the greatest industrial power in the world, the doctrine of isolationism remained strong. America came late to World War I—and recoiled after the war from the slaughter on the battlefield and the power politics of the victorious allies. Only with World War II did the nation begin to change its traditional foreign and defense policy, and it was in the immediate postwar years that the great transformation in American international relations occurred. Then, in the Cold War era, some of Hamilton's dreams were finally fulfilled, and some of the Anti-federalists' fears finally came true.

THE DEMOCRATIC DEBATE OVER THE COLD WAR

The **Cold War** was a forty-year struggle (lasting from the late 1940s to the late 1980s) between the United States and its allies, championing the cause of democracy and capitalism, and the Soviet Union (USSR) and its allies, championing the cause of communism. It was called a "cold" war because the two principal adversaries, the United States and the Soviet Union, armed themselves to the teeth, yet never actually engaged in direct combat with each other. But the Cold War became a "hot" war in many places, with major armed conflicts in Korea and Vietnam and numerous smaller armed conflicts around the globe. The Cold War was also waged with nonmilitary weapons ranging from political manipulation and economic pressure to propaganda and espionage.

Most Americans would agree with the triumphant rhetoric of President Bush: "From the fall of the Berlin Wall to the last gasp of imperial communism, from the four decades of the cold war to the 40 days of Desert Storm, America has led the way. We won the cold war . . . because we Americans never shirked responsibility."[9] Conventional wisdom now relegates the Cold War to the past and regards American Cold War policy as vindicated by the successful outcome. Nevertheless, the Cold War remains essential to study not only because it shaped foreign and defense policy until very recently but also because it fundamentally transformed this policy.

For most of American history, foreign policy was isolationist, and the peacetime military establishment was small. Presidential power in this area was limited, with Congress and the public retaining a significant say. With the Cold War, the United States became an active and interventionist global superpower. It developed an enormous peacetime military establishment, armed with weaponry of previously unthinkable destructiveness. Presidents became the overwhelmingly dominant factors in policymaking and came to possess, among other resources, the capacity to operate in secret, employing new agencies of covert action like the CIA. Meanwhile, Congress and the public were reduced to a marginal role, expected to support but not to question American actions abroad. These developments gave rise to a **national security state,** a complex of executive, military, and secret powers previously unknown in the American republic. Even though the Cold War has now come to an end, this national security state remains.

The establishment of the national security state was a victory for elite democrats in their debate with popular democrats over American foreign and defense policy. Actually, for roughly the first half of the Cold War it was a very one-sided debate. Almost all Americans believed in the ideas and institutions of the Cold War. This early "Cold War consensus" derived in part from a general American loathing of communism. But this consensus was also a deliberate creation of elites, who sold the American public an exaggerated picture of the communist threat to the American way of life. Thus, President Truman, announcing in 1947 that America had to undertake a global struggle to contain the advance of communism, based his rhetoric on the advice of Republican Senator Arthur Vandenberg to "scare hell out of the country."[10]

The consensus finally cracked during the Vietnam War of the 1960s and early 1970s. It was in the protests against American policy in Vietnam that the popular democratic tradition of opposing a foreign and defense policy based on unchecked executive power, militarism, and secret, unaccountable institutions was revived. This opposition was expressed chiefly through mass movements. The antiwar movement of the 1960s attracted growing backing for its fundamental criticisms of the war in Vietnam. Mass movements of the 1980s levelled similar criticisms against President Reagan's policy in Central America and his nuclear arms build-up. Movement leaders such as Tom Hayden and Martin Luther King Jr. echoed Abraham Lincoln in questioning the moral justifications for American actions abroad. They were supported by some sympathetic political elites, such as Senators George McGovern (the Democrats' 1972 presidential candidate) and Edward Kennedy.

During the last half of the Cold War, the debate over foreign policy was intense. Elite democrats held to the essentials of their original perspective on the Cold War. Popular democrats fought to head off aggressive new Cold War moves, especially during the Reagan administration. Below, we consider more fully the perspectives of both sides in the democratic debate over the Cold War.

The Elite Democratic View of the Cold War

Most elite democrats admitted that the Cold War contained some unpleasant features and unfortunate episodes, but they insisted that it was a necessary, even heroic struggle. The advance of international communism had to be halted, they believed, if freedom and democracy were to survive in the world. And only a prudent and tough-minded elite could guide the complex and often nasty enterprise of containing communism until it collapsed of its own contradictions. Secretary of State Dean Acheson, one of the original architects of American Cold War policy, remarked that "the limitation imposed by democratic political practices makes it difficult to conduct our foreign affairs in the national interest."[11] For Acheson and other elite democratic managers of the new national security state, deviations from democracy were acceptable if needed to win the Cold War.

The elite case for the Cold War argued, first, that American policy had to have as its priority an opposition to aggression. The mistake of the Western allies before World War II—appeasing Adolf Hitler at Munich in 1938—must never again be repeated. According to elite democrats, only firm diplomatic opposition backed by massive military power could deter the Soviet Union from expanding communism by force and fraud. The United States organized a European alliance, the **North Atlantic Treaty Organization (NATO),** to block any Soviet expansion in Europe. Aggression by Soviet allies and clients in the Third World also had to be halted, a rationale that involved the United States in wars in Korea and Vietnam. In this view, the United States had built a national security state not to secure military supremacy but to keep peace in the world.

Second, elite democrats saw the American effort in the Cold War as a defense of freedom around the globe. In advocating a global American struggle for the **containment** of communism, President Truman declared, "I believe that it must be the policy of the United States to support free peoples who are resisting attempted subjugation by armed minorities or by outside pressures."[12] The strategy of containment, proclaimed in what came to be known as the Truman Doctrine, formed the basis of American policy throughout the Cold War and required that the United States and its European allies come to the assistance of governments in the less developed regions of the world when they were threatened by communist subversion or attack. To elite democrats, containment suffered several setbacks, particularly in Vietnam, but also achieved notable successes. For example, thanks to American military involvement the people of South Korea were spared the rule of a communist dictator, North Korea's Kim Il Sung.

Third, American policy in the Cold War aimed to lift the yoke of communist tyranny from peoples on whom it had been forcibly imposed, especially in Eastern Europe. The more conservative Cold Warriors argued for the "rollback" of communism in Eastern Europe (and in China as well) by military threats and measures. More cautious Cold War planners sought to erode Soviet control in Eastern European countries by encouraging nationalist tendencies and fostering economic links to the West. The limits to American power to challenge Soviet control in Eastern Europe were painfully evident in 1956, when the United States had to stand by helplessly as Soviet forces crushed a revolution in Hungary. But American hopes for freedom in Eastern Europe were finally realized in 1989 when the symbol of communist oppression, the Berlin Wall, came down and one Eastern European nation after another overthrew communist rule.

Fourth, the American Cold War policy was a prudent combination of force and diplomacy. The presidents who shaped this policy had to engage in a frightening arms race, but they always kept one eye on peace. President Eisenhower sought "peaceful coexistence" with the Russians. President Kennedy negotiated a ban on the testing of nuclear weapons in the atmosphere. President Nixon restored American ties to Communist China and signed a strategic arms limitation treaty with the Soviet Union. Even President Reagan, the harshest critic of the Soviet Union among Cold War executives, agreed to an intermediate nuclear forces treaty with Soviet leader Mikhail Gorbachev.[13]

Fifth, the Cold War had the support of the American people. The Cold War required elite dominance of American foreign and defense policy. It necessitated a shift of power from Congress to the president, a huge and expensive military establishment, and agencies of secret action outside the constitutional system of public accountability. Yet, elite democrats argued, Americans understood that they were in a difficult struggle with a dangerous, undemocratic enemy, and they accepted the fact that this struggle could not always be conducted in accordance with democratic political practices.

The Popular Democratic View of the Cold War

Popular democrats agreed with elite democrats that communism had to be opposed. But they believed that the threat posed by the communists to the freedom of other nations and to the United States itself was often exaggerated by elite democrats in the presidency, the military, and the CIA because such exaggerations increased their own power and resources. Further, popular democrats favored more peaceful and open methods to block communism, methods more in keeping with democratic practices and values. In the eyes of popular democrats, American Cold War policy as run by elite democrats purchased whatever successes it achieved at a high price.

The most haunting price of Cold War policy, in the eyes of popular democrats, was the war in Vietnam. In the name of containing the aggressive expansionism of the Soviet and Chinese communists, elite democratic managers of the national security state plunged the United States into what was actually a Vietnamese

A badly wounded American soldier awaits evacuation after being ambushed in Vietnam. The war in Vietnam scarred Americans psychologically as well as physically.

civil war. By the time the United States pulled all of its troops out of Vietnam, almost sixty thousand Americans had died, along with hundreds of thousands of Vietnamese soldiers and civilians. The Vietnamese countryside bore terrible ecological scars, as did Vietnamese society and economy. Americans, too, were scarred by the war, especially in psychological traumas that persist to this day.[14]

Vietnam was an unparalleled disaster for America, but it was not, popular democrats insisted, an aberration for American foreign policy. A second price of Cold War policy was American backing of dictators and military regimes that repressed their own people in the name of anticommunism. Although President Truman had promised to assist "free peoples" resisting communism, the policy of containment he initiated led the United States to support some rather dubious representatives of freedom. Thus, the CIA overthrew a nationalist government in Iran in 1953 and restored the autocratic shah to power. For the next twenty-five years, the shah was the recipient of lavish American aid, including CIA training of his ruthless secret police, SAVAK. When he was overthrown in 1979—by Islamic fundamentalists rather than communists—Iran became a bitter foe of the United States.[15] Similarly, the Reagan administration backed the military-dominated government of El Salvador with financial aid and combat advisers for its struggle against left-wing guerrillas. But it was right-wing death squads connected to the Salvadorean military that brutally murdered thousands of civilian opponents.[16]

A third price of Cold War policy was that the United States, the global sponsor of democracy, schemed to overthrow democracies abroad if they infringed on American political and economic interests and to replace them with authoritarian governments that would do what the national security managers wanted. The most important case of this type was Chile in the early 1970s. Employing the CIA, President Nixon and his national security adviser, Henry Kissinger, tried to block the election of socialist Salvador Allende as president of Chile. When this failed, they worked secretly to disrupt Chile's economy and to foment political opposition to the Allende government. They also courted the Chilean military, which finally undertook a coup in 1973 in which Allende was killed and his supporters were arrested. The result of American policy in Chile was a military government that executed or tortured thousands of Allende followers, refused to hold democratic elections for the next decade and a half, and favored American corporate interests at the expense of its own nation's workers and poor people.[17]

Claiming to champion democracy in a global campaign against communism, American Cold War policy damaged democracy at home as well as abroad. In the popular democratic view, a fourth price paid for the Cold War was the damage done to the constitutional system of checks and balances. With the emergence of a national security state, a government that was supposed to be open and accountable to the people began to classify massive amounts of information as secret and to conduct numerous operations concealed from public view. Executive power swelled to previously unknown proportions in international relations, taking on the character of an "imperial presidency." Presidents manipulated the public with rhetorical fear-mongering, deceived the public with false information, and engaged in illegal acts when the public would not support their foreign policies. Two major threats to the Constitution, the Watergate affair under Nixon and the Iran/*contra* affair under Reagan, could be traced to the mentality of the imperial presidency during the Cold War.

According to popular democrats, the public support for Cold War policies that elite democrats claimed was engineered in substantial part through manipulation and even coercion. Thus, the fifth price paid for American Cold War policy was the damage done to democratic debate in America. In the early Cold War years, the small minority of dissenters from the Cold War consensus, including pacifists, progressives, and socialists as well as communists, were intimidated by McCarthyism (see Chapter 16). Even after McCarthyism faded, questioning of fundamental Cold War premises was taboo if a person wanted to hold political office. American political leaders did not dare appear "soft on communism" and often adopted bellicose language and gestures to ward off accusations that they were not tough enough for the Cold War. (Recall 1988 Democratic presidential candidate Michael Dukakis riding in a tank.)

A sixth price paid for American Cold War policy, in the eyes of popular democrats, was the damage done to economic progress and social justice in America. The Cold War arms race introduced distortions into the economy, leaving the United States at a disadvantage in many areas of civilian production compared to the nonmilitarized economies of West Germany and Japan. Equally damaging was the impact on spending for social needs. The arms race was often used to justify the country's failure to address adequately the needs of its own poor and disadvantaged. The one extensive effort to meet these needs, President Johnson's War on Poverty and Great Society programs, was cut back because of the mushrooming costs of the war in Vietnam. President Eisenhower, the Cold War president who best understood the tragic cost of the arms race, eloquently made the popular democrats' point: "Every gun that is made, every warship launched, every rocket fired signifies, in the final sense, a theft from those who hunger and are not fed, those who are cold and are not clothed."[18]

The End of the Cold War

The Cold War came to a sudden and surprising end in the late 1980s. In an attempt to reform the decrepit structure of the Soviet state, Gorbachev only managed to expose its fatal weaknesses. The global power of the Soviet Union slipped away in 1989 when Gorbachev refused to respond with force as popular upheavals toppled communist regimes in Eastern Europe. The Soviet Union itself crumbled in 1991 after a botched coup against Gorbachev by hard-line communists. Soon Gorbachev himself was swept from power in peaceful fashion, and the Soviet state was dismantled, with Boris Yeltsin and other leaders of the Soviet republics proclaiming their independence in a loosely knit federation.

The United States and its allies exulted in the Cold War's demise. Indeed, the whole world breathed easier now that the frightening prospect of a third world war and a nuclear holocaust had been removed. Yet celebration was bound to be brief, for the post–Cold War world already contains new problems and violent conflicts. Nonetheless, there are new opportunities as well, new openings to address fundamental issues of economic progress, human rights, and environmental protection. At the same time, the institutions of the national security state are groping to redefine their roles in an era that lacks the simplifying assumption of a global communist enemy.

FOREIGN AND DEFENSE POLICY: INSTITUTIONS

The presidency is the dominant institution in the making of foreign and defense policy, and in the first half of the Cold War era it controlled this area with few checks from anywhere else. But the disastrous presidential war in Vietnam sparked Congress to reassert its constitutional role in shaping American policy abroad. Since Vietnam, foreign and defense policy has often been the subject of struggle between presidents and Congress.

Agencies of the executive branch are central to the formulation and implementation of national security policy. Presidents have considerable latitude to use these agencies as they see fit, so the role of each agency and the structure of the foreign policy process itself have varied from one administration to the next. National security agencies are subordinate units that advise and assist the president, yet they shape how the United States understands and operates in international affairs.

The National Security Council

The **National Security Council (NSC)** was created in 1947, at the dawn of the Cold War, to serve as a coordinating mechanism for foreign and defense policy at the highest level. The president, vice president, secretary of state, and secretary of defense are statutory members of the NSC; the director of central intelligence and the chair of the Joint Chiefs of Staff are statutory advisers (see Table 19.1). In theory, NSC members and their hand-picked advisers meet together to set the basic guidelines for American global policy and to respond when overseas crises erupt.

In practice, however, presidents have found NSC meetings to be a ponderous instrument. The importance of the NSC has come to reside, instead, in the head of its staff, the president's **national security adviser.** President Kennedy was the first to transform this position from bureaucratic assistant to the council to personal adviser to the president; his national security adviser, McGeorge Bundy, came to overshadow his secretary of state, Dean Rusk, in influence. Subsequent national security advisers expanded on Bundy's role. None dominated American foreign policy so thoroughly as Henry Kissinger. Under Presidents Nixon and Ford, Kissinger was the basic architect of American foreign policy and its most celebrated spokesperson in the media.

TABLE 19.1

Composition of the
National Security
Council

Statutory Members of the NSC
President
Vice president
Secretary of state
Secretary of defense
Statutory Advisers to the NSC
Director of central intelligence
Chairman, Joint Chiefs of Staff
Other Attendees
Chief of staff to the president
Assistant to the president for national security affairs
Secretary of the treasury
Attorney general
Others as invited

Source: Reproduced by permission of the publisher, F.E. Peacock Publishers, Inc., Itasca, Illinois. From James M. McCormick, AMERICAN FOREIGN POLICY AND PROCESS, 2nd Ed., 1992 copyright, p. 371.

National security advisers are in a strong position to exert influence. They have an advantage over secretaries of state in physical proximity to the president, working in the White House and briefing the president frequently on developments around the globe. National security advisers and their small staffs filter the massive amounts of information flowing into the White House from American diplomatic, military, and intelligence personnel throughout the world and can tailor what they report to fit the president's interests more effectively than the larger and more bureaucratic State Department can. A president who relies more on the national security adviser than on the secretary of state retains greater personal control over American foreign policy.[19]

However, criticism in the media and among foreign policy experts that NSC advisers had grown too powerful has led recent presidents to downgrade the adviser's role somewhat. Occupants of the position are now expected to act mainly as coordinators and facilitators and *not* to compete with the secretary of state for public attention. Brent Scowcroft, national security adviser to President Bush, and Anthony Lake, national security adviser to President Clinton, have operated in this manner.

Department of State

The **Department of State** is the oldest department in the president's cabinet and the traditional organ of American diplomacy. For most of American history, the secretary of state was the president's principal foreign policy adviser. State

Department personnel, stationed in embassies and consulates in nations with which the United States maintained diplomatic relations, were America's principal point of contact with the rest of the world.

During the Cold War, however, the Department of State was eclipsed in influence by other institutions. The national security adviser often had greater influence with the president than did the secretary of state. The Department of Defense grew vastly larger than the Department of State in budget and personnel and played a more central role in overseas conflicts. The Department of State also suffered from its reputation as a rigidly bureaucratic institution whose recommendations to the president were overly cautious and uncreative.[20]

Even State's role as the American representative to the world was partially undermined during the Cold War. Personnel from the department's Foreign Service still make up the principal staff at the approximately three hundred embassies, consulates, and other offices that the United States maintains in other nations. American missions abroad are no longer, however, purely diplomatic outposts; military attachés and CIA spies use them as a base to conduct the overseas business of the national security state. In countries where Cold War struggles have been aggressively waged, representatives from the military and from CIA "stations" have frequently played a more important role than Foreign Service officers.

With the end of the Cold War, the Department of State may be making a comeback. President Bush selected his closest political friend and counsellor, James Baker, as secretary of state. President Clinton has indicated that his secretary of state, Warren Christopher, is his principal foreign policy adviser. Christopher's role appears to be even larger than Baker's because Clinton, unlike Bush, prefers to spend his time dealing with domestic policy. In the post–Cold War era, the standing of the Department of State should benefit from the fact that diplomatic, rather than military, approaches to international problems seem more appropriate.

Department of Defense

The end of the Cold War has not been so beneficial to the **Department of Defense.** During that era, this umbrella organization for the armed forces, symbolized by its massive headquarters, the Pentagon, was the most powerful agency of the national security state.

The Department of Defense has a dual leadership structure: civilian and military. The secretary of defense heads the department and maintains the American tradition of civilian control of the military. Below the secretary on the civilian side are several assistant secretaries for specialized functions, along with civilian secretaries for the army, navy, and air force. Secretaries of defense have varied considerably in their approaches to the military. Some, such as President Kennedy's secretary, Robert McNamara, have seen their role as imposing organizational rationality on the military, especially by setting limits to the services' unceasing request for costly new weapons systems. Others, such as

President Reagan's secretary, Caspar Weinberger, have been zealous advocates for rapid increases in defense spending.

Each of the military services also has a commanding officer from among its ranks. The top uniformed leaders come together in the **Joint Chiefs of Staff (JCS),** headed by a chair. The JCS conveys the military's point of view to the president and the secretary of defense. The JCS's influence with civilian officials often has been diminished by the perception that its advice is biased toward military priorities. President Kennedy thus was highly skeptical of JCS recommendations. President Reagan was more friendly but reportedly could not remember the name of one of his JCS chairs. The JCS did reach a peak of prestige after President Bush appointed as its chair General Colin Powell, the highest-ranking African American in the history of the armed forces.

The enormous expansion of the American military during the Cold War was built on claims, at times deliberately exaggerated, of a communist campaign to take over the entire planet. Concealed beneath the rhetoric about the communist threat was a different fuel for military expansion: interservice rivalry. Each branch of the services was eager to grow larger, more powerful, and better armed; each was fearful that the others would encroach on its central missions (see Chapter 14 for an example). Each service pushed for its own preferred new weapons system, even when the result was overlap and duplication in weaponry. Every time the Air Force developed a new model fighter plane, for instance, the Navy had to have a new fighter plane to match, and vice versa.

Cold War expansion of the military was facilitated by the growth of the *military-industrial complex*. Coined by President Eisenhower, the term refers to the potentially dangerous influence of the political alliance between the Pentagon and the corporations that manufacture its arms. Expensive new weapons systems are mutually rewarding to the armed forces and to companies, especially in such fields as aircraft, electronics, and shipbuilding, for which defense contracts can bring in several billion dollars a year in guaranteed sales. Defense contractors thus place their financial muscle and lobbying resources behind Pentagon budget requests.

Throughout the Cold War, the Pentagon was always eager to obtain costly new weapons. It was not, however, always eager to use them. Vietnam was a searing experience for the American military, which felt angry that it had not been allowed to go all-out and embarrassed that it had lost a war for the first time in American history. After Vietnam, Pentagon officials tended to oppose the use of American troops abroad unless first assured of congressional and public support and promised that massive force could be employed. In the 1980s, it was the Department of Defense that was reluctant to get militarily engaged in Central America and Lebanon, while the Department of State pushed for such involvement.

The Persian Gulf War showed the American military at its most impressive and provided a shot in the arm for its prestige. But the euphoria of a high-tech military machine faded quickly, especially after the grim realities of the federal deficit came back into view. Now the Pentagon is engaged in a defensive battle to hold down cuts in its force levels, termination of funding for its new weapons systems, and closing of its bases. In a nation that no longer feels militarily threatened, the Department of Defense is struggling to define new roles for a standing army in the post–Cold War world.

The Intelligence Community

One of the central features of the national security state is a large and diverse *intelligence community*. A number of U.S. agencies gather intelligence (information) about military, political, and economic developments in other countries (see Figure 19.1). Some of the institutions in this community specialize in high-tech intelligence-gathering: among these is the National Security Agency, which

FIGURE 19.1

The Intelligence Community

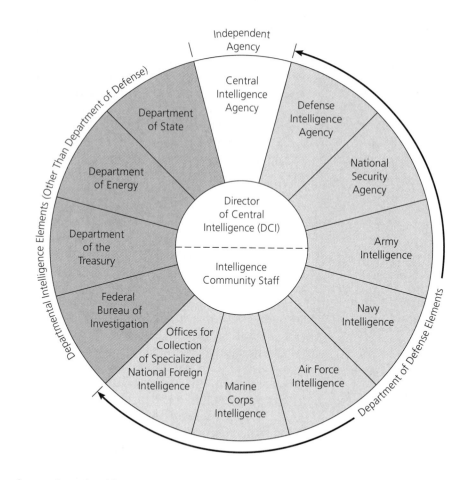

Source: Reproduced by permission of the publisher, F.E. Peacock Publishers, Inc., Itasca, Illinois. From James M. McCormick, AMERICAN FOREIGN POLICY AND PROCESS, 2nd Ed., 1992 copyright, p. 407.

employs the most advanced computer technology and spy satellites to monitor communications around the world. Each branch of the armed forces maintains its own intelligence unit. But the preeminent force in the intelligence community is the **Central Intelligence Agency.** The head of the CIA is also director of central intelligence for the entire government and the most influential figure in the highly secretive world of intelligence.

When Congress created the CIA, it thought it was establishing an agency to gather intelligence by various means ranging from analyses of foreign newspapers to espionage. Yet a vague phrase in the 1947 law referring to "other functions and duties" was seized on by the CIA to establish a unit that had little to do with intelligence-gathering.[21] This was the **covert action** wing of the CIA, which specialized in secret operations that could not be traced to the U.S. government. Covert action became a secret weapon for presidents, allowing them to conduct a hidden as well as a public foreign policy by, for example, bribing foreign politicians, stirring up economic unrest in other nations, or pushing for military coups to overthrow governments considered unfriendly.

Covert action became the hallmark of the CIA and was usually supported by the argument that the nation's communist enemies were employing the same kinds of "dirty tricks" to advance their sinister objectives. Few covert operations, as it turned out, actually hurt the communists or furthered American national security. Many backfired, making more enemies than friends in the long run; the Iranian people's continuing hostility to America is a prime example.[22]

It is not the ineffectiveness of covert action, however, that has made the CIA the national security agency that most disturbs popular democrats. They are even more worried about the incompatibility of covert action with American democracy. Political scientist Loch Johnson notes that whereas democracy requires open government, public debate, the rule of law, and ethical behavior, covert action requires "the use of tactics or 'dirty tricks' that are far removed from the accepted philosophical tenets of democratic theory—lying, sabotage, even clandestine warfare and assassination in times of peace."[23]

Revelations in the mid-1970s of CIA abuses, including spying on American citizens as well as assassination plots, led to the formation of intelligence committees in the House and Senate to monitor and occasionally veto covert operations. Through these congressional committees, there is now at least some measure of CIA public accountability.[24] Yet the CIA has found ways to evade accountability. President Reagan's director of the CIA, William Casey, misled the congressional committees about the agency's covert actions against the government of Nicaragua. When Congress later prohibited the Reagan administration from using the CIA to fund and direct the *contras*, which were fighting to overthrow that government, Casey turned to the NSC staff and Lieutenant Colonel Oliver North to carry out this mission—a covert action that led to the Iran/*contra* scandal.

Even today, the intelligence community remains shrouded in a protective cloak of secrecy. Despite the urgings of legislative leaders, its budget, estimated at nearly $30 billion for 1994, is still hidden in the spending figures for the

Pentagon and thus is protected from congressional and public debate.[25] Deprived of a communist enemy, the CIA is ripe for a renewed democratic debate. A strong case can be made that the United States will continue to require effective intelligence-gathering in the post–Cold War world to forewarn American foreign policy makers about political and military developments in other nations. Some in the CIA also are focusing on new intelligence fields, such as economic spying and counterspying. But the rationale for a covert action wing of the CIA has become increasingly dubious.

FOREIGN POLICY AND ECONOMIC POWER

Although military concerns were uppermost for American foreign policy makers during the Cold War, economic concerns were by no means forgotten. The United States emerged from World War II as an unchallenged economic giant, its superiority all the greater because its rivals had been physically or economically devastated by the war. To restore the shattered economies of Europe as trading partners (and to prevent European nations from falling prey to communist subversion), the United States undertook a massive program of economic aid, the Marshall Plan. During the first several decades of the Cold War, the United States was the hegemonic (predominant) power in the capitalist part of the world, setting the rules on international economic relations. American overseas investments and trade boomed during these decades.

But this hegemonic power finally weakened, eroded both by the economic resurgence of Western Europe and Japan and by the heavy burden of the arms race against the Soviet Union (a burden that America's capitalist competitors largely escaped). Starting in 1971, the United States began to run up a trade deficit, importing more from other countries than it sold to them. This deficit grew to huge proportions, and by the mid-1980s the U.S. had become the world's largest debtor. Rather than being able to set the rules, America now had to engage in extended—and frequently frustrating—multinational negotiations to bring down tariff barriers or open up foreign markets.[26]

Private interests play a significant role in American foreign economic policy. Labor unions are active, especially in seeking to restrict imports from low-wage nations because they eliminate American jobs. Farm groups press for greater government efforts to promote agricultural exports. The most influential private force is the corporate sector. Individuals in the top decision-making echelon of the national security state often have been recruited into temporary government service from large corporations, investment banks, and corporate law firms.[27] Regardless of economic background, American foreign policy makers have generally subscribed to the proposition that what advances the interests of American corporations and banks abroad advances the American national interest.

It is difficult at times to disentangle economic interests from political interests in the history of Cold War policy. Consider two cases already mentioned concerning the CIA: Iran and Chile. In Iran, the CIA's role in putting the shah in

Selling the Persian Gulf War

Since the war in Vietnam, the American people have been fearful of becoming involved again in a large-scale military conflict. So how did the 1991 Persian Gulf War, during which the United States led a multinational coalition in a rout of the Iraqi invaders of Kuwait, become so popular?

The popularity of the Gulf War stemmed, in part, from the kind of dramatic moral contrasts that have traditionally appealed to Americans. In Saddam Hussein, the Iraqi dictator, the United States faced a genuinely ruthless and brutal foe. With the Iraqi invasion of tiny, oil-rich Kuwait, the United States was opposing a case of naked aggression. The impressive ability of President Bush to rally a multinational coalition to drive Hussein out of Kuwait demonstrated both American leadership and international commitment to deny aggressors the object of their crimes.

But even these appealing elements were not enough, in the eyes of the White House and the military, to persuade the American people to fight a war in the Persian Gulf. The Gulf War had to be sold to the American people, they believed, with hype and myth. Consider the uses of babies and bombs to sell the war.

A shocking story of Iraqi brutality helped convince many Americans that the country had to go to war to rescue the suffering people of Kuwait. A fifteen-year-old Kuwaiti girl, identified only by her first name, Nayirah, appeared before a congressional caucus and related in a tearful voice how she had witnessed Iraqi soldiers take Kuwaiti babies out of their hospital incubators and leave them on the floor to die. The incubator story was widely repeated by President Bush and others. After the war, it was revealed that Nayirah was in fact the daughter of Kuwait's ambassador to the United States and that the incubator story had been devised by an American public-relations firm in the pay of the Kuwaiti government. Reporters seeking evidence of the incubator tragedy found none and concluded that this notorious Iraqi atrocity had never happened.

Once the war began, the White House and the Pentagon kept a tight control over independent reporting by the press while feeding the media dramatic footage of military triumphs. The undisputed favorite for most Americans were Pentagon videos of laser-guided "smart" bombs homing in on Iraqi targets with incredible accuracy. Watching these videos on TV, viewers could easily believe that the war was a marvel of American technological genius and was humane to boot since smart bombs hit only military targets and spared civilians. After the war, however, the air force revealed that only 7 percent of the explosives it dropped were smart bombs. The rest were conventional dumb bombs, which landed off target 75 percent of the time, sometimes in areas populated by civilians.

There is an old saying that "in a war, truth is the first casualty." The American people had less than the truth to go on when they responded enthusiastically to the Persian Gulf War. They were skillfully manipulated by political and military elites that wanted unquestioning support. The selling of the Persian Gulf War should teach both journalists and citizens that in the face of wartime secrecy and propaganda, they must struggle to keep alive a democratic debate.

Source: John R. MacArthur, *Second Front: Censorship and Propaganda in the Gulf War* (New York: Hill and Wang, 1992); Cecil V. Crabb Jr. and Kevin V. Mulcahy, "The Elitist Presidency: George Bush and the Management of Operation Desert Storm," in Richard W. Waterman, ed., *The Presidency Reconsidered* (Itasca, Ill.: Peacock, 1993), pp. 275–300.

power not only established an anticommunist bastion in the Middle East; it also opened up Iran as a profitable field of operations for American oil companies. In Chile, American-owned corporations were just as zealous as Nixon and Kissinger in getting rid of President Allende. Fearful that Allende might nationalize their properties, the International Telephone and Telegraph Corporation and other American businesses offered the CIA $1.5 million for its covert campaign against him.[28]

FOREIGN POLICY AND PUBLIC OPINION

Until recently, scholars presented a picture of American public opinion in foreign policy that was closely in line with the perspective of elite democracy. Their studies suggested that the mass of Americans lacked interest in or knowledge of foreign affairs, were subject to emotional reactions to foreign events, and tended to defer to elites, especially presidents, in the determination of foreign policies. This view implied that it was fortunate for U.S. foreign policy that elites had the upper hand and that ordinary citizens had relatively little influence.

An important piece of evidence for this view is the rally-around-the-flag phenomenon. When presidents make dramatic moves abroad, Americans tend to back them—and the flag they represent—in overwhelming numbers. It does not seem to matter what a president's move has been. Thus, President Johnson's popularity went up both after he increased the bombing of North Vietnam and after he decreased it. Nor does it seem to matter whether the president's move has been successful. The popularity of President Kennedy rose after he sponsored the disastrous Bay of Pigs invasion of Cuba in 1961.

New and more extensive research by political scientists has altered this picture substantially.[29] The view of public opinion that has emerged is more favorable to the perspective of popular democracy. Although public knowledge of foreign affairs may fall short of the standard held by foreign policy experts, the newest research shows public opinion about foreign policy to be sensible and stable. The public responds rationally to the information it receives. It rallies behind a president who monopolizes the dissemination of information in a foreign crisis. But it may turn against the White House when alternative sources of information become available.

According to the new research, the public seldom has a direct impact on *specific* foreign policy decisions. But it can establish a climate of opinion that policymakers have to take into account. During the era of Cold War consensus, elites enjoyed a permissive climate for dispatching American troops to overseas conflicts. In the 1970s and 1980s, however, the majority of Americans were affected by a "Vietnam syndrome," an apprehension about sending troops abroad that constrained decision-makers. President Reagan tried to overcome this syndrome with a guaranteed military victory in Grenada. Yet his efforts were not very successful: Public opinion constrained the Reagan administration from sending troops to attack the Sandinista government of Nicaragua and pressured the president to resume arms control negotiations with the Soviet Union.[30] President Bush claimed that he had finally vanquished the Vietnam syndrome in the Persian Gulf war. Yet public fears about sending American forces "in harm's way" continue to limit President Clinton's options abroad.

Rather than always deferring to foreign policy elites, public opinion can, if it becomes strong and intense, compel elites to change their policies. Neither the president nor Congress is likely to hold out long once public opinion moves sharply in a new direction. Robert Shapiro and Benjamin Page found that when public opinion changed significantly, American foreign policy subsequently changed with it about two-thirds of the time. The more that public unhappiness over American casualties in the war in Vietnam mounted, for example, the faster the president withdrew American forces from the conflict.[31]

That public opinion on foreign policy is rational *and* influential is encouraging to advocates of popular democracy. Also encouraging is what the new research has demonstrated about the content of popular beliefs. In the words of Shapiro and Page, "A strong aversion to using U.S. troops and a preference for negotiated settlements, arms control, and cooperative relations run through decades of public opinion data. The American public is willing to fight when it perceives a clear threat to U.S. interests but is very reluctant to do so unless there is no alternative."[32]

POST-COLD WAR FOREIGN POLICY AND THE DEMOCRATIC DEBATE

If there was ever a fitting moment to introduce an "End of the Cold War Act" into Congress, 1991 was it. With communism in collapse almost everywhere, Senator Daniel Patrick Moynihan of New York proposed that the prime symbol of Cold War secrecy—the CIA—be abolished, its functions folded into the Defense and State Departments. "The law of nations," argued Moynihan, "somewhere got lost in the fog of the Cold War. . . . The task of purging the Cold War from our institutions is enormous. It will require a sustained and determined effort."[33]

As Moynihan spoke, the Bush administration was engaging in a different kind of "determined effort." The national security state was arrayed in battle gear for the Persian Gulf War, with half a million troops poised to oust Iraqi forces from Kuwait. President Bush spoke of a new challenge for the American military and for America's allies. The brutality and aggression of Iraqi dictator Saddam Hussein, Bush proclaimed, must not be rewarded. Hussein's defeat would initiate a "new world order," in which the threat of "chaos" and "instability" would be banished by a strengthened international community led by the United States.[34]

Neither Moynihan's nor Bush's version of American foreign policy for the post–Cold War era has been put into effect. The CIA has not been abolished, and the Pentagon is still massive. Despite some cuts in weapons systems and troop levels, the U.S. government still spends $260 billion annually for the military, about as much (considering inflation) as was spent in the late 1970s before President Reagan's military build-up. Indeed, as Figure 19.2 shows, the United States now spends about four times as much on the military as all of its potential adversaries do *combined*.[35] Although the Cold War may be over, the conversion of a permanent war economy to civilian purposes still seems remote.

President Bush's new world order has not fared much better. Operation Desert Storm seemed to be a great victory at the time, but it left the man Bush had called the Adolf Hitler of the Middle East still in power in Iraq. The victory was also tarnished when Hussein used his remaining weapons (many of them supplied by American sources) to crush rebellious Kurdish and Shi'ite minorities.

After Desert Storm, the use of American forces to keep order abroad became increasingly unpopular at home. In Bosnia, the U.S. and its European allies did little militarily to stop the slaughter of Muslims by Serbs. In Somalia, American forces, originally sent by Bush on a humanitarian mission to feed the starving, became targets in a civil war. Gruesome pictures on television of American casualties forced President Clinton to order the withdrawal of troops. Clinton was able to use military power effectively in nearby Haiti. Facing an imminent American invasion, Haiti's military dictators agreed to give up their power. American troops took over the island and began the arduous task of dismantling the structures of repression that had terrorized the Haitian people. Jean-Bertrand Aristide, the democratically elected president exiled by a military coup in 1991, returned in October 1994 to a joyous welcome by Haiti's masses.

Addressing the United Nations General Assembly in 1993, President Clinton

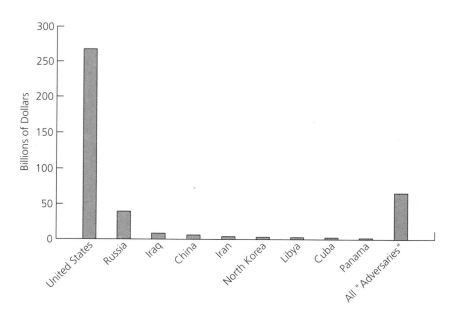

FIGURE 19.2

The United States vs. Potential Adversaries: 1992 Military Spending

Source: Reprinted from STATE OF THE UNION, by Richard Caplan and John Feffer, eds., 1994, by permission of Westview Press, Boulder, Colorado.

When American troops landed on the beaches of Somalia in December, 1992, they found television crews waiting for them. In the post–Cold War era, the media often play an influential role in foreign policy crises.

called the post–Cold War era "a magic moment" ripe with new opportunities as well as potential dangers. Few would disagree. More than at any time since World War II, however, simply defining foreign policy choices has become the subject of debate. Without the glue of anticommunism, American foreign policy has become fragmented. Older issues of military security and economic strength have been joined by newer issues of human rights and environmental protection, bringing into the foreign policy debate dissenting voices that previously had been locked out. Public opinion, concerned about America's economic future and hostile to endangering American lives abroad in long-term military engagements, is an increasingly potent factor in the debate.[36]

Military Force and National Security

For the first time since Franklin Roosevelt's administration, the United States faces no known enemies capable of invading Europe or North America or obliterating either in a nuclear attack. Why, then, keep a military of Cold War size? An important group of Pentagon planners and foreign policy experts has perceived new military threats to national security. They argue that maintaining and readjusting the country's vast military power should be the top foreign policy priority.[37] The influence of these "new militarists" has been enhanced by the fact that President Clinton, on the defensive in military matters because he avoided the draft during the Vietnam War, has not been willing to challenge them.

The new militarists construct many frightening scenarios. The proliferation of nuclear and chemical weapons means that countries like Pakistan or North Korea could threaten their neighbors. Civil wars in the Balkans and the former Soviet Union could spiral beyond present borders. A newly unified Germany could conflict with its traditional enemy, Russia. Japan and China could threaten each other. Third World leaders with ambitions like those of Saddam Hussein could attempt to control commodities, such as oil, that are essential for the wealthy countries. International terrorism and crime could reign unpunished. Accordingly, the new militarists call for a defense shift from the "high-intensity conflict" between Cold War superpowers to the ostensible "low- and medium-intensity conflicts" of the post–Cold War era.[38]

Popular democrats respond to this frightening picture with skepticism. Pentagon planners, they suggest, will always find threats to justify their bloated budget requests. In the popular democratic view, the United States can effectively safeguard its national security with a much smaller military than the Cold War version. Besides, the post–Cold War world requires a mode of thinking that stops defining threats to security exclusively in military terms and begins to recognize that economic, political, and environmental problems pose security issues as well. Expressing this perspective, Michael Shuman and Hal Harvey write:

> The time has surely come for the United States to lead the world beyond the habits of the Cold War. . . . At a time when military force is less and less relevant to global politics, a security policy that continues to focus on force will pillage the U.S. economy, weaken its international influence, erode its democratic decisionmaking, and damage its moral standing.[39]

Economic Security and Foreign Policy

During the 1980s, the United States rolled up huge budget and trade deficits, saw its lead in the field of high technology overtaken by Japan, and stood by as its workers' wages, literacy, and skills stagnated. In response to these developments, many now view the American position in the world economy as the central issue of national security. Surveys of the public find greater worries about international economics than about military threats; among most corporate elites and foreign policy experts a similar concern prevails. In place of megatons and firepower as measurements of America's global standing, many now propose to use export totals, the strength of the dollar, and the level of American wages.

Those who stress international economics as the new key to national security generally praise free markets. But the Clinton administration has brought a new emphasis on government's role as an innovator, negotiator, and facilitator in international economic relations. It stresses public-private partnerships designed to develop new technologies and products as a foreign policy priority. Experts outside the administration echo its call for reversing many of the practices of the Reagan-Bush years. At a time when government spending needs to be limited, a Carnegie Foundation report calls for a new foreign policy to alter the emphasis from military to economic strength. Instead of spending so heavily on the military, this approach advocates public investments in the health, education, and retraining of American workers and in physical infrastructure—research centers, electronic superhighways, and other public works programs—as the way to enhance America's competitive position in the global economy.[40]

Putting the economy first in foreign policy, however, raises as many questions as it answers. The bitter 1993 debate over the North American Free Trade Agreement (NAFTA) is an instructive example. On the side of free trade in this debate stood President Clinton; his most active backers were large corporations that stood to benefit from the agreement because it increased their ability to export and import. The opposition to NAFTA brought together the labor, environmental, and other movements, which argued that the agreement was bad for both Americans and Mexicans since it would keep wages low and environmental regulations unenforced on both sides of the border. Congress passed NAFTA by a narrow margin. President Clinton immediately went on to promote further lowering of global trade barriers, first in meetings with the Pacific Rim nations and then at international meetings to update the General Agreement on Tariffs and Trade.

The call to reorient American foreign policy toward economic security draws support from both elite and popular democrats. But as the struggle over NAFTA suggests, the two differ in their priorities. In the elite democratic perspective, the United States can remain competitive in world markets only if corporate experts make the important decisions and American workers accept the inevitable dislocations and hardships that economic restructuring brings. Popular democrats, on the other hand, favor public policies that will help the United States remain competitive without sacrificing the future of American workers or of the environment.

Environmental Security and Foreign Policy

Throughout the Cold War, environmental issues were virtually absent from the foreign policy debate, at least among the elites that usually dominated that debate. But it has become increasingly difficult to see what national security can mean in a future where the earth's ozone layer is depleted, its energy sources are diminished, or its crops are withered by the heat of the "greenhouse effect." Since the United States and other rich countries are huge energy guzzlers and serve as ready markets for the timber and agricultural products of destroyed rain forests, world environmental issues are bound to redefine how we think about security in foreign policy.

Often, as in the NAFTA debate, environmental concerns are intertwined with economic issues. The national security state of the Cold War era has left us with its own share of environmental problems. For example, millions of pounds of reactor fuel, used to make nuclear bombs, have sat for so long in storage pools at government weapons centers that they are rusting and releasing radioactivity into the environment. The cost of cleaning up this and other environmental hazards of the nuclear arms race is expected to run to tens of billions of dollars.[41]

It has chiefly been through the actions of domestic groups, such as the Sierra Club, and international organizations, such as Greenpeace, that environmental issues have joined the foreign policy agenda. A foreign policy that takes the environment into account now enjoys wide public support. When President Bush, attending an earth summit in Brazil in 1992, succeeded in weakening a treaty on global warming and refused to sign another treaty safeguarding biodiversity, he was roundly criticized back home. Shortly after taking office, President Clinton signed the biodiversity treaty that Bush had rejected.

Democracy, Human Rights, and National Security

American foreign policy during the Cold War tended to concentrate on human rights abuses only in communist countries. The government ignored—and in some cases abetted—repression by anticommunist allies in countries from Iran to Chile to El Salvador.

Although the United States continues to support some repressive governments, foreign policy makers now pay at least some attention to human rights concerns. In 1993, President Clinton promised to make American-Chinese trade conditional on Chinese progress in human rights. Under heavy pressure from American business interests, however, he backed away from this human rights stance a year later. Human rights concerns often continue to be subordinated to military or economic considerations. Yet American foreign policy makers are under greater pressure than they were during the Cold War era to live up to their pronouncements about the importance of democracy.

CONCLUSION: A MORE DEMOCRATIC FOREIGN POLICY?

In the confusing new world of the post–Cold War era, many Americans, echoing the old popular democratic strain, wish to cut back on international involvement and turn inward. This impulse may be taken too far when it advocates a new isolationism. The United States is too intertwined with the rest of the world, and has too much at stake in international economic, military, political, and environmental issues, to return to the isolationism of the past. In upholding their traditional standard of internationalism, as against isolationism, foreign policy elites have an important case to make to the American people.

Nevertheless, the popular democratic tradition has much to offer American policy for a post–Cold War world. Popular democrats have long argued that American strength in the world depends, above all, on a healthy economy and society at home. They have believed that America should seek peaceful commercial relations with other nations and support democratic progress around the globe. They have warned of a large, expensive, and aggressive military and emphasized the distortions it introduces into the economy and political system.

For popular democrats, the end of the Cold War is a blessing. Its familiar argument that democratic goals must be sacrificed to the imperatives of superpower rivalry has collapsed. Now American foreign policy can be reoriented to furthering democracy. The United States can pursue economic progress for its own people in ways that do not undermine economic progress for other peoples, especially in poorer nations. It can stand for human rights and democratic elections in nations struggling to cast off the legacy of authoritarianism, whether of the left or of the right. And it can find common cause with other nations in combatting the environmental dangers that threaten everyone.

Popular democrats seek to widen the democratic debate over foreign policy. To open up this debate, the secretive habits of the national security state, including excessive classification of information and covert action, must be terminated. Foreign policy experts in the executive branch and the Pentagon must not monopolize the discussion; voices in Congress and in citizen groups also must be heard. Because the United States must speak to the rest of the world in a clear and coherent fashion, presidential leadership in foreign policy will remain necessary. But in the post–Cold War world, presidents should not be the sole masters of foreign policy. Their approach to the world should emerge from a democratic dialogue over the goals and instruments of American foreign policy.

KEY TERMS

isolationism
expansion
Cold War
national security state
North Atlantic Treaty Organization (NATO)
containment

National Security Council (NSC)
national security adviser
Department of State
Department of Defense
Joint Chiefs of Staff (JCS)
Central Intelligence Agency (CIA)
covert action

SUGGESTED READINGS

Richard J. Barnet, *The Rockets' Red Glare: When America Goes to War—The Presidents and the People* (New York: Simon and Schuster, 1990). A narrative history of American decisions to fight abroad, told from a popular democratic perspective.

Loch K. Johnson, *America's Secret Power: The CIA in a Democratic Society* (New York: Oxford University Press, 1989). Focuses on congressional efforts to hold the CIA accountable for its covert activities.

Henry Kissinger, *Diplomacy* (New York: Simon and Schuster, 1994). Diplomatic history as viewed by a central figure in the elite democratic tradition.

James M. McCormick, *American For-*

eign Policy and Process, Second Edition (Itasca, IL: Peacock Publishers, 1992). A comprehensive text on the history and institutions of American foreign policy.

Michael H. Shuman and Hal Harvey, *Security Without War: A Post–Cold War Foreign Policy* (Boulder, CO: Westview Press, 1993). Provocative proposals for an American foreign policy that relies on military force less than we have in the past.

Afterword: The Prospects for Popular Democracy

Throughout this book, we have examined the tension in American politics between elite democracy and popular democracy. Where is the democratic debate heading? Is elite democracy likely to predominate in the world of high-tech economics and politics? What are the prospects for popular democracy?

Clearly, the forces of elite democracy are powerful. Nowhere is this more true than in the case of the political economy. Given their enormous monetary resources, central role in capital investment, and ideological status as the champions of the free market, corporations hold a privileged position in the political economy. With the onset of intensified global competition, they present themselves as America's front line in the defense of our standard of living and warn that attempts to impose popular democratic controls over private economic forces will undercut our competitive standing and injure all of us in the long run.

Political elites look almost as powerful. They are closely connected to economic elites through campaign contributions and lobbying. And they have found numerous methods to insulate themselves from democratic accountability. Members of Congress are the most accountable, but many have mastered the fundraising and image-making techniques that practically guarantee them reelection and preserve their status as a privileged elite. Presidents also must be responsive to some extent to public opinion, but their royal lifestyle, engagement in elite decision-making circles, and powers of secrecy link them more to elite democracy than to popular democracy. Although bureaucrats and judges sometimes uphold important democratic values, neither are directly accountable to the public.

The many points of connection between private power and political power create a policy process that works, more often than not, to favor elite democracy. Government policies tend to reflect the existing, unequal distribution of power. Rather than fostering greater equality in resources and opportunities, they promote further economic inequality.

Of course, elites do not like to admit that their power comes from money, position, or techniques of manipulation. In their view, it is the growing complexity of the modern world that makes elite guidance of politics a necessity. In an era when change is rapid, many-sided, and often bewildering, ordinary citizens, it often seems, cannot hope to control their own fates directly. Even though citizens should hold ultimate authority through the electoral process, elite democrats assert, actual decision-making must remain in the hands of sophisticated elites, which should not be sidetracked by interference from an ill-informed public.

Elite democracy has been, and is sure to remain, a strong force in American political life. In "normal" times, elites have most of the political advantages. Periodically, however, popular democratic mobilizations challenge the power of elites. When popular democratic forces become active, as in the movements of the 1960s, elite democracy suddenly becomes vulnerable. Why is elite democracy so susceptible to criticism and challenge? What are the strengths of popular democracy?

Although elite democrats build their best case on their superior expertise, elites often make big mistakes. Usually, it is ordinary citizens who pay for these mistakes—and know they do. It was the elite managers of the national security state who planned the Vietnam War—and ordinary American soldiers who were its physical and psychological casualties. It was the secretive White House of Richard Nixon and Ronald Reagan that undermined democratic accountability in the Watergate and Iran-*contra* scandals respectively. It was corporate elites, with their short-sighted pursuit of profit, that polluted the environment and devastated communities through plant closings and layoffs. Recent revelations of Cold War experiments, in which government officials and scientists exposed unwitting Americans to atomic radiation, are only one more demonstration that the people are not served well when elites make important decisions without democratic controls.

Elite wisdom and power are called into question by American political values. The idea that concentrated power is dangerous to liberty and damaging to ordinary citizens is central to the American political tradition. The American Revolution was a grand experiment in bringing government under popular control. Although elite power made a comeback in the Constitution, it was tempered by concessions to popular democracy and limited by the Bill of Rights won by the Anti-federalists. Throughout the course of American history, mass movements have revived the revolutionary spirit of protest and reasserted the popular democratic doctrine that ordinary people are competent to govern their own affairs.

Not only in the United States but around the globe as well, the logic of democracy has become increasingly difficult for elites to resist. This inclusionary logic—the strongest advantage that popular democrats enjoy in the democratic debate—holds that every citizen, regardless of class, race, gender, or specialized education, has a rightful say in the processes of public decision-making. The popular democratic emphasis on equality and the popular democratic commitment to the dignity and competence of ordinary citizens have largely won the battle for rhetorical and symbolic preeminence; even elite democrats have to pay at least lip service to them. When these popular democratic values are put into political action, elites are put on the defensive. Accustomed to mass apathy, they are surprised and even frightened by instances of popular democratic activism.

Popular democrats cannot hope to match elite democrats in money or privileged access to the inner councils of government. Yet popular democracy in America has enduring strengths. The American tradition is rich in ideas and activities that show, contrary to the assumption of elite democrats, that people can get beyond a narrow self-interest when they participate in the affairs of society. There is the republican tradition, with its ideal of virtuous citizens deliberating together on how to advance the common good. There is the diversity of religious faiths, almost all of which teach service to others over self-seeking. There is the experience of countless neighborhoods and communities in which people have joined together to bring improvement and harmony. There are the inspiring efforts of racial minorities and women to claim their equal share of the democratic promise.

All of these rest on—and sustain—the most fundamental assumption of popular democracy: that people can be sociable rather than self-centered and can make their lives better and more meaningful when they are involved in public life. Against the elite democratic claim that mass apathy is natural, popular democrats argue that given the opportunity, people will participate in public affairs and will learn from their participation how they can gain in both power and dignity. Evidence for this argument can be found in the major policy victories won by popular democrats in such areas as collective bargaining for labor, civil rights, women's rights, and environmental protection.

Popular democrats concede that the complexity of modern society requires experts to play a significant role in the political process. They do not concede that the role of expertise must be as great as elite democrats would have it. Our modern high-tech society may in fact make possible a diffusion of expertise to citizens that will enhance popular democracy. With the rise of more diverse and interactive media, with the spread of personal computers, and with other new developments that place almost every conceivable kind of information within the public's grasp, the gap between elites and ordinary citizens can be narrowed. The end of the Cold War also favors popular democracy by reducing the need to keep so much information about the world secret in the name of national security.

As political scientists, we wrote this book to explain how American politics can be understood as a debate between elite democracy and popular democracy. As citizens who came of age politically in the mass movements of the 1960s and 1970s, we wrote this book because we care particularly about the fate of popular democracy. It is easy to become cynical about the possibilities of a genuine popular democracy, and in the course of this book we have noted many obstacles to moving American political life farther in this direction. Yet we are struck by the continued vibrancy of the popular democratic tradition in the United States.

Too often, we believe, elite democrats have sold American democracy short. And sometimes they have persuaded ordinary Americans of the need to accept the guidance of a "superior" few. In writing this book, we join an enduring

American tradition, stretching back to the revolutionaries and Anti-federalists, that calls on ordinary citizens to have confidence in their capacity for self-government. We hope that the book stimulates thought and action on your part about the meaning of American democracy.

APPENDIXES

The Declaration of Independence in Congress   July 4, 1776

The unanimous declaration of the thirteen United States of America

When, in the course of human events, it becomes necessary for one people to dissolve the political bonds which have connected them with another, and to assume, among the powers of the earth, the separate and equal station to which the laws of nature and of nature's God entitle them, a decent respect to the opinions of mankind requires that they should declare the causes which impel them to the separation.

We hold these truths to be self-evident: That all men are created equal; that they are endowed by their Creator with certain unalienable rights; that among these are life, liberty, and the pursuit of happiness; that, to secure these rights, governments are instituted among men, deriving their just powers from the consent of the governed; that whenever any form of government becomes destructive of these ends, it is the right of the people to alter or to abolish it, and to institute new government, laying its foundation on such principles, and organizing its powers in such form, as to them shall seem most likely to effect their safety and happiness. Prudence, indeed, will dictate that governments long established should not be changed for light and transient causes; and accordingly all experience hath shown that mankind are more disposed to suffer, while evils are sufferable, than to right themselves by abolishing the forms to which they are accustomed. But when a long train of abuses and usurpations, pursuing invariably the same object, evinces a design to reduce them under absolute despotism, it is their right, it is their duty, to throw off such government, and to provide new guards for their future security. Such has been the patient sufferance of these colonies; and such is now the necessity which constrains them to alter their former systems of government. The history of the present King of Great Britain is a history of repeated injuries and usurpations, all having in direct object the establishment of an absolute tyranny over these states. To prove this, let facts be submitted to a candid world.

He has refused his assent to laws, the most wholesome and necessary for the public good.

He has forbidden his governors to pass laws of immediate and pressing importance, unless suspended in their operation till his assent should be obtained; and, when so suspended, he has utterly neglected to attend to them.

He has refused to pass other laws for the accommodation of large districts of people, unless those people would relinquish the right of representation in the legislature, a right inestimable to them, and formidable to tyrants only.

He has called together legislative bodies at places unusual, uncomfortable, and distant from the depository of their public records, for the sole purpose of fatiguing them into compliance with his measures.

He has dissolved representative houses repeatedly, for opposing, with manly firmness, his invasions on the rights of the people.

He has refused for a long time, after such dissolutions, to cause others to be elected; whereby the legislative powers, incapable of annihilation, have returned to the people at large for their exercise; the state remaining, in the mean time, exposed to all the dangers of invasions from without and convulsions within.

He has endeavored to prevent the population of these

states; for that purpose obstructing the laws for naturalization of foreigners; refusing to pass others to encourage their migration hither, and raising the conditions of new appropriations of lands.

He has obstructed the administration of justice, by refusing his assent to laws for establishing judiciary powers.

He has made judges dependent on his will alone, for the tenure of their offices, and the amount and payment of their salaries.

He has erected a multitude of new offices, and sent hither swarms of officers to harass our people and eat out their substance.

He has kept among us, in times of peace, standing armies, without the consent of our legislatures.

He has affected to render the military independent of, and superior to, the civil power.

He has combined with others to subject us to a jurisdiction foreign to our constitution, and unacknowledged by our laws, giving his assent to their acts of pretended legislation:

For quartering large bodies of armed troops among us;

For protecting them, by a mock trial, from punishment for any murders which they should commit on the inhabitants of these states;

For cutting off our trade with all parts of the world;

For imposing taxes on us without our consent;

For depriving us, in many cases, of the benefits of trial by jury;

For transporting us beyond seas, to be tried for pretended offenses;

For abolishing the free system of English laws in a neighboring province, establishing therein an arbitrary government, and enlarging its boundaries, so as to render it at once an example and fit instrument for introducing the same absolute rule into these colonies;

For taking away our charters, abolishing our most valuable laws, and altering fundamentally the forms of our governments;

For suspending our own legislatures, and declaring themselves invested with power to legislate for us in all cases whatsoever.

He has abdicated government here, by declaring us out of his protection and waging war against us.

He has plundered our seas, ravaged our coasts, burned our towns, and destroyed the lives of our people.

He is at this time transporting large armies of foreign mercenaries to complete the works of death, desolation, and tyranny already begun with circumstances of cruelty and perfidy scarcely paralleled in the most barbarous ages, and totally unworthy the head of a civilized nation.

He has constrained our fellow-citizens, taken captive on the high seas, to bear arms against their country, to become the executioners of their friends and brethren, or to fall themselves by their hands.

He has excited domestic insurrection among us, and has endeavored to bring on the inhabitants of our frontiers the merciless Indian savages, whose known rule of warfare is an undistinguished destruction of all ages, sexes, and conditions.

In every stage of these oppressions we have petitioned for redress in the most humble terms; our repeated petitions have been answered only by repeated injury. A prince, whose character is thus marked by every act which may define a tyrant, is unfit to be the ruler of a free people.

Nor have we been wanting in our attentions to our British brethren. We have warned them, from time to time, of attempts by their legislature to extend an unwarrantable jurisdiction over us. We have reminded them of the circumstances of our emigration and settlement here. We have appealed to their native justice and magnanimity; and we have conjured them, by the ties of our common kindred, to disavow these usurpations, which would inevitably interrupt our connections and correspondence. They, too, have been deaf to the voice of justice and of consanguinity. We must, therefore, acquiesce in the necessity which denounces our separation, and hold them, as we hold the rest of mankind, enemies in war, in peace friends.

We, therefore, the representatives of the United States of America, in General Congress assembled, appealing to the Supreme Judge of the world for the rectitude of our intentions, do, in the name and by the authority of the good people of these colonies, solemnly publish and declare, that these United Colonies are, and of right ought to be, FREE AND INDEPENDENT STATES; that they are absolved from all allegiance to the British crown, and that all political connection between them and the state of Great Britain is, and ought to be, totally dissolved; and that, as free and independent states, they have full power to levy war, conclude peace, contract alliances, establish commerce, and do all other acts and things which independent states may of right do. And for the support of this declaration, with a firm reliance on the protection of Divine Providence, we mutually pledge to each other our lives, our fortunes, and our sacred honor.

JOHN HANCOCK
and fifty-five others

The Constitution of the United States of America*

Preamble

We the people of the United States, in order to form a more perfect union, establish justice, insure domestic tranquillity, provide for the common defense, promote the general welfare, and secure the blessings of liberty to ourselves and our posterity, do ordain and establish this Constitution for the United States of America.

Article 1

Section 1 All legislative powers herein granted shall be vested in a Congress of the United States, which shall consist of a Senate and a House of Representatives.

Section 2 The House of Representatives shall be composed of members chosen every second year by the people of the several States, and the electors in each State shall have the qualifications requisite for electors of the most numerous branch of the State Legislature.

No person shall be a Representative who shall not have attained to the age of twenty-five years, and been seven years a citizen of the United States, and who shall not, when elected, be an inhabitant of that State in which he shall be chosen.

Representatives and direct taxes shall be apportioned among the several States which may be included within this Union, according to their respective numbers, *which shall be determined by adding to the whole number of free persons, including those bound to service for a term of years and excluding Indians not taxed, three-fifths of all other persons.* The actual enumeration shall be made within three years after the first meeting of the Congress of the United States, and within every subsequent term of ten years, in such manner as they shall by law direct. The number of Representatives shall not exceed one for every thirty

thousand, but each State shall have at least one Representative; *and until such enumeration shall be made, the State of New Hampshire shall be entitled to choose three, Massachusetts eight, Rhode Island and Providence Plantations one, Connecticut five, New York six, New Jersey four, Pennsylvania eight, Delaware one, Maryland six, Virginia ten, North Carolina five, South Carolina five, and Georgia three.*

When vacancies happen in the representation from any State, the Executive authority thereof shall issue writs of election to fill such vacancies.

The House of Representatives shall choose their Speaker and other officers; and shall have the sole power of impeachment.

Section 3 The Senate of the United States shall be composed of two Senators from each State, *chosen by the legislature thereof,* for six years; and each Senator shall have one vote.

Immediately after they shall be assembled in consequence of the first election, they shall be divided as equally as may be into three classes. The seats of the Senators of the first class shall be vacated at the expiration of the second year, of the second class at the expiration of the fourth year, and of the third class at the expiration of the sixth year, so that one-third may be chosen every second year; and if vacancies happen by resignation or otherwise, during the recess of the legislature of any State, the Executive thereof may make temporary appointments until the next meeting of the legislature, which shall then fill such vacancies.

No person shall be a Senator who shall not have attained to the age of thirty years, and been nine years a citizen of the United States, and who shall not, when elected, be an inhabitant of that State for which he shall be chosen.

The Vice-President of the United States shall be President of the Senate, but shall have no vote, unless they be equally divided.

The Senate shall choose their other officers, and also a President *pro tempore*, in the absence of the Vice-President, or when he shall exercise the office of President of the United States.

The Senate shall have the sole power to try all impeachments. When sitting for that purpose, they shall be on oath or affirmation. When the President of the United States is tried, the Chief Justice shall preside: and no person shall be convicted without the concurrence of two-thirds of the members present.

Judgment in cases of impeachment shall not extend

*Passages no longer in effect are printed in italic type.

further than to removal from the office, and disqualification to hold and enjoy any office of honor, trust or profit under the United States: but the party convicted shall nevertheless be liable and subject to indictment, trial, judgment and punishment, according to law.

Section 4   The times, places and manner of holding elections for Senators and Representatives shall be prescribed in each State by the legislature thereof; but the Congress may at any time by law make or alter such regulations, except as to the places of choosing Senators.

The Congress shall assemble at least once in every year, and such meeting *shall be on the first Monday in December, unless they shall by law appoint a different day.*

Section 5   Each house shall be the judge of the elections, returns and qualifications of its own members, and a majority of each shall constitute a quorum to do business; but a smaller number may adjourn from day to day, and may be authorized to compel the attendance of absent members, in such manner, and under such penalties, as each house may provide.

Each house may determine the rules of its proceedings, punish its members for disorderly behavior, and with the concurrence of two-thirds, expel a member.

Each house shall keep a journal of its proceedings, and from time to time publish the same, excepting such parts as may in their judgment require secrecy; and the yeas and nays of the members of either house on any question shall, at the desire of one-fifth of those present, be entered on the journal.

Neither house, during the session of Congress, shall, without the consent of the other, adjourn for more than three days, nor to any other place than that in which the two houses shall be sitting.

Section 6   The Senators and Representatives shall receive a compensation for their services, to be ascertained by law and paid out of the treasury of the United States. They shall in all cases except treason, felony and breach of the peace, be privileged from arrest during their attendance at the session of their respective houses, and in going to and returning from the same; and for any speech or debate in either house, they shall not be questioned in any other place.

No Senator or Representative shall, during the time for which he was elected, be appointed to any civil office under the authority of the United States, which shall have been created, or the emoluments whereof shall have been increased, during such time; and no person holding any office under the United States shall be a member of either house during his continuance in office.

Section 7   All bills for raising revenue shall originate in the House of Representatives; but the Senate may propose or concur with amendments as on other bills.

Every bill which shall have passed the House of Representatives and the Senate, shall, before it become a law, be presented to the President of the United States; if he approve he shall sign it, but if not he shall return it with objections to that house in which it originated, who shall enter the objections at large on their journal, and proceed to reconsider it. If after such reconsideration two-thirds of that house shall agree to pass the bill, it shall be sent, together with the objections, to the other house, by which it shall likewise be reconsidered, and, if approved by two-thirds of that house, it shall become a law. But in all such cases the votes of both houses shall be determined by yeas and nays, and the names of the persons voting for and against the bill shall be entered on the journal of each house respectively. If any bill shall not be returned by the President within ten days (Sundays excepted) after it shall have been presented to him, the same shall be a law, in like manner as if he had signed it, unless the Congress by their adjournment prevent its return, in which case it shall not be a law.

Every order, resolution, or vote to which the concurrence of the Senate and House of Representatives may be necessary (except on a question of adjournment) shall be presented to the President of the United States; and before the same shall take effect, shall be approved by him, or being disapproved by him, shall be repassed by two-thirds of the Senate and House of Representatives, according to the rules and limitations prescribed in the case of a bill.

Section 8   The Congress shall have power

To lay and collect taxes, duties, imposts, and excises, to pay the debts and provide for the common defense and general welfare of the United States; but all duties, imposts and excises shall be uniform throughout the United States;

To borrow money on the credit of the United States;

To regulate commerce with foreign nations, and among the several States, and with the Indian tribes;

To establish an uniform rule of naturalization, and uniform laws on the subject of bankruptcies throughout the United States;

To coin money, regulate the value thereof, and of foreign coin, and fix the standard of weights and measures;

To provide for the punishment of counterfeiting the securities and current coin of the United States;

To establish post offices and post roads;

To promote the progress of science and useful arts by securing for limited times to authors and inventors the exclusive right to their respective writings and discoveries;

To constitute tribunals inferior to the Supreme Court;

To define and punish piracies and felonies committed on the high seas and offenses against the law of nations;

To declare war, grant letters of marque and reprisal, and make rules concerning captures on land and water;

To raise and support armies, but no appropriation of money to that use shall be for a longer term than two years;

To provide and maintain a navy;

To make rules for the government and regulation of the land and naval forces;

To provide for calling forth the militia to execute the laws of the Union, suppress insurrections, and repel invasions;

To provide for organizing, arming, and disciplining the militia, and for governing such part of them as may be employed in the service of the United States, reserving to the States respectively the appointment of the officers, and the authority of training the militia according to the discipline prescribed by Congress;

To exercise exclusive legislation in all cases whatsoever, over such district (not exceeding ten miles square) as may, by cession of particular States, and the acceptance of Congress, become the seat of government of the United States, and to exercise like authority over all places purchased by the consent of the legislature of the State, in which the same shall be, for erection of forts, magazines, arsenals, dockyards, and other needful buildings;—and

To make all laws which shall be necessary and proper for carrying into execution the foregoing powers, and all other powers vested by this Constitution in the government of the United States, or in any department or officer thereof.

Section 9   *The migration or importation of such persons as any of the States now existing shall think proper to admit shall not be prohibited by the Congress prior to the year 1808; but a tax or duty may be imposed on such importation, not exceeding $10 for each person.*

The privilege of the writ of habeas corpus shall not be suspended, unless when in cases of rebellion or invasion the public safety may require it.

No bill of attainder or ex post facto law shall be passed.

No capitation, or other direct, tax shall be laid, unless in proportion to the census or enumeration herein before directed to be taken.

No tax or duty shall be laid on articles exported from any State.

No preference shall be given by any regulation of commerce or revenue to the ports of one State over those of another; nor shall vessels bound to, or from, one State, be obliged to enter, clear, or pay duties in another.

No money shall be drawn from the treasury, but in consequence of appropriations made by law; and a regular statement and account of the receipts and expenditures of all public money shall be published from time to time.

No title of nobility shall be granted by the United States: and no person holding any office of profit or trust under them, shall, without the consent of the Congress, accept of any present, emolument, office, or title, of any kind whatever, from any king, prince, or foreign state.

Section 10   No State shall enter into any treaty, alliance, or confederation; grant letters of marque and reprisal; coin money; emit bills of credit; make anything but gold and silver coin a tender in payment of debts; pass any bill of attainder, ex post facto law, or law impairing the obligation of contracts, or grant any title of nobility.

No State shall, without the consent of Congress, lay any imposts or duties on imports or exports, except what may be absolutely necessary for executing its inspection laws: and the net produce of all duties and imposts, laid by any State on imports or exports, shall be for the use of the treasury of the United States; and all such laws shall be subject to the revision and control of the Congress.

No State shall, without the consent of Congress, lay any duty of tonnage, keep troops or ships of war in time of peace, enter into any agreement or compact with another State, or with a foreign power, or engage in war, unless actually invaded, or in such imminent danger as will not admit of delay.

Article II

Section 1   The executive power shall be vested in a President of the United States of America. He shall hold his office during the term of four years, and, together with the Vice-President, chosen for the same term, be elected as follows:

Each State shall appoint, in such manner as the legislature thereof may direct, a number of electors, equal to the whole number of Senators and Representatives to which the State may be entitled in the Congress; but no Senator or Representative, or person holding an office of trust or profit under the United States, shall be appointed an elector.

The electors shall meet in their respective States, and vote by ballot for two persons, of whom one at least shall not be an inhabitant of the same State with themselves. And they shall make a list of all the persons voted for, and of the number of votes for each; which list they shall sign and certify, and transmit sealed to the seat of government of the United States, directed to the President of the Senate. The President of the Senate shall, in the presence of the Senate and House of Representatives, open all the certificates, and the votes shall then be counted. The person having the greatest number of votes shall be the President, if such number be a majority of the whole number of electors appointed; and if there be more than one who have such majority, and have an equal number of votes, then the House of Representatives shall immediately choose by ballot one of them for President; and if no person have a majority, then from the five highest on the list said house shall in like manner choose the President. But in choosing the President the votes shall be taken by States, the representation from each State having one vote; a quorum for this purpose shall consist of a member or members from two-thirds of the States, and a majority of all the States shall be necessary to a choice. In every case, after the choice of the President, the person having the greatest number of votes of the electors shall be the Vice-President. But if there should remain two or more who have equal votes, the Senate shall choose from them by ballot the Vice-President.

The Congress may determine the time of choosing the electors and the day on which they shall give their votes; which day shall be the same throughout the United States.

No person except a natural-born citizen, *or a citizen of the United States at the time of the adoption of this Constitution*, shall be eligible to the office of President; neither shall any person be eligible to that office who shall not have attained to the age of thirty-five years, and been fourteen years a resident within the United States.

In cases of the removal of the President from office or of his death, resignation, or inability to discharge the powers and duties of the said office, the same shall devolve on the Vice-President, and the Congress may by law provide for the case of removal, death, resignation, or inability, both of the President and Vice-President, declaring what officer shall then act as President, and such officer shall act accordingly, until the disability be removed, or a President shall be elected.

The President shall, at stated times, receive for his services a compensation, which shall neither be increased nor diminished during the period for which he shall have been elected, and he shall not receive within that period any other emolument from the United States, or any of them.

Before he enter on the execution of his office, he shall take the following oath or affirmation:— "I do solemnly swear (or affirm) that I will faithfully execute the office of the President of the United States, and will to the best of my ability preserve, protect and defend the Constitution of the United States."

Section 2   The President shall be commander in chief of the army and navy of the United States, and of the militia of the several States, when called into the actual service of the United States; he may require the opinion, in writing, of the principal officer in each of the executive departments, upon any subject relating to the duties of their respective offices, and he shall have power to grant reprieves and pardons for offenses against the United States, except in cases of impeachment.

He shall have power, by and with the advice and consent of the Senate, to make treaties, provided two-thirds of the Senators present concur; and he shall nominate, and by and with the advice and consent of the Senate, shall appoint ambassadors, other public ministers and consuls, judges of the Supreme Court, and all other officers of the United States, whose appointments are not herein otherwise provided for, and which shall be established by law: but Congress may by law vest the appointment of such inferior officers, as they think proper, in the President alone, in the courts of law, or in the heads of departments.

The President shall have power to fill up all vacancies that may happen during the recess of the Senate, by granting commissions which shall expire at the end of their next session.

Section 3   He shall from time to time give to the Congress information of the state of the Union, and recommend to their consideration such measures as he shall judge necessary and expedient; he may, on extraordinary occasions, convene both houses, or either of them, and in case of disagreement between them, with respect to the time of adjournment, he may adjourn them to such time as he shall think proper; he shall receive ambassadors and other public ministers; he shall take care that the laws be faithfully executed, and shall commission all the officers of the United States.

Section 4   The President, Vice-President and all civil officers of the United States shall be removed from office on impeachment for, and on conviction of, treason, bribery, or other high crimes and misdemeanors.

Article III

Section 1   The judicial power of the United States shall be vested in one Supreme Court, and in such inferior courts as the Congress may from time to time ordain and establish. The judges, both of the Supreme and inferior courts, shall hold their offices during good behavior, and shall, at stated times, receive for their services a compensation which shall not be diminished during their continuance in office.

Section 2   The judicial power shall extend to all cases, in law and equity, arising under this Constitution, the laws of the United States, and treaties made, or which shall be made, under their authority;—to all cases affecting ambassadors, other public ministers and consuls;—to all cases of admiralty and maritime jurisdiction;—to controversies to which the United States shall be a party;—to controversies between two or more States;—*between a State and citizens of another State;*—between citizens of different States;—between citizens of the same State claiming lands under grants of different States, and between a State, or the citizens thereof, and foreign states, citizens or subjects.

In all cases affecting ambassadors, other public ministers and consuls, and those in which a State shall be party, the Supreme Court shall have original jurisdiction. In all the other cases before mentioned, the Supreme Court shall have appellate jurisdiction, both as to law and fact, with such exceptions, and under such regulations, as the Congress shall make.

The trial of all crimes, except in cases of impeachment, shall be by jury; and such trial shall be held in the State where said crimes shall have been committed; but when not committed within any State, the trial shall be at such place or places as the Congress may by law have directed.

Section 3   Treason against the United States shall consist only in levying war against them, or in adhering to their enemies, giving them aid and comfort. No person shall be convicted of treason unless on the testimony of two witnesses to the same overt act, or on confession in open court.

The Congress shall have power to declare the punishment of treason, but no attainder of treason shall work corruption of blood, or forfeiture except during the life of the person attainted.

Article IV

Section 1   Full faith and credit shall be given in each State to the public acts, records, and judicial proceedings of every other State. And the Congress may by general laws prescribe the manner in which such acts, records, and proceedings shall be proved, and the effect thereof.

Section 2   The citizens of each State shall be entitled to all privileges and immunities of citizens in the several States.

A person charged in any State with treason, felony, or other crime, who shall flee from justice, and be found in another State, shall on demand of the executive authority of the State from which he fled, be delivered up, to be removed to the State having jurisdiction of the crime.

No person held to service or labor in one State, under the laws thereof, escaping into another, shall, in consequence of any law or regulation therein, be discharged from such service or labor, but shall be delivered up on claim of the party to whom such service or labor may be due.

Section 3   New States may be admitted by the Congress into this Union; but no new State shall be formed or erected within the jurisdiction of any other State; nor any State be formed by the junction of two or more States, or parts of States, without the consent of the legislatures of the States concerned as well as of the Congress.

The Congress shall have power to dispose of and make all needful rules and regulations respecting the territory or other property belonging to the United States; and nothing in this Constitution shall be so construed as to prejudice any claims of the United States, or of any particular State.

Section 4   The United States shall guarantee to every State in this Union a republican form of government, and shall protect each of them against invasion; and on application of the legislature, or of the executive (when the legislature cannot be convened), against domestic violence.

Article V

The Congress, whenever two-thirds of both houses shall deem it necessary, shall propose amendments to this Constitution, or, on the application of the legislatures of two-thirds of the several States, shall call a convention for proposing amendments, which, in either case, shall be valid to all intents and purposes, as part of this Constitution, when ratified by the legislatures of three-fourths of the several States, or by conventions in three-fourths thereof, as the one or the other mode of ratification may be proposed by the Congress; provided *that no amendments which may be made prior to the year one thousand eight hundred and eight shall in any manner affect the first and fourth clauses in the ninth section of the first article;* and that no State, without its consent, shall be deprived of its equal suffrage in the Senate.

Article VI

All debts contracted and engagements entered into, before the adoption of this Constitution, shall be as valid against the United States under this Constitution, as under the Confederation.

This Constitution, and the laws of the United States which shall be made in pursuance thereof; and all treaties made, or which shall be made, under the authority of the United States, shall be the supreme law of the land; and the judges in every State shall be bound thereby, anything in the Constitution or laws of any State to the contrary notwithstanding.

The Senators and Representatives before mentioned, and the members of the several State legislatures, and all executive and judicial officers, both of the United States and of the several States, shall be bound by oath or affirmation to support this Constitution; but no religious test shall ever be required as a qualification to any office or public trust under the United States.

Article VII

The ratification of the conventions of nine States shall be sufficient for the establishment of this Constitution between the States so ratifying the same.

Done in Convention by the unanimous consent of the States present, the seventeenth day of September in the year of our Lord one thousand seven hundred and eighty-seven and of the Independence of the United States of America the twelfth. In witness whereof we have hereunto subscribed our names.

GEORGE WASHINGTON
and thirty-seven others

Amendments to the Constitution*

Amendment I

Congress shall make no law respecting an establishment of religion, or prohibiting the free exercise thereof; or abridging the freedom of speech, or of the press; or the right of the people peaceably to assemble, and to petition the government for a redress of grievances.

Amendment II

A well-regulated militia being necessary to the security of a free State, the right of the people to keep and bear arms shall not be infringed.

Amendment III

No soldier shall, in time of peace, be quartered in any house without the consent of the owner, nor in time of war, but in a manner to be prescribed by law.

Amendment IV

The right of the people to be secure in their persons, houses, papers, and effects, against unreasonable searches and seizures, shall not be violated, and no warrants shall issue but upon probable cause, supported by oath or affirmation, and particularly describing the place to be searched, and the persons or things to be seized.

Amendment V

No person shall be held to answer for a capital, or otherwise infamous crime, unless on a presentment or indictment of a grand jury, except in cases arising in the land or naval forces, or in the militia, when in actual service in time of war or public danger; nor shall any person be subject for the same offense to be twice put in jeopardy of life or limb; nor shall be compelled in any criminal case to be a witness against himself, nor be deprived of life, liberty, or property, without due process of law; nor shall private property be taken for public use without just compensation.

*The first ten amendments (the Bill of Rights) were adopted in 1791.

Amendment VI

In all criminal prosecutions, the accused shall enjoy the right to a speedy and public trial, by an impartial jury of the State and district wherein the crime shall have been committed, which district shall have been previously ascertained by law, and to be informed of the nature and cause of the accusation; to be confronted with the witnesses against him; to have compulsory process for obtaining witnesses in his favor, and to have the assistance of counsel for his defense.

Amendment VII

In suits at common law, where the value in controversy shall exceed twenty dollars, the right of trial by jury shall be preserved, and no fact tried by a jury shall be otherwise reexamined in any court of the United States, than according to the rules of the common law.

Amendment VIII

Excessive bail shall not be required, nor excessive fines imposed, nor cruel and unusual punishments inflicted.

Amendment IX

The enumeration in the Constitution, of certain rights, shall not be construed to deny or disparage others retained by the people.

Amendment X

The powers not delegated to the United States by the Constitution, nor prohibited by it to the States, are reserved to the States respectively, or to the people.

Amendment XI   *[Adopted 1798]*

The judicial power of the United States shall not be construed to extend to any suit in law or equity, commenced or prosecuted against one of the United States by citizens of another State, or by citizens or subjects of any foreign state.

Amendment XII   *[Adopted 1804]*

The electors shall meet in their respective States, and vote by ballot for President and Vice-President, one of whom, at least, shall not be an inhabitant of the same State with themselves; they shall name in their ballots the person voted for as President, and in distinct ballots the person voted for as Vice-President, and they shall make distinct lists of all persons voted for as President, and of all persons voted for as Vice-President, and of the number of votes for each, which lists they shall sign and certify, and transmit sealed to the seat of government of the United States, directed to the President of the Senate;—the President of the Senate shall, in the presence of the Senate and House of Representatives, open all the certificates and the votes shall then be counted;—the person having the greatest number of votes for President shall be the President, if such number be a majority of the whole number of electors appointed; and if no person have such majority, then from the persons having the highest numbers not exceeding three on the list of those voted for as President, the House of Representatives shall choose immediately, by ballot, the President. But in choosing the President, the votes shall be taken by States, the representation from each State having one vote; a quorum for this purpose shall consist of a member or members from two-thirds of the States, and a majority of all the States shall be necessary to a choice. And if the House of Representatives shall not choose a President whenever the right of choice shall devolve upon them, before *the fourth day of March* next following, then the Vice-President shall act as President, as in the case of the death or other constitutional disability of the President.

The person having the greatest number of votes as Vice-President shall be the Vice-President, if such number be a majority of the whole number of electors appointed; and if no person have a majority, then from the two highest numbers on the list the Senate shall choose the Vice-President; a quorum for the purpose shall consist of two-thirds of the whole number of Senators, and a majority of the whole number shall be necessary to a choice. But no person constitutionally ineligible to the office of President shall be eligible to that of Vice-President of the United States.

Amendment XIII   *[Adopted 1865]*

Section 1   Neither slavery nor involuntary servitude, except as a punishment for crime whereof the party shall have been duly convicted, shall exist within the United States, or any place subject to their jurisdiction.

Section 2   Congress shall have power to enforce this article by appropriate legislation.

Amendment XIV   *[Adopted 1868]*

Section 1   All persons born or naturalized in the United States, and subject to the jurisdiction thereof, are citizens of the United States and of the State wherein they reside. No State shall make or enforce any law which shall abridge the privileges or immunities of citizens of the United States; nor shall any State deprive any person of life, liberty, or property, without due process of law; nor deny to any person within its jurisdiction the equal protection of the laws.

Section 2   Representatives shall be apportioned among the several States according to their respective numbers, counting the whole number of persons in each State, excluding Indians not taxed. But when the right to vote at any election for the choice of Electors for President and Vice-President of the United States, Representatives in Congress, the executive and judicial officers of a State, or the members of the legislature thereof, is denied to any of the male inhabitants of such State, being twenty-one years of age and citizens of the United States, or in any way abridged, except for participation in rebellion, or other crime, the basis of representation therein shall be reduced in the proportion which the number of such male citizens shall bear to the whole number of male citizens twenty-one years of age in such State.

Section 3   No person shall be a Senator or Representative in Congress, or Elector of President and Vice-President, or hold any office, civil or military, under the United States, or under any State, who, having previously taken an oath, as a member of Congress, or as an officer of the United States, or as a member of any State legislature, or as an executive or judicial officer of any State, to support the Constitution of the United States, shall have engaged in insurrection or rebellion against the same, or given aid or comfort to the enemies thereof. Congress may, by a vote of two-thirds of each house, remove such disability.

Section 4   The validity of the public debt of the United States, authorized by law, including debts incurred for payment of pensions and bounties for services in suppressing insurrection or rebellion, shall not be questioned. But neither the United States nor any State shall assume or pay any debt or obligation incurred in aid of insurrec-

tion or rebellion against the United States, or any claim for the loss of emancipation of any slave; but all such debts, obligations, and claims shall be held illegal and void.

Section 5   The Congress shall have power to enforce, by appropriate legislation, the provisions of this article.

Amendment XV   *[Adopted 1870]*

Section 1   The right of citizens of the United States to vote shall not be denied or abridged by the United States or by any State on account of race, color, or previous condition of servitude.

Section 2   The Congress shall have power to enforce this article by appropriate legislation.

Amendment XVI   *[Adopted 1913]*

The Congress shall have power to lay and collect taxes on incomes, from whatever source derived, without apportionment among the several States, and without regard to any census or enumeration.

Amendment XVII   *[Adopted 1913]*

Section 1   The Senate of the United States shall be composed of two Senators from each State, elected by the people thereof, for six years; and each Senator shall have one vote. The electors in each State shall have the qualifications requisite for electors of [voters for] the most numerous branch of the State legislatures.

Section 2   When vacancies happen in the representation of any State in the Senate, the executive authority of such State shall issue writs of election to fill such vacancies: Provided, that the Legislature of any State may empower the executive thereof to make temporary appointments until the people fill the vacancies by election as the Legislature may direct.

Section 3   This amendment shall not be so construed as to affect the election or term of any Senator chosen before it becomes valid as part of the Constitution.

Amendment XVIII   *[Adopted 1919; Repealed 1933]*

Section 1   After one year from the ratification of this article the manufacture, sale, or transportation of intoxicating liquors within, the importation thereof into, or the exportation thereof from the United States and all territory subject to the jurisdiction thereof, for beverage purposes, is hereby prohibited.

Section 2   The Congress and the several States shall have concurrent power to enforce this article by appropriate legislation.

Section 3   This article shall be inoperative unless it shall have been ratified as an amendment to the Constitution by the legislatures of the several States, as provided by the Constitution, within seven years from the date of the submission thereof to the States by the Congress.

Amendment XIX   *[Adopted 1920]*

Section 1   The right of citizens of the United States to vote shall not be denied or abridged by the United States or by any State on account of sex.

Section 2   The Congress shall have power to enforce this article by appropriate legislation.

Amendment XX   *[Adopted 1933]*

Section 1   The terms of the President and Vice-President shall end at noon on the 20th day of January, and the terms of Senators and Representatives at noon on the 3rd day of January, of the years in which such terms would have ended if this article had not been ratified; and the terms of their successors shall then begin.

Section 2   The Congress shall assemble at least once in every year, and such meeting shall begin at noon on the 3d day of January, unless they shall by law appoint a different day.

Section 3   If, at the time fixed for the beginning of the term of the President, the President-elect shall have died, the Vice-President-elect shall become President. If a President shall not have been chosen before the time fixed for the beginning of his term, or if the President-elect shall have failed to qualify, then the Vice-President-elect shall act as President until a President shall have qualified; and the Congress may by law provide for the case wherein neither a President-elect nor a Vice-President-elect shall have qualified, declaring who shall then act as President, or the manner in which one who is to act shall be selected, and such persons shall act accordingly until a President or Vice-President shall have qualified.

Section 4   The Congress may by law provide for the case of the death of any of the persons from whom the House of Representatives may choose a President whenever the right of choice shall have devolved upon them, and for the case of the death of any of the persons from whom the Senate may choose a Vice-President whenever the right of choice shall have devolved upon them.

Section 5   Sections 1 and 2 shall take effect on the 15th day of October following the ratification of this article.

Section 6   This article shall be inoperative unless it shall have been ratified as an amendment to the Constitution by the Legislatures of three-fourths of the several States within seven years from the date of its submission.

Amendment XXI   *[Adopted 1933]*

Section 1   The eighteenth article of amendment to the Constitution of the United States is hereby repealed.

Section 2   The transportation or importation into any State, Territory, or Possession of the United States for delivery or use therein of intoxicating liquors, in violation of the laws thereof, is hereby prohibited.

Section 3   This article shall be inoperative unless it shall have been ratified as an amendment to the Constitution by conventions in the several States, as provided in the Constitution, within seven years from the date of submission thereof to the States by the Congress.

Amendment XXII   *[Adopted 1951]*

Section 1   No person shall be elected to the office of President more than twice, and no person who has held the office of President, or acted as President, for more than two years of a term to which some other person was elected President shall be elected to the office of President more than once. But this article shall not apply to any person holding the office of President when this article was proposed by the Congress, and shall not prevent any person who may be holding the office of President, or acting as President, during the term within which this article becomes operative from holding the office of President or acting as President during the remainder of such term.

Section 2   This article shall be inoperative unless it shall have been ratified as an amendment to the Constitution by the legislatures of three-fourths of the several States within seven years from the date of its submission to the States by the Congress.

Amendment XXIII   *[Adopted 1961]*

Section 1   The District constituting the seat of Government of the United States shall appoint in such manner as the Congress may direct:

A number of electors of President and Vice-President equal to the whole number of Senators and Representatives in Congress to which the District would be entitled if it were a State, but in no event more than the least populous State; they shall be in addition to those appointed by the States, but they shall be considered for the purposes of the election of President and Vice-President, to be electors appointed by a State; and they shall meet in the District and perform such duties as provided by the twelfth article of amendment.

Section 2   The Congress shall have the power to enforce this article by appropriate legislation.

Amendment XXIV   *[Adopted 1964]*

Section 1   The right of citizens of the United States to vote in any primary or other election for President or Vice-President, for electors for President or Vice-President, or for Senator or Representative in Congress, shall not be denied or abridged by the United States or any State by reason of failure to pay any poll tax or other tax.

Section 2   The Congress shall have the power to enforce this article by appropriate legislation.

Amendment XXV   *[Adopted 1967]*

Section 1   In case of the removal of the President from office or of his death or resignation, the Vice-President shall become President.

Section 2   Whenever there is a vacancy in the office of the Vice-President, the President shall nominate a Vice-President who shall take office upon confirmation by a majority vote of both Houses of Congress.

Section 3   Whenever the President transmits to the President pro tempore of the Senate and the Speaker of the House of Representatives his written declaration that he is unable to discharge the powers and duties of his office, and until he transmits to them a written declaration

to the contrary, such powers and duties shall be discharged by the Vice-President as Acting President.

Section 4   Whenever the Vice-President and a majority of either the principal officers of the executive departments or of such other body as Congress may by law provide, transmit to the President pro tempore of the Senate and the Speaker of the House of Representatives their written declaration that the President is unable to discharge the powers and duties of his office, the Vice-President shall immediately assume the powers and duties of the office as Acting President.

Thereafter, when the President transmits to the President pro tempore of the Senate and the Speaker of the House of Representatives his written declaration that no inability exists, he shall resume the powers and duties of his office unless the Vice-President and a majority of either the principal officers of the executive department[s] or of such other body as Congress may by law provide, transmit within four days to the President pro tempore of the Senate and the Speaker of the House of Representatives their written declaration that the President is unable to discharge the powers and duties of his office. Thereupon Congress shall decide the issue, assembling within forty-eight hours for that purpose if not in session. If the Congress, within twenty-one days after receipt of the latter written declaration, or, if Congress is not in session, within twenty-one days after Congress is required to assemble, determines by two-thirds vote of both Houses that the President is unable to discharge the powers and duties of his office, the Vice-President shall continue to discharge the same as Acting President; otherwise, the President shall resume the powers and duties of his office.

Amendment XXVI   *[Adopted 1971]*

Section 1   The right of citizens of the United States, who are eighteen years of age or older, to vote shall not be denied or abridged by the United States or by any State on account of age.

Section 2   The Congress shall have power to enforce this article by appropriate legislation.

Amendment XXVII   *[Adopted 1992]*

No law, varying the compensation for the services of the Senators and Representatives, shall take effect, until an election of Representatives shall have intervened.

Federalist No. 10,   1787

To the People of the State of New York: Among the numerous advantages promised by a well-constructed union, none deserves to be more accurately developed than its tendency to break and control the violence of faction. The friend of popular governments, never finds himself so much alarmed for their character and fate, as when he contemplates their propensity to this dangerous vice. He will not fail, therefore, to set a due value on any plan which, without violating the principles to which he is attached, provides a proper cure for it. The instability, injustice, and confusion introduced into the public councils, have, in truth, been the mortal diseases under which popular governments have everywhere perished; as they continue to be the favorite and fruitful topics from which the adversaries to liberty derive their most specious declamations. The valuable improvements made by the American constitutions on the popular models, both ancient and modern, cannot certainly be too much admired; but it would be an unwarrantable partiality, to contend that they have as effectually obviated the danger on this side, as was wished and expected. Complaints are everywhere heard from our most considerate and virtuous citizens, equally the friends of public and private faith, and of public and personal liberty, that our governments are too unstable; that the public good is disregarded in the conflicts of rival parties; and that measures are too often decided, not according to the rules of justice, and the rights of the minor party, but by the superior force of an interested and overbearing majority. However anxiously we may wish that these complaints had no foundation, the evidence of known facts will not permit us to deny that they are in some degree true. It will be found, indeed, on a candid review of our situation, that some of the distresses under which we labour have been erroneously charged on the operation of our governments; but it will be found, at the same time, that other causes will not alone account for many of our heaviest misfortunes; and, particularly, for that prevailing and increasing distrust of public engagements, and alarm for private rights, which are echoed from one end of the continent to the other. These must be chiefly, if not wholly, effects of the unsteadiness and injustice, with which a factious spirit has tainted our public administrations.

By a faction, I understand a number of citizens, whether amounting to a majority or minority of the whole, who are united and actuated by some common impulse of passion, or of interest, adverse to the rights of other citizens, or to the permanent and aggregate interests of the community.

There are two methods of curing the mischiefs of faction: The one, by removing its causes; the other, by controlling its effects.

There are again two methods of removing the causes of faction: The one, by destroying the liberty which is essential to its existence; the other, by giving to every citizen the same opinions, the same passions, and the same interests.

It could never be more truly said, than of the first remedy, that it was worse than the disease. Liberty is to faction what air is to fire, an aliment without which it instantly expires. But it could not be a less folly to abolish liberty, which is essential to political life, because it nourishes faction, than it would be to wish the annihilation of air, which is essential to animal life, because it imparts to fire its destructive agency.

The second expedient is as impracticable, as the first would be unwise. As long as the reason of man continues fallible, and he is at liberty to exercise it, different opinions will be formed. As long as the connection subsists between his reason and his self-love, his opinions and his passions will have a reciprocal influence on each other; and the former will be objects to which the latter will attach themselves. The diversity in the faculties of men, from which the rights of property originate, is not less an insuperable obstacle to an uniformity of interests. The protection of these faculties is the first object of government. From the protection of different and unequal faculties of acquiring property, the possession of different degrees and kinds of property immediately results; and from the influence of these on the sentiments and views of the respective proprietors, ensues a division of the society into different interests and parties.

The latent causes of action are thus sown in the nature of man; and we see them everywhere brought into different degrees of activity, according to the different circumstances of civil society. A zeal for different opinions concerning religion, concerning government, and many other points, as well as of speculation as of practice; an attachment to different leaders ambitiously contending for preeminence and power; or to persons of other descriptions whose fortunes have been interesting to the human passions, have, in turn, divided mankind into parties, inflamed them with mutual animosity, and rendered them much more disposed to vex and oppress each other, than to cooperate of their common good. So strong is this propensity of mankind, to fall into mutual animosities, that where no substantial occasion presents itself, the most frivolous and fanciful distinctions have been sufficient to kindle their unfriendly passions and excite their most violent conflicts. But the most common and durable source of factions, has been the various and unequal distribution of property. Those who hold, and those who are without property, have ever formed distinct interests in society. Those who are creditors, and those who are debtors, fall under a like discrimination. A landed interest, a manufacturing interest, a mercantile interest, a moneyed interest, with many lesser interests, grow up of necessity in civilized nations, and divide them into different classes, actuated by different sentiments and views. The regulation of these various and interfering interests forms the principal task of modern legislation, and involves the spirit of the party and faction in the necessary and ordinary operations of the government.

No man is allowed to be a judge in his own cause; because his interest will certainly bias his judgment, and, not improbably, corrupt his integrity. With equal, nay, with greater reason, a body of men are unfit to be both judges and parties at the same time; yet what are many of the most important acts of legislation, but so many judicial determinations, not indeed concerning the right of single persons, but concerning the rights of large bodies of citizens? And what are the different classes of legislators, but advocates and parties to the causes which they determine? Is a law proposed concerning private debts? It is a question to which the creditors are parties on one side, and the debtors on the other. Justice ought to hold the balance between them. Yet the parties are, and must be, themselves the judges; and the most numerous party, or, in other words, the most powerful faction, must be expected to prevail. Shall domestic manufactures be encouraged, and in what degree, by restrictions on foreign manufactures? are questions which would be differently decided by the landed and the manufacturing classes; and probably by neither with a sole regard to justice and the public good. The apportionment of taxes, on the various descriptions of property, is an act which seems to require the most exact impartiality; yet there is, perhaps, no legislative act, in which greater opportunity and temptation are given to a predominant party to trample on the rules of justice. Every shilling, with which they overburden the inferior number, is a shilling saved to their own pockets.

It is in vain to say, that enlightened statements will be able to adjust these clashing interests, and render them all subservient to the public good. Enlightened statesmen

will not always be at the helm: nor, in many cases, can such an adjustment be made at all, without taking into view indirect and remote considerations, which will rarely prevail over the immediate interest which one party may find in disregarding the rights of another, or the good of the whole.

The inference to which we are brought is, that the *causes* of faction cannot be removed; and that relief is only to be sought in the means of controlling its *effects*.

If a faction consists of less than a majority, relief is supplied by the republican principle, which enables the majority to defeat its sinister views, by regular vote. It may clog the administration, it may convulse the society; but it will be unable to execute and mask its violence under the forms of the constitution. When a majority is included in a faction, the form of popular government, on the other hand, enables it to sacrifice to its ruling passion or interest, both the public good and the rights of other citizens. To secure the public good, and private rights, against the danger of such a faction, and at the same time to preserve the spirit and the form of popular government, is then the great object to which our inquiries are directed. Let me add, that it is the great desideratum, by which alone this form of government can be rescued from the opprobrium under which it has so long laboured, and be recommended to the esteem and adoption of mankind.

By what means is this object attainable? Evidently by one of two only. Either the existence of the same passion or interest in a majority, at the same time, must be prevented; or the majority, having such coexistent passion or interest, must be rendered, by their number and local situation, unable to concert and carry into effect schemes of oppression. If the impulse and the opportunity be suffered to coincide, we well know that neither moral nor religious motives can be relied on as an adequate control. They are not found to be such on the injustice and violence of individuals, and lose their efficacy in proportion to the number combined together; that is, in proportion as their efficacy becomes needful.

From this view of the subject, it may be concluded, that a pure democracy, by which I mean a society consisting of a small number of citizens, who assemble and administer the government in person, can admit of no cure for the mischiefs of faction. A common passion or interest will, in almost every case, be felt by a majority of the whole; a communication and concert, results from the form of government itself; and there is nothing to check the inducements to sacrifice the weaker parts, or an obnoxious individual. Hence, it is, that such democracies have ever been spectacles of turbulence and contention; have ever been found incompatible with personal security, or the rights of property; and have in general been as short in their lives, as they have been violent in their deaths. Theoretic politicians, who have patronized this species of government, have erroneously supposed, that by reducing mankind to a perfect equality in their political rights, they would, at the same time, be perfectly equalized and assimilated in their possessions, their opinions, and their passions.

A republic, by which I mean a government in which the scheme of representation takes place, opens a different prospect, and promises the cure for which we are seeking. Let us examine the points in which it varies from pure democracy, and we shall comprehend both the nature of the cure and the efficacy which it must derive from the union.

The two great points of difference, between a democracy and a republic, are, first, the delegation of the government, in the latter, to a small number of citizens, elected by the rest; secondly, the greatest number of citizens, and greater sphere of country, over which the latter may be extended.

The effect of the first difference is, on the one hand, to refine and enlarge the public views, by passing them through the medium of a chosen body of citizens, whose wisdom may best discern the true interest of their country, and whose patriotism and love of justice, will be least likely to sacrifice it to temporary or partial considerations. Under such a regulation, it may well happen, that the public voice, pronounced by the representatives of the people, will be more consonant to the public good, than if pronounced by the people themselves, convened for the purpose. On the other hand the effect may be inverted. Men of factious tempers, of local prejudices, or of sinister designs, may by intrigue, by corruption, or by other means, first obtain the suffrages, and then betray the interest of the people. The question resulting is, whether small or extensive republics are most favourable to the election of proper guardians of the public weal; and it is clearly decided in favour of the latter by two obvious considerations.

In the first place, it is to be remarked that, however small the republic may be, the representatives must be raised to a certain number, in order to guard against the cabals of a few; and that however large it may be, they must be limited to a certain number, in order to guard against the confusion of a multitude. Hence, the number

of representatives in the two cases not being in proportion to that of the constituents, and being proportionally greatest in the small republic, it follows, that if the proportion of fit characters be not less in the large than in the small republic, the former will present a greater option, and consequently a greater probability of a fit choice.

In the next place, as each representative will be chosen by a greater number of citizens in the large than in the small republic, it will be more difficult for unworthy candidates to practice with success the vicious arts, by which elections are too often carried; and the suffrages of the people being more free, will be more likely to centre in men who possess the most attractive merit, and the most diffusive and established characters.

It must be confessed, that in this, as in most other cases, there is a mean, on both sides of which inconveniences will be found to lie. By enlarging too much the number of electors, you render the representatives too little acquainted with all their local circumstances and lesser interests; as by reducing it too much, you render him unduly attached to these, and too little fit to comprehend and pursue great and national objects. The federal constitution forms a happy combination in this respect; the great and aggregate interests being referred to the national, the local and particular to the state legislatures.

The other point of difference is, the greater number of citizens, and extent of territory, which may be brought within the compass of republican, than of democratic government; and it is this circumstance principally which renders factious combinations less to be dreaded in the former, than in the latter. The smaller the society, the fewer probably will be the distinct parties and interests composing it; the fewer the distinct parties and interests, the more frequently will a majority be found of the same party; and the smaller the number of individuals composing a majority, and the smaller the compass within which they are placed, the more easily will they concert and execute their plans of oppression. Extend the sphere, and you take in a greater variety of parties and interests; you make it less probable that a majority of the whole will have a common motive to invade the rights of other citizens; or if such a common motive exists, it will be more difficult for all who feel it to discover their own strength, and to act in unison with each other. Besides other impediments, it may be remarked, that where there is a consciousness of unjust or dishonorable purposes, communication is always checked by distrust, in proportion to the number whose concurrence is necessary.

Hence, it clearly appears, that the same advantage,

which a republic has over a democracy, in controlling the effects of faction, is enjoyed by a large over a small republic,—is enjoyed by the union over the states composing it. Does this advantage consist in the substitution of representatives, whose enlightened views and virtuous sentiments render them superior to local prejudices, and to schemes of injustice? It will not be denied that the representation of the union will be most likely to possess these requisite endowments. Does it consist in the greater security afforded by a greater variety of parties, against the event of any one party being able to outnumber and oppress the rest? In an equal degree does the increased variety of parties, comprised within the union, increase the security? Does it, in fine, consist in the greater obstacles opposed to the concert and accomplishment of the secret wishes of an unjust and interested majority? Here, again, the extent of the union gives it the most palpable advantage.

The influence of factious leaders may kindle a flame within their particular states, but will be unable to spread a general conflagration through the other states; a religious sect may degenerate into a political faction in a part of the confederacy; but the variety of sects dispersed over the entire face of it, must secure the national councils against any danger from that source: a rage for paper money, for an abolition of debts, for an equal division of property, or for any other improper or wicked project, will be less apt to pervade the whole body of the union than a particular member of it; in the same proportion as such a malady is more likely to taint a particular county or district, than an entire state.

In the extent and proper structure of the union, therefore, we behold a republican remedy for the diseases most incident to republican government. And according to the degree of pleasure and pride we feel in being republicans, ought to be our zeal in cherishing the spirit, and supporting the character of federalists.

JAMES MADISON

Federalist No. 51,   1788

To the People of the State of New York: To what expedient then shall we finally resort for maintaining in practice the necessary partition of power among the several departments, as laid down in the constitution? The only

answer that can be given is, that as all these exterior provisions are found to be inadequate, the defect must be supplied, by so contriving the interior structure of the government, as that its several constituent parts may, by their mutual relations, be the means of keeping each other in their proper places. Without presuming to undertake a full development of this important idea, I will hazard a few general observations, which may perhaps place it in a clearer light, and enable us to form a more correct judgment of the principles and structure of the government planned by the convention.

In order to lay a due foundation for that separate and distinct exercise of the different powers of government, which to a certain extent, is admitted on all hands to be essential to the preservation of liberty, it is evident that each department should have a will of its own; and consequently should be so constituted, that the members of each should have as little agency as possible in the appointment of the members of the others. Were this principle rigorously adhered to, it would require that all the appointments for the supreme executive, legislative, and judiciary magistracies, should be drawn from the same fountain of authority, the people, through channels, having no communication whatever with one another. Perhaps such a plan of constructing the several departments would be less difficult in practice than it may in contemplation appear. Some difficulties however, and some additional expense, would attend the execution of it. Some deviations therefore from the principle must be admitted. In the constitution of the judiciary department in particular, it might be inexpedient to insist rigorously on the principle; first, because peculiar qualifications being essential in the members, the primary consideration ought to be to select that mode of choice, which best secures these qualifications; secondly, because the permanent tenure by which the appointments are held in that department, must soon destroy all sense of dependence on the authority conferring them.

It is equally evident that the members of each department should be as little dependent as possible on those of the others, for the emoluments annexed to their offices. Were the executive magistrate, or the judges, not independent of the legislature in this particular, their independence in every other would be merely nominal.

But the great security against a gradual concentration of the several powers in the same department, consists in giving to those who administer each department, the necessary constitutional means, and personal motives, to resist encroachments of the others. The provision for defense must in this, as in all other cases, be made commensurate to the danger of attack. Ambition must be made to counteract ambition. The interest of the man must be connected with the constitutional rights of the place. It may be a reflection on human nature, that such devices should be necessary to control the abuses of government. But what is government itself but the greatest of all reflections on human nature? If men were angels, no government would be necessary. If angels were to govern men, neither external nor internal controls on government would be necessary. In framing a government which is to be administered by men over men, the great difficulty lies in this: You must first enable the government to control the governed; and in the next place, oblige it to control itself. A dependence on the people is no doubt the primary control on the government; but experience has taught mankind the necessity of auxiliary precautions.

This policy of supplying by opposite and rival interests, the defect of better motives, might be traced through the whole system of human affairs, private as well as public. We see it particularly displayed in all the subordinate distributions of power; where the constant aim is to divide and arrange the several offices in such a manner as that each may be a check on the other; that the private interest of every individual, may be a sentinel over the public rights. These inventions of prudence cannot be less requisite in the distribution of the supreme powers of the state.

But it is not possible to give to each department an equal power of self defense. In republican government the legislative authority, necessarily, predominates. The remedy for this inconveniency is, to divide the legislature into different branches; and to render them by different modes of election, and different principles of action, as little connected with each other, as the nature of their common functions, and their common dependence on the society, will admit. It may even be necessary to guard against dangerous encroachments by still further precautions. As the weight of the legislative authority requires that it should be thus divided, the weakness of the executive may require, on the other hand, that it should be fortified. An absolute negative, on the legislature, appears at first view to be the natural defense with which the executive magistrate should be armed. But perhaps it would be neither altogether safe, nor alone sufficient. On ordinary occasions, it might not be exerted with the requisite firmness; and on extraordinary occasions, it might be perfidiously abused. May not this defect of an absolute negative be supplied, by some qualified connection between this weaker department, and the weaker

branch of the stronger department, by which the latter may be led to support the constitutional rights of the former, without being too much detached from the rights of its own department?

If the principles on which these observations are founded be just, as I persuade myself they are, and they be applied as a criterion, to the several state constitutions, and to the federal constitution, it will be found, that if the latter does not perfectly correspond with them, the former are infinitely less able to bear such a test.

There are moreover two considerations particularly applicable to the federal system of America, which place that system in a very interesting point of view.

First. In a single republic, all the power surrendered by the people, is submitted to the administration of a single government; and usurpations are guarded against by a division of the government into distinct and separate departments. In the compound republic of America, the power surrendered by the people, is first divided between two distinct governments, and then the portion allotted to each, subdivided among distinct and separate departments. Hence a double security arises to the rights of the people. The different governments will control each other; at the same time that each will be controlled by itself.

Second. It is of great importance in a republic, not only to guard the society against the oppression of its rulers; but to guard one part of the society against the injustice of the other part. Different interests necessarily exist in different classes of citizens. If a majority be united by a common interest, the rights of the minority will be insecure. There are but two methods of providing against this evil: The one by creating a will in the community independent of the majority, that is, of the society itself; the other by comprehending in the society so many separate descriptions of citizens, as will render an unjust combination of a majority of the whole, very improbable, if not impracticable. The first method prevails in all governments possessing an hereditary or self appointed authority. This at best is but a precarious security; because a power independent of the society may as well espouse the unjust views of the major, as the rightful interests, of the minor party, and may possibly be turned against both parties. The second method will be exemplified in the federal republic of the United States. While all authority in it will be derived from and dependent on the society, the society itself will be broken into so many parts, interests and classes of citizens, that the rights of individuals or of the minority, will be in little danger from interested combinations of the majority. In a free government, the security for civil rights must be the same as for religious rights. It consists in the one case in the multiplicity of interests, and in the other in the multiplicity of sects. The degree of security in both cases will depend on the number of interests and sects; and this may be presumed to depend on the extent of country and number of people comprehended under the same government. This view of the subject must particularly recommend a proper federal system to all the sincere and considerate friends of republican government: Since it shows that in exact proportion as the territory of the union may be formed into more circumscribed confederacies or states, oppressive combinations of a majority will be facilitated; the best security under the republican form, for the rights of every class of citizens, will be diminished; and consequently, the stability and independence of some member of the government, the only other security, must be proportionally increased. Justice is the end of government. It is the end of civil society. It ever has been, and ever will be pursued, until it be obtained, or until liberty be lost in the pursuit. In a society under the forms of which the stronger faction can readily unite and oppress the weaker, anarchy may as truly be said to reign, as in a state of nature where the weaker individual is not secured against the violence of the stronger: And as in the latter state even the stronger individuals are prompted by the uncertainty of their condition, to submit to a government which may protect the weak as well as themselves: So in the former state, will the more powerful factions or parties be gradually induced by a like motive, to which for a government which will protect all parties, the weaker as well as the more powerful. It can be little doubted, that if the state of Rhode Island was separated from the confederacy, and left to itself, the insecurity of rights under the popular form of government within such narrow limits, would be displayed by such reiterated oppression of factious majorities, that some power altogether independent of the people would soon be called for by the voice of the very factions whose misrule had proved the necessity of it. In the extended republic of the United States, and among the great variety of interests, parties and sects which it embraces, a coalition of a majority of the whole society could seldom take place on any other principles than those of justice and the general good; and there being thus less danger to a minor from the will of the major party, there must be less pretext also, to provide for the security of the former, by introducing into the government a will not dependent on the latter; or in other words,

a will independent of the society itself. It is no less certain that it is important, notwithstanding the contrary opinions which have been entertained, that the larger the society, provided it lie within a practicable sphere, the more duly capable it will be of self government. And happily for the *republican cause*, the practicable sphere may be carried to a very great extent, by a judicious modification and mixture of the *federal principle*.

JAMES MADISON

Antifederalist Paper   18 October 1787

To the Citizens of the State of New-York.

When the public is called to investigate and decide upon a question in which not only the present members of the community are deeply interested, but upon which the happiness and misery of generations yet unborn is in great measure suspended, the benevolent mind cannot help feeling itself peculiarly interested in the result.

In this situation, I trust the feeble efforts of an individual, to lead the minds of the people to a wise and prudent determination, cannot fail of being acceptable to the candid and dispassionate part of the community. Encouraged by this consideration, I have been induced to offer my thoughts upon the present important crisis of our public affairs.

Perhaps this country never saw so critical a period in their political concerns. We have felt the feebleness of the ties by which these United-States are held together, and the want of sufficient energy in our present confederation, to manage, in some instances, our general concerns. Various expedients have been proposed to remedy these evils, but none have succeeded. At length a Convention of the states has been assembled, they have formed a constitution which will now, probably, be submitted to the people to ratify or reject, who are the fountain of all power, to whom alone it of right belongs to make or unmake constitutions, or forms of government, at their pleasure. The most important question that was ever proposed to your decision, or to the decision of any people under heaven, is before you, and you are to decide upon it by men of your own election, chosen specially for this purpose. If the constitution, offered to your acceptance, be a wise one, calculated to preserve the invaluable blessings of liberty, to secure the inestimable rights of mankind, and promote human happiness, then, if you accept it, you will lay a lasting foundation of happiness for millions yet unborn; generations to come will rise up and call you blessed. You may rejoice in the prospects of this vast extended continent becoming filled with freemen, who will assert the dignity of human nature. You may solace yourselves with the idea, that society, in this favored land, will fast advance to the highest point of perfection; the human mind will expand in knowledge and virtue, and the golden age be, in some measure, realized. But if, on the other hand, this form of government contains principles that will lead to the subversion of liberty—if it tends to establish a despotism, or, what is worse, a tyrannic aristocracy; then, if you adopt it, this only remaining asylum for liberty will be shut up, and posterity will execrate your memory.

Momentous then is the question you have to determine, and you are called upon by every motive which should influence a noble and virtuous mind, to examine it well, and to make up a wise judgment. It is insisted, indeed, that this constitution must be received, be it ever so imperfect. If it has its defects, it is said, they can be best amended when they are experienced. But remember, when the people once part with power, they can seldom or never resume it again but by force. Many instances can be produced in which the people have voluntarily increased the powers of their rulers; but few, if any, in which rulers have willingly abridged their authority. This is a sufficient reason to induce you to be careful, in the first instance, how you deposit the powers of government.

With these few introductory remarks, I shall proceed to a consideration of this constitution:

The first question that presents itself on the subject is, whether a confederated government be the best for the United States or not? Or in other words, whether the thirteen United States should be reduced to one great republic, governed by one legislature, and under the direction of one executive and judicial; or whether they should continue thirteen confederated republics, under the direction and control of a supreme federal head for certain defined national purposes only?

This enquiry is important, because, although the government reported by the convention does not go to a perfect and entire consolidation, yet it approaches so near to it, that it must, if executed, certainly and infallibly terminate in it.

This government is to possess absolute and uncontroulable power, legislative, executive and judicial, with respect to every object to which it extends, for by the last clause of section 8th, article 1st, it is declared "that the Congress shall have power to make all laws which shall be necessary and proper for carrying into execution the foregoing powers, and all other powers vested by this constitution, in the government of the United States; or in any department or office thereof." And by the 6th article, it is declared "that this constitution, and the laws of the United States, which shall be made in pursuance thereof, and the treaties made, or which shall be made, under the authority of the United States, shall be the supreme law of the land; and the judges in every state shall be bound thereby, any thing in the constitution, or law of any state to the contrary notwithstanding." It appears from these articles that there is no need of any intervention of the state governments, between the Congress and the people, to execute any one power vested in the general government, and that the constitution and laws of every state are nullified and declared void, so far as they are or shall be inconsistent with this constitution, or the laws made in pursuance of it, or with treaties made under the authority of the United States.—The government then, so far as it extends, is a complete one, and not a confederation. It is as much one complete government as that of New-York or Massachusetts, has as absolute and perfect powers to make and execute all laws, to appoint officers, institute courts, declare offenses, and annex penalties, with respect to every object to which it extends, as any other in the world. So far therefore as its powers reach, all ideas of confederation are given up and lost. It is true this government is limited to certain objects, or to speak more properly, some small degree of power is still left to the states, but a little attention to the powers vested in the general government, will convince every candid man, that if it is capable of being executed, all that is reserved for the individual states must very soon be annihilated, except so far as they are barely necessary to the organization of the general government. The powers of the general legislature extend to every case that is of the least importance—there is nothing valuable to human nature, nothing dear to freemen, but what is within its power. It has authority to make laws which will affect the lives, the liberty, and property of every man in the United States; nor can the constitution or laws of any state, in any way prevent or impede the full and complete execution of every power given. The legislative power is competent to lay taxes, duties, imposts, and excises;—there is no limitation to this power, unless it be said that the clause which directs the use to which those taxes, and duties shall be applied, may be said to be a limitation: but this is no restriction of the power at all, for by this clause they are to be applied to pay the debts and provide for the common defence and general welfare of the United States; but the legislature have authority to contract debts at their discretion; they are the sole judges of what is necessary to provide for the common defence, and they only are to determine what is for the general welfare; this power therefore is neither more nor less, than a power to lay and collect taxes, imposts, and excises, at their pleasure; not only [is] the power to lay taxes unlimited, as to the amount they may require, but it is perfect and absolute to raise them in any mode they please. No state legislature, or any power in the state governments, have any more to do in carrying this into effect, than the authority of one state has to do with that of another. In the business therefore of laying and collecting taxes, the idea of confederation is totally lost, and that of one entire republic is embraced. It is proper here to remark, that the authority to lay and collect taxes is the most important of any power that can be granted; it connects with it almost all other powers, or at least will in process of time draw all other after it; it is the great mean of protection, security, and defence, in a good government, and the great engine of oppression and tyranny in a bad one. This cannot fail of being the case, if we consider the contracted limits which are set by this constitution, to the late [state?] governments, on this article of raising money. No state can emit paper money—lay any duties, or imposts, on imports, or exports, but by consent of the Congress; and then the net produce shall be for the benefit of the United States: the only mean therefore left, for any state to support its government and discharge its debts, is by direct taxation; and the United States have also power to lay and collect taxes, in any way they please. Every one who has thought on the subject, must be convinced that but small sums of money can be collected in any country, by direct taxe[s], when the federal government begins to exercise the right of taxation in all its parts, the legislatures of the several states will find it impossible to raise monies to support their governments. Without money they cannot be supported, and they must dwindle away, and, as before observed, their powers absorbed in that of the general government.

It might be here shewn, that the power in the federal legislative, to raise and support armies at pleasure, as well in peace as in war, and their controul over the militia, tend, not only to a consolidation of the government, but the destruction of liberty.—I shall not, however, dwell upon these, as a few observations upon the judicial power of this government, in addition to the preceding, will fully evince the truth of the position.

The judicial power of the United States is to be vested in a supreme court, and in such inferior courts as Congress may from time to time ordain and establish. The powers of these courts are very extensive; their jurisdiction comprehends all civil causes, except such as arise between citizens of the same state; and it extends to all cases in law and equity arising under the constitution. One inferior court must be established, I presume, in each state, at least, with the necessary executive officers appendant thereto. It is easy to see, that in the common course of things, these courts will eclipse the dignity, and take away from the respectability, of the state courts. These courts will be, in themselves, totally independent of the states, deriving their authority from the United States, and receiving from them fixed salaries; and in the course of human events it is to be expected, that they will swallow up all the powers of the courts in the respective states.

How far the clause in the 8th section of the 1st article may operate to do away all idea of confederated states, and to effect an entire consolidation of the whole into one general government, it is impossible to say. The powers given by this article are very general and comprehensive, and it may receive a construction to justify the passing almost any law. A power to make all laws, which shall be *necessary and proper*, for carrying into execution, all powers vested by the constitution in the government of the United States, or any department or officer thereof, is a power very comprehensive and definite [indefinite?], and may, for ought I know, be exercised in a such manner as entirely to abolish the state legislatures. Suppose the legislature of a state should pass a law to raise money to support their government and pay the state debt, may the Congress repeal this law, because it may prevent the collection of a tax which they may think proper and necessary to lay, to provide for the general welfare of the United States? For all laws made, in pursuance of this constitution, are the supreme law of the land, and the judges in every state shall be bound thereby, any thing in the constitution or laws of the different states to the contrary notwithstanding.—By such a law, the government of a particular state might be overturned at one stroke, and thereby be deprived of every means of its support.

It is not meant, by stating this case, to insinuate that the constitution would warrant a law of this kind; or unnecessarily to alarm the fears of the people, by suggesting, that the federal legislature would be more likely to pass the limits assigned them by the constitution, than that of an individual state, further than they are less responsible to the people. But what is meant is, that the legislature of the United States are vested with the great and uncontrollable powers, of laying and collecting taxes, duties, imposts, and excises; of regulating trade, raising and supporting armies, organizing, arming, and disciplining the militia, instituting courts, and other general powers. And are by this clause invested with the power of making all laws, *proper and necessary*, for carrying all these into execution; and they may so exercise this power as entirely to annihilate all the state governments, and reduce this country to one single government. And if they may do it, it is pretty certain they will; for it will be found that the power retained by individual states, small as it is, will be a clog upon the wheels of the government of the United States; the latter therefore will be naturally inclined to remove it out of the way. Besides, it is a truth confirmed by the unerring experience of ages, that every man, and every body of men, invested with power, are ever disposed to increase it, and to acquire a superiority over every thing that stands in their way. This disposition, which is implanted in human nature, will operate in the federal legislature to lessen and ultimately to subvert the state authority, and having such advantages, will most certainly succeed, if the federal government succeeds at all. It must be very evident then, that what this constitution wants of being a complete consolidation of the several parts of the union into one complete government, possessed of perfect legislative, judicial, and executive powers, to all intents and purposes, it will necessarily acquire in its exercise and operation.

Let us now proceed to enquire, as I at first proposed, whether it be best the thirteen United States should be reduced to one great republic, or not? It is here taken for granted, that all agree in this, that whatever government we adopt, it ought to be a free one; that it should be so framed as to secure the liberty of the citizens of America, and such an one as to admit of a full, fair, and equal representation of the people, The question then will be, whether a government thus constituted, and founded on such principles, is practicable, and can be exercised over the whole United States, reduced into one state?

If respect is to be paid to the opinion of the greatest and wisest men who have ever thought or wrote on the science of government, we shall be constrained to con-

clude, that a free republic cannot succeed over a country of such immense extent, containing such a number of inhabitants, and these encreasing in such rapid progression as that of the whole United States. Among the many illustrious authorities which might be produced to this point, I shall content myself with quoting only two. The one is the baron de Montesquieu, spirit of laws, chap. xvi. vol. I [book VIII]. "It is natural to a republic to have only a small territory, otherwise it cannot long subsist. In a large republic there are men of large fortunes, and consequently of less moderation; there are trusts too great to be placed in any single subject; he has interest of his own; he soon begins to think that he may be happy, great and glorious, by oppressing his fellow citizens; and that he may raise himself to grandeur on the ruins of his country. In a large republic, the public good is sacrificed to a thousand views; it is subordinate to exceptions, and depends on accidents. In a small one, the interest of the public is easier perceived, better understood, and more within the reach of every citizen; abuses are of less extent, and of course are less protected." Of the same opinion is the marquis Beccarari.

History furnishes no example of a free republic, any thing like the extent of the United States. The Grecian republics were of small extent; so also was that of the Romans. Both of these, it is true, in process of time, extended their conquests over large territories of country; and the consequence was, that their governments were changed from that of free governments to those of the most tyrannical that ever existed in the world.

Not only the opinion of the greatest men, and the experience of mankind, are against the idea of an extensive republic, but a variety of reasons may be drawn from the reason and nature of things, against it. In every government, the will of the sovereign is the law. In despotic governments, the supreme authority being lodged in one, his will is law, and can be as easily expressed to a large extensive territory as to a small one. In a pure democracy the people are the sovereign, and their will is declared by themselves; for this purpose they must all come together to deliberate, and decide. This kind of government cannot be exercised, therefore, over a country of any considerable extent; it must be confined to a single city, or at least limited to such bounds as that the people can conveniently assemble, be able to debate, understand the subject submitted to them, and declare their opinion concerning it.

In a free republic, although all laws are derived from

the consent of the people, yet the people do not declare their consent by themselves in person, but by representatives, chosen by them, who are supposed to know the minds of their constituents, and to be possessed of integrity to declare this mind.

In every free government, the people must give their assent to the laws by which they are governed. This is the true criterion between a free government and an arbitrary one. The former are ruled by the will of the whole, expressed in any manner they may agree upon; the latter by the will of one, or a few. If the people are to give their assent to the laws, by persons chosen and appointed by them, the manner of the choice and the number chosen, must be such, as to possess, be disposed, and consequently qualified to declare the sentiments of the people; for if they do not know, or are not disposed to speak the sentiments of the people, the people do not govern, but the sovereignty is in a few. Now, in a large extended country, it is impossible to have a representation, possessing the sentiments, and of integrity, to declare the minds of the people, without having it so numerous and unwieldy, as to be subject in great measure to the inconveniency of a democratic government.

The territory of the United States is of vast extent; it now contains near three millions of souls, and is capable of containing much more than ten times that number. Is it practicable for a country, so large and so numerous as they will soon become, to elect a representation, that will speak their sentiments, without their becoming so numerous as to be incapable of transacting public business? It certainly is not.

In a republic, the manners, sentiments, and interests of the people should be similar. If this be not the case, there will be a constant clashing of opinions; and the representatives of one part will be continually striving against those of the other. This will retard the operations of government, and prevent such conclusions as will promote the public good. If we apply this remark to the condition of the United States, we shall be convinced that it forbids that we should be one government. The United States includes a variety of climates. The productions of the different parts of the union are very variant, and their interests, of consequence, diverse. Their manners and habits differ as much as their climates and productions; and their sentiments are by no means coincident. The laws and customs of the several states are, in many respects, very diverse, and in some opposite; each would be in favor of its own interests and customs, and, of consequence, a legislature, formed of representatives from

the respective parts, would not only be too numerous to act with any care or decision, but would be composed of such heterogenous and discordant principles, as would constantly be contending with each other.

The laws cannot be executed in a republic, of an extent equal to that of the United States, with promptitude.

The magistrates in every government must be supported in the execution of the laws, either by an armed force, maintained at the public expense for that purpose; or by the people turning out to aid the magistrate upon his command, in case of resistance.

In despotic governments, as well as in all the monarchies of Europe, standing armies are kept up to execute the commands of the prince or the magistrate, and are employed for this purpose when occasion requires: But they have always proved the destruction of liberty, and [are] abhorrent to the spirit of a free republic. In England, where they depend upon the parliament for their annual support, they have always been complained of as oppressive and unconstitutional, and are seldom employed in executing of the laws; never except on extraordinary occasions, and then under the direction of a civil magistrate.

A free republic will never keep a standing army to execute its laws. It must depend upon the support of its citizens. But when a government is to receive its support from the aid of the citizens, it must be so constructed as to have the confidence, respect, and affection of the people. Men who, upon the call of the magistrate, offer themselves to execute the laws, are influenced to do it either by affection to the government, or from fear; where a standing army is at hand to punish offenders, every man is actuated by the latter principle, and therefore, when the magistrate calls, will obey: but, where this is not the case, the government must rest for its support upon the confidence and respect which the people have for their government and laws. The body of the people being attached, the government will always be sufficient to support and execute its laws, and to operate upon the fears of any faction which may be opposed to it, not only to prevent an opposition to the execution of the laws themselves, but also to compel the most of them to aid the magistrate; but the people will not be likely to have such confidence in their rulers, in a republic so extensive as the United States, as necessary for these purposes. The confidence which the people have in their rulers, in a free republic, arises from their knowing them, from their being responsible to them for their conduct, and from the power they have of displacing them when they misbehave: but in a republic of the extent of this continent, the people in general would be acquainted with very few of their rulers: the people at large would know little of their proceedings, and it would be extremely difficult to change them. The people in Georgia and New-Hampshire would not know one another's mind, and therefore could not act in concert to enable them to effect a general change of representatives. The different parts of so extensive a country could not possibly be made acquainted with the conduct of their representatives, nor be informed of the reasons upon which measures were founded. The consequence will be, they will have no confidence in their legislature, suspect them of ambitious views, be jealous of every measure they adopt, and will not support the laws they pass. Hence the government will be nerveless and inefficient, and no way will be left to render it otherwise, but by establishing an armed force to execute the laws at the point of the bayonet—a government of all others the most to be dreaded.

In a republic of such vast extent as the United-States, the legislature cannot attend to the various concerns and wants of its different parts. It cannot be sufficiently numerous to be acquainted with the local condition and wants of the different districts, and if it could, it is impossible it should have sufficient time to attend to and provide for all the variety of cases of this nature, that would be continually arising.

In so extensive a republic, the great officers of government would soon become above the controul of the people, and abuse their power to the purpose of aggrandizing themselves, and oppressing them. The trust committed to the executive offices, in a country of the extent of the United-States, must be various and of magnitude. The command of all the troops and navy of the republic, the appointment of officers, the power of pardoning offenses, the collecting of all the public revenues, and the power of expending them, with a number of other powers, must be lodged and exercised in every state, in the hands of a few. When these are attended with great honor and emolument, as they always will be in large states, so as greatly to interest men to pursue them, and to be proper objects for ambitious and designing men, such men will be ever restless in their pursuit after them. They will use the power, when they have acquired it, to the purposes of gratifying their own interest and ambition, and it is scarcely possible, in a very large republic, to call them to account for their misconduct, or to prevent their abuse of power.

These are some of the reasons by which it appears, that a free republic cannot long subsist over a country of the great extent of these states. If then this new constitution is calculated to consolidate the thirteen states into one, as it evidently is, it ought not to be adopted.

Though I am of opinion, that it is a sufficient objection to this government, to reject it, that it creates the whole union into one government, under the form of a republic, yet if this objection was obviated, there are exceptions to it, which are so material and fundamental, that they ought to determine every man, who is a friend to the liberty and happiness of mankind, not to adopt it. I beg the candid and dispassionate attention of my countrymen while I state these objections—they are such as have obtruded themselves upon my mind upon a careful attention to the matter, and such as I sincerely believe are well founded. There are many objections, of small moment, of which I shall take no notice—perfection is not to be expected in any thing that is the production of man—and if I did not in my conscience believe that this scheme was defective in the fundamental principles—in the foundation upon which a free and equal government must rest— I would hold my peace.

Brutus.

Presidents of the United States

	Party	Term
1. George Washington (1732–1799)	Federalist	1789–1797
2. John Adams (1735–1826)	Federalist	1797–1801
3. Thomas Jefferson (1743–1826)	Democratic-Republican	1801–1809
4. James Madison (1751–1836)	Democratic-Republican	1809–1817
5. James Monroe (1758–1831)	Democratic-Republican	1817–1825
6. John Quincy Adams (1767–1848)	Democratic-Republican	1825–1829
7. Andrew Jackson (1767–1845)	Democratic	1829–1837
8. Martin Van Buren (1782–1862)	Democratic	1837–1841
9. William Henry Harrison (1773–1841)	Whig	1841
10. John Tyler (1790–1862)	Whig	1841–1845
11. James K. Polk (1795–1849)	Democratic	1845–1849
12. Zachary Taylor (1784–1850)	Whig	1849–1850
13. Millard Fillmore (1800–1874)	Whig	1850–1853
14. Franklin Pierce (1804–1869)	Democratic	1853–1857
15. James Buchanan (1791–1868)	Democratic	1857–1861
16. Abraham Lincoln (1809–1865)	Republican	1861–1865
17. Andrew Johnson (1808–1875)	Union	1865–1869
18. Ulysses S. Grant (1822–1885)	Republican	1869–1877
19. Rutherford B. Hayes (1822–1893)	Republican	1877–1881
20. James A. Garfield (1831–1881)	Republican	1881
21. Chester A. Arthur (1830–1886)	Republican	1881–1885
22. Grover Cleveland (1837–1908)	Democratic	1885–1889
23. Benjamin Harrison (1833–1901)	Republican	1889–1893
24. Grover Cleveland (1837–1908)	Democratic	1893–1897
25. William McKinley (1843–1901)	Republican	1897–1901
26. Theodore Roosevelt (1858–1919)	Republican	1901–1909
27. William Howard Taft (1857–1930)	Republican	1909–1913
28. Woodrow Wilson (1856–1924)	Democratic	1913–1921
29. Warren G. Harding (1865–1923)	Republican	1921–1923
30. Calvin Coolidge (1871–1933)	Republican	1923–1929
31. Herbert Hoover (1874–1964)	Republican	1929–1933
32. Franklin Delano Roosevelt (1882–1945)	Democratic	1933–1945
33. Harry S Truman (1884–1972)	Democratic	1945–1953
34. Dwight D. Eisenhower (1890–1969)	Republican	1953–1961
35. John F. Kennedy (1917–1963)	Democratic	1961–1963
36. Lyndon B. Johnson (1908–1973)	Democratic	1963–1969
37. Richard M. Nixon (1913–1994)	Republican	1969–1974
38. Gerald R. Ford (b. 1913)	Republican	1974–1977
39. Jimmy Carter (b. 1924)	Democratic	1977–1981
40. Ronald Reagan (b. 1911)	Republican	1981–1989
41. George Bush (b. 1924)	Republican	1989–1993
42. Bill Clinton (b. 1946)	Democratic	1993–

GLOSSARY

administrative adjudication   The quasi-judicial powers delegated to executive agencies to try individuals or organizations that have violated legally binding agency rules.

administrative state   A national government involved in regulating or supporting almost every form of social activity by means of a large, complex, and diverse bureaucracy.

affirmative action   Positive steps taken to award educational opportunities or jobs to racial minorities or women because these groups have been the victims of prior discrimination.

agenda-setting   The ability to determine what issues are considered legitimate, or even worthy of discussion, within the political arena.

American Civil Liberties Union (ACLU)   An organization that defends the civil liberties and civil rights of many individuals and groups in court challenges.

Anti-federalists   Opponents of the Constitution during the ratification debates of 1787–88.

appellate court   A court that possesses the power to review the decisions of lower courts.

Articles of Confederation   The first written U.S. Constitution, ratified by the states in 1781, establishing a loose confederation among the former colonies under a weak national government.

autonomy   Greater freedom on the part of executive agencies from control by external forces.

Bill of Rights   The first ten amendments to the Constitution, which spell out the basic rights to which Americans are entitled.

block grants   The consolidation of a number of related categorical grants into one larger grant that provides recipients with the ability to spend the money as they see fit within the broad purposes of the grant.

Brown* v. *Board of Education of Topeka   The 1954 case in which the Supreme Court rejected the separate but equal doctrine in the field of education and thereby began the end of legal racial segregation.

Budget and Impoundment Control Act of 1974   A law that reasserted congressional authority in budget-making by creating new budget committees and the Congressional Budget Office and requiring annual timelines for the budgetary process.

bureaucracy   Units of the executive branch, organized in a hierarchical fashion, governed through formal rules, and distinguished by their specialized functions.

bureaucratic politics   The conflict that arises when an agency seeking to carry out its core mission is threatened by another agency promoting its core mission.

business confidence factor   The extent to which political officials anticipate and consider the future investment and spending habits of corporations when making political decisions.

bystander   A citizen who lacks consistent views about political issues, is generally uninterested in political events, and generally does not vote or participate in public affairs.

cabinet departments   The fourteen major divisions of the executive branch, each responsible for a broad area of governmental operations.

candidate-centered campaign   Election contests in which candidates base their support on their personality, distinctive record, and self–developed organization rather than on their party affiliations.

capitalism   An economic system in which individuals and corporations, not the government, own the principal means of production and pursue profits.

casework   The help given individual constituents by congressional staffs.

casino economy An economy characterized by a high number of speculative sales, purchases, and mergers of corporations during the 1980s.

categorical grant Federal money to state and local governments that requires recipients to apply for funding under specific categories, detailing exactly how the money will be spent, and subject themselves to strict federal monitoring.

Central Intelligence Agency (CIA) The chief government intelligence-gathering agency, which has two primary functions: espionage and covert action.

civil disobedience The deliberate violation of the law by persons willing to accept the law's punishment in order to dramatize a cause.

civil liberties The basic freedoms embodied in the Bill of Rights, such as speech and religion, which individuals enjoy and government cannot invade.

civil rights Constitutional guarantees, such as the right to vote and equal treatment under the law, that belong to people because of their status as citizens.

Civil Rights Act of 1964 A law that made racial discrimination in public accommodations (hotels and restaurants) and employment illegal.

Civil War amendments The Thirteenth, Fourteenth, and Fifteenth Amendments to the Constitution, which extended the Bill of Rights to and emphasized equality in the treatment of the former slaves.

clear and present danger test A Supreme Court standard stating that the government can prohibit political speech only if it can bring about an immediate evil that Congress has a right to prevent.

cloture A Senate procedure for terminating debate and ending a filibuster, which requires a three-fifths vote of the membership.

Cold War A worldwide political, economic and ideological struggle between the United States and the Soviet Union that lasted from 1945 to 1989.

collective action problem The difficulty in getting individuals to act collectively to obtain a common good when everyone in a group will benefit regardless of whether she or he contributes to the collective action.

committee system The division of the legislative workload among several congressional bodies assigned specific issues.

concurrent powers The constitutional authority granted to both the federal and state governments, such as the authority to tax.

concurring opinion A written statement by a Supreme Court justice about why he or she agrees with the decision reached in a case by the majority of the Court but not with the majority reasoning.

Confidence and trust gap The decline in favorable popular opinion about the behavior and performance of government and social institutions, such as organized religion, corporations, and unions. Most observers date such decline from the late 1960s and early 1970s.

conservative A person who advocates streamlined government, a business sector free from government regulation, a return to traditional social values, and a priority on military over social needs.

containment A Cold War policy, also known as the Truman Doctrine, of a global American struggle to restrict the spread of communism.

core beliefs The long-standing, consistent general attitudes that Americans share, such as support for freedom of speech and democracy.

corporate capitalism The developed or advanced stage of capitalism in which large corporations dominate the means of production and often the political system as well.

corporate image advertising The promotion of a company's public persona rather than its products in order to create favorable public opinion about the role of the company in society.

cost-benefit analysis A method of determining if the dollar benefits of proposed government regulation are greater than the dollar costs.

Council of Economic Advisers A body of professional economists who provide the president with regular assistance.

court-packing plan A failed attempt by President Franklin Roosevelt in 1937 to change the direction of the Supreme Court, by giving the president the power to name one new justice to the Court for each current justice over the age of seventy.

covert action   Secret CIA activities that cannot be traced to the U.S. government.

creative federalism   The attempt by President Lyndon Johnson to solve the problems of urban poverty by having the federal government bypass state and city governments and give grants directly to community and nonprofit organizations in the ghettos.

culture of poverty   The theory that people are poor because they have certain values, passed from generation to generation, that cause them to miss or ignore opportunities to advance themselves economically.

dealignment   The weakening of the party system caused by growing popular indifference to the parties themselves.

Declaration of Independence   The document written by Thomas Jefferson and adopted by the Continental Congress on July 4, 1776, in which the American colonies announced themselves to be free and independent from Great Britain and set forth the revolutionary principle of democracy.

deficit spending   Government expenditures in excess of tax revenues.

delegate   A representative who comes from a particular district or state and is supposed to reflect the opinions, feelings, and interests of the voters in this district or state.

Department of Defense   The cabinet department that coordinates and controls American military activities and is headed by a civilian secretary.

Department of State   The cabinet department that is the traditional organ of American diplomacy and is headed by a secretary.

deregulation   The reduction or elimination of government control of the conduct or activities of private citizens amd organizations.

deserving poor   Those people, such as single mothers with young children, who through no fault of their own cannot achieve a basic minimum standard of living by working.

direct democracy   The face-to-face meeting of all citizens in one place to vote on all important issues.

direct marketing   The targeted solicitation of individuals for political support, sometimes by phone but more often by mail.

discretion   The latitude that administrators have in carrying out their agency's mission.

disinformation campaign   CIA activity to disseminate misleading or false reports about opponents of the U.S. government's activities.

dissenting opinion   A written statement by a Supreme Court justice about why he or she disagrees with the decision reached in a case by the majority of the Court.

downsizing   Reducing the numbers of employees of a company by a conscious strategy of layoffs, firings, and retirements.

Dred Scott* v. *Sandford   The infamous 1857 case in which the Supreme Court decided that blacks were not citizens and that slaves were property protected by the Constitution.

dual federalism   The system created at the founding of the Constitution in which the national and state governments each have separate spheres of authority and are supreme within their own sphere.

economic cycles   The tendency of the world and national economy to vacillate between periods of economic expansion and recession or economic booms and busts.

economic individualism   The belief that hard work is the major determining factor in individual economic success and that economic opportunities are widely available to individuals who seek them.

Economic Recovery Tax Act of 1981   Reagan administration legislation that dramatically cut taxes to encourage capital investment and economic growth.

economic regulation   Control by an independent regulatory commission of a specific industry that focuses on prices, quality of services, and the ability to enter or leave the industry.

efficacy   In politics, an individual's feeling or sense that her or his participation can affect public policy.

elite democracy   A political system in which the privileged classes acquire the power to decide by a competition for the people's votes and have substantial freedom between elections to rule as they see fit.

employee stock ownership plan (ESOP)   A legal arrangement, encouraged by federal legislation, which enables workers to gradually acquire shares of the companies they work for.

Employment Act of 1946   A law giving the federal government responsibility to promote free enterprise, avoid economic fluctuations, and maintain jobs, production, and purchasing power.

entitlement   A social benefit, such as social security in which all who pay into it have a right to the benefits; one does not have to apply for the program or show that one deserves help.

enumerated powers   The authority specifically granted to the federal government in the Constitution under Article I, section 8.

equality of opportunity   The idea that there should be no discriminatory barriers placed on an individual's access to economic success.

Equal Time Provision   An FCC broadcasting regulation that requires radio and television stations that sell time to one political candidate to also sell to others.

Establishment Clause   That part of the First Amendment that forbids Congress to make any law instituting a religion; the central component of the separation of church and state.

exclusionary rule   A doctrine, based on the Fourth Amendment's guarantee against unreasonable searches and seizures, in which the Supreme Court established that material seized in an illegal search cannot be introduced as evidence in a criminal case.

Executive Office of the President (EOP)   The complex of support agencies designed to assist the chief executive, including the White House staff, the Office of Management and Budget, the Council of Economic Advisers, and the National Security Council.

expansion   Nineteenth–century activities by the United States to extend the nation to the Pacific Ocean and to gain territorial acquisitions in Latin America and Asia.

expertise   The specialized knowledge of administrators about their particular areas of responsibility.

externalities   The involuntary or unforeseen effects on people of a voluntary exchange between buyers and sellers in the capitalist marketplace.

Fairness Rule   An FCC regulation requiring broadcasters to provide reasonable time for expression of opposing views on controversial issues.

Federal Communications Commission (FCC)   The governmental regulatory agency charged with encouraging competition in radio and in television. The FCC licenses these media and regulates the private ownership of broadcast stations.

federal foundations and endowments   Organizations that enable the federal government to sponsor scientific and cultural activities.

federalism   A system in which power is divided between the central government and the states.

Federalist   Supporters of the Constitution during the Constitutional Convention of 1787 and the ratification debates of 1787–1788.

Federal Register   The daily government publication of all national administrative regulations.

feminization of poverty   The increased proportion of women, especially single women with children, who fall below the poverty line.

filibuster   The Senate tradition whereby a senator can try to delay or defeat a vote on legislation by talking the bill to death.

fiscal policy   The manipulation of components of the national budget, taxes, and spending to regulate the economy.

5-5-10 rule   A Federal Communications Commission regulation requiring broadcasters to devote a minimum of 5 percent of airtime to local affairs, 5 percent to news and public affairs, and 10 percent to nonentertainment programming.

flexible specialization   An innovative form of production that enables companies to develop new products and produce them in smaller batches to respond to specialized niches in the market system.

focus group   A selected sample of voters intensively interviewed by campaign consultants to gain knowledge about reactions to particular candidates and their campaign messages and themes.

footnote four   A footnote in a 1938 Supreme Court decision that sets out three conditions under which the Court will not grant government action the presumption of constitutionality: when the action falls under the prohibitions of the Bill of Rights or Fourteenth Amendment, when the action restricts the democratic process, or when the action is harmful to particular religions or national or racial minorities.

franking privilege   The benefit enjoyed by members of Congress of free postage to send mass mailings to their constituents.

Freedom Summer   A intensive campaign of direct action launched in the summer of 1964 by major civil rights organizations to press for federal intervention to eliminate racial segregation and discrimination in the southern states.

Free Exercise Clause   That part of the First Amendment that states that Congress shall make no law prohibiting the practice of religion.

fundamentalist   A conservative Christian, groups of whom gained political power in the 1980's. They often promote family and religious themes and attack homosexuality, feminism, and pro-choice stands on abortion.

gender gap   Distinctions between the attitudes, voting behavior, and outlooks of men and women.

general revenue sharing   Federal grants to states and localities without the stringent requirements associated with categorical grants.

Gibbons v. Ogden   The 1824 case in which the Supreme Court broadly defined the congressional power to "regulate commerce among the states," thereby establishing the supremacy of the federal government over the states in matters involving interstate commerce.

governmental gridlock   The sense that government is unable to act coherently or energetically due to bickering and impasses created by split party control of Congress and the White House.

grant-in-aid   Money provided by one level of government to another to perform certain functions.

grassroots campaign   A run for office that emphasizes volunteer efforts, person-to-person contact, and voter organization over paid advertising, extensive polling, and other costly activities managed by a central staff.

Great Compromise   An agreement, also known as the Connecticut Compromise, in which the Constitutional Convention of 1787 resolved that Congress would be bicameral, with the Senate composed of two members from each state and the House of Representatives apportioned according to each state's population.

hearing   A congressional committee session in which witnesses for and against a proposed bill make statements and answer questions.

horse race journalism   The tendency of the media to report election campaigns in terms of who is winning and losing rather than in terms of what issues are at stake.

ideological bloc   A group of two or more Supreme Court justices who vote the same way with a high degree of regularity on the basis of a shared legal philosophy.

ideological party   A political group whose leaders and members have strong roots in a distinctive philosophical tradition or doctrine.

ideology   A specific set of beliefs for making sense of issues and actions, a consistent pattern of opinion used to justify political behavior.

implied powers   The authority of Congress to enact all laws that are "necessary and proper" to carry out the powers enumerated in Article I of the Constitution.

income inequality   The gap in yearly earnings between those groups and individuals with the highest and those with the lowest incomes.

incorporation   The doctrine that the Supreme Court used to apply the Bill of Rights to the states under the 14th Amendment Due Process Clause.

independent agency   An executive branch organization that stands outside of and generally handles more narrow areas of governmental operation than the cabinet departments.

independent regulatory commission   A governmental body that controls a sector of the economy and is directed by commissioners who are appointed by the president, have long terms, and are exempt from presidential removal so that the agency is distanced from political pressures.

information superhighway   New technology allowing individuals and institutions with computers to communicate directly with each other and with commercial, educational, and other institutions via the Internet and profit-making operations such as Prodigy and America On-line.

insider strategy   The use by an interest group of face-to-face, one-on-one persuasion to convince decision makers in Washington that the interest group's position makes sense.

interest-group politics   Any attempt by an organization to influence the policies of government through normal extra electoral channels, such as lobbying, writing letters, testifying before legislative committees, or advertising.

intergovernmental relations   The modern system of federalism in which relations between the different levels of government are worked out by specific legislation and negotiations, rather than through the formal distinction of separate spheres of authority that characterized dual federalism.

isolationism   The idea that apart from commercial relations, the United States should stay out of the political and military quarrels of the rest of the world; the core principle of American foreign and defense policy from the founding until World War II.

Joint Chiefs of Staff (JCS)   A body composed of the commanding officer of each military service, and headed by a chair, that conveys the military's point of view to the president and the secretary of defense.

joint stock ownership   The pooling of resources of a number of investors in a corporation, all of whom can freely buy and sell their shares.

judicial review   The power of the courts to invalidate legislative or executive actions because they conflict with the Constitution.

jurisprudence of original intention   The argument that Supreme Court justices should restrict their constitutional interpretation to the precise words of the Constitution and the known intentions of the men who drafted it.

Laffer curve   The representational graph that argues that decreasing tax rates below a certain point actually increases total tax revenues.

laissez-faire   The idea that government should not be involved in running the private economy.

legislative liaison staff   The group of people responsible for keeping the president informed of the political maneuvering and likely vote lineup in Congress for important bills and for providing small favors to members of Congress in the hopes that they will later return these favors to the president with their votes.

legislative term limit   The placement of restrictions on the number of consecutive terms that a legislator may serve; a proposed remedy for the ills of Congress and the state legislatures.

Lemon test   The standard used by the Supreme Court in cases involving government aid to religion, which states that government assistance is constitutional only if it has a secular purpose, its effect does not advance or inhibit religion, and it does not entangle government and religious institutions in each other's affairs.

liberal   A person who advocates an active government, supports social welfare programs and expanded individual rights and liberties, tolerates social change and diversity, and opposes "excessive" military spending and action.

libertarian   A person who objects to governmental "interference" in both business activity and personal lifestyles.

mail order politics   The modern tendency for some to participate in politics through monetary contributions to Washington lobbying groups.

majority leader   The head of the majority party in the House of Representatives or Senate.

manufactured consent   Those instances when the government is able to manipulate public opinion because it controls access to information and public knowledge is either low or accepting.

Marbury v. *Madison*   The 1803 case in which the Supreme Court established that it had the right to exercise judicial review even though that power was not stated in the Constitution.

market failures   Occasions when the capitalist economy diverges from the competition and voluntary cooperation said to be characteristic of it. Examples include economic repressions and the formation of monopolies.

markup   A session in which a congressional committee drafts the actual language of a bill.

mass movement   The participation of large numbers of previously passive bystanders in a political protest action.

matching grants   Money given by the federal government to lower levels of government to fulfill certain functions, requiring that the recipients put up some of their own money and meet minimal federal standards for the program.

McCarthyism   The practice, named after Senator Joseph McCarthy, of falsely accusing individuals of being disloyal or subversive in order to gain publicity or suppress opposition.

means–tested benefits   The method of granting public assistance that forces people to prove their inability to support themselves in order to secure that assistance.

Medicaid   Means-tested health insurance for the poor.

Medicare   Health insurance for the elderly, comprising compulsory insurance for hospital services for people sixty five and older and voluntary insurance for medical services.

member of a responsible party   The model of representation in which people vote for a representative based on his or her belonging to a disciplined party with a coherent program for governance.

military-industrial complex   The network of ties among large corporations, the Department of Defense, the armed services, and their key political supporters in Congress and the executive branch.

minority leader   The head of the minority party in the House of Representatives or Senate.

Miranda warnings   The requirement that police inform all criminal suspects of their rights before taking them into custody.

mission   The central task to which the members of a government agency are committed.

monetarism   An economic philosophy that believes steady growth can be achieved if the money supply grows only as fast as the economy's productivity.

monetary policy   A method of economic management that regulates the supply of money in the economy.

Motor-Voter bill   Legislation passed in 1993 that allows people to register to vote when they apply for a driver's license, thereby making voter registration easier and more accessible, especially for youth, the group most likely not to vote.

name recognition   The extent to which a candidate's or potential candidate's name is known by voters.

National Association for the Advancement of Colored People (NAACP)   An organization that fights for the rights of black Americans.

national security adviser   The personal counselor to the president in foreign policy and defense matters.

National Security Council (NSC)   A governmental body created in 1947 to advise the president and coordinate foreign and defense policy.

national security state   A complex of executive, military, and secret powers that shaped American international relations in the Cold War and largely excluded Congress and the public from decisions about the country's security.

new federalism   The attempt by President Richard Nixon to weaken the power of liberal political lobbies in Washington and reverse the trend toward centralization of authority and control in Washington, by placing more power, monies, and responsibility for government programs in the hands of the states.

New Jersey Plan   The proposal submitted by the New Jersey delegation at the Constitutional Convention of 1787 to reform the Articles of Confederation but maintain most governmental power in the states.

new liberal   Individuals who favor strong environmentalist and feminist positions, and defend civil liberties for nonconforming groups. New liberals are also critics of Cold War American foreign policy and large military budgets.

newspaper chain   The ownership of many local newspapers by one corporation.

new working class   Those who make wages and labor in subordinate positions in the service industries that have grown rapidly in the past two decades.

nondecision making   The ability to prevent certain issues from even being considered for action by government.

North Atlantic Treaty Organization (NATO)   The military alliance among the United States, Canada, and the Western European states, created to oppose Soviet aggression in the Cold War period.

nullification   The doctrine that the states have the right to declare invalid any federal legislation that they believe violates the Constitution.

obscenity   Sexually explicit material that lacks serious literary, artistic, political, or scientific value and that appeals to a "prurient" interest; one of the categories of unprotected speech.

Office of Management and Budget (OMB)   The agency responsible for preparing the annual presidential budget and for scrutinizing legislative proposals originating in the agencies of the executive branch to ensure that these proposals are in accord with the president's legislative program.

oral argument   The spoken presentation of each side of a case to the justices of the Supreme Court.

original jurisdiction   The power of a court to hear a case at its inception.

outsider strategy   The mobilization by an interest group of forces outside Washington to put pressure on decision makers to act in ways favorable to the interest group.

outsourcing   The ability of large companies to avoid wage and benefit costs by contracting out many of their operations to smaller companies that hire cheaper, often part-time labor.

oversight   Congressional attempts to exercise control over the activities of executive branch agencies through a variety of techniques, including hearings and investigations.

pack journalism   The development by a group of reporters of similar views after receiving the same information and insights from the same sources.

party caucus   A public meeting held within a political party to select delegates pledged to the nomination of a particular candidate.

party identification   A person's psychological identification with or tie to a particular political party.

party system   Long–lasting forms, themes, and rules that dominate interparty competition and dialogue, usually established by realigning elections and usually featuring a dominant issue.

patronage   The power of elected officials to increase their political strength by appointing people of their choice to governmental or public jobs; one of the methods that political machines use to guarantee loyalty.

pluralism   The elite democratic theory that views the interest-group system as a political marketplace in which power is dispersed among many interest groups competing for influence through a process of bargaining and compromising.

Political Action Committee (PAC)   A voluntary organization that funnels monies from individuals in corporations, trade associations, labor unions, and other groups into political campaigns or coffers.

political machine   An organization of political professionals able to win elections through intensive follower organization and loyalty which is usually garnered by providing jobs and services to followers and denying them to opponents.

political socialization   The ways in which individuals obtain their ideas about human nature, politics, and political institutions.

poll bias   Conscious or unconscious mistakes in sampling technique or question wording that serve to mischaracterize or misinterpret public opinion.

popular democracy   A political system in which the citizens are involved as much as possible in making the decisions that affect their lives.

populist   A person who advocates regulating the excesses of corporations and redistributing wealth but opposes relaxing social morals or being too lenient on crime.

Populist party   The political party formed by southern and western farmers in the late 1880s to rally against the alleged advantages given to big business and banking interests.

precedent   A previous decision by a court that is treated as a rule for future cases.

preemption   The ability of the federal government to assume total or partial responsibility for a function where there is concurrent authority for both the federal government and the states to act.

presidential power of secrecy   The ability of the chief executive to make foreign policy and national security decisions that are not subject to public scrutiny.

president's cabinet   The executive body composed of the appointed heads of the fourteen major executive departments, plus any others designated by the chief executive.

primary   An election in which voters decide which of a party's candidates will be nominated to run for office in the general election. Closed primaries permit only those requested in a particular party to participate. Open primaries leave the balloting open to non–party registrants.

prior restraint   The First Amendment prohibition against government officials preventing information from being published.

privatization   The turning over of governmental functions to the private sector when it can perform functions more cheaply than government agencies.

progressive tax   A tax that takes a higher proportion of income as income increases.

Progressivism   An early-twentieth-century American reform doctrine that advocated limits to the power of political machines, expert and efficient bureaucracies, and a politics free of allegedly corrupt influences from party politicians, especially those representing urban immigrants.

protest politics   Political actions designed to broaden conflicts and activate outside parties to pressure the bargaining process in ways favorable to the protestors.

proxy   The right to vote shares of corporate stock in elections held by corporations.

public corporation   A government agency that engages in business activities.

public-interest group   Any association seeking government action, the achievement of which will not principally benefit the members of the association.

public opinion   The average person's ideas and views on political issues.

Rainbow Coalition   A name applied to the political organization and strategy developed by the Rev. Jesse Jackson, emphasizing the organization and power of political outcasts among racial minorities, the poor, women, and others.

rational actor approach   A theory of voter behavior that argues that individual voters attempt to calculate, on the basis of available information, the party or candidate least and best able to benefit them personally.

Reagan Democrats   Traditional, usually white, working class Democrats who supported Ronald Reagan in the 1980 and 1984 presidential elections for his stance on race, crime, and taxes.

realigning election   An election that shapes entire electoral eras; it features increased voter turnout and a reshuffling of the social groups that support each party, and results in the domination of one party in succeeding elections.

reelection motive   The primary incentive of legislators: to be returned to office.

regressive tax   A tax that takes a smaller proportion of income as income increases.

regulation   A process by which the government imposes restrictions on the conduct of private citizens and organizations.

relative deprivation   The theory that people mobilize politically not when they are worst off, but when they perceive that they are deprived unjustly, relative to other groups in the population.

republicanism   The eighteenth–century body of political thought, based on the ideas of liberty versus power, legislatures versus executives, civic virtue, and the small republic, that shaped the political activities of colonial Americans and infused them with the revolutionary "spirit of '76."

reserved powers   The authority not given to the federal government and left to the states by the Tenth Amendment.

responsible two-party system   A scholarly ideal in which parties fulfill their democratic character by forming consistent and meaningful ideologies and programs that become well known to the voters and in which the winning party is held accountable by voters for implementation of programs and their consequences.

retrospective voting   The tendency of voters to cast ballots on the basis of the perceived performance of the incumbent while in office or the condition of the economy rather than on the candidates' policy positions or traditional voting allegiances.

revolving door   The phenomenon whereby people working in Congress or in an executive branch agency become lobbyists or journalists once they leave government service, using their experience and knowledge for the benefit of their clients.

right of privacy   The freedom to be left alone implied in the Constitution.

Roe v. *Wade*   The 1973 Supreme Court case that established a woman's right to choose abortion and rendered unconstitutional all state laws that made abortion a crime.

rule   A statement issued by the House Rules Committee indicating how much time will be devoted to floor debate on a particular bill and what kinds of amendments will be allowed on the floor.

rule-making authority   The power of an executive agency to issue regulations that carry the force of law.

rule of four   An informal Supreme Court standard whereby if any four justices vote that a case deserves consideration, the Court will grant certiorari.

salience   An issue's perceived degree of significance in public opinion.

satyagraha   "Truth Force"; or the belief of the Indian pacifist Mahatma Gandhi that a carefully orchestrated civil disobedience plan can persuade one's opponents of the justice of one's cause.

senatorial courtesy   The Senate's withholding of consent to the nomination of a district court judge if the senior senator of the president's party from the nominee's state objects to that nomination.

seniority   The congressional norm that dictates that the member from the majority party who has the most years of continuous service on a committee becomes its chair.

separate but equal   The doctrine established by the Supreme Court in the 1896 case of *Plessey* v. *Ferguson*, that separate equivalent facilities for whites and blacks did not violate the Fourteenth Amendment's guarantee of equal protection of the laws, thereby providing the legal basis for segregation of the races.

single-member district system   A type of representation that allows the person who wins the most votes in a district's election to represent the entire district.

social class   A groups differentiated by occupation, income, wealth, power, and social and cultural outlook.

social mobility   The ability of a group or individual to move from one social class to another, thereby achieving greater or lesser income, wealth, or power.

social regulation   Executive agency rules that cover all industries and focus on such matters as environmental protection, safety, health, and nondiscrimination.

social rights   The popular democratic belief that all citizens should be entitled to basic educational and health services and minimum income benefits.

soft money   Campaign funds raised by national political parties under state laws and used to influence federal elections, while often circumventing federal regulations on campaign spending.

sound bite   A very short, supposedly representative quote from a public official presented in advertising or the news.

Speaker of the House of Representatives   The presiding officer of the House of Representatives, who is chosen by the majority party in the House, and is second, after the vice president, in the line of presidential succession.

split-ticket voting   The tendency of many voters to vote for the candidate of one party for a particular office and that of another party for other offices in the same election.

spoils system   The awarding of political jobs to political supporters and friends.

stagflation   The simultaneous existence of high inflation and high unemployment.

strict scrutiny   A Supreme Court standard in civil liberties or civil rights cases of striking down a law unless the government can demonstrate a "compelling interest" that necessitates such a law.

supply-side economics   The economic theory used by the Reagan administration to justify reducing taxes on investment, profits, and income and reducing government regulation of industry to promote economic prosperity.

Supremacy Clause   Article VI of the Constitution, which states that when the national and state governments conflict, the national laws shall supersede the state laws.

swing voter   A voter who is least committed to either political party and thus is more easily convinced to switch his or her votes.

symbolic speech   Protected political expression that communicates with visual symbols instead of words.

think tanks   Nonprofit institutions, funded primarily by foundations and corporate grants, that conduct public policy research.

transactional leader   A party or interest-group leader whose leadership is based on brokering beneficial exchanges with followers.

transforming leader   A mass movement leader who engages the full personalities of followers, helping them to go beyond self-interest and participate in direct political action.

trustee   A model of representation in which voters choose legislators for their integrity and good judgment and expect them to do what they think is best.

unitary government   A system in which all significant powers rest in the hands of the central government.

unprotected speech   Communication that is not protected by the First Amendment either because its social value is insignificant or because it verges on conduct that is harmful to others.

upscale demographics   The tendency of advertisers and media outlets to communicate with high-income, big-spending consumers.

valence issue   The goals, symbols, or conditions that are almost universally approved or disapproved by voters.

veto   The constitutional power of the president to reject legislation passed by Congress, subject to a two-thirds override by both houses.

Virginia Plan   The proposal submitted by the Virginia delegation at the Constitutional Convention of 1787, to create a strong national government.

Voting Rights Act of 1965   The law that removed the barriers that southern officials had placed in the way of black Americans who sought to register to vote.

Wagner Act   Also known as the National Labor Relations Act of 1935 and named for its sponsor, New York Senator Robert Wagner; legislation affirming the rights of workers to form unions and bargain with employers. The act established the National Labor Relations Board (NLRB).

War Powers Resolution of 1973   An attempt by Congress to reassert its constitutional authority in the area of war-making.

wealth inequality   The gap in net money worth among various population groups.

wedge issue   A topic used to divide and split off one formerly loyal constituency of a political party from other groups in that party's coalition.

welfare state   The array of social policies in advanced industrial countries designed to redistribute wealth and assist those who cannot support themselves in the private marketplace.

White House staff   The president's personal aides and advisers along with their numerous assistants.

whip   One who assists a party's leaders in the House and Senate by gathering information about how party members plan to vote on forthcoming issues and by encouraging partisan loyalty through persuasion and personal attention.

yellow journalism   A form of reporting pioneered in the late nineteenth century by the Hearst and Pulitzer newspaper chains, emphasizing entertaining and often lurid scandals as news.

ENDNOTES

CHAPTER 1

1. Joseph A. Schumpeter, *Capitalism, Socialism and Democracy*, 3rd ed. (New York: Harper and Row, 1950), p. 269. In Part IV Schumpeter makes one of the classic defenses of elite democracy. For critiques of the elite theory of democracy from a popular democratic viewpoint, see Jack L. Walker, "A Critique of the Elitist Theory of Democracy," *American Political Science Review*, 60 (1966): 285–95; and Peter Bachrach, *The Theory of Democratic Elitism: A Critique* (Boston: Little, Brown, 1967).

2. The most influential political scientist who has written on the ideas of elite and popular democracy is Robert A. Dahl. Dahl began his career by defending a version of elite democracy in *A Preface to Democratic Theory* (Chicago: University of Chicago Press, 1956); and *Who Governs? Democracy and Power in an American City* (New Haven, Conn.: Yale University Press, 1961). In his later works, Dahl shifted dramatically to a more popular democratic position. See *A Preface to Economic Democracy* (Berkeley: University of California Press, 1985); and *Democracy and Its Critics* (New Haven, Conn.: Yale University Press, 1989).

3. James Madison, Federalist 10, in Clinton Rossiter, ed., *The Federalist Papers* (New York: New American Library, 1961).

4. See Ralph Ketcham, ed., *The Anti-Federalist Papers and the Constitutional Convention Debates* (New York: New American Library, 1986), p. 213.

5. We are not the first to present a cyclical view of American politics in which participatory upsurges are followed by periods of elite consolidation. See Arthur M. Schlesinger, Jr., *Paths to the Present* (New York: Macmillan, 1949); Arthur M. Schlesinger, Jr., *The Cycles of American History* (Boston: Houghton Mifflin, 1986); and Albert O. Hirschman, *Shifting Involvements: Private Interest and Public Action* (Princeton: Princeton University Press, 1982).

6. Voting turnout rates taken from U.S. Bureau of the Census, *Statistical Abstract of the United States: 1993* (Washington, D.C.: U.S. Government Printing Office, 1993), p. 284.

7. George Will, "In Defense of Nonvoting," *Newsweek*, October 10, 1983, 96.

CHAPTER 2

1. Gordon S. Wood, *The Radicalism of the American Revolution* (New York: Alfred A. Knopf, 1992), pp. 11–92.

2. For an excellent account of this political dynamic, see Pauline Maier, *From Resistance to Revolution: Colonial Radicals and the Development of American Opposition to Britain, 1765–1776* (New York: Vintage Books, 1974).

3. Sidney Hook, ed., *The Essential Thomas Paine* (New York: New American Library, 1969), pp. 48, 33.

4. On republicanism and the origins of the American Revolution, see Bernard Bailyn, *The Ideological Origins of the American Revolution* (Cambridge: Harvard University Press, 1967); and Gordon S. Wood, *The Creation of the American Republic, 1776–1787* (New York: W. W. Norton, 1972), pp. 3–124.

5. On the place of the Declaration of Independence in American political thought, see especially two books by Garry Wills: *Inventing America: Jefferson's Declaration of Independence* (New York: Vintage Books, 1978); and *Lincoln at Gettysburg: The Words That Remade America* (New York: Simon and Schuster, 1992).

6. Roy P. Basler, ed., *The Collected Works of Abraham Lincoln*, vol. 3 (New Brunswick, N.J.: 1953), p. 375.

7. The Declaration of Independence was creatively used by Elizabeth Cady Stanton to advance the cause of women and by W. E. B. DuBois and Martin Luther King, Jr., to promote equality for African Americans.

8. On the state constitutions of 1776, see Wood, *Creation of the American Republic*, pp. 127–255.

9. For the Virginia Bill of Rights, see Samuel Eliot Morison, ed., *Sources and Documents Illustrating the American Revolution, 1764–1788* (New York: Oxford University Press, 1965), pp. 149–51. See also Robert Allen Rutland, *The Birth of the Bill of Rights, 1776–1791* (New York: Collier Books, 1962), pp. 38–48.

10. On the economic legislation of the 1780s, see Merrill Jensen, *The New Nation: A History of the United States During the Confederation, 1781–1789* (New York: Vintage Books, 1950), pp. 302–26.

11. Jackson Turner Main, "Government by the People: The American Revolution and the Democratization of the Legislatures," in Jack P. Greene, ed., *The Reinterpretation of the American Revolution, 1763–1789* (New York: Harper and Row, 1968) pp. 322–38.

12. Marvin Meyers, ed., *The Mind of the Founder: Sources of the Political Thought of James Madison*, rev. ed. (Hanover, N.H.: University Press of New England, 1981), p. 62.

13. Alfred A. Young, "Conservatives, the Constitution, and the 'Spirit of Accommodation,' " in Robert A. Goldwin and William A. Schambra, eds., *How Democratic Is the Constitution?* (Washington, D.C.: American Enterprise Institute, 1980), pp. 118, 138.

14. Max Farrand, ed., *The Records of the Federal Convention of 1787*, vol. 1 (New Haven, Conn.: Yale University Press, 1937), p. 422.

15. Ibid., pp. 65, 66.

16. Ibid., p. 51.

17. Farrand, ed., *Records of the Federal Convention*, vol. 2, p. 370.

18. Herbert J. Storing, *What the Anti-Federalists Were For* (Chicago: University of Chicago Press, 1981), p. 72.

19. Clinton Rossiter, ed., *The Federalist Papers* (New York: New American Library, 1961), p. 79.

20. Ibid., p. 54.

21. Ibid., p. 346.

22. Ibid., p. 414.

23. On the Anti-Federalist conception of virtue, see Storing, *What the Anti-Federalists Were For*, pp. 19–23.

24. Ralph Ketcham, ed., *The Anti-Federalist Papers and the Constitutional Convention Debates* (New York: New American Library, 1986), p. 202.

25. Rossiter, ed., *Federalist Papers*, p. 83.

26. See Storing, *What the Anti-Federalists Were For*, pp. 16–23.

27. Herbert J. Storing, ed., *The Anti-Federalist* (Chicago: University of Chicago Press, 1985), p. 116.

28. Rossiter, ed., *Federalist Papers*, p. 82.

29. Storing, ed., *Anti-Federalist*, p. 340.

30. Rossiter, ed., *Federalist Papers*, p. 322.

31. Ibid., p. 423.

32. Ketcham, ed., *Anti-Federalist Papers*, p. 213.

33. Rossiter, ed., *Federalist Papers*, p. 78.

34. Ibid., p. 88.

35. Ketcham, ed., *Anti-Federalist Papers*, pp. 207–8.

36. Rossiter, ed., *Federalist Papers*, p. 314.

37. Merrill D. Peterson, ed., *The Portable Thomas Jefferson* (New York: Penguin, 1975), p. 417. For an excellent discussion of the conflicting perspectives on stability and change, see Michael Lienesch, *New Order of the Ages: Time, the Constitution, and the Making of Modern American Political Thought* (Princeton, N.J.: Princeton University Press, 1988), pp. 63–81.

38. Jackson Turner Main, *The Anti-Federalists: Critics of the Constitution, 1781–1788* (New York: W. W. Norton, 1974), p. 133.

39. On Madison and the Bill of Rights, see Robert A. Rutland, *James Madison: The Founding Father* (New York: Macmillan, 1987), pp. 59–65.

CHAPTER 3

1. Justice William J. Brennan, Jr., "Federal Judges Properly and Inevitably Make Law Through 'Loose' Constitutional Construction," in Peter Woll, ed., *Debating American Government*, 2nd ed. (Glenview, Ill.: Scott, Foresman, 1988), p. 338.

2. Clinton Rossiter, ed., *The Federalist Papers* (New York: New American Library, 1961), #10.

3. Edward S. Corwin, "The Passing of Dual Federalism," *Virginia Law Review*, 36:1 (1950): 4.

4. *The Federalist Papers*, #45.

5. "The Address and Reasons of Dissent of the Minority of the Convention of Pennsylvania to Their Constituents" (December 18, 1787); as reported in

Ralph Ketcham, ed., *The Anti-Federalist Papers and the Constitutional Convention Debates* (New York: New American Library, 1986), p. 242.

6. A national bank was first proposed during George Washington's administration by Secretary of the Treasury Alexander Hamilton, who wrote a detailed opinion arguing that the authority to establish a national bank was reasonably implied by the enumerated powers of Congress in the U.S. Constitution. Thomas Jefferson, Washington's Secretary of State, strenuously opposed a national bank on the grounds that it was an unconstitutional exercise of federal powers at the expense of the states. Washington followed the advice of Hamilton over Jefferson and the First Bank of the United States was chartered in 1791.

7. *McCulloch* v. *Maryland*, 4 Wheat. 316 (1819).

8. *Dred Scott* v. *Sanford*, 19 How. 393 (1857).

9. *Wabash, St. Louis and Pac. Ry.* v. *Illinois, 118 U.S. 557.*

10. Gabriel Kolko, *Railroads and Regulation: 1877–1916* (Princeton: Princeton University Press, 1965), p. 232.

11. *Pollock* v. *Farmers' Loan and Trust Co., 157 U.S. 429 (1895).*

12. *Cincinnati N.O. & T.P. Railway Co.* v. *Interstate Commerce Commission, 162 U.S. 184 (1896).*

13. *Hammer* v. *Dagenhart, 247 U.S. 251 (1918).*

14. Ralph Nader, Mark Green, and Joel Seligman, *Taming the Giant Corporation* (New York: W. W. Norton, 1976), p. 37. The following account, unless otherwise noted, is based on this useful book.

15. Quoted in Nader, Green, and Seligman, *Taming the Giant*, p. 43.

16. Nader, Green, and Seligman, *Taming the Giant*, p. 47.

17. William L. Cary, *Corporations: Cases and Materials*, 4th ed. (Mineloa, N.Y.: Foundation Press, 1970), p. 10.

18. David B. Robertson and Dennis R. Judd, *The Development of American Public Policy: The Structure of Policy Restraint* (Glenview, Ill.: Scott, Foresman, 1989), p. 45.

19. Quoted in Nader, Green, and Seligman, *Taming the Giant*, p. 44.

20. Raymond T. Zillmer, "State Laws: Survival of the Unfit," *University of Pennsylvania Law Review*, 62 (1914): 509–24.

21. See Paul Peterson, *City Limits* (Chicago: University of Chicago Press, 1981).

22. "A Counterattack in the War Between the States," *Business Week*, June 21, 1976.

23. Bryan D. Jones and Lynn W. Bachelor, *The Sustaining Hand: Community Leadership and Corporate Power*, 2nd ed. (Lawrence: University Press of Kansas, 1993), p. 80.

24. Ibid., p. 215.

25. Thomas J. Lueck, "Chase, with $235 Million Incentive Package, Picks Brooklyn," *New York Times*, November 10, 1988.

26. The research on the effectiveness of state and local tax incentives is vast. For an introduction to the literature, see Thomas R. Dye, *American Federalism: Competition Among Governments* (Lexington, Mass.: Lexington Books, 1990), chap. 7.

27. Advisory Commission on Intergovernmental Relations, *The Federal Role in the Federal System: The Dynamics of Growth, Public Assistance: The Growth of a Federal Function* (Washington, D.C.: Advisory Commission on Intergovernmental Relations, 1980), p. 6.

28. James A. Maxwell, *The Fiscal Impact of Federalism in the United States* (Cambridge, Mass.: Harvard University Press, 1946), p. 135.

29. Josephine Chapin Brown, *Public Relief 1929–1939* (New York: Henry Holt & Company, 1940), pp. 14–15; as cited in Francis Fox Piven and Richard A. Cloward, *Regulating the Poor: The Functions of Public Welfare* (New York: Random House, 1971), p. 47.

30. In fact, in 1929 ten states authorized no outdoor relief at all. (Outdoor relief allows people to stay in their homes while they receive aid, like the present welfare system.) Advisory Commission on Intergovernmental Relations, *Federal Role*, p. 7.

31. Piven and Cloward, *Regulating the Poor*, p. 60.

32. Mark I. Gelfand, *A Nation of Cities: The Federal Government and Urban America 1933–1965* (New York: Oxford University Press, 1975), pp. 32–33.

33. *Congressional Record*, vol. 75, p. 11597; as quoted in Maxwell, *Fiscal Impact*, p. 138.

34. Quoted in Walter I. Trattner, *From Poor Law to Welfare State: A History of Social Welfare in America*, 3rd ed. ((New York: Free Press, 1984), pp. 261–2.

35. *Schechter Poultry Corp.* v. *United States, 295 U.S. 495 (1935).*

36. David B. Robertson and Dennis R. Judd, *The Development of American Public Policy: The Structure of Policy Restraint* (Glenview, Ill.: Scott, Foresman, 1989), p. 105.

37. *The United States* v. *Butler et al., 297 U.S. 1 (1936).*

38. *New State Ice Company* v. *Liebmann, 285 U.S. 262 (1932).*

39. *Massachusetts* v. *Mellon;* as quoted in Robertson and Judd, *American Public Policy*, p. 138.

40. Maxwell, *Fiscal Impact*, p. 26.

41. *Steward Machine Co.* v. *Davis, 301 U.S. 548 (1937)* and *Helvering et al.* v. *Davis, 301 U.S. 619 (1937).*

42. Maxwell, *Fiscal Impact*, p. 136.

43. Johnson's remark to Bill Moyers; quoted in Thomas Byrne Edsall and Mary D. Edsall, *Chain Reaction: The Impact of Race, Rights, and Taxes on American Politics* (New York: W. W. Norton, 1991), p. 37.

44. Piven and Cloward, *Regulating the Poor*, p. 295.

45. David B. Walker, *Toward a Functioning Federalism* (Cambridge, Mass.: Winthrop Publishers, 1981), p. 193.

46. Jeffrey L. Pressman and Aaron Wildavsky, *Implementation*, 3rd ed. (Berkeley: University of California Press, 1984).

47. Nicholas Lemann, *The Promised Land: The Great Black Migration and How It Changed America* (New York: Knopf, 1991), p. 188.

48. Not all federal grant programs targeted the poor. Many large federal grants, such as those for interstate highways and the construction of sewer and water systems, primarily benefitted the suburban middle class.

49. Edsall and Edsall, *Chain Reaction*, p. 106.

50. Ibid., pp. 75–76.

51. Quoted in Timothy Conlan, *New Federalism: Intergovernmental Reform from Nixon to Reagan* (Washington, D.C.: The Brookings Institution, 1988), p. 31.

52. Conlan, *New Federalism*, p. 154.

53. Ibid., p. 215.

54. Joseph F. Zimmerman, *Contemporary American Federalism: The Growth of National Power* (New York: Praeger, 1992), p. 67.

55. Paul E. Peterson and Mark C. Rom, *Welfare Magnets: A New Case for a National Standard* (Washington, D.C.: The Brookings Institution, 1990).

56. Ann O'M. Bowman and Richard C. Kearney, *State and Local Government*, 2nd ed. (Boston: Houghton Mifflin, 1993), pp. 12–13.

57. Richard P. Nathan et al., *Reagan and the States* (Princeton: Princeton University Press, 1987), chap. 5.

58. See Peter K. Eisinger, *The Rise of the Entrepreneurial State: State and Local Economic Development Policy in the United States* (Madison: University of Wisconsin Press, 1988); and David Osborne, *Laboratories of Democracy* (Boston: Harvard University Press, 1988).

59. Larry C. Ledebur and William R. Barnes, *City Distress, Metropolitan Disparities and Economic Growth* (Washington, D.C.: National League of Cities, 1992), p. 2 and appendix.

60. Robertson and Judd, *American Public Policy*, p. 380.

CHAPTER 4

1. For a good account of the home and market economy of early America, see Louis Wright and Elaine Fowler, *Everyday Life in the New Nation* (New York: G. P. Putnam's Sons, 1972).

2. See William Serrin, *The Company and the Union: The "Civilized Relationship" of the General Motors Corporation and the United Automobile Workers* (New York: Vintage, 1974); and James R. Green, *The World of the Worker* (New York: Hill and Wang, 1980), chap. 7. For discussion of GM, see "What Went Wrong?" *Time*, November 9, 1992, 36–42.

3. There are scores of works tracing this great transformation. Among the best are Herbert Gutman, *Work, Culture and Society in Industrializing America: Essays in American Working-Class and Social History* (New York: Vintage Books, 1977); and Robert Heilbroner, *Between Capitalism and Socialism*, Part I (New York: Random House, 1970).

4. Quote from Adam Smith, *The Wealth of Nations* (New York: Penguin, 1973).

5. While Smith is a hero to many modern elite democrats, it is interesting to contrast and compare him with Milton Friedman, *Capitalism and Freedom* (Chicago: University of Chicago Press, 1964); and Irving Kristol, *Two Cheers for Capitalism* (New York: Basic Books, 1978). The quote is from Milton Friedman and Rose Friedman, *Free to Choose* (New York: Harcourt, Brace, Jovanovich, 1980), p. 6.

6. There is no single work that contains all these arguments. For an excellent short analysis and critique of markets, see Kenneth Dolbeare, *Democracy at Risk* (Chatham, N.J.: Chatham House, 1986). Another important overview is Samuel Bowles, David M. Gordon, and Thomas Weisskopf, *Beyond the Wasteland: A Democratic Alternative to Economic Decline* (New York: Doubleday/Anchor, 1983); and, by the same authors, *After the Wasteland* (Armonk, N.Y.: M. E. Sharpe, 1990).

7. For a discussion of non-decision making and agenda setting, see Peter Bachrach and Morton S. Baratz, "Two Faces of Power," *American Political Science Review*, 56: 4 (1962) 947–52; and E. E. Schattschneider, *The Semi-Sovereign People: A Realist's View of Democracy* (New York: Holt, Rinehart and Winston, 1960).

8. *Christian Science Monitor*, April 29, 1991; as reported in Kevin Phillips, *Boiling Point: Democrats, Republicans, and the Decline of Middle Class Prosperity* (New York: Random House, 1993), p. 21.

9. On income stagnation, see Center for Popular Economics, *A Field Guide to the U.S. Economy*, (Amherst, Mass.: The Center for Popular Economics, 1988), table 2.5.

10. See Center for Popular Economics, *Field Guide*, table 1.2, and Edward Pessen, "Status and Social Class in America," in Luther Luedtke, ed., *Making America* (Washington, D.C.: U.S. Information Agency, 1987), p. 276.

11. See Katherine S. Newman, *Declining Fortunes: The Withering of the American Dream* (New York: Basic Books, 1993); Kevin Phillips, *The Politics of Rich and Poor* (New York: Random House, 1990) p. 25.

12. Donald Bartlett and James Steele, *America: What Went Wrong?* (Kansas City: Andrew and McMeel, 1992), p. 5 (figures not adjusted for inflation). For further evidence on increasing income inequality in the United States, see Lester Brown et al., *State of the World* (New York: W. W. Norton, 1988); Frank Levy, *Dollars and Dreams: The Changing American Income Distribution* (New York: W. W. Norton, 1988); and Robert B. Reich, *The Work of Nations* (New York: Random House, 1990).

13. Joint Economic Committee of Congress, *The Concentration of Wealth in the United States* (Washington, D.C.: U.S. Government Printing Office, 1986); Kevin Phillips, *The Politics of Rich and Poor* (New York: Random House, 1990) Chap. 11 and appendix B.

14. Estimates on women's hours and the annual hours of full-time employees by Juliet B. Schor, *The Overworked American: The Unexpected Decline of Leisure* (New York: Basic Books, 1992), pp. 21, 29.

15. Figures for economic insecurity from Bowles, Gordon, and Weisskopf, *After the Wasteland*, p. 141; Phillips, *Politics of Rich and Poor*, p. 22.

16. U.S. Bureau of the Census, *Statistical Abstract of the United States: 1992*, 112th ed. (Washington, D.C.: U.S. Government Printing Office, 1992), pp. 427, 458.

17. John E. Schwarz and Thomas J. Volgy, *The Forgotten Americans* (New York: W. W. Norton, 1992), p. 70.

18. *U.S. Bureau of the Census, Statistical Abstract of the United States, 1991*, p. 459; Center for Popular Economics, *Field Guide*, tables 7.3–7.6.

19. Figures on female and male income are from U.S. Bureau of the Census, *Statistical Abstract of the United States, 1992* (Washington, D.C.: U.S. Government Printing Office, 1992), p. 452.

20. See Arthur M. Okun, *Equality and Efficiency: The Big Tradeoff* (Washington, D.C.: The Brookings Institution, 1975).

21. For evidence on mortgage redlining and popular democratic efforts to correct it, see Gregory D. Squires, ed., *From Redlining to Reinvestment: Community Responses to Urban Disinvestment* (Philadelphia: Temple University Press, 1992).

22. In an otherwise obscure decision on railroad regulation, the Supreme Court declared that corporations have the same rights as individuals. *Santa Clara County* v. *Southern Pacific R.R.*, 118 U.S. 394 (1886).

23. Charles Lindblom, *Politics and Markets: The World's Political-Economic Systems* (New York: Basic Books, 1977), p. 356.

24. For a history of the emergence of the modern corporation as a hierarchy, see Martin Sklar, *The Corporate Reconstruction of American Capitalism, 1890–1916* (Cambridge: Cambridge University Press, 1988); and R. Jeff Lustig, *Corporate Liberalism: The Origins of Modern American Political Theory, 1890–1920* (Berkeley: University of California Press, 1982). See also Alfred Chandler, *The Visible Hand: The Managerial Revolution in American Business* (Cambridge, Mass.: Belknap Press, 1977); Louis Galambos and Joseph Pratt, *The Rise of the Corporate Commonwealth* (New York: Basic Books, 1988).

25. Center for Popular Economics, *Field Guide*, tables 1.13, 1.14; see also Jeremy Rifkin and Randy Barber, *The North Will Rise Again: Pensions, Power and Politics in the 1980s* (Boston: Beacon Press, 1979); Richard A. Ippolito, *Pensions, Economics and Public Policy* (Homewood, Ill.: Dow Jones-Irwin, 1986).

26. Center for Popular Economics, *Field Guide*, table 1.3; see also Lawrence Mishel and Jacqueline Simon, *The State of Working America* (Washington, D.C.: The Economic Policy Institute, 1988).

27. U.S. Central Intelligence Agency, *World Fact Book* (Washington, D.C.: U.S. Central Intelligence Agency, 1990), as cited in Edward S. Greenberg and Benjamin Page, *The Struggle for Democracy* (New York: HarperCollins, 1993), p. 226.

28. Michael Goldfield, *The Decline of Organized Labor in the United States* (Chicago: University of Chicago Press, 1987). For an entertaining insider's account of the decline of labor unions, see Thomas Geoghegan, *Which Side Are You On? Trying to Be for Labor When It's Flat on Its Back* (New York: Plume, 1991).

29. The classic case for the separation of ownership and control in the modern corporation is made by Gardiner Means and Adolph Berle, *The Corporation and Private Property* (New York: Macmillan and Co, 1948). For a modification of it, see Robert Kuttner, "The Corporation in America: Is It Socially Redeemable?" *Dissent*, Winter 1993, 35–49.

30. Lindblom, *Politics and Markets*, p. 154.

31. The most important work about the functions of the mature corporation is John Kenneth Galbraith, *The New Industrial State* (Boston: Houghton Mifflin, 1985).

32. Galbraith, *New Industrial State*, p. xxi.

33. Excellent accounts of this period include Alan Wolfe, *The Limits of Legitimacy* (New York: Free Press, 1977); David Halberstam, *The Reckoning* (New York: Morrow, 1986); and Bowles, Gordon, and Weisskopf, *After the Wasteland*, pp. 47–97.

34. The source for this account is the Gannett *Citizen-Register*, printed in White Plains, Westchester County, New York, in March and April 1992. See also, for GM executives, "What Went Wrong?" *Time*, November 9, 1992, 41. See also "Tarrytown GM," *New York Times*, November 21, 1993, Westchester supplement.

35. See Barry Bluestone and Bennett Harrison, *The Great U Turn* (New York: Basic Books, 1988), pp. 69–75. There is much evidence that restructuring the workplace in this way is the major contributor to increases in racial and gender inequality. See Saskia Sassen, *Global Cities* (Princeton, N.J.: Princeton University Press, 1990); and Robert Kuttner, "The Declining Middle," *Atlantic Monthly*, July 1983.

36. See Michael J. Piore and Charles F. Sabel, *The Second Industrial Divide: Possibilities for Prosperity* (New York: Basic Books, 1984).

37. Reich, *The Work of Nations*, p. 83.

38. Ibid., p. 95.

39. Quote from Norman Jonas, "The Hollow Corporation," *Business Week*, 3: 1987. The essentials of this strategy and the phrase "if you can't beat 'em" are used by Bluestone and Harrison, *Great U Turn*, pp. 26–38. See also Joseph Grunwald and Kenneth Flamm, *The Global Factory: Foreign Assembly in International Trade* (Washington, D.C.: The Brookings Institution, 1985).

40. The term *casino society* was originated by Susan Strange in *The Casino Society* (London: Basil Blackwell, 1984). For figures on mergers, see Center for Popular Economics, *Field Guide*, table 1.8. For the best story of corporate raiders, see Bryan Burrough and John Helyar, *Barbarians at the Gate: The Fall of RJR Nabisco* (New York: Harper and Row, 1990).

41. See Seymour Melman, *Profits Without Production* (New York: Alfred A. Knopf, 1983).

42. This point is made by Lindblom in *Politics and Markets*, final chapter. For an earlier and succinct account of corporate organization in government, see Grant McConnell, *Private Power and American Democracy*, (New York: Atheneum, 1967).

43. Figures cited in Phillips, *Politics of Rich and Poor*, p. 113.

44. Quoted in Phillips, *Politics of Rich and Poor*, p. 80.

45. See James Weinstein, *The Corporate Ideal in the Liberal State* (Boston: Beacon Press, 1968); and Sklar, *Corporate Reconstruction*, chap. 1.

46. John Maynard Keynes, *General Theory of Employment, Interest and Money* (New York: Harcourt, Brace, 1965). About Keynes, see Robert Skidelsky, *John Maynard Keynes: A Biography* (New York: Viking, 1986). The influence of Keynes is vast. See Robert Lekachman, *The Age of Keynes* (New York: McGraw Hill, 1975).

47. Kevin Phillips argues that "the genius of American politics" is that about once in a generation the tensions associated with capitalist development are managed through electoral realignments that restructure political power. Phillips suggests that the country is ready for another electoral correction, driven by "the accumulation of wealth by a relatively narrow elite" under the Republicans. See Phillips, *Politics of Rich and Poor*, p. 33.

48. Francis Fox Piven and Richard A. Cloward argue that the power of the poor depends more on their ability to protest and to disrupt the system than on their power at the ballot box. See *Regulating the Poor: The Functions of Public Welfare* (New York: Vintage Books, 1971).

49. John Schwarz, *America's Hidden Success* (New York: Norton, 1988) p. 24. For the idea of economic rights see Frances Fox Piven and Richard Cloward, *Poor People's Movements* (New York: Pantheon, 1977) and, by the same authors, *The New Class War* (New York: Pantheon, 1982).

50. For further analysis of this question, see Chapter 18 of this book.

CHAPTER 5

1. Turnout figures on party primaries are provided in M. Margaret Conway, *Political Participation in the United States* (Washington, D.C.: Congressional Quarterly, 1991) pp. 156–72; Ross K. Baker, "The Presidential Nominations" in Gerald Pomper, ed., *The Election of 1992* (Chatham, N.J.: Chatham House, 1993) pp. 49–50.

2. See, for example, "Election Results for New York City Council," *New York Times*, Sept. 13, 1991, B4; for Los Angeles, "Bradley Victory," April 13, 1989; Todd Swanstrom and Dennis Judd, *City Politics*, (New York: HarperCollins, 1993) pp. 251–53.

3. This way of analyzing elections is suggested by Walter Dean Burnham, "The Future of American Politics" in Ellis Sandoz and Cecil Crabb, Jr., eds., *Election '84* (New York: New American Library, 1985), pp. 204–60.

4. George F. Will, "In Defense of Non-Voting," *Newsweek*, October 10, 1983, 96.

5. See Raymond Wolfinger and Steven Rosenstone, *Who Votes?* (New Haven: Yale University Press, 1978) pp. 1–12. Two founding works in the tradition are Anthony Downs, *An Economic Theory of Democracy* (New York: Harper and Row, 1978); V. O. Key, *The Responsible Electorate* (New York: Cambridge University Press, 1966). One of the most well-known works is Morris Fiorina, *Retrospective Voting in American National Elections* (New Haven: Yale University Press, 1981).

6. See George Will, *Statecraft as Soulcraft* (New York: Simon and Schuster, 1983), p. 16.

7. See Frances Fox Piven and Richard Cloward, *Why Americans Don't Vote* (New York: Pantheon, 1987), p. 16.

8. See G. Bingham Powell, "Voter Turnout in Comparative Perspective," *American Political Science Review*, 80:1 (1986); Wolfinger and Rosenstone, *Who Votes?*, pp. 61–88; and Walter Dean Burnham, "The Appearance and Disappearance of the American Voter," in Burnham, *The Current Crisis in American Politics* (New York: Oxford University Press, 1982). See Ruy Teixeira, *The Disappearing American Voter*, (Washington, D.C.: The Brookings Institution, 1992). Details of the Motor-Voter bill taken from *International Herald Tribune*, May 11, 1993, 3, and "Senate Approves Motor Voter with Concessions to the GOP," *Congressional Quarterly Weekly Report*, March 20, 1993, 664.

9. See Hanes Walton, *Black Politics* (New York: Lippincott, 1972); and Manning Marable, *Black American Politics* (London: Verso Books, 1985); Doug McAdam, *Freedom Summer* (New York: Harper, 1988).

10. For Hamer's story, see Nicolaus Mills, *Like a Holy Crusade* (Chicago: Ivan Dee, 1992) pp. 47–63.

11. See Roman Hedges and Carl Carlucci, "The Implementation of the Voting Rights Act: The Case

Of New York," unpublished paper, 1986; Jim Sleeper, *The Closest of Strangers* (New York: Norton, 1990).

12. Theodore Lowi and Benjamin Ginsberg, *The Democrats Return to Power* (New York: Norton, 1993), p. 46.

13. See David Montgomery, *The Fall of the House of Labor* (New York: Oxford University Press, 1988) for an account of the richness of late-nineteenth-century labor associations. For the Alliance and Populism, see Lawrence Goodwyn, *The Populist Moment in America*, (New York: Oxford University Press, 1976). For a brilliant analysis of public "third places" in America, see Ray Oldenburg, *The Great Good Place* (New York: Paragon House, 1989), pp. 66–85.

14. See Conway, *Political Participation*, p. 114.

15. Conway, *Political Participation*, and Kenneth Dolbeare, *Democracy at Risk* (Chatham, N.J.: Chatham House, 1986), chap. 7. For quote, see "Participation in Politics Declines," *Boston Globe*, March 7, 1993, 6. For data, see Steven Rosenstone and John Mark Hansen, *Mobilization, Participation and Democracy in America* (New York: Macmillan, 1993), chap. 3.

16. Burnham, "The Future of American Politics," in Sandoz and Crabbe, *Election of '84*.

17. This perspective is suggested by Howard Reiter, *Parties and Elections in Corporate America* (New York: St. Martin's, 1987), chap. 8, as well as by many works in recent urban sociology, including Jonathan Rieder's *Canarsie* (Cambridge: Harvard University Press, 1989); Lillian Rubin, *Worlds of Pain* (New York: Harper and Row, 1976). See also "Unions and Community Mobilization: The 1988 Massachusetts Prevailing Wage Campaign," *Labor Studies Journal*, Winter 1989, 18–39. Citation from Oldenburg, *The Great Good Place*, p. 163.

18. One of the most extensive surveys was conducted in 1976 by Hart Research Associates, Inc., for the Committee for the Study of the American Electorate in Washington, D.C. See also CBS News–*New York Times* poll of November 21, 1988, and the Times/Mirror polls of September through November 1988. For 1992, see "The Generations Divide: Campaign '92" (Washington, D.C.: Times/Mirror Center for the People and the Press, 1992). The most extensive academic studies are conducted by the University of Michigan's Center for Political Studies. See also Wolfinger and Rosenstone, *Who Votes?*, and Arthur Hadley,

The Empty Polling Booth (Englewood Cliffs, N.J.: Prentice-Hall, 1978).

19. University of Michigan, Center for Political Studies, American National Election Studies, 1984; CBS News–*New York Times* poll, *New York Times*, November 21, 1988, A5; "The Generations Divide," Times/Mirror, 34–35.

20. William Maddox and Stuart Lilie, *Beyond Liberal and Conservative: Reassessing the Political Spectrum* (Washington, D.C.: The Cato Institute, 1984).

21. Dolbeare, *Democracy at Risk*, pp. 209–25.

22. The definitive account is Paul Kleppner, *Chicago; The Making of a Black Mayor* (DeKalb, Ill.: Northern Illinois University Press, 1984), chap. 6.

23. Kleppner, *Chicago*, chaps. 7–8.

24. See, for 1984, Thomas Cavanagh and Lorn Foster, *Jesse Jackson's Campaign: The Primaries and the Caucuses* (Washington, D.C.: Joint Center for Political Studies, Report 2, 1984); for 1988, data compiled from Abramson et al., *change*, chap. 1.

25. A good account of the 1992 election is Gerald Pomper, ed., *The Election of 1992* (Chatham, N.J.: Chatham House, 1993) (Will's quote is from Wilson Carey McWilliams, "The Meaning of the Election" in Pomper, ed. *Election of 1992*, p. 201). See also Michael Nelson, ed., *The Elections of 1992* (Washington, D.C.: Congressional Quarterly, 1993).

26. See Howard Fineman, "Ross Perot's New Army: How He's Building His Army Behind the Scenes," *Newsweek*, June 7, 1993, 24–25; Jack Germond and Jules Witcover, "Perot Is Expanding His Local Base," *National Journal*, June 5, 1993, 1371.

27. Data from Gerald Pomper, "The Presidential Election," in Pomper, ed., *Election of 1992*, pp. 140–42.

28. Wilson Carey McWilliams, "The Meaning of the Election," in Pomper, ed., *Election of 1992*, p. 197.

CHAPTER 6

1. *American National Election Study* (Ann Arbor: University of Michigan, Center for Political Studies, 1986, 1988, 1992); CBS News–*New York Times* poll, *New York Times*, April 6, 1986, A1.

2. Hamilton's cite from Clinton Rossiter, ed., *The Federalist Papers* (New York: New American Library,

1961), p. 432. From Phillip Converse, "The Nature of Belief Systems in Mass Publics," in David Apter, ed., *Ideology and Discontent* (New York: Free Press, 1964), pp. 243–45.

3. See Walter Lippmann, *The Phantom Public* (New York: Harcourt Brace Jovanovich, 1925), pp. 13, 155.

4. John Dewey, *The Public and Its Problems* (Chicago: Swallow Press, 1927).

5. See James Miller, *Democracy Is in the Streets* (New York: Simon and Schuster, 1987), chap. 8, for an extended discussion in the context of the 1960s.

6. See Robert Bellah et al., *Habits of the Heart* (Berkeley: University of California Press, 1987), pp. 256–71, for an extended discussion of these ideas.

7. See Donald J. Devine, *The Political Culture of the United States* (Boston: Little, Brown, 1972); Samuel Huntington, *American Politics: The Promise of Disharmony* (Cambridge: Harvard University Press, 1981); Herbert McCloskey and John Zaller, *The American Ethos* (Cambridge: Harvard University Press, 1984).

8. *Eurobarometre*, Opinion poll, Brussels, Belgium, 1990; Laurence Parisot, "Attitudes About the Media," *Public Opinion*, January/February 1988, 18.

9. See Herbert McCloskey and Alida Brill, *Dimensions of Tolerance: What Americans Believe About Civil Liberties* (New York: Russell Sage Foundation, 1983).

10. Samuel Stouffer, *Communism, Conformity and Civil Liberties* (New York: Doubleday, 1955).

11. Times/Mirror Center for the People and the Press, "The Generations Divide," July 1992, 29.

12. Thomas Dye and Harmon Ziegler, *The Irony of Democracy* (Monterey: Brooks Cole, 1987), pp. 137, 143.

13. For the story of COINTELPRO, see Bob Woodward and Carl Bernstein, *All the President's Men*. For surveys during the Nixon years, see Jonathan Schell, *The Time of Illusion* (New York: Pantheon, 1985). See also Barry Sussman, *What Americans Really Think: And Why Our Politicians Pay No Attention* (New York: Pantheon, 1988).

14. Michael Rogin, *The Intellectuals and McCarthy* (Cambridge: MIT Press, 1970); Ann Meiklejohn, *The Cold War Against Labor* (San Francisco: Meiklejohn Institute, 1988); Ellen Schrecker, *No Ivory Tower* (New York: Oxford University Press, 1986).

15. Stanley Feldman, "Structure and Consistency in Public Opinion: The Role of Core Beliefs and Values," *American Journal of Political Science*, Spring 1988, 416–38.

16. J. Huber and W. H. Form, *Income and Ideology* (New York: Free Press, 1973); Times/Mirror, "Generations," 23, 32.

17. See James Kluegel and Eliot Smith, *Beliefs About Inequality* (New York: Aldine de Gruyter, 1986), chaps. 1, 11; Times/Mirror, "Generations," 23, 32.

18. Kluegel and Smith, *Beliefs*, chaps. 3, 4. For a subtle account of the difference between agreement with the class structure and acquiescence to it, see Jennifer Hochschild, *What's Fair?* (Cambridge: Harvard University Press, 1981).

19. See Angus Campbell, *The Sense of Well Being in America* (New York: McGraw-Hill, 1981); Feldman, "Structure and Consistency," p. 438.

20. See Seymour Martin Lipset and William Schneider, *The Confidence Gap* (New York: Free Press, 1983), chap. 1; CBS News–*New York Times* poll, March 1992, for sentiments about government in an election year.

21. Harold Stanley and Richard Niemi, *Vital Statistics in American Politics* (Washington, D.C.: Congressional Quarterly, 1993), p. 169.

22. See Chapter 13 for the public reputation of the bureaucracy; for Congress, see CBS News–*New York Times* poll, *New York Times*, April 2, 1992.

23. Roper Organization Surveys, 1982–88; *American National Election Study*, 1988); Lipset and Schneider, *Confidence Gap*, chap. 12; CBS News–*New York Times* poll, March 26, 1992.

24. Leon P. Baradat, *Political Ideologies: Their Origins and Impact* (Englewood Cliffs, N.J.: Prentice-Hall, 1979), pp. 30–37; Hochschild, *What's Fair?*

25. Eric R. A. N. Smith, *The Unchanging American Voter* (Berkeley: University of California Press, 1989); Converse, "Nature of Belief Systems," in Apter, ed., *Ideology;* Angus Campbell, Phillip Converse, Warren Miller, and Donald Stokes, *The American Voter* (New York: Wiley, 1960).

26. See Sidney Blumenthal, *Pledging Allegiance: The Last Campaign of the Cold War* (New York: HarperCollins 1989), for reports on these incidents. See Linda Medcalf and Kenneth Dolbeare, *American*

Political Ideas in the 1980s (New York: Random House, 1985); and for a discussion of Clinton on this score, see Barbara Ehrenreich, "Lurch to the Left? You're Kidding," *Time*, June 21, 1993, 78.

27. The populist label is used by Stuart Lilie and William Maddox, *Beyond Liberalism and Conservatism* (Washington, D.C.: Cato Institute, 1984); and Kevin Phillips, *The Politics of Rich and Poor* (New York: Random House, 1990). The other ideological categories derive from combining, and in some cases renaming, the subdivisions in public opinion designed by the Times/Mirror Center for the People and the Press. For the listing and justification of these categories, see Times/Mirror, "Generations," 63–65.

28. See Paul Light, *The Baby Boomers* (New York: W. W. Norton, 1987); Phillips, *Politics of Rich and Poor*; "new liberals" are called "sixties Democrats" and "seculars" in the Times/Mirror categories.

29. In Times/Mirror studies, "libertarians" are called "upbeats and enterprisers," p. 64.

30. See Medcalf, *American Politics*, chaps. 8 and 9. The Times/Mirror survey calls this opinion bloc "moralists." Some enterprisers also fit in the new conservative category. See the discussion of the new conservatism in Kevin Phillips, *Post-Conservative America* (New York: Random House, 1985). See also E. J. Dionne, *Why Americans Hate Politics* (New York: HarperCollins, 1992).

31. M. Kent Jennings and Richard Niemi, *The Political Character of Adolescence* (Princeton: Princeton University Press, 1974).

32. E. L. Dey et al., *The American Freshman: Twenty Five Year Trends* (Los Angeles: Higher Education Institute, University of California–Los Angeles, 1991).

33. See Richard Sennett and Jonathan Cobb, *The Hidden Injuries of Class* (New York: Vintage, 1974).

34. See Charles Lindblom, *Politics and Markets* (New York: Harper and Row, 1978).

35. Werner Sombart, *Why Is There No Socialism in the United States?* Patricia Hocking and C. T. Husbands, trans. (White Plains, N.Y.: M. E. Sharpe, 1976).

36. M. R. Jackman and R. W. Jackman, *Class Awareness in the United States* (Berkeley: University of California Press, 1983); Sidney Verba and Gary Oren, *Equality in America* (Cambridge: Harvard University Press, 1986); Louis Harris, *Inside America* (New York: Vintage

Books, 1987); CBS News–*New York Times* poll, *New York Times*, March 1992.

37. See William Julius Wilson, *The Truly Disadvantaged* (Chicago: University of Chicago Press, 1987); Thomas Byrne Edsall and Mary Edsall, *Chain Reaction: The Impact of Race, Rights and Taxes on American Politics* (New York: W. W. Norton, 1991); Manning Marable, *Black American Politics: From the Washington Marches to Jesse Jackson* (New York: Verso Books, 1985).

38. Lawrence Bobo, Charlotte Steen, Howard Schuman, *Racial Trends in America: Trends and Interpretations* (Cambridge: Harvard University Press, 1985), p. 135.

39. Bobo et al., *Racial Trends*, chap. 4.

40. "Whites Retain Negative Views of Minorities, a Survey Finds," *New York Times*, January 10, 1991, B10; Times/Mirror, "Generations," 20; Bobo et al., *Racial Trends*, p. 113.

41. Times/Mirror, "Generations," p. 20; Bobo et al., *Racial Trends*, chap. 5.

42. Kluegel and Smith, *Beliefs*, pp. 135–43.

43. Quote from Andrew Hacker, *Two Nations* (New York: Ballantine, 1992), p. 52; see Mary Jackman and Michael Muha, "Education and Intergroup Attitudes: Moral Enlightenment, Superficial Democratic Commitment or Ideological Refinement?" *American Sociological Review*, 49:6 (1984): 751–69. See also Jim Sleeper, *The Closest of Strangers* (New York: W. W. Norton, 1991).

44. Robert Shapiro and Hapreet Mahajan, "Gender Differences in Policy Preferences: A Summary of Trends from the 1960s to the 1980s," *Public Opinion Quarterly*, 50:1 (1986): 42–61.

45. Barbara Farah and Ethel Klein, "Public Opinion Trends," in Gerald Pomper, ed., *The Election of 1988* (Chatham, N.J.: Chatham House, 1989); CBS News–*New York Times* poll, November 5, 1992, B9.

46. Shapiro and Mahajan, "Gender," 42–61. Robert Wuthnow, ed., *The New Religious Right* (New York: Aldine de Gruyter, 1987); Robert Wuthnow, *The Struggle for America's Self: Evangelicals, Liberalism and Secularism* (New York: Eerdman's, 1989); Bellah et al., *Habits*, chap. 9.

47. Quoted in Christopher Hitchens, "Voting in the Passive Voice," *Harpers*, April 1992, 46.

48. Hitchens, "Voting," 52.

49. Hitchens "Voting," 52. For a systematic critique of polling, see David Moore, *The Superpollsters: How*

They Measure and Manipulate Public Opinion in America (Durham, N.C.: Four Walls Eight Windows, 1992).

50. Noam Chomsky and Edward Herman, *Manufacturing Consent* (New York: Pantheon, 1989). D. Behar and G. Harris, *Invasion: The American Destruction of the Noriega Regime in Panama* (New York: The Americas Group, 1990); Jacqueline Sharkey report, "All Things Considered," National Public Radio, January 18, 1992; Richard Knight, *The First Casualties*, 1991; "Coverage of the Gulf War," in *Extra!*, May 1991; John Mueller, *Policy and Opinion in the Gulf War* (Chicago: University of Chicago Press, 1993).

51. See the discussion in Benjamin Page and Robert Shapiro, *The Rational Public* (Chicago: University of Chicago Press, 1992), chap. 5.

52. For a discussion of the tax revolt of the 1970s, see Robert Kuttner, *Revolt of the Haves* (New York: Harper and Row, 1980). For figures on the effects of tax reform, see Edsall and Edsall, *Chain Reaction*, p. 205; Phillips, *Politics of Rich and Poor*, chaps. 3–5; James Bartlett and Donald Steele, *America: What Went Wrong?* (Kansas City: Andrews and McNeel, 1992), pp. 48–49.

53. Benjamin Page and Robert Shapiro, "Effects of Public Opinion on Policy," *American Political Science Review*, March 1983, 175–90.

54. Robert Spitzer, *The Right to Life Movement and Third Party Politics* (Westport, Conn.: Greenwood Press, 1987).

55. See William Freudenberg and Eugene Rosa, *Public Reactions to Nuclear Power* (Boulder, Colo.: Westview Press, 1984), chap. 1.

56. Freudenberg and Rosa, *Public Reactions*, p. 9.

57. Freudenberg and Rosa, *Public Reactions*, pp. 334–41; S. Nealey, B. Melber, and W. Rankin, *Public Opinion and Nuclear Energy* (Lexington, Ky.: Lexington Books, 1983), chap. 3; Charles Piller, *The Fail-Safe Society* (New York: Norton, 1991), p. 9, for post-Chernobyl polls. See also Joseph Rees, *Hostages of Each Other* (Chicago: University of Chicago Press, 1993).

58. See Bryan Jones and Frank Baumgartner, "Image and Agenda in Urban Politics," paper presented at the Second Annual Conference on Public Policy, State University of New York, Albany, 1989. Spencer Weart, *Nuclear Fear: A History of Images* (Cambridge: Harvard University Press, 1988); Piller, *Fail-Safe*, chap. 1. See also the story of the Hanford atomic weapons site in Michael D'Antonio, *Atomic Harvest* (New York: Crown, 1993).

CHAPTER 7

1. C. Wright Mills, *The Power Elite* (New York: Oxford University Press, 1956), pp. 298–305; Ben Bagdikian, *The Media Monopoly* (Boston: Beacon Press, 1981), chap. 1; William Greider, *Who Will Tell the People?* (New York: Simon and Schuster, 1992), pp. 306–7.

2. See Jim Lehrer, *A Bus of My Own: A Memoir* (New York: New American Library, 1992); Dan Rather and Mickey Herskowitz, *The Camera Never Blinks: Adventures of a TV Journalist* (New York: Ballantine Books, 1987).

3. "Nothing Against Your Baby, Ms. Brown," *New York Times*, September 21, 1992, A14. See also L. Brent Bozell and Brent Baker, eds., *And That's the Way It Isn't* (Alexandria, Va.: Media Research Center, 1990).

4. For a variety of these criticisms see Todd Gitlin, *The Whole World Is Watching* (Berkeley: University of California Press, 1980); Austin Ranney, *Channels of Power: The Impact of Television on American Politics* (New York: Basic Books, 1983); Bozell and Baker, *And That's the Way*.

5. Thomas C. Leonard, *The Power of the Press* (New York: Oxford University Press, 1986).

6. Michael Schudson, *Discovering the News* (New York: Basic Books, 1978).

7. Frank Luther Mott, *American Journalism: 1660–1960* (New York: Macmillan, 1962), p. 529; for an account of Hearst's life, see W. A. Swanberg, *Citizen Hearst* (New York: Scribner's, 1961).

8. For figures, see Ronald Berkman and Laura Kitch, *The Politics of the Mass Media* (New York: St. Martin's Press, 1990), p. 42.

9. For Murrow's story at CBS, see Alexander Kendrick, *Prime Time: The Life of Edward R. Murrow* (Boston: Little, Brown, 1969).

10. Reuven Frank, *Out of Thin Air: The Invention and History of TV Network News* (New York: Simon and Schuster, 1991).

11. On TV coverage of the 1960s, see Edward Epstein, *News from Nowhere* (New York: Random

House, 1973); Everett Carl Ladd, *The American Polity* (New York: W. W. Norton, 1988); Robert Cirino, *Don't Blame the People* (New York: Vintage, 1971); Michael Arlen, *The Living Room War* (New York: Viking, 1969).

12. See Bill Carter, "500-Channel TV; The Vision Recedes," *New York Times,* January 3, 1994, C11; for viewership data, see Times/Mirror Center for the People and the Press, "The Age of Indifference: A Study of Young Americans and How They View the News," press release (Washington, D.C.: 1990), 20.

13. For the 1940s, see Paul Lazarsfeld, Bernard Berelson, and Hazel Gaudet, *The People's Choice* (New York: Columbia University Press, 1948); Thomas Patterson and Robert McClure, *The Unseeing Eye: The Myth of Television Power in National Elections* (New York: G. P. Putnam, 1976), p. 90.

14. See Maxwell McCombs and Donald Shaw, *The Emergence of American Political Issues: The Agenda Setting Functions of the Press* (St. Paul: West, 1977); Shanto Iyengar and Donald Kinder, *News That Matters* (Chicago: University of Chicago Press, 1987), chap. 1; Thomas Patterson, *Out of Order* (New York: Alfred Knopf, 1993). See also Chapters 6, 8, and 9 of this book.

15. S. Iyengar, M. Peters, and D. Kinder, "Experimental Demonstrations of the 'Not So Minimal' Consequences of Television News Programs," *American Political Science Review,* 24:1 (1980).

16. For monopolization, see Bagdikian, *Media,* chaps. 2–5; others of more recent vintage include Noam Chomsky and Edward Herman, *Manufacturing Consent: The Political Economy of the Mass Media* (New York: Pantheon, 1988); Herbert Schiller, *Culture, Inc.: The Corporate Takeover of Public Expression* (New York: Oxford University Press, 1989). For the information superhighway, see C. Edwin Baker, "Tollbooths on the Information Superhighway," *New York Times,* October 23, 1993, A21.

17. Martin A. Lee and Norman Solomon, *Unreliable Sources* (New York: Carol, 1991), p. 71.

18. Lee and Solomon, *Unreliable,* p. 82.

19. See *INFACT Brings GE to Light,* handout (New York: INFACT, 1989); "The French Lesson," NBC documentary, March 1987.

20. *Facts on File,* February 11, 1993, p. 85; and Doron Levin, "GM Makes Case," *New York Times,* April 30, 1993, D2.

21. Quoted in Lee and Solomon, *Unreliable,* p. 61.

22. See Stephen Farber, *New York Times Magazine,* April 7, 1989; Erik Barnouw, *The Sponsor: Notes on a Modern Potentate* (New York: Oxford University Press, 1978).

23. Doris Graber, *The Mass Media in American Politics* (Washington, D.C.: Congressional Quarterly, 1984), p. 38; Lee and Solomon, *Unreliable,* p. 86; Pat Aufderheide, *The Progressive,* January, 1988; Tom Burnes, "The Organization of Public Opinion," in James Curran, ed., *Mass Communications and Society,* (Beverly Hills, Calif.: Sage, 1978).

24. See Erwin Krasnow, Lawrence Longley, and Herbert Terry, *The Politics of Broadcast Regulation* (New York: St. Martin's Press, 1982); and Graber, *Mass Media,* pp. 47–52.

25. See Berkman and Kitch, *Politics,* pp. 50–59; Lee and Solomon, *Unreliable,* p. 75; David Burnham, "FCC Eases Rules for Broadcast TV," *New York Times,* June 28, 1984; Ben Bagdikian, "Journalism of the 1980s," *Mother Jones,* May/June 1992; Edmund Andrews, "A Merger of Giants," *New York Times,* October 14, 1993, D10.

26. See Fred Landis, "El Mercurio and the CIA," *Covert Action Information Bulletin,* March 1982; see also Martha Honey, "Contra Coverage—Paid For by the CIA," *Columbia Journalism Review,* March/April 1987; "CIA Back In," *Common Cause Magazine,* September/October 1986; Lee and Solomon, *Unreliable,* pp. 117–120.

27. Athan Theoharris, *The Boss: J. Edgar Hoover and the Great American Inquisition* (Philadelphia: Temple University Press, 1988); Joseph Trento and Nicholas E. Roman, "Copley and the FBI," *Penthouse,* August 1977; Nelson Blackstock, *COINTELPRO: The FBI's Secret War on Press Freedom* (New York: Vintage, 1976).

28. Clarence Page, *Chicago Tribune,* February 12, 1989; William Hoynes and David Croteau, "Are You on the *Nightline* Guest List?" *Extra!* Winter 1990; Marc Cooper and Lawrence Soley, "All the Right Sources," *Mother Jones,* Feb/March, 1990, 21–47.

29. *Extra!* "Special Issue on the Persian Gulf War," May 1991, 3–25.

30. National Public Radio, "All Things Considered," March 19, 1992.

31. Bozell and Baker, *And That's the Way,* chap. 1; Stanley Rothman and Linda Lichter, "Media and Business Elites," *Public Opinion,* November 1981.

32. David Weaver and G. Cleveland Wilhoit, "The American Journalist in the 1990s," (Arlington, Va: Freedom Forum, 1992), 7.

33. Howard Reiter, *Parties and Elections in Corporate America* (New York: St. Martin's Press, 1986), p. 179; Weaver and Wilhoit, "The American Journalist," 12.

34. Weaver and Wilhoit, "The American Journalist," 12–13.

35. See Herbert Gans, *Deciding What's News* (New York: Vintage, 1980); Leon Sigal, *Reporters and Officials: The Organization and Politics of Newsmaking* (Lexington, Ky.: Heath, 1973); Michael Parenti, *Inventing Reality: The Politics of the News Media* (New York: St. Martin's Press, 1986); Chomsky and Herman, *Manufacturing Consent*, p. 22.

36. Robert Entman, *Democracy Without Citizens: Media and the Decay of American Politics* (New York: Oxford University Press, 1989), p. 20. See also Walter Karp, "All the Congressman's Men: How Capitol Hill Controls the Press," *Harper's*, June 1989.

37. Entman, *Democracy*, pp. 36–37; William Greider, *Who Will Tell the People? The Betrayal of American Democracy* (New York: Simon and Schuster, 1992).

38. Joe Foote and Michael Steele, "Degree of Conformity in Lead Stories in Early Evening Network TV Newscasts," *Journalism Quarterly*, Winter 1986, 21.

39. Timothy Crouse, *The Boys on the Bus* (New York: Random House, 1973), p. 44.

40. Graber, *Mass Media*, p. 74.

41. Such studies include Thomas Patterson, *The Mass Media Election* (New York: Praeger, 1980); and *Out of Order* (New York: Alfred Knopf, 1993); James David Barber, *The Pulse of Politics: Electing Presidents in the Media Age* (New York: W. W. Norton, 1980); Michael Robinson and Margaret Sheehan, *Over the Air and on TV* (New York: Russell Sage, 1983). See also Reiter, *Parties*, p. 180.

42. Berkman and Kitch, *Politics*, p. 126.

43. Marjorie Randon Hershey, "The Campaign and the Media," in Gerald Pomper, ed., *The Election of 1988* (Chatham, N.J.: Chatham House, 1989).

44. Douglas Lowenstein, "Covering the Primaries," *Washington Journalism Review*, September 1980; "Sex, Polls and Campaign Strategy: How the Press Misses the Issues of the '92 Election," *Extra!* June 1992.

45. Carter quote from James McCartney, "The Triumph of Junk News," *Columbia Journalism Review*, January/February 1977, 18; Hershey, "Campaign," 92.

46. James Boylan, "Where Have All the People Gone?" *Columbia Journalism Review*, May/June 1991, 33.

47. See, for example, Larry Sabato, *Feeding Frenzy: How Attack Journalism Has Transformed American Politics* (New York: Free Press, 1991).

48. Russell Baker, *New York Times*, March 14, 1992, A25.

49. See Christopher Arterton, "Campaign '92: Strategies and Tactics," in Gerald Pomper, ed., *The Election of 1992* (Chatham, N.J.: Chatham House, 1993), pp. 85–93.

50. See "Old News Reconstructed," *The Economist*, October 31, 1992, 23.

51. Times/Mirror Center for the People and the Press, "Campaign '92, Voters Say Thumbs Up," November 15, 1992, table 3.

52. Wilson Carey McWilliams, "The Meaning of the Election," in Pomper, ed., *Election of 1992*, p. 199. For an insider account, see Tom Rosenstiel, *Strange Bedfellows: How Television and the Presidential Candidates Changed American Politics, 1992* (New York: Hyperion, 1993).

53. Boylan, "Where?" 35.

54. Austin Runney, quoted in Ladd, *American Polity*, p. 557.

55. Michael Grossman and Martha Kumar, *Portraying the President: The White House and the News Media* (Baltimore: Johns Hopkins University Press, 1981), p. 34.

56. Grossman and Kumar, *Portraying*, pp. 254–55.

57. Benjamin Page and Robert Shapiro, "Presidents as Opinion Leaders: Some New Evidence," *Policy Studies Journal*, June 1984; Lance Bennett, *News: The Politics of Illusion* (New York: Longman, 1988).

58. See Sabato, *Feeding*, chap. 6.

59. Iyengar and Kinder, *News*, p. 126.

CHAPTER 8

1. *Topeka Advocate*, 1892; cited in Michael McGerr, *The Decline of Popular Politics* (New York: Oxford University Press, 1986), p. 216; Sidney Blumenthal, *Pledging Allegiance: The Last Campaign of the Cold War* (New York: HarperCollins, 1991), p. 301.

2. Lawrence Goodwyn, *The Populist Moment in America* (New York: Oxford University Press, 1976).

3. This point is best made in Maurice Duverger's classic, *Political Parties* (New York: Wiley and Sons, 1954); Max Weber, "Politics As a Vocation" in Hans Gerth and C. Wright Mills, *From Max Weber* (New York: Oxford University Press, 1958), pp. 77–128; see also the classic by E. E. Schattschneider, *Party Government* (New York: Holt, Rinehart and Winston, 1942). See also Walter Dean Burnham, "The End of American Party Politics," *Transaction*, December 1969; Sidney Verba, Norman Nie, and Jae-on Kim, *Participation and Political Equality* (New York: Cambridge University Press, 1979).

4. Leon Epstein, "The Scholarly Commitment to Parties," in Ada Finifter, ed., *Political Science* (Washington, D.C.: American Political Science Association, 1983).

5. Overviews include Ronald Formisano, *The Transformation of Political Culture: Massachusetts Parties 1790–1840* (New York: W. W. Norton, 1983); Paul Kleppner, ed., *The Evolution of American Electoral Systems* (Westport, Conn.: Greenwood Press, 1981); Everett Carll Ladd, *American Political Parties* (New York: W. W. Norton, 1970); James Sundquist, *Dynamics of the Party System* (Washington, D.C.: Congressional Quarterly, 1983).

6. Samuel Huntington, "The Visions of the Democratic Party," *The Public Interest*, Spring 1985, 64.

7. Angus Campbell, Phillip Converse, Warren Miller, and Donald Stokes, *The American Voter* (New York: Wiley and Sons, 1960).

8. Walter Dean Burnham and William Nisbet Chambers, eds., *The American Party Systems* (New York: Oxford University Press, 1967); Paul Kleppner, *Who Voted? The Dynamics of Electoral Turnout 1870–1980* (New York: Harper and Row, 1983).

9. This is somewhat less true of current European parties. See Joel Krieger and Mark Kesselman, eds., *European Politics in Transition* (Boston: Heath, 1987), especially the contribution by Stephen Hellman about Italy.

10. See the discussion in Walter Dean Burnham, *The Current Crisis in American Politics* (New York: Oxford University Press, 1983).

11. William Riordon, *Plunkitt of Tammany Hall* (New York: Dutton, 1963); Milton Rakove, *Don't Make No Waves . . . Don't Back No Losers: An Insider's Account of the Daley Machine* (Bloomington: Indiana University Press, 1975); and Steven Erie, *Rainbow's End* (Berkeley: University of California Press, 1988).

12. William Riker, "The Two Party System and Duverger's Law," *American Political Science Review*, 76-4 (1982): 753–66. See also Douglas Amy, *Real Choices/New Voices: The Case for Proportional Representation in the United States* (New York: Columbia University Press, 1993).

13. Giovanni Sartori, *Parties and Party Systems* (Cambridge: Cambridge University Press, 1976), p. 42.

14. See McGerr, *The Decline*, pp. 12–42.

15. Walter Dean Burnham, *Critical Elections and the Mainsprings of American Politics* (New York: W. W. Norton, 1967). *Critical elections* and *surrogate for revolution* are Burnham's terms. See also Jerome Clubb, Nancy Zingale, and William Flanigan, *Partisan Realignment: Voters, Party and Government in American History* (Beverly Hills: Sage, 1980).

16. Frances Fox Piven and Richard Cloward, *Why Americans Don't Vote* (New York: Pantheon, 1987).

17. See Richard Jensen, *The Winning of the Midwest: Social and Political Conflict 1888–1896* (Chicago: University of Chicago Press, 1971).

18. See Walter Dean Burnham, "The Appearance and Disappearance of the American Voter," in Burnham, ed., *The Current Crisis in American Politics* (New York: Oxford University Press, 1982), pp. 142–60.

19. For accounts of the period, see Robert Wiebe, *The Search for Order 1877–1920* (New York: Hill and Wang, 1967); McGerr, *Decline*, pp. 52–68; Piven and Cloward, *Why*, chaps. 3–5.

20. Samuel Hays, *The Response to Industrialism* (Chicago: University of Chicago Press, 1957), p. 156.

21. V. O. Key, *Southern Politics* (New York: Alfred Knopf, 1949), final chap.

22. See Sundquist, *Dynamics;* Bruce Stave, *The New Deal and the Last Hurrah* (Pittsburgh: University of Pittsburgh Press, 1970). See also Steve Fraser and Gary Gerstle, eds., *The Rise and Fall of the New Deal Order 1930–1980* (Princeton: Princeton University Press, 1989); Sidney Milkis, *The Modern Presidency and the Transformation of the American Party System* (New York: Oxford University Press, 1993); Stephen Skowronek, *The Politics Presidents Make* (Cambridge: Harvard University Press, 1993).

23. E. E. Schattschneider, quoted in Leon Epstein, *Political Parties in the American Mold* (Madison: University of Wisconsin Press, 1986), p. 32; Clinton Rossiter, *Parties and Politics in America* (Ithaca: Cornell University Press, 1957), p. 64.

24. The idea that parties are still strong can be found in Xandra Kayden and Eddie Mahe, Jr., *The Party Goes On* (New York: Basic Books, 1985).

25. See Times/Mirror Center for the People and the Press, "The People, the Press and Politics: Campaign '92," Press-release, November 15, 1992, 6.

26. Data found in Paul Abramson, John Aldrich, and David Rohde, *Change and Continuity in the 1988 Elections* (Washington, D.C.: Congressional Quarterly Press, 1990); Margaret Conway, *Political Participation in the United States* (Washington, D.C.: CQ Press, 1991); Warren Miller, *American National Elections Data Sourcebook* (Ann Arbor: University of Michigan Press, 1988).

27. Thomas Edsall, *The New Politics of Inequality* (New York: W. W. Norton, 1984), p. 71; Gerald Pomper, "The Presidential Election," in Pomper, ed., *The Election of 1988* (Chatham, N.J.: Chatham House, 1989).

28. Abramson et al., *Change*, chap. 5; CBS News–*New York Times* poll, "Portrait of the Electorate," *New York Times*, November 5, 1992.

29. Abramson et al., *Change*, p. 127 and chap. 5; figures on Clinton from CBS News–*New York Times* poll, "Portrait."

30. Alan Matusow, *The Unraveling of America* (New York: Harper and Row, 1984), p. 427; Hugh Davis Graham, *The Civil Rights Era* (New York: Oxford University Press, 1990).

31. Thomas Edsall and Mary Edsall, *Chain Reaction* (New York: Norton, 1991); William Julius Wilson, *The Truly Disadvantaged* (Chicago: University of Chicago Press, 1987); Frances Fox Piven and Richard Cloward, *Regulating the Poor* (New York: Vintage Books, 1977).

32. Godfrey Hodgson, *America in Our Time* (New York: Pantheon, 1977); John Petrocik, *Realignment and the Decay of the New Deal Party System* (Chicago: University of Chicago Press, 1981); Todd Gitlin, *The Sixties* (New York: Simon and Schuster, 1989).

33. James Davison Hunter, *Culture Wars: The Struggle to Define America* (New York: Basic Books, 1990).

34. Kevin Phillips, *The Emerging Republican Majority* (New Rochelle, N.Y.: Arlington House, 1969).

35. Edsall, *New Politics*, chap. 4; Robert Kuttner, *Life of the Party* (New York: Simon and Schuster, 1988).

36. Thomas Ferguson and Joel Rogers, eds., *The Hidden Election* (New York: Pantheon, 1981).

37. Kevin Phillips, *The Politics of Rich and Poor* (New York: Random House, 1990), p. 43.

38. For complete accounts, see two fine collections: Gerald Pomper, ed., *The Election of 1992* (Chatham, N.J.: Chatham House, 1993); and Michael Nelson, ed., *The Elections of 1992* (Washington, D.C.: Congressional Quarterly Press, 1993). See also Richard Berke, "Tides That Brought Democrats to GOP Have Turned," *New York Times*, February 20, 1994, Ideas section, 3.

39. Jesse Jackson quoted in *Washington Post*, November 5, 1992, A30.

40. See Times/Mirror Center for the People and the Press, "Campaign '92: Voters Say Thumbs Up to Campaign, Process and Coverage," press release, November 15, 1992, 5–6.

41. Times Mirror Center, *The New Political Landscape*, October , 1994, pp. 5, 22, 42; Kevin Phillips, "Under the Electoral Volcano", *New York Times*, November 7, 1994, A19; *New York Times*, November 10, 1994, B1–B4.

42. Walter Dean Burnham, "The Future of American Politics," in E. Sandoz and C. Crabb, eds., *Election '84* (New York: New American Library, 1985).

43. See Frank Sorauf and Paul Allen Beck, *Party Politics in America* (Glenview, Ill.: Scott, Foresman, 1988).

44. The story comes from William Greider's *Who Will Tell the People? The Betrayal of American Democracy* (New York: Touchstone, 1993), pp. 246–48. For a contrasting view generally optimistic about grassroots parties, see William Crotty, ed., *Political Parties in Local Areas* (Knoxville: University of Tennessee Press, 1986).

45. For further examination of the increasingly negative and indifferent attitudes about parties, see Martin Wattenberg, *The Decline of Political Parties 1952–1988* (Cambridge: Cambridge University Press, 1990); Times/Mirror Center for the People and the Press, "The Generations Divide," press release, July 8, 1992, 43; Howard Reiter, *Parties and Elections in Corporate America* (New York: St. Martin's Press, 1987).

46. For this account, see Thomas Ferguson and Joel Rogers, *Right Turn* (New York: Pantheon, 1986).

47. See Morris Fiorina, *Retrospective Voting in American National Elections* (New Haven, Conn.: Yale University Press, 1981).

48. See Martin Shefter and Ben Ginsberg, *Politics by Other Means* (New York: W. W. Norton, 1991).

CHAPTER 9

1. Martin Wattenberg, *The Rise of Candidate-Centered Politics* (Cambridge: Harvard University Press, 1991).

2. "President Clinton: How He Won," *Special Election Report, Newsweek,* November 16, 1992, 24–40. For good accounts of presidential campaigns, see Steven Wayne, *The Road to the White House 1992* (New York: St. Martin's Press, 1992); Ryan Barilleaux and Randall Adkins, "The Nominations: Process and Patterns," in Michael Nelson, ed., *The Elections of 1992* (Washington, D.C.: Congressional Quarterly, 1993).

3. See "President Clinton," *Newsweek,* 38 and Ross Baker, "Sorting Out and Suiting Up: The Presidential Nominations," in Gerald Pomper, ed., *The Election of 1992* (Chatham, N.J.: Chatham House, 1993).

4. Sidney Blumenthal, *The Permanent Campaign* (New York: Harper and Row, 1981); and David Mayhew, *Congress: The Electoral Connection* (New Haven, Conn.: Yale University Press, 1974).

5. Common Cause, "Campaign Finance Activities of 1992 House and Senate General Election Candidates," May 1993.

6. Federal Election Commission report, October 23, 1992.

7. William Greider, *Who Will Tell The People?* (New York: Simon and Schuster, 1992); Thomas Byrne Edsall, *The New Politics of Inequality* (New York: Norton, 1986), p. 84; Figures on leadership PACs from "PAC Pollution," *New York Times,* March 21, 1994, A16.

8. Michael Barone and Grant Ujifusa, *Almanac of American Politics,* (Washington, D.C.: National Journal, 1991); Ross Baker, *The New Fat Cats: Members of Congress as Political Benefactors* (New York: Twentieth Century Fund, 1990); Common Cause, "Campaign Finance Activities."

9. Ross Baker, "The Congressional Elections," in Gerald Pomper, ed., *The Election of 1988* (Chatham, N.J.: Chatham House, 1989), p. 167. See Chapter 12 for a discussion of the House banking scandal.

10. Gary Jacobson, *The Politics of Congressional Elections* (New York: HarperCollins, 1992), pp. 47–48; Alan Abramowitz, "Incumbency, Campaign Spending and the Decline of Competition in US House Elections," *Journal of Politics,* 53 (February 1991): 47–9.

11. For figures on Congressional popularity, see "Congress, My Congressman," *Public Perspective,* 3 (May/June 1992), p. 102. Incumbent victories, defeats and retirements are chronicled in *Congressional Quarterly Weekly Report,* November 7, 1992, p. 3579. Money figures from Marjorie Randon Hershey, "The Congressional Elections," in Pomper, ed., *The Election,* p. 177; Glenn R. Simpson, "Why Did So Few Incumbents Lose Nov. 3?" *Roll Call,* November 1992.

12. Beth Donovan, "Freshman Focus on the Product, Not on Legislative Process," *Congressional Quarterly Weekly Report,* 14, November 1992, 3626.

13. Common Cause, Press Release, October 28, 1994; Richard Berke, "Americans in Surveys," November 10, 1994, B1–4. Thanks to Michael Malbin for additional info. Peter Kostmayer, "The Price of Politics," *Korea Herald,* May 31, 1993, 6. Potential changes in election laws are discussed at the end of the chapter.

14. For the Nixon story and historical background, see Herbert Alexander, *Financing Politics: Money, Elections and Political Reform,* (Washington, D.C.: Congressional Quarterly Press, 1984); Herbert Alexander, *Financing the 1988 Election* (Boulder: Westview Press, 1991); Brooks Jackson, *Honest Graft* (New York: Knopf, 1988).

15. Michael Malbin, *Money and Politics in the United States,* (Washington, D.C.: AEI, 1984); Elizabeth Drew, *Politics and Money,* (New York: Macmillan, 1984); Fred Wertheimer, "Pressing Forward," *Common Cause Magazine,* Summer 1993, 46.

16. Gary Jacobson, *The Politics of Congressional Elections* (Boston: Little Brown, 1992).

17. For this line of analysis, see James Q. Wilson, *American Government* (Lexington, Mass.: Heath, 1990), p. 231.

18. Edsall, *New Politics,* p. 104.

19. Federal Elections Commission, *Contributions,* 1990.

20. Harper's Index, *Harper's,* July 1992; Greider, *Who?* pp. 65, 253.

21. Edsall, *New Politics,* p. 105; *New York Times,* June 11, 1992, 11; Donald Bartlett and James B. Steele, *America: What Went Wrong?* (Kansas City: Andrews and McMeel, 1992).

22. *American National Election Study*, (Center for Political Studies, University of Michigan, 1988); Citizen Participation Project data, reported in *Boston Globe*, February 1993.

23. Harper's Index, *Harper's*, July 1992, 14.

24. Quoted in Frank Sorauf, "Political Action Committees in the United States: An Overview" (New York: Twentieth Century Fund, 1984), p. 96; see also Sorauf, *Money in American Elections*, (Glenview, Ill.: Scott, Foresman, 1988).

25. Greider, *Who?* p. 66.

26. Steven Salmore and Barbara Salmore, *Candidates, Parties, and Campaigns* (Washington, D.C.: Congressional Quarterly Press, 1990), pp. 261–71.

27. Drew, *Politics*, p. 14; Howard Reiter, *Parties and Elections in Corporate America* (New York: St. Martin's Press, 1988), p. 174. See also Stephen Labaton, "Democrats Awash in Money While GOP Coffers Suffer," *New York Times*, September 13, 1992.

28. Common Cause Report on Soft Money, reported on "All Things Considered," National Public Radio, June 18, 1992; Christopher Arterton, "Campaign '92: Strategies and Tactics," in Pomper, ed., *The Election*, p. 105.

29. Larry Sabato, *The Rise of Political Consultants* (New York: Basic Books, 1981).

30. Kenneth J. Godwin, *One Billion Dollars of Influence: The Direct Marketing of Politics* (Chatham, N.J.: Chatham House, 1988). See also Matthew McCubbins, ed., *Under the Watchful Eye: Managing Presidential Campaigns in the Television Era* (Washington, D.C.: Congressional Quarterly Press, 1992).

31. Christopher Hitchens, "Voting in the Passive Voice: What Polling Has Done to American Democracy," *Harper's*, April 1992.

32. Recorded in Sabato, *The Rise*, p. 149.

33. Salmore and Salmore, *Candidates, Parties, Campaigns*, p. 271.

34. See Christopher Arterton, "Campaign '92," in Pomper, ed., *The Election*, pp. 85–93.

35. See discussion in Robert Lineberry et al., *Government in America: People, Power and Policy* (New York: HarperCollins, 1991); Joe McGinness, *The Selling of the President, 1968* (New York: Trident, 1969).

36. See "Citizens and Politics: The View from Main Street" (Dayton: Kettering Foundation, 1991).

37. See Sidney Blumenthal, *Pledging Allegiance: The Last Campaign of the Cold War* (New York: HarperCollins, 1990); David Runkel, ed., *Campaign for President: The Managers Look at '88* (Dover, Mass.: Auburn House Publishing, 1989).

38. Times/Mirror Center for the People and the Press, "Voters Say Thumbs Up to Campaign, Process and Coverage," news release, November 15, 1992, 3–4.

39. See Kathleen Hall Jamieson, *Dirty Politics* (New York: Oxford University Press, 1992).

40. Wilson Carey McWilliams, "The Meaning of the Election," in Pomper, ed., *The Election of 1988* (Chatham, N.J.: Chatham House, 1989), p. 191.

41. "60 Seconds to Victory: Six Political Ad Men in Search of a Willie Horton in '92," *Harper's*, July 1992, 36–37; see also Times/Mirror, "The Generations Divide," press release, May 15, 1992.

42. Survey data from Times/Mirror, "Voters Say Thumbs Up," 7–10. Good overviews of the presidential election include chapters by Kathleen Frankovic, Gerald Pomper, and Wilson Carey McWilliams in Pomper, ed., *The Election;* and Paul Quirk and Jon Dalager, "A New Democrat and a New Kind of Political Campaign," in Michael Nelson, ed., *The Elections of 1992* (Washington, D.C.: Congressional Quarterly Press, 1993).

43. Gerald Mazorati, "From Tocqueville to Perotville," *New York Times*, June 28, 1992, E17; George Will, "Ross Perot: America's Rohrschach Test," *Washington Post National Weekly*, June 14, 1992.

44. Wertheimer, "Pressing," *Common Cause*, Summer, 1993, 45; Beth Donovan, "Democrats Prepare Final Push for Bill to President," *Congressional Quarterly Weekly Report*, April 9, 1994, 834; "The Reformer Vanishes," *New York Times*, May 31, 1994, A16.

45. Greider, *Who?*, p. 14.

CHAPTER 10

1. Michael Wines, "Congress's Twists and Turns Reshape Bill on Energy Tax," *New York Times*, June 2, 1993.

2. Office of the Clerk, U.S. House of Representatives; as cited in W. Lance Bennett, *Inside the System: Cul-*

ture, Institutions, and Power in American Politics (Fort Worth, Tex.: Harcourt Brace Jovanovich, 1994), pp. 8–44.

3. Cited in Mark P. Petracca, "The Rediscovery of Interest Group Politics," in Petracca, ed., *The Politics of Interests: Interest Groups Transformed* (Boulder, Colo.: Westview, 1992), p. 14.

4. See Ester R. Fuchs, *Mayors and Money: Fiscal Policy in New York and Chicago* (Chicago: University of Chicago Press, 1992), chap. 7.

5. Quoted in Jeffrey H. Birnbaum and Alan S. Murray, *Showdown at Gucci Gulch: Lawmakers, Lobbyists, and the Unlikely Triumph of Tax Reform* (New York: Random House, 1987), pp. 178–79.

6. Kay Lehman Schlozman and John T. Tierney, "More of the Same Washington Pressure Group Activity in a Decade of Change," *Journal of Politics*, 45 (1988): 351–75.

7. Quoted in Kay Lehman Schlozman and John T. Tierney, *Organized Interests and American Society* (New York: Harper and Row, 1986), p. 85.

8. For the top 1,100 employees in the executive branch, President Clinton, in 1993, raised the ban on lobbying their former agencies to five years.

9. Benjamin Ginsberg and Martin Shefter, *Politics by Other Means: The Declining Importance of Elections in America* (New York: Basic Books, 1990).

10. Schlozman and Tierney, *Organized Interests*, p. 75.

11. Allen J. Cigler and Burdett A. Loomis, "The Changing Nature of Interest Group Politics," in William Lasser, ed., *Perspectives on American Government: A Comprehensive Reader* (Lexington, Mass.: Heath, 1992), pp. 305–6.

12. See David Truman, *The Governmental Process* (New York: Knopf, 1951); Robert Dahl, *A Preface to Democratic Theory* (Chicago: University of Chicago Press, 1956); and Dahl, *Who Governs? Democracy and Power in an American City* (New Haven, Conn.: Yale University Press, 1961).

13. Schlozman and Tierney, *Organized Interests*, p. 70.

14. *The Gallup Poll: Public Opinion 1981* (Wilmington, Delaware: Scholarly Resources Inc., 1982), p. 179. The survey did not include unions, which in 1990 represented about 16 percent of workers.

15. E. E. Schattschneider, *The Semi-Sovereign People: A Realist's View of Democracy in America* (New York:

Holt, Rinehart and Winston, 1960), p. 35. For critiques of pluralist theory as a form of democratic elitism, see Jack Walker, "A Critique of the Elitist Theory of Democracy," *American Political Science Review*, 60 (1966): 285–95; and Peter Bachrach, *The Theory of Democratic Elitism: A Critique* (Boston: Little, Brown, 1967).

16. See Mancur Olson, Jr., *The Logic of Collective Action: Public Goods and the Theory of Groups* (New York: Schocken, 1968).

17. Schlozman and Tierney, *Organized Interests*, p. 76.

18. The following account of Nader's life and accomplishments relies on Robert F. Buckhorn, *Nader: The People's Lawyer* (Englewood Cliffs, N.J.: Prentice-Hall, 1972); Jay Acton and Alan LeMond, *Ralph Nader: A Man and a Movement* (New York: Warner Books, 1972); and Charles McCarry, *Citizen Nader* (New York: Saturday Review Press, 1972).

19. Buckhorn, *Nader*, p. 36.

20. Ralph Nader, *Unsafe at Any Speed: The Designed-in Dangers of the American Automobile* (New York: Grossman, 1966).

21. From court documents filed when Nader sued GM. Quoted in Nader, *Unsafe*, p. 14.

22. Quoted in Nader, *Unsafe*, p. 36.

23. Ralph Nader, "How to Put the Punch Back in Politics," *Mother Jones*, July/August 1990, 26.

24. Jeffrey M. Berry, *Lobbying for the People* (Princeton: Princeton University Press, 1977).

25. William Greider, *Who Will Tell the People: The Betrayal of American Democracy* (New York: Simon and Schuster, 1992), p. 48.

26. Schlozman and Tierney, *Organized Interests*, pp. 77–78.

27. Greider, *Who Will Tell*, p. 50.

28. Samuel Huntington called this the "democratic distemper." See his article, "The United States," in Michel J. Crozier, Huntington, and Joji Watanuki, *The Crisis of Democracy: Report on the Governability of Democracies to the Trilateral Commission* (New York: New York University Press, 1975), pp. 59–118.

29. Subcommittee on Commerce, Consumer and Monetary Affairs of the House Government Operations Committee; as reported in Thomas Byrne Edsall, *The New Politics of Inequality* (New York: Norton, 1984), p. 116.

30. Advertisement, "Progress and the Environment," *New York Times*, December 3, 1981; quoted in Jeffrey M. Berry, *The Interest Group Society* (Boston: Little, Brown, 1984), p. 140.

31. James T. Bennett, *Patterns of Corporate Philanthropy: Ideas, Advocacy and the Corporation* (Capital Research Center, 1989); as reported in Greider, *Who Will Tell*, p. 48.

32. Edsall, *New Politics*, p. 117.

33. R. Kenneth Godwin, *One Billion Dollars of Influence: The Direct Marketing of Politics* (Chatham, N.J.: Chatham House, 1988), p. 2.

34. Schlozman and Tierney, *Organized Interests*, pp. 94–95.

35. Cited in Schlozman and Tierney, *Organized Interests*, p. 22.

36. Godwin, *One Billion Dollars*, p. 3. The bill would have made it legal for unions not involved in a strike to support another union by refusing to cross picket lines.

37. Stephen Englemberg, "A New Breed of Hired Hands Cultivates Grass-Roots Anger," *New York Times*, March 17, 1993.

38. Quoted in Greider, *Who Will Tell*, p. 38.

39. Hugh Heclo, "Issue Networks and the Executive Establishment," in Anthony King, ed., *The New American Political System* (Washington, D.C.: American Enterprise Institute, 1978), pp. 87–124.

40. Edsall, *New Politics*, p. 112.

41. Schlozman and Tierney, *Organized Interests*, p. 41.

42. Ibid., p. 115.

CHAPTER 11

1. The following account of the Montgomery bus boycott is based on Taylor Branch, *Parting the Waters: America in the King Years 1954–63* (New York: Simon and Schuster, 1988); and Juan Williams, *Eyes on the Prize: America's Civil Rights Years 1954–1965* (New York: Penguin, 1987).

2. Michael Lipsky, *Protest in City Politics: Rent Strikes, Housing and the Power of the Poor* (Chicago: Rand McNally, 1970), p. 2. We draw freely in this chapter on Lipsky's analysis of protest as a political resource.

3. Quoted in Williams, *Eyes on the Prize*, p. 78.

4. Paul Kleppner, *Who Voted? The Dynamics of Electoral Turnout* (New York: Praeger, 1982), p. 116; as cited in Frances Fox Piven and Richard A. Cloward, *Why Americans Don't Vote* (New York: Pantheon, 1989), p. 144.

5. Quoted in William Greider, *Who Will Tell the People? The Betrayal of American Democracy* (New York: Simon and Schuster, 1992), p. 17.

6. For a contemporary elite democratic critique of mass politics, see Samuel P. Huntington, *American Politics: The Promise of Disharmony* (Cambridge, Mass.: Harvard University Press, 1981).

7. For a critique of the populist/progressive movements along these lines, see Richard Hofstadter, *The Age of Reform: From Bryan to F.D.R.* (New York: Vintage, 1955).

8. Michael Paul Rogin, *The Intellectuals and McCarthy: The Radical Specter* (Cambridge, Mass.: M.I.T. Press, 1967). Rogin's book is a carefully researched popular democratic defense of mass movements.

9. Merril D. Peterson, ed., *The Portable Thomas Jefferson* (New York: Penguin, 1975), p. 417.

10. T. R. Gurr, *Why Men Rebel* (Princeton: Princeton University Press, 1970).

11. John D. McCarthy and Mayer N. Zald, "Resource Mobilization and Social Movements: A Partial Theory," *American Journal of Sociology*, 82:6, 1212–41.

12. Sara M. Evans and Harry C. Boyte, *Free Spaces: The Sources of Democratic Change in America* (Chicago: University of Chicago Press, 1992).

13. For an insightful account of the populist movement that stresses the formation of a movement culture, see Lawrence Goodwyn, *The Populist Moment* (New York: Oxford University Press, 1978).

14. Quoted in Sara Evans, *Personal Politics: The Roots of Women's Liberation in the Civil Rights Movement and the New Left* (New York: Vintage Books, 1980), p. 87.

15. The concepts of transactional and transformational leaders are developed in James MacGregor Burns, *Leadership* (New York: Harper & Row, 1978).

16. For an analysis of Stanton as a dissenting movement leader, see Bruce Miroff, *Icons of Democracy: American Leaders as Heroes, Aristocrats, Dissenters, & Democrats* (New York: Basic Books, 1993), chap. 4.

17. Quoted in Williams, *Eyes on the Prize*, p. 76.

18. Saul D. Alinsky, *Reveille for Radicals* (New York: Random House, 1969), p. 132.

19. Henry David Thoreau, "Civil Disobedience," in Milton Meltzer, ed., *Thoreau: People, Principles, and Politics* (New York: Hill and Wang, 1963), p. 38.

20. Frances Fox Piven and Richard A. Cloward, *Poor People's Movements: Why They Succeed, How They Fail* (New York: Pantheon, 1977).

21. *Report of the National Advisory Commission on Civil Disorders* (New York: Bantam Books, 1968).

22. Murray Edelman, *The Symbolic Uses of Politics* (Urbana, Ill.: University of Illinois Press, 1967); see also Edelman's *Constructing the Political Spectacle* (Chicago: University of Chicago Press, 1988).

23. On repression see Alan Wolfe, *The Seamy Side of Democracy* (New York: David McKay, 1978); David Caute, *The Great Fear* (New York: Simon and Schuster, 1978); and Robert Justin Goldstein, *Political Repression in Modern America* (Cambridge, Mass.: Schenkman, 1978).

24. In 1977 a Federal District Court ordered all tapes, transcripts, and other FBI information on King's private life to be impounded for fifty years under the seal of secrecy. Branch, *Parting the Waters*, p. 872.

25. Tom Wolfe, *Radical Chic and Mau-Mauing the Flak Catchers* (New York: Bantam Books, 1971), pp. 117–18.

26. "No Guardrails," editorial, *Wall Street Journal*, March 18, 1993.

27. Samuel P. Huntington, "The United States," in Michel J. Crozier, Huntington, and Joji Watanuki, *The Crisis of Democracy: Report on the Governability of Democracies to the Trilateral Commission* (New York: New York University Press, 1975), pp. 59–118.

28. See Richard Rose, ed., *Challenge to Governance: Studies in Overloaded Politics* (Beverly Hills, Calif.: Sage, 1980).

29. Samuel P. Huntington, *American Politics: The Promise of Disharmony* (Cambridge, Mass.: Harvard University Press, 1981), p. 219.

30. Thomas R. Dye and Harmon Ziegler, *The Irony of Democracy: An Uncommon Introduction to American Politics*, 9th ed. (Belmont, Calif.: Wadsworth, 1993), p. 17.

31. For a gripping account of the events in Chicago, see James Miller, *"Democracy Is in the Streets": From Port Huron to the Siege of Chicago* (New York: Simon and Schuster, 1987), chap. 12.

32. *Rights in Conflict: The Violent Confrontation of Demonstrators and Police in the Parks and Streets of Chicago During the Week of the Democratic National Convention of 1968*, report submitted by Daniel Walker, director of the Chicago Study Team, to the National Commission on the Causes and Prevention of Violence, 1968.

33. Most Americans, 57 percent according to one poll, felt that the police had used the right amount of force or too little. John P. Robinson, "Public Reaction to Political Protest: Chicago 1968," *Public Opinion Quarterly*, 34 (Spring 1970): 1–9.

34. Joint Center for Political and Economic Studies, *Black Elected Officials: A National Roster* (Washington, D.C.: Joint Center for Political and Economic Studies, 1990), p. 10.

35. Jo Freeman, *The Politics of Women's Liberation* (New York: David McKay, 1975), p. 53.

36. Ethel Klein, *Gender Politics: From Consciousness to Mass Politics* (Cambridge, Mass.: Harvard University Press, 1984), p. 30.

37. Figures on salaries and political representation computed from U.S. Bureau of the Census, *Statistical Abstract of the United States: 1989* (Washington, D.C.: Government Printing Office, 1989), pp. 448, 511; *Statistical Abstract of the United States: 1993* (Washington, D.C.: Government Printing Office, 1993), pp. 277, 465.

38. Clinton did 5 percent better among women than among men (46 percent versus 41 percent), CBS News–*New York Times* poll based on a nationwide sample of voters leaving the polls on election day, *New York Times*, November 5, 1992.

CHAPTER 12

1. Alexander Hamilton, James Madison, and John Jay, *The Federalist Papers* (New York: New American Library, 1961), p. 384.

2. Data on the social composition of the 103rd Congress are drawn from *CQ Guide to Current American Government, Spring 1993* (Washington, D.C.: CQ Press, 1993), pp. 61–64; and *New York Times*, January 5, 1993.

3. Hamilton et al., *Federalist Papers*, p. 353.

4. These examples are drawn from Gary C. Jacobson, *The Politics of Congressional Elections*, 3rd ed. (New York: HarperCollins, 1992), pp. 85–86.

5. See Jacobson, *Politics*, pp. 27–28; and *CQ Guide*, pp. 40–49.

6. Jacobson, *Politics*, p. 141.

7. On Congressman Leggett, see Gary C. Jacobson and Samuel Kernell, *Strategy and Choice in Congressional Elections*, 2nd ed. (New Haven, Conn.: Yale University Press, 1983), p. 48.

8. David R. Mayhew, *Congress: The Electoral Connection* (New Haven, Conn.: Yale University Press, 1974).

9. Morris P. Fiorina, *Congress: Keystone of the Washington Establishment*, 2nd ed. (New Haven, Conn.: Yale University Press, 1989), pp. 46–47.

10. Richard E. Fenno, Jr., *Home Style: House Members in Their Districts* (Boston: Little, Brown, 1978).

11. On the independent effect of institutions, see James G. March and Johann P. Olsen, "The New Institutionalism: Organizational Factors in Political Life," *American Political Science Review*, 78, September 1984: 734–49.

12. On differences between the House and the Senate, see Ross K. Baker, *House and Senate* (New York: W. W. Norton, 1989).

13. Quoted in Baker, *House and Senate*, p. 50.

14. Roger H. Davidson and Walter J. Oleszek, *Congress and Its Members*, 4th ed. (Washington, D.C.: CQ Press, 1994), p. 203.

15. Michael J. Malbin, *Unelected Representatives: Congressional Staff and the Future of Representative Government* (New York: Basic Books, 1980).

16. Lawrence C. Dodd and Bruce I. Oppenheimer, "Maintaining Order in the House: The Struggle for Institutional Equilibrium," in Dodd and Oppenheimer, eds., *Congress Reconsidered*, 5th ed. (Washington, D.C.: CQ Press, 1993), p. 51.

17. Steven S. Smith and Christopher J. Deering, *Committees in Congress*, 2nd ed. (Washington, D.C.: CQ Press, 1990), p. 216.

18. Norman J. Ornstein, Thomas E. Mann, and Michael J. Malbin, *Vital Statistics on Congress, 1993–1994* (Washington, D.C.: CQ Press, 1994), pp. 201–2.

19. See Barbara Sinclair, "The Emergence of Strong Leadership in the 1980s House of Representatives," *Journal of Politics*, 54, August 1992: 657–84.

20. See Norman J. Ornstein, Robert L. Peabody, and David W. Rohde, "The U.S. Senate in an Era of Change," in Dodd and Oppenheimer, eds., *Congress Reconsidered*, pp. 27–30.

21. Baker, *House and Senate*, p. 71.

22. For a portrait of the generation that transformed Congress into a more egalitarian institution, see Burdett Loomis, *The New American Politician: Ambition, Entrepreneurship, and the Changing Face of Political Life* (New York: Basic Books, 1988).

23. Barbara Sinclair, *The Transformation of the U.S. Senate* (Baltimore: Johns Hopkins University Press, 1989), p. 85.

24. John W. Kingdon, *Congressmen's Voting Decisions*, 3rd ed. (Ann Arbor: University of Michigan Press, 1989). The discussion in the following paragraphs draws from Kingdon's book.

25. See R. Douglas Arnold, *The Logic of Congressional Action* (New Haven, Conn.: Yale University Press, 1990), especially pp. 119–46.

26. On heightened warfare between the branches under Reagan and Bush, see Benjamin Ginsberg and Martin Shefter, *Politics by Other Means: The Declining Significance of Elections* (New York: Basic Books, 1990). For a contrary view, see David Mayhew, *Divided We Govern: Party Control, Lawmaking, and Investigations, 1946–1990* (New Haven, Conn.: Yale University Press, 1991).

27. James A. Thurber, "The Impact of Budget Reform on Presidential and Congressional Governance," in Thurber, ed., *Divided Democracy: Cooperation and Conflict Between the President and Congress* (Washington, D.C.: CQ Press, 1991), p. 148.

28. Eileen Burgin, "Congress and Foreign Policy: The Misperceptions," in Dodd and Oppenheimer, eds., *Congress Reconsidered*, pp. 333–63.

29. See Philip Brenner and William LeoGrande, "Congress and Nicaragua: The Limits of Alternative Policy Making," in Thurber, ed., *Divided Democracy*, pp. 219–53.

30. Joel D. Aberbach, *Keeping a Watchful Eye: The Politics of Congressional Oversight* (Washington: D.C.: The Brookings Institution, 1990), pp. 191–93.

31. On term limits, see Gerald Benjamin and Michael J. Malbin, eds., *Limiting Legislative Terms* (Washington, D.C.: CQ Press, 1992).

CHAPTER 13

1. Alexander Hamilton et al., *The Federalist Papers* (New York: New American Library, 1961), p. 423. For a recent Hamiltonian argument, see Terry Eastland, *Energy in the Executive: The Case for the Strong Presidency* (New York: Free Press, 1992).

2. Ralph Ketcham, ed., *The Anti-Federalist Papers* (New York: New American Library, 1986), p. 211.

3. Max Farrand, ed., *The Records of the Federal Convention of 1787, Vol. 1* (New Haven, Conn.: Yale University Press, 1937), p. 112.

4. Almost all texts on the presidency start from the premise that the American political system requires strong presidential leadership.

5. Hamilton et al., *Federalist Papers*, p. 424.

6. George E. Reedy, *The Twilight of the Presidency* (New York: New American Library, 1971), p. 18.

7. Arthur Schlesinger, Jr., *The Imperial Presidency* (Boston: Houghton Mifflin, 1973).

8. Edward Pessen, *The Log Cabin Myth: The Social Backgrounds of the Presidents* (New Haven, Conn.: Yale University Press, 1984), pp. 170–71.

9. Richard A. Watson and Norman C. Thomas, *The Politics of the Presidency*, 2nd ed. (Washington, D.C.: CQ Press, 1988), p. 127.

10. Ibid., pp. 131–32.

11. Theodore Lowi, *The Personal President* (Ithaca, N.Y.: Cornell University Press, 1985), pp. 67–133.

12. For a lengthy treatment of the White House staff, see John Hart, *The Presidential Branch* (New York: Pergamon, 1987).

13. See Thomas E. Cronin, *The State of the Presidency*, 2nd ed. (Boston: Little, Brown, 1980), pp. 223–51.

14. See Reedy, *Twilight*, pp. x–xiii.

15. See Hugh Heclo, "OMB and the Presidency: The Problem of 'Neutral Competence,' " *The Public Interest* (1975): 80–98.

16. Cronin, *State of the Presidency*, pp. 276–78.

17. Quoted in Richard E. Neustadt, *Presidential Power and the Modern Presidents* (New York: Free Press, 1990), p. 10.

18. Richard P. Nathan, *The Administrative Presidency* (New York: Wiley, 1983). Also see Terry M. Moe, "The Politicized Presidency," in James P. Pfiffner, ed., *The Managerial Presidency* (Pacific Grove, Calif.: Brooks/ Cole, 1991), pp. 135–57.

19. For the story of the Reagan administration and OSHA, see William F. Grover, *The President as Prisoner: A Structural Critique of the Carter and Reagan Years* (Albany, N.Y.: SUNY Press, 1989), pp. 112–23.

20. Hamilton et al., *Federalist Papers*, p. 322.

21. See George C. Edwards III, *At the Margins: Presidential Leadership of Congress* (New Haven, Conn.: Yale University Press, 1989), pp. 39–46.

22. For the story of Clinton's 1993 budget battle in Congress, see Richard E. Cohen, *Changing Course in Washington: Clinton and the New Congress* (New York: Macmillan, 1994), pp. 70–86, 190–212.

23. *Washington Post*, November 18, 1993.

24. Theodore C. Sorensen Papers, John F. Kennedy Library.

25. Ibid.

26. *United States v. Curtiss-Wright Corp.*, 299 U.S. 304 (1936).

27. For an example, see Theodore Lowi, *The End of Liberalism*, 2nd ed. (New York: W. W. Norton, 1979), pp. 127–63.

28. Eve Pell, "White House Secret Powers: The Backbone of Hidden Government," *The Nation*, June 19, 1989, 833, 848–53.

29. For a vivid account of repression in the Nixon administration, see Jonathan Schell, *The Time of Illusion* (New York: Vintage, 1976).

30. For a good analysis of the framers' view of the president, see Jeffrey K. Tulis, *The Rhetorical Presidency* (Princeton: Princeton University Press, 1987), pp. 25–45.

31. Samuel Kernell, *Going Public: New Strategies of Presidential Leadership*, 2nd ed. (Washington, D.C.: CQ Press, 1993), pp. 90–91.

32. On public expectations of presidents, see Cronin, *State of the Presidency*, pp. 2–25; and Stephen J. Wayne, "Great Expectations: What People Want from Presidents," in Thomas E. Cronin, ed., *Rethinking the Presidency* (Boston: Little, Brown, 1982), pp. 185–99.

33. The fullest analysis of this relationship is Michael Baruch Grossman and Martha Joynt Kumar, *Portraying the President: The White House and the News Media* (Baltimore: The Johns Hopkins University Press, 1981).

34. Material on Reagan and the media is drawn from Mark Hertsgaard, *On Bended Knee: The Press and the Reagan Presidency* (New York: Farrar, Strauss, and Giroux, 1988); and Ronald Berkman and Laura Kitch, *The Politics of the Mass Media* (New York: St. Martin's Press, 1990).

35. *New York Times*, January 31, 1993.

36. Jann S. Wenner and William Greider, "The Rolling Stone Interview: President Clinton," *Rolling Stone*, December 9, 1993, 81.

37. *New York Times*, January 24, 1993.

38. See Steven Stark, "The First Post-Modern Presidency," *Atlantic Monthly*, April 1993.

39. Bruce Miroff, "Monopolizing the Public Space: The President as a Problem for Democratic Politics," in Cronin, ed., *Rethinking the Presidency*, pp. 218–32.

40. Material in the following paragraphs is adapted from Bruce Miroff, *Icons of Democracy: American Leaders as Heroes, Aristocrats, Dissenters, and Democrats* (New York: Basic Books, 1993), pp. 300–5.

41. Quoted in Miroff, *Icons*, p. 304.

CHAPTER 14

1. Clinton Rossiter, ed., *The Federalist Papers* (New York: New American Library, 1961), p. 174.

2. On the administrative apparatus under Washington and Hamilton, see Leonard D. White, *The Federalists: A Study in Administrative History, 1789–1801* (New York: Free Press, 1948).

3. Quoted in James A. Morone, *The Democratic Wish: Popular Participation and the Limits of American Government* (New York: Basic Books, 1990), p. 87.

4. Matthew A. Crenson, *The Federal Machine: Beginnings of Bureaucracy in Jacksonian America* (Baltimore: Johns Hopkins University Press, 1975), p. 4.

5. On late-nineteenth-century state builders, see Stephen Skowronek, *Building a New American State: The Expansion of National Administrative Capacities, 1877–1920* (New York: Cambridge University Press, 1982), esp. pp. 42–45.

6. Morone, *The Democratic Wish*, p. 98.

7. George McJimsey, *Harry Hopkins* (Cambridge, Mass.: Harvard University Press, 1987), p. 114.

8. Quoted in McJimsey, *Harry Hopkins*, p. 63.

9. Quoted in McJimsey, *Harry Hopkins*, p. 97.

10. Quoted in McJimsey, *Harry Hopkins*, p. 66.

11. Quoted in Charles T. Goodsell, *The Case for Bureaucracy*, 2nd ed. (Chatham, N.J.: Chatham House, 1985), p. 166.

12. Goodsell, *The Case for Bureaucracy*, p. 166.

13. Data on government employment are taken from Charles H. Levine, B. Guy Peters, and Frank J. Thompson, *Public Administration: Challenges, Choices, Consequences* (Glenview, Ill.: Scott, Foresman, 1990), p. 30.

14. Goodsell, *The Case for Bureaucracy*, p. 83.

15. B. Guy Peters, "Public Bureaucracy in the American Political System," in Gillian Peele, Christopher J. Bailey, and Bruce Cain, eds., *Developments in American Politics* (New York: St. Martin's Press, 1992), p. 170.

16. See Levine et al., *Public Administration*, pp. 348–49.

17. Goodsell, *The Case for Bureaucracy*, p. 103.

18. Reported in Goodsell, *The Case for Bureaucracy*, pp. 23–24.

19. See James Q. Wilson, *Bureaucracy: What Government Agencies Do and Why They Do It* (New York: Basic Books, 1989), pp. 179–95.

20. Ibid., pp. 113–36.

21. See John A. Rohr, *To Run a Constitution: The Legitimacy of the Administrative State* (Lawrence: University Press of Kansas, 1986), pp. 59–89.

22. Francis E. Rourke, *Bureaucracy, Politics, and Public Policy*, 2nd ed. (Boston: Little, Brown, 1976), p. 16.

23. Ibid., p. 46.

24. Wilson, *Bureaucracy*, p. 251.

25. See Eugene Lewis, *Public Entrepreneurship: Toward a Theory of Bureaucratic Political Power* (Bloomington: Indiana University Press, 1980), pp. 116–18.

26. Richard Gid Powers, *Secrecy and Power: The Life of J. Edgar Hoover* (New York: Free Press, 1987), p. 216.

27. David J. Garrow, *The FBI and Martin Luther King, Jr.* (New York: Penguin Books, 1983), pp. 125–34.

28. Levine et al., *Public Administration*, pp. 52–53.

29. Morton H. Halperin, *Bureaucratic Politics and Foreign Policy* (Washington, D.C.: Brookings Institution, 1974), p. 43.

30. Wilson, *Bureaucracy*, p. 257. For a historical account of this rivalry, see Skowronek, *Building a New American State*, pp. 165–292.

31. Michael D. Reagan, *Regulation: The Politics of Policy* (Boston: Little, Brown, 1987), p. 15.

32. The most famous—and controversial—of the revisionist histories of economic regulation is Gabriel Kolko, *The Triumph of Conservatism* (Chicago: Quadrangle Books, 1967).

33. For a critique of the capture thesis, see Wilson, *Bureaucracy*, pp. 83–88.

34. Reagan, *Regulation*, pp. 86–88.

35. See E. S. Savas, *Privatizing the Public Sector: How to Shrink Government* (Chatham, N.J.: Chatham House, 1982).

36. Cited in William T. Gormley, Jr., *Taming the Bureaucracy: Muscles, Prayers, and Other Strategies* (Princeton: Princeton University Press, 1989), p. 71.

37. Ibid., p. 89.

38. Charles Noble, *Liberalism at Work: The Rise and Fall of OSHA* (Philadelphia: Temple University Press, 1986), p. 34.

39. Ibid., p. 201.

CHAPTER 15

1. *Smith* v. *United States*, 113 S. Ct. 2050 (1993).

2. David M. O'Brien, *Storm Center: The Supreme Court in American Politics*, 3rd ed. (New York: Norton, 1993), p. 14.

3. Edwin Meese, Address to the D.C. Chapter of the Federalist Society Lawyers Division, November 15, 1985, in Paul G. Cassell, ed., *The Great Debate: Interpreting Our Written Constitution* (Washington, D.C.: Federalist Society, 1986), p. 37.

4. Edwin Meese, Address to the American Bar Association, July 9, 1985, in Cassell, *The Great Debate*, p. 9.

5. Ibid.

6. Ibid., p. 1.

7. Ibid., p. 10.

8. Justice William Brennan, Jr., Address to the Text and Teaching Symposium, Georgetown University, October 12, 1985, in Cassell, *The Great Debate*, p. 14.

9. Ibid., p. 15.

10. Ibid., p. 17.

11. Meese in Cassell, *The Great Debate*, p. 9.

12. Brennan in Cassell, *The Great Debate*, p. 11.

13. John Brigham, *The Cult of the Court* (Philadelphia: Temple University Press, 1987), p. 53.

14. For an illuminating treatment of the conflicting theories of democracy that have been utilized by different justices on the modern Supreme Court, see Martin Edelman, *Democratic Theories and the Constitution* (Albany: State University of New York Press, 1984).

15. Robert H. Bork, *The Tempting of America: The Political Seduction of the Law* (New York: Free Press, 1990), p. 130.

16. Kermit L. Hall, *The Magic Mirror: Law in American History* (New York: Oxford University Press, 1989), pp. 78–79.

17. *Marbury* v. *Madison*, 1 Cranch 137 (1803).

18. Robert G. McCloskey, *The American Supreme Court* (Chicago: University of Chicago Press, 1960), p. 57.

19. *Dred Scott* v. *Sandford*, 19 How. (60 U.S.) 393 (1857).

20. Michael Les Benedict, "History of the Court: Reconstruction, Federalism, and Economic Rights," in Kermit L. Hall et al., eds., *The Oxford Companion to the Supreme Court of the United States* (New York: Oxford University Press, 1992), p. 388.

21. O'Brien, *Storm Center*, p. 107.

22. Stephen Labaton, "Clinton Expected to Change Makeup of Federal Courts," *New York Times*, March 8, 1993.

23. On the difference a single new appointee can make, see Laurence H. Tribe, *God Save This Honorable Court: How the Choice of Supreme Court Justices Shapes Our History* (New York: New American Library, 1986), pp. 36–48.

24. O'Brien, *Storm Center*, p. 92.

25. See Tribe, *God Save This Honorable Court*, pp. 60–92.

26. See John Massaro, *Supremely Political: The Role of Ideology and Presidential Management in Unsuccessful Supreme Court Nominations* (Albany: State University of New York Press, 1990).

27. Data on female and minority appointments to the district courts are taken from Sheldon Goldman, "Bush's Judicial Legacy: The Final Imprint," *Judicature*, vol. 76, no. 6 (April–May 1993): 287.

28. Phillip J. Cooper, *Hard Judicial Choices: Federal District Court Judges and State and Local Officials* (New York: Oxford University Press, 1988), p. 328. For a contrary view of judicial "interventionism," see Jeremy Rabkin, *Judicial Compulsions: How Public Law Distorts Public Policy* (New York: Basic Books, 1989).

29. Stephen L. Wasby, *The Supreme Court in the Federal Judicial System*, 4th ed. (Chicago: Nelson-Hall Publishers, 1993), p. 58.

30. *Brown* v. *Allen*, 344 U.S. 443 (1953).

31. On the Court's flexibility in setting its own agenda through case selection, see Wasby, *The Supreme Court in the Federal Judicial System*, pp. 204–6.

32. Bryan A. Garner, "Style of Opinions," in Hall et al., *The Oxford Companion to the Supreme Court*, p. 610.

33. O'Brien, *Storm Center*, p. 276.

34. For a scathing portrayal of Chief Justice Burger, see Bob Woodward and Scott Armstrong, *The Brethren: Inside the Supreme Court* (New York: Avon Books, 1981), esp. pp. 27–29, 179–81, 199–201, 220–23, 303–4, 372–73.

35. Walter Murphy, *Elements of Judicial Strategy* (Chicago: University of Chicago Press, 1964), p. 209.

36. Changes in voting behavior by sitting justices may sometimes reinforce the ideological impact of membership changes. See Lawrence Baum, "Membership Change and Collective Voting Change in the United States Supreme Court," *Journal of Politics*, vol. 54, no. 1 (February 1992): 3–24.

37. See Lawrence Baum, *The Supreme Court*, 4th ed. (Washington, D.C.: CQ Press, 1992), pp. 144–56.

38. Compare Linda Greenhouse, "Moderates on Court Defy Predictions," *New York Times*, July 5, 1992; and Linda Greenhouse, "The Court's Counter-revolution Comes in Fits and Starts," *New York Times*, July 4, 1993.

39. Wasby, *The Supreme Court in the Federal Judicial System*, p. 349.

40. See Gregory A. Caldeira, "Neither the Purse Nor the Sword: Dynamics of Public Confidence in the Supreme Court," *American Political Science Review*, vol. 80, no. 4 (December 1986): 1209–226.

CHAPTER 16

1. *West Virginia State Board of Education* v. *Barnette*, 319 U.S. 624 (1943).

2. *Texas* v. *Johnson*, 491 U.S. 397 (1989).

3. Charles G. Curtis, Jr., and Shirley S. Abrahamson, "William Joseph Brennan, Jr.," in Kermit L. Hall et al., eds., *The Oxford Companion to the Supreme Court of the United States* (New York: Oxford University Press, 1992), pp. 86–89.

4. Peter Irons, *The Courage of Their Convictions: Sixteen Americans Who Fought Their Way to the Supreme Court* (New York: Penguin Books, 1990), pp. 63–79.

5. Ibid., pp. 153–78.

6. See Samuel Walker, *In Defense of American Liberties: A History of the ACLU* (New York: Oxford University Press, 1990).

7. Actually, twelve amendments passed Congress. One was rejected by the states; the other, which required that congressional pay raises not take effect until after an election, did not receive enough state ratifications to pass. Resurrected in the early 1980s, this amendment finally was passed by enough states to become the Twenty-seventh Amendment in 1992—over two hundred years after it was originally proposed!

8. *United States* v. *Carolene Products Co.*, 304 U.S. 144 (1938).

9. On the double standard, see Henry J. Abraham, *Freedom and the Court: Civil Rights and Liberties in the United States*, 4th ed. (New York: Oxford University Press, 1982), pp. 8–27.

10. *Palko* v. *Connecticut*, 302 U.S. 319 (1937).

11. See Alan Wolfe, *The Seamy Side of Democracy: Repression in America* (New York: David McKay, 1973).

12. *Schenck* v. *United States*, 249 U.S. 47 (1919).

13. *Brandenburg* v. *Ohio*, 395 U.S. 444 (1969).

14. *Tinker* v. *Des Moines Independent Community School District*, 393 U.S. 503 (1969).

15. *Roth* v. *United States*, 354 U.S. 476 (1957).

16. *Miller* v. *California*, 413 U.S. 15 (1973).

17. *F.C.C.* v. *Pacifica Foundation*, 438 U.S. 726 (1978).

18. Garry Wills, *Under God: Religion and American Politics* (New York: Simon and Schuster, 1990), p. 16.

19. *Rochin* v. *California*, 342 U.S. 165 (1952). For the gory details, see Abraham, *Freedom and the Court*, pp. 103–7.

20. See the classic account by Anthony Lewis, *Gideon's Trumpet* (New York: Vintage Books, 1964).

21. See Thomas Y. Davies, "Exclusionary Rule," in Hall et al., *The Oxford Companion to the Supreme Court*, pp. 264–66.

22. See Yale Kamisar, "*Miranda* v. *Arizona*," in Hall et al., *The Oxford Companion to the Supreme Court*, pp. 552–55.

23. Davies, "Exclusionary Rule," p. 266.

24. *Jencks* v. *United States*, 353 U.S. 657 (1957).

25. *Olmstead* v. *United States*, 277 U.S. 438 (1928).

26. *Griswold* v. *Connecticut*, 381 U.S. 479 (1965).

27. See Barbara Hinkson Craig and David M. O'Brien, *Abortion and American Politics* (Chatham, N.J.: Chatham House, 1993), pp. 35–68.

28. *Bowers* v. *Hardwick*, 478 U.S. 186 (1986).

29. *Plessy* v. *Ferguson*, 163 U.S. 537 (1896).

30. For the indignities inflicted on George McLaurin, see Richard Kluger, *Simple Justice* (New York: Knopf, 1976), pp. 266–69.

31. *Brown* v. *Board of Education of Topeka*, 347 U.S. 483 (1954).

32. For a brief and vivid account of these struggles, see Juan Williams, *Eyes on the Prize: America's Civil Rights Years, 1954–1965* (New York: Penguin Books, 1988).

CHAPTER 17

1. David Bensman and Roberta Lynch, *Rusted Dreams: Hard Times in a Steel Community* (Berkeley and Los Angeles: University of California Press, 1988).

2. Ira C. Magaziner and Robert B. Reich, *Minding America's Business: The Decline and Rise of the American Economy* (New York: Harcourt Brace Jovanovich, 1982), p. 2.

3. Sylvia Nasar, "The American Economy, Back on Top," *New York Times*, February 27, 1994.

4. U.S. Department of Commerce figures as cited in Paul Krugman, *The Age of Diminished Expectations: U.S. Economic Policy in the 1990s* (Cambridge, Mass.: MIT Press, 1992), p. 40.

5. Quoted in Alfred L. Malabre, *Lost Prophets: An Insider's History of the Modern Economists* (Boston: Harvard Business School Press, 1994), p. 183. See Jude Wanniski, *The Way the World Works* (New York: Basic Books, 1978).

6. William A. Niskanen, *Reaganomics: An Insider's Account of the Policies and the People* (New York: Oxford University Press, 1988), p. 4.

7. See Barry Bosworth, *Tax Incentives and Economic Growth* (Washington, D.C.: Brookings Institution, 1984); and Charles R. Hulten and Isabel V. Sawhill, eds., *The Legacy of Reaganomics: Prospects for Long-term Growth* (Washington, D.C.: Urban Institute Press, 1984).

8. Krugman, *The Age of Diminished Expectations*, pp. 66–67.

9. William Greider, *The Education of David Stockman and Other Americans* (New York: Dutton, 1982), p. 55.

10. *Pollock* v. *Farmers' Loan & Trust Co.*, 157 U.S. 429, 158 U.S. 601 (1895).

11. Quoted in Benjamin I. Page, *Who Gets What from Government* (Berkeley and Los Angeles: University of California Press, 1983), p. 21.

12. Stanley S. Surrey and Paul R. McDaniel, *Tax Expenditures* (Cambridge, Mass.: Harvard University Press, 1985), p. 34.

13. U.S. Bureau of the Census, *Statistical Abstract of United States 1993* (Washington, D.C.: GPO, 1993), Table 515.

14. Figures from U.S. Bureau of the Census, *Statistical Abstract of the United States 1990* (Washington; D.C.: GPO, 1990), p. 308. The concept of fiscal welfare is examined in Michael Peter Smith, *City, State & Market: The Political Economy of Urban Society* (Cambridge, Mass.: Basil Blackwell, 1988), chap. 2.

15. Surrey and McDaniel, *Tax Expenditures*, pp. 77–78.

16. Joseph A. Pechman, *Who Paid the Taxes, 1966–1985?* (Washington, D.C.: Brookings Institution, 1985), p. 10.

17. Francis X. Clines, "Gambling, Pariah No More," *New York Times*, December 5, 1993.

18. Kevin Phillips, *Boiling Point: Democrats, Republicans, and the Decline of Middle-Class Prosperity* (New York: Random House, 1993), chap. 4.

19. Donald L. Barlett and James B. Steele, *America: What Went Wrong?* (Kansas City, Missouri: Andrews and McMeel, 1992), p. 6.

20. As reported in *Facts on File*, Vol. 53, No. 2750 (August 12, 1993), p. 588.

21. Robert B. Reich, *The Work of Nations* (New York: Vintage Books, 1992), p. 27.

22. Quoted in David E. Rosenbaum, "Critics Want Fed's Power Under More Accountability," *New York Times*, November 14, 1991.

23. The Federal Reserve reports are cited in William Greider, *Secrets of the Temple: How the Federal Reserve Runs the Country* (New York: Simon and Schuster, 1987), p. 39.

24. Richard Syron as quoted in ibid. p. 54.

25. Quoted in ibid., p. 47.

26. Quoted in ibid.

27. See Milton Friedman, *Capitalism and Freedom* (Chicago: University of Chicago Press, 1982).

28. Quoted in Greider, *Secrets of the Temple*, p. 217.

29. Ibid., p. 593.

30. Quoted in Osha Gray Davidson, *Broken Heartland: The Rise of America's Rural Ghetto* (New York: Free Press, 1990), p. 21.

31. Quoted in Greider, *Secrets of the Temple*, p. 676.

32. Ibid., p. 682.

33. Ibid., p. 579.

34. Sylvia Nasar, "Fed Gives New Evidence of 80's Gains by Richest," *New York Times*, April 21, 1992.

35. Donald F. Kettl, *Leadership at the Fed* (New Haven, Conn.: Yale University Press, 1986).

36. Quoted in Greider, *Secrets of the Temple, p. 51.*

37. Ibid., p. 313.

38. Bensman and Lynch, *Rusted Dreams*, p. 1.

39. Barry Bluestone and Bennett Harrison, *The Deindustrialization of America: Plant Closings, Community Abandonment, and the Dismantling of Basic Industry* (New York: Basic Books, 1982), p. 9.

40. Kenneth M. Dolbeare, *Democracy at Risk: The Politics of Economic Renewal*, rev. ed. (Chatham, N.J.: Chatham House, 1981).

41. Statistics cited in Bensman and Lynch, *Rusted Dreams*, pp. 206–7.

42. Ann Markusen and Catherine Hill, *Converting the Cold War Economy: Investing in Industries, Workers, and Communities* (Washington, D.C.: Economic Policy Institute, 1992), p. 15.

43. Quoted in Dolbeare, *Democracy at Risk*, p. 112.

44. The terms *sunset* and *sunrise industries* originated with Lester Thurow, *The Zero-Sum Society: Distribution and the Possibilities for Economic Change* (New York: Penguin Books, 1981).

45. See Samuel Bowles, David M. Gordon, and Thomas E. Weiskopf, *Beyond the Wasteland: A Democratic Alternative to Economic Decline* (New York: Doubleday, 1983); and *After the Wasteland: A Democratic Economics for the Year 2000* (Armonk, New York: Sharpe, 1990).

46. Quoted in Bensman and Lynch, *Rusted Dreams*, p. 2.

47. Bowles, Gordon, and Weiskopf, *Beyond the Wasteland*, ch. 7.

48. See Bowles, Gordon, and Weisskopf, *Beyond the Wasteland*, pp. 262–73; Robert Kuttner, *The Economic Illusion* (Boston: Houghton Mifflin, 1984), pp. 46–48; and Arnold J. Heidenheimer, Hugh Heclo, and Carolyn Adams, *Comparative Public Policy: The Politics of Social Choice in America, Europe, and Japan*, 3rd ed. (New York: St. Martin's Press, 1990), p. 164.

49. Bowles, Gordon, and Weiskopf, *After the Wasteland*, p. 176.

50. Franklin D. Roosevelt, "An Economic Bill of Rights [January 11, 1944]" in Henry Steele Commager, ed. *Documents of American History* (New York: Appleton-Century-Crofts, 1963), p. 482.

51. Dolbeare, *Democracy at Risk*, pp. 147–48.

52. Bowles, Gordon, and Weisskopf, *Beyond the Wasteland*, p. 294.

53. In 1988, President Reagan reluctantly signed a weak version of plant-closing legislation that requires employers of 100 or more workers to give sixty days' advance notice of major plant closings or layoffs.

54. See Ann Markusen and Joel Yudken, *Dismantling the Cold War Economy* (New York: Basic Books, 1992).

55. See Sylvia Nasar, "The American Economy, Back on Top."

CHAPTER 18

1. Jonathan Kozol, *Rachel and Her Children: Homeless Families in America* (New York: Crown, 1988), p. 34.

2. Figures taken from U.S. Bureau of the Census, *Statistical Abstract of the United States 1993* (Washington, D.C.: GPO 1993), pp. 471, 473.

3. Fascism, with its dangerous emphasis on the inferiority of certain races, discredited the genetic approach. Genetic explanations of poverty were revived in the 1960s, prompting an angry debate about poverty, race, and the wisdom of egalitarian social policies. For a recent effort to revive genetic explanations of poverty, see Richard J. Herrnstein and Charles Murray, *The Bell Curve: Intellligence and Class Structure in American Life* (New York: The Free Press, 1994).

4. For a good example of the culture of poverty argument, see Edward Banfield, *The Unheavenly City*, 2nd ed. (Boston: Little, Brown, 1970).

5. Quoted in Andrew Rosenthal, "Quayle Says Riots Arose from Burst of Social Anarchy," *New York Times*, May 20, 1992.

6. The concept of social rights, or social citizenship, was first developed by T. H. Marshall in a well-known essay first published in 1949: "Citizenship and Social Class," in *Class, Citizenship, and Social Development* (New York: Doubleday, 1964).

7. For a review of the arguments linking social rights to democracy, see Desmond S. King and Jeremy Waldron, "Citizenship, Social Citizenship and the Defense of Welfare Provision," *British Journal of Political Science*, 18 (1988): 415–43.

8. See Bruce S. Jansson, *The Reluctant Welfare State: A History of American Social Welfare Policies*, 2nd ed. (Pacific Grove, Calif.: Brooks/Cole, 1993).

9. James MacGregor Burns, *Roosevelt: The Lion and the Fox, 1882—1940* (New York: Harcourt, Brace and World, 1956), pp. 212–13.

10. Theda Skocpol, "Targeting Within Universalism: Politically Viable Policies to Combat Poverty in the United States," in Christopher Jencks and Paul E. Peterson, eds., *The Urban Underclass* (Washington, D.C.: Brookings Institution, 1991), p. 425.

11. Robert C. Lieberman, "Race and the Organization of Social Policy," a paper presented at the Annual Meeting of the American Political Science Association, Chicago, Illinois, September 3–6, 1992.

12. Timothy Smeeding, "Why the U.S. Antipoverty System Doesn't Work Very Well," *Challenge* (January-February 1992): 33.

13. U.S. Bureau of the Census as cited in Theresa Amott, "The Disenfranchised: Eliminating Poverty," in Richard Caplan and John Feffer, eds., *State of the Union 1994* (Boulder, Colo.: Westview Press, 1994), p. 171.

14. Charles Murray, *Losing Ground: American Social Policy, 1950–1980* (New York: Basic Books, 1984).

15. Milton Friedman and Rose Friedman, *Free to Choose* (New York: Avon Books, 1981), p. 98.

16. The official poverty line is established by the federal government based on the amount of money needed to purchase an "emergency" diet (a diet that provides minimal adequate nutrition). This amount is then multiplied by three, based on the assumption that food takes about one-third of the average family's budget.

17. Jason DeParle, "Why Marginal Changes Don't Rescue the Welfare System," *New York Times*, March 1, 1992.

18. Christopher Jencks, *Rethinking Social Policy: Race, Poverty, and the Underclass* (New York: HarperCollins, 1992).

19. Cited in John E. Schwarz, *America's Hidden Success: A Reassessment of Public Policy from Kennedy to Reagan*, rev. ed. (New York: Norton, 1993), p. 32.

20. For a review of the evidence on the relationship between welfare and the rise of single-parent families, see William Julius Wilson, *The Truly Disadvantaged: The Inner City, the Underclass, and Public Policy* (Chicago: University of Chicago Press, 1987), chap. 3.

21. DeParle, "Why Marginal Changes Don't Rescue the Welfare System."

22. Wilson, *The Truly Disadvantaged*.

23. Theresa Funiciello, *Tyranny of Kindness: Dismantling the Welfare System to End Poverty in America* (New York: Atlantic Monthly Press, 1993), p. 285.

24. Arnold J. Heidenheimer, Hugh Heclo, and Carolyn Teich Adams, *Comparative Public Policy: The Politics of Social Choice in America, Europe, and Japan*, 3rd ed. (New York: St. Martin's Press, 1990), p. 249.

25. In 1973, the Supreme Court ruled that education is not right guaranteed equal protection under the U.S. Constitution. See *Rodriguez* v. *San Antonio Independent School District*, 411 U.S. 1 (1973). Many state constitutions, however, do guarantee equal educational opportunity, and lawsuits have successfully forced changes in the unequal funding of schools in many states.

26. Jonathan Kozol, *Savage Inequalities: Children in America's Schools* (New York: HarperCollins, 1991).

27. Paul E. Peterson and Mark C. Rom, *Welfare Magnets: A New Case for a National Standard* (Washington, D.C.: Brookings Institution, 1990).

28. See Frances Fox Piven and Richard A. Cloward, *Regulating the Poor: The Functions of Public Welfare* (New York: Random House, 1971).

29. Quoted in Jonathan Rieder, *Canarsie: The Jews and Italians of Brooklyn against Liberalism* (Cambridge, Mass.: Harvard University Press, 1985), p. 102.

30. Quoted in Gwen Ifill, "Clinton Offers Plan for Overhaul of Welfare, with Stress on Work," *New York Times*, September 10, 1992.

31. Quoted in Robert Suro, "Duke Campaigns on Distorted Facts Despite Rebuttals and Clarifications," *New York Times*, November 12, 1991.

32. See Funiciello, *Tyranny of Kindness.*

33. See Barbara Ehrenreich, "The New Right Attack on Social Welfare," in Fred Block et al., eds., *The Mean Season: The Attack on the Welfare State* (New York: Pantheon Books, 1987), pp. 161–95.

34. Funiciello, *Tyranny of Kindness*, p. 268.

35. Quoted in Jason DeParle, "When Giving Up Welfare for a Job Just Doesn't Pay," *New York Times*, July 8, 1992.

36. Richard P. Nathan, *Turning Promises into Performance: The Management Challenge of Implementing Workfare* (New York: Columbia University Press, 1993), p. 8.

37. Quoted in Daniel Patrick Moynihan, *The Politics of a Guaranteed Annual Income* (New York: Random House, 1973), pp. 540–41.

38. Amott, "The Disenfranchised," p. 175.

39. The speechwriter was William Safire. The term *workfare* was coined by Charles Evers of Mississippi. See Nathan, *Turning Promises into Performance*, p. 14.

40. Findings of the Manpower Demonstration Research Program as reported in Jason DeParle, "A Law Meant to Shift People on Welfare to Jobs Pays Off," *New York Times*, April 23, 1992.

41. Jan L. Hagen and Irene Lurie, *Implementing JOBS: Initial State Choices* (Albany, N.Y.: Rockefeller Institute of Government, March 1992).

42. Cited in Amott, "The Disenfranchised," p. 168.

43. Cited in Robert Reich, *The Work of Nations* (New York: Vintage Books, 1992), p. 206.

44. See Laurence E. Lynn Jr., "Ending Welfare Reform as We Know It," *American Prospect* (Fall 1993); 83–92.

45. See Douglas Jehl, "President Offers Delayed Proposal to Redo Welfare," *New York Times* (June 15, 1994); and Jason DeParle, "Change in Welfare Is Likely to Need Big Jobs Program," *New York Times*, January 30, 1994.

46. Paul Starr, *The Social Transformation of American Medicine: The Rise of a Sovereign Profession and the Making of a Vast Industry* (New York: Basic Books, 1982), p. 237.

47. The following account of the role of the medical profession in health policy relies heavily on Starr's insightful history (ibid.).

48. Quoted in ibid., p. 279.

49. Quoted in ibid., p. 285. (The Library of Congress was never able to locate the quotation in Lenin's writings.)

50. Reported in Schwarz, *America's Hidden Success*, p. 38.

51. U.S. Bureau of the Census, *Statistical Abstract of the United States 1993*, p. 849.

52. Reported in Ellen R. Shaffer and Paul D. Wellstone, "Providing Comprehensive Coverage," in Richard Caplan and John Feffer, eds., *State of the Union 1994* (Boulder, Colo.: Westview Press, 1994), p. 153.

53. *The President's Health Security Plan: The Complete Draft and Final Reports of the White House Domestic Policy Council* (New York: Random House, 1993), p. 4.

54. Ibid., p. 10.

55. Heidenheimer, Heclo, and Adams, *Comparative Public Policy*, p. 89.

56. Shaffer and Wellstone, "Providing Comprehensive Coverage," p. 154.

57. Lisa W. Forderaro, "In Harlem, Children Reflect the Ravages U.N. Seeks to Relieve," *New York Times*, September 30, 1990.

58. *New York Times*/CBS News Poll, September 16–19, 1993.

59. Poll results reported in R. W. Apple, Jr., "Going from a Good Bet to (Maybe) Even Money," *New York Times* (August 4, 1994).

60. Based on research by Darrell M. West and Diane J. Heith of Brown University, as reported in Robin Toner, "The Art of Reprocessing the Democratic Process," *New York Times* (September 4, 1994).

61. Quoted in Robert Pear, "Doctors Rebel Over Health Plan in Major Challenge to President," *New York Times* (September 30, 1993).

62. Yankelovich poll as reported in *U.S. News and World Report*, October 5, 1992, p. 40.

CHAPTER 19

1. The story of CIA plots against Castro is drawn from U.S. Senate, Select Committee to Study Governmental Operations with Regard to Intelligence Activities, *Alleged Assassination Plots Involving Foreign Leaders* (Washington, D.C.: GPO, 1975).

2. See especially Hamilton's arguments in *Federalist Papers* #6 and #11.

3. Clinton Rossiter, ed., *The Federalist Papers* (New York: New American Library, 1961), p. 424.

4. Richard H. Kohn, *Eagle and Sword: The Federalists and the Creation of the Military Establishment in America, 1783–1802* (New York: Free Press, 1975).

5. Ibid., p. 9.

6. Richard J. Barnet, *The Rockets' Red Glare: When America Goes to War—The Presidents and the People* (New York: Simon and Schuster, 1990), p. 82.

7. Ibid., pp. 111–15, 125–38; Bruce Miroff, *Icons of Democracy: American Leaders as Heroes, Aristocrats, Dissenters, and Democrats* (New York: Basic Books, 1993), pp. 182–87.

8. Roy P. Basler, ed., *The Collected Works of Abraham Lincoln* (New Brunswick, N.J.: Rutgers University Press, 1953–1955), vol. 3, p. 357.

9. George Bush, "Remarks at the Bush-Quayle Campaign Kick-Off," *Weekly Compilation of Presidential Documents, February 24, 1992* (Washington, D.C.: GPO, 1992).

10. Quoted in Bert Cochran, *Harry Truman and the Crisis Presidency* (New York: Funk and Wagnalls, 1973), p. 187.

11. Quoted in Barnet, *The Rockets' Red Glare*, p. 15.

12. Quoted in Ralph B. Levering, *The Cold War, 1945–1987* (Arlington Heights, Ill.: Harlan Davidson, 1988), p. 30.

13. Of all the Cold War presidents, Eisenhower probably had the deepest interest in peace. See Robert A. Divine, *Eisenhower and the Cold War* (New York: Oxford University Press, 1981), pp. 105–55.

14. George C. Herring, *America's Longest War: The United States and Vietnam, 1950–1975*, 2nd ed. (New York: Knopf, 1986).

15. John Prados, *Presidents' Secret Wars: CIA and Pentagon Covert Operations Since World War II* (New York: William Morrow, 1986), pp. 91–98.

16. Walter La Feber, *Inevitable Revolutions: The United States in Central America* (New York: Norton, 1984), pp. 274–78, 284–93.

17. Seymour M. Hersh, *The Price of Power: Kissinger in the Nixon White House* (New York: Summit Books, 1983), pp. 258–96.

18. Quoted in Divine, *Eisenhower and the Cold War*, p. 108.

19. James M. McCormick, *American Foreign Policy and Process*, 2nd ed. (Itasca, Ill.: Peacock, 1992), pp. 377–80.

20. Ibid., pp. 361–69.

21. Loch K. Johnson, *America's Secret Power: The CIA in a Democratic Society* (New York: Oxford University Press, 1989), pp. 16–17.

22. Prados, *Presidents' Secret Wars*, pp. 402–13.

23. Johnson, *America's Secret Power*, p. 10.

24. Ibid., pp. 107–10, 118–29, 207–33.

25. Tim Weiner, "Disclosure Urged for Secret Budget," *New York Times*, November 25, 1993.

26. Charles W. Kegley, Jr., and Eugene R. Wittkopf, *World Politics*, 4th ed. (New York: St. Martin's Press, 1993), pp. 214–50.

27. Richard J. Barnet, *Roots of War* (New York: Penguin Books, 1973), pp. 179–82.

28. Johnson, *America's Secret Power*, p. 22.

29. See Thomas W. Graham, "Public Opinion and U.S. Foreign Policy Decision Making," in David A. Deese, ed., *The New Politics of American Foreign Policy* (New York: St. Martin's Press, 1994), pp. 190–215.

30. McCormick, *American Foreign Policy and Process*, pp. 498–505.

31. Robert Y. Shapiro and Benjamin I. Page, "Foreign Policy and Public Opinion," in Deese, *The New Politics of American Foreign Policy*, pp. 229–33.

32. Ibid., p. 220.

33. Quoted in William Greider, *Who Will Tell the People?* (New York: Simon and Schuster, 1992), p. 359.

34. Quoted in Walter Russell Mead, "An American Grand Strategy," *World Policy Journal* (Spring 1993): 9–37.

35. Robert L. Borosage, "Meeting Real Security Needs," in Richard Caplan and John Feffer, eds., *State of the Union 1994: The Clinton Administration and the Nation in Profile* (Boulder, Col.: Westview Press, 1994), pp. 68–69; Lawrence J. Korb, "Shock Therapy for the Pentagon," *New York Times*, February 15, 1994.

36. Times-Mirror Center for the People and the Press, *Foreign Policy Survey*, November 2, 1993 (press release).

37. Christopher Layne and Benjamin Schwartz, "American Hegemony—Without an Enemy," *Foreign Policy* (Fall 1993): 10.

38. Ibid.; Michael Klare, "The Two-War Strategy," *The Nation*, October 4, 1993, pp. 347–50.

39. Michael H. Shuman and Hal Harvey, *Security Without War: A Post–Cold War Foreign Policy* (Boulder, Col.: Westview Press, 1993), p. 22.

40. Martin Walker, "The Establishment Reports," *Foreign Policy* (Winter 1992): 82–95.

41. Matthew Wald, "Uranium Rusting in Storage Pools is Troubling U.S.," *New York Times*, December 8, 1993.

Funiciello, Theresa, Ch. 18 n. 23, 32, 34

Galambos, Louis, Ch. 4 n. 24
Galbraith, John Kenneth, Ch. 4 n. 31, 32
Gans, Herbert, Ch. 7 n. 35
Garner, Bryan A., Ch. 15 n. 32
Garrow, David J., Ch. 14 n. 27
Gaudet, Hazel, Ch. 7 n. 13
Gelfand, Mark I., Ch. 3 n. 32
Geoghegan, Thomas, Ch. 4 n. 28
Georges, Christopher, Ch. 7 n. 59
Germond, Jack, Ch. 5 n. 26
Gerstle, Gary, Ch. 8 n. 22
Ginsberg, Benjamin, Ch. 5 n. 12; Ch. 8 n. 47; Ch. 10 n. 9; Ch. 12 n. 26
Gitlin, Todd, Ch. 7 n. 4; Ch. 8 n. 32
Godwin, Kenneth J., Ch. 9 n. 30; Ch. 10 n. 33, 36
Goldfield, Michael, Ch. 4 n. 28
Goldman, Sheldon, Ch. 15 n. 27
Goldstein, Robert Justin, Ch. 11 n. 23
Goldwin, Robert A., Ch. 2 n. 13
Goodsell, Charles T., Ch. 14 n. 11, 12, 14, 17
Goodwyn, Lawrence, Ch. 5 n. 13; Ch. 8 n. 2; Ch. 11 n. 13
Gordon, David M., Ch. 4 n. 6, 15, 33; Ch. 17 n. 45, 47, 48, 49, 52
Gormley, William T., Ch. 14 n. 36, 37
Graber, Doris, Ch. 7 n. 23, 24, 40
Graham, Hugh Davis, Ch. 8 n. 30
Graham, Thomas W., Ch. 19 n. 29
Green, James R., Ch. 4 n. 2
Green, Mark, Ch. 3 n. 14, 15, 16, 19
Greenberg, Edward S., Ch. 4 n. 27
Greene, Jack P., Ch. 2 n. 11
Greenhouse, Linda, Ch. 15 n. 38
Greider, William, Ch. 7 n. 1, 37; Ch. 8 n. 44; Ch. 9 n. 7, 20, 25,

27, 45; Ch. 10 n. 25, 27, 31, 38; Ch. 11 n. 5; Ch. 13 n. 36; Ch. 17 n. 9, 23, 28, 29, 31, 32, 33, 36, 37; Ch. 19 n. 33
Grossman, Michael, Ch. 7 n. 55, 56; Ch. 13 n. 33
Grover, William F., Ch. 13 n. 19; Ch. 18 n. 15
Grunwald, Joseph, Ch. 4 n. 39
Gurr, T.R., Ch. 11 n. 10
Gutman, Herbert, Ch. 4 n. 3

Hacker, Andrew, Ch. 6 n. 43
Hadley, Arthur, Ch. 5 n. 18
Hagen, Jan L., Ch. 18 n. 41
Halberstam, David, Ch. 4 n. 33
Hall, Kermit L., Ch. 15 n. 16, 20; Ch. 16 n. 3, 21
Halperin, Morton H., Ch. 14 n. 29
Hamilton, Alexander, Ch. 12 n. 1, 3; Ch. 13 n. 1, 5, 20; Ch. 19 n. 2
Hansen, John Mark, Ch. 5 n. 15
Harper's Index, Ch. 9 n. 20, 23
Harris, G., Ch. 6 n. 50
Harris, Louis, Ch. 6 n. 36
Harrison, Bennett, Ch. 4 n. 35, 39
Hart, John, Ch. 13 n. 12
Harvey, Hal, Ch. 19 n. 39
Hays, Samuel, Ch. 8 n. 20
Heith, Diane J., Ch. 19 n. 60
Heclo, Hugh, Ch. 10 n. 39; Ch. 13 n. 15; Ch. 17 n. 48; Ch 18 n. 24, 25
Hedges, Roman, Ch. 5 n. 11
Heidenheimer, Arnold J., Ch. 17 n. 48; Ch. 18 n. 24, 55
Heilbroner, Robert, Ch. 4 n. 3
Helyar, John, Ch. 4 n. 40
Herman, Edward, Ch. 6 n. 50; Ch. 7 n. 16, 35
Hernstein, Richard J., Ch. 18 n. 63
Herring, George C., Ch. 19 n. 14
Hersh, Seymour M., Ch. 19 n. 17
Hershey, Marjorie Randon, Ch. 7 n. 43, 45; Ch. 9 n. 11
Herskowitz, Mickey, Ch. 7 n. 2

Hertsgaard, Mark, Ch. 7 n. 58; Ch. 13 n. 34
Hill, Catherine, Ch. 17 n. 42
Hirschman, Albert O., Ch. 1 n. 5
Hitchens, Christopher, Ch. 6 n. 47, 48, 49; Ch. 9 n. 31
Hochschild, Jennifer, Ch. 6 n. 18, 24
Hodgson, Godfrey, Ch. 8 n. 32
Hofstadter, Richard, Ch. 11 n. 7
Honey, Martha, Ch. 7 n. 26
Hook, Sidney, Ch. 2 n. 3
Hoynes, William, Ch. 7 n. 28
Huber, J., Ch. 6 n. 16
Hulten, Charles R., Ch. 17 n. 7
Hunter, James Davison, Ch. 8 n. 33
Huntington, Samuel, Ch. 6 n. 7; Ch. 8 n. 6; Ch. 10 n. 28; Ch. 11 n. 6, 27, 29

Ifill, Gwen, Ch. 18 n. 30
INFACT (New York, 1989) Ch. 7 n. 19
Ippolito, Richard A., Ch. 4 n. 25
Irons, Peter, Ch. 16 n. 4, 5
Iyengar, Shanto, Ch. 7 n. 14, 15, 59

Jackman, M.R., Ch. 6 n. 36, 43
Jackman, R.W., Ch. 6 n. 36
Jackson, Brooks, Ch. 9 n. 14
Jackson, Jesse, Ch. 8 n. 39
Jacobson, Gary, Ch. 9 n. 10, 16; Ch. 12 n. 4, 5, 6, 7
Jamieson, Kathleen Hall, Ch. 9 n. 39
Jansson, Bruce S., Ch. 18 n. 8
Jay, John, Ch. 12 n. 1, 3; Ch. 13 n. 1, 5, 20
Jehl, Douglas, Ch. 18 n. 45
Jencks, Christopher, Ch. 18 n. 10, 18
Jennings, M. Kent, Ch. 6 n. 31
Jensen, Merrill, Ch. 2 n. 10
Jensen, Richard, Ch. 8 n. 17

Smart bombs, 561
Smith, Adam, 83
Smith, Christopher E., 428n
Smith, Connie, 280
Smith, John Angus, 413
Smith, Melancton, 39
Smith, Steven, 336
Smith Act, 456
Smith v. United States, 413
Smokeless Tobacco Council, 283
Smokeless tobacco law, 283
SNCC, see Student Nonviolent
    Coordinating Committee
"Snick," see Student Nonviolent
    Coordinating Committee
Snowcroft, Brent, 555
Snuff, lobbying for, 283
Social bias, in Congressional
    makeup, 322–323
Social Bill of Rights, 515
Social class
    income and interest-group
        participation, 276
    interest-group bias and, 275
    and public opinion, 154–156
Social differences, and American
    public opinion, 154–160
Social insurance entitlements,
    517
Social issues, religious right and,
    222
Socialization, political, 154
Social mobility, 87–88
Social movements, 220–221
Social policies
    economic policy and, 508–510
    effect on children and elderly,
        520
    health care, 529–534
    president and, 366
    spending in, 523
    welfare state and, 512–541
Social regulation, 401, 403–405
Social resources, of mass
    movements, 301–302
Social rights, 515
Social Security Act (1935), 62, 107
Social Security System, 518
    health care and, 73

means-tested public assistance
    and, 518–519
    payments of, 489–490
    welfare state and, 516
Social services, cuts in, 71
Social tensions, in revolutionary
    coalition, 27
Sodomy, privacy rights and, 470
Soft money, 239
    campaign funding and, 248–250
Solid South, 213
Somalia, 377
    U.S. forces in, 564, 565
Sombart, Werner, 155
Somoza, Anastasio, 164
Sons of Liberty, 19
Sorensen, Theodore, 369–370
Sound bites, 196
Sources, news making and,
    190–191
Souter, David H., 425, 426, 468
South (region)
    Democratic domination in, 211
    nonvoting in, 113–114
    racism in, 62
    Roosevelt, Franklin D.,
        compromise with, 62
    slavery and, 33
    voter registration in, 124–126
    voting rights in, 63
    welfare payments in, 62
South Africa, foreign policy and,
    345
Southern Christian Leadership
    Conference (SCLC), 294, 473
Southern Politics (Key), 212
Southern whites
    party identification of, 215
    shift to GOP of, 216
Southwest, Mexican Americans
    in, 135
Southwest Voter Registration
    Project (SWVRP), 135
Sovereignty, consumer, 83–84
Soviet Union (USSR)
    civil wars in former, 566
    Cold War and, 548
    disinformation about, 186
    expansionism of, 551

Spanish-American war, 547
Speaker of the House of
    Representatives, 337
Specialization, 102
Speech
    freedom of, 455–458
    unprotected, 458–459
Spencer Roberts (firm), 251
Spending
    deficit, 106
    fiscal policies and, 106
Spirit of '76, 20–21
Split level contributions, 246
Split-ticket voting, 231
Spoils system, 206, 384–385
Stability, Federalists vs. Anti-
    federalists on, 41–42
Staff aides, to congressional
    committees, 335
Stagflation, 483–484
    prosperity to, 482–490
Stalinism, as ideology, 150
Stamp Act, 19
Standard Oil
    of New Jersey, 55
    of Ohio, 54, 55
Standing committees, 332
Stanley, Harold W., 115n, 149n,
    157n, 177n, 519n
Stanton, Elizabeth Cady, 475
    as transformational leader, 302
    women's declaration of
        independence by, 9–10
Stark, Pete, 270
State Department, 371
State government
    federally-mandated
        expenditures of, 70
    regressive taxation and, 494
States
    administration of federal
        funding, 60
    Bill of Rights and, 452
    bills of rights in, 24
    competition for power, 54–57
    constitutions in, 23–24
    control of corporations by, 54
    corporate growth and, 54–55
    federal supremacy over, 420